John Koenig Jr.
Alexandria, Va.
10/23/79

JOHNSONIAN MISCELLANIES

G. BIRKBECK HILL

VOL. I.

JOHNSONIAN MISCELLANIES

ARRANGED AND EDITED

BY

GEORGE BIRKBECK HILL, D.C.L., LL.D.

HONORARY FELLOW OF PEMBROKE COLLEGE, OXFORD

EDITOR OF 'BOSWELL'S LIFE OF JOHNSON'
AND OF 'THE LETTERS OF SAMUEL JOHNSON'

IN TWO VOLUMES

VOL. I

BARNES & NOBLE, Inc.
NEW YORK
PUBLISHERS & BOOKSELLERS SINCE 1873

First published in 1897
by The Clarendon Press

Reprinted 1966
in the United States of America
by Barnes & Noble Inc, New York
and in Great Britain
by Constable & Co. Ltd, London
through special arrangement with
The Clarendon Press

L. C. Catalog Card Number: 66-28308

Reprinted, 1970

Printed in the United States of America

TO

THE REVEREND

BARTHOLOMEW PRICE

D.D., F.R.S., F.R.A.S.

CANON OF GLOUCESTER

MASTER OF PEMBROKE COLLEGE, OXFORD

SEDLEIAN PROFESSOR OF NATURAL PHILOSOPHY

IN COMMEMORATION OF HIS LONG AND HONOURABLE CONNEXION

WITH THAT 'LITTLE COLLEGE' WHICH JOHNSON LOVED

THIS WORK IS DEDICATED

PREFACE

IN the Preface to the *Letters of Samuel Johnson* I spoke of the hope I entertained that I should live to complete the main work of my life as a scholar by a new edition of the *Lives of the Poets*. I have been turned away from my purpose, at least for a time, by a letter which I received from Mr. Leslie Stephen. He asked me to edit all those writings which have long been included under the general title of *Johnsoniana*. The task that he proposed seemed pleasant in itself. Even had it been irksome, I should have hesitated much before I declined such a request, coming as it did from a man to whom every student of the literature, biography, and history of our country is so deeply indebted. It gratified me greatly to know that my labours had been of real service to the first editor of the *Dictionary of National Biography*.

These two volumes of *Johnsonian Miscellanies* would have been ready for publication three years earlier had I not been delayed by illness, and by the necessity I have been under of passing all my winters abroad. On the banks of the Lake of Geneva, or on the shores of the Mediterranean, an editor, however much he may be supported by the climate, has to struggle against difficulties which might almost overwhelm him. Many

a day

a day he 'casts a long look' towards the Bodleian and the British Museum. Many a day he thinks with idle regret of his own study, where he is surrounded by those books to which he has often to refer. The cost of carriage and the time lost in transport hinder him from taking backwards and forwards more than a few of the most needful works. Last year I sent off from London a box of books to Alassio, on the Italian Riviera, three weeks before I myself started for that pleasant little town. It was not till full five weeks after my arrival that they reached me. Fifty-nine days had they spent in traversing little more than a thousand miles. They had advanced at the rate of about three-quarters of a mile an hour. Towards Clarens, on the Lake of Geneva, where I passed three winters, they used to creep at a somewhat faster pace, for in every four-and-twenty hours they moved at least five-and-twenty miles. It is scarcely likely that Gibbon, when he transported his great library to Lausanne, had his patience as sorely tried as mine. The Kentish carrier, who, leaving Rochester betimes, delivered that same day a gammon of bacon and two razes of ginger as far as Charing Cross, was certainly more expeditious.

Had I been in England while the book was passing through the press the disadvantages which arose from my earlier absence would have been greatly lessened. It has so happened that of the eleven months during which it has been in the printer's hands I have spent nearly ten abroad. In the six volumes of the *Life*, and in the two volumes of the *Letters*, there is scarcely a quotation or a reference in my notes which I did not verify in the proof by a comparison with the original authority. I never trusted my own copy. The labour was great, but it was not more than a man should be ready to undergo who

ventures

ventures to edit an English classic. Tillemont's accuracy may, as Gibbon says, be inimitable; but none the less, inspired by the praise which our great historian bestows on mere accuracy, a scholar should never lose the hope of imitation.

In such a variety of material as is comprised in these two volumes, where much the same ground is frequently travelled over by different writers, I have found it difficult to exclude idle repetitions. Wherever there are two original authorities for the same anecdote, repetition may not only be justifiable, but even necessary. In many cases, however, one writer borrows from another without owning the obligation. William Seward, for instance, who knew Johnson well, from whose *Anecdotes of Distinguished Persons* and *Biographiana* I have quoted, had taken not a few passages from Mrs. Piozzi's *Anecdotes* without the change of a single word. Some of these thefts I only discovered in correcting the proof-sheets. It might be thought that plagiarism such as this would be easily detected by one who was so familiar with the subject. It was this very familiarity which made detection difficult. Every anecdote I had long known so well that frequently I could not be sure whether I was not for the second time including in my selection what had been included before.

The imperfections of such a piece of work as this are often more clearly seen by the editor than even by the most sharp-sighted reviewer. They are discovered too late for correction, but not for criticism. Were the whole book in type at the same time, and were the cost of correction of no moment, what improvements could be made! I have never yet finished an index without wishing that by the help of it I could at once re-edit my own editing.

I had

I had at first thought of giving extracts from Madame D'Arblay's *Diary*. Reflection soon convinced me that it is too good a piece of work to be hacked in pieces. He who wishes to see Johnson's 'fun, and comical humour, and love of nonsense, of which,' she says, 'he had about him more than almost anybody she ever saw'; he who would know 'Gay Sam, agreeable Sam, pleasant Sam,' must turn to her pages. It is a great pity that her *Diary* has never had a competent editor. In its present form it is not altogether as she originally wrote it, or even as she left it on her death. Some of the alterations, made partly by herself, partly by her niece, were unwarrantable. By the help of the manuscript, which is still in existence, though not, I believe, in a perfect condition, the original entries could in most cases be restored. Miss Seward's *Letters* I have passed over for a different reason: they are untrustworthy.

In the *Dicta Philosophi* at the end of the book, I have given a second concordance of Johnson's sayings. Neither in extent nor in quality is this collection quite equal to the first, which was gathered from the *Life* and *The Journal of a Tour to the Hebrides*. 'Boswell's long head,' as Mrs. Thrale said, 'was equal to short-hand.' In his tablets the point of his master's wit was not blunted, and the strength of his wisdom was not weakened. 'It is not every man that can carry a *bon mot*.' Johnson, if I am not mistaken, in the frequency with which he is quoted, comes next to the Bible and Shakespeare. By the help of my concordances he should suffer much less than formerly from inaccuracy of quotation.

In these two volumes I am able to make some additions to Johnsonian lore. By collating the text of *Prayers and Meditations*

tions

tions with the original manuscript preserved in the library of Pembroke College, Oxford, I have made some corrections in the text, and supplied some omissions. On one entry which had been suppressed I wish light could be thrown. Who was 'dying Jenny' for whose spiritual comfort Johnson provided [1]? Was she some poor outcast, like the wretched woman he carried home and nursed there for thirteen weeks [2]?

An interesting collection of manuscripts which had once belonged to Miss Reynolds I am allowed to use by the kindness of Lady Colomb, of Dronquinna, Kenmare, a descendant of Sir Joshua's sister, Mary. Most of them are given in Croker's edition, but not all. I have revised his version, and have supplied omissions, and corrected the text where it was faulty [3]. Some letters which he had not seen or had passed over are now printed for the first time [4], as well as the corrections which Johnson made in 'Renny's' verses when he 'mended some bad rhymes [5].'

To my friend, Mr. Robert B. Adam, of Buffalo, whose Johnsonian collection far surpasses any we have on this side of the Atlantic, I am greatly indebted for the liberality with which he has placed all his treasures at my service. I wish every collector of autographs were like him, free from that petty selfishness which makes a man hug some famous author's letter as a miser hugs his gold, rejoicing in it all the more as he keeps it entirely to himself.

My kinsman, Mr. Horatio Percy Symonds, of Beaumont Street, Oxford, has allowed me to make use of the curious manuscript notes on the margin of a copy of the first edition

[1] Vol. i. p. 124. [2] Vol. ii. p. 168.
[3] See vol. ii. p. 449, *n.* 3, for the correction of some curious blunders.
[4] Vol. ii. pp. 455-460. [5] Vol. ii. p. 279, *n.* 4.

of

of the *Life*, which his father, a Johnsonian collector, purchased many years ago. They were written, I have no doubt, by the Rev. John Hussey, 'who,' as Boswell tells us, 'had long been in habits of intimacy with Johnson[1].'

Messrs. J. Pearson & Co., of 5 Pall Mall Place, London, I have to thank for permission to print some hitherto unpublished letters of Johnson which were in their possession.

To Mr. John Murray, of Albemarle Street, the publisher of *The Life of Reynolds* by C. R. Leslie and Tom Taylor, I am indebted for permission to reprint an interesting paper by Sir Joshua on Johnson's character.

Mr. G. K. Fortescue, of the British Museum, has once more greatly lessened my labours by the assistance he has so kindly given me when I have been working in the Library. His friends rejoice in his well-earned promotion, much as they must miss him in his old place in the Reading Room.

It only remains for me to express the hope that the kind welcome which was given by scholars on both sides of the Atlantic to my editions of the *Life* and *Letters* will be extended also to these two volumes.

G. B. H.

VILLA VENUSTA, ALASSIO,
February 7, 1897.

[1] *Life*, vol. iii. p. 369.

FOREWORD

Within a few years after it was published, *Johnsonian Miscellanies* (1897) had become one of the classics of English literature. By far the richest supplement to Boswell's *Life of Johnson,* it gives us a variety of close personal glimpses of a man of whom—whether we already know much of him or very little—we are always eager to hear more.

No writer since Shakespeare, at least no writer in the English-speaking world, has appealed to so many different kinds of people. How do we explain the magnetic attraction Johnson has had, during almost two centuries, not only for writers of every sort but also for statesmen, teachers, financiers, lawyers, or physicians? A part of the explanation is that there were few subjects in which Johnson himself was not interested. He could move easily through classical and most modern literature, was widely read in philosophy, theology, and law, and knew something of chemistry and medicine. The practical application of knowledge always fascinated him; and he could talk well of navigation, the process of tanning, or the making of whey or gunpowder. Richard Arkwright (said George Steevens in one of the "Anecdotes" presented in the present volume) considered Johnson "the only person who, on a first view, understood the principle and powers of his most complicated piece of machinery," the spinning-jenny. In the *Tour to Hebrides,* Boswell tells of his successful attempt to draw out Johnson on a subject as "far out of the way of a philosopher and poet" as any he could imagine—that of a butcher. Again: "He this morning gave us all the operation of coining, and at night . . . the operation of brewing spirits." It is partly the range of his active curiosity and notice that makes Johnson so great as a moralist, a psychologist, and a critic of literature. "After the distribution of particular arts and sciences" into separate compartments, said Bacon, men "abandon universality," forgetting that "no large discovery can be made upon a flat or level; neither is it possible to discover the more remote and deeper parts of any science, if you stand but upon the level of the *same* science."

But if Johnson (as his friend Thomas Tyers said) "belongs" to no one field of learning but rather "to the world at large," it is not simply through his horizontal range of interests, though this is an important element. There have been other polymaths whose names are now forgotten except by scholars. The deeper appeal is that he is always returning centripetally to the essential claims of the human heart—its hopes and fears, its hunger for meaning, for happiness, for re-assurance. And he does so with an honesty, a relevance, and a refreshing humor that cut through all the "cant," all the loose talk and pretense with which most of us complicate life for ourselves and others. "He may be said to have formed my mind," said Sir Joshua Reynolds, "and to have *brushed from it a great deal of rubbish*"; and Reynolds' tribute has been echoed by thousands of people in the past two centuries. Finally, there is the novelty and readiness of expression. He said even "the most common things," wrote Thomas Tyers, "in the *newest* manner." They can never be predicted. Yet when we read them, they seem altogether typical. "Promptitude of thought, indeed, and quickness of expression," said Mrs. Piozzi, "were among the peculiar felicities of Johnson: his notions rose up like the dragon's teeth sowed by Cadmus already clothed, and in bright armour too, fit for immediate battle."

It is to Johnson's writing on life and literature—the moral essays, *Rasselas,* the *Lives of the Poets*—that our own generation has begun increasingly to turn. But it is still true that his writing, however superlative it can be, is only a part of the man. As Sir Walter Raleigh said, he is "great by his reserves"; "his books are mere outworks." So many other writers whom we approach hopefully turn out to have compressed economically everything they had or were into their writings; and we find remaining, as Raleigh said, only the "husk" of the man. In Johnson there is always abundance left.

If the memoirs of Johnson are easily the most complete for any writer before the twentieth century, it is because his own contemporaries were so aware of this abundance and tried to record something of their own experience of it. Soon after George Birkbeck Hill completed his great edition of Boswell's *Life of Johnson* (1887), he had the happy thought of bringing together and editing the present collection. There is only one major omission, the sections of Fanny Burney's *Diary* concerned with Johnson (an omission Hill explains in his Preface). Otherwise we have almost everything else —anecdotes or accents from over thirty different people—and so beautifully edited that no attempt has since been made to duplicate Hill's collection.

A few words should be added about George Birkbeck Hill, to whom everyone interested in Johnson owes at least as much as to any scholar of the past century and a half.

Hill's family had for two generations been closely identified with political and social reform. His father, Arthur Hill, was the headmaster of a school at Bruce Castle, Tottenham, Middlesex. There the boy was born (June 7, 1834) and educated, and then sent to Pembroke College, Oxford (1855). A severe case of typhoid prevented him from graduating highly (1858). He returned to teach in his father's school, married, and ten years later succeeded his father as headmaster, by which time Hill was thirty-four. During the following year occurred a memorable event in his life. In a book-shop where he was browsing, he bought a second-hand copy of Boswell's *Life of Johnson.* He had read in Boswell as a boy but had scarcely opened the book since then. At Pembroke College, to be sure, he had "loved to think that Johnson had been there before me," and, interested primarily in their style, had read in many of the major prose writers of the eighteenth century. Fascinated now by the great biography, he began in spare moments to note parallel passages and allusions. His health became very uncertain, and in 1869 he resigned from the school, wrote frequently for the press, and continued to study the literature of the eighteenth century. After editing his *Dr. Johnson: His Friends and His Critics* (1878) and Boswell's *Journal of a Tour to Corsica* (1879), he was asked to write a life of his uncle Sir Rowland Hill (1880) and also his still remembered *Colonel Gordon in Central Africa* (1880). The work helped, as he said, to train him as an editor; and he now (1881) proposed to the Clarendon Press a new edition, on a really majestic scale, of the *Life of Johnson.* The plan was accepted; much of the work had already been done; and in 1887, the great edition of six volumes appeared. No nineteenth-century edition of any classic has better stood the test of time; and, revised by L. F. Powell (1934-1950), it is not only the standard edition but almost certain to remain so for another century. Hill had hoped to turn next to a new edition of Johnson's *Lives of the Poets*, but persuaded by Sir Leslie Stephen, he fortunately turned aside to edit *Johnsonian Miscellanies* (1897), work on which was delayed by illness and the necessity of spending winters abroad. Meanwhile, on the side, he continued to publish other works.* The present-day scholar cannot help but feel humbled before the achievements of scholars of Hill's generation or of the nineteenth century generally. They were repeatedly delayed by illness, by a variety of tasks that consumed twelve hours a day, and yet, every three or four years, brought out a work that now seems to demand ten or fifteen years of leisure. But the truth is that, when we look back to that age of giants, we tend to regard them as a norm when they were really very much an exception. Hill is one of these great exceptions.

He died in February, 1901, but was able to complete beforehand the spaciously edited three volumes (published posthumously in 1905) of Johnson's *Lives of the Poets.*

Walter Jackson Bate

Harvard University
May, 1966

* Works or editions concerned simply with Johnson, or Johnson's circle, include: *Dr. Johnson: His Friends and His Critics* (1878), Boswell's *Correspondence with Erskine and His Journal of a Tour to Corsica* (1879), Boswell's *Life of Johnson* (6 vols., 1887), *Rasselas* (1887), *Wit and Wisdom of Samuel Johnson* (1888), *Select Essays of Johnson* (2 vols., 1889), *Footsteps of Dr. Johnson* (1890), *Letters of Samuel Johnson* (2 vols., 1892), *Johnsonian Miscellanies* (2 vols., 1897), and Johnson's *Lives of the Poets* (3 vols., 1905). Other works or editions include the books, mentioned above, on Sir Rowland Hill (2 vols., 1880) and Colonel Gordon (1880), Hume's letters to Strahan (1888), selections from Chesterfield (1891), *Harvard College by an Oxonian* (1894), Rossetti's letters to Allingham (1897), *Unpublished Letters of Dean Swift* (1899), Gibbon's *Memoirs* (1900), and *Letters Written by a Grandfather* (1903). A memoir of Hill, written by his nephew, Harold Spencer Scott, is prefixed to Vol. I of Hill's edition of the *Lives of the Poets* (1905).

TABLE OF CONTENTS

VOLUME I

PAGE

Prayers and Meditations, composed by Samuel Johnson, LL.D. . . 1

Annals: An Account of the Life of Dr. Samuel Johnson, from his Birth to his Eleventh Year, written by himself 125

Anecdotes of the late Samuel Johnson, LL.D., during the Last Twenty Years of his Life, by Hesther Lynch Piozzi 141

An Essay on the Life and Genius of Samuel Johnson, LL.D., by Arthur Murphy 353

VOLUME II

Apophthegms, &c., from Hawkins's Edition of Johnson's Works . . 1

Extracts from James Boswell's Letters to Edmond Malone . . . 21

Anecdotes from the Rev. Dr. Thomas Campbell's Diary of a Visit to England in 1775 39

Anecdotes from Pennington's Memoirs of Mrs. Carter 58

Anecdotes from Joseph Cradock's Memoirs 61

Anecdotes from Richard Cumberland's Memoirs 72

Extracts from Sir John Hawkins's Life of Johnson 79

Anecdotes from Miss Hawkins's Memoirs 139

Narrative by John Hoole of Johnson's end 145

Anecdotes from the Life of Johnson published by Kearsley . . . 161

Anecdotes by Lady Knight 171

Anecdotes from Hannah More's Memoirs 177

Anecdotes by Bishop Percy 208

Sir Joshua Reynolds on Johnson's Character 219

Sir Joshua Reynolds on Johnson's Influence 229

PAGE

Sir Joshua Reynolds's Two Dialogues in Imitation of Johnson s Style of Conversation—
- Dialogue I 232
- Dialogue II 237

Recollections of Dr. Johnson by Miss Reynolds 250
Anecdotes by William Seward 301
Anecdotes by George Steevens 312
Anecdotes from the Rev. Percival Stockdale's Memoirs 330
A Biographical Sketch of Dr. Samuel Johnson by Thomas Tyers . . 335
Narrative of the Last Week of Dr. Johnson's Life by the Right Hon. William Windham 382

MINOR ANECDOTES—
- By Robert Barclay 389
- By H. D. Best 390
- By Sir Brooke Boothby 391
- By the Rev. W. Cole 392
- By William Cooke 393
- From the European Magazine 394
- By Richard Green 397
- By T. Green 399
- By Ozias Humphry 400
- By Dr. Lettsom 402
- From Croker's Edition of Boswell's Life of Johnson 403
- By Dr. John Moore 408
- By John Nichols 409
- By the Rev. Mr. Parker 413
- By William Weller Pepys 416
- By the Rev. Hastings Robinson 417
- By Mrs. Rose 419
- From Shaw's History of Staffordshire 422
- Adam Smith on Dr. Johnson 423
- Dugald Stewart on Boswell's Anecdotes 425
- From Gilbert Stuart's History of the Rise of the Arts of Design in the United States 425
- By the Rev. Richard Warner 426
- By Mr. Wickins 427
- Styan Thirlby, by Dr. Johnson 430

PAGE

LETTERS OF DR. JOHNSON—
To Samuel Richardson 435
To Samuel Richardson 436
To Samuel Richardson 438
To Dr. George Hay 439
To the Rev. Thomas Percy 440
To the Rev. Thomas Percy 441
To the Rev. Edward Lye 441
To William Strahan 442
To James Macpherson 446
To —— 447
To the Rev. Dr. Taylor 447
To Miss Reynolds 448
To Miss Reynolds 449
To Miss Reynolds 450
To Miss Porter 450
To the Rev. Mr. Allen 451
To Miss Thrale 451
To the Rev. Dr. Taylor 452
To the Rev. James Compton 453
To Miss Reynolds 453
To Francesco Sastres 454
To Griffith Jones 454
To Miss Reynolds (enclosing a letter to be sent in her name to Sir Joshua Reynolds) 455

Sir Joshua Reynolds to Miss Reynolds 456
James Boswell to Sir Joshua Reynolds 457
James Boswell to Lord Thurlow 459
Sir Joshua Reynolds to James Boswell 460
Dr. Adams to Dr. Scott 460

ADDENDA 463

INDEX 469

DICTA PHILOSOPHI 511

PRAYERS AND MEDITATIONS

[Composed by SAMUEL JOHNSON, LL.D., and published from his manuscripts by GEORGE STRAHAN, D.D., Prebendary of Rochester, and Vicar of Islington in Middlesex. The fifth edition. LONDON: printed for T. CADELL, and W. DAVIES, in the Strand. 1817.]

PRAYERS AND MEDITATIONS

[THE title of *Prayers and Meditations* was not sufficiently comprehensive to describe this work, including as it did long passages from Johnson's journal. Many of his papers, which in no respect differ from those printed in this collection, fell into other hands than those of the editor. Some of these were printed by Hawkins and Boswell; others have appeared from time to time in various publications. One or two, which had remained hidden in the cabinets of collectors, see the light for the first time in the present volumes.

I have collated Strahan's edition with the original manuscripts preserved in the Library of Pembroke College, Oxford. Johnson's spelling I have carefully preserved, and some passages which had been struck out, but not obliterated, I have restored. There are, however, many lines so thoroughly scored out that not a single word can be deciphered. This, it can scarcely be doubted, was done by Johnson himself.

That he should have wished his friend to publish all that is included in these *Prayers and Meditations* almost passes belief. Most likely, when in the weakness of his last days he placed these papers in his hands, he forgot how much they contained that was meant for no eye but his own. Nevertheless his character gains much more than it loses by this full publication. If we are grieved by the pettiness of the records about the milk that he did, or did not put into his tea on Good Friday, on the other hand, our reverence for him is increased by the tenderness of heart and the humility which are seen in so many passages, and by the patience and courage with which he bore his grievous illnesses.]

PREFACE TO THE FIRST EDITION IN 1785.

THESE Posthumous Devotions of Dr. Johnson will be, no doubt, welcomed by the Public, with a distinction similar to that which has been already paid to his other Works.

During many years of his life, he statedly observed certain days[1] with a religious solemnity; on which, and other occasions, it was his custom to compose suitable Prayers and Meditations; committing them to writing for his own use, and, as he assured me, without any view to their publication. But being last summer on a visit to Oxford to the Reverend Dr. Adams[2], and that Gentleman urging him repeatedly to engage in some work of this kind, he then first conceived a design to revise these pious effusions, and bequeath them, with enlargements, to the use and benefit of others.

Infirmities, however, now growing fast upon him, he at length changed this design, and determined to give the Manuscripts, without revision, in charge to me, as I had long shared his intimacy, and was at this time his daily attendant. Accordingly, one morning, on my visiting him by desire at an early hour, he put these Papers into my hands, with instructions for committing them to the Press, and with a promise to prepare a sketch of his own life to accompany them. But the performance of this promise also was prevented, partly by his hasty destruction of some private memoirs, which he afterwards lamented, and partly by that incurable sickness, which soon ended in his dissolution.

. . . . .

That the authenticity of this Work may never be called in question, the original manuscript will be deposited in the library of Pembroke College in Oxford. . . . .

GEORGE STRAHAN.

ISLINGTON,
August 6, 1785.

[1] Viz., New Year's Day; March 28, the day on which his wife, Mrs. Elizabeth Johnson, died; Good Friday; Easter Day; and September the 18th, his own birthday.

[2] *Life*, iv. 293.

PRAYERS AND MEDITATIONS

1.

Oct. 1729. Desidiae valedixi; syrenis istius cantibus surdam posthac aurem obversurus [1].

2.

1729, *Dec.* S. J. Oxonio rediit [2].

3.

1732, *Julii* 15. Undecim aureos deposui, quo die quicquid ante matris funus (quod serum sit precor) de paternis bonis sperari licet, viginti scilicet libras, accepi. Usque adeo mihi fortuna fingenda est. Interea, ne paupertate vires animi languescant, nec in flagitia egestas abigat, cavendum [3].

[1] *Life*, i. 74. 'I bid farewell to Sloth, being resolved henceforth not to listen to her syren strains.' 'Vitanda est improba Siren Desidia.' HORACE, 2 *Satires*, iii. 14. Sir Walter Scott, early in his struggles with his load of debt, has this saying of Johnson's in mind. On March 2, 1826, he records:—'I would have given something to have lain still this morning and made up for lost time. But *desidiae valedixi*'; and on July 17:—'Desidiae tandem [1] valedixi.' Lockhart's *Scott*, ed. 1839, viii. 275, 382. '"Leisure and I," said Wesley, "have taken leave of one another."' Southey's *Wesley*, ed. 1846, ii. 383.

[2] Hawkins's *Johnson*, p. 16. For Johnson's departure from Oxford, see *Life*, i. 78, *n*. 2.

[3] *Life*, i. 80. 'I layed by eleven guineas on this day, when I received twenty pounds, being all that I have reason to hope for out of my father's effects, previous to the death of my mother; an event which I pray GOD

[1] In the *Journal of Sir Walter Scott*, ed. 1891, p. 228, not *tandem* but *longum*. Lockhart, I have observed, not unfrequently tacitly corrected Scott, especially in his misuse of *will* for *shall*.

Julii

4.

Julii 16 [? 1732]. Bosvortiam pedes petii [1].

5.

Friday, *August* 27 [1734], 10 at night. This day I have trifled away, except that I have attended the school in the morning. I read to-night in Rogers's sermons. To-night I began the breakfast law (*sic*) anew [2].

6.

Sept. 7, 1736 [3]. I have this day entered upon my 28th year. Mayest thou, O God, enable me for Jesus Christ's sake

may be very remote. I now therefore see that I must make my own fortune. Meanwhile, let me take care that the powers of my mind may not be debilitated by poverty, and that indigence do not force me into any criminal act.' *Ib.* Johnson left his father's freehold house in the possession of his mother till her death in 1759. *Letters*, i. 19, *n.* 1, 82. He had been driven from Oxford by his poverty; no public maintenance had been provided there for the poor scholar, though 'he had gained great applause' by his Latin version of Pope's *Messiah*. Two years after he entered upon his inheritance of twenty pounds, twenty thousand pounds of public money were spent on the voyage of the Princess Royal to the Hague. Lord Hervey's *Memoirs*, i. 437.

[1] *Life*, i. 84. Johnson went on foot to Market-Bosworth to fill the office of usher in the school of that town. Jonathan Boucher, who became usher in St. Bees' School in 1756, writes:—'My salary from the head-master was £10 a year; and entrances and cock-pennies amounted to as much more. The second year I got nearly £30.' *Letters of Radcliffe and James*, Preface, p. vii. 'The cock-penny was a customary payment at Shrovetide, formerly made to the schoolmaster in certain schools in the north of England. Originally applied to defray the expense of cock-fighting or cock-throwing.' *New Eng. Dict.* ii. 576. W. B. Scott, who was born in 1811, describing his childhood near Edinburgh, says:—'Our uncle still possessed the Bible his game-cock had won at the breaking-up time on the floor of the school.' *Life of W. B. Scott*, 1892, i. 30.

[2] Hawkins's *Johnson*, p. 163. Johnson stayed only a few months at Market-Bosworth. In 1734 he was again living in Lichfield. Rogers's sermons were probably *Sermons at Boyle's Lectures*, 1727, by the Rev. John Rogers, D.D.

[3] He was born on Sept. 7, Old Style—Sept. 18, New Style. The New Style was introduced on Sept. 3, 1752, which day was called the 14th. Unless that year he advanced his birthday and kept it on the 18th he did not observe the anniversary. With his dislike of keeping the day, he was perhaps glad to have it for once disappear. On Jan. 1, 1753, he notes down that he shall for the future use the New Style. *Post*, p. 13.

to

to spend this in such a manner that I may receive comfort from it at the hour of death and in the day of judgement. Amen.

I intend to-morrow to review the rules I have at any time laid down, in order to practise them [1].

7.

A PRAYER ON MY BIRTHDAY.

Sept. 7, 1738 [2].

O God, the Creatour and Preserver of all Mankind, Father of all mercies, I thine unworthy servant do give Thee most humble thanks, for all thy goodness and lovingkindness to me. I bless Thee for my Creation, Preservation, and Redemption, for the knowledge of thy Son Jesus Christ, for the means of Grace and the Hope of Glory. In the days of Childhood and Youth, in the midst of weakness, blindness, and danger, Thou hast protected me; amidst Afflictions of Mind, Body, and Estate, Thou hast supported me; and amidst vanity and Wickedness Thou hast spared me. Grant, O merciful Father, that I may have a lively sense of thy mercies. Create in me a contrite Heart, that I may worthily lament my sins and acknowlege my wickedness, and obtain Remission and forgiveness, through the satisfaction of Jesus Christ. And, O Lord, enable me, by thy Grace, to redeem the time which I have spent in Sloth, Vanity, and wickedness; to make use of thy Gifts to the honour of thy Name; to lead a new life in thy Faith, Fear, and Love; and finally to obtain everlasting Life. Grant this, Almighty Lord, for the merits and through the mediation of our most holy and blessed Saviour Jesus Christ; to whom, with Thee and the Holy Ghost, Three Persons and one God, be all honour and Glory, World without end. Amen.

Tr[anscribed] June 26, 1768 [3].

This is the first solemn [4] prayer, of which I have a copy. Whether I composed any before this, I question.

[1] Hawkins's *Johnson*, p. 163, and *Life*, i. 70.

[2] This was the first birthday after his settlement in London.

[3] *Post*, under 1768.

[4] He uses solemn, I conjecture, somewhat in the sense of the first of his definitions of that word in his *Dictionary—anniversary; observed once a year with religious ceremonies.* This paragraph is not in the manuscript.

PRAYER

8.

Prayer on Newyear's Day.

Jan. 1, $174\frac{4}{5}$.

Almighty and everlasting God, in whose hands are life and death, by whose will all things were created, and by whose providence they are sustained, I return thee thanks that Thou hast given me life, and that thou hast continued it to this time, that thou hast hitherto forborn to snatch me away in the midst of Sin and Folly, and hast permitted me still to enjoy the means of Grace, and vouchsafed to call me yet again to Repentance. Grant, O merciful Lord, that thy Call may not be vain, that my Life may not be continued to encrease my Guilt, and that thy gracious Forbearance may not harden my heart in wickedness. Let me remember, O my God, that as Days and Years pass over me, I approach nearer to the Grave, where there is no repentance[1], and grant, that by the assistance of thy Holy Spirit, I may so pass through this Life, that I may obtain Life everlasting, for the Sake of our Lord Jesus Christ. Amen.

9.

Jan. 1, $174\frac{7}{8}$.

Almighty and most merciful Father, who hast not yet suffered me to fall into the Grave, grant that I may so remember my past Life, as to repent of the days and years which I have spent in forgetfulness of thy mercy, and neglect of my own Salvation, and so use the time which thou shalt yet allow me, as that I may become every day more diligent in the duties which in thy Providence shall be assigned me, and that when at last I shall be called to judgement I may be received as a good and faithful servant into everlasting happiness, for the sake of Jesus Christ our Lord. Amen.

[1] Nevertheless he later on thought it possible, and perhaps even probable, that the dead might receive benefit from the prayers of the living. *Post*, pp. 14, 15.

Almighty

10.

Jan. 1, $17\frac{49}{50}$, after 3 in the morning.

Almighty God, by whose will I was created, and by whose Providence I have been sustained, by whose mercy I have been called to the knowledge of my Redeemer, and by whose Grace whatever I have thought or acted acceptable to thee has been inspired and directed, grant, O Lord, that in reviewing my past life, I may recollect [1] thy mercies to my preservation [2], in whatever state thou preparest for me, that in affliction I may remember how often I have been succoured, and in Prosperity may know and confess from whose hand the blessing is received. Let me, O Lord, so remember my sins, that I may abolish them by true repentance, and so improve the Year to which thou hast graciously extended my life, and all the years which thou shalt yet allow me, that I may hourly become purer in thy sight; so that I may live in thy fear, and die in thy favour, and find mercy at the last day, for the sake of Jesus Christ. Amen.

11.

Prayer on the Rambler [3].

Almighty God, the giver of all good things, without whose help all Labour is ineffectual, and without whose grace all wisdom is folly, grant, I beseech Thee, that in this my undertaking, thy Holy Spirit may not be withheld from me, but that I may promote thy glory, and the Salvation both of myself and others; grant this, O Lord, for the sake of Jesus Christ. Amen.

[1] *improve*, scored out.

[2] *support and comfort*, scored out.

[3] Quoted in the *Life*, i. 202.

The first paper of the *Rambler* was published on March 20, 1749-50. In the original manuscript there is written after this prayer:—'Lord bless me. So be it.' Through these words a pen has been drawn.

In the last paragraph of the last *Rambler*, Johnson says:—'The essays professedly serious, if I have been able to execute my own intentions, will be found exactly conformable to the precepts of Christianity, without any accommodation to the licentiousness and levity of the present age. I therefore look back on this part of my work with pleasure, which no blame or praise of man shall diminish or augment.'

12.

PRAYERS COMPOSED BY ME ON THE DEATH OF MY WIFE[1], AND REPOSITED AMONG HER MEMORIALS, MAY 8, 1752[2].

Deus exaudi.—Heu!

April 24, 1752.

Almighty and most merciful Father, who lovest those whom Thou punishest, and turnest away thy anger from the penitent, look down with pity upon my sorrows, and grant that the affliction which it has pleased Thee to bring upon me, may awaken my conscience, enforce my resolutions of a better life, and impress upon me such conviction of thy power and goodness, that I may place in Thee my only felicity, and endeavour to please Thee in all my thoughts, words, and actions. Grant, O Lord, that I may not languish in fruitless and unavailing sorrow[3], but that I may consider from whose hand all good and evil is received, and may remember that I am punished for my sins, and hope for comfort only by repentance. Grant, O merciful God, that by the assistance of thy Holy Spirit I may repent, and be comforted, obtain that peace which the world cannot give, pass the residue of my life in humble resignation and cheerful obedience; and when it shall please Thee to call me from this mortal state, resign myself into thy hands with faith and confidence, and finally obtain mercy and everlasting happiness, for the sake of Jesus Christ our Lord. Amen.

13.

April 25, 1752.

O Lord, our heavenly Father, almighty and most merciful God, in whose hands are life and death, who givest and takest away, castest down and raisest up, look with mercy on the affliction of thy unworthy servant, turn away thine anger from me, and speak peace to my troubled soul. Grant me the

[1] She had died on March 17, O. S. (March 28, N. S.) of this year. *Life*, i. 234.

[2] The following prayers to that of April 22, 1753, are not in the Pembroke College MSS.

[3] For his exhortations against unavailing sorrow, see *Letters*, ii. 4, *n.* 1, 215.

assistance

assistance and comfort of thy Holy Spirit, that I may remember with thankfulness the blessings so long enjoyed by me in the society of my departed wife; make me so to think on her precepts and example, that I may imitate whatever was in her life acceptable in thy sight, and avoid all by which she offended Thee. Forgive me, O merciful Lord, all my sins, and enable me to begin and perfect that reformation which I promised her, and to persevere in that resolution, which she implored Thee to continue, in the purposes which I recorded in thy sight, when she lay dead before me[1], in obedience to thy laws, and faith in thy word. And now, O Lord, release me from my sorrow, fill me with just hopes, true faith, and holy consolations, and enable me to do my duty in that state of life to which Thou hast been pleased to call me, without disturbance from fruitless grief, or tumultuous imaginations; that in all my thoughts, words, and actions, I may glorify thy Holy Name, and finally obtain, what I hope Thou hast granted to thy departed servant, everlasting joy and felicity, through our Lord Jesus Christ. Amen.

14.

April 26, 1752, being after 12 at Night of the 25th.

O Lord! Governour of heaven and earth, in whose hands are embodied and departed Spirits, if thou hast ordained the Souls of the Dead to minister to the Living, and appointed my departed Wife to have care of me, grant that I may enjoy the good effects of her attention and ministration, whether exercised by appearance, impulses, dreams or in any other manner agreeable to thy Government. Forgive my presumption, enlighten my ignorance, and however meaner agents are employed, grant me the blessed influences of thy holy Spirit, through Jesus Christ our Lord. Amen[2].

[1] See *post*, p. 25, for his resolution 'to consult the resolves on Tetty's coffin.' 'Tetty or Tetsey is provincially used as a contraction for Elisabeth.' *Life*, i. 98.

[2] *Life*, i. 235.

'The universal attention which has been paid to dreams in all ages, proves that the superstition is natural; and I have heard too many well-attested facts (facts to which belief could not be refused upon any known laws of evidence) not to believe that impressions are some-

O Lord

15.

May 6, 1752.

O Lord, our heavenly Father, without whom all purposes are frustrate, all efforts are vain, grant me the assistance of thy Holy Spirit, that I may not sorrow as one without hope, but may now return to the duties of my present state with humble confidence in thy protection, and so govern my thoughts and actions, that neither business may withdraw my mind from Thee, nor idleness lay me open to vain imaginations; that neither praise may fill me with pride, nor censure with discontent; but that in the changes of this life, I may fix my heart upon the reward which Thou hast promised to them that serve Thee, and that whatever things are true, whatever things are honest, whatever things are just, whatever are pure, whatever are lovely, whatever are of good report, wherein there is virtue, wherein there is praise, I may think upon and do[1], and obtain mercy and everlasting happiness. Grant this, O Lord, for the sake of Jesus Christ. Amen.

Our Father, &c.—The grace, &c.

May 6. I used this service, written *April* 24, 25, *May* 6, as preparatory to my return to life to-morrow.

Μακάριοι οἱ νεκροὶ οἱ ἐν Κυρίῳ ἀποθνήσκοντες ἀπάρτι[2].

Apoc. xiv. 13.

16.

Before any new Study.

November.

Almighty God, in whose hands are all the powers of man; who givest understanding, and takest it away; who, as it seemeth

times made in this manner, and forewarnings communicated, which cannot be explained by material philosophy or mere metaphysics.' Southey. *Life of Wesley*, i. 359. Coleridge, in his copy of this work, wrote in the margin opposite the last line:—'Would it not have been *safer* to have said, "which *have not been*, instead of *cannot be*"?'

[1] 'Finally brethren, whatsoever things are true, whatsoever things are honest, whatsoever things are just, whatsoever things are pure, whatsoever things are lovely, whatsoever things are of good report; if there be any virtue and if there be any praise, think on these things.' *Philippians*, iv. 8.

[2] 'Blessed are the dead which die in the Lord from henceforth.'

good

good unto Thee, enlightenest the thoughts of the simple, and darkenest the meditations of the wise, be present with me in my studies and enquiries.

Grant, O Lord, that I may not lavish away the life which Thou hast given me on useless trifles, nor waste it in vain searches after things which Thou hast hidden from me.

Enable me, by thy Holy Spirit, so to shun sloth and negligence, that every day may discharge part of the task which Thou hast allotted me; and so further with thy help that labour which, without thy help, must be ineffectual, that I may obtain, in all my undertakings, such success as will most promote thy glory, and the salvation of my own soul, for the sake of Jesus Christ. Amen.

17.

AFTER TIME NEGLIGENTLY AND UNPROFITABLY SPENT.

November 19.

O Lord, in whose hands are life and death, by whose power I am sustained, and by whose mercy I am spared, look down upon me with pity. Forgive me, that I have this day neglected the duty which Thou hast assigned to it, and suffered the hours, of which I must give account, to pass away without any endeavour to accomplish thy will, or to promote my own salvation. Make me to remember, O God, that every day is thy gift, and ought to be used according to thy command. Grant me, therefore, so to repent of my negligence, that I may obtain mercy from Thee, and pass the time which Thou shalt yet allow me, in diligent performance of thy commands, through Jesus Christ. Amen.

18.

Jan. 1, 1753, N. S. which I shall use for the future.

Almighty God, who hast continued my life to this day, grant that, by the assistance of thy Holy Spirit, I may improve the time which thou shalt grant me, to my eternal salvation. Make me to remember, to thy glory, thy judgements and thy mercies. Make me so to consider the loss of my wife, whom thou hast taken from me, that it may dispose me, by thy grace, to lead

the

the residue of my life in thy fear. Grant this, O Lord, for Jesus Christ's sake. Amen [1].

19.

March 28, 1753. I kept this day as the anniversary of my Tetty's death, with prayer and tears in the morning. In the evening I prayed for her conditionally, if it were lawful [2].

20.

Apr. 3, 1753. I began the second vol. of my Dictionary, room being left in the first for Preface, Grammar, and History, none of them yet begun.

O God, who hast hitherto supported me, enable me to proceed in this labour, and in the whole task of my present state; that when I shall render up, at the last day, an account of the talent

[1] *Life*, i. 251.

Boswell in his *Hebrides* (*Life*, v. 53) says that Johnson, on starting from Edinburgh, left behind in an open drawer in Boswell's house 'one volume of a pretty full and curious diary of his life of which I have a few fragments.' He also states (*ib.* iv. 405):—'I owned to him, that having accidentally seen them [two quarto volumes of his *Life*] I had read a great deal in them.' It would seem that he had also transcribed a portion, for he says that the above entry he 'transcribed from that part of the diary which Johnson burnt a few days before his death.'

[2] *Life*, i. 236.

Following the change of style he kept the 28th instead of the 17th.

For prayers for the dead and the doctrine of a middle state, see *Life*, i. 240; ii. 104, 162; v. 356. 'John Rolland (writes Ramsay of Ochtertyre) showed me an excerpt from one of Boswell's settlements, in which he requests the prayers of all good Christians for his soul after its departure—which, he says, may benefit it, and cannot possibly do it harm.' *Scotland and Scotsmen in the Eighteenth Century*, i. 175.

Hume, writing of the articles of faith decided by Convocation in 1536, says:—'The article with regard to purgatory contains the most curious jargon, ambiguity, and hesitation, arising from the mixture of opposite tenets. It was to this purpose:—"Since according to due order of charity and the book of Maccabees and divers ancient authors it is a very good and charitable deed to pray for souls departed, and since such a practice has been maintained in the Church from the beginning; all bishops and teachers should instruct the people not to be grieved for the continuance of the same. But since the place where departed souls are retained before they reach Paradise, as well as the nature of their pains, is left uncertain by Scripture, all such questions are to be submitted to God, to whose mercy it is meet and convenient to commend the deceased, trusting that he accepteth our prayers for them.' *Hist. of Eng.* ed. 1773, iv. 167.

committed

committed to me, I may receive pardon, for the sake of Jesus Christ. Amen[1].

21.

PRAYER ON EASTER DAY.

Ap. 22, 1753.

O Lord, who givest the grace of Repentance, and hearest the prayers of the penitent, grant, that by true contrition, I may obtain forgiveness of all the sins committed, and of all duties neglected, in my union with the Wife whom thou hast taken from me, for the neglect of joint devotion, patient exhortation, and mild instruction. And, O Lord, who canst change evil to good, grant that the loss of my Wife may so mortify all inordinate affections in me, that I may henceforth please thee by holiness of Life.

And, O Lord, so far as it may be lawful for me, I commend to thy fatherly goodness the Soul of my departed wife[2]; beseeching thee to grant her whatever is best in her present state, and finally to receive her to eternal happiness. All this I beg for Jesus Christ's sake, whose death I am now about to commemorate. To whom, &c. Amen[3].

This I repeated sometimes at church.

22.

April 23, 1753. I know not whether I do not too much indulge the vain longings of affection; but I hope they intenerate my heart, and that when I die like my Tetty, this affection will be acknowledged in a happy interview, and that in the mean time I am incited by it to piety. I will, however, not deviate too much from common and received methods of devotion[4].

[1] *Life*, i. 255.

[2] He had begun to write wife with a capital letter, but scored it out.

[3] Most of this prayer is quoted in the *Life*, i. 240.

[4] *Life*, i. 237. It was, no doubt, in his conditional prayers for his wife that he deviated from 'the common and received methods of devotion.'

A few weeks after Johnson made this entry Gibbon joined the Church of Rome. 'On the eighth of June, 1753, I solemnly, though privately, abjured the errors of heresy.' Gibbon's *Misc. Writ.* i. 64.

[Undated

23.

[Undated; probably 1753.]

I do not remember that since I left Oxford I ever rose early by mere choice, but once or twice at Edial, and two or three times for the *Rambler*[1].

24.

Fl. Lacr.[2] *March* 28, in the Morning.

O God, who on this day wert pleased to take from me my dear Wife, sanctify to me my sorrows and reflections. Grant, that I may renew and practise the resolutions which I made when thy afflicting hand was upon me. Let the remembrance of thy judgements by which my wife is taken away awaken me to repentance, and the sense of thy mercy by which I am spared, strengthen my hope and confidence in Thee, that by the assistance and comfort of thy holy spirit I may so pass through things temporal, as finally to gain everlasting happiness, and to pass by a holy and happy death, into the joy which thou hast prepared for those that love thee. Grant this, O Lord, for the sake of Jesus Christ. Amen.

The melancholy of this day hung long upon me.

Of the resolutions made this day[3] I, in some measure kept that of breaking from indolence.

25.

March 28, 1754, at Night.

Almighty God, vouchsafe to sanctify unto me the reflections and resolutions of this day[3], let not my sorrow be unprofitable; let not my resolutions be vain. Grant that my grief may produce true repentance, so that I may live to please thee, and when the time shall come that I must die like her whom thou hast taken from me, grant me eternal happiness in thy presence, through Jesus Christ our Lord. Amen.

[1] *Life*, ii. 143.
'Burton's *Anatomy of Melancholy*, he said, was the only book that ever took him out of bed two hours sooner than he wished to rise.' *Ib.* ii. 121.

[2] 'We presume to interpret *flentibus lacrymis*.' *Gent. Mag.* 1785, ii. 731.

[3] He at first wrote: Almighty God, by whose grace I have this day endeavoured.

July

26.

July 13, 1755. Having lived not without an habitual reverence for the Sabbath, yet without that attention to its religious duties which Christianity requires, [I resolve]

1. To rise early, and in order to it, to go to sleep early on Saturday.

2. To use some extraordinary devotion in the morning.

3. To examine the tenour of my life, and particularly the last week; and to mark my advances in religion, or recession from it.

4. To read the Scripture methodically with such helps as are at hand.

5. To go to church twice.

6. To read books of Divinity, either speculative or practical.

7. To instruct my family.

8. To wear off by meditation any worldly soil contracted in the week[1].

27.

ON THE STUDY OF PHILOSOPHY, AS AN INSTRUMENT OF LIVING[2].

July.

O Lord, who hast ordained labour to be the lot of man, and seest the necessities of all thy creatures, bless my studies and endeavours; feed me with food convenient for me; and if it shall be thy good pleasure to intrust me with plenty, give me

[1] *Life*, i. 303. 'Sunday (said Johnson) was a heavy day to me when I was a boy. My mother confined me on that day, and made me read *The Whole Duty of Man*, from a great part of which I could derive no instruction.' *Ib.* i. 67. See *post*, under April 16, 1781. For his unwillingness to attend church see *Life*, i. 67, *n.* 2, and for the observance of Sunday, *ib.* ii. 72, 376; v. 69.

[2] This prayer is not in the Pembroke College MSS. See *Life*, i. 302.

The *Dictionary* on which he had been working for nearly eight years had been published in the previous April. He was now casting about for fresh employment. Though he did not, he says, pursue the study of philosophy, nevertheless in the imaginary University which he and Boswell planned, he was to teach 'logick, metaphysicks, and scholastick divinity.' *Life*, v. 109.

Hume wrote in 1764: 'Civil employments for men of letters can scarcely be found: all is occupied by men of business or by parliamentary interest.' Burton's *Hume*, ii. 187.

a compassionate heart, that I may be ready to relieve the wants of others; let neither poverty nor riches estrange my heart from Thee, but assist me with thy grace so to live as that I may die in thy favour, for the sake of Jesus Christ. Amen.

This study was not persued.

Transcribed June 26, 1768 [1].

28.

Jan. 1, 1756, Afternoon.

Almighty and everlasting God, in whom we live and move, and have our being, glory be to thee, for my recovery from sickness, and the continuance of my Life [2]. Grant O my God that I may improve the year which I am now begining, and all the days which thou shalt add to my life, by serious repentance and diligent obedience, that, by the help of thy holy Spirit I may use the means of Grace to my own salvation, and at last enjoy thy presence in eternal happiness, for Jesus Christ's sake. Amen.

29.

HILL BOOTHBY'S DEATH [3].

January, 1756.

O Lord God, almighty disposer of all things, in whose hands are life and death, who givest comforts and takest them away, I return Thee thanks for the good example of Hill Boothby, whom Thou hast now taken away, and implore thy grace, that I may improve the opportunity of instruction which Thou hast afforded me, by the knowledge of her life, and by the sense of her death; that I may consider the uncertainty of my present state, and apply myself earnestly to the duties which Thou hast set before me, that living in thy fear, I may die in thy favour, through Jesus Christ our Lord. Amen.

I commend, &c. W. and H. B.[4]

Transcribed June 26, 1768.

[1] See *post*, under 1768.

[2] For his illness see *Letters*, i. 45–52.

[3] This prayer is not in the Pembroke College MSS.

[4] For Hill Boothby see *Letters*, i. 45–53. She died on Jan. 16. 'I have heard Baretti say,' writes Mrs. Piozzi, 'that when this lady died Johnson was almost distracted with his grief.' Piozzi's *Anecdotes*, p. 161. William was a common name in the Boothby family. Perhaps 'W. and H. B.' stands for William and Hill Boothby.

WHEN

30.

When my Eye was restored to its Use.

February 15, 1756[1].

Almighty God, who hast restored light to my eye[2], and enabled me to persue again the studies which Thou hast set before me; teach me, by the diminution of my sight, to remember that whatever I possess is thy gift, and by its recovery, to hope for thy mercy: and, O Lord, take not thy Holy Spirit from me; but grant that I may use thy bounties according to thy will, through Jesus Christ our Lord. Amen.

31.

Introductory Prayer.

O God who desirest not the death of a Sinner, look down with mercy upon me now daring to call upon thee. Let thy Holy Spirit so purify my affections, and exalt my desires that my prayer may be acceptable in thy sight, through Jesus Christ. Amen.

March 25, 1756.

32.

March 28, —56, about two in the morning.

Almighty God, our heavenly father whose judgments terminate in mercy grant, I beseech Thee, that the remembrance of my Wife, whom Thou hast taken from me, may not load my soul with unprofitable sorrow, but may excite in me true repentance of my sins and negligences, and by the operation of thy Grace may produce in me a new life pleasing to thee. Grant that the loss of my Wife may teach me the true use of the Blessings which are yet left me; and that, however bereft of worldly comforts[3], I may find peace and refuge in thy service through Jesus Christ our Lord. Amen.

[1] This prayer is not in the Pembroke College MSS.

[2] Four days later he wrote: 'The inflammation is come again into my eye.' *Letters*, i. 57. See also *Life*, i. 305.

[3] At first he wrote: 'that however solitary.'

33.

Jan. 1, 1757, at two in the Morning.

Almighty God, who hast brought me to the beginning of another year, and by prolonging my life invitest to repentance, forgive me that I have mispent the time past, enable me from this instant to amend my life according to thy holy Word, grant[1] me thy Holy Spirit, that I may so pass through things temporal as not finally to lose the things eternal. O God, hear my prayer for the sake of Jesus Christ. Amen.

34.

EASTER EVE, 1757.

Almighty God, heavenly Father, who desirest not the death of a sinner, look down with mercy upon me depraved with vain imaginations, and entangled in long habits of sin. Grant me that grace without which I can neither will nor do what is acceptable to thee. Pardon my sins, remove the impediments that hinder my obedience. Enable me to shake off sloth, and to redeem the time mispent in idleness and sin by a diligent application of the days yet remaining to the duties which thy Providence shall allot me. O God, grant me thy Holy Spirit that I may repent and amend my life, grant me contrition, grant me resolution for the sake of Jesus Christ, to whose covenant I now implore admission, of the benefits of whose death I implore participation. For his sake have mercy on me, O God; for his sake, O God, pardon and receive me. Amen.

35.

PRAYER.

Sept. 18, 1757.

Almighty and most merciful Father by whose providence my life has been prolonged, and who hast granted me now to begin another year of probation, vouchsafe me such assistance of thy Holy Spirit, that the continuance of my life may not add to the measure of my guilt, but that I may so repent of the days and years passed in neglect of the duties which thou hast set before

[1] The rest of the prayer he at first scored through, but afterwards added 'Stet.'

me

me, in vain thoughts, in sloth, and in folly, that I may apply my heart to true wisdom, by diligence redeem the time lost, and by repentance obtain pardon, for the sake of JESUS CHRIST. Amen [1].

36.

EASTER DAY, *March* 26, 1758.

Almighty and most merciful Father, who hast created me to love and to serve thee, enable [me] so to partake of the sacrament in which the Death of Jesus Christ is commemorated that I may henceforward lead a new life in thy faith and fear. Thou who knowest my frailties and infirmities strengthen and support me. Grant me thy Holy Spirit, that after all my lapses I may now continue stedfast in obedience, that after long habits of negligence and sin, I may, at last, work out my salvation with diligence and constancy, purify my thoughts from pollutions, and fix my affections on things eternal. Much of my time past has been lost in sloth, let not what remains, O Lord, be given me in vain, but let me from this time lead a better life and serve thee with a quiet mind through Jesus Christ our Lord. Amen.

37.

March 28, 1758.

Almighty and eternal God, who givest life and takest it away, grant that while thou shalt prolong [2] my continuance on earth, I may live with a due sense of thy mercy and forbearance, and let the remembrance of her whom thy hand has separated from me, teach me to consider the shortness and uncertainty of life, and to use all diligence to obtain eternal happiness in thy presence. O God enable me to avoid sloth, and to attend heedfully and constantly to thy word and worship. Whatever was good in the example of my departed wife, teach me to follow; and whatever was amiss give me grace to shun, that my affliction may be sanctified, and that remembering how much every day brings me nearer to the grave, I may every day purify my mind, and amend my life, by the assistance of

[1] At the foot of the page he had written but scored out: 'Idleness —intemperate sleep—dilatoriness, inmethodical life. Negligence of Worship.'

[2] He had at first written: 'Make me to enjoy the time for which thou shalt' &c.

thy

thy holy Spirit, till at last I shall be accepted by Thee, for Jesus Christ's sake. Amen.

38.

Sept. 18, 1758, horâ primâ matutinâ.

Almighty and most merciful Father, who yet sparest and yet supportest me, who supportest me in my weakness, and sparest me in my sins, and hast now granted to me to begin another year, enable me to improve the time which is yet before me, to thy glory and my own Salvation. Impress upon my Soul such repentance of the days mispent in idleness and folly, that I may henceforward diligently attend to the business of my station in this world [1], and to all the duties which thou hast commanded. Let thy Holy Spirit comfort and guide me that in my passage through the pains or pleasures of the present state, I may never be tempted to forgetfulness of Thee. Let my life be useful, and my death be happy [2]; let me live according to thy laws, and dye with just confidence in thy mercy for the sake of Jesus Christ our Lord. Amen.

This year I hope to learn diligence [3].

39.

Jan. 23, 1759.

The day on which my dear Mother was buried. Repeated on my fast, with the addition [4].

Almighty God, merciful Father, in whose hands are life and death, sanctify unto me the sorrow which I now feel. Forgive me whatever I have done unkindly to my Mother, and whatever I have omitted to do kindly. Make me to remember her good precepts, and good example, and to reform my life according to

[1] At first he had written: 'the duties which thou shalt assign me, and to the duties by which.'

[2] At first he had written 'useful.'

[3] This line is quoted in the *Life*, i. 331.

[4] For the death of his mother see *Life*, i. 339, and *Letters*, i. 75-81. The fast was held on March 24, as the next entry shows.

It is a striking illustration of the way in which different generations overlap each other that Jeremy Bentham's mother died about a fortnight before Johnson's mother. Bentham's *Works*, x. 26. Mrs. Johnson was born nine years after the Restoration, and Bentham died the day before the first Reform Bill was carried.

thy

thy holy word, that I may lose no more opportunities of good; I am sorrowful, O Lord, let not my sorrow be without fruit. Let it be followed by holy resolutions, and lasting amendment, that when I shall die like my mother, I may be received to everlasting life.

I commend, O Lord, so far as it may be lawful, into thy hands, the soul of my departed Mother, beseeching Thee to grant her whatever is most beneficial to Her in her present state.

O Lord, grant me thy Holy Spirit, and have mercy upon me for Jesus Christ's sake. Amen.

And, O Lord, grant unto me that am now about to return to the common comforts and business of the world, such moderation in all enjoyments, such diligence in honest labour, and such purity of mind, that, amidst the changes, miseries, or pleasures of life, I may keep my mind fixed upon thee, and improve every day in grace, till I shall be received into thy kingdom of eternal happiness.

I returned thanks for my mother's good example, and implored pardon for neglecting it.

I returned thanks for the alleviation of my sorrow.

The dream of my brother[1] I shall remember.

40.

jej.[2]

March the 24, 1759, rather 25, after 12 at night.

Almighty God, heavenly Father, who hast graciously prolonged my life to this time, and by the change of outward things which I am now to make[3], callest me to a change of inward affections, and to a reformation of my thoughts words and practices. Vouchsafe merciful Lord that this call may not be vain. Forgive me whatever has been amiss in the state which I am now leaving, Idleness, and neglect of thy word and worship. Grant me the grace of thy Holy Spirit, that the course which I am now begining may proceed according to thy laws, and end

[1] His brother died in 1737. *Life*, i. 90.

[2] *Jej.* I conjecture is put for *Jejunus, fasting.*

[3] He had moved on the 23rd from Gough Square to Staple Inn. *Letters*, i. 86. See also *Life*, i. 350.

in the enjoyment of thy favour [1]. Give me, O Lord, pardon and peace, that I may serve thee with humble confidence, and after this life enjoy thy presence in eternal Happiness.

And, O Lord, so far as it may be lawful for me, I commend to thy Fatherly goodness, my Father, my Brother, my Wife, my Mother. I beseech thee to look mercifully upon them, and grant them whatever may most promote their present and eternal joy.

O Lord, hear my prayers for Jesus Christs sake, to whom, with Thee and the Holy Ghost three persons and one God be all honour and glory world without end. Amen [2].

O Lord, let the change which I am now making in outward things, produce in [me] such a change of manners, as may fit me for the great change through which my Wife has passed [3].

41.

EASTER DAY, *April* 15, 1759 [4].

Almighty and most merciful Father, look down with pity upon my sins. I am a sinner, good Lord; but let not my sins burthen me for ever. Give me thy grace to break the chain of evil custom. Enable me to shake off idleness and sloth; to will and to do what thou hast commanded; grant me chaste [5] in thoughts, words and actions; to love and frequent thy worship, to study and understand thy word; to be diligent in my calling, that I may support myself and relieve others.

Forgive me, O Lord, whatever my mother has suffered by my fault, whatever I have done amiss, and whatever duty I have neglected. Let me not sink into useless dejection; but so sanctify my affliction, O Lord, that I may be converted and

[1] This paragraph is quoted in the *Life*, i. 350.

[2] Boswell adduces this prayer as proof of Johnson's 'orthodox belief in the sacred mystery of the Trinity.' *Life*, ii. 254.

[3] The following words are scored out:—

At the place where I commended her.

At the place where she died.

As much of the prayer as I can remember of Easter 17 [*sic*].

Use the lines on this page.

On another page is written:—

Uxbridge, 13. 9.

Wicombe, 10. 6.

Tetsworth, 10. 6.

If my mother had lived till March, she would have been eighty-nine.

[4] Croker's *Boswell*, x. 130.

[5] Johnson does not give in his *Dictionary* such a construction as 'grant me chaste.'

healed

healed; and that, by the help of thy holy spirit, I may obtain everlasting life through Jesus Christ our Lord.

And, O Lord, so far as it may be lawful, I commend unto thy fatherly goodness my father, brother, wife, and mother, beseeching thee to make them happy for Jesus Christ's sake. Amen.

42.

Sept. 18, 1760, resolved D. j.[1]

To combat notions of obligation[2].
To apply to study.
To reclaim imagination.
To consult the resolves on Tetty's coffin[3].
To rise early.
To study Religion.
To go to Church.
To drink less strong liquors[4].
To keep Journal.
To oppose laziness, by doing what is to [be] done to morrow.
Rise as early as I can.
Send for books for Hist. of war[5].
Put books in order[6].
Scheme life[7].

[1] Deo juvante.

[2] He had, I conjecture, been tempted to bind himself by a vow in order to force himself to do what he thought he ought to do. Against vows he more than once strongly protested. 'Do not accustom yourself,' he wrote to Boswell, 'to enchain your volatility by vows; they will sometime leave a thorn in your mind, which you will perhaps never be able to extract or eject.' *Life*, ii. 21. 'A vow is a horrible thing, it is a snare for sin.' *Ib.* iii. 357. See also *Letters*, i. 217. See *post*, p. 30, where he records:—'I resolved in the presence of God but without a vow' &c. This would seem to show that he had once made vows.

[3] *Ante*, p. 11.

[4] For his use of strong liquors and his long periods of abstinence, see *Life*, i. 103, *n*. 3.

[5] Boswell assumes that he meant to write a history of the war that the first Pitt was carrying on in a succession of triumphs. It is possible that it was a history of war in general that he had in view. *Ib.* i. 354.

[6] 'On Wednesday, April 3, [1776], in the morning I found him very busy putting his books in order, and as they were generally very old ones clouds of dust were flying around him. He had on a pair of large gloves such as hedgers use. His present appearance put me in mind of my uncle Dr. Boswell's description of him, "A robust genius, born to grapple with whole libraries."' *Life*, iii. 7.

[7] 'I have,' he said, 'from the

O Almighty

O Almighty God, merciful Father, who hast continued my life to another year grant that I may spend the time which thou shalt yet give me in such obedience to thy word and will that finally, I may obtain everlasting life. Grant that I may repent and forsake my sins before the miseries of age fall upon me, and that while my strength yet remains I may use it to thy glory and my own salvation, by the assistance of thy Holy Spirit, for Jesus Christ's sake. Amen.

43.

EASTER EVE, 1761.

Since the Communion of last Easter I have led a life so dissipated and useless, and my terrours and perplexities have so much encreased, that I am under great depression and discouragement, yet I purpose to present myself before God to-morrow with humble hope that he will not break the bruised reed,

Come unto me all ye that travail.

I have resolved, I hope not presumptuously, till I am afraid to resolve again. Yet hoping in God I stedfastly purpose to lead a new life. O God, cnable me, for Jesus Christ's sake.

My purpose is

To avoid Idleness.

To regulate my sleep as to length and choice of hours.

To set down every day what shall be done the day following.

To keep a Journal.

To worship God more diligently.

To go to Church every Sunday.

To study the Scriptures.

To read a certain portion every week.

Almighty and most merciful Father look down upon my misery with pity, strengthen me that I may overcome all sinful habits, grant that I may with effectual faith commemorate the death of thy Son Jesus Christ, so that all corrupt desires may be extinguished, and all vain thoughts may be dispelled. Enlighten

earliest time almost that I can remember been forming schemes of a better life.' *Post*, p. 31. The evening before he was struck with the palsy, he was still 'planning schemes of life.' *Life*, iv. 230.

me

me with true knowledge, animate me with reasonable hope, comfort me with a just sense of thy love, and assist me to the performance of all holy purposes, that after the sins, errours, and miseries of this world, I may obtain everlasting happiness for Jesus Christ's sake. To whom, &c. Amen.

I hope to attend on God in his ordinances to-morrow.

Trust in God O my soul. O God, let me trust in Thee[1].

44.

March, 28, 1762.

God grant that I may from this day
Return to my studies.
Labour diligently.
Rise early.
Live temperately.
Read the Bible.
Go to church.

O God, Giver and Preserver of all life, by whose power I was created, and by whose providence I am sustained, look down upon me [with] tenderness and mercy, grant that I may not have been created to be finally destroyed, that I may not be preserved to add wickedness to wickedness[2], but may so repent me of my sins, and so order my life to come, that when I shall be called hence like the wife whom Thou hast taken from me, I may dye in peace and in thy favour, and be received into thine everlasting kingdom through the merits and mediation of Jesus Christ thine only Son our Lord and Saviour. Amen.

45.

[1764.]

Almighty and most merciful Father, who by thy son Jesus Christ hast redeemed man from Sin and Death, grant that the commemoration of his passion may quicken my repentance, encrease my hope, and strengthen my faith and enlarge my Charity; that I may lament and forsake my sins and for the time which thou shalt yet grant me, may avoid Idleness, and neglect of thy word and worship. Grant me strength to be

[1] The last clause has been added in pencil.

[2] Quoted in the *Life*, iv. 397.

diligent in the lawful employments which shall be set before me; Grant me purity of thoughts, words, and actions. Grant me to love and study thy word, and to frequent thy worship with pure affection. Deliver and preserve me from vain terrours, and grant that by the Grace of thy Holy Spirit I may so live that after this life ended, I may be received to everlasting happiness for the sake of Jesus Christ our Lord. Amen.

46.

April 20, 1764, GOOD FRYDAY.

I have made no reformation, I have lived totally useless, more sensual in thought and more addicted to wine and meat [1], grant me, O God, to amend my life for the sake of Jesus Christ. Amen.

I hope

To put my rooms in order *.

I fasted all day.

*Disorder I have found one great cause of idleness [2].

47.

April 21, 1764,-3-m.

My indolence, since my last reception of the Sacrament [3], has sunk into grosser sluggishness, and my dissipation spread into wilder negligence. My thoughts have been clouded with sensuality, and, except that from the beginning of this year I have in some measure forborn excess of Strong Drink my appetites have predominated over my reason. A kind of strange oblivion has overspread me, so that I know not what has become of the last year, and perceive that incidents and intelligence pass over me without leaving any impression.

This is not the life to which Heaven is promised [4]. I purpose

[1] Quoted in the *Life*, i. 482.

[2] 'We cannot but reflect on that inertness and laxity of mind which the neglect of order and regularity in living, and the observance of stated hours, in short the waste of time, is apt to lead men to: this was the source of Johnson's misery throughout his life; all he did was by fits and starts, and he had no genuine impulse to action, either corporal or mental.' *Hawkins*, p. 205.

[3] In only two or three instances is mention made of his reception of the Sacrament on any other day but Easter Sunday. See *post*, under April 18, 1779.

[4] The whole of the above passage is quoted in the *Life*, i. 482.

to

to approach the altar again to morrow. Grant, O Lord, that I may receive the Sacrament with such resolutions of a better life as may by thy grace be effectual, for the sake of Jesus Christ. Amen.

48.

April 21. I read the whole Gospel of St. John. Then sat up till the 22d.

My Purpose is from this time

To reject or expel sensual images, and idle thoughts.

To provide some useful amusement for leisure time.

To avoid Idleness.

To rise early.

To study a proper portion of every day.

To Worship God diligently.

To read the Scriptures.

To let no week pass without reading some part.

To write down my observations.

I will renew my resolutions made at Tetty's death.

I perceive an insensibility and heaviness upon me. I am less than commonly oppressed with the sense of sin, and less affected with the shame of Idleness. Yet I will not despair. I will pray to God for resolution, and will endeavour to strengthen my faith in Christ by commemorating his death.

I prayed for Tett.

49.

Ap. 22, Easter Day.

Having before I went to bed composed the foregoing meditation and the following prayer, I tried to compose myself but slept unquietly. I rose, took tea, and prayed for resolution and perseverance. Thought on Tetty, dear poor Tetty, with my eyes full.

I went to church, came in at the first of the Psalms [1], and endeavoured to attend the service which I went through without perturbation. After sermon I recommended Tetty in a prayer by herself, and my Father, Mother, Brother, and Bathurst [2], in another

[1] All his resolutions often—perhaps generally—failed to get him to church in time.

[2] For his friend Dr. Bathurst, who had died of fever in the Havannah, 'of whom he hardly ever spoke without tears in his eyes,' see *Life*, i. 190, 242, and *Letters*, i. 32. Accord-

another. I did it only once, so far as it might be lawful for me.

I then prayed for resolution and perseverance to amend my Life. I received soon, the communicants were many. At the altar it occurred to me that I ought to form some resolutions. I resolved, in the presence of God, but without a vow, to repel sinful thoughts to study eight hours daily, and, I think, to go to church every Sunday [1], and read the Scriptures. I gave a shilling, and seeing a poor girl at the Sacrament in a bedgown [2], gave her privately a crown, though I saw Hart's hymns [3] in her hand. I prayed earnestly for amendment, and repeated my prayer at home. Dined with Miss W.[4] went to Prayers at church; went to Davies's, spent the evening not pleasantly. Avoided wine and tempered a very few glasses with Sherbet [5]. Came home, and prayed.

I saw at the Sacrament a man meanly dressed whom I have always seen there at Easter [6].

ing to Chetwood (*History of the Stage*, ed. 1749, p. 41), a company of players went to Jamaica in 1733. They acted the *Beggars' Opera.* Within the space of two months they buried their third Polly.

[1] See *post*, where he records on April 6, 1777:—'I have this year omitted church on most Sundays, intending to supply the deficience in the week. So that I owe twelve attendances on worship.' See also *Life*, i. 67, *n.* 2; iii. 401.

[2] *Bedgown* is not in Johnson's *Dictionary.* Dr. Murray defines it as '1. A woman's night-gown or night-dress. 2. A kind of jacket worn by women of the working class in the north.'

[3] *Hymns composed on Various Subjects.* By J. Hart. London 1759.

In the Preface, Hart describes his 'Experience'—his sins and 'the Clouds of Horror with which he was overwhelmed till Whitsunday 1757; when' he says, 'I happened to go to the Moravian Chapel in Fetter Lane, where I had been several times before ... I was hardly got home, when I felt myself melting away into a strange Softness of Affection ... Thenceforth I enjoyed sweet Peace in my Soul.' In the hymn entitled *The Author's own Confession* (p. 40), he says:—

'I strove to make my Flesh decay
With foul Disease and wasting Pain.
I strove to fling my Life away,
And damn my Soul—but strove in vain.'

This Hymn-book was so popular that in 1811 it reached its twentieth edition.

[4] Miss Williams. He often dined in a tavern, though he always took tea with her. *Life*, i. 421.

[5] Johnson defines *Sherbet* as 'the juice of lemons or oranges mixed with water and sugar.'

[6] *Post*, p. 35.

Almighty

50.

Easter Day, *April* 22, 1764, at 3 m.

Almighty and most merciful Father, who hast created and preserved me, have pity on my weakness and corruption. Deliver me from habitual wickedness and idleness, enable me to purify my thoughts, to use the faculties which Thou hast given me with honest diligence, and to regulate my life by thy holy word.

Grant me, O Lord, good purposes and steady resolution, that I may repent my sins, and amend my life. Deliver me from the distresses of vain terrour, and enable me by thy Grace to will and to do what may please thee, that when I shall be called away from this present state I may obtain everlasting happiness through Jesus Christ our Lord. Amen.

51.

Sept. 18, 1764, about 6 evening.

THIS is my fifty-sixth birth-day, the day on which I have concluded fifty five years.

I have outlived many friends. I have felt many sorrows. I have made few improvements. Since my resolution formed last Easter I have made no advancement in knowledge or in goodness; nor do I recollect that I have endeavoured it. I am dejected but not hopeless.

O God for Jesus Christ's Christ's sake have mercy upon me.

52.

7 in the evening.

I went to church prayed *to be loosed from the chain of my sins* [1].

I have now spent fifty five years in resolving, having from the earliest time almost that I can remember been forming schemes of a better life [2]. I have done nothing, the need of doing there-

[1] 'Though we be tied and bound with the chain of our sins, yet let the pitifulness of thy great mercy loose us.' *Book of Common Prayer.*

[2] Johnson was but fifty-five years old, so that he began resolving, it seems, from his birth.

Prescott, the historian, made resolutions from one end of his life to the other. One of his friends writes of him:—'The practice, I apprehend, must have reached its acme about the time when he informed me one day that he had just made a new

fore

fore is pressing, since the time of doing is short. O God grant me to resolve aright, and to keep my resolutions for Jesus Christ's sake. Amen [1].

Haec limina vitae. STAT.[2]

I resolve

to study the Scriptures. I hope in the original Languages. Six hundred and forty verses every Sunday will nearly comprise the Scriptures in a year [3].

To read good books. To study Theology.

to treasure in my mind passages for recollection [4].

to rise early. Not later than six if I can I hope sooner, but as soon as I can [5].

to keep a journal both of employment and of expences. to keep accounts [6].

to take of my health by such means as I have designed.

to set down at night some plan for the morrow.

Last year I prayed on my birth-day by accommodating the Morning collect for Grace [7], putting *year* for *day*. This I did this day.

53.

Sept. 7[8], 1764.

O God, heavenly Father, who desirest not the death of a Sinner, grant that I may turn from my Wickedness and live.

resolution, which was—since he found he could not keep those which he had made before—that he would never make another resolution as long as he lived.' Ticknor's *Life of Prescott*, Boston, 1864, p. 17.

[1] This passage is quoted in the *Life*, i. 483.

[2] Quis tibi, parve, Deus tam magni pondera fati
Sorte dedit? tune hoc vix prima ad limina vitae
Hoste iaces?
STATIUS, *Thebais*, v. 534.

[3] For his plans of 'a methodical course of study according to computation,' see *Life*, i. 72.

[4] For the distinction between *remembering* and *recollecting*, see *Life*, iv. 127, *n.* 1.

[5] The next Easter he purposed to rise at eight. 'I often lye till two,' he adds. *Post*, p. 33.

[6] See *Life*, iv. 177, where he said of a lady:—'Sir, it is fit she should keep an account because her husband wishes it, but I do not see its use'; and *ib.* iv. 362 where he wrote to Langton:—I am a little angry at you for not keeping minutes of your own *acceptum et expensum*, and think a little time might be spared from Aristophanes for the *res familiares*.'

[7] In the *Book of Common Prayer*.

[8] In the margin he has written '18th.'

Enable

Enable me to shake off all impediments of lawful action, and so to order my life, that increase of days may produce increase of grace, of tranquillity of thought, and vigour in duty. Grant that my resolves may be effectual to a holy life, and a happy death, for Jesus Christs sake. Amen.

To morrow I purpose to regulate my room.

54.

EASTER DAY, *Apr.* 7, 1765, about 3 in the morning.

I purpose again to partake of the blessed Sacrament, yet when I consider how vainly I have hitherto resolved at this annual commemoration of my Saviour's deathe, to regulate my life by his laws, I am almost afraid to renew my resolutions. Since the last Easter I have reformed no evil habits, my time has been unprofitably spent, and seems as a dream that has left nothing behind. My memory grows confused, and I know not how the days pass over me.

Good Lord deliver me [1].

I will call upon God to morrow for repentance and amendment. O heavenly Father, let not my call be vain, but grant me to desire what may please thee, and fulfill those desires for Jesus Christs sake. Amen.

My resolutions, which God perfect, are,

1. to avoid loose thoughts.
2. to rise at eight every morning.

I hope to extend these purposes to other duties, but it is necessary to combat evil habits singly. I purpose to rise at eight because though I shall not yet rise early it will be much earlier than I now rise, for I often lye till two, and will gain me

[1] The whole of this entry is quoted in the *Life*, i. 487.

Boswell, under date of 1764, says:—'About this time Johnson was afflicted with a very severe return of the hypochondriack disorder.' *Ib.* i. 483. On this Percy remarks that 'he cannot believe this could possibly happen in the year 1764, or the hypochondriacal fit must have been very short; for he saw him in the spring, summer and winter of that year, and never found him more cheerful or conversible.' Anderson's *Johnson*, ed. 1815, p. 300. The year of his attack was probably 1766. *Life*, i. 521.

much time, and tend to a conquest over idleness, and give time for other duties. I hope to rise yet earlier [1].

Almighty and most merciful Father, who hatest nothing that thou hast made, nor desirest the Death of a Sinner, look down with mercy upon me, and grant that I may turn from my wickedness and live. Forgive the days and years which I have passed in folly, idleness, and sin. Fill me with such sorrow for the time mispent, that I may amend my life according to thy holy word; Strengthen me against habitual idleness, and enable me to direct my thoughts to the performance of every duty; that while I live I may serve thee in the state to which thou shalt call me, and at last by a holy and happy death be delivered from the struggles and sorrows of this life, and obtain eternal happiness by thy mercy, for the sake of Jesus Christ our Lord. Amen.

O God, have mercy upon me.

At church I purpose

before I leave the pew to pray the occasional prayer, and read my resolutions [2].

To pray for Tetty and the rest [3]

the like after Communion.

at intervals to use the collects of Fourth after Trinity, and First and Fourth after Epiphany and to meditate.

After church, 3 p.m.

This was done, as I purposed, but with some distraction. I came in at the Psalms [4], and could not well hear. I renewed my resolutions at the altar. God perfect them. When I came home I prayed, and have hope, grant O Lord for the sake of Jesus Christ that my hope may not be in vain.

[1] 'No man (said Johnson) practises so well as he writes. I have all my life long been lying till noon; yet I tell all young men, and tell them with great sincerity, that nobody who does not rise early will ever do any good.' *Ib.* v. 210. 'Johnson, Langton told us, did not get up till some one called to rouse him, whether it was ten, eleven, twelve, or one o'clock.' *Life of W. Wilberforce*, ed. 1838, ii. 179.

[2] Perhaps the resolutions made when his wife lay dead before him. *Ante*, pp. 11, 25.

[3] The previous Easter he had joined with her his father, mother, brother, and Bathurst. *Ante*, p. 29.

[4] *Ante*, p. 29, *n.* 1.

I invited

I invited home with me the man whose pious behaviour I had for several years observed on this day, and found him a kind of Methodist, full of texts, but ill-instructed [1]. I talked to him with temper, and offered him twice wine, which he refused. I suffered him to go without the dinner which I had purposed to give him. I thought this day that there was something irregular and particular [2] in his look and gesture, but having intended to invite him to acquaintance, and having a fit opportunity by finding him near my own seat after I had missed him, I did what I at first designed, and am sorry to have been so much disappointed. Let me not be prejudiced hereafter against the appearance of piety in mean persons, who, with indeterminate notions, and perverse or inelegant conversation perhaps are doing all that they can.

At night I used the occasional prayer with proper collects.

55.

July 2. I paid Mr. Simpson ten guineas, which he had formerly lent me in my necessity and for which Tetty expressed her gratitude.

July 8. I lent Mr. Simpson ten guineas more.

July 16. I received seventy-five pounds. Lent Mr. Davis twenty-five [3].

56.

Sept. 26, 1765.

Before the Study of Law [4].

Almighty God, the Giver of wisdom, without whose help resolutions are vain, without whose blessing study is ineffectual, enable me, if it be thy will, to attain such knowledge as may qualify me to direct the doubtful, and instruct the ignorant, to

[1] *Ante*, p. 30.

[2] Johnson defines 'particular' in one of its significations as 'Odd; having something that eminently distinguishes him from others. This is commonly used in a sense of contempt.' Richardson often uses the word without any sense of contempt.

[3] *Life*, i. 488. Joseph Simpson was 'a schoolfellow of Dr. Johnson's, a barrister-at-law, of good parts, but who fell into a dissipated course of life.' *Ib.* iii. 28. See *ib.* i. 346, Piozzi's *Anecdotes*, p. 120, and Hayward's *Piozzi*, i. 322, for an account of his improvidence. The money received was one quarter's pension. *Life*, i. 376.

[4] At an earlier time of his life he had wished to practise in Doctors' Commons. *Ib.* i. 134.

prevent wrongs, and terminate contentions; and grant that I may use that knowledge which I shall attain, to thy glory and my own salvation, for Jesus Christ's sake. Amen.

57.

Oct. 1765.

At church, Oct. —65[1].

To avoid all singularity[2]; *Bonaventura*[3].

To come in before service, and compose my mind by meditation, or by reading some portions of scripture. *Tetty.*

If I can hear the sermon, to attend it, unless attention be more troublesome than useful.

To consider the act of prayer as a reposal of myself upon God, and a resignation of all into his holy hand.

58.

Engaging in Politicks with H—n[4].

Nov. 1765.

Almighty God, who art the Giver of all Wisdom, enlighten my understanding with knowledge of right, and govern my will by thy laws, that no deceit may mislead me, nor temptation corrupt me, that I may always endeavour to do good, and to hinder evil. Amidst all the hopes and fears of this world, take not thy Holy Spirit from me, but grant that my thoughts may be fixed on thee, and that I may finally attain everlasting happiness, for Jesus Christs sake. Amen.

Endorsed. Prayer on Politicks, Nov. — 65, No. 51 E.

59.

Jan. 1, [1766] after two in the morning.

Almighty and most merciful Father, I again appear in thy presence the wretched mispender of another year which thy mercy has allowed me. O Lord let me not sink into total depravity, look down upon me, and rescue me at last from

[1] *Life*, i. 500.

[2] For Johnson's dislike of singularity, see *ib.* ii. 74.

[3] 'He was probably proposing to himself the model of this excellent person, who for his piety was named the *Seraphic Doctor*.' BOSWELL.

[4] William Gerard Hamilton. For my note on the connexion between him and Johnson, see *Life*, i. 518.

the

the captivity of Sin[1]. Impart to me good resolutions, and give me strength and perseverance to perform them. Take not from me thy Holy Spirit, but grant that I may redeem the time lost, and that by temperance and diligence, by sincere repentance and faithful Obedience I may finally obtain everlasting happiness, for the sake of Jesus Christ our Lord. Amen.

60.

March 3. I have never, I thank God, since new year's day deviated from the practice of rising. In this practice I persisted till I went to Mr. Thrale's some time before Midsummer: the irregularity of that family broke my habit of rising. I was there till after Michaelmas[2].

61.

March 7, 1766.

ENTRING N. M. [NOVUM MUSEUM[3].]

Almighty and most merciful Father, who hast graciously supplied me with new conveniences for study, grant that I may use thy gifts to thy glory. Forgive me the time mispent, relieve my perplexities, strengthen my resolution, and enable me to do my duty with vigour and constancy; and when the fears and hopes, the pains and pleasures of this life shall have

[1] Quoted in the *Life*, iv. 397.

[2] Hawkins's *Johnson*, p. 458 *n.* This entry was, I believe, made at two different times. On March 9, 1766, Johnson wrote to Langton:—'Burke is a great man by nature, and is expected soon to attain civil greatness. I am grown greater too, for I have maintained the newspapers these many weeks; and what is greater still, I have risen every morning since New-year's day, at about eight; when I was up, I have indeed done but little; yet it is no slight advancement to obtain for so many hours more, the consciousness of being.' *Life*, ii. 16. See also *post*, pp. 40, 48. It was therefore in the spring of 1766 that he made the first part of the entry. His visit to Mr. Thrale's was paid in the following summer. *Post*, p. 43.

[3] In the letter to Langton, quoted in the last note, he says:—'I wish you were in my new study; I am now writing the first letter in it. I think it looks very pretty about me.' Hawkins describes it as 'an upper room, which had the advantages of a good light and free air.' Hawkins's *Johnson*, p. 452. Johnson had moved into 'a good house in Johnson's Court, Fleet Street,' in the latter part of 1765. *Life*, ii. 5; iii. 406.

an end, receive me to everlasting happiness, for the sake of Jesus Christ our Lord. Amen.

Endorsed Novum Museum, March 7, —66.

Transcribed, June 26, —68.

62.

Good Friday. *March* 28, 1766[1]. On the night before I used proper Collects, and prayed when I arose in the morning. I had all the week an awe upon me, not thinking on Passion week till I looked in the almanack[2]. I have wholly forbone M [? meat] and wines, except one glass on Sunday night.

In the morning I rose, and drank very small tea[3] without milk, and had nothing more that day.

This was the day on which Tetty died. I did not mingle much men [? mention] of her with the devotions of this day, because it is dedicated to more holy subjects. I mentioned her at church, and prayed once solemnly at home. I was twice at church, and went through the prayers without perturbation, but heard the sermons imperfectly. I came in both times at the second lesson, not hearing the bell.

When I came home I read the Psalms for the day, and one sermon in Clark[4]. Scruples distract me, but at church I had hopes to conquer them[5].

[1] From the autograph record by Johnson of Good Friday, March 28, Easter Sunday, March 30, and May 4, and the copy of the record of Saturday, March 29, preserved in the Bodleian Library (Select Autographs, Montagu). These entries are given in Appendix A to my edition of the *Life*, ii. 476.

[2] Apparently he had 'omitted church' of late.

[3] This use of *small* applied to tea on the analogy of *small-beer* was, I think, uncommon.

[4] Dr. Samuel Clarke, of whose sermons, though he was 'a condemned heretic as to the doctrine of the Trinity,' Johnson thought highly. 'He had made it a rule not to admit his name in his Dictionary'; nevertheless he recommended them on his death-bed, 'because he is fullest on the propitiatory sacrifice.' *Life*, iii. 248; iv. 416. Clarke's *Scripture Doctrine of the Trinity* had been condemned by the Lower House of Convocation. Smollett's *Hist. of Eng.* ii. 303.

[5] Johnson warned Boswell against scruples. 'I am afraid of scruples,' he wrote. *Life*, ii. 421. 'Let me warn you very earnestly against scruples.' *Ib.* ii. 423. 'I am no friend to scruples.' *Ib.* v. 62. On his death-bed, he said: 'Scruples made many men miserable, but few men good.' Croker's *Boswell*, p. 844. See *Post*, p. 93.

I bore

I bore abstinence this day not well, being at night insupportably heavy, but as fasting does not produce sleepyness, I had perhaps rested ill the night before. I prayed in my study for the day, and prayed again in my chamber. I went to bed very early—before eleven.

After church I selected collects for the Sacraments.

Finding myself upon recollection very ignorant of religion, I formed a purpose of studying it.

I went down and sat to tea, but was too heavy to converse.

63.

Saturday, 29. I rose at the time now usual, not fully refreshed. Went to tea. A sudden thought of restraint hindered me. I drank but one dish. Took a purge for my health. Still uneasy. Prayed, and went to dinner. Dined sparingly *on fish* [added in different ink] about four. Went to Simpson[1]. Was driven home by my physick. Drank tea, and am much refreshed. I believe that if I had drank tea again yesterday, I had escaped the heaviness of the evening. Fasting that produces inability is no duty, but I was unwilling to do less than formerly.

I had lived more abstemiously than is usual the whole week, and taken physick twice, which together made the fast more uneasy.

Thus much I have written medically, to show that he who can fast long must have lived plentifully[2].

64.

Saturday, *March* 29, 1766. I was yesterday very heavy. I do not feel myself to-day so much impressed with awe of the approaching mystery. I had this day a doubt, like Baxter, of my state, and found that my faith, though weak, was yet faith[3]. O God! strengthen it.

[1] *Ante*, p. 35.

[2] 'He told me,' writes Boswell, 'that he had fasted two days without inconvenience.' *Life*, i. 468; iii. 306; v. 284.

[3] Baxter describes the doubts of his own salvation which exercised him many years. *Reliquiae Baxterianae*, ed. 1696, p. 6.

Since

Since the last reception of the sacrament I hope I have no otherwise grown worse than as continuance in sin makes the sinner's condition more dangerous.

Since last New Year's Eve I have risen every morning by eight, at least not after nine, which is more superiority over my habits than I have ever before been able to obtain. Scruples still distress me. My resolution, with the blessing of God, is to contend with them, and, if I can, to conquer them.

My resolutions are—

To conquer scruples.
To read the Bible this year.
To try to rise more early.
To study Divinity.
To live methodically.
To oppose idleness.
To frequent Divine worship.

Almighty and most merciful Father! before whom I now appear laden with the sins of another year, suffer me yet again to call upon Thee for pardon and peace.

O God! grant me repentance, grant me reformation. Grant that I may be no longer distracted with doubts, and harassed with vain terrors. Grant that I may no longer linger in perplexity, nor waste in idleness that life which Thou hast given and preserved. Grant that I may serve Thee in firm faith and diligent endeavour, and that I may discharge the duties of my calling with tranquillity and constancy. Take not, O God, Thy holy Spirit from me: but grant that I may so direct my life by Thy holy laws, as that, when Thou shalt call me hence, I may pass by a holy and happy death to a life of everlasting and unchangeable joy, for the sake of Jesus Christ our Lord. Amen.

I went to bed (at) one or later; but did not sleep, tho' I knew not why.

65.

Easter Day, *March* 30, 1766. I rose in the morning. Prayed. Took my prayer book to tea; drank tea; planned my devotion for the church. I think prayed again. Went to church, was early

early. Went through the prayers with fixed attention. Could not hear the sermon. After sermon, applied myself to devotion. Troubled with Baxter's scruple, which was quieted as I returned home. It occurred to me that the scruple itself was its own confutation [1].

I used the prayer against scruples in the foregoing page in the pew, and commended (so far as it was lawful) Tetty, dear Tetty, in a prayer by herself, then my other friends. What collects I do not exactly remember. I gave a shilling. I then went towards the altar that I might hear the service. The communicants were more than I ever saw. I kept back; used again the foregoing prayer; again commended Tetty, and lifted up my heart for the rest. I prayed in the collect for the fourteen S. after Trinity for encrease of Faith, Hope, and Charity, and deliverance from scruples; this deliverance was the chief subject of my prayers. O God, hear me. I am now to try to conquer them. After reception I repeated my petition, and again when I came home. My dinner made me a little peevish; not much [2]. After dinner I retired, and read in an hour and a half the seven first chapters of St. Matthew in Greek. Glory be to God. God grant me to proceed and improve, for Jesus Christ's sake. Amen.

I went to Evening Prayers, and was undisturbed. At church in the morning it occurred to me to consider about example of good any of my friends had set me. This is proper, in order to the thanks returned for their good examples.

My attainment of rising [3] gives me comfort and hope. O God, for Jesus Christ's sake, bless me. Amen.

After church, before and after dinner, I read Rotheram on Faith [4].

[1] 'He cou'd raise scruples dark and nice,
And after solve 'em in a trice;
As if Divinity had catch'd
The itch on purpose to be scratch'd.'
Hudibras, i. 1. 164.

[2] Dr. Rutty, 'at whose self-condemning minutes Johnson laughed heartily,' recorded one day that he was 'snappish on fasting.' *Life*, iii. 171.

[3] His early rising. *Ante*, p. 37.

[4] *On the Origin of Faith*, A Sermon preached before the University of Oxford in 1761. Nichols's *Lit. Anec.* viii. 193. Rotheram was a Fellow of University College. In 1767 he was

After

After evening prayer I retired, and wrote this account.

I then repeated the prayer of the day, with collects, and my prayer for night, and went down to supper at near ten.

May 4, —66. I have read since the noon of Easter day the Gospels of St. Matthew and St. Mark in Greek.

I have read Xenophon's Cyropædia.

66.

Sept. 18, 1766, at Streatham.

I have this day completed my fifty seventh year. O Lord, for Jesus Christ's sake, have mercy upon me.

Almighty and most merciful Father, who hast granted me to prolong my life to another year, look down upon me with pity. Let not my manifold sins and negligences avert from me thy fatherly regard. Enlighten my mind that I may know my duty that I may perform it, strengthen my resolution. Let not another year be lost in vain deliberations; let me remember, that of the short life of man, a great part is already past, in sinfulness and sloth. Deliver me, gracious Lord, from the bondage of evil customs, and take not from me thy Holy Spirit; but enable me so to spend my remaining days, that, by performing thy will I may promote thy glory, and grant that after the troubles and disappointments of this mortal state I may obtain everlasting happiness for the sake of Jesus Christ our Lord. Amen.

Added,

The Fourteenth S. after Tr.

The Morning collect.

The beginning of this (day) year [1].

Purposes,

To keep a journal. to begin this day.

succeeded in his Fellowship by John Scott, then a youth of sixteen, afterwards Earl of Eldon. Twiss's *Life of Lord Eldon*, ed. 1846, i. 40.

[1] He added the Collect for the fourteenth Sunday after Trinity, and the third Collect at Morning Prayer in the Book of Common Prayer. This latter prayer he 'accommodated' (*post*, p. 54) by altering *day* into *year* and *us* into *me*. It begins: 'O Lord, our heavenly Father, Almighty and everlasting God, who hast safely brought us to the beginning of this day.'

To spend four hours every day in study, and as much more as I can.

To read a portion of the Scriptures in Greek every Sunday.

To rise at eight.

Oct. 3, —66. Of all this I have done nothing.

I returned from Streatham, Oct. 1, —66, having lived there more than three months [1].

67.

Jan. 1, 1767, imâ mane scripsi.

Almighty and most merciful Father, in whose hand are life and death, as thou hast suffered me to see the beginning of another year, grant, I beseech thee, that another year may not be lost in Idleness, or squandered in unprofitable employment. Let not sin prevail on the remaining part of life, and take not from me thy Holy Spirit, but as every day brings me nearer to my end, let every day contribute to make my end holy and happy. Enable me O Lord, to use all enjoyments with due temperance, preserve me from unseasonable and immoderate sleep, and enable me to run with diligence the race that is set before me, that, after the troubles of this life, I may obtain everlasting happiness, through Jesus Christ our Lord. Amen.

68.

August 2, 1767.

I have been disturbed and unsettled for a long time, and have been without resolution to apply to study or to business, being hindered by sudden snatches [2].

I have for some days forborn wine and suppers. Abstinence is not easily practised in another's house [3]; but I think it fit to try.

I was extremely perturbed in the night, but have had this day (9.24 p.m.) more ease than I expected. D. gr. [4]. Perhaps

[1] For his residence at Streatham, see *Life*, i. 490-6, 520.

[2] Quoted in the *Life*, ii. 44. Johnson defines *snatch* in its second signification as *a short fit of vigorous action*, and in its fourth as *a broken or interrupted action; a short fit.*

[3] He was staying at Lichfield in his step-daughter's house. *Letters*, i. 128.

[4] Deo gratias.

this

this may be such a sudden relief as I once had by a good night's rest in Fetter lane[1].

The shortness of the time which the common order of nature allows me to expect is very frequently upon my mind. God grant that it may profit me.

69.

August 17.

From that time, by abstinence, I have had more ease. I have read five books of Homer[2], and hope to end the sixth to-night. I have given Mrs. Le Clerc [?] a guinea.

By abstinence from wine and suppers I obtained sudden and great relief, and had freedom of mind restored to me, which I have wanted for all this year, without being able to find any means of obtaining it.

70.

August 17, 1767.

I am now about to receive with my old friend Kitty Chambers[3] the sacrament, preparatory to her death. Grant, O God, that it may fit me. I purpose temperance for my resolution. O God, enable me to keep my purpose to thy glory.

5.32 p.m. I have communicated with Kitty, and kissed her. I was for some time distracted but at last more composed. I commended my friends and Kitty. Lucy and I were much affected. Kitty is, I think, going to heaven.

[1] See *post*, under April 6, 1777, for two other good nights. He lodged in Fetter Lane some time between 1741 and 1749. *Life*, iii. 406 *n.* Lord Eldon, writing of the year 1766, when he came from Newcastle to London on his way to Oxford, says 'my brother, now Lord Stowell, met me at the White Horse in Fetter Lane, Holborn, then the great Oxford house, as I was told. He took me to see the play at Drury Lane. When we came out of the house it rained hard. There were then few hackney coaches, and we got both into one sedan-chair. Turning out of Fleet Street into Fetter Lane there was a sort of contest between our chairmen and some persons who were coming up Fleet Street, whether they should first pass Fleet Street, or we in our chair first get out of Fleet Street into Fetter Lane. In the struggle the sedan-chair was overset with us in it.' Twiss's *Life of Eldon*, ed. 1846, i. 39.

[2] He never read the *Odyssey* through in the original. Windham's *Diary*, p. 17.

[3] His mother's servant. Johnson had allowed her to stay on in his house at Lichfield. *Letters*, i. 76, 82–6, 125.

O God,

O God, grant that I may practise such temperance in Meat, Drink, and Sleep, and all bodily enjoyments, as may fit me for the duties to which thou shalt call me, and by thy blessing procure me freedom of thought and quietness of mind, that I may so serve Thee in this short and frail life, that I may be received by Thee at my death to everlasting happiness. Take not O Lord thy Holy Spirit from me, deliver me not up to vain fears, but have mercy on me, for the sake of Jesus Christ our Lord. Amen.

O God who desirest not the Death, &c.

O Lord grant us encrease—

O God,—pardon and Peace.

O God who knowest our necessities[1].

Our Father.

71.

Oct. 18, 1767, Sunday.

Yesterday, *Oct.* 17, at about ten in the morning I took my leave for ever[2] of my dear old friend Catherine Chambers, who came to live with my mother about 1724, and has been but little parted from us since. She buried my Father, my Brother, and my Mother. She is now fifty-eight years old.

I desired all to withdraw, then told her that we were to part for ever, that as Christians we should part with prayer, and that I would, if she was willing say a short prayer beside her. She expressed great desire to hear me, held up her poor hands, as she lay in bed, with great fervour, while I prayed kneeling by her, nearly in the following words:

Almighty and most merciful Father, whose loving-kindness is over all thy works, behold, visit, and relieve this thy Servant, who is grieved with sickness. Grant that the sense of her weakness may add strength to her faith, and seriousness to her Repentance. And grant that by the help of thy Holy Spirit after the pains and labours of this short life, we may all obtain

[1] He has apparently in mind the Absolution and the Collects for the fourteenth and twenty-first Sundays after Trinity and the last Collect but one in the Communion Service in the Book of Common Prayer.

[2] He was returning to London, whence he dates a letter on Oct. 24. *Life*, ii. 30.

everlasting

everlasting happiness through Jesus Christ our Lord, for whose sake hear our prayers. Amen. Our Father.

I then kissed her. She told me that to part was the greatest pain that she had ever felt, and that she hoped we should meet again in a better place. I expressed with swelled eyes and great emotion of tenderness the same hopes. We kissed, and parted. I humbly hope, to meet again, and to part no more [1].

72.

BED-TIME.

Lent 2[2], [1768.]

Almighty God, who seest that I have no power of myself to help myself; keep me both outwardly in my body, and inwardly in my soul, that I may be defended from all adversities that may happen to the body, and from all evil thoughts which may assault and hurt the soul, through Jesus Christ our Lord. Amen.

This prayer may be said before or after the entrance into bed, as a preparative for sleep.

When I transcribed this Prayer, it was my purpose to have made this book [3] a Collection.

73.

SCRUPLES.

O Lord, who wouldst that all men should be saved, and who knowest that without thy grace we can do nothing acceptable to thee, have mercy upon me. Enable me to break the chain of my sins, to reject sensuality in thought, and to overcome and suppress vain scruples; and to use such diligence in lawful employment as may enable me to support myself and do good to others. O Lord, forgive me the time lost in idleness; pardon the sins which I have committed, and grant that I may redeem the time misspent, and be reconciled to thee by true repentance, that I may live and die in peace, and be received to everlasting

[1] Quoted in the *Life*, ii. 43.

[2] The following prayer, which is not in the Pembroke College MSS., is an 'accommodation' of the Collect for the Second Sunday in Lent.

[3] A parchment book containing such of these Prayers as are marked *transcribed*. Note by G. Strahan.

happiness

happiness. Take not from me, O Lord, thy Holy Spirit, but let me have support and comfort for Jesus Christ's sake. Amen.

Transc. June 26, 1768. Of this prayer there is no date, nor can I conjecture when it was composed [1].

74.

STUDY OF TONGUES.

Almighty God, giver of all knowledge, enable me so to pursue the study of tongues, that I may promote thy glory and my own salvation.

Bless my endeavours, as shall seem best unto Thee; and if it shall please Thee to grant me the attainment of my purpose, preserve me from sinful pride; take not thy Holy Spirit from me, but give me a pure heart and humble mind, through Jesus Christ. Amen.

Of this Prayer there is no date, nor can I tell when it was written; but I think it was in Gough-square, after the Dictionary was ended [2]. I did not study what I then intended.

Transcribed June 26, 1768.

75.

July 26, 1768. I shaved my nail by accident in whetting the knife, about an eighth of an inch from the bottom, and about a fourth from the top. This I measure that I may know the growth of nails; the whole is about five eighths of an inch [3].

76.

Sept. 18, 1768, at night.
Townmalling, in Kent [4].

I have now begun the sixtieth year of my life. How the last year has past I am unwilling to terrify myself with thinking.

[1] Croker's *Boswell*, ed. 1844, x. 130.

[2] This prayer is not in the Pembroke College MSS. See *Ante*, p. 17, for his prayer 'on the Study of Philosophy as an Instrument of Living,' made after the Dictionary was ended.

[3] *Life*, iii. 398.

[4] He was staying with Mr. Francis Brooke, 'an eminent attorney-at-law.' 'His house,' Johnson wrote, 'is one of my favourite places. His water is very commodious, and the whole place has the true appearance of a little country town.' *Letters*, ii. 23. 'His water' was, no doubt, 'the square canals which drop into one another.' *Ib. n.* 2.

This

This day has been past in great perturbation, I was distracted at church in an uncommon degree, and my distress has had very little intermission. I have found myself somewhat relieved by reading, which I therefore intend to practise when I am able.

This day it came into my mind to write the history of my melancholy. On this I purpose to deliberate. I know not whether it may not too much disturb me [1].

I this day read a great part of Pascal's Life [2].

O Lord, who hast safely brought me, &c.[3]

Almighty and most merciful Father, Creator and Preserver of mankind, look down with pity upon my troubles and maladies. Heal my body, strengthen my mind, compose my distraction, calm my inquietude, and relieve my terrours, that if it please thee, I may run the race that is set before me with peace patience constancy and confidence. Grant this O Lord, and take not from me thy Holy Spirit, but pardon and bless me for the sake of Jesus Christ our Lord.

77.

Jan. 1, 1769, 24 after 12.

I am now about to begin another year, how the last has past, it would be in my state of weakness [4] perhaps not prudent too solicitously to recollect. God will I hope turn my sufferings to my benefit, forgive me whatever I have done amiss, and having vouchsafed me great relief, will by degrees heal and restore both my mind and body, and permit me when the last year of my life shall come, to leave the world in holiness and tranquillity.

I am not yet in a state to form many resolutions; I purpose and hope to rise early in the morning, at eight, and by degrees at six; eight being the latest hour to which Bedtime can be properly extended, and six the earliest that the present system of life requires [5].

[1] He wrote to Boswell, twelve years later:—'Make it an invariable and obligatory law to yourself never to mention your own mental diseases; if you are never to speak of them you will think on them but little, and if you think little of them they will molest you rarely.' *Life*, iii. 421.

[2] He gave Boswell *Les Pensées de Pascal.* *Post*, p. 87.

[3] *Ante*, p. 42, *n.* 1.

[4] On his next birthday he records:—'The last year has been wholly spent in a slow progress of recovery.'

[5] Six years later, in the month of June, he wrote to Mrs. Thrale from

Almighty

78.

Jan. 1, 1769.

Almighty and most merciful Father, who hast continued my life from year to year, grant that by longer life I may become less desirous of sinful pleasures, and more careful of eternal happiness[1]. As age comes upon me let my mind be more withdrawn from vanity and folly, more enlightened with the knowledge of thy will, and more invigorated with resolution to obey it. O Lord, calm my thoughts, direct my desires, and fortify my purposes. If it shall please thee give quiet to my latter days, and so support me with thy grace that I may dye in thy favour for the sake of Jesus Christ our Lord. Amen.

Safely brought us to the beginning of this year[2].

79.

Sept. 18, 1769.

This day completes the sixtieth year of my age. What I have done and what I have left undone the unsettled state of my mind makes all endeavours to think improper. I hope to survey my life with more tranquillity, in some part of the time which God shall grant me.

The last year has been wholly spent in a slow progress of recovery. My days are easier, but the perturbation of my nights is very distressful. I think to try a lower diet. I have grown fat too fast. My lungs seems incumbered, and my breath fails me, if my strength is in any unusual degree exerted, or my motion accelerated. I seem to myself to bear exercise with more difficulty than in the last winter. But though I feel all those decays of body, I have made no preparation for the grave. What shall I do to be saved?

Almighty and most merciful Father, I now appear in thy presence, laden with the sins, and accountable for the mercies of another year. Glory be to thee, O God, for the mitigation of my troubles, and for the hope of health both of mind and body

Oxford :—'Don't suppose that I live here as we live at Streatham. I went this morning to the chapel at six.' *Letters*, i. 323.

[1] This passage is quoted in the *Life*, iv. 397.

[2] *Ante*, p. 42, *n.* 1.

which thou hast vouchsafed me. Most merciful Lord, if it seem good unto thee, compose my mind, and relieve my diseases; enable me to perform the duties of my station, and so to serve thee, as that, when my hour of departure from this painful life shall be delayed no longer, I may be received to everlasting happiness, for the sake of Jesus Christ our Lord. Amen.

O Lord, without whose help all the purposes of man are vain, enable me to use such temperance as may heal my body, and strengthen my mind, and enable me to serve Thee. Grant this, O Lord, for the sake of Jesus Christ our Saviour. Amen.

Who hast safely brought me to, &c.

80.

Sept. 19.

Yesterday, having risen from a disturbed and wearisome night, I was not much at rest the whole day. I prayed with the collect, *to the beginning*[1], in the night and in the morning. At night I composed my prayer and wrote my reflection. Reviewing them I found them both weakly conceived and imperfectly expressed, and corrected the prayer this morning. I am glad that I have not omitted my annual practice. I hope that by rigid temperance, and moderate exercise I may yet recover. I used the prayer again at night, and am now to begin, by the permission of God, my sixty first year.

81.

November 5, 1769.

Almighty God, merciful Father, whose providence is over all thy works, look down with pity upon the diseases of my body, and the perturbations of my mind. Give thy Blessing, O Lord, to the means which I shall use for my relief, and restore ease to my body, and quiet to my thoughts. Let not my remaining life be made useless by infirmities, neither let health, if thou shalt grant it, be employed by me in disobedience to thy laws; but give me such a sense of my pains, as may humble me before thee; and such remembrance of thy mercy as may produce honest industry, and holy confidence. And, O Lord, whether

[1] *Ante*, p. 42, *n.* 1.

Thou

Thou ordainest my days to be past in ease or anguish, take not from me thy Holy Spirit; but grant that I may attain everlasting life, for the sake of Jesus Christ our Lord. Amen.

This I found Jan. 11, —72; and believe it written when I began to live on milk. I grew worse with forbearance of solid food.

82.

Primâ mane, *Jan.* 1, 1770.

Almighty God by whose mercy I am permitted to behold the beginning of another year, succour with thy help and bless with thy favour, the creature whom Thou vouchsafest to preserve. Mitigate, if it shall seem best unto thee, the diseases of my body, and compose the disorders of my mind. Dispel my terrours; and grant that the time which thou shalt yet allow me, may not pass unprofitably away. Let not pleasure seduce me, Idleness lull me, or misery depress me[1]. Let me perform to thy glory, and the good of my fellow creatures the work which thou shalt yet appoint me. And grant that as I draw nearer to my dissolution, I may, by the help of thy Holy Spirit feel my knowledge of Thee encreased, my hope exalted, and my Faith strengthened, that, when the hour which is coming shall come, I may pass by a holy death to everlasting happiness, for the sake of Jesus Christ our Lord. Amen.

83.

1770, *March* 28, Wednesday.

This is the day on which in —52, I was deprived of poor dear Tetty. Having left off the practice of thinking on her with some particular combinations, I have recalled her to my mind of late less frequently, but when I recollect the time in which we lived together, my grief for her departure is not abated, and I have less pleasure in any good that befals me, because she does not partake it[2]. On many occasions I think what she would have said or done. When I saw the sea at Brighthelmston, I wished

[1] The following words he had struck out:—'Let my remaining days be innocent and useful.'

[2] When five years later he entered the Palais Bourbon at Paris, he recorded in his Journal:—'As I entered my wife was in my mind; she would have been pleased. Having now nobody to please I am little pleased.' *Life*, ii. 393.

for her to have seen it with me[1]. But with respect to her no rational wish is now left, but that we may meet at last where the mercy of God shall make us happy, and perhaps make us instrumental to the happiness of each other. It is now eighteen years.

84.

1770, *April* 11. Cupped[2].

85.

1770, *April* 14.

This week is Passion week.

I have for some weeks past been much afflicted with the Lumbago, or Rheumatism in the Loins, which often passes to the muscles of the belly, where it causes equal, if not greater pain. In the day the sunshine mitigates it, and in cold or cloudy weather such as has for some time past remarkably prevailed the heat of a strong fire suspends it. In the night it is so troublesome, as not very easily to be borne. I lye wrapped in Flannel with a very great fire near my bed, but whether it be that a recumbent posture encreases the pain, or that expansion by moderate warmth excites what a great heat dissipates, I can seldom remain in bed two hours at a time without the necessity of rising to heat the parts affected at the fire.

One night, between the pain and the spasms in my stomach I was insupportably distressed. On the next night, I think, I laid a blister to my back, and took opium; my night was tolerable, and from that time the spasms in my stomach which disturbed me for many years, and for two past harassed me almost to distraction, have nearly ceased; I suppose the breast is relaxed by the opium.

Having passed Thursday in Passion Week at Mr. Thrales[3],

[1] Johnson visited Brighton in 1765 (*Letters*, i. 120) when he was fifty-six years old. This seems to have been his first sight of the sea. His wife had never seen it. 'George III had never seen the sea, nor ever been thirty miles from London at the age of thirty-four.' Walpole's *Memoirs of the Reign of George III*, iv. 327. Goethe was thirty-seven years old when he first saw the sea. It was at Venice. Lewes's *Life of Goethe*, ed. 1890, p. 297.

[2] For his recourse to bleeding, see *Life*, iii. 152, *n*. 3.

[3] At Mr. Thrale's house in Southwark.

I came

I came home on Fryday morning, that I might pass the day unobserved. I had nothing but water once in the morning and once at bed-time. I refused tea after some deliberation in the afternoon. They did not press it. I came home late, and was unwilling to carry my Rheumatism to the cold church in the morning, unless that were rather an excuse made to myself. In the afternoon I went to Church but came late, I think at the Creed. I read Clarkes Sermon on the Death of Christ, and the Second Epistle to Timothy in Greek, but rather hastily. I then went to Thrale's, and had a very tedious and painful night. But the Spasms in my Throat are gone and if either the pain or the opiate which the pain enforced has stopped them the relief is very cheaply purchased. The pain harasses me much, yet many have the disease perhaps in a much higher degree with want of food, fire, and covering, which I find thus grievous with all the succours that riches and kindness can buy and give.

On Saturday I was not hungry and did not eat much breakfast. There was a dinner and company at which I was persuaded, or tempted to stay [1]. At night I came home sat up, and composed the prayer, and having ordered the maid to make the fire in my chamber at eight went to rest, and had a tolerable night.

86.

EASTER DAY, *Apr.* 15 [1770], in the morning.

Almighty and everlasting God, who hast preserved me by thy fatherly care through all the years of my past Life, and now permittest me again to commemorate the sufferings and the merits of our Lord and Saviour Jesus Christ grant me so to partake of this holy Rite, that the disquiet of my mind may be appeased, that my Faith may be encreased, my hope strengthened, and my Life regulated by thy Will. Make me truly thankful for that portion of health which thy mercy has restored, and enable me to use the remains of Life to thy glory and my own salvation. Take not from me O Lord thy Holy Spirit. Extinguish in my mind all sinful and inordinate desires. Let me resolve to do

[1] Two years later, he wrote to Dr. Taylor who had asked him to dinner on Easter Eve:—'On the last day of Lent I do not willingly go out, and shall be glad to change to-morrow for Monday,' &c. *Letters*, i. 188.

that

that which is right, and let me by thy help keep my resolutions. Let me, if it be best for me, at last know peace and comfort, but whatever state of life Thou shalt appoint me let me end it by a happy death, and enjoy eternal happiness in thy presence, for the sake of Jesus Christ our Lord. Amen.

87.

1 in the afternoon, EASTER DAY.

I am just returned from the communion having been very little interrupted in my duty by bodily pain.

I was very early at church and used this prayer, I think, before service with proper collects. I was composed during the service. I went to the table to hear the prefatory part of the office, then returned to my pew, and tried to settle some resolutions.

I resolved to form this day, some plan for reading the Scriptures.

To rise by eight, or earlier.

To form a plan for the regulation of my daily life.

To excite in myself such a fervent desire of pleasing God as should suppress all other passions.

I prayed through all the collects of meditation [1], with some extemporary prayers; recommended my friends living and dead [2]. When I returned to the table I staid till most had communicated, and in the mean time tried to settle my mind prayed against bad and troublesome thoughts, resolved to oppose sudden incursions of them, and, I think had —— thrown into my mind at the general confession. When I went first to the table, the particular series of my thoughts I cannot recollect.

When I came home I returned thanks by accommodating the general thanksgiving [3], and used this prayer again, with the collects, after receiving. I hope God has heard me.

[1] Johnson, *Post*, p. 66, mentions these 'collects of meditation.' See *ante*, p. 34, where he resolves 'at church to use the collects of Fourth after Trinity, and First and Fourth after Epiphany, and to meditate.' It may be the case, though it is not likely, that he made use of one of the books of private devotion common in his time, in which the Communion Service is printed with appropriate prayers and meditations. Such meditations Jeremy Taylor gives in his *Worthy Communicant*.

[2] *Ante*, p. 29.

[3] For his 'accommodative' prayers, see *Ante*, p. 42.

Shall

Shall I ever receive the Sacrament with tranquillity? Surely the time will come.

Some vain thoughts stole upon me while I stood near the table, I hope I ejected them effectually so as not to be hurt by them.

I went to prayers at seven having fasted; read the two morning lessons in Greek. At night I read Clarke's Sermon of the Humiliation of our Saviour.

88.

1 Sunday after Easter.

I have been recovering from my rheumatism slowly yet sensibly. But the last week has produced little good. Uneasy nights have tempted me to lye long in the morning. But when I wake in the night the release which still continues from the spasms in my throat, gives me great comfort.

The plan which I formed for reading the Scriptures was to read 600 verses in [the] Old Testament, and 200 in the New every week[1]. The Old Testament in any language, the New in Greek.

This day I began to read the Septuagint but read only 230 verses the nine first chapters of Genesis.

On this evening I repeated the prayer for Easter day[2], changing the future tense to the past.

89.

1770, *June* 1.

Every man naturally persuades himself that he can keep his resolutions, nor is he convinced of his imbecillity but by length of time and frequency of experiment. This opinion of our own constancy is so prevalent that we always despise him who suffers his general and settled purpose to be overpowered by an occasional desire. They therefore whom frequent failures have made desperate cease to form resolutions, and they who are become cunning do not tell them. Those who do not make them, are very few, but of their effect little is perceived, for scarcely any man persists in a course of life planned by choice, but as he is restrained from deviation by some external power. He who may live as he will, seldom lives long in the observation of his

[1] *Ante*, p. 32. [2] His Prayer. *Ante*, p. 53.

own

own rules[1]. I never yet saw a regular family unless it were that of Mrs. Harriots[2], nor a regular man except Mr. Campbel[3], whose exactness I know only by his own report, and Psalmanazar[4], whose life was I think, uniform.

90.

EASTER DAY, *March* 31, —71.

Almighty and most merciful Father, I am now about to commemorate once more in thy presence, the redemption of the world by our Lord and Saviour thy Son Jesus Christ. Grant, O most merciful God, that the benefit of his sufferings may be extended to me. Grant me Faith, grant me Repentance. Illuminate me with thy Holy Spirit. Enable me to form good purposes, and to bring these purposes to good effect. Let me so dispose my time, that I may discharge the duties to which thou shalt vouchsafe to call me, and let that degree of health, to which thy mercy has restored me be employed to thy Glory. O God, invigorate my understanding, compose my perturbations, recal my wanderings, and calm my thoughts, that having lived while thou shalt grant me life, to do good and to praise Thee, I may when thy call shall summon me to another state, receive mercy from thee, for Jesus Christ's sake. Amen.

91.

1771, *September* 18, 9 at night.

I am now come to my sixty-third year. For the last year I have been slowly recovering both from the violence of my last illness, and, I think, from the general disease of my life. My Breath is less obstructed, and I am more capable of motion and exercise. My mind is less encumbered, and I am less interrupted in mental employment. Some advances I hope have been made towards regularity. I have missed Church since Easter only two Sundays, both which I hope I have endeavoured to supply by attendance on Divine Worship in the following week[5]. Since Easter, my Evening devotions have been lengthened. But

[1] Quoted in the *Life*, ii. 113.

[2] Mrs. Harriots was a relation of Johnson's mother.

[3] Perhaps Dr. John Campbell. But see *Life*, iii. 243, for his drinking.

[4] *Ib.* iii. 443.

[5] *Post*, p. 81.

Indolence

Indolence and indifference has been neither conquered nor opposed. No plan of Study has been pursued or formed, except that I have commonly read every week, if not on Sunday, a stated portion of the New Testament in greek. But what is most to be considered I have neither attempted nor formed any scheme of Life by which I may do good, and please God.

One great hindrance is want of rest, my nocturnal complaints grow less troublesome towards morning, and I am tempted [to] repair the deficiencies of the night[1]. I think however to try to rise every day by eight, and to combat indolence as I shall obtain strength. Perhaps Providence has yet some use for the remnant of my life[2].

Almighty and everlasting God, whose mercy is over all thy works, and who hast no pleasure in the Death of a Sinner, look with pity upon me, succour and preserve me; enable me to conquer evil habits, and surmount temptations. Give me Grace so to use the degree of health which Thou hast restored to my Mind and Body, that I may perform the task thou shalt yet appoint me. Look down, O gracious Lord upon my remaining part of Life; grant, if it please thee, that the days few or many which thou shalt yet allow me, may pass in reasonable confidence, and holy tranquillity. Withhold not thy Holy Spirit from me, but strengthen all good purposes till they shall produce a life pleasing to Thee. And when thou shalt call me to another state, forgive me my sins, and receive me to Happiness, for the Sake of Jesus Christ our Lord. Amen.

Safely brought us, &c.[3]

92.

Sept. 23, 1771.

On the 18th, in the morning, before I went to Bed, I used the general prayer [beginning of this year]. When I rose, I came home from Mr. Thrale's that I might be more master of my hours[4]. I went to Church in the Morning, but came in to the

[1] Quoted in the *Life*, ii. 143.

[2] *The Lives of the Poets* had yet to be written.

[3] *Ante*, p. 42, *n.* 1.

[4] He sat up on the eve of his birthday till after midnight. On Jan. 1, 1770, he uttered his New Year's Day prayer 'prima mane'—in the first hour after midnight. 'The general prayer' was, I conjecture, his 'accommodation' of the Third Collect. *Ante*, p. 42, *n.* 1.

Litany.

Litany. I have gone voluntarily to Church on the week day but few times in my Life. I think to mend.

At night I composed and used the prayer, which I have used since in my devotions one morning. Having been somewhat disturbed, I have not yet settled in any plan, except that yesterday I began to learn some verses in the Greek Testament for a Sundays recital. I hope by Trust in God to amend my Life.

93.

Jan. 1, 1772, 2 in the morning.

Almighty God, who hast permitted me to see the beginning of another year, enable me so to receive thy mercy, as that it may raise in me stronger desires of pleasing thee by purity of mind and holiness of Life. Strengthen me, O Lord, in good purposes, and reasonable meditations. Look with pity upon all my disorders of mind, and infirmities of body. Grant that the residue of my life may enjoy such degrees of health as may permit me to be useful, and that I may live to thy Glory; and O merciful Lord when it shall please thee to call me from the present state, enable me to dye in confidence of thy mercy, and receive me to everlasting happiness, for the sake of Jesus Christ our Lord. Amen.

To rise in the morning.

94.

EASTER EVE, *Apr.* 18, 1772.

I am now again preparing by Divine Mercy to commemorate the Death of my gracious Redeemer, and to form, as God shall enable me, resolutions and purposes of a better life.

When I review the last year, I am able to recollect so little done, that shame and sorrow, though perhaps too weakly, come upon me [1]. Yet I have been generally free from local pain, and my strength has seemed gradually to increase. But my sleep has generally been unquiet, and I have not been able to rise early. My mind is unsettled, and my memory confused. I have of late turned my thoughts, with a very useless earnestness, upon past incidents. I have yet got no command over my thoughts;

[1] Quoted in the *Life*, ii. 143.

an

an unpleasing incident is almost certain to hinder my rest [1]. This is the remainder of my last illness. By sleepless or unquiet nights and short days, made short by late rising the time passes away uncounted and unheeded. Life so spent is useless.

I hope to cast my time into some stated method.

To let no hour pass unemployed.

To rise by degrees more early in the morning.

To keep a Journal.

I have, I think, been less guilty of neglecting public worship than formerly. I have commonly on Sunday gone once to church, and if I have missed, have reproached myself.

I have exerted rather more activity of body. These dispositions I desire to improve.

I resolved, last Easter, to read within the year, the whole Bible, a very great part of which I had never looked upon. I read the Greek Testament without construing, and this day concluded the Apocalypse [2]. I think that no part was missed.

My purpose of reading the rest of the Bible was forgotten, till I took by chance the resolutions of last Easter in my hand. I began it the first day of lent; and, for a time read with some regularity. I was then disturbed or seduced, but finished the old Testament last Thursday.

I hope to read the whole Bible once a year as long as I live.

Yesterday I fasted, as I have always, or commonly done, since the death of Tetty. The Fast was more painful than it has formerly been, which I imputed to some medicinal evacuations

[1] Quoted in the *Life*, ii. 190. He wrote to Dr. Taylor on August 31 of this year:—'I had formerly great command of my attention, and what I did not like could forbear to think on. But of this power, which is of the highest importance to the tranquillity of life, I have been some [*sic*] much exhausted, that I do not go into a company towards night, in which I foresee any thing disagreeable, nor enquire after any thing to which I am not indifferent, lest something, which I know to be nothing, should fasten upon my imagination, and hinder me from sleep.' *Letters*, i. 190.

[2] Boswell writes of this Easter:—'I paid him short visits both on Friday and Saturday, and seeing his large folio Greek Testament before him beheld him with a reverential awe, and would not intrude upon his time.' *Life*, ii. 189.

in the beginning of the week, and to a meal of cakes on the forgoing day. I cannot now fast as formerly.

I devoted this week to the perusal of the Bible, and have done little secular business. I am this night easier than is customary on this anniversary, but am not sensibly enlightened.

95.

EASTER DAY, after 12 at night.

The Day is now begun, on which I hope to begin a new course ὥσπερ ἀφ' ὑσπλήγγων [1].

My hopes are from this time,

To rise early.

To waste less time.

To appropriate something to charity [2].

Almighty God, merciful Father, who hatest nothing that thou hast made, look down with pity on my sinfulness and weakness. Strengthen, O Lord, my mind, deliver me from needless terrours. Enable me to correct all inordinate desires, to eject all evil thoughts, to reform all sinful habits, and so to amend my life [3], that when at the end of my days thou shalt call me hence, I may depart in peace, and be received into everlasting happiness, for the sake of Jesus Christ our Lord. Amen.

96.

9 in the morning.

Glory be to Thee, O Lord God, for the deliverance which Thou hast granted me from diseases of mind and body [4]. Grant, O gracious God, that I may employ the powers which thou vouchsafest me to thy Glory, and the Salvation of my soul, for the sake of Jesus Christ. Amen.

[1] As if from the starting-place.

[2] 'Johnson's charity to the poor was uniform and extensive, both from inclination and principle.' *Life*, iv. 132. 'His liberality in giving his money to persons in distress was extraordinary.' *Ib.* p. 191.

[3] In another version of this prayer he thus varies these words:—'to eject all wicked thoughts, to break off all sinful habits, and so to regulate my life that,' &c.

[4] On March 15 of this year he wrote to Boswell:—'My health grows better, yet I am not fully recovered. I believe it is held that men do not recover very fast after threescore.' *Life*, ii. 145.

I was

97.

April 26.

I was some way hinderd from continuing this contemplation in the usual manner, and therefore try at the distance of a week to review the last Sunday.

I went to Church early having first, I think, used my prayer. When I was there I had very little perturbation of mind. During the usual time of Meditation, I considered the Christian Duties under the three principles of Soberness; Righteousness; and Godliness; and purposed to forward Godliness by the *annual perusal of the Bible*; Righteousness *by settling something for Charity*, and Soberness *by early hours.* I commended as usual with preface of permission, and, I think, mentioned Bathurst [1]. I came home, and found Paoli and Boswel waiting for me [2]. What devotions I used after my return home I do not distinctly remember. I went to prayers in the evening; and, I think, entred late.

I have this week endeavoured every day but one to rise early, and have tried to be diligent, but have not performed what I required from myself.

On Good Fryday, I paid Peyton [3] without requiring work.

Since Easter —71 I have added a collect to my Evening devotion.

I have been less indulgent to corporal inactivity. But I have done little with my mind.

It is a comfort to me, that at last, in my sixty-third year, I have attained to know, even thus hastily, confusedly, and imperfectly, what my Bible contains.

May the good God encrease and sanctify my knowledge.

I have never yet read the apocrypha. When I was a boy I have read or heard Bel and the dragon, Susannah, some of Tobit, perhaps all. Some at least of Judith, and some of Ecclesiasticus; and I suppose, the Benedicite. I have some

[1] *Ante*, p. 29. [2] *Life*, ii. 190.

[3] Peyton, who had been one of his amanuenses when he was writing the *Dictionary*, was now assisting him in the preparation of the fourth edition. *Life*, ii. 155. 'Peyton and Macbean are both starving,' he wrote in 1775, 'and I cannot keep them.' *Letters*, i. 319. For Peyton's melancholy end, see *ib.* i. 385.

time

time looked into the Maccabees, and read a chapter containing the question, *Which is the strongest?*[1] I think in Esdras.

In the afternoon of Easter day, I read Pococke's commentary[2].

I have this last week scarcely tried to read, nor have I read any thing this day.

I have had my mind weak and disturbed for some weeks past.

Having missed Church in the morning I went this evening, and afterwards sat with Southwel[3].

Having not used the prayer[4], except on the day of communion; I will offer it this night, and hope to find mercy. On this day little has been done and this is now the last hour. In life little has been done, and life is very far advanced. Lord, have mercy upon me.

98.

1773, *Jan.* 1, mane 1. 33.

Almighty God, by whose mercy my life has been yet prolonged to another year, grant that thy mercy may not be vain. Let not my years be multiplied to encrease my guilt, but as age advances, let me become more pure in my thoughts, more regular in my desires, & more obedient to thy laws[5]. Let not the cares of the world distract me, nor the evils of age overwhelm me. But continue and encrease thy loving kindness towards me, and when thou shalt call me hence, receive me to everlasting happiness, for the sake of Jesus Christ, our Lord. Amen.

99.

Good Friday, *April* 9, 1773.

On this day I went twice to Church and Boswel was with me[6]. I had forborn to attend Divine Service for some time in the winter,

[1] 'The first [of three young men that were of the guard that kept the king's body] wrote, Wine is the strongest.

The second wrote, The king is the strongest.

The third wrote, Women are strongest: but above all things Truth beareth away the victory.' 1 Esdras iii. 10.

[2] Edward Pococke's *Commentary on Micah, Malachi, Hosea and Joel*, 1677-91. 'At the time when Johnson's pension was granted to him he said, with a noble literary ambition, "Had this happened twenty years ago I should have gone to Constantinople to learn Arabick as Pococke did."' *Life*, iv. 27.

[3] *Letters*, i. 205, *n.* 3.

[4] *Ante*, p. 53.

[5] Quoted in the *Life*, iv. 397.

[6] 'On the 9th of April, being Good Friday, I breakfasted with him on

winter, having a cough which would have interrupted both my own attention and that of others, and when the cough grew less troublesome I did not regain the habit of going to church, though I did not wholly omit it. I found the service not burthensome nor tedious, though I could not hear the lessons. I hope in time to take pleasure in public Worship[1].

On this whole day I took nothing of nourishment but one cup of tea without milk, but the fast was very inconvenient. Towards night I grew fretful, and impatient, unable to fix my mind, or govern my thoughts, and felt a very uneasy sensation both in my stomach and head, compounded as it seemed of laxity and pain.

From this uneasiness, of which when I was not asleep I was sensible all night, I was relieved in the morning by drinking tea, and eating the soft part of a penny loaf.

This I have set down for future observation.

100.

Saturday *Apr.* 10, I dined on cakes and found myself filled and satisfied.

Saturday 10. Having offered my prayers to God, I will now review the last year.

Of the Spring and Summer, I remember that I was able in those seasons to examine and improve my dictionary[2], and was

tea and cross-buns. . . . . He carried me with him to the church of St. Clement Danes, where he had his seat; and his behaviour was, as I had imaged to myself, solemnly devout. I never shall forget the tremulous earnestness with which he pronounced the awful petition in the Litany: "In the hour of death, and in the day of judgement, good Lord deliver us."' *Life*, ii. 214.

'Nov. 24, 1782. I preached at St. Clement's in the Strand (the largest church I ever preached in at London, except perhaps St. Sepulchre's) to an immense congregation.' Wesley's Journal, ed. 1830, iv. 241.

[1] For 'his great reluctance to go to church,' see *Life*, i. 67.

[2] On Aug. 29, 1771, he wrote to Boswell:—'I am engaging in a very great work, the revision of my *Dictionary*.' *Life*, ii. 142. On March 23, 1772, Boswell found him busy on the work. *Ib.* p. 155. On Oct. 6 he wrote to Dr. Taylor:—'I am now within a few hours of being able to send the whole dictionary to the press, and though I often went sluggishly to the work I am not much delighted at the completion.' *Letters*,

seldom

seldom withheld from the work but by my own unwillingness. Of my Nights I have no distinct remembrance but believe that as in many foregoing years they were painful and restless.

A little before Christmas I had caught cold, of which at first, as is my custom, I took little notice, but which harrassed me as it grew more violent, with a cough almost incessant, both night and day. I was let blood three times, and after about ten weeks, with the help of warm weather I recovered. From this time I have been much less troubled with nocturnal flatulencies, and have had some nights of that quiet and continual sleep, which I had wanted till I had almost forgotten it.

O God, grant that I may not mispend or lose the time which thou shalt yet allow me. For Jesus Christs sake have mercy upon me.

My purpose is to attain in the remaining part of the year as much knowledge as can easily be had of the Gospels and Pentateuch. Concerning the Hebrew I am in doubt. I hope likewise to enlarge my knowledge of Divinity, by reading at least once a week some sermon or small theological tract, or some portion of a larger work.

To this important and extensive study, my purpose is to appropriate (libere) part of every Sunday, Holyday, Wednesday, and Friday, and to begin with the Gospels. Perhaps I may not be able to study the Pentateuch before next year.

My general resolution to which I humbly implore the help of God is to methodise my life; to resist sloth. I hope from this time to keep a Journal [1].

i. 191. On Feb. 24, 1773, he wrote to Boswell :—'A new edition of my great *Dictionary* is printed, from a copy which I was persuaded to revise; but having made no preparation, I was able to do very little. Some superfluities I have expunged, and some faults I have corrected, and here and there have scattered a remark; but the main fabrick of the work remains as it was. I had looked very little into it since I wrote it, and, I think, I found it full as often better, as worse, than I expected.' *Life*, ii. 205.

[1] 'On his thirty-eighth birthday, being February 18, 1597, Casaubon resolved, as many literary men have resolved, to keep a diary. But he continued to keep it with the same perseverance which he carried into everything, daily, till within a fortnight of his death in 1614. It is literally "*nulla dies sine linea.*" I recollect but one other example of such regularity, that of Joseph

N. B.

N.B. On Friday I read the first of Mark, and Clarks sermon on Faith.

On Saturday I read little, but wrote the foregoing account, and the following prayer.

Almighty God, by whose mercy I am now about to commemorate the death of my Redeemer, grant that from this time I may so live as that his death may be efficacious to my eternal happiness. Enable me to conquer all evil customs. Deliver me from evil and vexatious thoughts. Grant me light to discover my duty, and Grace to perform it. As my life advances, let me become more pure, and more holy. Take not from me thy Holy Spirit, but grant that I may serve thee with diligence and confidence; and when thou shalt call me hence, receive me to everlasting happiness, for the sake of Jesus Christ our Lord. Amen.

Apr. 10, near midnight.

101.

EASTER SUNDAY, *April* 11.

I had more disturbance in the night than has been customary for some weeks past. I rose before nine in the morning, and prayed and drank tea. I came, I think, to church in the beginning of the prayers. I did not distinctly hear the Psalms, and found that I had been reading the Psalms for Good Friday. I went through the Litany, after a short disturbance with tolerable attention.

After sermon I perused my prayer in the pew, then went nearer the altar[1] and being introduced into another pew, used my prayer again, and recommended my relations with Bathurst and Boothby[2], then my Wife again by herself. Then I went

Priestley, who began to keep a diary of his studies, aet. 22, and continued it till within three or four days of his death, aet. 71. . . . Priestley's diary shared the fate of all his collections, and became the victim of the savages of one of our great cities.' Pattison's *Casaubon*, 2nd ed., p. 89.

[1] Johnson's pew was in the gallery. The reviewer of his *Prayers*, &c., in the *Gentleman's Magazine* for 1785, p. 731, objects to the use of the word *altar* by 'so exact a philologist and so rational a protestant.' Johnson in his *Dictionary* gives as the second meaning of *altar*, 'the table in Christian churches where the communion is administered.'

[2] Miss Hill Boothby. *Ante*, p. 18.

nearer the altar, and read the collects chosen for meditation. I prayed for Salusbury [1] and I think the Thrales. I then communicated with calmness, used the collect for Easter day, and returning to the first pew, prayed my prayer the third time. I came home, again used my prayer and the Easter Collect. Then went into the study to Boswel [2], and read the Greek Testament. Then dined, and when Boswel went away ended the four first chapters of St. Matthew, and the Beatitudes of the fifth.

I then went to Evening prayers, and was composed.

I gave the Pewkeepers each *5s. 3d.* [3]

Apr. 12 near one in the morning. I used my prayer with my ordinary devotions, and hope to lead henceforward a better life.

102.

June 18, 1773, Friday.

This day after dinner died Mrs. Salusbury, she had for some days almost lost the power of speaking. Yesterday as I touched her hand and kissed it, she pressed my hand between her two hands, which she probably intended as the parting caress [4]. At night her speech returned a little; and she said among other things to her daughter, I have had much time, and I hope I have used it. This morning being called about nine to feel her pulse I said at parting God bless you, for Jesus Christs sake. She smiled, as pleased. She had her senses perhaps to the dying moment.

103.

July 22, —73.

This day I found this book [5] with the resolutions, some of which I had forgotten, but remembered my design of reading the Pentateuch and Gospels, though I have not perused it.

[1] Mrs. Salusbury, Mrs. Thrale's mother, who was dying of cancer. *Letters*, i. 196, *n.* 5.

[2] 'To my great surprise,' writes Boswell, 'he asked me to dine with him on Easter-day. I never supposed that he had a dinner at his house; for I had not then heard of any one of his friends having been entertained at his table.' *Life*, ii. 215.

[3] The fourth part of a guinea.

[4] Writing of her a few weeks earlier he said:—'Part we must at last, but the last parting is very afflictive. When I see her I shall torment her with caressing her.' *Letters*, i. 213.

[5] A book in which this, and the

Of

Of the time past since these resolutions were made I can give no very laudable account. Between Easter and Whitsuntide, having always considered that time as propitious to study [1], I attempted to learn the low Dutch Language [2], my application was very slight, and my memory very fallacious, though whether more than in my earlier years, I am not very certain. My progress was interrupted by a fever, which, by the imprudent use of a small print, left an inflammation in my useful eye [3], which was not removed but by two copious bleedings, and the daily use of catharticks for a long time. The effect yet remains.

My memory has been for a long time very much confused. Names, and Persons, and Events, slide away strangely from me. But I grow easier.

The other day looking over old papers, I perceived a resolution to rise early always occurring. I think I was ashamed, or grieved, to find how long and how often I had resolved, what yet except for about one half year I have never done [4]. My Nights are now such as give me no quiet rest, whether I have not lived resolving till the possibility of performance is past, I know not. God help me, I will yet try.

104.

Talisker [5] in Skie, *Sept.* 24, 1773.

On last Saturday was my sixty fourth birthday. I might perhaps have forgotten it had not Boswel told me of it, and, what pleased me less, told the family at Dunvegan [6].

preceding Meditations on Good Friday and Easter Sunday are written. Note by G. Strahan.

[1] For the influence that weather and seasons have on study, see *Life*, i. 332.

[2] Quoted in *Life*, ii. 263. He seems to have twice taken up the study of Dutch. *Ib.* iv. 21, *n.* 3.

[3] *Letters*, i. 57, *n.* 5, 220.

[4] *Ante*, p. 37.

[5] *Life*, v. 250-6; *Letters*, i. 268; *Footsteps of Dr. Johnson in Scotland*, pp. 206-11.

[6] On Sept. 21 Johnson wrote to Mrs. Thrale:—'Boswell, with some of his troublesome kindness, has informed this family and reminded me that the 18th of September is my birthday. The return of my birth-day, if I remember it, fills me with thoughts which it seems to be the general care of humanity to escape. I can now look back upon threescore and four years, in which little has been done, and little has been enjoyed; a life diversified by misery, spent part in the sluggishness of penury, and part under the violence of pain, in gloomy discontent or importunate distress. But perhaps I am better than I should have been

The

The last year is added to those of which little use has been made. I tried in the summer to learn Dutch, and was interrupted by an inflammation in my eye. I set out in August on this Journey to Skie. I find my memory uncertain, but hope it is only by a life immethodical and scattered [1]. Of my body I do not perceive that exercise, or change of air has yet either encreased the strength or activity. My Nights are still disturbed by flatulencies.

My hope is, for resolution I dare no longer call it, to divide my time regularly, and to keep such a journal of my time, as may give me comfort in reviewing it. But when I consider my age, and the broken state of my body, I have great reason to fear lest Death should lay hold upon me, while I am yet only designing to live [2]. But I have yet hope.

Almighty God, most merciful Father, look down upon me with pity; Thou hast protected me in childhood and youth, support me, Lord, in my declining years. Preserve me from the dangers of sinful presumption. Give me, if it be best for me, stability of purposes, and tranquillity of mind. Let the year which I have now begun, be spent to thy glory, and to the furtherance of my salvation. Take not from me thy holy Spirit, but as Death approaches, prepare me to appear joyfully in thy presence for the sake of Jesus Christ our Lord. Amen.

if I had been less afflicted. With this I will try to be content.' *Letters*, i. 249. See also *Life*, v. 222, and *post*, p. 92. He was staying at Dunvegan in Sky with the Laird of Macleod.

[1] Four years later he said:—'There must be a diseased mind where there is a failure of memory at seventy. A man's head, Sir, must be morbid if he fails so soon.' *Life*, iii. 191.

Macaulay in his fifty-fifth year entered in his journal:—'My memory I often try, and find it as good as ever; and memory is the faculty which it is most easy to bring to decisive tests, and also the faculty which gives way first.' Trevelyan's *Macaulay*, ed. 1877, ii. 386.

[2] 'Those that lie here stretched before us,' said Rasselas, 'the wise and the powerful of ancient times, warn us to remember the shortness of our present state, they were perhaps snatched away while they were busy like us in the choice of life.' *Rasselas*, chap. 48.

1773.

105.

1773[1]. Inchoavi lectionem Pentateuchi—Finivi lectionem Conf. Fab Burdonum[2].—Legi primum actum Troadum[3].—Legi Dissertationem Clerici postremam de Pent.[4]—2 of Clark's Sermons.—L. Appolonii pugnam Betriciam[5].—L. centum versus Homeri

106.

1774, *Jan.* 1, near 2 in the morning.

Almighty God, merciful Father, who hatest nothing that thou hast made, but wouldest that all should be saved, have mercy upon me. As thou hast extended my Life, encrease my strength, direct my purposes, and confirm my resolution, that I may truly serve Thee, and perform the duties which Thou shalt allot me.

Relieve, O gracious Lord, according to thy mercy the pains and distempers of my Body, and appease the tumults of my Mind. Let my Faith and Obedience encrease as my life advances, and let the approach of Death incite my desire to please Thee, and invigorate my diligence in good works, till at last, when Thou shalt call me to another state, I shall lie down in humble hope, supported by thy Holy Spirit, and be received to everlasting happiness, through Jesus Christ our Lord. Amen.

The beginning, &c.[6]

I hope

To read the Gospels before Easter.

[1] 'These notes of his studies appear on different days in his manuscript diary of this year.' *Life*, ii. 263.

[2] Accurata Burdonum [i. e. Scaligerorum] Fabulae Confutatio. *Brit. Mus. Catalogue* (auctore I. R.). Lugduni Batavorum. Apud Ludovicum Elzevirium MDCXVII.

[3] For Johnson's study of Euripides, see *Life*, i. 70, 72; iv. 311.

[4] 'JOHNSON. I should recommend Dr. Clarke's sermons, were he orthodox. However it is very well known *where* he was not orthodox, which was upon the doctrine of the Trinity, as to which he is a condemned heretik.' *Ib.* iii. 248, and *ante*, p. 38, *n.* 4.

[5] The Rev. H. E. D. Blakiston of Trinity College, Oxford, informs me that in the second book of Apollonius's *Argonautica* there is the fight of Polydeuces with Amycus, King of the Bebryces, which Johnson might have latinised as *pugna Bebrycia* or *Bebricia*, misprinted *Betricia*.

[6] *Ante*, p. 42, *n.* 1.

To rise at eight.

To be temperate in Food.

This year has past with so little improvement, that I doubt whether I have not [rather] impaired than encreased my Learning [1]. To this omission some external causes have contributed. In the Winter I was distressed by a cough, in the Summer an inflammation fell upon my useful eye from which it has not yet, I fear, recovered. In the Autumn I took a journey to the Hebrides, but my mind was not free from perturbation [2]. Yet the chief cause of my deficiency has been a life immethodical and unsettled, which breaks all purposes, confounds and suppresses memory, and perhaps leaves too much leisure to imagination [3]. O Lord, have mercy upon me.

Jan. 9, 1774.

107.

Nov. 27. Advent Sunday. I considered that this day, being the beginning of the ecclesiastical year, was a proper time for a new course of life. I began to read the Greek Testament regularly at 160 verses every Sunday. This day I began the Acts.

In this week I read Virgil's *Pastorals*. I learned to repeat the *Pollio* and *Gallus*. I read carelessly the first *Georgick* [4].

108.

Apr. 13 [1775], MAUNDY THURSDAY [5].

Of the use of time or of my commendation of myself I thought no more, but lost life in restless nights and broken days, till this week awakened my attention.

[1] Quoted in the *Life*, ii. 271.

[2] 'He said to me often,' writes Boswell, 'that the time he spent in this tour was the pleasantest part of his life.' *Ib.* v. 405.

[3] He wrote to Boswell on Nov. 16, 1776:—'I believe it is best to throw life into a method, that every hour may bring its employment, and every employment have its hour... I have not practised all this prudence myself, but I have suffered much for want of it.' *Ib.* iii. 94.

[4] *Life*, ii. 288.

[5] The day before Good Friday. Johnson in his *Dictionary* gives *Maundy* as the spelling, and quotes Spelman's derivation 'from *mande*, a hand-basket, in which the king was accustomed to give alms to the poor.' Mr. Skeat, in his *Etymological Dictionary*, deriving the word

This

This year has passed with very little improvement perhaps with diminution of knowledge. Much time I have not left. Infirmities oppress me. But much remains to be done. I hope to rise at eight or sooner in the morning.

109.

Apr. 14, GOOD FRIDAY.

Boswel came in before I was up. We breakfasted, I only drank tea without milk or bread[1]. We went to Church, saw Dr. Wetherel[2] in the pew, and by his desire took him home with us. He did not go very soon, and Boswel staid. Dilly and Millar called[3]. Boswel and I went to Church, but came very late. We then took tea, by Boswel's desire, and I eat one bun, I think, that I might not seem to fast ostentatiously. Boswel sat with me till night; we had some serious talk[4]. When he went I gave Francis[5] some directions for preparation to communicate. Thus has passed hitherto this awful day.

110.

10° 30′ p.m.

When I look back upon resolutions of improvement and amendments, which have year after year been made and broken, either by negligence, forgetfulness, vicious idleness, casual interruption, or morbid infirmity, when I find that so much of my life has stolen unprofitably away, and that I can descry by retrospection scarcely a few single days properly and vigorously employed[6], why do I yet try to resolve again? I try because

from *mandatum*, says, 'Spelman's guess is as false as it is readily believed.'

[1] 'On Friday, April 14, being Good-Friday, I repaired to him in the morning, according to my usual custom on that day, and breakfasted with him. I observed that he fasted so very strictly, that he did not even taste bread, and took no milk with his tea; I suppose because it is a kind of animal food.' *Life*, ii. 352.

[2] Nathan Wetherell, D.D., Master of University College, Oxford, and Dean of Hereford. *Ib.* ii. 356.

[3] This passage is scored out in the original. Dilly and Millar were the two publishers. Boswell mentions two gentlemen calling, one of whom uttered a 'common-place complaint' which Johnson ridiculed. *Ib.* ii. 357.

[4] *Ib.*

[5] His black servant. *Ib.* ii. 359.

[6] Grotius at the end of life exclaimed: 'Heu! vitam perdidi; operose nihil agendo.' Chalmers's *Brit. Essayists*, vol. xvi. p. lix.

Reformation

Reformation is necessary and despair is criminal. I try in humble hope of the help of God.

As my life has from my earliest years been wasted in a morning bed my purpose is from Easter day to rise early, not later than eight.

11° 15′ p.m. D. j.

111.

Apr. 15, EASTER EVE.

I rose more early than is common after a night disturbed by flatulencies though I had taken so little. I prayed, but my mind was unsettled, and I did not fix upon the book. After the bread and tea I trifled, and about three ordered coffee and bunns for my dinner. I find more faintness and uneasiness in fasting than I did formerly.

While coffee was preparing, Collier[1] came in, a man whom I had not seen for more than twenty years, but whom I consulted about Macky's books. We talked of old friends and past occurrences and eat and drank together.

I then read a little in the Testament, and tried Fiddes's B. of Divinity[2], but did not settle.

I then went to Evening prayer, and was tolerably composed. At my return I sat awhile, then retired, but found reading uneasy.

11 p.m.

These two days in which I fasted, I have not been sleepy, though I rested ill.

[1] According to the *Gentleman's Magazine*, 1785, p. 731, Dr. Collier of Doctors' Commons; but he did not die till May 23, 1777 (*Letters*, ii. 69), whereas Johnson records on April 7, 1776 (*post*, p. 73), 'Collier is dead.' Joseph Collyer, an author, died on Feb. 20, 1776. *Gent. Mag.* 1776, p. 95.

[2] Richard Fiddes, 1671–1725. His *Body of Divinity* is in two volumes folio; vol. i is entitled *Theologia Speculativa*; vol. ii, *Theologia Practica*, 1718–20. He was presented with the living of Halsham in Yorkshire. 'Here he was so unhappy as to be deprived in a great measure of his speech, till which misfortune he had been admired for the sweetness of his voice and the gracefulness of his delivery.' He thereupon 'resolved to apply himself entirely to writing.' Bayle's *General Dictionary*, 1737, v. 238. See also Hearne's *Remains*, ed. 1869, ii. 223.

Almighty

112.

EASTER DAY, *Apr.* 16, 12° 3′.

Almighty God, heavenly Father, whose mercy is over all thy works, look with pity on my miseries and sins. Suffer me to commemorate in thy presence my redemption by thy Son Jesus Christ. Enable me so to repent of my mispent time that I may pass the residue of my life in thy fear and to thy glory. Relieve, O Lord, as seemeth best unto thee, the infirmities of my body, and the perturbations of my mind. Fill my thoughts with awful love of thy Goodness, with just fear of thine Anger, and with humble confidence in thy Mercy. Let me study thy laws, and labour in the duties which thou shalt set before me. Take not from me thy Holy Spirit, but incite in me such good desires as may produce diligent endeavours after thy Glory and my own salvation; and when, after hopes and fears, and joys and sorrows thou shalt call me hence, receive me to eternal happiness, for the Sake of Jesus Christ our Lord. Amen.

Collier is dead[1]. April 7, 1776.

Transcribed from a former book with a slight emendation or two. With that book I parted perhaps unnecessarily by a Catch[2].

113.

Sept. 18, 1775.

O God by whom all things were created and are sustained, who givest and takest away, in whose hands are life and death, accept my imperfect thanks for the length of days which thou hast vouchsafed to grant me, impress upon my mind such repentance of the time mispent in sinfulness and negligence, that I may obtain forgiveness of all my offences, and so calm my mind and strengthen my resolutions that I may live the remaining part of my life in thy fear, and with thy favour. Take not thy Holy Spirit from me, but let me so love thy laws, and so obey them, that I may finally be received to eternal happiness, through Jesus Christ our Lord. Amen.

[1] *Ante*, p. 72.

[2] I do not know in what sense he uses this word. Perhaps he means by a sudden impulse, or by some scruple that caught hold of him. Dr. Murray in the *New English Dictionary* gives as one of its significations, 'a catching or entangling question.'

Composed

Composed at Calais in a sleepless night, and used before the morn at Nôtre Dame [1], written at St. Omers.

114.

Jan. 1, 1776.

Almighty God, merciful Father, who hast permitted me to see the beginning of another year, grant that the time which thou shalt yet afford me may be spent to thy glory, and the salvation of my own Soul. Strengthen all good resolutions. Take not from me thy Holy Spirit, but have mercy upon me, and shed thy Blessing both on my soul and body, for the sake of Jesus Christ our Lord. Amen.

115.

1776, *Apr.* 7, Easter Day.

The time is again at which, since the death of my poor dear Tetty, on whom God have mercy, I have annually commemorated the mystery of Redemption, and annually purposed to amend my life. My reigning sin, to which perhaps many others are appendant, is waste of time, and general sluggishness, to which I was always inclined, and in part of my life have been almost compelled by morbid melancholy and disturbance of mind. Melancholy has had in me its paroxisms and remissions, but I have not improved the intervals, nor sufficiently resisted my natural inclination, or sickly habits. I will resolve henceforth to rise at eight in the morning, so far as resolution is proper [2], and will pray that God will strengthen me. I have begun this morning.

Though for the past week I have had an anxious design of communicating to-day, I performed no particular act of devotion, till on Friday I went to Church. My design was to pass part of the day in exercises of piety, but Mr. Boswel interrupted me;

[1] For his journey to Paris see *Life*, ii. 384-404. He wrote to Levett from Paris:—'We are here in France after a very pleasing passage of no more than six hours.' *Ib.* p. 385. Mrs. Piozzi, when she crossed to Calais nineteen years later, took twenty-six hours on the passage. She describes the start from the inn for Paris:—'Postillions with greasy night-caps and vast jack-boots, driving your carriage harnessed with ropes, and adorned with sheep-skins.' *Journey through France*, i. 1, 5.

[2] *Ante*, p. 67.

of

of him, however, I could have rid myself, but poor Thrale, orbus et exspes, came for comfort and sat till seven when we all went to Church [1].

In the morning I had at Church some radiations of comfort.

I fasted though less rigorously than at other times. I by negligence poured milk into the tea, and, in the afternoon drank one dish of coffee with Thrale [2]; yet at night, after a fit of drowsiness I felt myself very much disordered by emptiness, and called for tea with peevish and impatient eagerness. My distress was very great.

Yesterday I do not recollect that to go to Church came into my thoughts, but I sat in my chamber, preparing for preparation; interrupted, I know not how. I was near two hours at dinner.

I go now with hope

To rise in the morning at eight.

To use my remaining time with diligence.

To study more accurately the Christian Religion.

Almighty and most merciful Father, who hast preserved me by thy tender forbearance, once more to commemorate thy Love in the Redemption of the world, grant that I may so live the residue of my days, as to obtain thy mercy when thou shalt call me from the present state. Illuminate my thoughts with knowledge, and inflame my heart with holy desires. Grant me to resolve well, and keep my resolutions. Take not from me thy

[1] Thrale had lost his only surviving son on March 23 of this year. *Life*, ii. 468; *Letters*, i. 381. Baretti shows how he was both *orbus et exspes*. 'Having now lost the strong hope of being one day succeeded in the profitable Brewery by the only son he had left, he gave himself silently up to his grief and fell in a few years a victim to it.' *Ib.* i. 384, *n.* 2. Boswell records on this Good Friday:—'Mr. Thrale called upon Dr. Johnson, and appeared to bear the loss of his son with a manly composure. There was no affectation about him, and he talked, as usual, upon indifferent subjects.' *Life*, iii. 18.

[2] 'We sat together till it was too late for the afternoon service. Thrale said he had come with intention to go to church with us. We went at seven to evening prayers at St. Clement's church, after having drank coffee; an indulgence, which I understood Johnson yielded to on this occasion, in compliment to Thrale.' *Ib.* iii. 24.

Holy

Holy Spirit, but in life and in death have mercy on me for Jesus Christs sake. Amen.

acts of forgiveness [1].

p.m. In the pew I read my prayer and commended my friends, and those that θ[2] this year. At the Altar I was generally attentive, some thoughts of vanity came into my mind while others were communicating, but I found when I considered them, that they did not tend to irreverence of God. At the altar I renewed my resolutions. When I received, some tender images struck me. I was so mollified by the concluding address to our Saviour that I could not utter it [3]. The Communicants were mostly women. At intervals I read collects, and recollected, as I could, my prayer. Since my return I have said it. 2 p.m.

May 21.

These resolutions I have not practised nor recollected. O God grant me to begin now for Jesus Christ's Sake. Amen.

116.

July 25, 1776.

O God who hast ordained that whatever is to be desired, should be sought by labour, and who, by thy Blessing, bringest

[1] In Jeremy Taylor's *Holy Living*, under the heading of *A prayer of preparation or address to the holy sacrament*, we find *An act of love; An act of desire; An act of contrition; An act of faith.* I do not find in the *Dictionaries* any definition of *act* as here used.

[2] Strahan prints 'died,' though 'died' it certainly is not. What Johnson wrote was the Greek letter θ. For an explanation of this see *post*, p. 89.

[3] 'O Lord, the only begotten Son Jesu Christ; O Lord God, Lamb of God, Son of the Father, that takest away the sins of the world, have mercy upon us. Thou that takest away the sins of the world, have mercy upon us. Thou that takest away the sins of the world, receive our prayer. Thou that sittest at the right hand of God the Father, have mercy upon us.

For thou only art holy; Thou only art the Lord; Thou only, O Christ, with the Holy Ghost, art most high in the glory of God the Father.'

Johnson defines *to mollify* 'to appease; to pacify; to quiet.' Here he must use *mollified* in the sense of *affected* or *touched*.

Boswell, who, 'according to his usual custom' on Easter Sunday, visited him after morning service, records:—'It seemed to me that there was always something peculiarly mild and placid in his manner upon this holy festival.' *Life*, iii. 25.

honest labour to good effect; look with mercy upon my studies and endeavours. Grant me, O Lord, to design only what is lawful and right, and afford me calmness of mind, and steadiness of purpose, that I may so do thy will in this short life, as to obtain happiness in the world to come, for the sake of Jesus Christ our Lord. Amen.

When I purposed to apply vigorously to study particularly of the Greek and Italian tongues[1].

Repeated July 3, —77 about 12 at night.

117.

2 p.m., *Jan.* 1, 1777.

Almighty Lord, merciful Father vouchsafe to accept the thanks which I now presume to offer thee for the prolongation of my life. Grant, O Lord, that as my days are multiplied, my good resolutions may be strengthened, my power of resisting temptations encreased, and my struggles with snares and obstructions invigorated. Relieve the infirmities both of my mind and body. Grant me such strength as my duties may require and such diligence as may improve those opportunities of good that shall be offered me. Deliver me from the intrusion of evil thoughts. Grant me true repentance of my past life, and as I draw nearer and nearer to the grave, strengthen my Faith, enliven my Hope, extend my Charity, and purify my desires, and so help me by thy Holy Spirit that when it shall be thy pleasure to call me hence, I may be received to everlasting happiness, for the sake of thy Son Jesus Christ our Lord. Amen.

Our Father.

118.

1777, *March* 28.

This day is Good Friday. It is likewise the day on which my poor Tetty was taken from me.

My thoughts were disturbed in bed. I remembered that it was

[1] Quoted in the *Life*, iii. 90.

Not four months before his death he wrote to Mr. Sastres:—'I have hope of standing the English winter, and of seeing you and of reading Petrarch at Bolt Court.' *Letters*, ii. 417.

my

my Wife's dying day, and begged pardon for all our sins, and commended her; but resolved to mix little of my own sorrows or cares with the great Solemnity. Having taken only tea without milk, I went to church, had time before service to commend my wife, and wished to join quietly in the service, but I did not hear well, and my mind grew unsettled and perplexed. Having rested ill in the night[1], I slumbered at the sermon, which, I think, I could not as I sat, perfectly hear.

I returned home, but could not settle my mind. At last I read a Chapter. Then went down, about six or seven and eat two cross buns[2], and drank tea. Fasting for some time has been uneasy and I have taken but little.

At night I had some ease. L. D.[3] I had prayed for pardon and peace.

I slept in the afternoon.

119.

29, EASTER EVE.

I rose and again prayed with reference to my departed Wife. I neither read nor went to Church, yet can scarcely tell how I have been hindered. I treated with booksellers on a bargain, but the time was not long[4].

120.

30, EASTER DAY, 1ma mane.

The day is now come again in which, by a custom which since the death of my wife I have by the Divine assistance always observed, I am to renew the great covenant with my Maker and my Judge. I humbly hope to perform it better. I hope for more efficacy of resolution, and more diligence of endeavour. When I survey my past life, I discover nothing but a barren waste of time with some disorders of body, and disturbances of the mind very near to madness, which I hope he that made me, will suffer to extenuate many faults, and excuse many deficiencies.

[1] On March 19 he had written to Mrs. Thrale:—'You are all young and gay and easy; but I have miserable nights and know not how to make them better.'—*Letters*, ii. 5.

[2] Neither cross-bun nor bun is in Johnson's *Dictionary*.

[3] *Laus Deo.*

[4] Quoted in the *Life*, iii. 109. The treaty was about the *Lives of the Poets*. *Ib.*

deficiencies[1]. Yet much remains to be repented and reformed. I hope that I refer more to God than in former times, and consider more what submission is due to his dispensations. But I have very little reformed my practical life, and the time in which I can struggle with habits cannot be now expected to be long. Grant O God, that I may no longer resolve in vain, or dream away the life which thy indulgence gives me, in vacancy and uselessness.

9nâ mane.

I went to bed about two, had a disturbed night, though not so distressful as at some other times.

Almighty and most merciful Father, who seest all our miseries, and knowest all our necessities, Look down upon me, and pity me. Defend me from the violent incursions of evil thoughts, and enable me to form and keep such resolutions as may conduce to the discharge of the duties which thy Providence shall appoint me, and so help me by thy Holy Spirit, that my heart may surely there be fixed where true joys are to be found, and that I may serve Thee with pure affection and a cheerful mind. Have mercy upon me, O God, have mercy upon me; years and infirmities oppress me, terrour and anxiety beset me. Have mercy upon me, my Creatour and my Judge. In all dangers protect me, in all perplexities relieve and free me, and so help me by thy Holy Spirit, that I may now so commemorate the death of thy Son our Saviour Jesus Christ as that when this short and painful life shall have an end, I may for his sake be received to everlasting happiness. Amen[2].

121.

April 6 [1777].

By one strange hindrance or another, I have been withheld from the continuation of my thoughts to this day, the Sunday following Easter day.

[1] Quoted in the *Life*, iii. 99.
For 'the disturbances of the mind' see *Life*, i. 65; v. 215; and *Letters*, i. 39. 'Folly, melancholy, madness are but one disease. *Delirium* is a common name to all.' *Anatomy of Melancholy*, ed. 1660, Introduction, p. 18.

[2] Quoted in the *Life*, iii. 99.

On

On Easter day I was at Church early, and there prayed over my Prayer, and commended Tetty and my other Friends. I was for some time much distressed, but at last obtained, I hope from the God of peace, more quiet than I have enjoyed for a long time. I had made no resolution, but as my heart grew lighter, my hopes revived and my courage increased, and I wrote with my pencil in my common prayer book,

Vita ordinanda.
Biblia legenda.
Theologiæ opera danda.
Serviendum et lætandum[1].
Scrupulis obsistendum.

I then went to the altar, having I believe, again read my prayer. I then went to the table and communicated, praying for some time afterwards, but the particular matter of my prayer I do not remember.

I dined by an appointment with Mrs. Gardiner[2], and passed the afternoon with such calm gladness of Mind as it is very long since I felt before. I came home and began to read the Bible. I passed the night in such sweet uninterrupted sleep, as I have not known since I slept at Fort Augustus[3].

On Monday I dined with Sheward[4], on Tuesday with Paradise[5]; the mornings have been devoured by company, and one intrusion has through the whole week succeeded to another.

At the beginning of the year I proposed to myself a scheme of life, and a plan of study, but neither life has been rectified nor study followed. Days and months pass in a dream, and I am afraid that my memory grows less tenacious, and my observation less attentive. If I am decaying, it is time to make haste. My nights are restless and tedious, and my days drowsy. The flatulence which torments me, has sometimes so obstructed my

[1] Quoted in the *Life*, iii. 99.

[2] 'The wife of a tallow-chandler on Snow Hill, not in the learned way, but a worthy good woman.' *Ib.* i. 242.

[3] Where he arrived after a ride of thirty-two miles on Aug. 30, 1773. *Ib.* v. 134. For another good night's rest see *ante*, p. 44.

[4] Mentioned *post*, p. 102. Johnson twice mentions a Mrs. Sheward in his *Letters*, ii. 310, 314.

[5] *Life*, iv. 364, and *Letters*, i. 314.

breath,

breath, that the act of respiration became not only voluntary but laborious in a decumbent posture[1]. By copious bleeding I was relieved, but not cured[2].

I have this year omitted church on most Sundays, intending to supply the deficience in the week. So that I owe twelve attendances on worship[3]. I will make no more such superstitious stipulations, which entangle the mind with unbidden obligations[4].

My purpose once more, O Thou merciful Creatour that governest all our hearts and actions, βιοτῆς ὄιηκα κυβερνῶν[5], let not my purpose be vain—My purpose once more is

To rise at eight.

1. To keep a journal.
2. To read the whole Bible in some language before Easter.
3. To gather the arguments for Christianity[6].
4. To worship God more frequently in publick.

122.

Sept. 18, 1777, Ashbourn[7].

Almighty and most merciful Father, who hast brought me to the beginning of another year, grant me so to remember thy

[1] *Voluntary* is a strange term to use of breathing. *Decumbent* is not in Johnson's *Dictionary*.

[2] *Life*, iii. 104; *Letters*, ii. 1-2; and *ante*, p. 64.

[3] There had been but fourteen Sundays so far in this year. See *ante*, p. 56.

[4] *Ante*, p. 25. Cowper wrote on Aug. 27, 1785:—'If it be fair to judge of a book by an extract I do not wonder that you were so little edified by Johnson's journal. It is even more ridiculous than was poor ——s of flatulent memory [Dr. Rutty, *Life*, iii. 171]. The portion of it given us in this day's paper contains not one sentiment worth one farthing; except the last, in which he resolves to bind himself with no more unbidden obligations. Poor man! one would think that to pray for his dead wife and to pinch himself with church fasts had been almost the whole of his religion.' Cowper's *Works*, ed. 1836, v. 157.

[5] Steering the helm of life.

[6] Boswell on the Sunday evening which he and Johnson spent in Aberdeen in August, 1773, records:—'I said he should write expressly in support of Christianity; for that, although a reverence for it shines through his works in several places, that is not enough. "You know (said I) what Grotius has done, and what Addison has done. You should do also." He replied, "I hope I shall."' *Life*, v. 89.

[7] He spent his birthday with Boswell at Dr. Taylor's. *Ib.* iii. 157; *Letters*, ii. 33.

 gifts,

gifts, and so to acknowledge thy goodness, as that every year and day which thou shalt yet grant me, may be employed in the amendment of my life, and in the diligent discharge of such duties, as thy Providence shall allot me. Grant me, by thy Grace, to know and to do what Thou requirest. Give me good desires, and remove those impediments which may hinder them from effect. Forgive me my sins, negligences, and ignorances, and when at last thou shalt call me to another life, receive me to everlasting happiness, for the sake of Jesus Christ our Lord. Amen.

123.

'77 Sept. 21, Concio pro Tayloro [1].

124.

1778, *Apr.* 17, GOOD FRIDAY.

It has happened this week, as it never happened in Passion Week before, that I have never dined at home [2], and I have therefore neither practised abstinence nor peculiar devotion.

This Morning before I went to bed I enlarged my prayers, by adding some collects with reference to the day. I rested moderately and rose about nine, which is more early than is usual.

[1] Hawkins's *Johnson*, p. 392. Boswell, under date of Sunday, Sept. 21, says:—'I have no doubt that a good many sermons were composed for Taylor by Johnson. At this time I found upon his table a part of one which he had newly begun to write.' *Life*, iii. 181. See also *Ib.* vi; *Addenda*, p. 66. In an interleaved copy of the first edition of the *Life* in the possession of Mr. Horatio Symonds of Beaumont Street, Oxford, I have found the following note made (with many others) I have no doubt by the Rev. John Hussey, 'who had long been in habits of intimacy with Johnson.' (*Life*, iii. 369). 'Johnson not only told me that he had written, he believed, forty sermons, but that several of them had been published. Upon my expressing some surprise that the preachers of them should hazard such an imposition, he replied, "Nay, Sir, there was no hazard, if they kept their own counsel; they might be very sure I should not claim them; indeed I had no right to them after I had been paid for them." He also added that they were generally copied in his own study by those that employed him, and when finished he always destroyed the original in their presence.'

[2] In Passion Week three years later he dined on Wednesday at one Bishop's, and on Thursday at another Bishop's. Boswell describes 'the admirable sophistry' with which he defended his conduct. *Life*, iv. 89.

usual. I think I added something to my morning prayers. Boswel came in to go to church [1]; we had tea, but I did not eat. Talk lost our time, and we came to Church late, at the second lesson. My mind has been for some time feeble and impressible, and some trouble it gave me in the morning, but I went with some confidence and calmness through the prayers.

In my return from Church, I was accosted by Edwards, an old fellow Collegian, who had not seen me since —29. He knew me, and asked if I remembered one Edwards, I did not at first recollect the name, but gradually as we walked along recovered it, and told him a conversation that had passed at an alehouse between us [2]. My purpose is to continue our acquaintance.

We sat till the time of worship in the afternoon, and then came again late at the Psalms. Not easily, I think, hearing the sermon, or not being attentive, I fell asleep. When we came home we had tea and I eat two buns, being somewhat uneasy with fasting, and not being alone. If I had not been observed I should probably have fasted.

125.

April 19, EASTER DAY, after 12 at night.

O Lord have mercy upon me.

Yesterday (18) I rose late having not slept ill. Having promised a Dedication, I thought it necessary to write, but for some time neither wrote nor read. Langton came in and talked. After dinner I wrote. At tea Boswel came in and wrote to Macaulay about his son [3]. He staid till nearly twelve [4].

[1] 'It was a delightful day: as we walked to St. Clement's church, I again remarked that Fleet-street was the most cheerful scene in the world. "Fleet-street (said I,) is in my mind more delightful than Tempé." JOHNSON. "Ay, Sir; but let it be compared with Mull."' *Life*, iii. 302.

[2] *Ib.* iii. 304.

[3] These words are scored out in the original. Johnson had promised to get a servitorship at Oxford for the son of the Rev. Kenneth Macaulay. *Life*, ii. 380; v. 122.

[4] He stayed so late in spite of 'the horrible shock' which Johnson gave him. 'We talked of a gentleman who was running out his fortune in London; and I said, "We must get him out of it. All his friends must quarrel with him, and that will soon drive him away." JOHNSON. "Nay, Sir; we'll send

I purposed to have gone in the evening to Church but missed the hour.

Edwards observed how many we have outlived [1]. I hope, yet hope, that my future life shall be better than my past.

From the year 1752, the year in which my poor dear Tetty died, upon whose soul may God have had mercy for the sake of Jesus Christ, I have received the sacrament every year at Easter. My purpose is to receive it now. O Lord God, for the sake of Jesus Christ, make it effectual to my salvation.

My purposes are

To study Divinity, particularly the Evidences of Christianity.

To read the New Testament over in the year with more use than hitherto of Commentators.

To be diligent in my undertakings.

To serve and trust God, and be cheerful [2].

Almighty and most merciful Father, suffer me once more to commemorate the death of thy Son Jesus Christ, my Saviour and Redeemer, and make the memorial of his death profitable to my salvation, by strengthening my Faith in his merits, and quickening my obedience to his laws. Remove from me, O God, all inordinate desires, all corrupt passions, & all vain terrours; and fill me with zeal for thy glory, and with confidence in thy mercy. Make me to love all men, and enable me to use thy gifts, whatever thou shalt bestow, to the benefit of my fellow creatures. So lighten the weight of years, and so mitigate the

you to him. If your company does not drive a man out of his house, nothing will."' *Life*, iii. 316.

[1] 'EDWARDS. "Ah, Sir! we are old men now." JOHNSON (who never liked to think of being old), "Don't let us discourage one another."' *Ib.* p. 302. 'Mr. Edwards, when going away, again recurred to his consciousness of senility, and looking full in Johnson's face said to him, "You'll find in Dr. Young,

O my coevals! remnants of yourselves."

Johnson did not relish this at all; but shook his head with impatience.' *Ib.* p. 306.

[2] *Inservi Deo et laetare*—Serve God and be cheerful—is the motto round the picture of Hacket, Bishop of Lichfield and Coventry. *Life*, i. 344, *n.* 4.

Perhaps Johnson was reminded of the duty of cheerfulness by Edwards who had said:—'You are a philosopher, Dr. Johnson. I have tried too in my time to be a philosopher; but, I don't know how, cheerfulness was always breaking in.' *Ib.* p. 305.

afflictions

afflictions of disease that I may continue fit for thy service, and useful in my station. And so let me pass through this life by the guidance of thy Holy Spirit, that at last I may enter into eternal joy, through Jesus Christ our Lord. Amen.

126.

Having gone to bed about two I rose about nine, and, having prayed, went to Church. I came early and used this prayer. After sermon I again used my Prayer; the collect for the day I repeated several times, at least the petitions. I recommended my friends. At the altar I prayed earnestly, and when I came home prayed for pardon and peace; repeated my own prayer, and added the petitions of the Collect.

O God have mercy upon me, for the sake of Jesus Christ. Amen.

At my return home, I returned thanks for the opportunity of Communion.

I was called down to Mrs. Nollikens[1]. Boswel came in[2]; then Dinner. After dinner which I believe was late, I read the First Epistle to Thess.; then went to Evening prayers; then came to tea, and afterwards tried Vossius de Baptismo[3]. I was sleepy.

127.

Monday, *Apr.* 20 [1778].

After a good night, as I am forced to reckon, I rose seasonably, and prayed, using the collect for yesterday.

In reviewing my time from Easter —77, I find a very melancholy and shameful blank. So little has been done that

[1] Mrs. Nollekens, the wife of Joseph Nollekens, 'the statuary,' who made a bust of Johnson. *Letters*, ii. 59, 62. She was the daughter of Johnson's friend, Saunders Welch, the magistrate. *Life*, iii. 216. "I have heard Mr. Nollekens say that Dr. Johnson, when joked about Mary Welch, observed, "Yes, I think Mary would have been mine, if little Joe had not stepped in."" *Nollekens and his Times*, by J. T. Smith, i. 126. Smith gives many instances of her meanness.

[2] *Life*, iii. 316.

[3] The 443rd lot in the sale catalogue of Johnson's library was 'Vossii dissertationes, Amst. 1642,' in six volumes.

days

days and months are without any trace [1]. My health has indeed been very much interrupted. My nights have been commonly not only restless but painful and fatiguing. My respiration was once so difficult, that an asthma was suspected [2]. I could not walk but with great difficulty, from Stowhill to Greenhill [3]. Some relaxation of my breast has been procured, I think, by opium, which, though it never gives me sleep, frees my breast from spasms [4].

I have written a little of the Lives of the poets, I think with all my usual vigour [5]. I have made sermons, perhaps as readily as formerly [6]. My memory is less faithful in retaining names, and, I am afraid, in retaining occurrences. Of this vacillation and vagrancy of mind I impute a great part to a fortuitous and unsettled life, and therefore purpose to spend my time with more method.

This year, the 28th of March passed away without memorial. Poor Tetty, whatever were our faults and failings, we loved each other. I did not forget thee yesterday. Couldest thou have lived !——

I am now, with the help of God, to begin a new life.

[1] Macaulay recorded in his Journal in 1857:—'How the days steal away and nothing done! I think often of Johnson's lamentations repeated every Easter over his own idleness. But the cases differ. Often I have felt this morbid incapacity to work; but never so long and so strong as of late; the natural effect of age and ease.' Trevelyan's *Macaulay*, ed. 1877, ii. 447. It was much more the effect of ill-health.

[2] In the last year of his life he suffered greatly from spasmodic asthma. *Life*, iv. 255.

[3] Two gentle eminences on the outskirts of Lichfield. *Letters*, i. 160, 363.

[4] For his 'horror of opiates' see *Letters*, ii. 367, 376, 383. Nevertheless Hawkins says that 'he had a strong propensity to the use of opium, which increased as he advanced in years . . . It was the means of positive pleasure, and as such was resorted to by him whenever any depression of spirits made it necessary.' *Life of Johnson*, p. 320.

[5] He had a proof-sheet of his *Life of Waller* on Good Friday, though he would not look at it on that day. *Life*, iii. 313. He seems to have finished first the *Lives of Denham, Butler and Waller*. *Cowley* he had sent to the printer by the end of the following July. *Milton* was not yet begun by that time, though 'in *Dryden* he was very far advanced.' *Letters*, ii. 68.

[6] *Life*, v. 67.

Almighty

128.

Jan. 1, 1779, before one in the morning.

Almighty God, merciful Father, who hast granted to me the beginning of another year, grant that I may employ thy gifts to thy glory, and my own salvation. Excite me to amend my life. Give me good resolutions, and enable me to perform them. As I approach the Grave let my Faith be invigorated, my Hope exalted, and my Charity enlarged. Take not from me thy Holy Spirit, but in the course of my life protect me, in the hour of death sustain me, and finally receive me to everlasting happiness, for the sake of Jesus Christ. Amen.

129.

1779, GOOD FRIDAY, *Apr.* 2.

After a night restless and oppressive, I rose this morning somewhat earlier than is usual, and having taken tea which was very necessary to compose the disorder in my breast, having eaten nothing I went to church with Boswel[1]. We came late, I was able to attend the litany with little perturbation. When we came home I began the first to the Thess. having prayed by the collect for the right use of the Scriptures. I gave Boswel Les Pensées de Pascal that he might not interrupt me. I did not, I believe, read very diligently, and before I had read far, we went to Church again, I was again attentive. At home I read again, then drank tea with a bun and an half, thinking

[1] Boswell records of this visit, that 'finding that we insensibly fell into a train of ridicule upon the foibles of one of our friends, a very worthy man, I, by way of a check, quoted some good admonition from *The Government of the Tongue*, that very pious book.' *Life*, iii. 379. *Worthy* is almost always applied to Langton. His foibles were a common subject of their talk. *Ib.* iii. 48. Probably the book had been just given to Boswell by Langton, as may be inferred from the following inscription in a copy bought at the sale of the Auchinleck Library by my friend Mr. R. B. Adam of Buffalo:—

'James Boswell
London 1779.

Presented to me by my worthy freind Bennet Langton Esq: of Langton, as a Book by which I might be much improved, viz. by the Goverment of the Tongue. He gave me the Book and hoped I would read that treatise; but said no more. I have expressed in words what I beleive was his meaning. It was a delicate admonition.'

myself

myself less able to fast, than at former times; and then concluded the Epistle. Being much oppressed with drowsiness, I slept about an hour by the fire.

11 p.m.

I am now to review the last year, and find little but dismal vacuity, neither business nor pleasure; much intended and little done. My health is much broken; my nights afford me little rest. I have tried opium, but its help is counterbalanced with great disturbance; it prevents the spasms, but it hinders sleep[1]. O God, have mercy on me.

Last week I published the lives of the poets[2], written I hope in such a manner as may tend to the promotion of Piety[3].

In this last year I have made little acquisition, I have scarcely read any thing. I maintain Mrs. Desmoulins and her daughter[4], other good of myself I know not where to find, except a little Charity.

But I am now in my seventieth year; what can be done ought not to be delayed.

130.

Easter Eve, *April* 3, [1779], 11 p.m.

This is the time of my annual review, and annual resolution. The review is comfortless. Little done. Part of the life of Dryden and the Life of Milton have been written[5]; but my mind has neither been improved nor enlarged. I have read little, almost nothing[6]. And I am not conscious that I have gained any good, or quitted any evil habits.

Of resolutions I have made so many with so little effect, that I am almost weary, but, by the Help of God, am not yet hopeless.

[1] Dr. Brocklesby noticed what Johnson had told him, that 'an opiate was never destructive of his readiness in conversation.' *Letters*, ii. 437.

[2] The first four of the ten volumes. The last six were published in 1781.

[3] Quoted in the *Life*, iv. 34.

[4] *Ib.* iii. 222.

[5] He had written most of the *Life of Dryden* before the previous Easter. '*The Life of Milton* was begun in January, 1779, and finished in six weeks.' *Gentleman's Magazine*, 1785, p. 9, *n.* 1.

[6] For Johnson's use of the phrase *almost nothing* see *Life*, ii. 446, *n.* 3. Beattie reckoned it as a Scotticism. *Scotticisms*, ed. 1787, p. 9.

hopeless. Good resolutions must be made and kept[1]. I am almost seventy years old, and have no time to lose. The distressful restlessness of my nights, makes it difficult to settle the course of my days. Something however let me do.

131.

EASTER DAY, *Apr.* 4, 1779.

I rose about half an hour after nine, transcribed the prayer written last night, and by neglecting to count time sat too long at Breakfast, so that I came to Church at the first lesson. I attended the litany pretty well, but in the pew could not hear the communion service, and missed the prayer for the Church militant. Before I went to the altar I prayed the occasional prayer. At the altar I commended my Θ. Φ.[2] and

[1] More than twenty years earlier he had written:—'I believe most men may review all the lives that have passed within their observation without remembering one efficacious resolution, or being able to tell a single instance of a course of practice suddenly changed in consequence of a change of opinion, or an establishment of determination.' *Idler*, No. 27. See *ante*, p. 31.

[2] A writer in the *Gentleman's Magazine*, 1785, p. 731, deciphered these letters as 'θανοντας φιλους, deceased friends'; another ridiculously as 'Thrale friends.' *Ib.* 1838, ii. 364. The following letter by Dr. Henry Jackson, published in the *Athenaeum*, June 18, 1887, gives, no doubt, the true explanation.

'Trinity College, Cambridge, June 14, 1887.

'"Mr. Croker has favoured us," writes Macaulay in his essay on Croker's 'Boswell,' "with some Greek of his own. 'At the altar,' says Dr. Johnson, 'I recommended my θ φ.' 'These letters,' says the editor, '(which Dr. Strahan seems not to have understood) probably mean θνητοι φιλοι, "departed friends."' Johnson was not a first-rate Greek scholar; but he knew more Greek than most boys when they leave school; and no schoolboy could venture to use the word θνητοι in the sense which Mr. Croker ascribes to it without imminent danger of a flogging."

'Macaulay's criticism of Croker's Greek is plainly just; θνητός never means anything except "mortal." But the great essayist had no other interpretation to offer. Accordingly a lively writer [Mr. Andrew Lang] in the *Daily News* of June 6th, admitting that "the Greek would be bad Greek," asks, "Would it not be good enough Greek shorthand for Dr. Johnson?" May I attempt another solution of the mystery?

'From the time of his wife's death on Tuesday, March 17, O.S., 1752, Johnson was in the habit of keeping Easter Day with special solemnity. In particular he "commended" in his prayers his wife, his father, his brother, his mother, and in some cases others, e.g. "Bathurst" and "Boothby." See Easter Day, 1759, again

again prayed the prayer, I then prayed the collects, and again my own prayer by memory. I left out a clause. I then received, I hope with earnestness, and while others received sat down, but thinking that posture, though usual, improper I rose and stood. I prayed again in the pew but with what prayer I have forgotten.

When I used the occasional prayer at the altar, I added a general purpose

To avoid Idleness.

I gave two shillings, to the plate.

Before I went I used, I think, my prayer and endeavoured to calm my mind. After my return I used it again, and the collect for the day. Lord have mercy upon me.

I have for some nights called Francis to prayers, and last night discoursed with him on the sacrament.

1764, 1770 ("friends living and dead"), 1773, 1777, 1778 [*ante*, pp. 24, 29, 54, 65, 80, 85], in his *Prayers and Meditations.*

'On Easter Day, April 4, 1779, occurs the phrase under discussion: "At the altar I commended my Θ Φ." But on Easter Day, 1781, he writes: "I commended my Θ friends, as I have formerly done." Strahan notes "*sic* MS." [*Post*, p. 98.]

'There can be no doubt, then, that Θ Φ means "dead friends," and very little that Φ stands for *φίλοι*.

'Now we know from Galen (Kühn's edition, XVII. i. 527) that in the case-book of a physician the letters *υ* and *θ* stood for *ὑγίεια* and *θάνατος* respectively: *ἐπὶ δὲ τῇ τελευτῇ τοῖς μὲν σωθεῖσιν υ προσγέγραπται, τὴν ὑγίειαν σημαῖνον, τοῖς δ' ἀποθανοῦσι τὸ θ, καὶ τοῦτο δηλονότι τὸν θάνατον ἐνδεικνύμενον.* And Forcellini quotes Rufinus, *Invect. in Hieron.*, ii. 36, to show that in the muster-roll of a Roman army the letter *θ* was affixed to the names of soldiers who were dead: "quod tale esset quale si quis accepto breviculo in quo militum nomina continentur nitatur inspicere quanti ex militibus supersint, quanti in bello ceciderint, et requirens qui inspicere missus et propriam notam . . . Θ ad uniuscuiusque defuncti nomen adscribat, et propria rursus nota [sc. v = vivit] superstitem signet." "Hinc etiam in vet. lapidibus," continues the lexicographer, "illud Θ videre est ap. *Marin. Frat. Arv.* p. 610." Thus, with the Romans, as well as with the Greeks, *θ* was a *symbol*, meaning "dead," or "died," or "is dead," and as such Johnson, I think, used it. In a word, it exactly corresponds to the cross (†) which is sometimes used in German books.

'Finally, Johnson may have learnt the symbol from Casaubon's note on *Persius*, iv. 13, "Nigrum vitio praefigere theta," where the passage from Rufinus is quoted. H. J.'

See *ante*, p. 76.

132.

EASTER DAY PRAYER, 1779.

Purposes, Apr. 4.

1. To rise at eight, or as soon as I can.
2. To read the Scriptures.
3. To study religion.

Almighty God, by thy merciful continuance of my life, I come once more to commemorate the sufferings and death of thy Son Jesus Christ, and to implore that mercy which for his sake thou shewest to sinners. Forgive me my sins, O Lord, and enable me to forsake them. Ease, if it shall please thee, the anxieties of my mind, and relieve the infirmities of my Body. Let me not be disturbed by unnecessary terrours, and let not the weakness of age make me unable to amend my life. O Lord, take not from me thy Holy Spirit, but receive my petitions, succour and comfort me, and let me so pass the remainder of my days, that when thou shalt call me hence I may enter into eternal happiness through Jesus Christ our Lord. Amen.

133.

Aug. 7, 1779. Partem brachii dextri carpo proximam et cutem pectoris circa mamillam dextram rasi, ut notum fieret quanto temporis pili renovarentur[1].

134.

September 18, 1779, h.p.m. 12 ma.

Almighty God, Creator of all things in whose hands are Life and death, glory be to thee for thy mercies, and for the prolongation of my Life to the common age of Man. Pardon me, O gracious God, all the offences which in the course of seventy years I have committed against thy holy Laws, and all negligences of those Duties which thou hast required. Look with pity upon me, take not from me thy Holy Spirit, but enable me

[1] *Life*, iii. 398. 'I shaved the part of my right arm that is next to the wrist and the skin of my chest round the right breast so that it might be seen how long it would take for the hair to grow again.'

to

to pass the days which thou shalt yet vouchsafe to grant me, in thy Fear and to thy Glory; and accept O Lord, the remains of a mispent life, that when Thou shalt call me to another state, I may be received to everlasting happiness for the sake of Jesus Christ our Lord. Amen.

135.

Epsom [1].

My Purpose is to communicate at least thrice a year [2].

To study the Scriptures.

To be diligent.

On the 17th, Mr. Chamier took me away with him from Streatham. I left the servants a guinea for my health, and was content enough to escape into a house where my Birth-day not being known could not be mentioned [3]. I sat up till midnight was past, and the day of a new year, a very awful day, began. I prayed to God, who had [safely brought me to the beginning of another year], but could not perfectly recollect the prayer, and supplied it [4]. Such desertions of memory I have always had [5].

When I rose on the 18th, I think I prayed again, then walked with my Friend into his grounds. When I came back after some time passed in the library, finding myself oppressed by sleepiness I retired to my chamber, where, by lying down, and a short imperfect slumber I was refreshed, and prayed as the night before.

[1] He was at the house of Andrew Chamier, a member of the Literary Club, at this time Under-Secretary of State. *Life*, i. 478, and *Letters*, ii. 109, *n*. 1.

[2] Apparently in most years he only communicated on Easter Sunday. Two years later he still has 'hope of participation of the Sacrament at least three times a year.' *Post*, p. 100. It would seem that before his wife's death he had not always communicated at Easter. *Ante*, p. 78, and *post*, p. 98.

[3] 'On the birthday of our eldest daughter,' writes Mrs. Piozzi, 'and that of our friend, Dr. Johnson, the 17th and 18th of September, we every year made up a little dance and supper to divert our servants and their friends.' Piozzi's *Anecdotes*, p. 211. See *ante*, p. 67.

[4] He could not perfectly recollect his 'accommodation' of the prayer (*ante*, p. 32) and supplied the deficiency by other words.

[5] 'JOHNSON. "Memory will play strange tricks. One sometimes loses a single word. I once lost *fugaces* in the Ode *Posthume, Posthume*."' *Life*, v. 68.

I then

I then dined and trifled in the parlour and library, and was freed from a scruple about Horace[1]. At last I went to Bed, having first composed a prayer.

19. Sunday. I went to Church, and attended the Service. I found at church a time to use my prayer, O Lord, have mercy.

136.

1780, *Jan.* 1, h. 1 a.m.[2]

Almighty God, my Creator and Preserver by whose mercy my life has been continued to the beginning of another year, grant me with encrease of days, encrease of Holiness, that as I live longer, I may be better prepared to appear before thee, when thou shalt call me from my present state.

Make me, O Lord, truly thankful for the mercy which Thou hast vouchsafed to shew me through my whole life; make me thankful for the health which thou hast restored in the last year, and let the remains of my strength and life be employed to thy glory and my own salvation.

Take not, O Lord, Thy holy Spirit from me; enable me to avoid or overcome all that may hinder my advancement in Godliness; let me be no longer idle, no longer sinful; but give me rectitude of thought and constancy of action, and bring me at last to everlasting happiness for the sake of Jesus Christ, our Lord and Saviour. Amen.

137.

Sunday, *June* 18, 1780.

In the morning of this day last year I perceived the remission of those convulsions in my breast which had distressed me for more than twenty years[3]. I returned thanks at Church for the mercy granted me, which has now continued a year.

THANKSGIVING.

Almighty God, our Creatour and Preserver, from whom proceedeth all good, enable me to receive with humble acknow-

[1] For his scruples, see *ante*, p. 41, and *post*, p. 113.

[2] *Hora prima ante meridiem*. One o'clock in the night.

[3] 'By removing that disorder,' he wrote to Mrs. Thrale, 'a great improvement was made in the enjoyment of life.' *Letters*, ii. 181. See also *ib.*, p. 143, *n.* 3.

ledgment

ledgment of thy unbounded benignity, and with due consciousness of my own unworthiness, that recovery and continuance of health which thou hast granted me, and vouchsafe to accept the thanks which I now offer. Glory be to Thee, O Lord, for this and all thy mercies. Grant, I beseech Thee, that the health and life which thou shalt yet allow me, may conduce to my eternal happiness. Take not from me thy Holy Spirit, but so help and bless me, that when Thou shalt call me hence I may obtain pardon and salvation, for the sake of Jesus Christ our Lord. Amen.

138.

Sept. 18, 1780.

I am now beginning the seventy second year of my life, with more strength of body and greater vigour of mind than, I think, is common at that age [1]. But though the convulsions in my breast are relieved, my sleep is seldom long. My Nights are wakeful, and therefore I am sometimes sleepy in the day. I have been attentive to my diet, and have diminished the bulk of my body [2]. I have not at all studied, nor written diligently. I have Swift and Pope yet to write, Swift is just begun [3].

I have forgotten or neglected my resolutions or purposes, [which] I now humbly and timorously renew. Surely I shall not spend my whole life with my own total disapprobation [4]. Perhaps God may grant me now to begin a wiser and a better life.

Almighty God, my Creator and Preserver, who hast permitted me to begin another year, look with mercy upon my wretchedness and frailty. Rectify my thoughts, relieve my perplexities,

[1] Quoted in the *Life*, iii. 440. Nearly six years earlier he had written to Dr. Taylor:—'You and I have had ill-health, yet in many respects we bear time better than most of our friends.' *Letters*, i. 305.

[2] On April 8 he had written:—'For some time past I have abated much of my diet, and am, I think, the better for abstinence.' *Ib.* ii. 135.

[3] He had written to Mrs. Thrale on May 30:—'I have been so idle that I know not when I shall get either to you or to any other place; for my resolution is to stay here till the work is finished . . . I hope however to see standing corn in some part of the earth this summer, but I shall hardly smell hay or suck clover flowers.' *Letters*, ii. 163.

[4] Quoted in the *Life*, iii. 440.

strengthen

strengthen my purposes, and reform my doings. Let encrease of years bring encrease of Faith, Hope, and Charity. Grant me diligence in whatever work thy Providence shall appoint me. Take not from me thy Holy Spirit but let me pass the remainder of the days which thou shalt yet allow me, in thy fear and to thy Glory; and when it shall be thy good pleasure to call me hence, grant me, O Lord, forgiveness of my sins, and receive me to everlasting happiness, for the Sake of Jesus Christ, our Lord. Amen.

10.40 p.m.

130.

1781.

Jan. 2. I was yesterday hindred by my old disease of mind, and therefore begin to day.

Jan. 1. Having sat in my chamber till the year began I used my accommodation of the morning prayer *to the beginning of this year*, and slept remarkably well, though I had supped liberally [1]. In the morning I went to Church. Then I wrote letters for Mrs. Desmoulins [2], then went to Streatham, and had many stops [3]. At night I took wine, and did not sleep well.

Jan. 2. I rose according to my resolution, and am now to begin another year. I hope with amendment of life.—I will not despair. Help me, help me, O my God. My hope is

1. To rise at eight or sooner.
2. To read the Bible through this year in some language.
3. To keep a Journal [4].
   To study Religion.
   To avoid Idleness.

Almighty God merciful Father, who hast granted me such continuance of Life, that I now see the beginning of another year, look with mercy upon me, as thou grantest encrease of

[1] See *Letters*, ii. 306, for 'a liberal dinner,' and *post*, p. 104, for 'I dined liberally.'

[2] Of these letters none have been published. See *Letters*, ii. 207, for one written two days earlier in which he recommends her for the post of 'matron of the Chartreux.'

[3] I conjecture that he means *obstructions or impediments in the mind*—part of what he calls 'my old disease of mind.'

[4] *Ante*, p. 64.

years,

years, grant encrease of Grace. Let me live to repent what I have done amiss, and by thy help so to regulate my future life, that I may obtain mercy when I appear before thee, through the merits of Jesus Christ. Enable me, O Lord, to do my duty with a quiet mind; and take not from me thy Holy Spirit, but protect and bless me, for the sake of Jesus Christ. Amen.

140.

Apr. 13, GOOD FRIDAY, 1781.

I forgot my Prayer and resolutions, till two days ago I found this paper.

Sometime in March I finished the lives of the Poets, which I wrote in my usual way, dilatorily and hastily, unwilling to work, and working with vigour and haste[1].

On Wednesday 11, was buried my dear Friend Thrale who died on Wednesday, 4; and with him were buried many of my hopes and pleasures. On Sunday 1st his Physician warned him against full meals, on Monday I pressed him to observance of his rules, but without effect, and Tuesday I was absent, but his Wife pressed forbearance upon him, again unsuccessfully. At night I was called to him, and found him senseless in strong convulsions. I staid in the room, except that I visited Mrs. Thrale twice[2]. About five(, I think), on Wednesday morning he expired; I felt almost the last flutter of his pulse, and looked for the last time upon the face that for fifteen years had never been turned upon me but with respect or benignity[3]. Farewel[4]. May God that delighteth in mercy, have had mercy on thee.

I had constantly prayed for him some time before his death.

[1] Macaulay recorded in his Journal in July, 1852:—'I could write a queer Montaignish essay on my morbidities. I sometimes lose months, I do not know how; accusing myself daily, and yet really incapable of vigorous exertion. I seem under a spell of laziness. Then I warm, and can go on working twelve hours at a stretch.' Trevelyan's *Macaulay*, ed. 1877, ii. 317.

[2] 'His servants (he said) would have waited upon him in this awful period, and why not his friend?' *Life*, iv. 84, *n.* 4. The advice which Johnson gave to Thrale was given by Taylor to Johnson three and a half years later. 'He extremely resented it from me,' wrote Taylor. *Letters*, ii. 426, *n.* 3.

[3] Quoted in the *Life*, iv. 84.

[4] Johnson, as I have shown in the Preface to his Letters (p. xv), often left out the second final consonant.

The decease of him from whose friendship I had obtained many opportunities of amusement, and to whom I turned my thoughts as to a refuge from misfortunes, has left me heavy. But my business is with myself.

Sept. 18. My first knowledge of Thrale was in 1765. I enjoyed his favour for almost a fourth part of my life [1].

141.

EASTER EVE, *Apr.* 14, 1781.

On Good Friday I took in the Afternoon some coffee and buttered cake, and to-day I had a little bread at breakfast, and potatoes and apples in the afternoon, the tea with a little toast, but I find myself feeble and unsustained, and suspect that I cannot bear to fast so long as formerly [2].

This day I read some of Clark's Sermons. I hope that since my last Communion I have advanced, by pious reflections in my submission to God, and my benevolence to Man, but I have corrected no external habits, nor have kept any of the resolutions made in the beginning of the year, yet I hope still to be reformed, and not to lose my whole life in idle purposes. Many years are already gone, irrevocably past, in useless Misery, that what remains may be spent better grant O God.

By this awful Festival is particularly recommended Newness of Life; and a new Life I will now endeavour to begin by more diligent application to useful employment, and more frequent attendance on public Worship.

I again with hope of help from the God of mercy, resolve

To avoid Idleness.

To read the Bible.

To study religion.

Almighty God, merciful Father, by whose Protection I have been preserved, and by whose clemency I have been spared,

[1] See *Life*, i. 520; iv. 85; and *Letters*, i. 142, 388; ii. 47, 100, 209, 211, 214.

[2] On Saturday in Passion Week in 1766 he recorded:—'I had lived more abstemiously than is usual the whole week, and taken physick twice, which together made the fast more uneasy.' *Ante*, p. 39. The present week, however, he had dined twice with Bishops, and therefore presumably dined well. He should have better borne to fast. See *Life*, iv. 88.

grant

grant that the life which thou hast so long continued may be no longer wasted in idleness or corrupted by wickedness. Let my future purposes be good, and let not my good purposes be vain. Free me O Lord from vain terrours, and strengthen me in diligent obedience to thy laws. Take not from me thy Holy Spirit, but enable me so to commemorate the death of my Saviour Jesus Christ, that I may be made partaker of his merits, and may finally, for his sake obtain everlasting happiness. Amen.

142.

EASTER SUNDAY, 1781.

I rose after eight, and breakfasted, then went early to church, and before service read the prayer for the Church Militant. I commended my Θ [1] friends as I have formerly done. I was one of the last that communicated. When I came home I was hindred by Visitants [2], but found time to pray before dinner. God send thy Blessing upon me.

143.

Monday, *Apr.* 16.

Yesterday at dinner was Mrs. Hall, Mr. Levet, Macbean, Boswel, Allen [3]. Time passed in talk after dinner. At seven I went with Mrs. Hall to Church, and came back to tea. At night I had some mental vellications, or revulsions [4]. I prayed in my chamber with Frank, and read the first Sunday in the Duty of Man, in which I had till then only looked by compulsion or by chance [5].

I paid the Pewkeepers.

This day I repeated my prayer, and hope to be heard.

I have, I thank God, received the Sacrament every year at Easter since the death of my poor dear Tetty. I once felt

[1] *Ante*, p. 89.

[2] He a second time (*post*, p. 105) uses *visitants* where we should use *visitors*. But *post*, p. 107, he speaks of *visitors*.

[3] For an account of this dinner, see *Life*, iv. 92.

[4] *Vellication* he defines as *twitchings, stimulation*; and *revulsion* as *the act of revolving or drawing humours from a remote part of the body*. See *ante*, p. 95, for his 'old disease of mind.'

[5] See *ante*, p. 17, *n*. 1. *The Whole Duty of Man* is divided into seventeen Sundays.

some

some temptation to omit it, but I was preserved from compliance. This was the thirtieth Easter. Sept. 18.

144.

1781, *June* 22.

Almighty God who art the Giver of all good enable me to remember with due thankfulness the comforts and advantages which I have enjoyed by the friendship of Henry Thrale, for whom, so far as is lawful, I humbly implore thy mercy in his present state. O Lord, since thou hast been pleased to call him from this world, look with mercy on those whom he has left, continue to succour me by such means as are best for me, and repay to his relations the kindness which I have received from him; protect them in this world from temptations and calamities, and grant them happiness in the world to come, for Jesus Christs sake. Amen.

145.

August 9, 3 P.M., ætat. 72, in the summer-house at Streatham.

After innumerable resolutions formed and neglected, I have retired hither, to plan a life of greater diligence, in hope that I may yet be useful, and be daily better prepared to appear before my Creator and my Judge, from whose infinite mercy I humbly call for assistance and support.

My purpose is,

To pass eight hours every day in some serious employment.

Having prayed, I purpose to employ the next six weeks upon the Italian language, for my settled study [1].

146.

Sept. 2, 1781.

When Thrales health was broken, for many months, I think before his death which happened Apr. [2], I constantly men-

[1] *Life*, iv. 134. The original is in the possession of Mr. Locker-Lampson of Rowfant. A picture of the summer-house by Clarkson Stanfield is given in Murray's *Johnsoniana*, ed. 1836, p. 68.

[2] Johnson left a blank, intending no doubt to fill it up. Thrale died on April 4, the seventh anniversary of Goldsmith's death.

tioned him in my prayers; and after his death have made particular supplication for his surviving family to this day, but having now recommended them to God in this particular address, which though written—[1]

147.

Sept. 18, 1781.

This is my seventy third birth-day an awful day. I said a preparatory prayer last night, and waking early made use in the dark, as I sat up in bed of the prayer [beginning of this year[2]]. I rose breakfasted, and gave thanks at Church[3] for my Creation, Preservation, and REDEMPTION. As I came home I thought I had never begun any period of life so placidly. I read the Second Epistle to the Thessalonians, and looked into Hammond's notes[4]. I have always [been] accustomed to let this day pass unnoticed, but it came this time into my mind that some little festivity was not improper. I had a dinner, and invited Allen and Levet[5].

What has passed in my thoughts on this anniversary is in stitched book K[6].

My purposes are the same as on the first day of this year, to which I add hope of

More frequent attendance on publick Worship.

Participation of the Sacrament at least three times a year[7].

148.

Sept. 18, Vesp. 10° 40′, circ.[8]

Almighty and most merciful Father, who hast added another year to my life, and yet permittest me to call upon thee,

[1] The rest of the sentence is missing.

[2] *Ante*, p. 42, *n.* 1.

[3] It was a week-day.

[4] Henry Hammond, D.D. Isaac Walton describes the discourse which Dr. Hammond and Dr. Sanderson had 'about those knotty points which are by the learned called the Quinquarticular Controversy.' Walton's *Lives*, ed. 1838, p. 372.

[5] For his unwillingness to have the day noticed, see *ante*, p. 67. In 1783 he again gave a dinner on his birthday. *Letters*, ii. 332. Allen was his neighbour and landlord. *Life*, iii. 141. For Levett, see *post*, p. 102.

[6] This book is not in the Editor's possession. Note by G. Strahan.

[7] *Ante*, p. 92, *n.* 2.

[8] *Vesperi* 10° 40′ *circiter*. About 10.40 at night.

Grant

Grant that the remaining days which thou shalt yet allow me may be past in thy fear and to thy glory, grant me good resolutions and steady perseverance. Relieve the diseases of my body and compose the disquiet of my mind. Let me at last repent and amend my life, and, O Lord, take not from me thy Holy Spirit, but assist my amendment, and accept my repentance, for the sake of Jesus Christ. Amen.

149.

Oct. 14, Sunday, [1781.]
(properly Monday morning [1].)

I am this day about to go by Oxford and Birmingham to Lichfield and Ashbourne. The motives of my journey I hardly know. I omitted it last year, and am not willing to miss it again. Mrs. Aston [2] will be glad, I think, to see me. We are both old, and if I put off my visit, I may see her no more; perhaps she wishes for another interview. She is a very good woman.

Hector is likewise an old friend, the only companion of my childhood that passed through the School with me. We have always loved one another [3]. Perhaps we may be made better by some serious conversation, of which however I have no distinct hope.

At Lichfield, my native place, I hope to shew a good example by frequent attendance on publick worship [4].

At Ashbourne I hope to talk seriously with Taylor [5].

[1] Part of this entry is quoted in the *Life*, iv. 135.

[2] One of the unmarried daughters of Sir Thomas Aston. She lived at Lichfield. *Life*, ii. 466.

[3] Hector was a Birmingham surgeon. *Life*, ii. 456; *Letters*, ii. 228.

[4] To make up perhaps for his shirking it in his boyhood. *Life*, i. 67.

[5] Taylor published in 1787 *A Letter to Samuel Johnson on the Subject of a Future State.* He writes that 'having heard that Johnson had said that he would prefer a state of torment to that of annihilation, he told him that such a declaration, coming from him, might be productive of evil consequences. Dr. J. desired him to arrange his thoughts on the subject.' Taylor says that Johnson's entry about the serious talk refers to this matter. *Gent. Mag.* 1787, p. 521. I believe that Johnson meant to warn Taylor about the danger *he* was running of 'entering the state of torment.'

January

150.

1782.

January 20, Sunday. Robert Levett was buried in the church-yard of Bridewell, between one and two in the afternoon. He died on Thursday 17, about seven in the morning, by an instantaneous death. He was an old and faithful friend; I have known him from about 46. *Commendavi.* May God have mercy on him. May he have mercy on me[1].

151.

1782, *March* 18.

Having been, from the middle of January, distressed by a cold which made my respiration very laborious, and from which I was but little relieved by being blooded three times, having tried to ease the oppression of my breast by frequent opiates, which kept me waking in the night and drowsy the next day, and subjected me to the tyranny of vain imaginations; Having to all this added frequent catharticks, sometimes with mercury; I at last persuaded Dr. Laurence on Thursday March 14 to let me bleed more copiously. Sixteen ounces were taken away, and from that time my breath has been free, and my breast easy. On that day I took little food, and no flesh[2]. On Thursday night I slept with great tranquillity. On the next night (15) I took diacodium[3] and had a most restless night. Of the next day I remember nothing but that I rose in the afternoon, and saw Mrs. Lennox[4] and Sheward[5].

[1] *Life*, iv. 137, where are quoted the beautiful lines which Johnson wrote on Levett. For Johnson's 'recommendation' of the dead, see *ante*, p. 14.

[2] He wrote to Mrs. Thrale on the day on which he was bled:—'I think the loss of blood has done no harm; whether it has done good time will tell. I am glad that I do not sink without resistance.' *Letters*, ii. 247. Miss Burney in the previous September had been alarmed at 'his strange discipline—starving, mercury, opium.' Mme. D'Arblay's *Diary*, ii. 107.

[3] Syrup of poppies. He considered *diacodium* an English word, for he gives it in his Dictionary.

[4] Mrs. Lennox he pronounced superior to Mrs. Carter, Hannah More, and Fanny Burney. *Life*, iv. 275. Miss Burney looked upon this statement as one of 'those occasional sallies of Dr. Johnson, which uttered from local causes and circumstances, but all retailed *verbatim* by Mr. Boswell are filling all sort of readers with amaze, except the small party to whom Dr. Johnson was known.' Mme. D'Arblay's *Diary*, v. 212.

[5] Mentioned *ante*, p. 80.

17 Sunday.

17 Sunday. I lay late, and had only Palfrey[1] to dinner. (d. 2*s*. 6.) I read part of Waller's Directory, a pious rational book, but in any except a very regular life difficult to practise[2].

It occurred to me that though my time might pass unemployed, no more should pass uncounted, and this has been written to-day in consequence of that thought. I read a Greek Chapter, prayed with Francis, which I now do commonly, and explained to him the Lord's Prayer, in which I find connection not observed, I think, by the expositors. I made punch[3] for Myself and my servants, by which in the night I thought both my breast and imagination disordered.

March 18. I rose late, looked a little into books. Saw Miss Reynolds and Miss Thrale, and Nicolaida[4], afterwards Dr. Hunter came for his catalogue[5]. I then dined on tea, &c.; then read over part of Dr. Laurence's book de Temperamentis[6], which seems to have been written with a troubled mind.

I prayed with Francis.

My mind has been for some time much disturbed. The Peace of God be with me.

[1] Strahan printed *palfrey*. A critic in *Notes and Queries*, March 2, 1867, suggested that Johnson wrote *pastry*. Palfrey, or Palfry (as Johnson writes the name, *post*, p. 106) was some poor man, to whom he gave (as 'd' probably signifies) on this day and on the 24th, two shillings and sixpence.

[2] *Divine Meditations upon Several Occasions with a Dayly Directory*. By the Excellent Pen of Sir William Waller, Kt. London, 1680. Waller was the Presbyterian general, the 'William the Conqueror' of the citizens of London. Clarendon's *History*, ed. 1826, iv. 114.

The day was strictly divided in the Directory, with frequent private prayers and meditations, and family prayers at noon and supper. 'In summer time I would be up by five; in winter by six. At Meals I would observe a moderation; a mean between eating by the ounce and by the pound.'

[3] In his *Dictionary* he describes *punch* as 'a cant word.'

[4] 'A learned Greek, nephew of the Patriarch of Constantinople, who had fled from a massacre of the Greeks.' Johnstone's *Works of Dr. Parr*, i. 84. See also *ib*. pp. 87-90, and *Life*, ii. 379.

[5] A little later was published an instalment of the Catalogue of Dr. William Hunter's Collection of Coins. It was written by Charles Combe. *Dict. of Nat. Biog*. xi. 427; xxviii. 304.

[6] Mr. Croker thinks that Lawrence had lent Johnson Galen's work *De Temperamentis et inequali temperie*. I conjecture that it was a work in manuscript by Lawrence, who wrote his medical books in Latin. The entries of the 19th and 26th support this view.

I hope

I hope to-morrow to finish Laurence, and to write to Mrs. Aston, and to Lucy.

19. I rose late. I was visited by Mrs. Thrale, Mr. Cotton[1], and Mr. Crofts[2]. I took Laurence's paper in hand, but was chill, having fasted yesterday, I was hungry and dined freely, then slept a little, and drank tea, then took candles and wrote to Aston and Lucy[3], then went on with Laurence of which little remains. I prayed with Francis.

Mens sedatior, laus DEO.

To-morrow Shaw[4] comes, I think to finish Laurence, and write to Langton.

Poor Laurence has almost lost the sense of hearing, and I have lost the conversation of a learned, intelligent, and communicative companion, and a friend whom long familiarity has much endeared. Laurence is one of the best men whom I have known.

Nostrum omnium miserere, Deus[5].

20. Shaw came; I finished reading Laurence. Steevens came. I dined liberally. Wrote a long letter to Langton[6], and designed to read but was hindered by Strahan[7]. The ministry is dissolved. I prayed with Fr. and gave thanks[8].

[1] Mrs. Thrale had cousins of that name. *Life*, v. 435, *n.* 2; *Letters*, ii. 394, *n.*

[2] It was not the Rev. Thomas Crofts, the owner of a famous library, for he had died in 1781. Nichols's *Literary Anecdotes*, viii. 482. See *Letters*, ii. 294, where his name is wrongly given as Croft. Perhaps Johnson's visitor was the Rev. Herbert Croft who had written for him the *Life of Young*. *Life*, iv. 58.

[3] The letter to Mrs. Aston has never been printed; for the letter to Miss Porter, see *Life*, iv. 142.

[4] William Shaw, the Gaelic scholar. *Life*, iii. 106; iv. 252.

[5] This passage about Dr. Lawrence is quoted in the *Life*, iv. 143.

[6] *Life*, iv. 145.

[7] William Strahan, the printer, M.P. for Malmesbury.

[8] Quoted by Boswell under date of Jan. 20. *Life*, iv. 139. On the afternoon of March 20 Lord North announced in the House of Commons 'that his Majesty's Ministers were no more.' *Parl. Hist.* xxii. 125. For Johnson's contempt of this ministry, see *Life*, iii. 1; iv. 139. On March 30 he wrote:—'The men are got in whom I have endeavoured to keep out, but I hope they will do better than their predecessors; it will not be easy to do worse.' *Letters*, ii. 248.

Fifty-one years later Macaulay described 'a splendid rout at Lord Grey's,' who was then Prime Minister. 'I mean,' he wrote, 'only to tell you one circumstance which struck and

To-morrow—To Mrs. Thrale—To write to Hector. To Dr. Taylor.

21. I went to Mrs. Thrale. Mr. Cox [1] and Paradise met me at the door and went with me in the coach. Paradise's loss [2]. In the evening wrote to Hector [3]. At night there were eleven visitants. Conversation with Mr. Cox. When I waked I saw the penthouses covered with snow.

22. I spent the time idly. Mens turbata. In the afternoon it snowed. At night I wrote to Taylor about the pot [4], and to Hamilton about the Fœdera [5].

23. I came home, and found that Desmoulins [6] had while

even affected me. I was talking to Lady Charlotte Lindsay, the daughter of Lord North, about the apartments, when she said with a good deal of emotion, "This is an interesting visit to me. I have never been in this house for fifty years. It was here that I was born; I left it a child when my father fell from power in 1782; and I have never crossed the threshold since."' Trevelyan's *Macaulay*, ed. 1877, i. 299.

[1] Mr. Cox was a solicitor. It was at his house in Southampton Buildings, Chancery Lane, that Burke and Johnson had argued with too much warmth over the management of the defence of Baretti on his trial for murder. 'Burke and I,' said Johnson, 'should have been of one opinion if we had had no audience.' *Life*, iv. 324. It was at the same house about thirteen years earlier that had taken place Jeremy Bentham's 'first conference with Dr. Markham,' the Headmaster of Westminster, afterwards Archbishop of York. 'It was,' said Bentham, 'an awful meeting—with three reverend doctors of divinity at once, in a large room, to whom a trembling lad was introduced, who had been talked of as a prodigy.' Bentham's *Works*, x. 27. See also *ib.*, p. 29, for the disquiet caused the boy by 'a tip' (to use his own word) of five guineas from Cox.

[2] 'John Paradise was born at Salonichi, brought up at Padua, and by far the greatest part of his life resided at London; was passionately fond of learned men, and opened his house to all descriptions of them.' *Annual Register*, 1795, ii. 49. See *Life*, iv. 364. A very large estate belonging to him in America 'had been attached by an order of the United States, who had threatened its confiscation unless the owner appeared in person to claim it.' Jones, the Orientalist, was on the point of sailing with him to America as his legal adviser, but the voyage was abandoned through Paradise's irresolution. Teignmouth's *Jones*, p. 247; Johnstone's *Parr*, i. 84-6.

[3] *Life*, iv. 147.

[4] This letter is not in print. On July 8 he wrote to Taylor:—'Have you settled about the silver coffee-pot? is it mine or Mrs. Fletcher's? I am yet afraid of liking it too well.' *Letters*, ii. 262.

[5] William Gerard Hamilton. The *Foedera* was no doubt the copy of Rymer's work, which Johnson 'sold on the 28th for Davies.' Davies had failed as a bookseller. *Life*, iii. 223.

[6] *Ante*, p. 88.

I was

I was away been in bed. Letters from Langton and Boswel. I promised Lowe[1] six guineas. Corrected proofs for Shaw.

24. Sunday. I rose not early. Visitors Allen[2], Davies[3], Windham[4], Dr. Horseley[5]. Palfry, 2*s*. 6*d*. Dinner at Strahan's. Came home and chatted with Williams[6], and read Romans ix. in Greek.

To-morrow begin again to read the Bible put rooms in order; copy Lowe's Letter.

25. M. I had from Strahan £78. At night of the Bible I read 11 p. and something more in 55′.

26. Tu. I copied Lowe's Letter. Then wrote to Mrs. Thrale[7]. Cox visited me. I sent home Dr. Laurence's papers with notes. I gave Desmoulins a guinea, and found her a gown.

27. W.—At Harley-street[8]. bad nights—in the evening Dr. Bromfield[9] and his Family. Merlin's steelyard[10] given me.

28. Th. I came home. Sold Rymer for Davies: wrote to Boswel[11]. Visitor Dr. Percy[12]. Mr. Crofts. I have in ten days written to Aston, Lucy, Hector, Langton, Boswel; perhaps to all by whom my Letters are desired.

The Weather, which now begins to be warm gives me great help. I have hardly been at Church this year, certainly not since the 15 of Jan. My Cough and difficulty of Breath would not permit it.

This is the day on which in 1752 dear Tetty died. I have

[1] *Life*, iv. 202; *Letters*, ii. 66, 274.

[2] *Ante*, p. 100.

[3] Thomas Davies the bookseller.

[4] Right Hon. William Windham. *Life*, iv. 407; *Letters*, ii. 439.

[5] Afterwards Bishop, first of St. David's, and next of Rochester. He was a member of Johnson's Essex Head Club. *Life*, iv. 254, 437. Gibbon (*Misc. Works*, i. 232) celebrates his 'mighty spear.' According to Jeremy Bentham 'he was a man of free conversation; he was proud and insolent . . . His discourse was such as none but an unbeliever could use. Wilberforce knew his character; he had a perfect abhorrence of him, and I have heard him call him "a dirty rascal" and "a dirty scoundrel."' Bentham's *Works*, x. 41.

[6] Miss Williams. *Post*, p. 114.

[7] This letter has not been published.

[8] Mrs. Thrale had taken a house in this street for three months of this year. Hayward's *Piozzi*, 2nd ed., i. 165.

[9] *Letters*, i. 178, *n*. 6.

[10] Mention is made of 'Mr. Merlin, the very ingenious mechanic' in the *Early Diary of Frances Burney*, ii. 58, 300. See also Mme. D'Arblay's *Diary*, ii. 6, 52.

[11] *Life*, iv. 148.

[12] Editor of the *Reliques*.

now

now uttered a prayer of repentance and c̄.[1]; perhaps Tetty knows that I prayed for her. Perhaps Tetty is now praying for me. God help me. Thou, God, art merciful, hear my prayers, and enable me to trust in Thee.

We were married almost seventeen years, and have now been parted thirty.

I then read 11 p. from Ex. 36. to Lev. 7. I prayed with Fr. and used the prayer for Good Friday.

29. Good Friday. After a night of great disturbance and solicitude, such as I do not remember, I rose, drank tea, but without eating, and went to Church. I was very composed, and coming home, read Hammond on one of the Psalms for the day[2]. I then read Leviticus. Scot[3] came in which hindred me from Church in the afternoon. A kind letter from Gastrel[4]. I read on, then went to Evening prayers, and afterwards drank tea with bunns; then read till I finished Leviticus 24 pages et sup.

To write to Gastrel to morrow.

To look again into Hammond.

30. Sat. Visitors Paradise and I think Horseley. Read 11 pages of the Bible. I was faint, dined on herrings and potatoes. At Prayers, I think, in the Evening. I wrote to Gastrel, and received a kind letter from Hector. At night Lowe. Pr.[5] with Francis.

31. Easter Day. Read 15 pages of the Bible. Cætera alibi[6].

[1] Contrition.

[2] He wrote from Lichfield on July 26, 1775:—'When I came I found Lucy at her book. She had Hammond's *Commentary on the Psalms* before her. He is very learned, she says, but there is enough that anybody may understand.' *Letters*, i. 357. Addison, quoting Fell's *Life of Hammond*, says:—'As this good man was troubled with a complication of distempers, when he had the gout upon him, he used to thank God that it was not the stone; and when he had the stone, that he had not both these distempers on him at the same time.' *The Spectator*, No. 574. Franklin, in a letter written in his old age, utters the same thanks.

[3] Scott had chambers hard by in the Temple, where Johnson and Boswell dined with him on April 10, 1778. *Life*, iii. 261.

[4] Mrs. Gastrell of Lichfield. *Life*, ii. 470. For Johnson's answer to her letter, see *Letters*, ii. 248.

[5] Prayed.

[6] The other book in which he made the remaining entries is, I fear, lost.

152.

At the Table.

Almighty God, by whose mercy I am now permitted to commemorate my Redemption by our Lord Jesus Christ; grant that this aweful remembrance may strengthen my Faith, enliven my Hope, and encrease my Charity; that I may trust in Thee with my whole heart, and do good according to my power. Grant me the help of thy Holy Spirit, that I may do thy will with diligence, and suffer it with humble patience; so that when Thou shalt call me to Judgement, I may obtain forgiveness and acceptance for the sake of Jesus Christ, our Lord and Saviour. Amen.

153.

At departure, or at home.

Grant, I beseech Thee, merciful Lord, that the designs of a new and better life, which by thy Grace I have now formed, may not pass away without effect. Incite and enable me by thy Holy Spirit, to improve the time which Thou shalt grant me; to avoid all evil thoughts words and actions; and to do all the duties which thou shalt set before me. Hear my prayer, O Lord, for the Sake of Jesus Christ. Amen.

These prayers I wrote for Mrs. Lucy Porter in the latter end of the year 1782, and transcribed them October 9, —84[1].

154.

[*On leaving Streatham*[2].]

October 6, 1782.

Almighty God, Father of all mercy, help me by thy Grace that I may with humble and sincere thankfulness remember the

[1] He was staying in her house at Lichfield on that day.

[2] Mrs. Thrale recorded in her Diary on Sept. 20 of this year:—'And now I am going to leave Streatham (I have let the house and grounds to Lord Shelburne, the expense of it eats me up) for three years.' Hayward's *Piozzi*, 2nd ed., i. 171. On July 28, 1790, she wrote:—'We have kept our seventh wedding-day and celebrated our return to this house [Streatham] with prodigious splendour and gaiety. Seventy people to dinner... Never was a pleasanter day seen, and at night the trees and front of the house were illuminated with coloured lamps, that called forth our neigh-

comforts

comforts and conveniences which I have enjoyed at this place, and that I may resign them with holy submission, equally trusting in thy protection when Thou givest and when Thou takest away. Have mercy upon me, O Lord, have mercy upon me.

To thy fatherly protection, O Lord, I commend this family. Bless, guide, and defend them, that they may so pass through this world as finally to enjoy in thy presence everlasting happiness, for Jesus Christs sake. Amen [1].

O Lord, so far as, &c.—Thrale [2].

Oct. 7. I was called early [3]. I packed up my bundles [4], and used the foregoing prayer, with my morning devotions somewhat, I think, enlarged. Being earlier than the family I read St. Pauls farewel in the Acts [5], and then read fortuitously in the Gospels, which was my parting use of the library.

155.

Sunday, went to church at Streatham. *Templo valedixi cum osculo* [6].

Oct. 6, Die Dominica, 1782.

Pransus sum Streathamiæ agninum crus coctum cum herbis (spinach) comminutis, farcimen farinaceum cum uvis passis, lumbos bovillos, et pullum gallinæ Turcicæ; et post carnes missas,

bours from all the adjacent villages to admire and enjoy the diversion.' *Ib.* p. 304.

In 1783 Jeremy Bentham visited Lord Shelburne at Streatham, who at that time was negotiating the Treaty of Peace with France. 'At one of the dinners Gibraltar was the topic, and Rayneval [one of the French negotiators] was very desirous it should be given up by the English. There were among the guests those who thought Gibraltar was not worth keeping.' The Viscount de Vergennes, the son of the Prime Minister of France, said to Bentham:—'Are there any such people in England as authors?' The portraits of 'the wits of the age' whom Reynolds had painted for Thrale were still hanging on the walls. Bentham, who had noticed them, perhaps, by way of answer, pointed out to the foolish Viscount the likenesses of Burke, Johnson, and Goldsmith. Bentham's *Works*, x. 118, 122; *Life*, iv. 158, *n.* 1.

[1] Quoted in the *Life*, iv. 158.

[2] *Ante*, p. 24.

[3] He was perhaps going that day with the Thrales to Brighton. He was there on the 10th. *Letters*, ii. 273. 'I came to Brighthelmston in a state of so much weakness that I rested four times in walking between the inn and the lodging.' *Life*, iv. 156.

[4] See *Letters*, ii. 319, where he says:—'I carried my *budget* myself.'

[5] *Acts* xx. 17–end.

[6] *Life*, iv. 159. 'I bade the church farewell with a kiss.'

missas, ficus, uvas, non admodum maturas, ita voluit anni intemperies, cum malis Persicis, iis tamen duris. Non lætus accubui, cibum modicè sumpsi, ne intemperantiâ ad extremum peccaretur. Si recte memini, in mentem venerunt epulæ in exequiis Hadoni celebratæ. Streathamiam quando revisam[1]?

[1] Oct. 6, Sunday, 1782. I dined at Streatham on a roast leg of lamb with spinach chopped fine, the stuffing of flour with raisins, a sirloin of beef, and a turkey poult; and after the first course figs, grapes not very ripe owing to the bad season, with peaches—hard ones. I took my place in no joyful mood, and dined moderately that I might not at the last fall into the sin of intemperance. If I am not mistaken, the banquet at the funeral of Hadon came into my mind. When shall I see Streatham again?

I have looked in vain in an old cookery-book for a recipe for 'farcimen farinaceum cum uvis passis.' See Piozzi's *Anec.*, p. 102, for Johnson's liking for 'veal-pie with plums and sugar.' Perhaps Mrs. Thrale had ordered his favourite sauce. It seems odd that the lamb, beef and turkey were not followed by a pudding or sweets. There is a passage in Miss Austen's *Pride and Prejudice* (ch. xx) which shows that a dinner, excluding the dessert, often consisted of but one course. 'Mrs. Bennet,' she writes, 'had been strongly inclined to ask them to stay and dine there that day; but, though she always kept a very good table, she did not think any thing less than two courses could . . . satisfy the appetite and pride of one who had ten thousand a year.' Johnson defines *dessert* as 'the last course at an entertainment; the fruit or sweetmeats set on the table after the meat.' Addison in the *Guardian*, No. 163, makes the tart and sweetmeats part of the dessert. It is in this sense that the word is still used in New England.

'Hadonus' is, I conjecture, Walter Haddon, who is mentioned in Johnson's *Life of Milton* (*Works*, vii. 68):—'Haddon and Ascham, the pride of Elizabeth's reign, however they have succeeded in prose, no sooner attempt verse than they provoke derision.'

The following description by Susan Burney shows what Johnson lost in losing Streatham:—

'We arrived at Streatham at a very little past eleven. As a *place* it surpassed all my expectations. The avenue to the house, plantations, &c. are beautiful; worthy of the charming inhabitants. It is a little Paradise, I think. Cattle, poultry, dogs, all running freely about, without annoying each other. Sam opened the chaise door, and told my father breakfast was not quite over, and I had no sooner got out than Mr. Thrale appeared at a window close to the door,—and, indeed, my dear Fanny, you did not tell me anything about him which I did not find *entirely* just. With regard to his reception of me, it was *particularly* polite. I followed my father into the library, which was much such a room as I expected;—a most charming one. There sat Mrs. Thrale and Dr. Johnson, the latter finishing his breakfast upon peaches. Mrs. Thrale immediately rose to meet me very sweetly, and to *welcome me* to Streatham. Dr. Johnson, too, rose. "*How do, dear lady?*" My father told him it was not *his* Miss, but another of his own bant-

1783,

156.

1783, *April* 5. I took leave of Mrs. Thrale. I was much moved. I had some expostulations with her. She said that she was likewise affected. I commended the Thrales with great good will to God; may my petition have been heard[1]!

157.

[In the Auction Catalogue of Messrs. Christie and Co., of June 5, 1888, Lot 67* is 'a leaf of Dr. Johnson's Memorandum Book for the year 1783, containing entries relating to his classical studies, &c.']

158.

June 16. I went to bed, and, as I conceive, about 3 in the morning I had a stroke of the palsy.

17. I sent for Dr. Heberden and Dr. Brocklesby. God bless them.

25. Dr. Heberden took leave[2].

159.

July 10. Dartford, Northfleet.

11. On the Medway.

12. Barber. 13. [Entries illegible.]

13. Church—Dryden.

lings. Dr. Johnson, however, looked at me with great kindness, and not at all in a *discouraging* manner.' *Early Diary of F. Burney*, ii. 256. 'Sam' was Samuel Greaves, at whose tavern, the Essex Head, Johnson started his last Club in 1783. *Life*, iv. 253; *Letters*, ii. 390.

[1] Hawkins's *Johnson*, p. 553. The next day Mrs. Thrale recorded in her Diary:—'I have been very busy preparing to go to Bath and save my money.' Hayward's *Piozzi*, 2nd ed., i. 204. See also *Life*, iv. 198, *n*. 4. Ten weeks later, after his stroke of palsy, Johnson wrote to her: 'I hope that what, when I could speak, I spoke of you and to you will be in a sober and serious hour remembered by you; and surely it cannot be remembered but with some degree of kindness. I have loved you with virtuous affection; I have honoured you with sincere esteem. Let not all our endearments be forgotten, but let me have in this great distress your pity and your prayers.' *Letters*, ii. 302.

[2] Hawkins's *Johnson*, p. 558. For his illness, see *Life*, iv. 227, and *Letters*, ii. 300.

14. Kad-[?]	1	6	6	expense of journey
	0	10	6	to Mr. Wright
	0	5	0	to Labourer
	2	2	0	

15. Receipt for pension April 5—75£. Salust imitates Plato. Longin 13 and Xenophon. Longin [1].

[1] I owe the copy of this entry and those of August 28 and 30 and September 17–18 to the kindness of Mr. Godfrey Locker-Lampson of Rowfant, where the original is preserved.

On July 10 Johnson went to Rochester to visit Bennet Langton who was quartered there as an officer of Militia. Dartford and Northfleet are on the road between Rochester and London.

Johnson wrote to Mrs. Thrale on July 23:—'While I was with Mr. Langton we took four little journies in a chaise, and made one little voyage on the Medway, with four misses and their maid, but they were very quiet.' *Letters*, ii. 320.

His pension was payable quarterly on the old quarter days, Jan. 5, April 5, July 5, Oct. 10. *Life*, i. 376, *n.* 2. Owing to the distressed state of the Treasury, brought about by the American War, payments no doubt were often at this time in arrears. Even in time of peace there had been great delays. Lord Chesterfield, on June 1, 1767, sending some money to his son who was envoy at Dresden, wrote:—'I believe it will come very seasonably, as all places, both foreign and domestic, are so far in arrears. They talk of paying you all up to Christmas. The King's inferior servants are almost starving.' Chesterfield's *Letters*, iv. 262.

Johnson, I conjecture, had found among Langton's books Longinus's *Treatise on the Sublime*. In Section 13 is quoted a passage from Plato's *Republic*, ix. 586 A. where it is said:—Οἱ ἄρα φρονήσεως καὶ ἀρετῆς ἄπειροι . . . βοσκημάτων δίκην κάτω ἀεὶ βλέποντες καὶ κεκυφότες εἰς γῆν καὶ εἰς τραπέζας βόσκονται χορταζόμενοι καὶ ὀχεύοντες. 'They who have no knowledge of wisdom and virtue . . . like beasts ever look downwards, and their heads are bent to the ground, or rather to the table; they feed full their bellies and their lusts' (*Longinus on the Sublime*, translated by H. L. Havell, 1890, p. 28). This recalled to him the opening lines in Sallust's *Catiline*:—'Omnes homines, qui sese student praestare ceteris animalibus, summa ope niti decet, ne vitam silentio transeant veluti pecora, quae natura prona atque ventri obedientia finxit.'

The passage in which Sallust imitated Xenophon was perhaps the following quoted in section 28 from the *Cyropaedia*, i. 5. 12:—Πόνον δὲ τοῦ ζῆν ἡδέως ἡγεμόνα νομίζετε· κάλλιστον δὲ πάντων καὶ πολεμικώτατον κτῆμα εἰς τὰς ψυχὰς συγκεκόμισθε· ἐπαινούμενοι γὰρ μᾶλλον ἢ τοῖς ἄλλοις ἅπασι χαίρετε. [This reading differs somewhat from the accepted text.]

'Labour you regard as the guide to a pleasant life, and you have laid up in your souls the fairest and most soldier-like of all gifts: in praise is your delight—more than in anything else.' Sallust says:—'Verum enimvero is demum mihi vivere atque frui anima videtur, qui aliquo negotio intentus praeclari facinoris aut artis bonae famam quaerit.' *Catilina*, cap. ii.

Almighty

160.

July 30.

Almighty God, Creator and Governor of the World, who sendest sickness and restorest health, enable me to consider, with a just sense of thy mercy, the deliverance which Thou hast lately granted me, and assist by thy Blessing, as is best for me, the means which I shall use for the cure of the disease with which I am now afflicted. Encrease my patience, teach me submission to thy will, and so rule my thoughts and direct my actions, that I may be finally received to everlasting happiness through Jesus Christ our Lord. Amen[1].

161.

Aug. 15, 1783. I cut from the vine 41 leaves, which weighed five oz. and a half, and eight scruples:—I lay them upon my book-case, to see what weight they will lose by drying[2].

162.

August 28. I came to Heale without fatigue.

30. I am entertained quite to my mind.

To endeavour to conquer scruples about,

Comedy.

Books in Garret.

Books on Shelves.

Hebrew. Pollution. [?]

Deus, juva[3].

[1] G. Strahan inserts this prayer among those of which it is not known in what year they were written. It belongs to 1783, at a time when Johnson had recovered from the stroke of the palsy, and 'was troubled with a complaint which threatened him with a surgical operation.' *Life*, iv. 239.

[2] *Life*, iii. 398, *n.* 3, where by mistake is given the date of Aug. 15, 1773.

The vine grew up his house in Bolt Court. Three years earlier he had written to Mrs. Thrale:—'I have three bunches of grapes on a vine in my garden.' *Letters*, ii. 193.

[3] From the original in the possession of Mr. Locker-Lampson of Rowfant. The first two lines of this entry are quoted in the *Life*, iv. 234.

For Johnson's visit to Heale, near Salisbury, see *Life*, iv. 234; *Letters*, ii. 328.

For his scruples, see *ante*, pp. 41, 93.

163.

PRAYER FOR MRS. WILLIAMS DURING HER ILLNESS PRECEDING HER DEATH IN 1783[1].

[*August*, 1783.]

Almighty God, who in thy late visitation hast shewn mercy to me, and now sendest to my companion disease and decay, grant me grace so to employ the life which thou hast prolonged, and the faculties which thou hast preserved, and so to receive the admonition which the sickness of my friend, by thy appointment, gives me, that I may be constant in all holy duties, and be received at last to eternal happiness.

Permit, O Lord, thy unworthy creature to offer up this prayer for Anna Williams now languishing upon her bed, and about to recommend herself to thy infinite mercy. O God, who desirest not the death of a sinner, look down with mercy upon her: forgive her sins and strengthen her faith. Be merciful, O Father of Mercy, to her and to me: guide us by thy holy spirit through the remaining part of life; support us in the hour of death, and pardon us in the day of judgement, for Jesus Christ's sake. Amen.

164.

September 6.

I had just heard of Williams's Death[2].

Almighty and most merciful Father, who art the Lord of life and death, who givest and who takest away, teach me to adore thy providence, whatever Thou shalt allot me; make me to remember, with due thankfulness, the comforts which I have received from my friendship with Anna Williams. Look upon her, O Lord, with mercy, and prepare me, by thy grace,

[1] From the fly-leaf of a copy of the fifth edition of *Prayers and Meditations* (1817) in the possession of Mr. C. E. Doble. There is nothing to show who transcribed the prayer or whence it was taken. The title is not Johnson's, for it begins 'Prayer of Dr. Johnson.' Moreover it is not correct, for though the prayer is partly for her it is still more for him.

[2] This prayer is not in the *Pembroke College MSS.* For Mrs. Williams's death, see *Life*, iv. 235, and *Letters*, ii. 331.

John Hoole wrote to Bishop Percy:—'We have here suffered great loss in the death of poor Mrs. Williams ... Mrs. Hoole and I shall miss her extremely. She was a very valuable woman—a hearty, sincere, and most intelligent friend.' Nichols, *Lit. Hist.* viii. 218.

to

to die with hope, and to pass by death to eternal happiness, through Jesus Christ our Lord. Amen.

165.

[*September* 18.]

Andover.
Whitchurch.
Overton.
Basingstoke.
Harford Bridge [Hartford Bridge].
Bagshot.
[Two entries illegible, ? Staines and Hounslow.]
Brentford [1].

166.

1784.

In Messrs. Sotheby & Co's Auction Catalogue of May 10, 1875, Lot 119 is 'a beautiful and most pious prayer in the autograph of Dr. Johnson, dated January 1, p.m. 11 1784.' It was sold for eight guineas.

167.

EASTER DAY, *Apr.* 11, 1784.

Almighty God, my Creator and my Judge, who givest life and takest it away, enable me to return sincere and humble thanks for my late deliverance from imminent death [2]. So govern my future life by the Holy Spirit, that every day which thou shalt permit to pass over me, may be spent in thy service, and leave me less tainted with wickedness, and more submissive to thy will.

[1] From the original in the possession of Mr. Locker-Lampson of Rowfant.

This is a record of some of the places on the road from Salisbury to London. Johnson reached home on Sept. 18 at noon. *Life*, iv. 239. He had taken about fifteen hours to go from London to Salisbury, a distance of eighty-two miles. *Ib.* p. 234. As Andover is sixty-four miles from London, unless he broke his journey in returning he must have travelled most of the night. At Hounslow the coach had halted for breakfast on the outward journey. *Letters*, ii. 328, *n.* 3.

[2] Ten days later he wrote to Mrs. Thrale :—'After a confinement of one hundred and twenty-nine days, more than the third part of a year, and no inconsiderable part of human life, I this day returned thanks to God in St. Clement's Church for my recovery.' *Letters*, ii. 392. See also *Life*, iv. 262-4, 271.

Enable me, O Lord, to glorify thee for that knowledge of my Corruption, and that sense of thy wrath, which my deasease and weakness, and danger awakened in my mind[1]. Give me such sorrow as may purify my heart, such indignation as may quench all confidence in myself, and such repentance as may by the intercession of my Redeemer obtain pardon. Let the commemoration of the sufferings and Death of thy Son which I am now, by thy favour, once more permitted to make[2], fill me with faith, hope, and charity. Let my purposes be good and my resolutions unshaken, and let me not be hindred or distracted by vain and useless fears, but through the time which yet remains guide me by thy Holy Spirit, and finally receive me to everlasting life, for the sake of Jesus Christ our Lord and Saviour. Amen.

168.

June 8, 9, and 10.

In Messrs. Sotheby & Co's Auction Catalogue of May 10, 1875, Lot 116 is 'brief autographic memoranda in Latin and English of Dr. Johnson's feelings &c. on the 8th, 9th, 10th, June 1784. "Very breathless and dejected" on the first date.'

It was sold for half a guinea[3].

[1] On March 20 he had written to Mrs. Thrale:—'Write to me no more about *dying with a grace*; when you feel what I have felt in approaching eternity—in fear of soon hearing the sentence of which there is no revocation, you will know the folly; my wish is, that you may know it sooner. The distance between the grave and the remotest point of human longevity, is but a very little; and of that little no path is certain. You knew all this, and I thought that I knew it too; but I know it now with a new conviction. May that new conviction not be vain!' *Letters*, ii. 384.

[2] The next day he wrote to Dr. Taylor:—'I could not have the consent of the physicians to go to church yesterday; I therefore received the holy sacrament at home, in the room where I communicated with dear Mrs. Williams a little before her death.' *Life*, iv. 270.

Hannah More says that 'in St. Clements she partook of the holy sacrament with Johnson, the last time he ever received it in public.' *Memoirs*, i. 397. This must have been after his return to London less than a month before his death.

[3] Johnson was during these days the guest of Dr. Adams, Master of Pembroke College, Oxford. It was on June 10 that he said:—'I would be a Papist if I could. I have fear enough; but an obstinate rationality prevents me. I shall never be a Papist, unless on the near approach of death, of which I have a very great terrour. I wonder that women are not all Papists.' BOSWELL. 'They

O God,

169.

August 1, 1784, Ashbourn.

O God, most merciful Father who by many diseases hast admonished me of my approach to the end of life, and by this gracious addition to my days hast given me an opportunity of appearing once more in thy presence to commemorate the sacrifice by which thy son Jesus Christ has taken away the sins of the world, assist me in this commemoration by thy Holy Spirit that I may look back upon the sinfulness of my life past with pious sorrow, and efficacious Repentance,‡ that my resolutions of amendment may be rightly formed and diligently exerted, that I may be freed from vain and useless scruples, and that I may serve thee with Faith, Hope, and Charity for the time which Thou shalt yet allow me, and finally be received to Everlasting Happiness for the sake of Jesus Christ, our Lord. Amen.

To work as I can.

To attempt a book of prayers.

To do good as occasion offers itself.

To review former resolutions.

At ‡ may be mentioned μ. χ. ἀισχ-νο κεν-β. M[1].

170.

Aug. 12, —84.

Against inquisitive and perplexing thoughts[2].

O Lord, my Maker and Protector, who hast graciously sent me

are not more afraid of death than men are.' JOHNSON. 'Because they are less wicked.' DR. ADAMS. 'They are more pious.' JOHNSON. 'No, hang 'em, they are not more pious. A wicked fellow is the most pious when he takes to it. He'll beat you all at piety.' *Life*, iv. 289.

[1] From the original in the possession of Mr. Robert McCheane, 90 Palace Gardens, London.

By the note which Johnson made at the word *Repentance* it is clear that he wished to recall certain faults when he was using the prayer; it is no less clear that in employing abbreviations in Greek he wished to secure secrecy, in case the prayer should fall into a stranger's hands.

My friend Mr. W. R. Morfill, Reader of the Slavonic Languages and Literature in the University of Oxford, ingeniously conjectures that the first three entries are *μέλαινα χολή*; *αἰσχρὰ νοήματα*; *κενὰ βουλεύματα* — melancholy; shameful thoughts; vain resolutions. His melancholy if he had indulged it, or if he had not taken the proper means to subdue it, he would have looked upon as sinful.

[2] Quoted in the *Life*, iv. 370.

me into this world, to work out my salvation, enable me to drive from me all such unquiet and perplexing thoughts as may mislead or hinder me in the practice of those duties which thou hast required. When I behold the works of thy hands and consider the course of thy providence, give me Grace always to remember that thy thoughts are not my thoughts, nor thy ways my ways. And while it shall please Thee to continue me in this world where much is to be done and little to be known, teach me by thy Holy Spirit to withdraw my mind from unprofitable and dangerous enquiries, from difficulties vainly curious, and doubts impossible to be solved. Let me rejoice in the light which thou hast imparted, let me serve thee with active zeal, and humble confidence, and wait with patient expectation for the time in which the soul which Thou receivest, shall be satisfied with knowledge. Grant this, O Lord, for Jesus Christ's sake. Amen [1].

171.

Aug. 28, 1784, Ashbourn.

Almighty and most merciful Father, who afflictest not willingly the children of Men, and by whose holy will [2]
now languishes in sickness and pain, make, I beseech [Thee,] this punishment effectual to those gracious purposes for which thou sendest it, let it, if I may presume to ask, end not in death, but in repentance, let him live to promote thy kingdom on earth by the useful example of a better life, but if thy will be to call him hence, let his thoughts be so purified by his sufferings, that he may be admitted to eternal Happiness. And, O Lord, by praying for him, let me be admonished to consider my own sins, and my own danger, to remember the shortness of life, and to use the time which thy mercy grants me to thy glory and my own salvation, for the sake of Jesus Christ our Lord. Amen.

[1] On the day on which he composed this prayer he wrote to one of his correspondents in London :—'As we cannot now see each other do not omit to write, for you cannot think with what warmth of expectation I reckon the hours of a post-day.' *Life*, iv. 354.

[2] The blank must be filled up by Taylor's name. Johnson wrote on Aug. 19 :—'My friend is sick himself, and the reciprocation of complaints and groans affords not much of either pleasure or instruction.' *Life*, iv. 365.

In

172.

Sept. 5.

In Messrs. Christie & Co's Auction Catalogue of June 5, 1888, Lot 38 is 'a Prayer in Dr. Johnson's autograph, dated Ashbourne, Sept. 5, 1784.' It was sold for five guineas. The same autograph was sold a few years later by Messrs. Sotheby & Co. for eight guineas. *The Bookman*, Dec. 1893, p. 75.

173.

Ashbourne, *September* 18, 1784.

Almighty God, merciful Father, who art the giver of all good enable me to return Thee due thanks for the continuance of my life and for the great mercies of the last year, for relief from the diseases that afflicted me, and all the comforts and alleviations by which they were mitigated; and O my gracious God make me truly thankful for the call by which thou hast awakened my conscience, and summoned me to Repentance. Let not thy call, O Lord, be forgotten or thy summons neglected, but let the residue of my life, whatever it shall be, be passed in true contrition, and diligent obedience. Let me repent of the sins of my past years and so keep thy laws for the time to come, that when it shall be thy good pleasure to call me to another state, I may find mercy in thy sight. Let thy Holy Spirit support me in the hour of death, and O Lord grant me pardon in the day of Judgement, for the sake of Jesus Christ, our Lord. Amen [1].

174.

PRECES.

Oct. 31, 1784 [2].

Against the incursion of evil thoughts.

[1] From the original in the possession of Mr. Alfred Morrison of Fonthill House. Published in my edition of the *Letters*, ii. 420.

[2] Croker's *Boswell*, p. 792.

These entries are perhaps the result of the following conversation recorded by Boswell in the previous June:—'On Friday, June 11, we talked at breakfast, of forms of prayer. JOHNSON. "I know of no good prayers but those in the *Book of Common Prayer*." DR. ADAMS (in a very earnest manner): "I wish, Sir, you would compose some family prayers." JOHNSON. "I will not compose prayers for you, Sir, because you can do it for yourself. But I have thought of getting together all the books of prayers which I could, selecting those which should appear to me the best, putting out some, inserting others, adding

Repentance

Repentance and pardon.—*Laud*[1].
In disease.
On the loss of friends—by death; by his own fault or friend's.
On the unexpected notice of the death of others.

Prayer generally recommendatory;
To understand their prayers;
Under dread of death;
Prayer commonly considered as a stated and temporary duty—performed and forgotten—without any effect on the following day.
Prayer—a vow.—*Taylor*[2].

SCEPTICISM CAUSED BY

1. Indifference about opinions.
2. Supposition that things disputed are disputable.
3. Demand of unsuitable evidence.
4. False judgement of evidence.

some prayers of my own, and prefixing a discourse on prayer." We all now gathered about him, and two or three of us at a time joined in pressing him to execute this plan. He seemed to be a little displeased at the manner of our importunity, and in great agitation called out, "Do not talk thus of what is so aweful. I know not what time GOD will allow me in this world. There are many things which I wish to do." Some of us persisted, and Dr. Adams said, "I never was more serious about any thing in my life." JOHNSON. "Let me alone, let me alone; I am overpowered." And then he put his hands before his face, and reclined for some time upon the table.' *Life*, iv. 293.

On August 1 (*ante*, p. 117) he had recorded his wish 'to attempt a book of prayers.' In November he passed a few days with Dr. Adams. 'We had much serious talk together,' wrote Adams to Boswell, 'for which I ought to be the better as long as I live. You will remember some discourse which we had in the summer upon the subject of prayer, and the difficulty of this sort of composition. He reminded me of this, and of my having wished him to try his hand, and to give us a specimen of the style and manner that he approved. He added, that he was now in a right frame of mind, and as he could not possibly employ his time better, he would in earnest set about it.' *Life*, iv. 376.

[1] My friend the Rev. W. H. Hutton, Fellow of St. John's College, Oxford, suggests that Johnson had in mind the second and third paragraphs of Laud's *Officium Quotidianum*. Laud's *Works*, ed. 1853, iii. 5.

[2] 'Be careful thou dost not speak a lie in thy prayers, which though not observed is frequently practised by careless persons, especially in the forms of confession, affirming things which they have not thought, professing sorrow which is not, making a vow they mean not.' Jeremy Taylor's *Works*, ed. 1865, vii. 622.

5. Complaint

5. Complaint of the obscurity of Scripture.
6. Contempt of fathers and of authority.
7. Absurd method of learning objections first.
8. Study not for truth, but vanity.
9. Sensuality and a vicious life.
10. False honour, false shame.
11. Omission of prayer and religious exercises.

175.

[The following Prayer was composed and used by Doctor Johnson previous to his receiving the Sacrament of the Lord's Supper, on Sunday December 5, 1784. Note by G. Strahan [1].]

Almighty and most merciful Father, I am now, as to human eyes it seems, about to commemorate, for the last time, the death of thy Son Jesus Christ our Saviour and Redeemer. Grant, O Lord, that my whole hope and confidence may be in his merits, and thy mercy; enforce and accept my imperfect repentance; make this commemoration available to the confirmation of my faith, the establishment of my hope, and the enlargement of my charity; and make the death of thy Son Jesus Christ effectual to my redemption. Have mercy upon me, and pardon the multitude of my offences. Bless my friends; have mercy upon all men. Support me, by the grace of thy Holy Spirit, in the days of weakness, and at the hour of death; and receive me, at my death, to everlasting happiness, for the sake of Jesus Christ. Amen [2].

176.

[The following Meditations and Prayers have no dates in the MS. Note by G. Strahan.]

I did not this week labour my preparation so much as I have sometimes done. My mind was not very quiet; and an anxious preparation makes the duty of the day formidable and burdensome. Different methods suit different states of mind, body and affairs. I rose this day, and prayed, then went to tea, and afterwards composed the Prayer, which I formed with great fluency.

[1] This prayer is not in Johnson's handwriting.

[2] Quoted in the *Life*, iv. 417. He died on December 13.

fluency. I went to church; came in at the Psalms; could not hear the reader in the lessons, but attended the prayers with tranquillity.

To read the New Testament once a year, in Greek.

177.

Receiving the Sacrament

I profess my Faith in Jesus.

I declare my resolution to obey him.

I implore in the highest act of worship, Grace to keep these resolutions.

I hope to rise to a new life this day.

178.

Prayer on the study of Religion.

Almighty God, our heavenly Father, without whose help labour is useless, without whose light search is vain, invigorate my studies and direct my enquiries, that I may, by due diligence and right discernment establish myself and others in thy holy Faith. Take not, O Lord, thy Holy Spirit from me, let not evil thoughts have dominion in my mind. Let me not linger in ignorance, but enlighten and support me, for the sake of Jesus Christ our Lord. Amen.

179.

O Lord God, in whose hand are the wills and affections of men, kindle in my mind holy desires, and repress sinful and corrupt imaginations; enable me to love thy commandments, and to desire thy promises; let me, by thy protection and influence, so pass through things temporal, as finally not to lose the things eternal; and among the hopes and fears, the pleasures and sorrows, the dangers and deliverances, and all the changes of this life, let my heart be surely fixed, by the help of thy Holy Spirit, on the everlasting fruition of thy presence, where true joys are to be found. Grant, O Lord, these petitions. Forgive, O merciful Lord, whatever I have done contrary to thy laws. Give me such a sense of my wickedness as may produce true contrition and effectual repentance, so that when

I shall

I shall be called into another state, I may be received among the sinners to whom sorrow and reformation have obtained pardon, for Jesus Christ's sake. Amen [1].

180.

Almighty and most merciful Father, whose clemency I now presume to implore, after a long life of carelessness and wickedness, have mercy upon me. I have committed many trespasses; I have neglected many duties. I have done what Thou hast forbidden, and left undone what Thou hast commanded. Forgive, merciful Lord, my sins, negligences, and ignorances, and enable me, by thy Holy Spirit, to amend my life according to thy Holy Word, for Jesus Christ's sake. Amen.

181.

O merciful God, full of compassion, long-suffering, and of great pity, who sparest when we deserve punishment, and in thy wrath thinkest upon mercy; make me earnestly to repent, and heartily to be sorry for all my misdoings; make the remembrance so burdensome and painful, that I may flee to Thee with a troubled spirit and a contrite heart; and, O merciful Lord, visit, comfort, and relieve me; cast me not out from thy presence, and take not thy Holy Spirit from me, but excite in me true repentance; give me in this world knowledge of thy truth, and confidence in thy mercy, and in the world to come life everlasting, for the sake of our Lord and Saviour, thy Son Jesus Christ. Amen [2].

182.

EJACULATION [3].

Imploring Diligence.

O God, make me to remember that *the night cometh when no man can work* [4].

[1] The last six lines are quoted in the *Life*, iv. 397.

[2] This prayer is not in the *Pembroke College MSS.*

[3] This ejaculation is not in the *Pembroke College MSS.*

[4] 'At this time I observed upon the dial-plate of his watch a short Greek inscription, taken from the New Testament, Νυξ γαρ ερχεται, being the first words of our SAVIOUR'S solemn admonition to the improvement of that time which is allowed us to prepare for eternity: "the night

[The

183.

[The following passage in the *Pembroke College MSS.* has been scored out. It bears no date, but the paper on which it is written follows one dated Easter, 1770. It cannot however belong to that year; for on Easter Eve, 1770, Johnson dined at Mr. Thrale's (*ante*, p. 53) and not, as he records below, at the Mitre.]

EASTER EVE.

I rose and breakfasted, eat little; gave orders that Mr.* Stainesby the Clergyman who is to give dying Jenny the Sacrament, shall have *5s. 3d.* Steevens was with me. Watson paid. Mrs. Otway. About Noon I grew faint by fasting, then dined on Fish and eggs at the Mitre.

I then came home, and read two of Rogers's Sermons. Between ten and eleven I was very weary, I think, by fasting, and a night rather unquiet. I was not much sleepy this day. O God for Jesus Christ's sake have mercy upon me. Amen.

* He came to Jenny very carefully.

cometh, when no man can work."' *Life*, ii. 57.

Sir Walter Scott put the same Greek inscription on the dial at Abbotsford. Near the close of his life, on a visit from home, hearing of the sudden death of a friend, who like himself had suffered from paralysis, he insisted on returning at once. 'He would listen to no persuasions. "No William," he said, "this is a sad warning. I must home to work while it is called day; for the night cometh when no man can work. I put that text many a year ago on my dial-stone; but it often preached in vain."' Lockhart's *Scott*, x. 88.

ANNALS

[An account of the life of DR. SAMUEL JOHNSON, from his birth to his eleventh year, written by himself. From the MSS. preserved by the Doctor; and now in Possession of RICHARD WRIGHT, Surgeon; Proprietor of the Museum of Antiquities, Natural and Artificial Curiosities, &c. Lichfield. LONDON: printed for RICHARD PHILLIPS, No. 6, Bridge-Street, Blackfriars; by NICHOLS and SON, Red Lion Passage, Fleet Street. 1805.]

PREFACE TO FIRST EDITION.

It will be expected, that the Editor of the following curious and interesting pages should give an account of the manner in which the original MSS. came into his possession.

Mr. Boswell, in his admirable Life of Dr. Johnson [1], thus observes:

'The consideration of numerous papers of which he was possessed seems to have struck Johnson's mind with a sudden anxiety; and, as they were in great confusion, it is much to be lamented that he had not intrusted some faithful and discreet person with the care and selection of them; instead of which, he, in a precipitate manner, burnt large masses of them, with little regard, as I apprehend, to discrimination. . . . . Two very valuable articles, I am sure, we have lost; which were two quarto volumes, containing a full, fair, and most particular account of his own life, from his earliest recollection.'

It does not appear, that the MS. from which the following short account of Dr. Johnson's early life is copied, was one of the two volumes to which Boswell alludes; although it is evident, from his enumeration of particular dates in the blank pages of the book, that he intended to have finished these Annals, according to this plan, with the same minuteness of description, in every circumstance and event.

This Volume was among that mass of papers which were ordered to be committed to the flames a few days before his death, thirty-two pages of which were torn out by himself, and destroyed; the contents of those which remain are here given with fidelity and exactness. Francis Barber, his black servant, unwilling that all the MSS. of his illustrious master should

[1] iv. 403.

be

be utterly lost, preserved these relicks from the flames. By purchase from Barber's widow they came into the possession of the Editor.

The original MSS. are deposited in the Museum of Antiquities and Natural Curiosities, belonging to the Editor; which is open to the inspection of the publick.

LICHFIELD,
March 2, 1805.

ANNALS

1.

Sept. 7 [1], 1709, I was born at Lichfield. My mother had a very difficult and dangerous labour, and was assisted by George Hector, a man-midwife of great reputation [2]. I was born almost dead, and could not cry for some time. When he had me in his arms, he said, 'Here is a brave boy [3].'

In a few weeks an inflammation was discovered on my buttock, which was at first, I think, taken for a burn; but soon appeared to be a natural disorder. It swelled, broke, and healed.

My Father [4], being that year Sheriff of Lichfield, and to ride the

[1] 18 of the present style. *Note by Dr. Johnson.*

Dr. Franklin wrote to his wife on Jan. 6, 1773:—'I feel some regard for this 6th of January as my old nominal birthday, though the change of style has carried the real day forward to the 17th.' Franklin's *Works*, ed. 1889, v. 86.

1709 was a year of great dearth. According to the table of the prices of wheat in the *Wealth of Nations*, ed. 1811, i. 357, there were only two dearer years—1648, 1649—between 1595 and 1764.

[2] Probably the father of Johnson's old schoolfellow Edmund Hector, the Birmingham surgeon. *Life*, ii. 456.

Accoucheur is not in Johnson's *Dictionary*. The earliest instance in the *New Eng. Dict.* is from *Tristram Shandy* in 1759:—'Nothing will serve you but to carry off the man-midwife.—*Accoucheur*, if you please, quoth Dr. Slop.'

[3] This was written in January, 1765. *Note by Wright.*

[4] I have copied the following entry from a document in the possession of my cousin, Mr. Horatio Symonds, of Beaumont Street, Oxford:—

'"Michaell the Sonne of William Johnson and Catherine his Wife was baptized Aprill the 20."

'Copied from the Register belonging to the parish of Cubley in Derbyshire.

'This part of the Register is so much injured by Time that it is uncertain whether the Date is Aprill the 20 or the 2. I think it is the 20.'

This extract is endorsed in Johnson's handwriting:—'Father's register.'

Michael Johnson was born in 1656. *Life*, iv. 393, *n.* 2.

The Rev. Cave Humfrey, Rector of Cubley, informs me that the Registers begin in 1566, but that several

circuit of the County[1] next day, which was a ceremony then performed with great pomp; he was asked by my mother, 'Whom he would invite to the Riding?' and answered, 'All the town now.' He feasted the citizens with uncommon magnificence, and was the last but one that maintained the splendour of the Riding[2].

I was, by my father's persuasion, put to one Marclew, commonly called Bellison[3], the servant, or wife of a servant of my father, to be nursed in George Lane[4], where I used to call when I was a bigger boy, and eat fruit in the garden, which was full of trees[5]. Here it was discovered that my eyes were bad; and an

pages are illegible. To his kindness I owe the following entries:—

Baptisms.

'Anno 1579.

'The — daie of August Edith Johnson daughter of —.'

'1657.

'— the Sonne of William Johnson and Catherine his wife baptized Aprill —.'

'1658.

'— the Sonne of William Johnson was Baptiz: Februarie the 14th.'

'1661.

'Andrew. The Sonne of William Johnson was baptiz: January 24th.'

'1701—Feb: 20—

'Samuel ye Sonn of William Johnson & his wife.'

Burials.

'1701.

'October 29. Avice Johnson. Wid. Buryed. Affid. made. Nov: ye 3d.'

Johnson's father served his apprenticeship at Leek in Staffordshire. *Life*, i. 37. A writer in *Notes and Queries*, 5th Ser., v. 335, says that in the Register of Burials in that town are found the names of two Samuel Johnsons—one who died in 1654 and the other in 1712. It is not unlikely that they were of Dr. Johnson's family.

'I can hardly tell who was my grandfather,' said Johnson. *Life*, ii. 261. He relates how some boatmen in the Hebrides, speaking of him, 'asked if the Englishman could recount a long genealogy. What answer was given them, the conversation being in Erse, I was not much inclined to examine.' *Works*, ix. 70.

[1] The City of Lichfield is a county in itself. Its circuit extends about sixteen miles.

[2] The Sheriff's 'Ride,' or perambulation of the City boundary, still takes place on September 8. The Sheriff, I am informed, on that day has about 250 guests to breakfast in the Guildhall. 'Various calls are made *en route* for refreshments,—chiefly at Freeford, where hospitality is dispensed by the owner, General Dyott.' For the family of Dyott see *Letters*, i. 342, *n*. 3.

[3] The name of Marklew, *alias* Bellison, is yet common in Lichfield, and is usually so distinguished. *Note by R. Wright.*

The last of this name in Lichfield, as it is believed, a very old innkeeper, died twenty years ago.

[4] *Letters*, i. 154.

[5] Perhaps Johnson had this garden in his mind when he wrote in his *Life of Swift*:—'Almost every boy eats as much fruit as he can get without any great inconvenience.' *Works*, viii. 194.

issue

issue was cut in my left arm[1]; of which I took no great notice, as I think my mother has told me, having my little hand in a custard.

It is observable, that, having been told of this operation, I always imagined that I remembered it, but I laid the scene in the wrong house. Such confusions of memory I suspect to be common.

My mother visited me every day, and used to go different ways, that her assiduity might not expose her to ridicule[2]; and often left her fan or glove behind her, that she might have a pretence to come back unexpected; but she never discovered any token of neglect. Dr. Swinfen[3] told me, that the scrofulous sores which afflicted me proceeded from the bad humours of the nurse, whose son had the same distemper, and was likewise short-sighted, but both in a less degree. My mother thought my diseases derived from her family.

In ten weeks I was taken home, a poor, diseased infant, almost blind.

I remember my aunt Nath. Ford[4] told me, when I was about . . . years old, that she would not have picked such a poor creature up in the street.

In . . . 67, when I was at Lichfield[5], I went to look for my

[1] How long this issue was continued I do not remember. I believe it was suffered to dry when I was about six years old. *Note by Johnson.*

[2] A curious instance of the brutality of the age.

[3] His godfather. *Life*, i. 34, *n.* 2.

[4] *Ib.* i. 49, *n.* 3.

[5] Benjamin West, in a curiously-spelt letter to a friend in Philadelphia, dated July 20, 1798, speaking of his recollections of that town, says:—'Early habits my friend make lasting impressions on our minds, and I am prosuaded were I to revisit those abodes, I should feel a greater joy than those felt by Dr. Johnson (that great luminary in the lettered world) whom I heard say at his Club, when a friend asked the Dr. then just returned from visiting the place of his Nativity after a space of 40 years absence, what gave him the greatest delight when there? Why Sir re-plyed the Dr. it was to jump over that Style when 70 years of age, which I had been accustom to jump over when I was a Boy going to the day school. From my feelings at the recollection of my juvinal foot-steps I am prosuaded the Dr. spoke the dictates of his heart.' *Pennsylvania Magazine*, July 1894, p. 221.

Johnson's first visit to Lichfield (not counting one of five days in the winter of 1761-2) was in 1767, thirty years after his removal to London. *Life*, iii. 452; *Letters*, i. 128-130.

nurse's house; and, inquiring somewhat obscurely, was told 'this is the house in which you were nursed.' I saw my nurse's son, to whose milk I succeeded, reading a large Bible, which my nurse had bought, as I was then told, some time before her death

Dr. Swinfen used to say, that he never knew any child reared with so much difficulty.

2.

1710–11.

In the second year I knew [? know] not what happened to me. I believe it was then that my mother carried me to Trysul[1], to consult Dr. Atwood, an oculist of Worcester. My father and Mrs. Harriots[2], I think, never had much kindness for each other. She was my mother's relation; and he had none so high to whom he could send any of his family. He saw her seldom himself, and willingly disgusted her, by sending his horses[3] from home on Sunday; which she considered, and with reason, as a breach of duty. My father had much vanity, which his adversity hindered from being fully exerted[4]. I remember, that, mentioning her legacy in the humility of distress, he called her *our good Cousin Harriots*. My mother had no value for his relations; those indeed whom we knew of were much lower than hers[5]. This contempt began, I know not on which side, very early: but, as my father was little at home, it had not much effect.

My father and mother had not much happiness from each other. They seldom conversed; for my father could not bear to talk of his affairs; and my mother, being unacquainted with books, cared not to talk of any thing else. Had my mother been more literate, they had been better companions. She might have sometimes introduced her unwelcome topick with

[1] Trysull, near Wolverhampton.

[2] *Ante*, p. 56.

[3] His business, as his son told Mrs. Thrale, 'led him to be much on horse-back.' *Post*, p. 148. The title-page of a book published by him shows that in 1687 he had shops at Lichfield, Uttoxeter, and Ashby-de-la-Zouch. *Life*, i. 36, *n*. 3. Besides, he attended book-sales in all the country round.

[4] 'My father,' he said, 'was a foolish old man; that is to say, foolish in talking of his children.' *Ib.* i. 40. For his 'distress' see *ib.* i. 78–80.

[5] They did not rise very high, for in 1773 Johnson wrote:—'Mr. Cornelius Harrison was the only one of my relations who ever rose in fortune above penury, or in character above neglect.' *Letters*, i. 225.

more

more success, if she could have diversified her conversation. Of business she had no distinct conception; and therefore her discourse was composed only of complaint, fear, and suspicion. Neither of them ever tried to calculate the profits of trade, or the expenses of living. My mother concluded that we were poor, because we lost by some of our trades; but the truth was, that my father, having in the early part of his life contracted debts, never had trade sufficient to enable him to pay them, and maintain his family; he got something, but not enough.

It was not till about 1768, that I thought to calculate the returns of my father's trade, and by that estimate his probable profits. This, I believe, my parents never did.

3.

1711–12.

This year, in Lent —12, I was taken to London, to be touched for the evil by Queen Anne[1]. My mother was at Nicholson's, the

[1] *Life*, i. 43, and *post*, p. 152.

Evelyn records on July 6, 1660:—'His Majesty began first to touch for the evil according to custom, thus: his Majesty sitting under his state [canopy] in the Banqueting-House the chirurgeons cause the sick to be brought or led, up to the throne, where they kneeling, the King strokes their faces or cheeks with both his hands at once, at which instant a chaplain in his formalities [solemn dress] says: "He put his hands upon them, and he healed them." This is said to every one in particular. When they have been all touched, they come up again in the same order, and the other chaplain kneeling, and having angel gold[1] strung on white ribbon on his arm, delivers them one by one to his Majesty, who puts them about the necks of the touched as they pass, while the first chaplain repeats, "That is the true light who came into the world." Then follows an Epistle (as at first a Gospel) with the Liturgy prayers for the sick, with some alteration; lastly the blessing; and then the Lord Chamberlain and the Comptroller of the Household bring a basin, ewer and towel for his Majesty to wash.' Evelyn's *Diary*, ed. 1872, i. 357.

Pepys, who saw the ceremony nine months later, says:—'The King did it with great gravity, and it seemed to me to be an ugly office and a simple one.' Pepys's *Diary*, ed. 1851, i. 212.

Hearne records on Aug. 3, 1728:—'Yesterday Mr. Gilman of St. Peter's parish in the east, Oxford (a lusty, heartick, thick, short man) told me that he is in the 85th year of his age, and that at the restoration of K. Charles ii, being much afflicted with the king's evil, he rode up to London behind his father, was touched on a Wednesday by that King, was in very good condition by that night, and by the Sunday night immediately following was perfectly recovered, and hath so continued ever since. He

[1] A piece of money impressed with an angel. It was rated at ten shillings. Johnson's *Dictionary*.

the famous bookseller, in Little Britain [1]. I always retained some memory of this journey, though I was then but thirty months old. I remembered a little dark room behind the kitchen, where the jack-weight fell through a hole in the floor, into which I once slipped my leg [2].

I remember a boy crying at the palace when I went to be touched. Being asked 'on which side of the shop was the counter?' I answered, 'on the left from the entrance,' many years after, and spoke, not by guess, but by memory. We went in the stage-coach, and returned in the waggon [3], as my mother said, because my cough was violent. The hope of saving a few shillings was no slight motive; for she, not having been accustomed to money, was afraid of such expenses as now seem very small. She sewed two guineas in her petticoat, lest she should be robbed.

hath constantly wore the piece of gold about his neck that he received of the King, and he had it on yesterday when I met him.' *Remains of Hearne*, ed. 1869, iii. 12.

Peter Wentworth wrote on April 23, 1714:—'The best news I can tell you in this is that the Queen is well, and grows better and better every day, has touch't twice a week.' *Wentworth Papers*, p. 375.

Hume says:—'The practice was first dropped by the present royal family, who observed that it could no longer give amazement even to the populace, and was attended with ridicule in the eyes of all men of understanding.' *History of England*, ed. 1773, i. 178.

Sully, writing of a letter which he had received from Henry IV, says:—'Il me mande, dans celle-ci, d'envoyer deux cents écus pour chacun des malades des écrouelles, que sa maladie avait empêché qu'il ne touchât, et qu'il n'avait pourtant pas voulu qu'on renvoyât.' *Mémoires de Sully*, ed. 1788, iv. 200.

[1] My mother, then with child, concealed her pregnancy, that she might not be hindered from the journey. *Note by Johnson.*

'Little Britain extends from Aldersgate Street to Duck Lane.' Dodsley's *London*, iii. 316. Roger North, writing of Little Britain soon after the Restoration, says:—'Then Little Britain was a plentiful and perpetual emporium of learned authors, and men went thither as to a market. This drew to the place a mighty trade, the rather because the shops were spacious, and the learned gladly resorted to them, where they seldom failed to meet with agreeable conversation. And the booksellers themselves were knowing and conversible men.' *Lives of the Norths*, ed. 1826, iii. 294.

[2] I seem to remember, that I played with a string and a bell, which my cousin Isaac Johnson gave me; and that there was a cat with a white collar, and a dog, called Chops, that leaped over a stick: but I know not whether I remember the thing, or the talk of it. *Note by Johnson.*

[3] In *Roderick Random*, chaps. xi–xiii, an account is given of a journey in the London and Newcastle wagon.

We

We were troublesome to the passengers; but to suffer such inconveniences in the stage-coach was common in these days to persons in much higher rank[1]. She bought me a small silver cup and spoon, marked SAM. I. lest if they had been marked S. I. which was her name, they should, upon her death, have been taken from me. She bought me a speckled linen frock, which I knew afterwards by the name of my London frock. The cup was one of the last pieces of plate which dear Tetty sold in our distress[2]. I have now the spoon. She bought at the same time two teaspoons, and till my manhood she had no more.

My ſather considered tea[3] as very expensive, and discouraged my mother from keeping company with the neighbours, and from paying visits or receiving them. She lived to say, many years after, that, if the time were to pass again, she would not comply with such unsocial injunctions.

I suppose that in this year I was first informed of a future state. I remember, that being in bed with my mother one morning, I was told by her of the two places to which the inhabitants of this world were received after death; one a fine place filled with happiness, called Heaven; the other a *sad* place, called Hell. That this account much affected my imagination, I do not remember. When I was risen, my mother bade me repeat what she had told me to Thomas Jackson[4]. When I told this afterwards to my mother, she seemed to wonder that she should begin such talk so late as that the first time could be remembered.

[1] I was sick; one woman fondled me, the other was disgusted. *Note by Johnson.*

[2] *Life*, i. 163.

[3] In January, 1731, the price of the cheapest tea in London was 10*s.* per pound, of the dearest 35*s. Gentleman's Magazine*, 1731, p. 39.

The Quakers of Aberdeen forbade the use of it. 'In 1715 the "fashionable using of tea" was ordered to be "avoided," "tea-tables to be laid aside as formerly advised."' R. Barclay's *Inner Life of the Religious Societies of the Commonwealth*, 1876, p. 498.

'Lord Bristol [writing in 1728] ascribes Lord Hervey's delicate health to the use of "that detestable and poisonous plant tea, which had once brought him to death's door, and, if persisted in, would carry him through it," and he implores him in the most pathetic terms to give it up.' Lord Hervey's *Memoirs*, vol. i, Preface, p. 27.

[4] Their man-servant. *Life*, i. 38. See *post*, p. 164.

[*Here*

[*Here there is a chasm of thirty-eight pages in the manuscript*[1].]

——— examination. We always considered it as a day of ease; for we made no preparation, and indeed were asked commonly such questions as we had been asked often before, and could regularly answer. But I believe it was of use at first.

On Thursday night a small portion of Æsop was learned by heart, and on Friday morning the lessons in Æsop were repeated; I believe, not those in Helvicus[2]. On Friday afternoon we learned *Quæ Genus*[3]; I suppose that other boys might say their repetition, but of this I have now no distinct remembrance. To learn *Quæ Genus* was to me always pleasing; and *As in Præsenti* was, I know not why, always disgusting.

When we learned our Accidence we had no parts, but, I think, two lessons. The boys that came to school untaught read the Accidence twice through before they learned it by heart.

When we learned *Propria quæ Maribus*, our parts were in the Accidence; when we learned *As in Præsenti*, our parts were in the Accidence and *Propria quæ Maribus*; when we learned *Syntaxis*, in the former three. *Propria quæ Maribus* I could repeat without any effort of recollection. I used to repeat it to my mother and Tom Johnson; and remember, that I once went as far as the middle of the paragraph, 'Mascula dicuntur monosyllaba,' in a dream.

On Saturday, as on Thursday, we were examined. We were sometimes, on one of those days, asked our Catechism[4], but with no regularity or constancy.

The progress of examination was this. When we learned *Propria quæ Maribus*, we were examined in the Accidence; particularly we formed Verbs, that is, went through the same person in all the Moods and Tenses. This was very difficult to

[1] What follows is the account of his studies at Lichfield School. See *Life*, i. 43.

[2] Christopher Helvicus (1581–1616) was Professor of Greek and Divinity at Giessen.

[3] 'Lady Booby, seeing a book in Dick's hand, asked him, if he could read. "Yes," cried Adams, "a little Latin, madam; he is just got into *Quae Genus*."' *Joseph Andrews*, Book iv. ch. 9.

Quae Genus, *As in Praesenti* and *Propria quae Maribus* are chapters in the Eton Latin Grammar.

[4] G. Hector never had been taught his Catechism. *Note by Johnson.*

me;

me; and I was once very anxious about the next day, when this exercise was to be performed, in which I had failed till I was discouraged. My mother encouraged me, and I proceeded better. When I told her of my good escape, 'We often,' said she, dear mother! 'come off best, when we are most afraid.' She told me, that, once when she asked me about forming verbs, I said, 'I did not form them in an ugly shape.' 'You could not,' said she, 'speak plain; and I was proud that I had a boy who was forming verbs.' These little memorials sooth my mind. Of the parts of Corderius[1] or Æsop, which we learned to repeat, I have not the least recollection, except of a passage in one of the Morals, where it is said of some man, that, when he hated another, he made him rich; this I repeated emphatically in my mother's hearing, who could never conceive that riches could bring any evil. She remarked it, as I expected.

I had the curiosity, two or three years ago, to look over Garretson's Exercises, Willymot's Particles[2], and Walker's Exercises; and found very few sentences that I should have recollected if I had found them in any other books. That which is read without pleasure is not often recollected nor infixed by conversation, and therefore in a great measure drops from the memory[3]. Thus it happens that those who are taken early from school, commonly lose all that they had learned.

When we learned *As in Præsenti*, we parsed *Propria quæ Maribus* by Hool's Terminations; and, when we learned *Syntaxis*, we parsed *As in Præsenti*; and afterwards *Quæ Genus*, by the same book; sometimes, as I remember, proceeding in order of the rules, and sometimes, particularly in *As in Præsenti*, taking words as they occurred in the Index.

[1] The ensign in *Tom Jones* (Bk. vii, c. 12) exclaimed:—'And there's Corderius, another d——d son of a whore that hath got me many a flogging.'

[2] 'It is not commonly known,' writes Malone, 'that the translation of Bacon's *Essays* into Latin, which was published in 1619, was done by the famous John Selden. One Willymot, a schoolmaster, was foolish enough to re-translate these *Essays* into English in the beginning of this [the eighteenth] century.' Prior's *Malone*, p. 424.

[3] 'A man,' said Johnson, 'ought to read just as inclination leads him; for what he reads as a task will do him little good.' *Life*, i. 428.

The

The whole week before we broke up, and the part of the week in which we broke up, were spent wholly, I know not why, in examination; and were therefore easy to both us and the master. The two nights before the vacation were free from exercise.

This was the course of the school, which I remember with pleasure; for I was indulged and caressed by my master, and, I think, really excelled the rest.

I was with Hawkins[1] but two years, and perhaps four months. The time, till I had computed it, appeared much longer by the multitude of novelties which it supplied, and of incidents, then in my thoughts important, it produced. Perhaps it is not possible that any other period can make the same impression on the memory.

4.

1719.

In the Spring of 1719, our class consisting of eleven, the number was always fixed in my memory, but one of the names I have forgotten, was removed to the upper school, and put under Holbrook[2], a peevish and ill-tempered man. We were removed sooner than had been the custom; for the head-master, intent upon his boarders, left the town-boys long in the lower school. Our removal was caused by a reproof from the Town-clerk; and Hawkins complained that he had lost half his profit. At this removal I cried. The rest were indifferent. My exercise in Garretson was somewhere about the Gerunds. Our places in Æsop and Helvicus I have totally forgotten.

At Whitsuntide Mrs. Longworth brought me a 'Hermes Garretsoni,' of which I do not remember that I ever could make much use. It was afterwards lost, or stolen at school. My exercise was then in the end of the Syntax. Hermes furnished me with the word *inliciturus*, which I did not understand, but used it.

This task was very troublesome to me; I made all the twenty-five exercises, others made but sixteen. I never shewed all mine; five lay long after in a drawer in the shop. I made an exercise in a little time, and shewed it my mother; but the task being long upon me, she said, 'Though you could make an

[1] 'The usher or under-master of Lichfield School; 'a man,' said Johnson, 'very skilful in his little way.' *Life*, i. 43.

[2] *Ib.* i. 44.

exercise

exercise in so short a time, I thought you would find it difficult to make them all as soon as you should.'

This Whitsuntide, I and my brother were sent to pass some time at Birmingham [1]; I believe, a fortnight. Why such boys were sent to trouble other houses, I cannot tell. My mother had some opinion that much improvement was to be had by changing the mode of life. My uncle Harrison was a widower; and his house was kept by Sally Ford, a young woman of such sweetness of temper, that I used to say she had no fault. We lived most at uncle Ford's, being much caressed by my aunt, a good-natured, coarse woman, easy of converse, but willing to find something to censure in the absent. My uncle Harrison did not much like us, nor did we like him. He was a very mean and vulgar man, drunk every night [2], but drunk with little drink, very peevish, very proud, very ostentatious, but, luckily, not rich. At my aunt Ford's I eat so much of a boiled leg of mutton, that she used to talk of it. My mother, who had lived in a narrow sphere, and was then affected by little things, told me seriously that it would hardly ever be forgotten. Her mind, I think, was afterwards much enlarged, or greater evils wore out the care of less.

I staid after the vacation was over some days; and remember, when I wrote home, that I desired the horses to come on Thursday of the first school week; and then, and not till then, they should be welcome to go. I was much pleased with a rattle to my whip, and wrote of it to my mother.

When my father came to fetch us home, he told the ostler, that he had twelve miles home [3], and two boys under his care. This offended me. He had then a watch, which he returned when he was to pay for it [4].

In making, I think, the first exercise under Holbrook, I perceived the power of continuity of attention, of application not suffered to wander or to pause. I was writing at the kitchen

[1] In 1700 the population of Birmingham was 15,032; in 1731, 23,286. *Gentleman's Magazine*, 1743, p. 539.

[2] 'I remember (said Dr. Johnson) when all the *decent* people in Lichfield got drunk every night and were not thought the worse of.' *Life*, v. 59.

[3] Lichfield was sixteen miles from Birmingham.

[4] Johnson, Hawkins believed, did not have a watch till he was in his fifty-ninth year. *Ib.* ii. 57, *n.* 4.

windows

windows, as I thought, alone, and turning my head saw Sally dancing. I went on without notice, and had finished almost without perceiving that any time had elapsed. This close attention I have seldom in my whole life obtained.

In the upper-school, I first began to point my exercise, which we made noon's business. Of the method I have not so distinct a remembrance as of the foregoing system. On Thursday morning we had a lesson, as on other mornings. On Thursday afternoon, and on Saturday morning, we commonly made examples to the Syntax.

We were soon raised from Æsop to Phædrus, and then said our repetition on Friday afternoon to Hunter. I remember the fable of the wolf and lamb, *to my draught—that I may drink.* At what time we began Phædrus, I know not. It was the only book which we learned to the end. In the latter part thirty lines were expected for a lesson. What reconciles masters to long lessons is the pleasure of tasking.

Helvicus was very difficult: the dialogue *Vestitus*, Hawkins directed us to omit, as being one of the hardest in the book. As I remember, there was another upon food, and another upon fruits, which we began, and were ordered not to pursue. In the dialogue of Fruits, we perceived that Holbrook did not know the meaning of *Uvæ Crispæ*[1]. That lesson gave us great trouble. I observed that we learned Helvicus a long time with very little progress. We learned it in the afternoon on Monday and Wednesday.

Gladiolus Scriptorius.—A little lapse[2], we quitted it. I got an English Erasmus.

In Phædrus we tried to use the interpretation, but never attempted the notes. Nor do I remember that the interpretation helped us.

In Phædrus we were sent up twice to the upper master to be punished. The second time we complained that we could not get the passage. Being told that we should ask, we informed him that we had asked, and that the assistant would not tell us.

[1] In the British Museum there are some of Helvicus's works, but not, I think, this one. Neither is there a copy of *Gladiolus Scriptorius.*

[2] This seems an unusual expression.

ANECDOTES

OF THE LATE

SAMUEL JOHNSON

LL.D.

DURING THE LAST TWENTY YEARS OF HIS LIFE

BY

HESTHER LYNCH PIOZZI

[The Fourth Edition. LONDON: Printed for T. CADELL
in the Strand. M DCC LXXXVI]

PIOZZI'S ANECDOTES

[MRS. PIOZZI writing in 1815, says:—'At Rome we received letters saying the book was bought with such avidity, that Cadell hadnot one copy left when the King sent for it at ten o'clock at night, and he was forced to beg one from a friend to supply his Majesty's impatience, who sate up all night reading it. I received £300, a sum unexampled in those days for so small a volume.' Hayward's *Piozzi*, ed. 1861, ii. 305.

Horace Walpole wrote on March 28, 1786 (*Letters*, ix. 46):—'Two days ago appeared Madame Piozzi's *Anecdotes of Dr. Johnson*. I am lamentably disappointed—in her, I mean; not in him. I had conceived a favourable opinion of her capacity. But this new book is wretched; a high-varnished preface to a heap of rubbish, in a very vulgar style, and too void of method even for such a farrago.' On April 30 he wrote:—'As she must have heard that the whole first impression was sold the first day, no doubt she expects, on her landing, to be received like the Governor of Gibraltar [after the siege], and to find the road strewed with branches of palm. She, and Boswell, and their Hero are the joke of the public.' *Ib*. p. 49.

According to the *Gentleman's Magazine* for March, 1786, p. 244:—'On the third morning after the book was published not a copy of it could be obtained.' At least four editions were issued in the first year of publication.

Hannah More wrote in April, 1786:—'The Bozzi &c. subjects are not yet exhausted though everybody seems heartily sick of them. Everybody, however, conspires not to let them drop. That, and the Cagliostro and the Cardinal's Necklace spoil all conversation; and destroyed a very good evening at Mr. Pepys's last night.' H. More's *Memoirs*, ii. 16. For the Cagliostro and the Cardinal's Necklace see Carlyle's Essays.

Malone says of these Anecdotes:—'On the whole the public is indebted to her for her lively, though very inaccurate and artful account of Dr. Johnson.' Prior's *Malone*, p. 364.]

PREFACE

I HAVE somewhere heard or read, that the Preface before a book, like the portico before a house, should be contrived, so as to catch, but not detain the attention of those who desire admission to the family within, or leave to look over the collection of pictures made by one whose opportunities of obtaining them we know to have been not unfrequent. I wish not to keep my readers long from such intimacy with the manners of Dr. Johnson, or such knowledge of his sentiments as these pages can convey. To urge my distance from England as an excuse for the book's being ill written, would be ridiculous; it might indeed serve as a just reason for my having written it at all; because, though others may print the same aphorisms and stories, I cannot *here* be sure that they have done so. As the Duke says however to the Weaver, in A Midsummer Night's Dream, 'Never excuse; if your play be a bad one, keep at least the excuses to yourself[1].'

I am aware that many will say, I have not spoken highly enough of Dr. Johnson; but it will be difficult for those who say so, to speak more highly, If I have described his manners as they were, I have been careful to shew his superiority to the common forms of common life. It is surely no dispraise to an oak that it does not bear jessamine; and he who should plant honeysuckle round Trajan's column, would not be thought to adorn, but to disgrace it.

When I have said, that he was more a man of genius than of learning, I mean not to take from the one part of his character that which I willingly give to the other. The erudition of Mr. Johnson proved his genius; for he had not acquired it by long or profound study: nor can I think those characters the greatest which have most learning driven into their heads, any

[1] 'Never excuse; for when the players are all dead there need none to be blamed.' Act v, sc. 1, l. 363.

more

more than I can persuade myself to consider the river Jenisca[1] as superior to the Nile, because the first receives near seventy tributary streams in the course of its unmarked progress to the sea, while the great parent of African plenty, flowing from an almost invisible source, and unenriched by any extraneous waters, except eleven nameless rivers[2], pours his majestic torrent into the ocean by seven celebrated mouths.

But I must conclude my Preface, and begin my book, the first I ever presented before the Public; from whose awful appearance in some measure to defend and conceal myself, I have thought fit to retire behind the Telamonian shield[3], and shew as little of myself as possible; well aware of the exceeding difference there is, between fencing in the school and fighting in the field.——Studious however to avoid offending, and careless of that offence which can be taken without a cause, I here not unwillingly submit my slight performance to the decision of that glorious country, which I have the daily delight to hear applauded in others, as eminently just, generous, and humane.

[1] The Yenisei. In Brookes's *Gazetteer* (1762) it is called the Jenisa.

[2] Had she read Johnson's translation of Lobo's *Abyssinia* she would not have made so absurd a statement.

[3] In this short Preface Johnson is an oak, Trajan's column, the Nile, and Ajax Telamonius. Mrs. Piozzi herself is the archer who retires behind his comrade's shield, because fencing in the school is so different from fighting in the field.

ANECDOTES

Too much intelligence is often as pernicious to Biography as too little; the mind remains perplexed by contradiction of probabilities, and finds difficulty in separating report from truth. If Johnson then lamented that so little had ever been said about Butler[1], I might with more reason be led to complain that so much has been said about himself; for numberless informers but distract or cloud information, as glasses which multiply will for the most part be found also to obscure. Of a life too, which for the last twenty years was passed in the very front of literature, every leader of a literary company, whether officer or subaltern, naturally becomes either author or critic, so that little less than the recollection that it was *once* the request of the deceased[2], and *twice* the desire of those whose will I ever delighted to comply with, should have engaged me to add my little book to the number of those already written on the subject. I used to urge another reason for forbearance, and say, that all the readers would, on this singular occasion, be the writers of his life: like the first representation of the Masque of Comus, which, by changing their characters from spectators to performers, was *acted* by the lords and ladies it was *written* to entertain[3]. This objection is however now at an end, as I have

[1] 'In the midst of obscurity passed the life of Butler, a man whose name can only perish with his language. The mode and place of his education are unknown, the events of his life are variously related; and all that can be told with certainty is that he was poor.' Johnson's *Works*, vii. 148.

[2] See *post*, p. 166.

[3] The Earl of Bridgewater's sons and daughter. As she was 'about

found friends, far remote indeed from literary questions, who may yet be diverted from melancholy by my description of Johnson's manners, warmed to virtue even by the distant reflexion of his glowing excellence, and encouraged by the relation of his animated zeal to persist in the profession as well as practice of Christianity.

SAMUEL JOHNSON was the son of Michael Johnson, a bookseller at Litchfield, in Staffordshire; a very pious and worthy man, but wrong-headed, positive, and afflicted with melancholy, as his son, from whom alone I had the information, once told me: his business, however, leading him to be much on horseback, contributed to the preservation of his bodily health, and mental sanity[1]; which, when he staid long at home, would sometimes be about to give way; and Mr. Johnson said, that when his work-shop, a detached building, had fallen half down for want of money to repair it, his father was not less diligent to lock the door every night, though he saw that any body might walk in at the back part, and knew that there was no security obtained by barring the front door. '*This* (says his son) was madness, you may see, and would have been discoverable in other instances of the prevalence of imagination, but that poverty prevented it from playing such tricks as riches and leisure encourage.' Michael was a man of still larger size and greater strength than his son; who was reckoned very like him[2], but did not delight in talking much of his family—'one has (says he) *so* little pleasure in reciting the anecdotes of beggary[3].' One day, however, hearing me praise a favourite friend with partial tenderness as well as true esteem; 'Why do you like that man's acquaintance so?' said he: Because, replied I, he is open and confiding, and tells me stories of his uncles and cousins; I love the light parts of a solid character. 'Nay, if you are for family history (says Mr. Johnson good-humouredly) *I* can fit you:

thirteen years of age and her two brothers were still younger,' it is absurd to describe them (even if there had been more than one lady) as 'the lords and ladies it was written to entertain.'

[1] *Life*, i. 35, and *ante*, p. 132.

[2] His likeness is given in Murray's *Johnsoniana*, ed. 1836, p. 464.

[3] *Ante*, p. 132.

I had

I had an uncle, Cornelius Ford, who, upon a journey, stopped and read an inscription written on a stone he saw standing by the way-side, set up, as it proved, in honour of a man who had leaped a certain leap thereabouts, the extent of which was specified upon the stone: Why now, says my uncle, I could leap it in my boots; and he did leap it in his boots. I had likewise another uncle, Andrew,' continued he, 'my father's brother, who kept the ring in Smithfield (where they wrestled and boxed) for a whole year[1], and never was thrown or conquered. Here now are uncles for you, Mistress[2], if that's the way to your heart.' Mr. Johnson was very conversant in the art of attack and defence by boxing, which science he had learned from his uncle Andrew, I believe; and I have heard him descant upon the age when people were received, and when rejected, in the schools once held for that brutal amusement, much to the admiration of those who had no expectation of his skill in such matters[3], from the sight of a figure which precluded all possibility of personal prowess[4]; though, because he saw Mr. Thrale one day

[1] By 'kept the ring' Johnson, no doubt, meant 'held it against all comers.' Smithfield had fallen in dignity from the days when Richard II charged heralds 'to publish in England, Scotland, Germany, Flanders, Brabant, Hainault and France that a great joust should be held in it on the Sunday after the Feast of St. Michael, which day was called "the Sunday of the Feast of Challenge."' Froissart's *Chronicles*, ed. 1816, iv. 170.

[2] 'He used to mention Mrs. Thrale by the epithets *Madam* or *my Mistress*.' *Life*, i. 494.

[3] 'I am sorry,' he said, 'that prize-fighting is gone out; every art should be preserved, and the art of defence is surely important.' *Ib.* v. 229.

Figg, the prize fighter, told Chetwood that he had not bought a shirt for more than twenty years. When he fought he sent round to a select number of his scholars to borrow one for the combat, and seldom failed of half a dozen from his prime pupils—of the nobility and young gentry: each one thought that it was in his shirt the battle was fought. He informed his lenders of linen of the chasms their shirts received, and promised to send them home. 'But,' said he, 'I seldom received any other answer than "Damn you, keep it."' R. W. Chetwood, *General History of the Stage*, 1749, p. 60.

Figg died in 1734. *Gentleman's Magazine*, 1734, p. 703. See *ib.* 1731, p. 172, for his 'amphitheatre.'

[4] 'Johnson told me that one night he was attacked in the street by four men, to whom he would not yield, but kept them all at bay till the watch came up, and carried both him and them to the Roundhouse.' *Life*, ii. 299.

Boswell wrote of him in 1773:—'Few men have his intrepidity, Her-

leap over a cabriolet stool [1], to shew that he was not tired after a chace of fifty miles or more, *he* suddenly jumped over it too; but in a way so strange and so unwieldy, that our terror lest he should break his bones, took from us even the power of laughing.

Michael Johnson was past fifty years old when he married his wife, who was upwards of forty; yet I think her son told me she remained three years childless before he was born into the world, who so greatly contributed to improve it. In three years more she brought another son, Nathaniel, who lived to be twenty-seven or twenty-eight years old [2], and of whose manly spirit I have heard his brother speak with pride and pleasure, mentioning one circumstance, particular enough, that when the company were one day lamenting the badness of the roads, he enquired where they could be, as he travelled the country more than most people, and had never seen a bad road in his life [3]. The two brothers did not, however, much delight in each other's company [4], being always rivals for the mother's fondness; and many of

culean strength, or presence of mind.' *Ib.* v. 329. Mrs. Piozzi says (*post*, p. 224):—'He had possessed an athletic constitution.' Perhaps she is now speaking of his state near the end of his life.

[1] A cabriolet (cut down into cab) was a late invention; the first instance of its use in the *New Eng. Dict.* being three years later than the publication of these *Anecdotes*. The stool, I conjecture, was used in getting into it.

[2] Michael Johnson was born in 1656, his wife in 1669; they were married in 1706. Samuel was born in 1709, and Nathanael in 1712. Nathanael died in 1737. *Life*, i. 35, *n.* 1; iv. 393, *n.* 2. The father was born under the Commonwealth, the son lived to be kept waiting for his dinner by the Prince of Wales who was afterwards George IV. *Ib.* iv. 270, *n.* 2. Michael was eighteen years old when Milton died; when Samuel died Wordsworth was fourteen.

[3] Cave, the proprietor of the *Gentleman's Magazine*, in the latter part of his life travelled a great deal on business. 'Time being more an object to him than expense, and the luxury of turnpike roads being then but little known, [he died in 1754] he generally used four horses.' Nichols's *Lit. Anec.* v. 43.

For Arthur Young's account in 1768 of the 'detestable' and 'infernal' roads see *Life*, iii. 135, *n.* 1. Of the bye-roads in Ireland he writes in 1780:—'They are the finest in the world.' *Tour in Ireland*, ed. 1892, i. 116. In 1787 he writes:—'If the French have not husbandry to shew us, they have roads.' *Travels in France*, ed. 1890, p. 7.

[4] Nathanael complained that his brother 'scarcely used him with common civility.' *Life*, i. 90, *n.* 3.

of the severe reflections on domestic life in Rasselas, took their source from its author's keen recollections of the time passed in his early years[1]. Their father Michael died of an inflammatory fever, at the age of seventy-six[2], as Mr. Johnson told me: their mother at eighty-nine, of a gradual decay. She was slight in her person, he said, and rather below than above the common size. So excellent was her character, and so blameless her life, that when an oppressive neighbour once endeavoured to take from her a little field she possessed, he could persuade no attorney to undertake the cause against a woman so beloved in her narrow circle[3]: and it is this incident he alludes to in the line of his Vanity of Human Wishes, calling her

The general favourite as the general friend.

Nor could any one pay more willing homage to such a character, though she had not been related to him, than did Dr. Johnson on every occasion that offered: his disquisition on Pope's epitaph placed over Mrs. Corbet, is a proof of that preference always given by him to a noiseless life over a bustling one[4]; for however

[1] 'Domestick discord,' answered the princess, 'is not inevitably and fatally necessary; but yet it is not easily avoided. We seldom see that a whole family is virtuous: the good and evil cannot well agree: and the evil can yet less agree with one another: even the virtuous fall sometimes to variance, when their virtues are of different kinds and tending to extremes.' *Rasselas*, ch. xxvi.

Admiring the harmony in the Burney family, Johnson wrote:—'Of this consanguineous unanimity I have had never much experience; but it appears to me one of the great lenitives of life.' *Letters*, ii. 237.

[2] He was seventy-five.

[3] Nevertheless Johnson never had a good word for an attorney. *Life*, ii. 126, *n*. 4.

[4] 'Here rests a woman, good without pretence,
Blest with plain reason and with sober sense:
No conquest she but o'er herself desir'd;
No arts essay'd, but not to be admir'd.
Passion and pride were to her soul unknown,
Convinc'd that virtue only is our own.
So unaffected, so compos'd a mind,
So firm, yet soft, so strong, yet so refin'd,
Heav'n as its purest gold by tortures try'd;
The saint sustain'd it, but the woman dy'd.'

Johnson, in his criticism on this epitaph, says:—'Domestick virtue, as it is exerted without great occasions or conspicuous consequences, in an even unnoted tenour, required the genius of Pope to display it in such a manner as might attract regard and enforce reverence.' *Works*, viii. 354.

taste

taste begins, we almost always see that it ends in simplicity; the glutton finishes by losing his relish for any thing highly sauced, and calls for his boiled chicken at the close of many years spent in the search of dainties; the connoisseurs are soon weary of Rubens [1], and the critics of Lucan [2]; and the refinements of every kind heaped upon civil life, always sicken their possessors before the close of it.

At the age of two years Mr. Johnson was brought up to London by his mother, to be touched by Queen Anne for the scrophulous evil, which terribly afflicted his childhood, and left such marks as greatly disfigured a countenance naturally harsh and rugged, beside doing irreparable damage to the auricular organs, which never could perform their functions since I knew him; and it was owing to that horrible disorder, too, that one eye was perfectly useless to him; that defect, however, was not observable, the eyes looked both alike. As Mr. Johnson had an astonishing memory, I asked him, if he could remember Queen Anne at all? 'He had (he said) a confused, but somehow a sort of solemn recollection of a lady in diamonds, and a long black hood [3].'

The christening of his brother he remembered with all its circumstances, and said, his mother taught him to spell and pronounce the words *little Natty*, syllable by syllable, making him say it over in the evening to her husband and his guests. The trick which most parents play with their children, of shewing off their newly-acquired accomplishments, disgusted Mr. Johnson beyond expression; he had been treated so himself, he said, till

[1] Sir Joshua Reynolds, writing four years earlier than Mrs. Piozzi, thus finishes his *Journey to Flanders and Holland*:—'To conclude, I will repeat in favour of Rubens, what I have before said in regard to the Dutch school,—that those who cannot see the extraordinary merit of this great painter either have a narrow conception of the variety of art, or are led away by the affectation of approving nothing but what comes from the Italian school.'

[2] 'Mrs. Thrale's learning,' said Johnson, 'is that of a school-boy in one of the lower forms.' *Life*, i. 494. The judgement passed by the critics on Lucan she had perhaps learnt from Addison in the *Guardian*, Nos. 115, 119.

[3] Quoted in the *Life*, i. 43.

he absolutely loathed his father's caresses, because he knew they were sure to precede some unpleasing display of his early abilities; and he used, when neighbours came o'visiting, to run up a tree that he might not be found and exhibited, such, as no doubt he was, a prodigy of early understanding. His epitaph upon the duck he killed by treading on it at five years old,

Here lies poor duck
  That Samuel Johnson trod on;
If it had liv'd it had been good luck,
  For it would have been an odd one;

is a striking example of early expansion of mind, and knowledge of language [1]; yet he always seemed more mortified at the recollection of the bustle [2] his parents made with his wit, than pleased with the thoughts of possessing it. 'That (said he to me one day) is the great misery of late marriages [3], the unhappy produce of them becomes the plaything of dotage: an old man's child

[1] Boswell made the following record in his note-book:—' Miss Porter told me in Johnson's presence at Litchfield, Monday, 25 March, 1776, that his mother told her, that when he was in petticoats he was walking by his father's side & carelessly trode upon a duck, one of thirteen, & killed it. So then this duck, it was said to him, must be buried, & he must make an epitaph for it. Upon which he made these lines:—

" Under this stone lyes Mr. Duck,
  Whom Samuel Johnson trode on;
He might have liv'd if he had luck,
  But then he'd been an odd one."

Dr. Johnson said that his father made one half of this epitaph. That he was a foolish old man, that is to say was foolish in talking of his children. But I trust to his mother's relation of what happened in his childhood rather than to his own recollection; and Miss Porter assured him, in my presence, upon his mother's authority, that he had made this epitaph himself. But he assures me, 21 Sept., 1777, that he remembers his father making it.' *Morrison Autographs*, second series, i. 367. See *Life*, i. 40.

Horace Walpole, with the words 'expansion of mind' in view, writes:—' The Signora talks of her Doctor's *expanded* mind, and has contributed her mite to show that never mind was narrower.' Walpole's *Letters*, ix. 48.

[2] *Bustle* was a favourite word of Johnson's. See *Letters*, i. 196; ii. 147, 164.

In his last note on *Coriolanus* he says:—' There is perhaps too much bustle in the first act and too little in the last.' Reynolds perhaps caught the word from him, when he write of one of Rubens's pictures:—' The bustle, which is in every part of the picture, makes a fine contrast to the character of resignation in the crucified Saviour.' Reynolds's *Works*, ed. 1824, ii. 216.

[3] *Life*, ii. 128.

(continued

(continued he) leads much such a life, I think, as a little boy's dog, teized with awkward fondness, and forced, perhaps, to sit up and beg, as we call it, to divert a company, who at last go away complaining of their disagreeable entertainment.' In consequence of these maxims, and full of indignation against such parents as delight to produce their young ones early into the talking world, I have known Mr. Johnson give a good deal of pain, by refusing to hear the verses the children could recite, or the songs they could sing; particularly one friend who told him that his two sons should repeat Gray's Elegy to him alternately, that he might judge who had the happiest cadence. 'No, pray Sir (said he), let the dears both speak it at once; more noise will by that means be made, and the noise will be sooner over.' He told me the story himself, but I have forgot who the father was[1].

Mr. Johnson's mother was daughter to a gentleman in the country, such as there were many of in those days, who possessing, perhaps, one or two hundred pounds a year in land, lived on the profits, and sought not to increase their income[2]: she was therefore inclined to think higher of herself than of her husband, whose conduct in money matters being but indifferent, she had a trick of teizing him about it, and was, by her son's account, very importunate with regard to her fears of spending more than they could afford, though she never arrived at knowing how much that was[3]; a fault common, as he said, to most women who pride themselves on their œconomy. They did not however, as I could understand, live ill together on the whole: 'my father (says he) could always take his horse and ride away for orders when things went badly.' The lady's maiden name was Ford; and the parson who sits next to the punch-bowl in Hogarth's Modern Midnight Conversation was her brother's son. This Ford was a man who chose to be eminent only for

[1] Perhaps Bennet Langton, who, it was said, would make his son repeat the Hebrew alphabet to a guest. Mme. D'Arblay's *Diary*, ii. 260.

[2] 'She was descended of an ancient race of substantial yeomanry.' *Life*, i. 35. (Boswell's use of *yeomanry* is incorrect; he should have said *yeomen*.) Johnson describes her as 'Antiqua Fordorum gente oriunda.' *Ib.* iv. 393, *n.* 2.

[3] *Ante*, p. 133.

vice,

vice, with talents that might have made him conspicuous in literature, and respectable in any profession he could have chosen: his cousin has mentioned him in the lives of Fenton and of Broome [1]; and when he spoke of him to me, it was always with tenderness, praising his acquaintance with life and manners, and recollecting one piece of advice that no man surely ever followed more exactly: 'Obtain (says Ford) some general principles of every science; he who can talk only on one subject, or act only in one department, is seldom wanted, and perhaps never wished for; while the man of general knowledge can often benefit, and always please [2].' He used to relate, however, another story less to the credit of his cousin's penetration, how Ford on some occasion said to him, 'You will make your way the more easily in the world, I see, as you are contented to dispute no man's claim to conversation excellence; they will, therefore, more willingly allow your pretensions as a writer.' Can one, on such an occasion, forbear recollecting the predictions of Boileau's father, when stroaking the head of the young satirist, *Ce petit bon homme* (says he) *n'à [sic] point trop d'esprit*, mais il ne *dira jamais mal de personne* [3]. Such are the prognostics formed by

[1] In the *Life of Fenton* he describes Ford as 'a clergyman at that time [1723] too well known, whose abilities, instead of furnishing convivial merriment to the voluptuous and dissolute, might have enabled him to excel among the virtuous and the wise.' *Works*, viii. 57. 'At his college Broome lived for some time in the same chamber with the well-known Ford.' *Ib.* p. 229. See *Life*, i. 49; iii. 348. Broome entered St. John's College, Cambridge, in 1708. In the *Gent. Mag.*, 1731, p. 354, is recorded the death on August 22 of 'The Rev. Mr. Ford, esteem'd for his polite, agreeable conversation.'

[2] 'Paschal had before enforced the same maxim. "You tell me that such a person is a good mathematician, but I have nothing to do with mathematics. You assert of another that he understands the art of war, but I have no wish to make war upon anybody. The world is full of wants, and loves only those who can satisfy them. It is false praise to say of any one that he is skilled in poetry, and a bad sign when he is quoted solely about verses."' *Quarterly Review*, No. 206, p. 306. See *Les Pensées de Pascal*, i. ix. 18.

[3] 'Il fut élevé jusqu'à l'âge de sept à huit ans dans la maison de son père, qui parcourant quelquefois les différens caractères de ses enfans, et surpris de l'extrême douceur, de la simplicité même qu'il croyait remarquer en celui-ci, disait ordinairement de lui, par une espèce d'opposition aux autres, *que c'était un bon garçon qui ne dirait jamais mal de personne.*' *Œuvres de Boileau*, ed. 1747, i. xxxiv.

men

men of wit and sense, as these two certainly were, concerning the future character and conduct of those for whose welfare they were honestly and deeply concerned; and so late do those features of peculiarity come to their growth, which mark a character to all succeeding generations.

Dr. Johnson first learned to read of his mother and her old maid Catharine, in whose lap he well remembered sitting while she explained to him the story of St. George and the Dragon. I know not whether this is the proper place to add, that such was his tenderness, and such his gratitude, that he took a journey to Litchfield fifty-seven years afterwards to support and comfort her in her last illness[1]; he had enquired for his nurse, and she was dead[2]. The recollection of such reading as had delighted him in his infancy, made him always persist in fancying that it was the only reading which could please an infant; and he used to condemn me for putting Newbery's books into their hands as too trifling to engage their attention. 'Babies do not want (said he) to hear about babies; they like to be told of giants and castles, and of somewhat which can stretch and stimulate their little minds.' When in answer I would urge the numerous editions and quick sale of Tommy Prudent or Goody Two Shoes[3]: 'Remember always (said he) that the parents *buy* the

[1] Mrs. Piozzi is speaking of Catherine Chambers, who died in 1767 (*ante*, p. 45). She and Johnson were of the same age; moreover it was not till 'about 1724,' when he was fifteen years old, that she came to live with his mother. *Ib.*

[2] *Ante*, p. 130.

[3] 'The author of *Caleb Williams* [William Godwin], who had been a child's publisher himself, had always a strong persuasion that Goldsmith wrote *Goody Two Shoes*.' Forster's *Goldsmith*, i. 346. Goldsmith introduces Newbery in the *Vicar of Wakefield*, ch. xviii, as 'the philanthropic bookseller in St. Paul's Church-yard, who has written so many little books for children: he called himself their friend, but he was the friend of all mankind.'

Johnson at Rochester maintained 'that *Jack the Giant-Killer*, *Parisenus and Parismenus*, and *The Seven Champions of Christendom* were fitter for children than Mrs. Barbauld and Mrs. Trimmer.' *Life*, iv. 8.

Boswell wrote on the fly-leaf of the first volume of a collection of Chap Books which he bought in 1763:— 'Having when a Boy been much entertained with *Jack the Giant Killer*, I went to the Printing office in Bow Churchyard and bought this collection. I shall certainly, some

books,

books, and that the children never read them.' Mrs. Barbauld however had his best praise, and deserved it; no man was more struck than Mr. Johnson with voluntary descent from possible splendour to painful duty [1].

At eight years old he went to school, for his health would not permit him to be sent sooner [2]; and at the age of ten years his mind was disturbed by scruples of infidelity, which preyed upon his spirits, and made him very uneasy; the more so, as he revealed his uneasiness to no one, being naturally (as he said) 'of a sullen temper and reserved disposition.' He scarched, however, diligently but fruitlessly, for evidences of the truth of revelation; and at length recollecting a book he had once seen in his father's shop, intitled, *De Veritate Religionis, &c.* he began to think himself highly culpable for neglecting such a means of information, and took himself severely to task for this sin, adding many acts of voluntary, and to others unknown, penance. The first opportunity which offered (of course) he seized the book with avidity; but on examination, not finding himself scholar enough to peruse its contents, set his heart at rest; and, not thinking to enquire whether there were any English books written on the subject, followed his usual amusements, and considered his

time or other, write a little Story Book in the style of these. I shall be happy to succeed, for he who pleases children will be remembered by men.' *Sale Catalogue of the Auchinleck Library*, Sotheby & Co., June 23, 1893, Lot 91.

[1] 'A voluntary descent from the dignity of science is perhaps the hardest lesson that humility can teach.' Johnson's *Works*, viii. 385. See also *ib.* vii. 99, 110 for 'a kind of humble dignity' which he praises in Milton. For his abuse of Mrs. Barbauld see *Life*, ii. 408.

Lamb wrote on Oct. 23, 1802:—'Mrs. Barbauld's stuff has banished all the old classics of the nursery; and the shopman at Newbery's hardly deigned to reach them off an old exploded corner of a shelf, when Mary asked for them. Mrs. Barbauld's and Mrs. Trimmer's nonsense lay in piles about. . . Science has succeeded to poetry no less in the little walks of children than with men.' Lamb's *Letters*, ed. 1888, i. 189.

[2] By the spring of 1719, when he was nine and a half, he had been in the Grammar School 'two years and perhaps four months.' *Ante*, p. 138. Before he went to this school he had been under Tom Brown, who 'published a spelling-book and dedicated it to the Universe,' and earlier still he had gone to Dame Oliver's school. *Life*, i. 43.

conscience

conscience as lightened of a crime. He redoubled his diligence to learn the language that contained the information he most wished for; but from the pain which guilt had given him, he now began to deduce the soul's immortality, which was the point that belief first stopped at; and from that moment resolving to be a Christian, became one of the most zealous and pious ones our nation ever produced[1]. When he had told me this odd anecdote of his childhood; 'I cannot imagine (said he) what makes me talk of myself to you so, for I really never mentioned this foolish story to any body except Dr. Taylor, not even to my *dear dear* Bathurst, whom I loved better than ever I loved any human creature; but poor Bathurst is dead!!![2]'—Here a long pause and a few tears ensued. Why Sir, said I, how like is all this to Jean Jaques Rousseau![3] as like, I mean, as the sensations of frost and fire, when my child complained yesterday that the ice she was eating *burned* her mouth. Mr. Johnson laughed at the incongruous ideas; but the first thing which presented itself to the mind of an ingenious and learned friend whom I had the pleasure to pass some time with here at Florence, was the same resemblance, though I think the two characters had little in common, further than an early attention to things beyond the capacity of other babies, a keen sensibility of right and wrong, and a warmth of imagination little consistent with sound and perfect health. I have heard him relate another odd thing of himself too, but it is one which every body has heard as well as I: how, when he was about nine years old, having got the play of Hamlet in his hand, and reading it quietly in his father's kitchen, he kept on steadily enough, till coming to the Ghost scene, he suddenly hurried up stairs to the street door that he might see people about him[4]: such an incident, as he was not unwilling to relate it, is probably in

[1] For Boswell's criticism of 'this strange fantastical account' see *Life*, i. 68, *n*. 3.

The book entitled *De Veritate Religionis* was, no doubt, Grotius's work.

[2] *Ante*, p. 29.

[3] In his *Confessions*.

[4] He told Boswell also of this terror that came upon him. *Life*, i. 70. In his *Observations on Macbeth* he says:—'He that peruses Shakespeare looks round alarmed, and starts to find himself alone.' *Works*, v. 71.

every

every one's possession now; he told it as a testimony to the merits of Shakespeare: but one day when my son was going to school, and dear Dr. Johnson followed as far as the garden gate, praying for his salvation[1], in a voice which those who listened attentively could hear plain enough, he said to me suddenly, 'Make your boy tell you his dreams: the first corruption that entered into my heart was communicated in a dream.' What was it, Sir? said I. '*Do* not ask me,' replied he with much violence, and walked away in apparent agitation. I never durst make any further enquiries. He retained a strong aversion for the memory of Hunter, one of his schoolmasters, who, he said once, was a brutal fellow: 'so brutal (added he), that no man who had been educated by him ever sent his son to the same school.' I have however heard him acknowledge his scholarship to be very great[2]. His next master he despised, as knowing less than himself, I found; but the name of that gentleman has slipped my memory[3]. Mr. Johnson was himself exceedingly disposed to the general indulgence of children, and was even scrupulously and ceremoniously attentive not to offend them[4]: he had strongly persuaded himself of the difficulty people always find to erase early impressions either of kindness or resentment, and said, 'he should never have so loved his mother when a man, had she not given him coffee[5] she could ill afford, to gratify his appetite when a boy.' If you had had children Sir, said I, would you have taught them any thing? 'I hope (replied he), that I should have willingly lived on bread and water to obtain

[1] For Johnson's love for the boy, who died early, see *Life*, ii. 468, and *Letters*, i. 383.

[2] Johnson said of him:—'Abating his brutality he was a very good master.' *Life*, ii. 146. See also *ib.* i. 44.

[3] Wentworth, master of Stourbridge school. According to Hawkins (p. 9) his real name was Winkworth, 'but affecting to be thought allied to the Strafford family, he assumed the name of Wentworth.' Johnson told Boswell that 'he was a very able man, but an idle man, and to me very severe. . . . Yet he taught me a great deal.' *Life*, i. 50.

[4] Boswell mentions 'Johnson's love of little children, which he discovered upon all occasions, calling them "pretty dears" and giving them sweetmeats.' *Ib.* iv. 126.

[5] In the list of prices given in the early numbers of the *Gentleman's Magazine*, though six or seven qualities of tea are included, I can find no mention of coffee.

instruction for them; but I would not have set their future friendship to hazard for the sake of thrusting into their heads knowledge of things for which they might not perhaps have either taste or necessity. You teach your daughters the diameters of the planets, and wonder when you have done that they do not delight in your company. No science can be communicated by mortal creatures without attention from the scholar; no attention can be obtained from children without the infliction of pain[1], and pain is never remembered without resentment.' That something should be learned, was however so certainly his opinion, that I have heard him say, how education had been often compared to agriculture, yet that it resembled it chiefly in this: 'that if nothing is sown, no crop (says he) can be obtained.' His contempt of the lady who fancied her son could be eminent without study, because Shakespeare was found wanting in scholastic learning, was expressed in terms so gross and so well known, I will not repeat them here.

To recollect, however, and to repeat the sayings of Dr. Johnson, is almost all that can be done by the writers of his life; as his life, at least since my acquaintance with him, consisted in little else than talking, when he was not absolutely employed in some serious piece of work; and whatever work he did, seemed so much below his powers of performance, that he appeared the idlest of all human beings; ever musing till he was called out to converse, and conversing till the fatigue of his friends, or the promptitude of his own temper to take offence, consigned him back again to silent meditation[2].

[1] 'Johnson upon all occasions expressed his approbation of enforcing instruction by means of the rod.' *Life*, i. 46.

[2] Most of this paragraph is quoted in the *Life*, iv. 343, 346.

For his musing see *ib.* v. 73 and *Letters*, i. 359, *n.* 2, 388, *n.* 2, and Piozzi's *Anecdotes*, p. 208.

Miss Burney describes how at a party at her father's house he took a book from the shelves 'and began, without further ceremony, to read to himself, all the time standing at a distance from the company. We were all very much provoked, as we perfectly languished to hear him talk; but it seems he is the most silent creature, when not particularly drawn out, in the world.' *Early Diary of F. Burney*, ii. 156.

The

The remembrance of what had passed in his own childhood, made Mr. Johnson very solicitous to preserve the felicity of children; and when he had persuaded Dr. Sumner to remit the tasks usually given to fill up boys' time during the holidays, he rejoiced exceedingly in the success of his negociation, and told me that he had never ceased representing to all the eminent schoolmasters in England, the absurd tyranny of poisoning the hour of permitted pleasure, by keeping future misery before the children's eyes, and tempting them by bribery or falsehood to evade it. 'Bob Sumner (said he), however, I have at length prevailed upon: I know not indeed whether his tenderness was persuaded, or his reason convinced, but the effect will always be the same.' Poor Dr. Sumner died, however, before the next vacation[1].

Mr. Johnson was of opinion, too, that young people should have *positive* not *general* rules given for their direction. 'My mother (said he) was always telling me that I did not *behave* myself properly; that I should endeavour to learn *behaviour*, and such cant[2]: but when I replied, that she ought to tell me what to do, and what to avoid, her admonitions were commonly, for that time at least, at an end.'

This, I fear, was however at best a momentary refuge, found out by perverseness. No man knew better than Johnson in how many nameless and numberless actions *behaviour* consists: actions which can scarcely be reduced to rule, and which come under no description. Of these he retained so many very strange ones,

[1] Sumner was Head Master of Harrow School. He died of apoplexy in 1771 at the age of forty-one. Among his pupils were Dr. Parr, Sir William Jones, and R. B. Sheridan. Field's *Life of Parr*, i. 16, 51, 58.

[2] See *Life*, iv. 221, *n.* 1, for instances of Johnson's use of the word *cant*. To these I would add the following:—'It is pleasant to remark how soon Pope learnt the cant of an author.' *Works*, viii. 238. 'Addison was not a man on whom such cant of sensibility could make much impression.' *Ib.* p. 248. 'The Persons of the Drama were first enumerated with all the cant of the modern stage by Mr. Rowe.' Johnson's *Shakespeare*, ii. 352. 'When he calls the girl *his only heaven on earth* he utters the common cant of lovers.' *Ib.* iii. 133.

 that

that I suppose no one who saw his odd manner of gesticulating, much blamed or wondered at the good lady's solicitude concerning her son's *behaviour*.

Though he was attentive to the peace of children in general, no man had a stronger contempt than he for such parents as openly profess that they cannot govern their children. 'How (says he) is an army governed? Such people, for the most part, multiply prohibitions till obedience becomes impossible, and authority appears absurd; and never suspect that they tease their family, their friends, and themselves, only because conversation runs low, and something must be said.'

Of parental authority, indeed, few people thought with a lower degree of estimation [1]. I one day mentioned the resignation of Cyrus to his father's will, as related by Xenophon, when, after all his conquests, he requested the consent of Cambyses to his marriage with a neighbouring princess; and I added Rollin's applause and recommendation of the example. 'Do you not perceive then (says Johnson), that Xenophon on this occasion commends like a pedant, and Pere [*sic*] Rollin applauds like a slave? If Cyrus by his conquests had not purchased emancipation, he had conquered to little purpose indeed. Can you bear to see the folly of a fellow who has in his care the lives of thousands, when he begs his papa permission to be married, and confesses his inability to decide in a matter which concerns no man's happiness but his own [2]?'—Mr. Johnson caught me another time

[1] It was parental tyranny that Johnson condemned. *Life*, i. 346, *n.* 2; iii. 377. For his lament over 'the general relaxation of reverence' see *ib.* iii. 262.

[2] Ascham, before Rollin, 'had applauded like a slave.' In his *Schoolmaster* (*Works*, 1864, iii. 121) he writes:—'And see the great obedience that was used in old time to fathers and governors. No son, were he never so old of years, never so great of birth, though he were a king's son, might marry but by his father's and mother's also consent. Cyrus the Great, after he had conquered Babylon and subdued rich King Croesus, with whole Asia Minor, coming triumphantly home, his uncle Cyaxares offered him his daughter to wife. Cyrus thanked his uncle and praised the maid; but for marriage, he answered him with these wise and sweet words, as they be uttered by Xenophon, &c.' See *Cyropaedia*, viii. 5. 20.

time reprimanding the daughter of my housekeeper for having sat down unpermitted in her mother's presence[1]. 'Why, she gets her living, does she not (said he), without her mother's help? Let the wench alone,' continued he. And when we were again out of the women's sight who were concerned in the dispute: 'Poor people's children, dear Lady (said he), never respect them: I did not respect my own mother, though I loved her: and one day, when in anger she called me a puppy, I asked her if she knew what they called a puppy's mother.' We were talking of a young fellow who used to come often to the house; he was about fifteen years old, or less, if I remember right, and had a manner at once sullen and sheepish. 'That lad (says Mr. Johnson) looks like the son of a schoolmaster; which (added he) is one of the very worst conditions of childhood: such a boy has no father, or worse than none; he never can reflect on his parent but the reflection brings to his mind some idea of pain inflicted, or of sorrow suffered[2].'

I will relate one thing more that Dr. Johnson said about babyhood before I quit the subject; it was this: 'That little people should be encouraged always to tell whatever they hear particularly striking, to some brother, sister, or servant, immediately before the impression is erased by the intervention of newer occurrences. He perfectly remembered the first time he ever heard of Heaven and Hell (he said), because when his mother had made out such a description of both places as she

[1] The following story is told of the 'proud' Duke of Somerset who died in 1748:—'His two youngest daughters were alternately obliged to stand and watch him during his afternoon siesta. On one occasion, Lady Charlotte, being fatigued, sat down, when the Duke awaking unexpectedly expressed his surprise at her disobedience, and declared he should remember her want of decorum in his will. He left this daughter £20,000 less than the other.' Addison's *Works*, v. 340, *n.* 3.

[2] See *Life*, i. 44, *n.* 2; ii. 144, *n.* 2, for the brutality of the masters of old. One of the characters in *Tom Jones* (bk. xi, ch. 7) represents her husband as asking her 'with the voice of a schoolmaster, or, what is often much the same, of a tyrant.' A happy change has taken place. I, at all events, the son of a schoolmaster, can honestly say that the reflection on my father does not bring to my mind a single idea of pain inflicted or of sorrow suffered.

thought likely to seize the attention of her infant auditor, who was then in bed with her, she got up, and dressing him before the usual time, sent him directly to call a favourite workman in the house, to whom she knew he would communicate the conversation while it was yet impressed upon his mind. The event was what she wished [1], and it was to that method chiefly that he owed his uncommon felicity of remembering distant occurrences, and long past conversations.'

At the age of eighteen Dr. Johnson quitted school [2], and escaped from the tuition of those he hated or those he despised. I have heard him relate very few college adventures. He used to say that our best accounts of his behaviour there would be gathered from Dr. Adams [3] and Dr. Taylor [4], and that he was sure they would always tell the truth. He told me however one day, how, when he was first entered at the university, he passed a morning, in compliance with the customs of the place, at his tutor's chambers; but finding him no scholar, went no more. In about ten days after, meeting the same gentleman, Mr. Jordan, in the street, he offered to pass by without saluting him; but the tutor stopped, and enquired, not roughly neither, What he had been doing? 'Sliding on the ice,' was the reply; and so turned away with disdain [5]. He laughed very heartily at the recollection

[1] Boswell, who had also heard this story from Johnson, thus concludes:—'She sent him to repeat it to Thomas Jackson, their man-servant; he not being in the way, this was not done.' *Life*, i. 38; *ante*, p. 135.

[2] According to Boswell he went to Stourbridge School at the age of fifteen, remained there little more than a year, and then spent two years at home before he entered college.' *Ib.* i. 49, 50, 56. This would make him in his nineteenth year when he entered; he was, however, in his twentieth. *Ib.* i. 58, *n.* 3.

[3] At that time one of the Fellows of Pembroke College; afterwards the Master. *Ib.* i. 59. A copy of his portrait has been lately hung in the Hall of the College.

[4] Johnson's schoolfellow and correspondent. *Ib.* i. 44.

[5] The tutor's name was Jorden. Johnson, in telling this story to Boswell, added:—'I had no notion that I was wrong or irreverent to my tutor.' *Ib.* i. 60. See also i. 272. According to Hawkins (*Life of Johnson*, p. 9) Johnson once said to the same tutor:—'Sir, you have sconced [fined] me twopence for non-attendance at a lecture not worth a penny.' Mr. Falconer Madan, one of the Sub-Librarians of the Bodleian, informs me that twopence was the

of

of his own insolence, and said they endured it from him with wonderful acquiescence, and a gentleness that, whenever he thought of it, astonished himself. He told me too, that when he made his first declamation, he wrote over but one copy, and that coarsely; and having given it into the hand of the tutor who stood to receive it as he passed, was obliged to begin by chance and continue on how he could, for he had got but little of it by heart; so fairly trusting to his present powers for immediate supply, he finished by adding astonishment to the applause of all who knew how little was owing to study [1]. A prodigious risque, however, said some one: 'Not at all (exclaims Johnson), no man I suppose leaps at once into deep water who does not know how to swim.'

I doubt not but this story will be told by many of his biographers, and said so to him when he told it me on the 18th of July 1773 [2]. 'And who will be my biographer (said he),

sconce in the middle ages. Johnson, in his *Dictionary*, calls *sconce* 'a low word which ought not to be retained.'

Adam Smith, who entered Oxford eleven years after Johnson left it, says:—'If the teacher happens to be a man of sense, it must be an unpleasant thing to him to be conscious, while he is lecturing his students, that he is either speaking or reading nonsense, or what is very little better than nonsense. It must, too, be unpleasant to him to observe that the greater part of his students desert his lectures; or, perhaps, attend upon them with plain enough marks of neglect, contempt, and derision.' *Wealth of Nations*, ed. 1811, iii. 171. 'No discipline,' he adds, 'is ever requisite to force attendance upon lectures which are really worth the attending, as is well known wherever any such lectures are given.' *Ib.* p. 172.

[1] He told Windham the same story. *Letters*, ii. 440. He was more careful with 'his first exercise at College,' for a 'certain apprehension arising from novelty made him write it twice over.' *Life*, i. 71; iv. 309.

[2] Even so early as this he knew that Boswell intended to write his life. On April 11 of this year Boswell records:—'I again solicited him to communicate to me the particulars of his early life. He said, "You shall have them all for two-pence. I hope you shall know a great deal more of me before you write my life."' *Ib.* ii. 217. See also *ib.* i. 25; ii. 166. In the autumn of the same year he read the following passage in Boswell's *Journal*:—'The Sunday evening that we sat by ourselves at Aberdeen, I asked him several particulars of his life, from his early years, which he readily told me; and I wrote them down before him. This day I proceeded in my inquiries, also writing them in his presence. I have them on detached sheets. I shall collect authentick materials for THE LIFE OF SAMUEL JOHNSON, LL.D.;

do

do you think?' Goldsmith, no doubt, replied I, and he will do it the best among us. 'The dog would write it best to be sure, replied he; but his particular malice towards me, and general disregard for truth, would make the book useless to all, and injurious to my character.' Oh! as to that, said I, we should all fasten upon him, and force him to do you justice[1]; but the worst is, the Doctor does not *know* your life; nor can I tell indeed who does, except Dr. Taylor of Ashbourne. 'Why Taylor (said he) is better acquainted with my *heart* than any man or woman now alive; and the history of my Oxford exploits lies all between him and Adams; but Dr. James[2] knows my very early days better than he. After my coming to London to drive the world about a little, you must all go to Jack Hawkesworth for anecdotes[3]: I lived in great familiarity with him (though I think there was not much affection) from the year 1753 till the time Mr. Thrale and you took me up[4]. I intend, however, to disappoint the rogues, and either make you write the life, with Taylor's intelligence; or, which is better, do it myself, after outliving you all. I am now (added he), keeping a diary, in hopes of using it for that purpose some time[5].' Here the conversation stopped, from my accidentally looking in an old magazine of the year 1768[6], where I saw the following lines with his name to them, and asked if they were his.

and, if I survive him, I shall be one who will most faithfully do honour to his memory.' *Life*, v. 312.

'Johnson found in James Boswell such a biographer as no man but himself ever had, or ever deserved to have. . . . His *Life of Johnson* may be termed without exception the best parlour-window book that was ever written.' Scott's *Misc. Works*, ed. 1834, iii. 260.

[1] See Forster's *Goldsmith*, ii. 380, for Forster's criticism of this passage.

[2] The inventor of the powder which bears his name. He had been at school with Johnson. *Life*, i. 81; iii. 4.

[3] For the sense in which Johnson used the word *anecdote* see *ib*. ii. 11, *n*. 1.

[4] *The Adventurer*, which Hawkesworth edited and to which Johnson contributed, was published in the years 1753–4. In the *Life of Swift* Johnson, mentioning Hawkesworth, speaks of 'the intimacy of our friendship.' *Works*, viii. 192. The Thrales 'took Johnson up' in 1765. *Life*, i. 490, 520.

[5] The greater part of this 'was consigned by him to the flames a few days before his death.' *Ib*. i. 25; iv. 405.

[6] *Gentleman's Magazine*, 1768, p. 439.

Verses

Verses said to be written by Dr. Samuel Johnson, at the request of a Gentleman to whom a Lady had given a Sprig of Myrtle.

What hopes, what terrors, does thy gift create,
Ambiguous emblem of uncertain fate:
The Myrtle, ensign of supreme command,
Consign'd by Venus to Melissa's hand,
Not less capricious than a reigning fair,
Now grants, and now rejects a lover's prayer[1].
In myrtle shades oft sings the happy swain,
In myrtle shades despairing ghosts complain:
The myrtle crowns the happy lovers' heads,
Th' unhappy lover's grave[2] the myrtle spreads:
O then the meaning of thy gift impart,
And ease the throbbings of an anxious heart!
Soon must this bough, as you shall fix his doom,
Adorn Philander's head, or grace his tomb.

'Why now, do but see how the world is gaping for a wonder! (cries Mr. Johnson;) I think it is now just forty years ago[3] that a young fellow had a sprig of myrtle given him by a girl he courted, and asked me to write him some verses that he might present her in return. I promised, but forgot; and when he called for his lines at the time agreed on—Sit still a moment (says I), dear Mund[4], and I'll fetch them thee—so stepped aside for five minutes, and wrote the nonsense you now keep such a stir about[5].'

Upon revising these Anecdotes, it is impossible not to be struck with shame and regret that one treasured no more of them

[1] In the *Gentleman's Magazine* this line is given:—
'Oft favours, oft rejects a lover's prayer.'

[2] 'Th' unhappy lovers graves.' *Ib.*; but Boswell, who had seen the original manuscript, gives it 'Th' unhappy lovers' grave.' *Life*, i. 92.

[3] It was in 1731. *Ib.* i. 93 *n.*

[4] It was Edmund Hector at whose request these verses were written. For Johnson's habit of contracting the names of his friends, see *ib.* ii. 258.

[5] Johnson told Nichols also that he had written these verses in five minutes. *Works*, i. 128 *n.*

Boswell, who in his first edition, on the authority of the mendacious Miss Seward, 'was induced to doubt the authenticity' of Mrs. Piozzi's anecdote, says in a note to the second:—'I am obliged in so many instances to notice Mrs. Piozzi's incorrectness of relation, that I gladly seize this opportunity of acknowledging, that however often, she is not always inaccurate.' *Life*, i. 93 *n.*

them up; but no experience is sufficient to cure the vice of negligence: whatever one sees constantly, or might see constantly, becomes uninteresting; and we suffer every trivial occupation, every slight amusement, to hinder us from writing down, what indeed we cannot chuse but remember; but what we should wish to recollect with pleasure, unpoisoned by remorse for not remembering more. While I write this, I neglect impressing my mind with the wonders of art, and beauties of nature, that now surround me; and shall one day, perhaps, think on the hours I might have profitably passed in the Florentine Gallery, and reflecting on Raphael's St. John at that time, as upon Johnson's conversation in this moment, may justly exclaim of the months spent by me most delightfully in Italy——

That I priz'd every hour that pass'd by,
  Beyond all that had pleas'd me before;
But now they are past, and I sigh,
  And I grieve that I priz'd them no more.
SHENSTONE[1].

Dr. Johnson delighted in his own partiality for Oxford; and one day, at my house, entertained five members of the other university with various instances of the superiority of Oxford, enumerating the gigantic names of many men whom it had produced, with apparent triumph[2]. At last I said to him, Why there happens to be no less than five Cambridge men in the room now. 'I did not (said he) think of that till you told me; but the wolf don't count the sheep.' When the company were retired, we happened to be talking of Dr. Barnard, the Provost of Eton, who died about that time[3]; and after a long and just eulogium on his wit, his learning, and his goodness of heart: 'He was the only man too (says Mr. Johnson quite seriously) that

[1] From *A Pastoral Ballad in four Parts.* Shenstone's *Poems*, ed. 1854, p. 150. Johnson quotes this verse in his *Life of Shenstone.* Mrs. Piozzi spoils the metre of the first line by adding 'that.'

[2] With the names of Bacon, Milton, and Newton even Johnson would have been overwhelmed.

[3] He died in Dec. 1781. Nichols's *Lit. Anec.* viii. 543. For the evening at Mrs. Vesey's when the company collected round him and Johnson 'four, if not five, deep,' see *Life*, iii. 425.

that did justice to my good breeding; and you may observe that I am well-bred to a degree of needless scrupulosity[1]. No man, (continued he, not observing the amazement of his hearers) no man is so cautious not to interrupt another; no man thinks it so necessary to appear attentive when others are speaking[2]; no man so steadily refuses preference to himself, or so willingly bestows it on another, as I do; no body holds so strongly as I do the necessity of ceremony, and the ill effects which follow the breach of it: yet people think me rude; but Barnard did me justice[3].' 'Tis pity, said I, laughing, that he had not heard you compliment the Cambridge men after dinner to-day. 'Why (replied he) I was inclined to *down*[4] them sure enough; but then a fellow *deserves* to be of Oxford that talks so.' I have heard him at other times relate how he used to sit in some coffee-house there, and turn M——'s C-r-ct-u-s into ridicule for the diversion of himself and of chance comers-in. 'The Elf—da (says he) was too exquisitely pretty; I could make no fun out of that[5].' When upon some occasions he would express his astonish-

[1] 'Every one,' says Lord Shaftesbury, 'thinks himself well-bred.' *Characteristicks*, ed. 1714, i. 65.

For instances of *scrupulosity*, see *Life*, iv. 5, *n.* 2, and *Letters*, ii. 144, *n.* 1. Richardson in *Sir Charles Grandison*, ed. 1754, v. 85, 90, puts it into the mouth of Mr. Selby who was remarkable for 'peculiarities of words.'

[2] 'He encouraged others, particularly young men, to speak, and paid a due attention to what they said.' Hawkins, p. 164.

'Bien écouter et bien répondre est une des plus grandes choses qu'on puisse avoir dans la conversation.' La Rochefoucauld, *Maximes*, No. 139.

[3] See *post*, p. 318. 'Every man of any education,' said Johnson, 'would rather be called a rascal than accused of deficiency in *the graces*.' *Life*, iii. 54. 'Sir,' said Johnson to Boswell, 'I look upon myself as a very polite man.' 'And he was right,' is Boswell's comment, 'in a proper manly sense of the word.' *Ib.* v. 363. 'Theoretically,' writes Sir Walter Scott, 'no man understood the rules of good breeding better than Dr. Johnson, or could act more exactly in conformity with them, when the high rank of those with whom he was in company for the time required that he should put the necessary constraint upon himself.' Scott's *Misc. Prose Works*, ed. 1834, iii. 268.

[4] See *Life*, iii. 335, where Johnson says:—'Robertson was in a mighty romantick humour, he talked of one whom he did not know; but I *downed* him with the King of Prussia.'

Percy says that Johnson's habit of depreciating Cambridge men 'was more affected than real.' Anderson's *Johnson*, ed. 1815, p. 486.

[5] Boswell, who 'ever entertained a warm admiration' for Mason's

ment

ment that he should have an enemy in the world [1], while he had been doing nothing but good to his neighbours, I used to make him recollect these circumstances: 'Why child (said he), what harm could that do the fellow [2]? I always thought very well of M——n for a *Cambridge* man; he is, I believe, a mighty blameless character.' Such tricks were, however, the more unpardonable in Mr. Johnson, because no one could harangue like him about the difficulty always found in forgiving petty injuries, or in provoking by needless offence. Mr. Jordan, his tutor, had much of his affection, though he despised his want of scholastic learning. 'That creature would (said he) defend his pupils to the last: no young lad under his care should suffer for committing slight improprieties, while he had breath to defend, or power to protect them. If I had had sons to send to college (added he), Jordan should have been their tutor [3].'

Sir William Browne the physician, who lived to a very extraordinary age, and was in other respects an odd mortal, with more genius than understanding, and more self-sufficiency than wit, was the only person who ventured to oppose Mr. Johnson, when he had a mind to shine by exalting his favourite university, and to express his contempt of the whiggish notions which prevail at Cambridge [4]. *He* did it once, however, with surprising felicity:

Caractacus and *Elfrida*, 'often wondered at Johnson's low estimation of his writings.' *Life*, ii. 335. Mason was a Cambridge man.

Johnson in his *Dictionary* calls *fun* 'a low cant [slang] word.' In *Sir Charles Grandison*, ed. 1754, i. 96–7, it is used by an illiterate gentleman.

[1] From a sick room he wrote to Mrs. Thrale in the last year but one of his life:—'I have in this still scene of life great comfort in reflecting that I have given very few reason to hate me.' *Letters*, ii. 314.

[2] See *Life*, iv. 280, where he asks, 'What harm does it do to any man to be contradicted?'

[3] When Johnson visited Oxford in 1754, 'he much regretted that his first tutor [Jorden] was dead, for whom he seemed to retain the greatest regard.' *Ib.* i. 272.

[4] Miss Burney records in May, 1772:—'I have just left the famous Sir William Browne in the parlour, a most extraordinary old man, who lives in the Square [Queen Square], and is here on a visit. He has been a very renowned physician; whether for saving or killing I cannot say. He is near eighty, and enjoys prodigious health and spirits, and is gallant to the ladies to a most ridiculous degree. He never comes without repeating some of his verses.'

his

his antagonist having repeated with an air of triumph the famous epigram written by Dr. Trapp [1],

> Our royal master saw, with heedful eyes,
> The wants of his two universities:
> Troops he to Oxford sent, as knowing why
> That learned body wanted loyalty:
> But books to Cambridge gave, as, well discerning,
> That that right loyal body wanted learning.

Which, says Sir William, might well be answered thus:

> The king to Oxford sent his troop of horse,
> For Tories own no argument but force;
> With equal care to Cambridge books he sent,
> For Whigs allow no force but argument [2].

Early Diary of Frances Burney, i. 177. He died on March 10, 1774, aged 82. *Gentleman's Magazine*, 1774, p. 142. See *ib.* 1775, p. 44 for the prizes of three gold medals which he founded at Cambridge for Greek and Latin verse.

[1] For a memoir of Dr. Joseph Trapp (1679–1747) see *Gentleman's Magazine*, 1786, pp. 381, 660. He was the first Professor of Poetry at Oxford. It is said that he was the original of Swift's 'little parson Dapper, who is the common relief to all the lazy pulpits in town. This smart youth has a very good memory, a quick eye, and a clean handkerchief. Thus equipped, he opens his text, shuts his book fairly, shows he has no notes in his Bible, opens both palms and shews all is fair there too.' *The Tatler*, No. 66. Swift's *Works*, viii. 163. I cannot find any evidence besides Mrs. Piozzi's that he wrote this epigram.

[2] In Nichols's *Lit. Anec.* iii. 330 the following versions are given:—

I.

> 'The King. observing with judicious eyes,
> The state of his two universities;
> To Oxford sent a troop of horse; and why?
> That learned body wanted loyalty;
> To Cambridge books, as very well discerning
> How much that loyal body wanted learning.'

II.

> 'The King to Oxford sent a troop of horse,
> For Tories own no argument but force;
> With equal skill to Cambridge books he sent,
> For Whigs admit no force but argument.'

George I, in September, 1715, gave 6,000 guineas for the library (30,000 volumes) of John Moore, Bishop of Ely, who had died the previous year, and presented it to the University of Cambridge. Willis and Clark's *Architectural History of Cambridge*, iii. 29. A little later 'an intercepted letter from an Oxford undergraduate to his friend in London boasts that "Here we fear nothing, but drink James's health every day." Colonel Owen and several other broken officers had taken shelter at the University, and were concerting measures

Mr.

Mr. Johnson did him the justice to say, it was one of the happiest extemporaneous productions he ever met with; though he once comically confessed, that he hated to repeat the wit of a whig urged in support of whiggism. Says Garrick to him one day, Why did not you make me a tory, when we lived so much together[1], you love to make people tories? 'Why (says Johnson, pulling a heap of halfpence from his pocket) did not the king make these guineas?'

Of Mr. Johnson's toryism the world has long been witness, and the political pamphlets written by him in defence of his party, are vigorous and elegant. He often delighted his imagination with the thoughts of having destroyed Junius, an anonymous writer who flourished in the years 1769, and 1770, and who kept himself so ingeniously concealed from every endeavour to detect him, that no probable guess was, I believe, ever formed concerning the author's name, though at that time the subject of general conversation[2]. Mr. Johnson made us all

with the Heads of Houses, and projecting an insurrection . . .; but Stanhope sent thither General Pepper with a squadron of dragoons. Marching all night, Pepper entered Oxford at day-break on the 6th of October, 1715.' Mahon's *History of England*, ed. 1839, i. 235.

[1] 'True to his King and the Constitution Garrick declined all disputes about Whig and Tory. Mr. Pelham was the minister whom he admired, as may be seen in his Ode on the death of that great man.' Murphy's *Garrick*, p. 379. For this *Ode* see *Life*, i. 269.

[2] Johnson attacked Junius in his pamphlet on *Falkland's Islands*, published in the early spring of 1771. *Life*, ii. 134; *Works*, vi. 198. The signature 'Junius' first appeared on Nov. 21, 1768. The first Junius of the collected edition appeared on Jan. 21, 1769; the last on Jan. 21, 1772. *Dict. Nat. Biog.*, xx. 173. 'Three men,' writes Horace Walpole, 'were especially suspected, Wilkes, Edmund Burke and W. G. Hamilton. Hamilton was most generally suspected.' *Memoirs of George III*, iii. 401. Johnson said, 'I should have believed Burke to be Junius, because I know no man but Burke who is capable of writing these letters, but Burke spontaneously denied it to me.' *Life*, iii. 376. Burke, writing on this subject to Charles Townshend on Oct. 17, 1771, says:—'My friends I have satisfied; my enemies shall never have any direct satisfaction from me.' Burke's *Correspondence*, i. 268. When Wilkes was charged with being the author '*Utinam scripsissem!*' he replied, 'Would to Heaven I could have written them.' Wraxall's *Memoirs*, ed. 1815, i. 460. Mrs. Piozzi, in a marginal note on Wraxall, says:—'I well remember when they [Junius's *Letters*] were most talked of—and N. [W] Seward

laugh

laugh one day, because I had received a remarkably fine Stilton cheese as a present from some person who had packed and directed it carefully, but without mentioning whence it came. Mr. Thrale, desirous to know who we were obliged to, asked every friend as they came in, but no body owned it: 'Depend upon it, Sir (says Johnson), it was sent by *Junius*.'

The False Alarm, his first and favourite pamphlet[1], was written at our house between eight o'clock on Wednesday night and twelve o'clock on Thursday night; we read it to Mr. Thrale when he came very late home from the House of Commons[2]: the other political tracts followed in their order. I have forgotten which contains the stroke at Junius; but shall for ever remember the pleasure it gave him to have written it. It was however in the year 1775 that Mr. Edmund Burke made the famous speech in parliament, that struck even foes with admiration, and friends with delight[3]. Among the nameless thousands who are contented to echo those praises they have not skill to invent, *I* ventured, before Dr. Johnson himself, to applaud, with rapture, the beautiful passage in it concerning Lord Bathurst and the Angel[4]; which, said our Doctor, had I been in the house, I would have answered *thus*:

said, "How the arrows of Junius were sure to wound and likely to stick." "Yes, sir," replied Dr. Johnson; "yet let us distinguish between the venom of the shaft and the vigour of the bow." At which expression Mr. Hamilton's countenance fell in a manner that to *me* betrayed the author. Johnson repeated the expression in his next pamphlet—and Junius wrote no more.' Hayward's *Piozzi*, 2nd ed., ii. 106. For Johnson's repetition of this expression see *Works*, vi. 205. Junius, however, continued to write.

[1] 'We talked of his two political pamphlets, *The False Alarm*, and *Thoughts concerning Falkland's Islands*. JOHNSON. "Well, Sir, which of them did you think the best?" BOSWELL. "I liked the second best." JOHNSON. "Why, Sir, I liked the first best; and Beattie liked the first best. Sir, there is a subtlety of disquisition in the first, that is worth all the fire of the second."' *Life*, ii. 147.

[2] He was member for Southwark from December, 1765, till the dissolution in 1780. *Parl. Hist.* xv. 1089; *Life*, iii. 442.

[3] On Conciliation with America, March 22, 1775.

[4] Burke, describing 'the growth of our national prosperity' through our trade with America, continues:—'It has happened within sixty-eight years. There are those alive whose memory might touch the two extremities.

'Suppose

'Suppose, Mr. Speaker, that to Wharton, or to Marlborough, or to any of the eminent whigs of the last age, the devil [1] had, not with any great impropriety, consented to appear; he would perhaps in somewhat like these words have commenced the conversation:

'You seem, my Lord, to be concerned at the judicious apprehension, that while you are sapping the foundations of royalty at home, and propagating here the dangerous doctrine of resistance; the distance of America may secure its inhabitants from your arts, though active: but I will unfold to you the gay prospects of futurity. This people, now so innocent and harmless, shall draw the sword against their mother country, and bathe its point in the blood of their benefactors; this people, now contented with a little, shall then refuse to spare what they themselves confess they could not miss [2]; and these men, now so honest and so grateful, shall, in return for peace and for protection, see [3] their vile agents in the house of parliament, there to sow the seeds of sedition, and propagate confusion, perplexity, and pain. Be not dispirited then at the contemplation of their present happy state: I promise you that anarchy, poverty, and death shall, by my care, be carried even

For instance, my Lord Bathurst might remember all the stages of the progress. . . . Suppose, Sir, that the angel of this auspicious youth . . . If amidst these bright and happy scenes of domestic honour and prosperity, that angel should have drawn up the curtain and unfolded the rising glories of his country, and, whilst he was gazing with admiration on the then commercial grandeur of England, the Genius should point out to him a little speck scarcely visible in the mass of the national interest, a small seminal principle, rather than a formed body, and should tell him—"Young man, there is America—which at this day serves for little more than to amuse you with stories of savage men and uncouth manners; yet shall, before you taste of death, show itself equal to the whole of that commerce which now attracts the envy of the world,"' &c. Payne's *Burke*, i. 172.

W. W. Pepys wrote to Hannah More:—'I once heard a man say of Burke, while he was pouring forth torrents of eloquence in the House of Commons, "How closely that fellow reasons in metaphor!"' More's *Memoirs*, iii. 377.

[1] 'I have always said the first Whig was the Devil.' *Life*, iii. 326.

[2] What they refused to spare was a contribution towards the expenses of the last French war.

[3] *See* I have little doubt is a misprint for *fee*.

across

across the spacious Atlantic, and settle in America itself, the sure consequences of our beloved whiggism.'

This I thought a thing so very particular, that I begged his leave to write it down directly, before any thing could intervene that might make me forget the force of the expressions[1]: a trick, which I have however seen played on common occasions, of sitting steadily[2] down at the other end of the room to write at the moment what should be said in company, either *by* Dr. Johnson or *to* him, I never practised myself, nor approved of in another. There is something so ill-bred, and so inclining to treachery in this conduct, that were it commonly adopted, all confidence would soon be exiled from society, and a conversation assembly-room would become tremendous as a court of justice[3]. A set of acquaintance joined in familiar chat may say a thousand things, which (as the phrase is) pass well enough at the time, though they cannot stand the test of critical examination; and as all talk beyond that which is necessary to the purposes of actual business is a kind of game[4], there will be ever found ways of playing fairly or unfairly at it, which distin-

[1] 'Mrs. Thrale,' writes Boswell, 'has published as Johnson's a kind of parody or counterpart of a fine poetical passage in one of Mr. Burke's speeches on American Taxation. It is vigorously but somewhat coarsely executed; and I am inclined to suppose, is not quite correctly exhibited. I hope he did not use the words "*vile agents*" for the Americans in the House of Parliament; and if he did so, in an extempore effusion, I wish the lady had not committed it to writing.' *Life*, iv. 317.

[2] Perhaps Mrs. Piozzi wrote *stealthily*. Mr. Barclay said that 'he had seen Boswell lay down his knife and fork, and take out his tablets in order to register a good anecdote.' *Post* in Mr. Barclay's *Anecdotes*.

[3] Bishop Percy in a note on Anderson's *Johnson*, p. 6, says of Boswell:—'It is surely an exception more than venial to violate one of the first and most sacred laws of society by publishing private and unguarded conversation of unsuspecting company into which he was accidentally admitted.' Percy had more than once suffered from this publication. *Life*, ii. 64; iii. 271.

[4] 'Sir, a game of jokes is composed partly of skill, partly of chance, a man may be beat at times by one who has not the tenth part of his wit.' *Ib.* ii. 231. 'And then also for men's reputation; and that either in point of wisdom or of wit. There is hardly anything which (for the most part) falls under a greater chance. . . . Nay, even where there is a real stock of wit, yet the wittiest sayings and sentences will be found in a great measure the issues of chance, and nothing else but so many lucky hits of a roving fancy.' South's *Sermons*, ed. 1823, i. 218–220.

guish

guish the gentleman from the juggler. Dr. Johnson, as well as many of my acquaintance, knew that I kept a common-place book[1]; and he one day said to me good-humouredly, that he would give me something to write in my repository. 'I warrant (said he) there is a great deal about me in it: you shall have at least one thing worth your pains; so if you will get the pen and ink, I will repeat to you Anacreon's Dove directly; but tell at the same time, that as I never was struck with any thing in the Greek language till I read *that*, so I never read any thing in the same language since, that pleased me as much. I hope my translation (continued he) is not worse than that of Frank Fawkes[2].' Seeing me disposed to laugh, 'Nay, nay (said he), Frank Fawkes had done them very finely.'

Lovely courier of the sky,
Whence and whither dost thou fly?
Scatt'ring, as thy pinions play,
Liquid fragrance all the way:
Is it business? is it love?
Tell me, tell me, gentle Dove.

[1] Boswell in his *Tour to the Hebrides*, which was published before the *Anecdotes*, had not attacked Mrs. Piozzi, so that her attack on him would seem unprovoked. She suspected him, however, of being the author of anonymous attacks in the newspapers. In the *Life*, iv. 343, he replies:—

'I have had occasion several times, in the course of this work, to point out the incorrectness of Mrs. Thrale, as to particulars which consisted with my own knowledge. But indeed she has, in flippant terms enough, expressed her disapprobation of that anxious desire of authenticity which prompts a person who is to record conversations, to write them down *at the moment*. Unquestionably, if they are to be recorded at all, the sooner it is done the better. . . . She boasts of her having kept a common-place book; and we find she noted, at one time or other, in a very lively manner, specimens of the conversation of Dr. Johnson, and of those who talked with him; but had she done it recently, they probably would have been less erroneous; and we should have been relieved from those disagreeable doubts of their authenticity, with which we must now peruse them.'

'From 1776 to 1809 Mrs. Piozzi kept a copious diary and note-book called *Thraliana*.' Hayward's *Piozzi*, i. 6.

[2] Francis Fawkes was the author of *The Brown Jug*. Campbell's *British Poets*, ed. 1845, p. 544. In 1761 he published *Original Poems and Translations*, for a copy of which on superfine paper Johnson subscribed. In conjunction with Woty, Fawkes published in 1763 *The Poetical Calendar*, to which Johnson contributed a character of Collins. *Life*, i. 382.

'Soft

'Soft Anacreon's vows I bear,
Vows to Myrtale the fair;
Grac'd with all that charms the heart,
Blushing nature, smiling art.
Venus, courted by an ode,
On the bard her Dove bestow'd.
Vested with a master's right
Now Anacreon rules my flight:
His the letters that you see,
Weighty charge consign'd to me:
Think not yet my service hard,
Joyless task without reward:
Smiling at my master's gates,
Freedom my return awaits;
But the liberal grant in vain
Tempts me to be wild again:
Can a prudent Dove decline
Blissful bondage such as mine?
Over hills and fields to roam,
Fortune's guest without a home;
Under leaves to hide one's head,
Slightly shelter'd, coarsely fed;
Now my better lot bestows
Sweet repast, and soft repose;
Now the generous bowl I sip
As it leaves Anacreon's lip;
Void of care, and free from dread,
From his fingers snatch his bread,
Then with luscious plenty gay,
Round his chamber dance and play;
Or from wine as courage springs,
O'er his face extend my wings;
And when feast and frolick tire,
Drop asleep upon his lyre.
This is all, be quick and go,
More than all thou canst not know;
Let me now my pinions ply,
I have chatter'd like a pye.'

When I had finished, 'But you must remember to add (says Mr. Johnson) that though these verses were planned, and even begun, when I was sixteen years old, I never could find time to make an end of them before I was sixty-eight [1].'

[1] He had perhaps shown these verses, or as many of them as were finished, to Miss Boothby in 1755; for writing to him in that year she

This facility of writing, and this dilatoriness ever to write, Mr. Johnson always retained, from the days that he lay a-bed and dictated his first publication [1] to Mr. Hector, who acted as his amanuensis, to the moment he made me copy out those variations in Pope's Homer which are printed in the Poets' Lives [2]: 'And now (said he, when I had finished it for him) I fear not Mr. Nichols [3] of a pin.'—The fine Rambler on the subject of Procrastination was hastily composed, as I have heard, in Sir Joshua Reynolds's parlour, while the boy waited to carry it to press [4]: and numberless are the instances of his writing under immediate pressure of importunity or distress. He told me that the character of *Sober* [5] in the Idler, was by himself intended as his own portrait; and that he had his own outset into life in his eye when he wrote the eastern story of Gelaleddin [6]. Of the allegorical papers in the Rambler, Labour and Rest [7] was his favourite; but Serotinus, the man who

says:—'I will tell you some time what I think of Anacreon.' *An Account of the Life of Dr. Johnson*, &c., 1805, p. 109.

[1] His translation of Lobo's *Abyssinia*. *Life*, i. 86.

[2] *Works*, viii. 256.

[3] The printer of the *Lives*. *Life*, iv. 36. *The Life of Pope* was one of the last to be written. *Letters*, ii. 196, *n*. 5. In the proof of the *Life of Johnson* I found 'the following sentence in one of Johnson's letters to Mrs. Thrale, "I have finished Prior; so a fig for Mr. Nichols."' Boswell struck it out.

[4] The *Rambler* on Procrastination, No. 134, was published on June 29, 1751. Reynolds left England for Italy in May, 1749, and returned in October, 1752 (Taylor's *Reynolds*, i. 35, 87), seven months after the last *Rambler* had appeared.

For Johnson's hasty composition, see *Life*, i. 203, 331; iii. 42. He wrote part of the *Lives of the Poets* in the parlour at Stow Hill, 'surrounded by five or six ladies engaged in work or conversation.' *Letters*, ii. 46 *n*. Miss Boothby wrote to him in 1754:—'You can write amidst the tattle of women, because your attention is so strong to sense that you are deaf to sound.' *An Account of the Life of Dr. Johnson*, &c., 1805, i. 80.

[5] *Idler*, No. 31. *Life*, iii. 398, *n*. 3.

[6] *Ib*. No. 75. Gelaleddin is a Persian student 'amiable in his manners and beautiful in his form, of boundless curiosity, incessant diligence, and irresistible genius, of quick apprehension and tenacious memory, accurate without narrowness and eager for novelty without inconstancy. . . . "I will instruct the modest," he said, "with easy gentleness, and repress the ostentatious by seasonable superciliousness." . . . He was sometimes admitted to the tables of the viziers, where he exerted his wit and diffused his knowledge; but he observed that where by endeavour or accident he had remarkably excelled he was seldom invited a second time.'

[7] No. 33. It contains a passage

who returns late in life to receive honours in his native country, and meets with mortification instead of respect, was by him considered as a masterpiece in the science of life and manners [1]. The character of Prospero in the fourth volume, Garrick took to be his [2]; and I have heard the author say, that he never forgave the offence. Sophron was likewise a picture drawn from reality [3]; and by Gelidus the philosopher, he meant to represent Mr. Coulson, a mathematician, who formerly lived at Rochester [4]. The man immortalised for purring like a cat was, as he told me, one Busby, a proctor in the Commons [5]. He who barked so ingeniously, and then called the drawer to drive away the dog, was father to Dr. Salter of the Charterhouse [6]. He who sung a song and by correspondent motions of his arm chalked out a giant on the wall, was one Richardson, an attorney [7]. The letter signed Sunday, was written by Miss Talbot [8]; and he

which being, I suspect, borrowed by Rogers suggested to Dickens, as he confessed, in his *Old Curiosity Shop*, 'the beautiful thought of Nell's grandfather wandering about after her death as if looking for her.' Johnson describes how where Rest came, 'Nothing was seen on every side but multitudes wandering about they knew not whither, in quest they knew not of what.' Rogers writes in his *Italy, Ginevra*:—

'And long was to be seen
An old man wandering as in quest
of something,
Something he could not find—he
knew not what.'

[1] No. 165. The rich man describing his deliberations about his return to his native town says:—'The acclamations of the populace I purposed to reward with six hogsheads of ale and a roasted ox, and then recommend to them to return to their work.'

[2] No. 200. *Life*, i. 216.

[3] *Idler*, No. 57.

[4] *Rambler*, No. 24; *Life*, i. 101.

[5] Doctors' Commons, the College of Civilians in London who practised in the Ecclesiastical Courts and the Court of Admiralty.

[6] Dr. Salter's father belonged to Johnson's Ivy Lane Club. *Life*, i. 191, *n*. 5. Hawkins describes him as 'a dignitary of the Church; he was well-bred, courteous and affable.' Hawkins's *Johnson*, p. 220.

[7] 'One I have known for fifteen years the darling of a weekly club because every night, precisely at eleven, he begins his favourite song, and during the vocal performance by corresponding motions of his hand chalks out a giant upon the wall. Another has endeared himself to a long succession of acquaintances by purring like a cat and then pretending to be frighted; and another by yelping like a hound and calling to the drawers to drive out the dog.' *Rambler*, No. 188.

[8] No. 30. For Miss Talbot, see *Carter and Talbot Correspondence*, vol. i. Preface, p. 6.

fancied

fancied the billets in the first volume of the Rambler, were sent him by Miss Mulso, now Mrs. Chapone[1]. The papers contributed by Mrs. Carter[2], had much of his esteem, though he always blamed me for preferring the letter signed Chariessa to the allegory, where religion and superstition are indeed most masterly delineated.

When Dr. Johnson read his own satire, in which the life of a scholar is painted, with the various obstructions thrown in his way to fortune and to fame, he burst into a passion of tears one day[3]: the family and Mr. Scott only were present, who, in a jocose way, clapped him on the back, and said, What's all this my dear Sir? Why you, and I, and *Hercules*, you know, were all troubled with *melancholy*. As there are many gentlemen of the same name, I should say, perhaps, that it was a Mr. Scott who married Miss Robinson, and that I think I have heard Mr. Thrale call him George Lewis, or George Augustus[4], I have forgot which. He was a very large man, however, and made out the trumvirate with Johnson and Hercules comically enough. The Doctor was so delighted at his odd sally, that he suddenly embraced him, and the subject was immediately changed. I never saw Mr. Scott but that once in my life.

Dr. Johnson was liberal enough in granting literary assistance to others, I think; and innumerable are the prefaces, sermons, lectures, and dedications which he used to make for people who begged of him[5]. Mr. Murphy related in his and my hearing

[1] No. 10. For Mrs. Chapone see *Life*, iv. 246.

[2] Nos. 44 and 100. For Mrs. Carter see *Life*, i. 122.

[3] *Vanity of Human Wishes*, ll. 135–164. 'The deep and pathetic morality of the *Vanity of Human Wishes*,' says Sir Walter Scott, 'has often extracted tears from those whose eyes wander dry over pages professedly sentimental.' Scott's *Misc. Works*, ed. 1834, iii. 264.

[4] George Lewis Scott, who had been sub-preceptor to George III, when Prince of Wales. *Life*, iii. 117, *n.* 4. Horace Walpole wrote on Nov. 19, 1750 (*Letters*, ii. 232):—'There is a new preceptor, one Scott, recommended by Lord Bolingbroke.' See also *ib.* p. 316.

Miss Robinson was Mrs. Montagu's sister. See *post* in *Anecdotes of Hannah More*.

[5] Boswell quotes this in the *Life*, iv. 344, in contrast with Mrs. Piozzi's assertion (*post*, p. 279) that 'Johnson would not stir a finger for the assistance of those to whom he was willing enough to give advice,' &c.

one

one day, and he did not deny it, that when Murphy joked him the week before for having been so diligent of late between Dodd's sermon and Kelly's prologue, that Dr. Johnson replied, 'Why, Sir, when they come to me with a dead stay-maker and a dying parson, what can a man do[1]?' He *said*, however, that 'he hated to give away literary performances, or even to sell them too cheaply[2]: the next generation shall not accuse me (added he) of beating down the price of literature: one hates, besides, ever to give that which one has been accustomed to sell; would not you, Sir (turning to Mr. Thrale), rather give away money than porter?'

Mr. Johnson had never, by his own account, been a close student[3], and used to advise young people never to be without a book in their pocket, to be read at bye-times when they had nothing else to do. 'It has been by that means (said he to a boy at our house one day) that all my knowledge has been gained, except what I have picked up by running about the world with my wits ready to observe, and my tongue ready to talk[4]. A man is seldom in a humour to unlock his book-case,

[1] In 1777 he wrote a Prologue to *A Word to the Wise* by Hugh Kelly—a play which had been *damned* in 1770, but was revived for one night for the benefit of the author's widow and children. *Life*, iii. 113. Kelly served his apprenticeship to a Dublin stay-maker. Chalmers's *Biog. Dict.* xix. 292.

The same summer Johnson wrote *The Convict's Address to his unhappy Brethren* for Dr. Dodd, who was under sentence of death. *Life*, iii. 141.

[2] 'No man but a blockhead,' he said, 'ever wrote except for money.' *Ib.* iii. 19. He often sold his own works far too cheaply. For the *Lives of the Poets* he asked only two hundred guineas. 'Had he asked one thousand, or even fifteen hundred guineas,' writes Malone, 'the booksellers would doubtless have readily given it.' *Ib.* iii. 111, *n.* 1. See also *ib.* i. 341, *n.* 3.

[3] 'Sir, in my early years I read very hard. It is a sad reflection, but a true one, that I knew almost as much at eighteen as I do now.' *Ib.* i. 445. 'I never knew a man who studied hard. I conclude indeed from the effects that some men have studied hard, as Bentley and Clarke.' *Ib.* i. 71. He told the King that 'he had read a great deal in the early part of his life, but having fallen into ill-health he had not been able to read much compared with others.' *Ib.* ii. 36. Nevertheless Adam Smith told Boswell that 'Johnson knew more books than any man alive.' *Ib.* i. 71.

[4] 'He said to me,' writes Boswell, 'that before he wrote the *Rambler* he had been "running about the

set

set his desk in order, and betake himself to serious study; but a retentive memory will do something, and a fellow shall have strange credit given him, if he can but recollect striking passages from different books, keep the authors separate in his head, and bring his stock of knowledge artfully into play[1]: How else (added he) do the gamesters[2] manage when they play for more money than they are worth?' His Dictionary, however, could not, one would think, have been written by running up and down; but he really did not consider it as a great performance; and used to say, 'that he might have done it easily in two years, had not his health received several shocks during the time[3].'

When Mr. Thrale, in consequence of this declaration, teized him in the year 1768 to give a new edition of it, because (said he) there are four or five gross faults[4]: 'Alas, Sir (replied

world," as he expressed it, more almost than any body.' *Life*, i. 215.

A writer in the *Monthly Review*, N. S. xx. p. 21, who had known Johnson, says:—'He always preferred conversation to reading, though it were with the lowest mechanics; and he constantly listened to professional men with respect. His disputes were chiefly with those pretenders to that knowledge and science of which he was himself at least equally qualified to judge.' Quoted in Anderson's *Johnson*, ed. 1815, p. 475.

[1] It was by this method that at Fort George he talked with the officers of granulating gunpowder, 'and made a very good figure upon these topicks.' *Life*, v. 124.

[2] *Gamester* has been long supplanted by *gambler*, under which word Johnson writes in his *Dictionary*, 'a cant word (I suppose) for *game* and *gamester*.'

[3] He told Dr. Adams that he expected to do it in three years. *Ib.* i. 186. He took seven or eight. We have no account of his ill-health during that time. His wife's long illness and death came in the midst, and so too did all his *Ramblers*.

[4] In the *Scots Magazine* for 1761, p. 693, is a short list of words with the following heading:—'A Scotch gentleman caused a friend wait of [*sic*] Mr. Johnson with a list of words suspected to be wrong accented in his dictionary; and was favoured with the following corrections marked by Mr. Johnson's own hand.' The errors seem to have been most, if not all, those of the printer.

When Reynolds asked him why he had not in his second edition corrected a certain error, he replied, 'No, they made so much of it that I would not flatter them by altering it.' *Life*, i. 293, *n.* 2. In the Abridgement which he made himself the erroneous definition of *pastern* remains, and *leeward* and *windward* are still both defined as *towards the wind*. In Murray's *Johnsoniana*, 1836, p. 467, an error in a reference is pointed out which has not been

Johnson

Johnson), there are four or five hundred faults, instead of four or five; but you do not consider that it would take me up three whole months labour, and when the time was expired, the work would not be done.' When the booksellers set him about it however some years after, he went cheerfully to the business, said he was well paid, and that they deserved to have it done carefully [1]. His reply to the person who complimented him on its coming out first [2], mentioning the ill success of the French in a similar attempt, is well known; and, I trust, has been often recorded: 'Why, what would you expect, dear Sir (said he), from fellows that eat frogs [3]?' I have however often thought Dr. Johnson more free than prudent in professing so loudly his little skill in the Greek language [4]: for though he considered it as a proof of a narrow mind to be too careful of literary reputation, yet no man could be more enraged than he, if an enemy, taking advantage of this confession, twitted him with his ignorance; and I remember when the king of Denmark was in England [5], one of his noblemen was brought by Mr. Colman [6]

corrected even in Todd's edition. 'It occurs in definition 13 of the verb *To sit*—'Asses are ye that sit in judgment,' Judges, v. 10. The verse is:—"Speak, ye that ride on white asses, ye that sit in judgment, and walk by the way."'

[1] It was published in 1773. *Life*, ii. 203. On March 4 of that year he wrote of it:—'I have mended some faults, but added little to its usefulness.' *Ib.* p. 209. I cannot account for the following advertisement which I found in the *London Chronicle* for Feb. 13-15, 1776. 'A New edition revised by the Author. This day was published in 2 vols. folio, price £4. 10, bound, the fourth edition of Mr. Samuel Johnson's *Dictionary*.'

[2] Mrs. Piozzi means of course 'who complimented him when it first came out.'

[3] When, on Johnson's undertaking to finish the *Dictionary* in three years, Dr. Adams pointed out that 'the French Academy, which consists of forty members, took forty years to compile their *Dictionary*,' he replied:—'Sir, thus it is. This is the proportion. Let me see; forty times forty is sixteen hundred. As three to sixteen hundred, so is the proportion of an Englishman to a Frenchman.' *Life*, i. 186.

[4] *Ib.* iv. 384.

[5] In August, 1768. Horace Walpole wrote on the 16th of that month:—'This great King is a very little one; not ugly, nor ill-made. He has the sublime strut of his grandfather [George II] or of a cock-sparrow; and the divine white eyes of all his family by the mother's side.' Walpole's *Letters*, v. 122.

[6] George Colman was to be Professor of Latin in the College which the Literary Club was to set up in St. Andrews. *Life*, v. 108.

to see Dr. Johnson at our country-house; and having heard, he said, that he was not famous for Greek literature, attacked him on the weak side; politely adding, that he chose that conversation on purpose to favour himself. Our Doctor, however, displayed so copious, so compendious a knowledge of authors, books, and every branch of learning in that language, that the gentleman appeared astonished. When he was gone home (says Johnson), 'Now for all this triumph, I may thank Thrale's Xenophon here, as, I think, excepting that *one*, I have not looked in a Greek book these ten years; but see what haste my dear friends were all in (continued he) to tell this poor innocent foreigner that I knew nothing of Greek! Oh, no, he knows nothing of Greek!' with a loud burst of laughing.

When Davies printed the Fugitive Pieces without his knowledge or consent [1]; How, said I, would Pope have raved, had he been served so? 'We should never (replied he) have heard the last on't, to be sure; but then Pope was a narrow man: I will however (added he) storm and bluster *myself* a little this time';—so went to London in all the wrath he could muster up. At his return I asked how the affair ended: 'Why (said he), I was a fierce fellow, and pretended to be very angry, and Thomas was a good-natured fellow, and pretended to be very sorry: so *there* the matter ended: I believe the dog loves me dearly. Mr. Thrale (turning to my husband), what shall you and I do that is good for Tom Davies? We will do something for him, to be sure [2].'

Of Pope as a writer he had the highest opinion, and once when a lady at our house talked of his preface to Shakespeare

[1] In Johnson's absence in Scotland Davies 'published two volumes, entitled *Miscellaneous and Fugitive Pieces*, which he advertised in the newspapers "By the Authour of the Rambler."' *Life*, ii. 270.

[2] 'Tom Davies had now unfortunately failed in his circumstances, and was much indebted to Dr. Johnson's kindness for obtaining for him many alleviations of his distress.' *Ib.* iii. 223. The Rev. John Hussey has the following manuscript marginal note on this passage:—'About this time I met poor Davies in the street, and enquiring earnestly after our common friend, Doctor Johnson (for I had been absent from Town four months), Davies burst into tears and replied, "God for ever bless him. I am beholden to that good man for the bread I eat and the bed I lie on."'

as

as superior to Pope's: 'I fear not, Madam (said he), the little fellow has done wonders[1].' His superior reverence of Dryden notwithstanding still appeared in his talk as in his writings[2]; and when some one mentioned the ridicule thrown on him in the Rehearsal, as having hurt his general character as an author: 'On the contrary (says Mr. Johnson), the greatness of Dryden's reputation is now the only principle of vitality which keeps the duke of Buckingham's play from putrefaction[3].'

It was not very easy however for people not quite intimate with Dr. Johnson, to get exactly his opinion of a writer's merit, as he would now and then divert himself by confounding those who thought themselves obliged to say to-morrow what he had said yesterday; and even Garrick, who ought to have been better acquainted with his tricks, professed himself mortified, that one time when he was extolling Dryden in a rapture that I suppose disgusted his friend[4], Mr. Johnson suddenly challenged him to produce twenty lines in a series that would not disgrace the poet and his admirer[5]. Garrick produced a passage that he had once heard the Doctor commend, in which he *now* found, if I remember rightly, sixteen faults, and made Garrick look silly at his own table. When I told Mr. Johnson the story, 'Why, what

[1] 'Pope's preface,' Johnson says, 'every editor has an interest to suppress but that every reader would demand its insertion.' *Works*, v. 137. also *ib.* viii. 272.

[2] For his estimate of Pope and Dryden see *Life*, ii. 5, 85, and *Works*, viii. 325.

[3] 'Talking of the Comedy of *The Rehearsal*, he said:—"It has not wit enough to keep it sweet." This was easy; he therefore caught himself, and pronounced a more round sentence; "It has not vitality enough to preserve it from putrefaction."' *Life*, iv. 320.

South says in his *Sermons*, iii. 398:—'They have souls so dull and stupid as to serve for little else but to keep their bodies from putrefaction.'

For *The Rehearsal* see Johnson's *Works*, vii. 272, and *Life*, ii. 168.

[4] 'I do not know for certain,' said Mrs. Thrale, 'what will please Dr. Johnson; but I know for certain that it will displease him to praise anything, even what he likes, extravagantly.' *Life*, iii. 225. One day he said to her:—'I know nobody who blasts by praise as you do; for whenever there is exaggerated praise everybody is set against a character.' *Ib.* iv. 81.

[5] 'Dryden's faults of negligence are beyond recital. Such is the unevenness of his compositions that ten lines are seldom found together without something of which the reader is ashamed.' *Works*, vii. 344.

a monkey

a monkey was David now (says he), to tell of his own disgrace!' And in the course of that hour's chat he told me, how he used to teize Garrick by commendations of the tomb scene in Congreve's Mourning Bride, protesting that Shakespeare had in the same line of excellence nothing as good: 'All which is strictly *true* (said he); but that is no reason for supposing Congreve is to stand in competition with Shakespeare[1]: these fellows know not how to blame, nor how to commend.' I forced him one day, in a similar humour, to prefer Young's description of Night to the so much admired ones of Dryden and Shakespeare, as more forcible, and more general. Every reader is not either a lover or a tyrant, but every reader is interested when he hears that

> Creation sleeps; 'tis as the general pulse
> Of life stood still, and nature made a pause;
> An awful pause—prophetic of its end[2].

[1] *Life*, ii. 85, 96. 'The noble passage which Johnson, both in writing and in conversation, extolled above any other in the English drama has suffered greatly in the public estimation from the extravagance of his praise.' Macaulay's *Essays*, ed. 1843, iii. 294.

[2] '*her* end.' *Night Thoughts*, i. 23.

'All things are hush'd, as Nature's self lay dead,
The Mountains seem to nod their drowsy head;
The little Birds in dreams their Songs repeat,
And sleeping Flowers beneath the night-dew sweat;
Ev'n Lust and Envy sleep, yet Love denies
Rest to my Soul and slumber to my Eyes.'

Dryden, *The Indian Emperour*, Act iii. sc. 2.

'Now o'er the one half-world
Nature seems dead, and wicked dreams abuse
The curtain'd sleep; now witchcraft celebrates
Pale Hecate's offerings, and wither'd murder,
Alarum'd by his sentinel, the wolf,
Whose howl 's his watch, thus with his stealthy pace,
With Tarquin's ravishing strides, towards his design
Moves like a ghost.'

Macbeth, ii. 1. 49.

Johnson in a note on this last passage says:—'Night is described by two great poets, but one describes a night of quiet, the other of perturbation. In the night of Dryden all the disturbers of the world are laid asleep; in that of Shakespeare nothing but sorcery, lust and murder is awake. He that reads Dryden finds himself lull'd with serenity, and disposed to solitude and contemplation. He that peruses Shakespeare looks round alarmed, and starts to find himself alone. One is the night of a lover, the other of a murderer.'

In his *Life of Dryden* he says of that poet's description of night that 'Rymer has made it famous by preferring it to those of all other poets.'

'This

'This (said he) is true; but remember that taking the compositions of Young in general, they are but like bright stepping-stones over a miry road: Young froths, and foams, and bubbles sometimes very vigorously; but we must not compare the noise made by your tea-kettle here with the roaring of the ocean [1].'

Somebody was praising Corneille one day in opposition to Shakespeare: 'Corneille is to Shakespeare (replied Mr. Johnson) as a clipped hedge is to a forest.' When we talked of Steele's Essays, 'They are too thin (says our Critic) for an Englishman's taste: mere superficial observations on life and manners, without erudition enough to make them keep, like the light French wines, which turn sour with standing a while for want of *body*, as we call it.'

Of a much admired poem, when extolled as beautiful (he replied), 'That it had indeed the beauty of a bubble: the colours are gay (said he), but the substance slight.' Of James Harris's Dedication to his Hermes I have heard him observe, that, though but fourteen lines long, there were six grammatical faults in it [2]. A friend was praising the style of Dr. Swift; Mr. Johnson did not find himself in the humour to agree with him

Works, vii. 249. 'Rymer at that time [1694],' says Dr. Warton, 'gave the Law to all writers, and was appealed to as a supreme judge of all works of Taste and Genius.' Pope's *Works*, ed. 1822, v. 173.

Wordsworth, writing of 'the poetry of the period intervening between the publication of the *Paradise Lost* and the *Seasons*,' says:—'To what a low state knowledge of the most obvious and important phenomena had sunk is evident from the style in which Dryden has executed a description of Night in one of his tragedies, and Pope his translation of the celebrated moonlight scene in the *Iliad*. . . . Dryden's lines are vague, bombastic and senseless; those of Pope, though he had Homer to guide him, are throughout false and contradictory. The verses of Dryden, once highly celebrated, are forgotten; those of Pope still retain their hold upon public estimation.' Wordsworth's *Works*, ed. 1857, vi. 370.

[1] 'Dr. Johnson said that there were very fine things in Young's *Night Thoughts*, though you could not find twenty lines together without some extravagance.' *Life*, v. 269.

[2] 'I looked into Harris's book,' said Johnson, 'and thought he did not understand his own system.' *Ib.* iii. 245. The Dedication as given in the second edition is more than thirty lines long. The chief fault in it seems to be the mixed use of 'Your Lordship' and 'you.'

him[1]: the critic was driven from one of his performances to the other. At length you *must* allow me, said the gentleman, that there are *strong facts* in the account of the Four last Years of Queen Anne: 'Yes surely Sir (replies Johnson), and so there are in the Ordinary of Newgate's account[2].' This was like the story which Mr. Murphy tells, and Johnson always acknowledged: How Dr. Rose of Chiswick, contending for the preference of Scotch writers over the English, after having set up his authors like nine-pins, while the Doctor kept bowling them down again; at last, to make sure of victory, he named Ferguson upon Civil Society, and praised the book for being written in a *new* manner[3]. 'I do not (says Johnson) perceive the value of this new manner; it is only like Buckinger, who had no hands, and so wrote with his feet[4].' Of a modern Martial[5] when it came out: 'There are in these verses (says Dr. Johnson) too much folly for madness, I think, and too much madness for folly.' If, however, Mr. Johnson lamented, that the nearer he approached to his own times, the more enemies he should make, by telling biographical truths

[1] For Johnson's opinion of Swift's style see *Life*, ii. 191, and *Works*, viii. 220.

[2] '"Surely, Sir, (said Dr. Douglas,) you must allow it has strong facts." JOHNSON: "Why yes, Sir; but what is that to the merit of the composition? In the Sessions-paper of the Old Bailey there are strong facts. Housebreaking is a strong fact; robbery is a strong fact; and murder is a *mighty* strong fact; but is great praise due to the historian of those strong facts? No, Sir. Swift has told what he had to tell distinctly enough, but that is all. He had to count ten, and he has counted it right."' *Life*, ii. 65.

[3] For Dr. Rose see *Letters*, ii. 325, *n*. 4, and for 'an imaginary victory' obtained by him over Johnson, *Life*, iv. 168 *n*.

Of Dr. Adam Fergusson's *Essay on the History of Civil Society* Gray says:—'His love of Montesquieu and Tacitus has led him into a manner of writing too short-winded and sententious.' Mason's *Gray*, 1807, ii. 223. See also *Life*, v. 42, *n*. 1, and Bentham's *Works*, x. 64.

[4] Horace Walpole describes a paper as being 'written in a hand as small as Buckinger's, who used to write the Lord's Prayer in the compass of a silver penny.' P. Cunningham, in a note on this, says:—'Matthew Buckinger, born 1674, without hands or feet, died 1722. There is a print of him drawn and written by himself, with the book of Psalms engraved on the curls of his large flowing periwig.' Walpole's *Letters*, iv. 159.

[5] By James Elphinston. 'His brother-in-law, Strahan, sent him a subscription of fifty pounds, and said he would send him fifty more, if he would not publish.' *Life*, iii. 258.

in

in his Lives of the later Poets[1], what may I not apprehend, who, if I relate anecdotes of Mr. Johnson, am obliged to repeat expressions of severity, and sentences of contempt? Let me at least soften them a little, by saying, that he did not hate the persons he treated with roughness, or despise them whom he drove from him by apparent scorn. He really loved and respected many whom he would not suffer to love him. And when he related to me a short dialogue that passed between himself and a writer of the first eminence in the world, when he was in Scotland, I was shocked to think how he must have disgusted him. Dr. —— asked me (said he) why I did not join in their public worship when among them? for (said he) I went to your churches often when in England. 'So (replied Johnson) I have read that the Siamese sent ambassadors to Louis Quatorze, but I never heard that the king of France thought it worth his while to send ambassadors from his court to that of *Siam*[2].' He was no gentler with myself, or those for whom I had the greatest regard. When I one day lamented the loss of a first cousin killed in America—'Prithee, my dear (said he), have done with canting: how would the world be worse for it, I may ask, if all your relations were at once spitted like larks, and roasted for Presto's supper[3]?' Presto was the dog that lay under the table

[1] 'The necessity of complying with times, and of sparing persons, is the great impediment of biography.... What is known can seldom be immediately told; and when it might be told, it is no longer known.... As the process of these narratives is now bringing me among my contemporaries, I begin to feel myself "walking upon ashes under which the fire is not extinguished," and coming to the time of which it will be proper rather to say "nothing that is false, than all that is true."' *Works*, vii. 444.

[2] It was at Allan Ramsay's house in London, more than four years after Johnson's tour in Scotland, that this 'short dialogue passed.' The eminent writer was Dr. Robertson. *Life*, iii. 336. For the King of Siam see Voltaire's *Siècle de Louis XIV*, ch. xiv.

[3] For Baretti's account of what was said see *Life*, iv. 347; also Prior's *Malone*, p. 398. For the name *Presto* see *Letters*, i. 151, *n*. 2. The dog is mentioned in the following anecdote told by Baretti of 'poor little Harry Thrale, some months before the boy died.' '"Harry," said his father to him on entering the room, "are you listening to what the Doctor and mamma are about?" "Yes, papa," answered the boy. "And," quoth Mr. Thrale, "what are they saying?" "They are disputing," replied Harry; "but mamma has just such a chance against Dr. Johnson as Presto would have if he

while

while we talked.—When we went into Wales together, and spent some time at Sir Robert Cotton's at Lleweny [1], one day at dinner I meant to please Mr. Johnson particularly with a dish of very young peas. Are not they charming? said I to him, while he was eating them.—'Perhaps (said he) they would be so—to a *pig* [2].' I only instance these replies, to excuse my mentioning those he made to others.

When a well-known author [3] published his poems in the year 1777: Such a one's verses are come out, said I: 'Yes (replied Johnson), and this frost has struck them in again. Here are some lines I have written to ridicule them: but remember that I love the fellow dearly, now—for all I laugh at him [4].

Wheresoe'er I turn my view,
All is strange, yet nothing new:
Endless labour all along,
Endless labour to be wrong;
Phrase that Time has flung away;
Uncouth words in disarray,
Trick'd in antique ruff and bonnet,
Ode, and elegy, and sonnet.'

were to fight Dash." Dash was a large dog, and Presto but a little one. The laugh this innocent observation produced was so very loud and hearty that Madam, unable to stand it, quitted the room in such a mood as was still more laughable than the boy's pertinent remark, though she muttered, "it was very impertinent."' Croker's *Boswell*, ed. 1844, x. 37.

[1] *Life*, v. 435.

[2] In a marginal note on this Mrs. Piozzi writes:—'meaning because they were too little boiled.' Hayward's *Piozzi*, ii. 295.

[3] Thomas Warton, who published a volume of poems in 1777. On Sept. 18 of that year Boswell records:—'Dr. Johnson observed, that a gentleman of eminence in literature had got into a bad style of poetry of late. "He puts," said he, "a very common thing in a strange dress, till he does not know it himself, and thinks other people do not know it."' *Life*, iii. 158.

Hume in his *History of England* (ed. 1773, v. 492, vi. 195) says:—'Several writers of late have amused themselves in copying the style of Spenser; and no imitation has been so indifferent as not to bear a great resemblance to the original: His manner is so peculiar that it is almost impossible not to transfer some of it into the copy . . . Raleigh is the best model of that ancient style which some writers would affect to revive at present.' See also Beattie's *Essays on Poetry and Music*, ed. 1779, p. 226.

[4] For Warton's estrangement, which 'Johnson lamented with tears in his eyes,' see *Life*, i. 270, *n.* 1.

When

When he parodied the verses of another eminent writer[1], it was done with more provocation, I believe, and with some merry malice. A serious translation of the same lines, which I think are from Euripides, may be found in Burney's History of Music[2].—Here are the burlesque ones:

Err shall they not, who resolute explore
Times gloomy backward with judicious eyes;
And scanning right the practices of yore,
Shall deem our hoar progenitors unwise.

They to the dome where smoke with curling play
Announc'd the dinner to the regions round,
Summon'd the singer blythe, and harper gay,
And aided wine with dulcet-streaming sound.

The better use of notes, or sweet or shrill,
By quiv'ring string, or modulated wind;
Trumpet or lyre—to their harsh bosoms chill,
Admission ne'er had sought, or could not find.

[1] Thomas Gray. Gray's friend Bonstetten was walking with him about the year 1769, 'when he exclaimed with bitterness, "Look, look, Bonstetten! the great bear! There goes *Ursa Major!*" This was Johnson. Gray could not abide him.' Sir Egerton Brydges's *Autobiography*, ii. 394.

[2] *Medea*, ll. 193-206.

The translation in Burney's *History of Music*, 1782, ii. 340, is also by Johnson. See *Works*, i. 142 *n.* It is as follows:—

'The rites deriv'd from ancient days
With thoughtless reverence we praise,
The rites that taught us to combine
The joys of music and of wine,
And bad the feast and song and bowl
O'erfill the saturated soul;
But n'er the Flute or Lyre apply'd
To cheer despair or soften pride,
Nor call'd them to the gloomy cells
Where Want repines and Vengeance swells,
Where Hate sits musing to betray
And Murder meditates his prey.
To dens of guilt and shades of care
Ye sons of Melody repair,
Nor deign the festive dome to cloy
With superfluities of joy.
Ah, little needs the Minstrel's pow'r
To speed the light convivial hour,
The board with varied plenty crown'd
May spare the luxuries of sound.'

A General History of Music, by Charles Burney.

'Mr. Norgate, the publisher, has a specimen of Porson's minute writing, comprising in a circle of an inch and a half in diameter the Greek verses on music from the Medea, with Johnson's translation of them, in all more than 220 words, with a considerable space left blank in the centre. It is written on vellum, a portion of a leaf which fell from the Photius which he copied.' J. S. Watson's *Porson*, p. 422.

Oh!

Oh! send them to the sullen mansions dun,
Her baleful eyes where Sorrow rolls around;
Where gloom-enamour'd Mischief loves to dwell,
And Murder, all blood-bolter'd, schemes the wound.

When cates luxuriant pile the spacious dish,
And purple nectar glads the festive hour;
The guest, without a want, without a wish,
Can yield no room to Music's soothing pow'r.

Some of the old legendary stories put in verse by modern writers provoked him to caricature[1] them thus one day at Streatham; but they are already well-known, I am sure.

The tender infant, meek and mild,
 Fell down upon the stone;
The nurse took up the squealing child,
 But still the child squeal'd on[2].

A famous ballad also, beginning *Rio verde*, *Rio verde*, when I commended the translation of it, he said he could do it better himself—as thus:

Glassy water, glassy water,
Down whose current clear and strong,
Chiefs confus'd in mutual slaughter,
Moor and Christian roll along[3].

[1] *Caricature* is not in Johnson's *Dictionary*.

[2] Wordsworth says of the imitators of the *Reliques*, and of Johnson's attack on the old ballads:—'The critic triumphed, the legendary imitators were deservedly disregarded, and as undeservedly, their ill-imitated models sank in this country into temporary neglect ... Dr. Percy was so abashed by the ridicule flung upon his labours . . . that, though while he was writing under a mask he had not wanted resolution to follow his genius into the regions of true simplicity and genuine pathos— . . . yet when he appeared in his own person and character as a poetical writer, he adopted, as in the tale of the *Hermit of Warkworth*, a diction scarcely in any one of its features distinguishable from the vague, the glossy, and unfeeling language of his day.' Wordsworth's *Works*, ed. 1857, vi. 372.

Percy himself described his *Reliques* as 'such a strange collection of trash.' Nichols's *Literary History*, vii. 577.

Johnson had helped Percy in the publication of the *Reliques*. *Life*, iii. 276, *n.* 2; *Letters*, i. 89.

[3] 'Rio verde, rio verde,
 Quanto cuerpo en ti se baña
De Cristianos y de Moros
 Muertos por la dura espada.'
'Gentle river, gentle river,
 Lo, thy streams are stain'd with gore!
Many a brave and noble captain
 Floats along thy willow'd shore.'

Reliques of Ancient English Poetry, vol. i. Bk. iii. No. 16.

But

But Sir, said I, this is not ridiculous at all. 'Why no (replied he), why should I always write ridiculously?—perhaps because I made these verses to imitate such a one, naming him:

Hermit hoar, in solemn cell,
Wearing out life's evening gray;
Strike thy bosom, sage! and tell
What is bliss, and which the way?
Thus I spoke, and speaking sigh'd,
Scarce repress'd the starting tear,
When the hoary Sage reply'd,
Come, my lad, and drink some beer[1].'

I could give another comical instance of caricatura imitation. Recollecting some day, when praising these verses of Lopez de Vega,

Se a quien los leones vence
Vence una muger hermosa
O el de flaco averguençe
O ella di ser mas furiosa,

more than he thought they deserved, Mr. Johnson instantly observed 'that they were founded on a trivial conceit; and that conceit ill-explained, and ill-expressed beside.——The lady, we all know, does nŏt conquer in the same manner as the lion does: 'Tis a mere play of words (added he), and you might as well say, that

If the man who turnips cries,
Cry not when his father dies,
'Tis a proof that he had rather
Have a turnip than his father.'

And this humour is of the same sort with which he answered the friend who commended the following line[2]:

Who rules o'er freemen should himself be free.

'To be sure (said Dr. Johnson),

Who drives fat oxen should himself be fat.'

[1] Boswell records the making of these verses. The third line runs:—'*Smite* thy bosom,' &c. 'BOSWELL. "But why smite his bosom, Sir?" JOHNSON. "Why to shew he was in earnest" (smiling).' *Hoary*, on Boswell's suggestion, he changed into *smiling*, 'both to avoid a sameness with the epithet in the first line and to describe the hermit in his pleasantry.' *Life*, iii. 159. See *ib.* ii. 136, *n.* 4, for another parody.

[2] In Brooke's *Earl of Essex*. *Life*, iv. 312, *n.* 5.

This readiness of finding a parallel, or making one, was shewn by him perpetually in the course of conversation.—When the French verses of a certain pantomime were quoted thus,

Je suis Cassandre descendue des cieux,
Pour vous fair [*sic*] *entendre, mesdames et messieurs,*
Que je suis Cassandre descendue des cieux;

he cried out gaily and suddenly, almost in a moment,

'I am Cassandra come down from the sky,
To tell each by-stander what none can deny,
That I am Cassandra come down from the sky.'

The pretty Italian verses too, at the end of Baretti's book, called 'Easy Phraseology,' he did *all' improviso*, in the same manner:

Viva! viva la padrona!
Tutta bella, e tutta buona,
La padrona è un angiolella
Tutta buona e tutta bella;
Tutta bella e tutta buona;
Viva! viva la padrona!

Long may live my lovely Hetty[1]!
Always young and always pretty,
Always pretty, always young,
Live my lovely Hetty long!
Always young and always pretty;
Long may live my lovely Hetty!

The famous distich too, of an Italian *improvisatore*, who, when the duke of Modena ran away from the comet in the year 1742 or 1743[2],

Se al venir vestro [*vostro*] *i principi sen' vanno*
Deh venga ogni dì—durate un' anno;

'which (said he) would do just as well in our language thus:

If at your coming princes disappear,
Comets! come every day—and stay a year.'

[1] Mrs. Thrale, whose name was Hester.

[2] A comet was seen in February and March, 1742. *Gentleman's Magazine*, 1742, pp. 106, 210. In May of that year the Duke of Modena withdrew from his dominions before the attack of the Sardinians. *Ib.* p. 334. Johnson wrote to Mrs. Thrale in 1783:—'Mr. Mudge tells me that the gout will secure me from everything paralytick: if this be true, I am ready to say to the arthritick pains, *Deh! venite ogni dì, durate un anno.*' *Letters*, ii. 338.

When

When some one in company commended the verses of M. de Benserade[1] *à son Lit*;

Théâtre des ris et des pleurs,
Lit! où je nais, et où je meurs,
Tu nous fais voir comment voisins,
Sont nos plaisirs, et nos chagrins.

To which he replied without hesitating,

'In bed we laugh, in bed we cry,
And born in bed, in bed we die;
The near approach a bed may shew,
Of human bliss to human woe.'

The inscription on the collar of Sir Joseph Banks's goat which had been on two of his adventurous expeditions with him, and was then, by the humanity of her amiable master, turned out to graze in Kent, as a recompence for her utility and faithful service, was given me by Johnson in the year 1777 I think, and I have never yet seen it printed.

Perpetui, [*Perpetua,*] *ambitâ bis terrâ, premia lactis,*
Hæc habet altrici Capra secunda Jovis[2].

The epigram written on Lord Anson's house many years ago, 'where (says Mr. Johnson) I was well received and kindly treated[3], and with the true gratitude of a wit ridiculed the master of the house before I had left it an hour,' has been falsely printed in many papers since his death. I wrote it down from his own lips one evening in August 1772, not neglecting the little preface, accusing himself of making so graceless a return for the civilities shewn him. He had, among other elegancies about the park and gardens, been made to observe a temple to the winds, when this thought naturally presented itself *to a wit.*

[1] 'Isaac de Benserade, 1612-1691. Sa petite maison de Gentilli, où il se retira sur la fin de sa vie, était remplie d'inscriptions en vers, qui valaient bien ses autres ouvrages; c'est dommage qu'on ne les ait pas recueillies.' *Œuvres de Voltaire*, ed. 1819, xvii. 49.

[2] It was in 1772 that Johnson made these lines. *Life*, ii. 144.

[3] Lord Anson died suddenly at his seat at Moor Park in Hertfordshire on June 6, 1762. *Gentleman's Magazine*, 1762, p. 264. His elder brother had been member for Lichfield. Burke's *Peerage*, under EARL OF LICHFIELD.

 Gratum

Gratum animum laudo; Qui debuit omnia ventis,
Quam bene ventorum surgere templa jubet[1]*!*

A translation of Dryden's epigram too, I used to fancy I had to myself.

Quos laudet vates, Graius, Romanus, et Anglus,
Tres tria temporibus secla dedere suis:
Sublime ingenium Graius; Romanus habebat
Carmen grande sonans; Anglus utrumque tulit.
Nil majus natura capit; clarare priores
Quae potuere duos tertius unus habet[2]*:*

from the famous lines written under Milton's picture:

Three poets in three distant ages born,
Greece, Italy, and England did adorn;
The first in loftiness of thought surpast,
The next in majesty; in both the last.
The force of Nature could no further go,
To make a third she join'd the former two.

One evening in the oratorio[3] season of the year 1771, Mr. Johnson went with me to Covent-Garden theatre; and though he was for the most part an exceedingly bad playhouse companion, as his person drew people's eyes upon the box, and the loudness of his voice made it difficult for me to hear any body but himself; he sat surprisingly quiet, and I flattered myself he was listening to the music[4]. When we were got home however he repeated

[1] A grateful mind I praise! All to the winds he owed;
And so upon the winds a temple he bestowed.

Horace Walpole wrote on June 18, 1744 (*Letters*, i. 306):—'Anson is returned with vast fortune, substantial and lucky. He has brought the Acapulca ship into Portsmouth, and its treasure is at least computed at five hundred thousand pounds. He escaped the Brest squadron by a mist.'

A photograph of the Temple is given in R. Bayne's *Moor Park*, 1871, p. 99.

[2] This translation Johnson made at Oxford, I suppose in his undergraduate days. *Life*, v. 86.

[3] *Oratorio* is not in Johnson's *Dictionary*. In the *Gentleman's Magazine* for 1733, p. 173, mention is made of a man 'who had contrived a thing that was better than an opera called an oratorio.'

[4] Boswell thus describes Johnson at Mrs. Abington's benefit at Drury Lane in 1775:—'He sat on the seat directly behind me; and as he could neither see nor hear at such a distance from the stage, he was wrapped up in grave abstraction, and seemed quite a cloud, amidst all the sunshine of glitter and gaiety.' *Life*, ii. 324.

these

these verses, which he said he had made at the oratorio, and he bid me translate them.

IN THEATRO.

Tertii verso quater orbe lustri
Quid theatrales tibi Crispe pompæ!
Quam decet canos male literatos
Sera voluptas!

Tene mulceri fidibus canoris?
Tene cantorum modulis stupere?
Tene per pictas oculo elegante
Currere formas?

Inter æquales sine felle liber,
Codices veri studiosus inter
Rectius vives; sua quisque carpat
Gaudia gratus.

Lusibus gaudet puer otiosis,
Luxus oblectat juvenem theatri,
At seni fluxo sapienter uti
Tempora [Tempore] restat.

I gave him the following lines in imitation, which he liked well enough, I think:

When threescore years have chill'd thee quite,
Still can theatric scenes delight?
Ill suits this place with learned wight,
May Bates [1] or Coulson cry.

The scholar's pride can Brent [2] disarm?
His heart can soft Guadagni [3] warm?
Or scenes with sweet delusion charm
The climacteric [4] eye?

[1] Bates was perhaps Joah Bates, a musician, in whose orchestra Herschel the astronomer played first violin. See *Dict. Nat. Biog.* under Bates. I do not know who Coulson was. It is possible that he was Johnson's friend, the Rev. John Coulson, Fellow of University College, Oxford (*Letters*, i. 323), and that Bates was another scholar.

[2] Charlotte Brent (d. 1802), afterwards Mrs. Pinto, 'was a favourite pupil of Dr. Arne, and for her he composed much of his later and more florid music.' *Dict. Nat. Biog.*

[3] Guadagni, in 1771, was engaged to sing in an unlicensed opera in Soho Square. Horace Walpole wrote on Feb. 22 (*Letters*, v. 283):—'Guadagni, who governed so haughtily at Vienna that, to pique some man of quality there, he named a minister to Venice, is not only fined, but was threatened to be sent to Bridewell, which chilled the blood of all the Caesars and Alexanders he had ever represented.'

[4] Johnson did not reach his grand climacteric till the next year when he was sixty-three years old.

The

The social club, the lonely tower,
Far better suit thy midnight hour [1];
Let each according to his power
In worth or wisdom shine!

And while play pleases idle boys,
And wanton mirth fond youth employs,
To fix the soul, and free from toys,
That useful task be thine.

The copy of verses in Latin hexameters, as well as I remember, which he wrote to Dr. Lawrence [2], I forgot to keep a copy of; and he obliged me to resign his translation of the song beginning, *Busy, curious, thirsty fly*, for him to give Mr. Langton [3], with a promise *not* to retain a copy. I concluded he knew why, so never enquired the reason. He had the greatest possible value for Mr. Langton, of whose virtue and learning he delighted to talk in very exalted terms [4]; and poor Dr. Lawrence had long been his friend and confident [5]. The conversation I saw them hold together in Essex-street one day in the year 1781 or 1782, was a melancholy one, and made a singular impression on my mind. He was himself exceedingly ill, and I accompanied him thither for advice. The physician was however, in some respects, more to be pitied than the patient: Johnson was panting under an asthma and dropsy; but Lawrence had been brought home that very morning struck with the palsy [6], from which he had, two hours before we came, strove to awaken himself by blisters: they were both deaf, and scarce able to speak besides; one from

[1] 'Or let my lamp at midnight hour
Be seen in some high lonely tower.'
Il Penseroso, l. 85.

[2] 'Ad Thomam Laurence, Medicum Doctissimum, cum filium peregre agentem desiderio nimis tristi prosequeretur.' *Works*, i. 165.

[3] He wrote to Langton on July 5, 1774:—'If you have the Latin version of *Busy, curious, thirsty fly*, be so kind as to transcribe and send it.' *Life*, ii. 281. See *Works*, i. 172.

[4] 'He said, "I know not who will go to Heaven, if Langton does not. Sir, I could almost say, *Sit anima mea cum Langtono*."' *Life*, iv. 280. 'It is to be feared that Averroes had not the right way of blessing himself, when in defiance of Christianity he wished, *Sit anima mea cum philosophis*.' South's *Sermons*, ii. 75. See also *ib.* iii. 203.

[5] 'Lawrence,' he wrote, 'is a friend whom long familiarity has much endeared. He is one of the best men whom I have known.' *Ante*, p. 104.

[6] *Life*, iv. 144, *n*. 3.

difficulty

difficulty of breathing, the other from paralytic debility. To give and receive medical counsel therefore, they fairly sate down on each side a table in the Doctor's gloomy apartment, adorned with skeletons, preserved monsters, &c. and agreed to write Latin billets to each other[1]. Such a scene did I never see! 'You (said Johnson) are *timidè* and *gelidè*[2];' finding that his friend had prescribed palliative not drastic remedies. It is not *me*, replies poor Lawrence in an interrupted voice; 'tis nature that is *gelidè* and *timidè*. In fact he lived but few months after I believe, and retained his faculties still a shorter time. He was a man of strict piety and profound learning, but little skilled in the knowledge of life or manners, and died without having ever enjoyed the reputation he so justly deserved[3].

Mr. Johnson's health had been always extremely bad since I first knew him, and his over-anxious care to retain without blemish the perfect sanity of his mind, contributed much to disturb it[4]. He had studied medicine diligently in all its branches[5]; but had given particular attention to the diseases of the imagination, which he watched in himself with a solicitude destructive of his own peace, and intolerable to those he trusted[6]. Dr. Lawrence told him one day, that if he would come and beat him once a week he would bear it; but to hear his complaints was more than *man* could support[7]. 'Twas therefore that he tried,

[1] See *Life*, iv. 143 for one of these letters.

[2] Johnson could not have said, 'You are *timide* and *gelide*.' On his death-bed he reproached Heberden with being *timidorum timidissimus*. *Ib*. iv. 400, *n*.

[3] Hawkins, who speaks highly of his skill, says that 'a vacuity of countenance very unfavourable to an opinion of his learning or sagacity stood in his way.' Hawkins's *Johnson*, p. 402.

[4] *Ante*, p. 78, and *post*, p. 234.

[5] 'He was a great dabbler in physic,' writes Boswell. *Life*, iii. 152. See also *ib*. iii. 22, and *Letters*, i. 49.

[6] See *ante*, p. 48, where he records:—'This day it came into my mind to write the history of my melancholy.' I believe that there is great exaggeration in Mrs. Piozzi's statement.

[7] 'I never knew any man who was less disposed to be querulous than Johnson. Whether the subject was his own situation, or the state of the publick, or the state of human nature in general, though he saw the evils, his mind was turned to resolution, and never to whining or complaint.' *Life*, ii. 357.

I suppose,

I suppose, and in eighteen years contrived to weary the patience of a *woman*[1]. When Mr. Johnson felt his fancy, or fancied he felt it, disordered, his constant recurrence was to the study of arithmetic[2]; and one day that he was totally confined to his chamber, and I enquired what he had been doing to divert himself; he shewed me a calculation which I could scarce be made to understand, so vast was the plan of it, and so very intricate were the figures: no other indeed than that the national debt, computing it at one hundred and eighty millions sterling, would, if converted into silver, serve to make a meridian of that metal, I forget how broad, for the globe of the whole earth, the real *globe*. On a similar occasion I asked him (knowing what subject he would like best to talk upon), How his opinion stood towards the question between Paschal and Soame Jennings[3] about number and numeration? as the French philosopher observes that infinity, though on all sides astonishing, appears most so when the idea is connected with the idea of number; for the notions of infinite number, and infinite number we know there is, stretches one's capacity still more than the idea of infinite space; 'Such a notion indeed (adds he) can scarcely find room in the human mind[4].' Our English author on the other hand exclaims, let no man give himself leave to talk about infinite number, for infinite number is a contradiction in terms; whatever is once numbered, we all see cannot be infinite[5]. 'I think (said Mr. Johnson after a pause) we must settle the matter thus: numeration is certainly infinite, for eternity might be employed in adding unit to unit; but every number is in itself finite, as the possibility of doubling

[1] See *post*, pp. 331, 341.

[2] Boswell tells how 'Johnson delighted in exercising his mind on the science of numbers.' *Life*, iii. 207. The only book which he took with him on his tour to the Hebrides was Cocker's *Arithmetic*. *Ib.* v. 138, *n.* 2. See *post*, p. 301.

[3] Soame Jenyns. Johnson reviewed his *Free Enquiry into the Nature and Origin of Evil*. *Life*, i. 315; *Works*, vi. 47.

[4] Mrs. Piozzi refers, I suppose, to the second article of the first part of Pascal's *Pensées*. In that case she does not give his meaning correctly.

[5] 'An infinite number is a contradiction in terms, and therefore everything that is infinite or eternal must exist in some manner which bears no manner of relation to Space or Time, and which must therefore be to us totally incomprehensible.' Jenyns's *Miscellaneous Pieces*, ed. 1761, ii. 209.

it easily

it easily proves: besides, stop at what point you will, you find yourself as far from infinitude as ever.' These passages I wrote down as soon as I had heard them, and repent that I did not take the same method with a dissertation he made one other day that he was very ill, concerning the peculiar properties of the number Sixteen, which I afterwards tried, but in vain, to make him repeat.

As ethics or figures, or metaphysical reasoning[1], was the sort of talk he most delighted in, so no kind of conversation pleased him less I think, than when the subject was historical fact or general polity. 'What shall we learn from *that* stuff (said he)[2]?

[1] He told Boswell that 'at Oxford the study of which he was the most fond was Metaphysicks, but he had not read much even in that way.' *Life*, i. 70. See *ante*, p. 17, for his prayer on the study of philosophy.

Mackintosh believed that he was withheld from metaphysics 'partly by a secret dread that it might disturb those prejudices in which his mind had found repose from the agitations of doubt.' *Life of Mackintosh*, ii. 171.

[2] In a note on the *Life*, iii. 206, I have stated that 'he was no doubt sick of the constant reference made by writers and public speakers to Rome.' It was the cant of the age. Voltaire says:—'Les membres du parlement d'Angleterre aiment à se comparer aux anciens Romains autant qu'ils le peuvent.' *Œuvres*, ed. 1819, xxiv. 33. Chesterfield writes to his son:—'Bring no precedents from the *virtuous Spartans, the polite Athenians, and the brave Romans.* Leave all that to futile pedants.' *Letters*, iii. 236.

Horace Walpole thus ridicules such talk as this (*Letters*, v. 235):—'I entertain myself with the idea of a future senate in Carolina and Virginia, where their future patriots will harangue on the austere and incorruptible virtue of the ancient English! will tell their auditors of our disinterestedness and scorn of bribes and pensions, and make us blush in our graves at their ridiculous panegyrics.'

Thomson's *Liberty* has a great deal of this cant about 'old virtuous Rome' (Part v. l. 229), and so has Bolingbroke's *Dissertation upon Parties*.

Johnson seriously thought of translating De Thou's *Historia sui Temporis*, 'which contains the history of only sixty-four years, yet, it has been calculated, would require twelve months, at four hours a day, for its perusal.' Pattison's *Isaac Casaubon*, ed. 1892, p. 59. In a list of books proper for a young man to study, drawn up by Johnson, many histories are included. *Life*, iv. 311. In the talk between him and Lord Monboddo on Aug. 21, 1773, Monboddo said:—'The history of manners is the most valuable. I never set a high value on any other history.' Johnson replied:—'Nor I; and therefore I esteem biography as giving us what comes near to ourself

let us not fancy like Swift that we are exalting a woman's character by telling how she

> Could name the ancient heroes round,
> Explain for what they were renown'd, &c.[1] '

I must not however lead my readers to suppose that he meant to reserve such talk for *men's* company as a proof of pre-eminence. 'He never (as he expressed it) desired to hear of the *Punic war*[2] while he lived: such conversation was lost time (he said), and carried one away from common life, leaving no ideas behind which could serve *living wight*[3] as warning or direction.'

> How I should act is not the case,
> But how would Brutus in my place?

'And now (cries Mr. Johnson, laughing with obstreperous violence), if these two foolish lines can be equalled in folly, except by the two succeeding ones[4]—shew them me.'

I asked him once concerning the conversation powers of a gentleman with whom I was myself unacquainted[5]—'He

selves, what we can turn to use.' *Life*, v. 79.

All this shows little of 'the fierce and boisterous contempt of ignorance' with which, according to Lord Macaulay, Johnson spoke of history. Macaulay's *Essays*, ed. 1843, i. 403.

[1] 'She nam'd the ancient heroes round,
Explain'd for what they were renown'd;
Then spoke with censure or applause
Of foreign customs, rites and laws.'
Cadenus and Vanessa. Swift's *Works*, ed. 1803, x. 128.

[2] Writing to Mrs. Thrale in July, 1775, he says:—'Therefore wherever you are and whatever you see talk not of the Punick War.' *Letters*, i. 343.

'The example of the *Romans* is eternally quoted from the Pamphleteer in the Garret to the Patriot in the Senate as extremely worthy of the Imitation of *Britons*.' *Four Tracts* by Josiah Tucker, D.D., 1774, p. 60.

[3] *Paradise Lost*, ii. 613.

[4] 'How shall I act is not the case;
But how would Brutus in my place?
In such a case would Cato bleed?
And how would Socrates proceed?'
To Stella, 1720. Swift's *Works*, x. 187.

[5] Mrs. Piozzi, in a marginal note, says it was Charles James Fox. Hayward's *Piozzi*, i. 292.

'I have heard Mr. Gibbon remark,' writes Boswell, 'that Mr. Fox could not be afraid of Dr. Johnson; yet he certainly was very shy of saying anything in Dr. Johnson's presence.' *Life*, iii. 267. See also *ib.* iv. 167.

talked

talked to me at club one day (replies our Doctor) concerning Catiline's conspiracy—so I withdrew my attention, and thought about Tom Thumb.'

Modern politics fared no better. I was one time extolling the character of a statesman, and expatiating on the skill required to direct the different currents, reconcile the jarring interests, &c. 'Thus (replies he) a mill is a complicated piece of mechanism enough, but the water is no part of the workmanship.'——On another occasion, when some one lamented the weakness of a then present minister[1], and complained that he was dull and tardy, and knew little of affairs,—'You may as well complain, Sir (says Johnson), that the accounts of time are kept by the clock; for he certainly does stand still upon the stair-head—and we all know that he is no great chronologer.'——In the year 1777, or thereabouts, when all the talk was of an invasion, he said most pathetically one afternoon, 'Alas! alas! how this unmeaning stuff spoils all my comfort in my friends' conversation! Will the people never have done with it; and shall I never hear a sentence again without the *French* in it? Here is no invasion coming, and you *know* there is none[2]. Let the vexatious and frivolous talk alone, or suffer it at least to teach you *one* truth; and learn by this perpetual echo of even unapprehended distress, how historians magnify events expected, or calamities endured; when you know they are at this very moment collecting all the big words they can find, in which to describe a consternation never felt, for a misfortune which never happened. Among all your lamentations, who eats the less[3]? Who sleeps the worse, for one general's ill success

[1] She means I suppose 'a minister of that time.' Perhaps it was the Duke of Grafton. Horace Walpole wrote of him on June 16, 1768:—'Because we are not in confusion enough he makes everything as bad as possible, neglecting on one hand, and taking no precaution on the other.' *Letters*, v. 106. Junius, in his Letter of April 10, 1769, described him as 'a singular instance of youth without spirit.'

[2] It was in 1778 and 1779 that there was a great panic about an invasion. *Life*, iii. 326; *Letters*, ii. 109.

[3] 'We are told that on the arrival of the news of the unfortunate battle of Fontenoy every heart beat and every eye was in tears. Now we know that no man eat his dinner the worse.' *Life*, i. 355.

success, or another's capitulation? *Oh, pray* let us hear no more of it!'——No man however was more zealously attached to his party; he not only loved a tory himself, but he loved a man the better if he heard he hated a whig. 'Dear Bathurst[1] (said he to me one day) was a man to my very heart's content: he hated a fool, and he hated a rogue, and he hated a *whig*; he was a very good *hater*.'

Some one mentioned a gentleman of that party for having behaved oddly on an occasion where faction was not concerned:—'Is he not a citizen of London, a native of North America, and a whig[2]? (says Johnson)—Let him be absurd, I beg of you: when a monkey is *too* like a man, it shocks one.'

Severity towards the poor was, in Dr. Johnson's opinion (as is visible in his Life of Addison[3] particularly), an undoubted and constant attendant or consequence upon whiggism; and he was not contented with giving them relief, he wished to add also indulgence. He loved the poor as I never yet saw any one else do, with an earnest desire to make them happy.—What signifies, says some one, giving halfpence to common beggars? they only lay it out in gin or tobacco. 'And why should they be denied such sweeteners of their existence (says Johnson)[4]? it is surely very savage to refuse them every possible

[1] *Ante*, p. 29.

[2] Alderman Lee (*Life*, iii. 78; *Letters*, i. 397) was all three.

[3] 'Steele had made Sir Andrew Freeport, in the true spirit of unfeeling commerce, declare that he "would not build an hospital for idle people."' *Works*, vii. 432. Johnson quoted from memory and quoted wrongly; for, 'Sir Andrew, after giving money to some importunate beggars, says:—'I ought to give to an hospital of invalids, to recover as many useful subjects as I can, but I shall bestow none of my bounties upon an almshouse of idle people.' *Spectator*, No. 232.

One evening at Mr. Thrale's Johnson said:—'Addison had made his Sir Andrew Freeport a true Whig, arguing against giving charity to beggars, and throwing out other such ungracious sentiments; but that he had thought better, and made amends by making him found an hospital for decayed farmers.' *Life*, ii. 212. *The Spectator*, No. 232, was written neither by Addison nor Steele; who wrote it is uncertain.

[4] 'He frequently gave all the silver in his pocket to the poor, who watched him between his house and the tavern where he dined.' *Ib.* ii. 119. 'You are much surer,' he said,

possible avenue to pleasure, reckoned too coarse for our own acceptance. Life is a pill which none of us can bear to swallow without gilding; yet for the poor we delight in stripping it still barer, and are not ashamed to shew even visible displeasure, if ever the bitter taste is taken from their mouths.' In consequence of these principles he nursed whole nests of people in his house, where the lame, the blind, the sick, and the sorrowful found a sure retreat from all the evils whence his little income could secure them[1]: and commonly spending the middle of the week at our house, he kept his numerous family in Fleet-street upon a settled allowance[2]; but returned to them every Saturday, to give them three good dinners, and his company, before he came back to us on the Monday night——treating them with the same, or perhaps more ceremonious civility, than he would have done by as many people of fashion——making the holy scriptures thus the rule of his conduct, and only expecting salvation as he was able to obey its precepts.

While Dr. Johnson possessed however the strongest compassion for poverty or illness, he did not even pretend to feel for those who lamented the loss of a child, a parent, or a friend[3].

'that you are doing good when you pay money to those who work, as the recompense of their labour, than when you give money merely in charity.' *Life*, iii. 56. 'It is an unhappy circumstance,' he said, 'that one might give away five hundred pounds in a year to those that importune in the streets, and not do any good.' *Ib.* iv. 3.

[1] There is great exaggeration in this passage. For some of the inmates of his house see *Ib.* iii. 222, 368, 461.

[2] To Levett he gave house-room and breakfast, and now and then a dinner on Sunday. *Ib.* i. 243, *n.* 3. Miss Williams was not wholly dependent on him. *Ib.* i. 393, *n.* 1; *Letters*, ii. 336. To Mrs. Desmoulins and her daughter and Miss Carmichael he gave a room; but they did not come to live with him till about the year 1777. To Mrs. Desmoulins he allowed also half-a-guinea a week. *Life*, iii. 222.

[3] 'The death of my mother,' he wrote, is one of the few calamities on which I think with terror.' *Letters*, i. 20. 'Of his friend Bathurst he hardly ever spoke without tears in his eyes.' Murphy's *Johnson*, p. 56. To Mr. Elphinston, who had lost his mother, he wrote:—'I read the letters in which you relate your mother's death to Mrs. Strahan, and I think I do myself honour when I tell you that I read them with tears.' *Life*,

'These

——'These are the distresses of sentiment (he would reply) which a man who is really to be pitied has no leisure to feel. The sight of people who want food and raiment is so common in great cities, that a surly fellow like me has no compassion to spare for wounds given only to vanity or softness[1].' No man, therefore, who smarted from the ingratitude of his friends, found any sympathy from our philosopher: 'Let him do good on higher motives next time,' would be the answer; 'he will then be sure of his reward.'——It is easy to observe, that the justice of such sentences made them offensive; but we must be careful how we condemn a man for saying what we know to be true, only because it *is* so. I hope that the reason our hearts rebelled a little against his severity, was chiefly because it came from a living mouth.—Books were invented to take off the odium of immediate superiority, and soften the rigour of duties prescribed by the teachers and censors of human kind—setting at least those who are acknowledged wiser than ourselves at a distance[2]. When we recollect however, that for this very reason *they* are

i. 212. Over the dying bed of Mrs. Thrale's mother 'he hung with the affection of a parent and the reverence of a son.' *Post*, p. 235. On the death of young Harry Thrale he wrote to his mother:—'Poor dear sweet little boy! When I read the letter this day to Mrs. Aston she said, "Such a death is the next to translation." Yet however I may convince myself of this the tears are in my eyes, and yet I could not love him as you loved him, nor reckon upon him for a future comfort as you and his father reckoned upon him.' *Letters*, i. 381. On the death of the boy's father he wrote to the widow:—'I am not without my part of the calamity. No death since that of my wife has ever oppressed me like this.' *Letters*, ii. 209. With Miss Burney he often had 'long and melancholy discourses about our dear deceased master, whom indeed he regrets incessantly.' Mme. D'Arblay's *Diary*, ii. 63.

Mrs. Piozzi says (*post*, p. 230):—'The truth is nobody suffered more from pungent sorrow at a friend's death than Dr. Johnson, though he would suffer no one else to complain of their losses in the same way.'

[1] It was the exaggeration of feeling that Johnson attacked. 'You will find these very feeling people,' he said, 'are not very ready to do you good. They *pay* you by *feeling*.' *Ib.* ii. 95.

[2] Johnson, in the *Rambler*, No. 87, entitled, 'The reasons why advice is generally ineffectual,' says:—'By the consultation of books, whether of dead or living authors, many temptations to petulance and opposition, which occur in oral conferences, are avoided . . . Books are seldom read with complete impartiality but by those from whom the writer is placed at such a distance that his life or death is indifferent.'

seldom

seldom consulted and little obeyed, how much cause shall his contemporaries have to rejoice that their living Johnson forced them to feel the reproofs due to vice and folly—while Seneca and Tillotson were no longer able to make impression—except on our shelves. Few things indeed which pass well enough with others would do with him: he had been a great reader of Mandeville[1], and was ever on the watch to spy out those stains of original corruption, so easily discovered by a penetrating observer even in the purest minds. I mentioned an event, which if it had happened would greatly have injured Mr. Thrale and his family——and then, dear Sir, said I, how sorry you would have been! 'I *hope* (replied he after a long pause)—I should have been *very* sorry;——but remember Rochefoucault's maxim[2].' ——I would rather (answered I) remember Prior's verses, and ask,

> What need of books these truths to tell,
> Which folks perceive that [who] cannot spell?
> And must we spectacles apply,
> To see [view] what hurts our naked eye[3]?

Will *any* body's mind bear this eternal microscope that you place upon your own so? 'I never (replied he) saw one that *would*, except that of my dear Miss Reynolds—and her's is very near to purity itself[4].'——Of slighter evils, and friends less distant than our own household, he spoke less cautiously. An acquaintance lost the almost certain hope of a good estate that had been long expected[5]. Such a one will grieve (said I) at her friend's disappointment. 'She will suffer as much perhaps (said he) as your horse did when your cow miscarried.'——I professed myself sincerely grieved when accumulated distresses crushed Sir George Colebrook's family; and I was so. 'Your own prosperity

[1] 'I read Mandeville,' he said, 'forty, or, I believe, fifty years ago. He did not puzzle me; he opened my views into life very much.' *Life*, iii. 292. Dr. Franklin describes Mandeville as 'a most facetious, entertaining companion.' Franklin's *Works*, ed. 1887, i. 89.

[2] 'Dans l'adversité de nos meilleurs amis nous trouvons toujours quelque chose qui ne nous déplaît pas.' See *Letters*, ii. 421, *n.* 2.

For the strong interest which Johnson took in Mr. Thrale's affairs see *ib.* i. 194, *n.*

[3] *Alma*, l. 1660.

[4] Boswell complained that 'her too nice delicacy would not permit Johnson's letters to her to be published.' *Life*, i. 486, *n.* 1.

[5] Mrs. Thrale herself suffered such a loss. *Letters*, i. 292, *n.* 5.

prosperity (said he) may possibly have so far increased the natural tenderness of your heart, that for aught I know you *may* be a *little sorry*; but it is sufficient for a plain man if he does not laugh when he sees a fine new house tumble down all on a sudden, and a snug cottage stand by ready to receive the owner, whose birth entitled him to do nothing better, and whose limbs are left him to go to work again with [1].'

I used to tell him in jest, that his morality was easily contented; and when I have said something as if the wickedness of the world gave me concern, he would cry out aloud against canting, and protest that he thought there was very little gross wickedness in the world [2], and still less of extraordinary virtue. Nothing indeed more surely disgusted Dr. Johnson than hyperbole [3]; he loved not to be told of sallies of excellence, which he said were seldom valuable, and seldom true. 'Heroic virtues (said he) are the *bons mots* of life; they do not appear often, and when they do appear are too much prized I think; like the aloe-tree, which shoots and flowers once in a hundred years. But life is made up of little things [4]; and that character is the best which does little but repeated acts of beneficence; as that conversation is the best which consists in elegant and pleasing thoughts expressed in natural and pleasing terms [5]. With regard to my own notions of moral virtue (continued he), I hope I have not lost my sensibility of wrong; but I hope likewise that I have lived long enough in the world, to prevent

[1] 'May 1, 1774. Sir George Colebrook, a citizen and martyr to what is called *speculation*, had his pictures sold by auction last week.' Walpole's *Letters*, vi. 81. As £80,000 had been settled on Lady Colebrook and her family the cottage was likely to be snug enough. *Gentleman's Magazine*, 1773, p. 248.

[2] Writing of Savage he says:—'The knowledge of life was his chief attainment; and it is not without some satisfaction that I can produce the suffrage of Savage in favour of human nature.' *Works*, viii. 188. See *post*, p. 262.

[3] *Life*, i. 309, *n.* 3.

[4] 'There is nothing, Sir, too little for so little a creature as man. It is by studying little things that we attain the great art of having as little misery and as much happiness as possible.' *Ib.* i. 433.

[5] 'That is the happiest conversation,' he said, 'where there is no competition, no vanity, but a calm quiet interchange of sentiments.' *Ib.* ii. 359. See also *Letters*, ii. 19.

me

me from expecting to find any action of which both the original motive and all the parts were good [1].'

The piety of Dr. Johnson was exemplary and edifying: he was punctiliously exact to perform every public duty enjoined by the church [2], and his spirit of devotion had an energy that affected all who ever saw him pray in private. The coldest and most languid hearers of the word must have felt themselves animated by his manner of reading the holy scriptures [3]; and to pray by his sick bed, required strength of body as well as of mind, so vehement were his manners, and his tones of voice so pathetic [4]. I have many times made it my request to heaven that I might be spared the sight of his death; and I was spared it [5]!

Mr. Johnson, though in general a gross feeder, kept fast in Lent [6], particularly the holy week, with a rigour very dangerous to his general health; but though he had left off wine (for religious motives as I always believed, though he did not own it [7]), yet he did not hold the commutation of offences by voluntary penance, or encourage others to practise severity upon themselves [8]. He

[1] Perhaps Mrs. Piozzi has in mind the following saying of Johnson's at Bath, where he was staying with her and Mr. Thrale:—'To act from pure benevolence is not possible for finite beings. Human benevolence is mingled with vanity, interest, or some other motive.' *Life*, iii. 48.

[2] Except the duty of going regularly to church and of receiving the sacrament at least three times a year. *Ante*, pp. 81, 92. It is likely however that on the Sundays that he passed at Streatham he was made regular by the regularity of the family.

[3] 'His recitation was grand and affecting.' *Life*, v. 115.

[4] *Ib.* iv. 409.

[5] She was spared it by deserting him. Eighteen months before his death, when attacked by palsy, he wrote to her:—'Let not all our endearments be forgotten, but let me have in this great distress your pity and your prayers. You see I yet turn to you with my complaints as a settled and unalienable friend; do not, do not drive me from you, for I have not deserved either neglect or hatred.' *Letters*, ii. 303.

[6] There is nothing besides this statement to show that he fasted in any part of Lent but Passion Week.

[7] 'I can't drink a little,' he said to Hannah More, 'and therefore I never touch it.' Hannah More's *Memoirs*, i. 251. He gave the same account to Boswell. *Life*, ii. 435. Religious motives had nothing to do with it. He did not disapprove of the use of wine by those who could be moderate. *Ib.* i. 103, *n.* 3. 'I hope you persevere in drinking,' he wrote to Dr. Taylor. *Letters*, i. 408.

[8] 'Austerities and mortifications are means by which the mind is

even once said, 'that he thought it an error to endeavour at pleasing God by taking the rod of reproof out of his hands.' And when we talked of convents, and the hardships suffered in them—'Remember always (said he) that a convent is an idle place, and where there is nothing to be *done* something must be *endured*[1]: mustard has a bad taste *per se* you may observe, but very insipid food cannot be eaten without it.'

His respect however for places of religious retirement was carried to the greatest degree of earthly veneration[2]: the Benedictine convent at Paris paid him all possible honours in return, and the Prior and he parted with tears of tenderness[3]. Two of that college sent to England on the mission some years after, spent much of their time with him at Bolt Court I know, and he was ever earnest to retain their friendship[4]; but though beloved by all his Roman Catholic acquaintance, particularly Dr. Nugent[5], for whose esteem he had a singular value, yet was Mr. Johnson a most unshaken church of England man[6]; and I think, or at

invigorated and roused, by which the attractions of pleasure are interrupted, and the claims of sensuality are broken..... Austerity is the proper antidote to indulgence; the diseases of mind as well as body are cured by contraries, and to contraries we should readily have recourse, if we dreaded guilt as we dread pain.' *Rambler*, No. 110.

For his penance in Uttoxeter market see *Life*, iv. 373.

[1] In the Benedictine convent in Paris he recorded:—'Benedictines may sleep eight hours.—Bodily labour wanted in monasteries.' *Ib.* ii. 390.

[2] Amidst the ruins at St. Andrews he said:—'I never read of a hermit, but in imagination I kiss his feet; never of a monastery, but I could fall on my knees, and kiss the pavement. But I think putting young people there, who know nothing of life, nothing of retirement, is dangerous and wicked.' *Ib.* v. 62. See also *ib.* i. 365.

'Goldsmith, who hated the prudery of Johnson's morals and the foppery of Hawkesworth's manners, yet warmly admired the genius of both, was in use to say among his acquaintance that Johnson would have made *a decent monk*, and Hawkesworth *a good dancing master*.' *Memoirs of the Life*, &c., *of Dr. Johnson*, 1785, p. 194.

[3] 'I was very kindly treated by the English Benedictines, and have a cell appropriated to me in their convent.' *Life*, ii. 402.

[4] *Letters*, i. 401, 406; ii. 39.

[5] Burke's father-in-law. *Post*, p. 230, and *Life*, i. 477.

[6] 'Of the Roman Catholic religion he said:—'. . . I would be a Papist if I could. I have fear enough; but an obstinate rationality prevents me.' *Ib.* iv. 289.

least

least I once *did* think, that a letter written by him to Mr. Barnard the King's librarian, when he was in Italy collecting books, contained some very particular advice to his friend to be on his guard against the seductions of the church of Rome [1].

The settled aversion Dr. Johnson felt towards an infidel he expressed to all ranks, and at all times, without the smallest reserve [2]; for though on common occasions he paid great deference to birth or title [3], yet his regard for truth and virtue never gave way to meaner considerations. We talked of a dead wit one evening, and somebody praised him—'Let us never praise talents so ill employed, Sir; we foul our mouths by commending such infidels' (said he). Allow him the *lumières* at least, intreated one of the company—'I do allow him, Sir (replied Johnson), just enough to light him to hell.'——Of a Jamaica gentleman, then lately dead [4]—'He will not, whither he is now gone (said Johnson), find much difference, I believe, either in the climate or the company.'——The Abbé Reynal probably remembers that, being at the house of a common friend in London, the master of it approached Johnson with that gentleman so much celebrated in his hand, and this speech in his mouth: Will you permit me, Sir, to present to you the Abbé Reynal? '*No, Sir*,' (replied the Doctor very loud) and suddenly turned away from them both [5].

[1] 'You are going into a part of the world divided, as it is said, between bigotry and atheism: such representations are always hyperbolical, but there is certainly enough of both to alarm any mind solicitous for piety and truth; let not the contempt of superstition precipitate you into infidelity, or the horror of infidelity ensnare you in superstition.' *Letters*, i. 147.

[2] See *Life*, i. 268 for his attack on that 'scoundrel and coward' Bolingbroke, and that 'beggarly Scotchman' Mallet; and ii. 95 for his attack on Foote, who, 'if he be an infidel, is an infidel as a dog is an infidel.' Of Hume he said something so rough that Boswell suppresses it. *Ib.* v. 30. 'He talked with some disgust of Gibbon's ugliness.' *Ib.* iv. 73.

[3] 'I have great merit,' he said, 'in being zealous for subordination and the honours of birth, for I can hardly tell who was my grandfather.' *Ib.* ii. 261.

[4] Perhaps Lord Mayor Beckford. *Ib.* iii. 76, 201.

[5] Hannah More (*Memoirs*, i. 394), records the same story, adding that Johnson put his hands behind his back. Romilly, who had formed the highest expectations of Raynal from

Though

Though Mr. Johnson had but little reverence either for talents or fortune, when he found them unsupported by virtue; yet it was sufficient to tell him a man was very pious, or very charitable, and he would at least *begin* with him on good terms, however the conversation might end[1]. He would, sometimes too, good-naturedly enter into a long chat for the instruction or entertainment of people he despised. I perfectly recollect his condescending to delight my daughter's dancing-master with a long argument about *his* art; which the man protested, at the close of the discourse, the Doctor knew more of than himself; who remained astonished, enlightened, and amused by the talk of a person little likely to make a good disquisition upon dancing[2]. I have sometimes indeed been rather pleased than vexed when Mr. Johnson has given a rough answer to a man who perhaps deserved one only half as rough, because I knew he would repent of his hasty reproof[3], and make us all amends by some conversation at once instructive and entertaining, as in the following cases: A young fellow asked him abruptly one day, Pray, Sir, what and where is Palmira? I heard somebody talk last night of the ruins of Palmira. ''Tis a hill in Ireland (replies Johnson), with palms growing on the top, and a bog at the bottom

his works, was greatly disappointed when he met him. 'I was filled at this time with horror at slavery and the slave-trade, and his history of the two Indies had served to enlighten these sentiments; but when I came to talk on these subjects with him he appeared to me so cold and so indifferent about them that I conceived a very unfavourable opinion of him.' *Memoirs of Romilly*, ed. 1840, i. 70.

In Grimm's *Correspondance*, ed. 1814, v. 390, under date of Sept. 1782, is the following entry:—'J'ai vu,' écrivit dernièrement le Roi de Prusse à M. d'Alembert, 'j'ai vu l'Abbé Raynal. À la manière dont il m'a parlé de la puissance, des ressources et des richesses de tous les peuples du globe, j'ai cru m'entretenir avec la Providence.... Je me suis bien gardé de révoquer en doute l'exactitude du moindre de ses calculs; j'ai compris qu'il n'entendrait pas raillerie, même sur un écu.'

[1] See *ante*, p. 35, where he invited 'a kind of Methodist' to his house on Easter Sunday, but did not keep him, as he had purposed, to dinner.

[2] He had had, he said, one or two lessons in dancing. *Life*, iv. 80, *n.* 2.

[3] Reynolds remarked that 'when upon any occasion Johnson had been rough to any person in company, he took the first opportunity of reconciliation by drinking to him, or addressing his discourse to him.' *Ib.* ii. 109. See also *ib.* ii. 256, and *post*, p. 269.

bottom and so they call it *Palm-mira.*' Seeing however that the lad thought him serious, and thanked him for the information, he undeceived him very gently indeed ; told him the history, geography, and chronology of Tadmor in the wilderness, with every incident that literature could furnish I think, or eloquence express, from the building of Solomon's palace to the voyage of Dawkins and Wood [1].

On another occasion, when he was musing over the fire in our drawing-room at Streatham, a young gentleman called to him suddenly, and I suppose he thought disrespectfully, in these words : Mr. Johnson, Would you advise me to marry? 'I would advise no man to marry, Sir (returns for answer in a very angry tone Dr. Johnson), who is not likely to propagate understanding ;' and so left the room [2]. Our companion looked confounded, and I believe had scarce recovered the consciousness of his own existence, when Johnson came back, and drawing his chair among us, with altered looks and a softened voice, joined in the general chat, insensibly led the conversation to the subject of marriage, where he laid himself out in a dissertation so useful, so elegant, so founded on the true knowledge of human life, and so adorned with beauty of sentiment, that no one ever recollected

[1] Horace Walpole makes the following use of this anecdote (*Letters*, ix. 48) :—'In fact the poor man is to be pitied: he was mad, and his disciples did not find it out, but have unveiled all his defects; nay, have exhibited all his brutalities as wit, and his lowest conundrums as humour. Judge! The Piozzi relates that, a young man asking him where Palmyra was, he replied, "In Ireland; it was a bog planted with palm-trees." . . . What will posterity think of us when it reads what an idol we adored?'

For 'Jamaica Dawkins' and the troop of Turkish horse which he hired to guard him and Wood on their way to Palmyra see *Life*, iv. 126.

[2] The young gentleman was Mr. Thrale's nephew, Sir John Lade, on whom Johnson wrote some lines on his coming of age. *Ib.* iv. 413; *Letters*, ii. 190. According to Mr. Hayward 'he married a woman of the town, and contrived to waste the whole of a fine fortune before he died.' Hayward's *Piozzi*, i. 78.

In the *Sporting Magazine* for 1796, p. 162, is the following entry :—'Another of Sir John Lade's estates is under the *hammer;* the money arising from which has been long appropriated; £200,000 have indiscreetly slipped through this baronet's fingers since he became possessed of his property.' He became of age in 1780. *Letters*, ii. 191, *n.* 1. See also *post*, p. 281.

recollected the offence, except to rejoice in its consequences. He repented just as certainly however, if he had been led to praise any person or thing by accident more than he thought it deserved; and was on such occasions comically earnest to destroy the praise or pleasure he had unintentionally given [1].

Sir Joshua Reynolds mentioned some picture as excellent. 'It has often grieved me, Sir (said Mr. Johnson), to see so much mind as the science of painting requires, laid out upon such perishable materials: why do not you oftener make use of copper? I could wish your superiority in the art you profess, to be preserved in stuff more durable than canvas.' Sir Joshua urged the difficulty of procuring a plate large enough for historical subjects, and was going to raise further objections: 'What foppish [2] obstacles are these! (exclaims on a sudden Dr. Johnson:) Here is Thrale has a thousand tun of copper; you may paint it all round if you will, I suppose; it will serve him to brew in afterwards: Will it not, Sir?' (to my husband who sat by). Indeed Dr. Johnson's utter scorn of painting was such, that I have heard him say, that he should sit very quietly in a room hung round with the works of the greatest masters, and never feel the slightest disposition to turn them if their backs were outermost, unless it might be for the sake of telling Sir Joshua that he *had* turned them [3]. Such speeches may

[1] 'It may be alleged that ... as a false satire ought to be recanted for the sake of him whose reputation may be injured, false praise ought likewise to be obviated, lest the distinction between vice and virtue should be lost,' &c. *Works*, viii. 126. See also *Life*, iv. 82, and *ante*, p. 185.

[2] Johnson defines *foppish* as—

(1) *Foolish, idle, vain.*

(2) *Vain in show; foolishly ostentatious; vain of dress.*

See *post*, p. 219 for 'foppish lamentations.'

[3] He wrote to Miss Reynolds on Oct. 19, 1779:—'You will do me a great favour if you will buy for me the prints of Mr. Burke, Mr. Dyer, and Dr. Goldsmith, as you know good impressions. If any of your own pictures are engraved buy them for me. I am fitting up a little room with prints.' *Letters*, ii. 107. Among his effects that were sold after his death were 146 portraits, of which 61 were framed and glazed. *Life*, iv. 441. See also *ib.* i. 363, *n.* 3.

Horace Walpole wrote on May 6, 1770 (*Letters*, v. 236):—'Another rage is for prints of English portraits; I have been collecting them above thirty years, and originally never gave for a mezzotinto above one or two shillings. The lowest are now a crown; most from half a guinea to a guinea.'

appear

appear offensive to many, but those who knew he was too blind to discern the perfections of an art which applies itself immediately to our eye-sight, must acknowledge he was not in the wrong.

He delighted no more in music than painting[1]; he was almost as deaf as he was blind: travelling with Dr. Johnson was for these reasons tiresome enough. Mr. Thrale loved prospects, and was mortified that his friend could not enjoy the sight of those different dispositions of wood and water, hill and valley, that travelling through England and France affords a man. But when he wished to point them out to his companion[2]: 'Never heed such nonsense,' would be the reply: a blade of grass is always a blade of grass, whether in one country or another: let us if we *do* talk, talk about something; men and women are my subjects of enquiry; let us see how these differ from those we have left behind.'

When we were at Rouen together[3], he took a great fancy to the Abbé Roffette, with whom he conversed about the destruction of the order of Jesuits, and condemned it loudly, as a blow to the general power of the church, and likely to be followed with many and dangerous innovations, which might at length become fatal to religion itself, and shake even the foundation of Christianity[4]. The gentleman seemed to wonder and delight in his conversation: the talk was all in Latin, which

[1] He said of music, 'it excites in my mind no ideas, and hinders me from contemplating my own.' Hawkins's *Johnson*, p. 319. See also *Life*, ii. 409.

[2] The more a man likes scenery the more he dislikes to have it pointed out to him. Johnson was not wholly insensible to scenery. In his *Tour to Wales* he describes how 'the way lay through pleasant lanes, and overlooked a region beautifully diversified with trees and grass.' *Ib.* v. 439. See *ib. n.* 2 for my note on his insensibility to nature, and *post*, p. 323.

[3] In September, 1775. *Life*, ii. 385.

[4] The order was suppressed in France in 1764, and generally in 1773. *Penny Cyclopaedia*, ed. 1839, xiii. 113.

Gibbon, during the alarm caused by the Reign of Terror, 'argued in favour of the Inquisition at Lisbon, and said he would not, at the present moment, give up even that old establishment.' Gibbon's *Misc. Works*, i. 328.

both

both spoke fluently[1], and Mr. Johnson pronounced a long eulogium upon Milton[2] with so much ardour, eloquence, and ingenuity, that the Abbé rose from his seat and embraced him. My husband seeing them apparently so charmed with the company of each other, politely invited the Abbé to England, intending to oblige his friend; who, instead of thanking, reprimanded him severely before the man, for such a sudden burst of tenderness towards a person he could know nothing at all of; and thus put a sudden finish to all his own and Mr. Thrale's entertainment from the company of the Abbé Roffette.

When at Versailles the people shewed us the theatre. As we stood on the stage looking at some machinery for playhouse purposes: Now we are here, what shall we act, Mr. Johnson,—The Englishman at Paris[3]? 'No, no (replied he), we will try to act Harry the Fifth.' His dislike of the French[4] was well known to both nations, I believe; but he applauded the number of their books and the graces of their style[5]. 'They have few sentiments (said he), but they express them neatly; they have little meat too, but they dress it well[6].' Johnson's own

[1] 'While Johnson was in France, he was generally very resolute in speaking Latin. It was a maxim with him that a man should not let himself down, by speaking a language which he speaks imperfectly.' *Life*, ii. 404. For instances of his colloquial Latin see *ib.* ii. 125, *n.* 5, 406.

[2] For Johnson's lofty praise of Milton see *ib.* i. 230.

[3] A comedy by Foote.

[4] In a note on *The Merry Wives of Windsor* he says:—'To be a foreigner was always in England, and I suppose everywhere else, a reason of dislike.' Johnson's *Shakespeare*, ii. 479. But according to Reynolds 'the prejudices he had to countries did not extend to individuals.' *Life*, iv. 169, *n.* 1. See also *ib.* iv. 15.

[5] 'He admitted that the French, though not the highest perhaps in any department of literature, yet in every department were very high.' *Ib.* ii. 125. 'He spoke often in praise of French literature. "The French are excellent in this, (he would say,) they have a book on every subject."' *Ib.* iv. 237. 'There is,' he said, 'perhaps, more knowledge circulated in the French literature than in any other. There is more original knowledge in English.' *Ib.* v. 310. In Macaulay's *Essay on Horace Walpole* (*Essays*, ed. 1843, ii. 107), there is an interesting expansion of the last passage.

[6] During his visit to Paris he says:—'Mr. Thrale keeps us a very fine table; but I think our cookery very bad.' *Life*, ii. 385. 'Their meals are gross.' *Ib.* p. 389. 'Mr.

notions

notions about eating however was nothing less than delicate; a leg of pork boiled till it dropped from the bone, a veal-pye with plums and sugar, or the outside cut of a salt buttock of beef, were his favourite dainties[1]: with regard to drink, his liking was for the strongest, as it was not the flavour, but the effect he sought for, and professed to desire[2]; and when I first knew him, he used to pour capillaire into his Port wine. For the last twelve years however, he left off all fermented liquors[3]. To make himself some amends indeed, he took his chocolate liberally, pouring in large quantities of cream, or even melted butter; and was so fond of fruit, that though he usually eat seven or eight large peaches of a morning before breakfast began[4], and treated them with proportionate attention after dinner again, yet I have heard him protest that he never had quite as much as he wished of wall-fruit, except once in his life, and that was when we were all together at Ombersley, the seat of my Lord Sandys[5]. I was saying to a friend one day, that I did not like

Thrale justly observed that the cookery of the French was forced upon them by necessity; for they could not eat their meat unless they added some taste to it.' *Life*, ii. 403. Arthur Young wrote:—'There is not better beef in the world than at Paris.' *Travels in France* (1792–4), 1890, p. 306. In 1769 there was a tax of fifty shillings upon every ox sold in Paris. Burke's *Works*, ed. 1808, ii. 88.

[1] By *plums* Mrs. Piozzi probably meant raisins. In Johnson's *Dictionary* the second definition of *plum* is *raisin*; *grape dried in the sun*. In the *Art of Cookery*, by a Lady, ed. 1748, p. 134, among the ingredients of a veal-pie are included 'some stoned raisins and currants washed clean, and some sugar.' Opposite the passage in the *Life* (i. 470) where Johnson says, 'This was a good dinner enough, to be sure; but it was not a dinner to *ask* a man to,' Mr. Hussey wrote on the margin of his copy:—'I have more than once allowed him to dine with me on a Buttock of Beef; but he could not expect more at my house.' For his gross feeding see *Life*, i. 467. For the plums with the veal pie see *ante*, p. 109, where he has 'farcimen farinaceum cum uvis passis.'

[2] 'Brandy,' he said, 'will do soonest for a man what drinking *can* do for him.' *Ib.* iii. 381.

[3] Three years before his death he was drinking wine at Mr. Thrale's house. *Ib.* iv. 72.

[4] Susan Burney, describing her visit to Streatham in 1779, says:—'There sat Mrs. Thrale and Dr. Johnson, the latter finishing his breakfast upon peaches. . . . He insisted upon my eating one of his peaches, and, when I had eat it, took a great deal of pains to persuade me to take another.' *Early Diary of F. Burney*, ii. 256.

[5] *Life*, v. 455. Johnson, a few months before his death, wrote to Dr. Brocklesby:—'What I consider as a goose

goose; one smells it so while it is roasting, said I: 'But you, Madam (replies the Doctor), have been at all times a fortunate woman, having always had your hunger so forestalled by indulgence, that you never experienced the delight of smelling your dinner beforehand.' Which pleasure, answered I pertly, is to be enjoyed in perfection by such as have the happiness to pass through Porridge-Island[1] of a morning. 'Come, come (says he gravely), let's have no sneering at what is so serious to so many: hundreds of your fellow-creatures, dear Lady, turn another way, that they may not be tempted by the luxuries of Porridge-Island to wish for gratifications they are not able to obtain: you are certainly not better than all of *them*; give God thanks that you are happier.'

I received on another occasion as just a rebuke from Mr. Johnson, for an offence of the same nature, and hope I took care never to provoke a third; for after a very long summer particularly hot and dry, I was wishing naturally but thoughtlessly for some rain to lay the dust as we drove along the Surry roads.

symptom of radical health, I have a voracious delight in raw summer fruit, of which I was less eager a few years ago.' *Life*, iv. 353.

[1] Porridge-Island is a mean street in London, filled with cook-shops for the convenience of the poorer inhabitants; the real name of it I know not, but suspect that it is generally known by, to have been originally a term of derision. *Note* by Mrs. Piozzi.

'The fine gentleman whose lodgings no one is acquainted with; whose dinner is served up under cover of a pewter plate from the cook's shop in Porridge Island, and whose annuity of a hundred pounds is made to supply a laced suit every year, and a chair every evening to a rout, returns to his bedroom on foot, and goes shivering and supperless to bed, for the pleasure of appearing among people of equal importance with the Quality of Brentford.' *The World*, Nov. 29, 1753, No. 48.

Charles Knight, describing a walk in 1812 from Covent Garden to Pimlico, says:—'We make our way to Charing Cross, deviating a little from the usual route, that I may see how some of the worthy electors of Westminster are lodged and fed. We are in the alleys known in the time of Ben Jonson as the Bermudas but since called the Caribbee Islands . . . Close at hand is Porridge Island, then famous for cook-shops, as in the middle of the previous century . . . We are out of the labyrinth, and are in a neglected open space, on the north of which stands the King's Mews. Trafalgar Square and the National Gallery have swept away these relics of the pride of the Crown and the low estate of the people.' *Passages of a Working Life*, i. 117.

'I cannot bear (replied he, with much asperity and an altered look), when I know how many poor families will perish next winter for want of that bread which the present drought will deny them, to hear ladies sighing for rain, only that their complexions may not suffer from the heat, or their clothes be incommoded by the dust;—for shame! leave off such foppish lamentations, and study to relieve those whose distresses are real.'

With advising others to be charitable however, Dr. Johnson did not content himself. He gave away all he had, and all he ever had gotten, except the two thousand pounds he left behind[1]; and the very small portion of his income which he spent on himself, with all our calculation, we never could make more than seventy, or at most fourscore pounds a year, and he pretended to allow himself a hundred. He had numberless dependents out of doors as well as in, 'who, as he expressed it, did not like to see him latterly unless he brought 'em money.' For those people he used frequently to raise contributions on his richer friends[2]; 'and this (says he) is one of the thousand reasons which ought to restrain a man from drony[3] solitude and useless retirement. Solitude (added he one day) is dangerous to reason, without being favourable to virtue: pleasures of some sort are necessary to the intellectual as to the corporeal health; and those who resist gaiety, will be likely for the most part to fall a sacrifice to appetite; for the solicitations of sense are always at hand, and a dram to a vacant and solitary person is a speedy and seducing relief. Remember (continued he) that the solitary mortal is certainly luxurious, probably superstitious, and possibly mad: the mind stagnates for want of employment, grows morbid, and is extinguished like a candle in foul air[4].'

[1] 'The amount of his property proved to be considerably more than he had supposed it to be.' *Life*, iv. 404.

[2] As for instance he wrote to Reynolds in June, 1784:—'I am ashamed to ask for some relief for a poor man, to whom, I hope, I have given what I can be expected to spare. The man importunes me, and the blow goes round.' *Ib.* iv. 283.

[3] *Dronish* is in Johnson's *Dictionary* but not *drony*.

[4] 'Solitude to Johnson,' wrote Reynolds, 'was horror; nor would he ever trust himself alone but when

It

It was on this principle that Johnson encouraged parents to carry their daughters early and much into company: 'for what harm can be done before so many witnesses? Solitude is the surest nurse of all prurient passions, and a girl in the hurry of preparation, or tumult of gaiety, has neither inclination nor leisure to let tender expressions soften or sink into her heart. The ball, the show, are not the dangerous places[1]: no, 'tis the private friend, the kind consoler, the companion of the easy vacant hour, whose compliance with her opinions can flatter her vanity, and whose conversation can just sooth, without ever stretching her mind, that is the lover to be feared: he who buzzes in her ear at court, or at the opera, must be contented to buzz in vain.' These notions Dr. Johnson carried so very far, that I have heard him say, 'if you would shut up any man with any woman, so as to make them derive their whole pleasure from each other, they would inevitably fall in love, as it is called, with each other; but at six months' end if you would throw them both into public life where they might change partners at pleasure, each would soon forget that fondness which mutual dependance, and the paucity of general amusement alone, had caused, and each would separately feel delighted by their release.'

In these opinions Rousseau apparently concurs with him exactly; and Mr. Whitehead's poem called *Variety*[2], is written solely to elucidate this simple proposition. Prior likewise advises the husband to send his wife abroad, and let her see the world as it really stands——

Powder, and pocket-glass, and beau[3].

employed in writing or reading.' *Life*, i. 144, *n.* 2. See also *ib.* iii. 27, 415.

[1] To Sir Adam Fergusson, 'who expressed some apprehension that the Pantheon would encourage luxury, "Sir (said Johnson), I am a great friend to public amusements, for they keep people from vice."' *Ib.* ii. 169.

'But whatever be the incentives to vice which are found at the theatre, public pleasures are generally less guilty than solitary ones.' Goldsmith's *Present State of Polite Learning*, ch. xii.

[2] This poem by William Whitehead is given in Campbell's *British Poets*, ed. 1845, p. 585.

[3] 'Dear angry friend, what must be done?
Is there no way? there is but one;

Mr.

Mr. Johnson was indeed unjustly supposed to be a lover of singularity. Few people had a more settled reverence for the world than he, or was less captivated by new modes of behaviour introduced, or innovations on the long-received customs of common life [1]. He hated the way of leaving a company without taking notice to the lady of the house that he was going; and did not much like any of the contrivances by which ease has been lately introduced into society instead of ceremony, which had more of his approbation. Cards [2], dress [3], and dancing however, all found their advocates in Dr. Johnson, who inculcated, upon principle, the cultivation of those arts, which many a moralist thinks himself bound to reject, and many a Christian holds unfit to be practised. 'No person (said he one day) goes under-dressed till he thinks himself of consequence enough to forbear carrying the badge of his rank upon his back [4].' And in

Send her abroad, and let her see
That all this mingled mass which she,
Being forbidden, longs to know,
Is a dull farce, an empty show,
Powder, and pocket-glass and beau.'

An English Padlock, l. 55. Prior's *Works*, ed. 1858, p. 85.

[1] See *Life*, ii. 75 for instances of Johnson's censure of singularity. In the *Tatler*, No. 103, it is thus attacked:—'The bearing to be laughed at for singularities teaches us insensibly an impertinent fortitude, and enables us to bear public censure for things which more substantially deserve it.'

Miss Byron says of Sir Charles Grandison's dress:—'*He* scruples not to modernize a little; but then you see that it is in compliance with the fashion, and to avoid singularity; a fault to which great minds are perhaps too often subject, tho' *he* is so much above it.' *Sir C. Grandison*, i. 324. 'Singularity is only pardonable in old age and retirement; I may now be as singular as I please, but you may not.' Chesterfield's *Letters to his Son*, iv. 78.

[2] 'He said, "I am sorry I have not learnt to play at cards. It is very useful in life; it generates kindness and consolidates society."' *Life*, v. 404. See *ib.* iii. 23.

[3] 'It is yet remembered of the learned and pious Nelson [the author of *Fasts and Festivals*] that he was remarkably elegant in his manners and splendid in his dress. He knew, that the eminence of his character drew many eyes upon him; and he was careful not to drive the young or the gay away from religion, by representing it as an enemy to any distinction or enjoyment in which human nature may innocently delight.' *Works*, iv. 138.

The portrait of Nelson, at the top of the staircase in the Bodleian, is of a splendidly-dressed man.

[4] 'You find the King of Prussia dresses plain because the dignity of his character is sufficient.' *Life*, ii. 475. 'Whoever differs from any general custom is supposed both to think and to proclaim himself wiser than the

answer

answer to the arguments urged by Puritans, Quakers, &c. against showy decorations of the human figure, I once heard him exclaim, 'Oh, let us not be found when our Master calls us, ripping the lace off our waistcoats, but the spirit of contention from our souls and tongues! Let us all conform in outward customs, which are of no consequence, to the manners of those whom we live among, and despise such paltry distinctions [1]. Alas, Sir (continued he), a man who cannot get to heaven in a green coat, will not find his way thither the sooner in a grey one.' On an occasion of less consequence, when he turned his back on Lord Bolingbroke in the rooms at Brighthelmstone, he made this excuse: 'I am not obliged, Sir (said he to Mr. Thrale, who stood fretting), to find reasons for respecting the rank of him who will not condescend to declare it by his dress or some other visible mark: what are stars and other signs of superiority made for?'

The next evening however he made us comical amends, by sitting by the same nobleman, and haranguing very loudly about the nature and use and abuse of divorces. Many people gathered round them to hear what was said, and when my husband called him away, and told him to whom he had been talking—received an answer which I will not write down [2].

rest of the world. . . . A young fellow is always forgiven, and often applauded, when he carries a fashion to an excess; but never if he stops short of it. The first is ascribed to youth and fire; but the latter is imputed to an affectation of singularity or superiority.' Chesterfield's *Letters to his Son*, iv. 23.

[1] 'He repeated his observation that the differences among Christians are really of no consequence.' *Life*, iii. 188.

[2] Mrs. Piozzi has noted in the margin:—'He said, "Why, Sir, I did not know the man. If he will put on no other mark of distinction let us make him wear his horns."' Hayward's *Piozzi*, i. 293. He was the nephew of the famous Lord Bolingbroke. He had been divorced from his wife, who thereupon married Topham Beauclerk. *Life*, ii. 246.

Johnson in a note on the last scene in the third act of *The Merry Wives of Windsor* says:—'There is no image which our author appears so fond of as that of a cuckold's horns. Scarcely a light character is introduced that does not endeavour to produce merriment by some allusion to horned husbands.'

Chesterfield wrote to his son on Feb. 11, 1766:—'Lord —, having parted with his wife, now keeps another w—e at a great expense. I fear he is totally undone.' *Letters*, iv. 238. 'Bolingbroke' is the name suppressed. See Mahon's edition, v. 472.

Though

Though no man perhaps made such rough replies as Dr. Johnson, yet nobody had a more just aversion to general satire [1]; he always hated and censured Swift for his unprovoked bitterness against the professors of medicine [2]; and used to challenge his friends, when they lamented the exorbitancy of physicians fees, to produce him one instance of an estate raised by physic in England [3]. When an acquaintance too was one day exclaiming against the tediousness of the law and its partiality; 'Let us hear, Sir (said Johnson), no general abuse; the law is the last result of human wisdom acting upon human experience for the benefit of the public.'

As the mind of Dr. Johnson was greatly expanded, so his first care was for general, not particular or petty morality; and those teachers had more of his blame than praise, I think, who seek to oppress life with unnecessary scruples [4]: 'Scruples would (as he observed) certainly make men miserable, and seldom make them good. Let us ever (he said) studiously fly from those instructors against whom our Saviour denounces heavy judgments, for having bound up burdens grievous to be borne, and laid them on the shoulders of mortal men.' No one had however higher notions of the hard task of true Christianity than Johnson, whose daily terror lest he had not done enough, originated in piety, but ended in little less than disease. Reason-

[1] *Life*, iv. 313. *Post*, p. 327.

[2] Of Dr. Arbuthnot, Swift wrote:—'O if the world had but a dozen Arbuthnots in it I would burn my travels.' Swift's *Works*, xvii. 212. In a poem entitled *In Sickness, Written in Ireland*, 1714, he laments that he is

'Remov'd from kind Arbuthnot's aid,
Who knows his art but not his trade.' *Ib.* x. 157.

Johnson, in his *Life of Swift*, says nothing of this 'unprovoked bitterness.' For his attacks on Swift see *Life*, ii. 65, 318; iv. 61; v. 44.

[3] The Library, the Infirmary and the Observatory at Oxford, which bear Dr. Radcliffe's name, as well as his foundations at University College, are a proof that one doctor at all events raised an estate by physic.

'Johnson,' says Boswell, 'had in general a peculiar pleasure in the company of physicians.' *Ib.* iv. 292. In the *Life of Garth* he says:—'I believe every man has found in physicians great liberality and dignity of sentiment, very prompt effusion of beneficence, and willingness to exert a lucrative art where there is no hope of lucre.' *Works*, vii. 402.

[4] *Ante*, p. 38.

able

able with regard to others, he had formed vain hopes of performing impossibilities himself; and finding his good works ever below his desires and intent, filled his imagination with fears that he should never obtain forgiveness for omissions of duty and criminal waste of time[1]. These ideas kept him in constant anxiety concerning his salvation; and the vehement petitions he perpetually made for a longer continuance on earth, were doubtless the cause of his so prolonged existence; for when I carried Dr. Pepys to him in the year 1782, it appeared wholly impossible for any skill of the physician or any strength of the patient to save him. He was saved that time however by Sir Lucas's prescriptions; and less skill on one side, or less strength on the other, I am morally certain, would not have been enough[2]. He had however possessed an athletic constitution, as he said the man who dipped people in the sea at Brighthelmstone acknowledged; for seeing Mr. Johnson swim[3] in the year 1766, Why Sir (says the dipper), you must have been a stout-hearted gentleman forty years ago.

Mr. Thrale and he used to laugh about that story very often: but Garrick told a better, for he said that in their young days, when some strolling players came to Litchfield, our friend had fixed his place upon the stage, and got himself a chair accordingly; which leaving for a few minutes, he found a man in it at his return, who refused to give it back at the first intreaty: Mr. Johnson however, who did not think it worth his while to make a second, took chair and man and all together, and threw them all at once into the pit. I asked the Doctor if this was a fact? 'Garrick has not *spoiled* it in the telling (said he), it is very *near* true to be sure[4].'

Mr. Beauclerc too related one day, how on some occasion he ordered two large mastiffs into his parlour, to shew a friend who

[1] *Life*, iv. 299.

[2] According to Mrs. Piozzi, it was only by his petitions to heaven that his life was prolonged, for nothing but Sir Lucas Pepys's skill and his own strength saved his life in 1782.

[3] *Life*, ii. 299; iii. 92, *n*. 1.

[4] Garrick gave much the same account to Boswell. *Ib*. ii. 299.

was

was conversant in canine beauty and excellence, how the dogs quarrelled, and fastening on each other, alarmed all the company except Johnson, who seizing one in one hand by the cuff of the neck, the other in the other hand, said gravely, 'Come, gentlemen! where's your difficulty? put one dog out at the door, and I will shew this fierce gentleman the way out of the window:' which, lifting up the mastiff and the sash, he contrived to do very expeditiously, and much to the satisfaction of the affrighted company. We inquired as to the truth of this curious recital. 'The dogs have been somewhat magnified, I believe Sir (was the reply): they were, as I remember, two stout young pointers; but the story has gained but little [1].'

One reason why Mr. Johnson's memory was so particularly exact, might be derived from his rigid attention to veracity; being always resolved to relate every fact as it stood [2], he looked even on the smaller parts of life with minute attention, and remembered such passages as escape cursory and common observers. 'A story (says he) is a specimen of human manners, and derives its sole value from its truth. When Foote [3] has told me something, I dismiss it from my mind like a passing shadow: when Reynolds tells me something, I consider myself as possessed of an idea the more.'

Mr. Johnson liked a frolic or a jest well enough; though he had strange serious rules about it too: and very angry was he if any body offered to be merry when he was disposed to be grave. 'You have an ill-founded notion (said he) that it is clever to turn matters off with a joke (as the phrase is); whereas nothing

[1] 'Topham Beauclerk told me,' writes Boswell, 'that at his house in the country, two large ferocious dogs were fighting. Dr. Johnson looked steadily at them for a little while; and then, as one would separate two little boys, who were foolishly hurting each other, he ran up to them, and cuffed their heads till he drove them asunder.' *Life*, v. 329.

[2] *Ib.* iii. 228 and *post*, p. 297. 'Some indulgence, however, to lying or fiction is given in *humorous* stories, because it is there really agreeable and entertaining, and truth is not of any importance.' Hume's *Essays*, ed. 1770, iv. 138.

[3] 'Foote,' said Johnson, 'is quite impartial, for he tells lies of everybody.' *Life*, ii. 434. See *post*, p. 265.

 produces

produces enmity so certain, as one person's shewing a disposition to be merry when another is inclined to be either serious or displeased.'

One may gather from this how he felt, when his Irish friend Grierson[1], hearing him enumerate the qualities necessary to the formation of a poet, began a comical parody upon his ornamented harangue in praise of a cook, concluding with this observation, that he who dressed a good dinner was a more excellent and a more useful member of society than he who wrote a good poem. 'And in this opinion (said Mr. Johnson in reply) all the dogs in the town will join you.'

Of this Mr. Grierson I have heard him relate many droll stories, much to his advantage as a wit, together with some facts more difficult to be accounted for; as avarice never was reckoned among the vices of the laughing world. But Johnson's various life, and spirit of vigilance to learn and treasure up every peculiarity of manner, sentiment, or general conduct, made his company, when he chose to relate anecdotes of people he had formerly known, exquisitely amusing and comical. It is indeed inconceivable what strange occurrences he had seen, and what surprising things he could tell when in a communicative humour[2]. It is by no means my business to relate memoirs of his acquaintance; but it will serve to shew the character of Johnson himself, when I inform those who never knew him, that no man told a story with so good a grace, or knew so well what would make an effect upon his auditors[3]. When he raised contributions for some distressed author, or wit in want, he often made us all more than amends by diverting descriptions of the lives they were then

[1] 'His Majesty's printer at Dublin, a gentleman of uncommon learning and great wit and vivacity.' *Life*, ii. 116.

[2] '"I have known all the wits," Dr. Johnson said, "from Mrs. Montagu down to Bet Flint." "Bet Flint!" cried Mrs. Thrale. "Pray, who is she?" "Oh, a fine character, madam. She was habitually a slut and a drunkard, and occasionally a thief and a harlot."' Mme. D'Arblay's *Diary*, i. 88.

[3] Hawkins (*Life*, p. 258) says, that 'in the talent of humour there hardly ever was Johnson's equal, except perhaps among the old comedians.'

passing

passing in corners unseen by any body but himself and that odd old surgeon whom he kept in his house to tend the out-pensioners[1], and of whom he said most truly and sublimely, that

> In misery's darkest caverns known,
> His useful care was ever nigh,
> Where hopeless anguish pours her groan,
> And lonely want retires to die[2].

I have forgotten the year, but it could scarcely I think be later than 1765 or 1766, that he was called abruptly from our house after dinner, and returning in about three hours, said, he had been with an enraged author, whose landlady pressed him for payment within doors, while the bailiffs beset him without; that he was drinking himself drunk with Madeira to drown care, and fretting over a novel which when finished was to be his whole fortune; but he could not get it done for distraction, nor could he step out of doors to offer it to sale. Mr. Johnson therefore set away the bottle, and went to the bookseller, recommending the performance, and desiring some immediate relief; which when he brought back to the writer, he called the woman of the house directly to partake of punch, and pass their time in merriment.

It was not till ten years after, I dare say, that something in Dr. Goldsmith's behaviour struck me with an idea that he was the very man, and then Johnson confessed that he was so; the novel was the charming Vicar of Wakefield[3].

[1] Robert Levett. There is no reason to believe that Johnson kept him for that purpose. Levett mainly supported himself by his practice. *Ante*, p. 205, *n.* 2. As Johnson says in his lines on him:—

> 'The modest wants of every day
> The toil of every day supplied.'
> *Life*, iv. 138.

[2] 'In Misery's darkest caverns known,
His ready help was ever nigh,
Where hopeless Anguish pour'd his groan,
And lonely want retir'd to die.'

[3] The 'extreme inaccuracy' of this anecdote is shown by Boswell. *Ib.* i. 416. Of one fact he was ignorant. Goldsmith sold the *Vicar of Wakefield* in 1762 (*ib.* i. 415, *n.* 1), two or three years before Johnson knew the Thrales. The price paid for it was £60. *Ib.* i. 416. 'A fine first edition in two vols. bound in red morocco, published in Salisbury in 1766' was sold in June, 1892, for £96. *Daily News*, July 1, 1892. An autograph letter of Goldsmith to Garrick referring to *She Stoops to Conquer* was sold by auction in 1885 for £34.

There was a Mr. Boyce too, who wrote some very elegant verses printed in the Magazines of five-and-twenty years ago [1], of whose ingenuity and distress I have heard Dr. Johnson tell some curious anecdotes; particularly, that when he was almost perishing with hunger, and some money was produced to purchase him a dinner, he got a bit of roast beef, but could not eat it without ketchup, and laid out the last half-guinea he possessed in truffles and mushrooms, eating them in bed too, for want of clothes, or even a shirt to sit up in.

Another man for whom he often begged, made as wild use of his friend's beneficence as these, spending in punch the solitary guinea which had been brought him one morning; when resolving to add another claimant to a share of the bowl, besides a woman who always lived with him, and a footman who used to carry out petitions for charity, he borrowed a chairman's watch, and pawning it for half a crown, paid a clergyman to marry him to a fellow-lodger in the wretched house they all inhabited, and got so drunk over the guinea bowl of punch the evening of his wedding-day, that having many years lost the use of one leg, he now contrived to fall from the top of the stairs to the bottom,

[1] Mrs. Piozzi places the publication of Samuel Boyse's verses about 1761; he died in 1749. In the *Annual Register*, 1764, ii. 54, a memoir of him is given. Having once pawned his clothes 'he sat up in bed with the blanket wrapt about him, through which he had cut a hole large enough to admit his arm, and placing the paper upon his knee scribbled in the best manner he could the verses he was obliged to make.' When he got some of his clothes out of pawn, to supply the want of a shirt, 'he cut some white paper to slips, which he tied round his wrists, and in the same manner supplied his neck. In this plight he frequently appeared abroad with the additional inconvenience of the want of breeches.' Fielding, in *Tom Jones* (bk. vii. ch. 1), which was published three or four months before Boyse's death, makes 'a very noble quotation' from his poem of *The Deity*.

Johnson told Nichols that 'Boyse translated well from the French, but if any one employed him, by the time one sheet of the work was done he pawned the original. If the employer redeemed it, a second sheet would be completed, and the book again be pawned, and this perpetually. He had very little learning, but wrote verse with great facility, as fast as most men write prose.' *Lit. Anec.* ix. 777. See also *Life*, iv. 408, 442, and *post* in John Nichols's *Anecdotes*.

and

and break his arm, in which condition his companions left him to call Mr. Johnson, who relating the series of his tragicomical distresses, obtained from the Literary Club [1] a seasonable relief [2].

Of that respectable society I have heard him speak in the highest terms, and with a magnificent panegyric on each member, when it consisted only of a dozen or fourteen friends [3]; but as soon as the necessity of enlarging it brought in new faces, and took off from his confidence in the company, he grew less fond of the meeting, and loudly proclaimed his carelessness *who* might be admitted, when it was become a mere dinner club [4].

[1] Steevens, in the *Gent. Mag.* for 1785, p. 98, under the signature of Aldebaran (see Nichols's *Lit. Hist.* v. 443) says:—'Since Mr. Garrick's funeral this association has been called (what I am told, it has never called itself) THE LITERARY CLUB.' Boswell apparently was pleased with the name. *Life*, i. 477; iv. 326; v. 109, *n.* 5.

Literary is not in Johnson's *Dictionary*.

[2] Mrs. Piozzi says this man was Joseph Simpson. Hayward's *Piozzi*, ii. 84. According to the account given of Simpson by Murphy, he was 'a schoolfellow of Dr. Johnson's, a barrister, of good parts, but who fell into a dissipated course of life.... Yet he still preserved a dignity in his deportment.' *Life*, iii. 28. See *ib.* i. 346 for Johnson's letter to him about his father's inexorability on his marriage.

[3] See *ib.* v. 108, where he and Boswell filled the chairs of an imaginary 'very capital University' with members of their Club.

[4] He wrote to Boswell on March 11, 1777:—'It is proposed to augment our club from twenty to thirty, of which I am glad; for as we have several in it whom I do not much like to consort with, I am for reducing it to a mere miscellaneous collection of conspicuous men, without any determinate character.' *Ib.* iii. 106.

Malone, writing about his attempt to get into the Literary club, says:—'I am not quite so anxious as Agmondesham Vesey was, who, I am told, had couriers stationed to bring him the quickest intelligence of his success.' *Hist. MSS. Com.* Twelfth Report, x. App. 344. Vesey was elected on April 2, 1773. Croker's *Boswell*, ed. 1844, ii. 326.

Reynolds wrote to Bishop Percy on Feb. 12, 1783:—'The Club seems to flourish this year; we have had Mr. Fox, Burke and Johnson very often. I mention those because they are, or have been, the greatest truants.' Nichols's *Lit. Hist.* viii. 205.

Macaulay wrote on March 20, 1839:—'I have this instant a note from Lord Lansdowne, who was in the chair of *the* Club yesterday night, to say that I am unanimously elected.' On April 9 he entered in his Diary:—'I went to the Thatched House, and was well pleased to meet the Club for the first time.... I was amused, in turning over the records of the Club, to come upon poor Bozzy's

I *think*

I *think* the original names, when I first heard him talk with fervor of every member's peculiar powers of instructing or delighting mankind, were Sir John Hawkins, Mr. Burke, Mr. Langton, Mr. Beauclerc, Dr. Percy, Dr. Nugent, Dr. Goldsmith, Sir Robert Chambers, Mr. Dyer, and Sir Joshua Reynolds, whom he called their Romulus [1], or said somebody else of the company called him so, which was more likely: but this was, I believe, in the year 1775 or 1776. It was a supper meeting then, and I fancy Dr. Nugent ordered an omelet sometimes on a Friday or Saturday night [2]; for I remember Mr. Johnson felt very painful sensations at the sight of that dish soon after his death, and cried, 'Ah, my poor dear friend! I shall never eat omelet with *thee* again!' quite in an agony. The truth is, nobody suffered more from pungent sorrow at a friend's death than Johnson, though he would suffer no one else to complain of their losses in the same way [3]; 'for (says he) we must either outlive

signature, evidently affixed when he was too drunk to guide his pen.' Trevelyan's *Macaulay*, ed. 1877, ii. 52.

In the winter of 1857-1858 Grote was invited to join the Club, but he refused. When Lord Overstone, after in vain urging him, was taking his leave, Mrs. Grote 'whispered to him, "Slip a shilling into his hand, and enlist him in the name of the Club."' 'Lord O. (ever alive to a joke) accomplished this "legerdemain" on shaking hands, and hurrying down the stairs left Grote laughing over this "impromptu" trick, and exclaiming, as he looked down at the coin, "How very absurd!" He surrendered at discretion and frequented the meetings of "The Club" with more and more relish as years rolled on, confessing that "it certainly was the best literary *talk* to be had in London."' *Life of George Grote*, 1873, p. 240.

[1] Percy, Chambers, and Dyer were not among the original members. Johnson and Chamier are omitted. According to Malone Reynolds 'started the first thought of the Club to Johnson at his own fireside.' *Life*, i. 477; Prior's *Malone*, p. 434. In the *Malone MSS.* in the British Museum, No. 36, is an account of a resolution of the Club to raise a subscription for a monument in St. Paul's to 'Sir J. Reynolds, one of the founders of the Club;' Johnson is mentioned as 'our other founder.'

[2] In 1766 Monday was the night of meeting. In 1772 it was changed to Friday. *Life*, i. 478, *n.* 3. It was no doubt at the Friday meetings that Nugent, who was a Roman Catholic, ordered an omelet. He died on Nov. 12, 1775. *Gentleman's Magazine*, 1775, p. 551.

The Friday Club instituted in Edinburgh, in June 1803, was founded, Lockhart believed, on the model of the Club. Among its original members were Sydney Smith, Scott, Brougham, and Jeffrey. Lockhart's *Scott*, iii. 240.

[3] *Ante*, p. 205.

our

our friends you know, or our friends must outlive us; and I see no man that would hesitate about the choice [1].'

Mr. Johnson loved late hours extremely, or more properly hated early ones [2]. Nothing was more terrifying to him than the idea of retiring to bed, which he never would call going to rest, or suffer another to call so. 'I lie down (said he) that my acquaintance may sleep; but I lie down to endure oppressive misery, and soon rise again to pass the night in anxiety and pain.' By this pathetic manner, which no one ever possessed in so eminent a degree, he used to shock me from quitting his company, till I hurt my own health not a little by sitting up with him when I was myself far from well: nor was it an easy matter to oblige him even by compliance, for he always maintained that no one forbore their own gratifications for the sake of pleasing another, and if one *did* sit up it was probably to amuse one's self. Some right however he certainly had to say so, as he made his company exceedingly entertaining when he had once forced one, by his vehement lamentations and piercing reproofs, not to quit the room, but to sit quietly and make tea for him, as I often did in London till four o'clock in the morning [3]. At Streatham indeed I managed better, having always

[1] 'He that lives must grow old; and he that would rather grow old than die has God to thank for the infirmities of old age.' *Life*, iv. 156. Horace Walpole writes (*Letters*, vi. 475):—'How often do our griefs become our comforts! I know what I wish to-day; not at all what I shall wish to-morrow. Sixty says, You did not wish for *me*, yet you would like to keep me. Sixty is in the right; and I have not a wordmore to say.'

[2] 'Whoever thinks of going to bed before twelve o'clock,' he said, 'is a scoundrel.' *Life*, iii. 1, *n.* 2.

[3] In a note on the King's soliloquy in *Henry V*, Act iv. sc. I. l. 247, he says:—'There is something very striking and solemn in this soliloquy, into which the King breaks immediately as soon as he is left alone. Something like this on less occasions every breast has felt. Reflection and seriousness rush upon the mind upon the separation of a gay company, and especially after forced and unwilling merriment.'

Hawkins records how Johnson, little more than a year before his death, when his three friends of the old Ivy Lane Club, who had met to dine at half an hour after three, could not be prevailed upon to stay beyond ten o'clock, 'left them with a sigh that seemed to come from his heart, lamenting that he was retiring to solitude and cheerless meditation.' *Life*, iv. 435.

some

some friend who was kind enough to engage him in talk, and favour my retreat [1].

The first time I ever saw this extraordinary man was in the year 1764 [2], when Mr. Murphy, who had been long the friend and confidential intimate of Mr. Thrale [3], persuaded him to wish for Johnson's conversation, extolling it in terms which that of no other person could have deserved, till we were only in doubt how to obtain his company, and find an excuse for the invitation. The celebrity of Mr. Woodhouse a shoemaker, whose verses were at that time the subject of common discourse [4], soon

[1] Dr. Burney told Boswell that in the year 1775, 'he very frequently met Dr. Johnson at Mr. Thrale's, at Streatham, where they had many long conversations, often sitting up as long as the fire and candles lasted, and much longer than the patience of the servants subsisted.' *Life*, ii. 407.

[2] In her *Thraliana* she had recorded:—'It was on the second Thursday of the month of January, 1765 that I first saw Mr. Johnson in a room. Murphy . . . so whetted our desire of seeing him soon that we were only disputing *how* he should be invited, *when* he should be invited, and what should be the pretence. At last it was resolved that one Woodhouse, a shoemaker, who had written some verses and been asked to some tables, should likewise be asked to ours, and made a temptation to Mr. Johnson to meet him: accordingly he came [to our house in Southwark] and Mr. Murphy at four o'clock brought Mr. Johnson to dinner. We liked each other so well that the next Thursday was appointed for the same company to meet, exclusive of the shoemaker, and since then Johnson has remained till this day our constant acquaintance, visitor, companion, and friend.' Hayward's *Piozzi*, 2nd ed. i. 13.

Had this passage been published in the first edition I might have spared my readers a note on Johnson's first acquaintance with the Thrales. *Life*, i. 520.

[3] 'They are very old friends,' wrote Miss Burney in 1779, 'and I question if Mr. Thrale loves any man so well.' Mme. D'Arblay's *Diary*, i. 210. For Murphy's introduction to Johnson, see *post*, p. 306.

[4] Mr. R. B. Adam of Buffalo has sent me a copy of the following letter of Woodhouse, dated July 28, 1809. To whom it was written is not apparent: 'I shall now answer your Request concerning the Anecdote relating to Dr. Johnson and myself, which is simply this—I was informed, at the Time, that Dr. Johnson's Curiosity was excited, by what was said of me in the literary World, as a kind of wild Beast from the Country, and express'd a Wish to Mr. Murphy, who was his intimate Friend, to see me. In consequence of which, Mr. Murphy, being acquainted with Mrs. Thrale, intimated to her that both might be invited to dine there; at the same Time; for, until then, Dr. Johnson had never seen Mrs. Thrale, who, no Doubt

afforded

afforded a pretence, and Mr. Murphy brought Johnson to meet him, giving me general cautions not to be surprised at his figure, dress, or behaviour. What I recollect best of the day's talk, was his earnestly recommending Addison's works to Mr. Woodhouse as a model for imitation. 'Give nights and days, Sir (said he), to the study of Addison, if you mean either to be a good writer, or what is more worth, an honest man.' When I saw something like the same expression in his criticism on that author, lately published [1], I put him in mind of his past injunctions to the young poet, to which he replied, 'That he wished the shoemaker might have remembered them as well.' Mr. Johnson liked his new acquaintance so much however, that from that time he dined with us every Thursday through the winter, and in the autumn of the next year he followed us to Brighthelmstone [2], whence we were gone before his arrival; so he was disappointed and enraged, and wrote us a letter expressive of anger [3], which we were very desirous to pacify, and to obtain his company again if possible. Mr. Murphy brought him back to us again very kindly, and from that time his visits grew more frequent, till in the year 1766 his health,

he also much desir'd to see. As a confirmation of this Statement, this Anecdote is related in the Introduction to one of the Folio Editions of the Drs. Dictionary; where I have seen it, or my Memory greatly deceives me. A close Intimacy having grown up betwixt the Dr. and Mrs. Thrale, I was a second Time invited to dine at her Table with the Dr. at which Time the Circumstances took Place which are recorded in your Remarks on the Drs. Works.'

For Johnson's 'contempt of the notice taken of Woodhouse' see *Life*, ii. 127. 'It is said that the solitary and meditative generation of cobblers have produced a larger list of murders and other domestic crimes than any other mechanical trade except the butchers; but the sons of Crispin have, to balance their account, a not less disproportionate catalogue of poets.' Lockhart's *Scott*, iii. 90.

[1] 'Whoever wishes to attain an English style, familiar but not coarse, and elegant but not ostentatious, must give his days and nights to the volumes of Addison.' *Works*, vii. 473. Dr. Beattie wrote to Sir W. Forbes on Sept. 10, 1776, more than five years before the *Life of Addison* was published, 'If I were to give advice to a young man on the subject of English style I would desire him to read Addison day and night.' Forbes's *Beattie*, ed. 1824, p. 237.

[2] *Letters*, i. 120.

[3] This letter has not been published.

which

which he had always complained of, grew so exceedingly bad, that he could not stir out of his room in the court[1] he inhabited for many *weeks* together, I think months.

Mr. Thrale's attentions and my own now became so acceptable to him, that he often lamented to us the horrible condition of his mind, which he said was nearly distracted; and though he charged *us* to make him odd solemn promises of secrecy on so strange a subject, yet when we waited on him one morning, and heard him, in the most pathetic terms, beg the prayers of Dr. Delap[2], who had left him as we came in, I felt excessively affected with grief, and well remember my husband involuntarily lifted up one hand to shut his mouth, from provocation at hearing a man so wildly proclaim what he could at last persuade no one to believe; and what, if true, would have been so very unfit to reveal.

Mr. Thrale went away soon after, leaving me with him, and bidding me prevail on him to quit his close habitation in the court and come with us to Streatham, where I undertook the care of his health, and had the honour and happiness of contributing to its restoration[3]. This task, though distressing enough sometimes, would have been less so had not my mother and he disliked one another extremely, and teized me often with

[1] Johnson's Court, Fleet-Street, into which he moved from Inner Temple Lane between July 15 and Oct. 2, 1765. *Letters*, i. 119, *n*. 2.

[2] Murphy calls Dr. Delap 'Rector of Lewes.' Murphy's *Johnson*, p. 99. In the *Gentleman's Magazine* for 1765, p. 592, is his preferment to the 'united vicarages of Iford and Kingston.' Both parishes are close to Lewes.

He was a poet and a play-wright. Kemble, writing about one of his pieces which was brought out at Drury Lane in 1786, says:—'The *Captives* were set at liberty last night amidst roars of laughter [It was a tragedy.] Cadell bought this sublime piece before it appeared for fifty pounds, agreeing to make it a hundred on its third representation. It has been played three times, and I dare say old Sanctimony will have no remorse in taking the other fifty.' Prior's *Malone*, p. 126.

[3] See *ante*, p. 43, where he records:—'I returned from Streatham, Oct. 1, —66, having lived there more than three months.' In his last letter to her he speaks of 'that kindness which soothed twenty years of a life radically wretched.' *Letters*, ii. 407.

perverse

perverse opposition, petty contentions, and mutual complaints. Her superfluous attention to such accounts of the foreign politics as are transmitted to us by the daily prints and her willingness to talk on subjects he could not endure, began the aversion; and when, by the peculiarity of his style, she found out that he teized her by writing in the newspapers concerning battles and plots which had no existence, only to feed her with new accounts of the division of Poland perhaps, or the disputes between the states of Russia and Turkey, she was exceedingly angry to be sure, and scarcely I think forgave the offence till the domestic distresses of the year 1772 [1] reconciled them to and taught them the true value of each other; excellent as *they both* were, far beyond the excellence of any other man and woman I ever yet saw. As her conduct too extorted his truest esteem, her cruel illness excited all his tenderness [2]; nor was the sight of beauty, scarce to be subdued by disease [3], and wit, flashing through the apprehension of evil, a scene which Dr. Johnson could see without sensibility. He acknowledged himself improved by her piety, and astonished at her fortitude, and hung over her bed with the affection of a parent, and the reverence of a son [4]. Nor did it give me less pleasure to see her sweet mind cleared of all its latent prejudices, and left at liberty to admire and applaud that force of thought and versatility of genius, that comprehensive soul and benevolent heart which attracted and commanded veneration from all, but inspired peculiar sensations of delight mixed with reverence in those who, like her, had the opportunity to observe these qualities, stimulated by gratitude, and actuated

[1] See *post*, in Sir B. Brookby's *Anecdotes*, for Johnson's fabrication of a battle between the Russians and Turks. The first mention in the *Gentleman's Magazine* of the division of Poland is in the number for July, 1772, p. 337, by which time Mrs. Salusbury had been at least a year dangerously ill. *Letters*, i. 172, 180. 'The domestic distresses of 1772' were money difficulties caused by the commercial panic of that year. *Ib.* i. 192, *n.* 3.

[2] Baretti, in a MS. Note on *Piozzi Letters*, i. 81, says that 'Johnson could not much bear Mrs. Salusbury, nor Mrs. Salusbury him, when they first knew each other. But her cancer moved his compassion, and made them friends.'

[3] It must have been a good deal subdued by age, for she was sixty-six when she died.

[4] *Ante*, p. 66.

by

by friendship[1]. When Mr. Thrale's perplexities disturbed his peace, dear Dr. Johnson left him scarce a moment, and tried every artifice to amuse as well as every argument to console him: nor is it more possible to describe than to forget his prudent, his pious attentions towards the man who had some years before certainly saved his valuable life, perhaps his reason, by half obliging him to change the foul air of Fleet-street for the wholesome breezes of the Sussex downs[2].

The epitaph engraved on my mother's monument[3] shews how deserving she was of general applause. I asked Johnson why he named her person before her mind: he said it was, 'because every body could judge of the one, and but few of the other.'

Juxta sepulta est HESTERA MARIA
Thomæ Cotton de Combermere baronetti Cestriensis filia,
Johannis Salusbury armigeri Flintiensis uxor[4].
Forma felix, felix ingenio;
Omnibus jucunda, suorum amantissima.
Linguis artibusque ita exculta
Ut loquenti nunquam deessent
Sermonis nitor, sententiarum flosculi,
Sapientiæ gravitas, leporum gratia:
Modum servandi adeo perita,
Ut domestica inter negotia literis oblectaretur,
Literarum inter delicias, rem familiarem sedulo curaret.
Multis illi multos annos precantibus
diri carcinomatis veneno contabuit,
nexibusque vitæ paulatim resolutis,
e terris—meliora sperans—emigravit.
Nata 1707. *Nupta* 1739. *Obiit* 1773.

Mr. Murphy, who admired her talents and delighted in her company, did me the favour to paraphrase this elegant inscription in verses which I fancy have never yet been published. His

[1] He wrote to Mrs. Thrale shortly before Mrs. Salusbury's death:—'Is it a good or an evil to me that she now loves me? It is surely a good; for you will love me better, and we shall have a new principle of concord; and I shall be happier with honest sorrow than with sullen indifference, and far happier still than with counterfeited sympathy.' *Letters*, i. 216.

[2] It was to Brighton that the Thrales frequently took him.

[3] In Streatham Church.

[4] For Mrs. Piozzi's pedigree see Hayward's *Piozzi*, ii. 6.

fame

fame has long been out of my power to increase as a poet [1]; as a man of sensibility perhaps these lines may set him higher than he now stands. I remember with gratitude the friendly tears which prevented him from speaking as he put them into my hand.

Near this place
Are deposited the remains of
HESTER MARIA,
The daughter of Sir Thomas Cotton of Combermere, in the county of Cheshire, Bart. the wife of
John Salusbury,
of the county of Flint, Esquire. She was born in the year 1707, married in 1739, and died in 1773.

A pleasing form, where every grace combin'd,
With genius blest, a pure enlighten'd mind;
Benevolence on all that smiles bestow'd,
A heart that for her friends with love o'erflow'd:
In language skill'd, by science form'd to please,
Her mirth was wit, her gravity was ease.
Graceful in all, the happy mien [*sic*] she knew,
Which even to virtue gives the limits due;
Whate'er employ'd her, that she seem'd to chuse,
Her house, her friends, her business, or the muse.
Admir'd and lov'd, the theme of general praise,
All to such virtue wish'd a length of days;
But sad reverse! with slow-consuming pains,
Th' envenom'd cancer revell'd in her veins;
Prey'd on her spirits—stole each power away;
Gradual she sunk, yet smiling in decay;
She smil'd in hope, by sore afflictions try'd,
And in that hope the pious Christian died.

The following epitaph on Mr. Thrale, who has now a monument close by her's in Streatham church, I have seen printed and commended in Maty's Review for April 1784 [2]; and a friend has favoured me with a translation.

[1] 'Speaking of Arthur Murphy, whom he very much loved, "I don't know (said Johnson) that Arthur can be classed with the very first dramatick writers; yet at present I doubt much whether we have any thing superiour to Arthur."' *Life*, ii. 127. It is probable that this was said before Goldsmith's plays were written, for Dr. Maxwell who reports it made Johnson's acquaintance in 1754. *Ib.* p. 116.

[2] *A New Review.* By Henry Maty, A.M., 1784, p. 269.

Hic

Hic conditur quod reliquum est
HENRICI THRALE,
Qui res seu civiles, seu domesticas, ita egit,
Ut vitam illi longiorem multi optarent;
Ita sacras,
Ut quam brevem esset habiturus præscire videretur;
Simplex, apertus, sibique semper similis,
Nihil ostentavit aut arte fictum aut cura
Elaboratum.
In senatu[1], *regi patriæque*
Fideliter studuit;
Vulgi obstrepentis contemptor animosus,
Domi inter mille mercaturæ negotia
Literarum elegantiam minimè neglexit[2].
Amicis quocunque modo laborantibus,
Consiliis, auctoritate, muneribus adfuit.
Inter familiares, comites, convivas, hospites,
Tam facili fuit morum suavitate
Ut omnium animos ad se alliceret;
Tam felici sermonis libertate
Ut nulli adulatus, omnibus placeret.
Natus 1724. *Ob.* 1781.
Consortes tumuli habet Rodolphum patrem[3], *strenuum*
fortemque virum, et Henricum filium unicum,
quem spei parentum mors inopina decennem
præripuit[4].
Ita
Domus felix et opulenta, quam erexit
Avus, auxitque pater, cum nepote decidit.
Abi viator[5]*!*
Et vicibus rerum humanarum perspectis,
Æternitatem cogita!

[1] He was member for Southwark for more than fourteen years.

[2] 'On Mr. Barclay becoming a partner in the brewery Johnson advised him not to allow his commercial pursuits to divert his attention from his studies. "A mere literary man," said the Doctor, "is a *dull* man; a man who is solely a man of business is a *selfish* man; but when literature and commerce are united they make a *respectable* man."' Croker's *Boswell*, ed. 1835, x. 122. For *respectable* see *Life*, iii. 241, *n.* 2.

[3] An account of Ralph Thrale is given in the *Life*, i. 490. He died on April 8, 1758, aged 60. Manning and Bray's *History of Sussex*, vol. xxiii. p. 392.

[4] *Life*, ii. 468. Another son, Ralph, had died in infancy. *Letters*, i. 353.

[5] In his *Essay on Epitaphs* (*Works*, v. 263), Johnson says:—'It is improper to address the epitaph to the passenger, a custom which an injudicious veneration for antiquity introduced again at the revival of letters.' He defines *passenger* as 'a traveller; one who is upon the road.'

Here

Here are deposited the remains of
HENRY THRALE,
Who managed all his concerns in the present
world, public and private, in such a manner
as to leave many wishing he had continued
longer in it;
And all that related to a future world,
as if he had been sensible how short a time he
was to continue in this.
Simple, open, and uniform in his manners,
his conduct was without either art or affectation.
In the senate steadily attentive to the true interests
of his king and country,
He looked down with contempt on the clamours
of the multitude:
Though engaged in a very extensive business,
He found some time to apply to polite literature:
And was ever ready to assist his friends
labouring under any difficulties,
with his advice, his influence, and his purse.
To his friends, acquaintance, and guests,
he behaved with such sweetness of manners
as to attach them all to his person:
So happy in his conversation with them,
as to please all, though he flattered none.
He was born in the year 1724, and died in 1781.
In the same tomb lie interred his father
Ralph Thrale, a man of vigour and activity,
And his only son Henry, who died before his father,
Aged ten years.
Thus a happy and opulent family,
Raised by the grandfather, and augmented by the
father, became extinguished with the grandson.
Go, Reader,
And reflecting on the vicissitudes of
all human affairs,
Meditate on eternity.

I never recollect to have heard that Dr. Johnson wrote inscriptions for any sepulchral stones, except Dr. Goldsmith's in Westminster abbey, and these two in Streatham church[1]. He made four lines once, on the death of poor Hogarth, which

[1] For his Latin epitaph on Goldsmith see *Life*, iii. 82; on his wife, *ib.* i. 241, *n.*, and for those on his parents and brother, *ib.* iv. 393. For his English epitaph on Mrs. Jane Bell see *Works*, i. 151.

were

were equally true and pleasing: I know not why Garrick's were preferred to them.

The hand of him here torpid lies,
That drew th' essential form of grace;
Here clos'd in death th' attentive eyes,
That saw the manners in the face [1].

Mr. Hogarth, among the variety of kindnesses shewn to me when I was too young to have a proper sense of them, was used to be very earnest that I should obtain the acquaintance, and if possible the friendship of Dr. Johnson, whose conversation was to the talk of other men, like Titian's painting compared to Hudson's [2], he said: but don't you tell people now, that I say so (continued he), for the connoisseurs and I are at war you know; and because I hate *them*, they think I hate *Titian*—and let them [3]!——Many were indeed the lectures I used to have in my

[1] Garrick consulted Johnson about an epitaph in three stanzas which he had made for Hogarth. Johnson replied:—'Suppose you worked upon something like this:—

'The Hand of Art here torpid lies
That traced the essential form of Grace:
Here death has closed the curious eyes
That saw the manners in the face.
If Genius warm thee, Reader, stay,
If Merit touch thee, shed a tear;
Be Vice and Dulness far away!
Great Hogarth's honour'd dust is here.'

Garrick cut down his own copy to two stanzas, which finally stood as follows:—

'Farewel! great Painter of mankind!
Who reach'd the noblest point of Art,
Whose pictur'd Morals charm the mind,
And thro' the eye correct the heart.
If thou hast Genius, Reader, stay,
If Nature touch thee, drop a tear;
If neither move thee, turn away,
For Hogarth's honour'd dust lies here.' *Letters*, i. 186.

[2] For Hogarth's mistaking Johnson for an idiot see *Life*, i. 146.

Hudson was for a time, 'for want of a better, the principal portrait painter in England.' Reynolds was apprenticed to him. Leslie and Taylor's *Reynolds*, i. 20.

[3] Horace Walpole wrote on May 5, 1761 (*Letters*, iii. 399):—'I went t'other morning to see a portrait Hogarth is painting of Mr. Fox. He told me he had promised, if Mr. Fox would sit as he liked, to make as good a picture as Vandyke or Rubens could. I was silent—"Why now," said he, "you think this very vain, but why should not one speak truth?"

very

very early days from dear Mr. Hogarth, whose regard for my father induced him perhaps to take notice of his little girl, and give her some odd particular directions about dress, dancing, and many other matters interesting now only because they were his. As he made all his talents, however, subservient to the great purposes of morality, and the earnest desire he had to mend mankind, his discourse commonly ended in an ethical dissertation, and a serious charge to me, never to forget his picture of the *Lady's last Stake*[1]. Of Dr. Johnson, when my father and he were talking together about him one day: That man (says Hogarth) is not contented with believing the Bible, but he fairly resolves, I think, to believe nothing *but* the Bible. Johnson (added he), though so wise a fellow, is more like king David than king Solomon; for he says in his haste that all men are liars. This charge, as I afterwards came to know, was but too well founded: Mr. Johnson's incredulity amounted almost to disease[2], and I have seen it mortify his companions exceedingly. But the truth is, Mr. Thrale had a very powerful influence over the Doctor, and could make him suppress many rough answers: he could likewise prevail on him to change his shirt, his coat, or his plate, almost before it came indispensably necessary to the comfortable feelings of his friends[3]: But as I never had any

This *truth* was uttered in the face of his own Sigismonda, which is exactly a maudlin w——, tearing off the trinkets that her keeper had given her, to fling at his head.'

[1] The picture was founded on Colley Cibber's play. Mrs. Thrale, according to Mr. Hayward, when a girl of fourteen, sat to Hogarth for the Lady in this picture. According to her account he said to her:—'You are not fourteen years old yet, I think, but you will be twenty-four, and this portrait will then be like you. 'Tis the lady's last stake; see how she hesitates between her money and her honour. Take you care; I see an ardour for play in your eyes and in your heart; don't indulge it.' Hayward's *Piozzi*, i. 44; ii. 309.

[2] 'He was indeed so much impressed with the prevalence of falsehood, voluntary or unintentional, that I never knew any person who upon hearing an extraordinary circumstance told, discovered more of the *incredulus odi*. He would say, with a significant look and decisive tone, "It is not so. Do not tell this again."' *Life*, iii. 229.

[3] According to Boswell, 'by associating with Mrs. Thrale Johnson's external appearance was much improved.' *Ib.* iii. 325. Her statement that it was her husband who brought about the change is confirmed by the two following passages in Johnson's letters to her:—'My ascendency

ascendency at all over Mr. Johnson, except just in the things that concerned his health, it grew extremely perplexing and difficult to live in the house with him when the master of it was no more[1]; the worse indeed, because his dislikes grew capricious; and he could scarce bear to have any body come to the house whom it was absolutely necessary for me to see[2]. Two gentlemen, I perfectly well remember, dining with us at Streatham in the Summer 1782, when Elliot's brave defence of Gibraltar was a subject of common discourse, one of these men naturally enough begun some talk about red-hot balls thrown with surprizing dexterity and effect[3]: which Dr. Johnson having listened some time to, 'I would advise you, Sir (said he with a cold sneer) never to relate this story again: you really can scarce imagine how *very poor* a figure you make in the telling of it.' Our guest being bred a Quaker[4], and I believe a man of an extremely gentle disposition, needed no more reproofs for the same folly; so if he ever did speak again, it was in a low voice to the friend who came with him. The check was given before dinner[5], and after

cloaths, Mr. Thrale says, must be made like other people's, and they are gone to the taylor.' *Letters*, i. 322. 'I will send directions to the taylor to make me some cloaths according to Mr. Thrale's direction.' *Ib.* ii. 39.

[1] 'I know no man (said Johnson) who is more master of his wife and family than Thrale. If he but holds up his finger he is obeyed.' *Life*, i. 494.

[2] Miss Burney writing of his conduct at Brighton in the late autumn of 1782 says:—'He has been in a terrible severe humour of late, and has really frightened all the people, till they almost ran from him. To me only I think he is now kind, for Mrs. Thrale fares worse than anybody.' Mme. D'Arblay's *Diary*, ii. 177. See also *Life*, iv. 159, *n.* 3.

[3] It was in the autumn of 1782 that the news of the defence reached England. Horace Walpole wrote on Oct. 1 (*Letters*, viii. 286):—'I have this minute received a letter from General Conway with these words:—"I have a piece of good news to tell you, which is the complete and entire defeat of the long-meditated attack on Gibraltar, which began on the 13th [of September] at 3 p.m., and before midnight all the famous batteries were either burnt or sunk by our red-hot balls."'

[4] This Quaker cannot have been Mr. Barclay the purchaser of the brewery, for 'he had never observed any rudeness or violence on the part of Johnson.' Croker's *Boswell*, ed. 1844, x. 123. Johnson told Boswell 'that he liked individuals among the Quakers, but not the sect.' *Life*, ii. 458.

[5] According to Barclay, 'Johnson, like many other men, was always in much better humour after dinner than before.' Croker's *Boswell*, x. 123.

coffee

coffee I left the room. When in the evening however our companions were returned to London, and Mr. Johnson and myself were left alone, with only our usual family about us, 'I did not quarrel with those Quaker fellows,' (said he, very seriously.) You did perfectly right, replied I; for they gave you no cause of offence. 'No offence! (returned he with an altered voice;) and is it nothing then to sit whispering together when *I* am present, without ever directing their discourse towards me, or offering me a share in the conversation?' That was, because you frighted him who spoke first about those hot balls. 'Why, Madam, if a creature is neither capable of giving dignity to falsehood, nor willing to remain contented with the truth, he deserves no better treatment.'

Mr. Johnson's fixed incredulity of every thing he heard, and his little care to conceal that incredulity, was teizing enough to be sure[1]: and I saw Mr. Sharp[2] was pained exceedingly, when relating the history of a hurricane that happened about that time in the West Indies[3], where, for aught I know, he had

[1] 'Talking of Dr. Johnson's unwillingness to believe extraordinary things, I ventured to say, "Sir, you come near Hume's argument against miracles, 'That it is more probable witnesses should lie, or be mistaken, than that they should happen.'"' *Life*, iii. 188. For Hume's argument see *ib.* i. 444, *n.* 3.

'The wisest and most experienced are generally the least credulous. But the man scarce lives who is not more credulous than he ought to be. . . . The natural disposition is always to believe. It is acquired wisdom and experience only that teach incredulity, and they very seldom teach it enough.' Adam Smith's *Moral Sentiments*, ed. 1801, ii. 326.

'It is the business of history to distinguish between the *miraculous* and the *marvellous*; to reject the first in all narrations merely profane and human; to doubt the second; and when obliged by unquestionable testimony, . . . to admit of something extraordinary, to receive as little of it as is consistent with the known facts and circumstances.' Hume's *History of England*, ed. 1773, iii. 143.

[2] Perhaps Richard Sharpe, commonly known as 'Conversation Sharpe.' H. C. Robinson (*Diary*, ii. 412) wrote of him in 1829:—'In his room were five most interesting portraits, all of men he knew—Johnson, Burke and Reynolds, by Reynolds, Henderson by Gainsborough, and Mackintosh by Opie.' Among those present at Johnson's Funeral was a Mr. Sharp. *Letters*, ii. 434. Samuel Sharp, the author of *Letters from Italy* (*Life*, iii. 55), died in 1778.

[3] Probably the hurricane of Oct. 3, 1780, described in the *Annual Register*, 1780, i. 292.

himself

himself lost some friends too, he observed Dr. Johnson believed not a syllable of the account: 'For 'tis *so* easy (says he) for a man to fill his mouth with a wonder, and run about telling the lie before it can be detected, that I have no heart to believe hurricanes easily raised by the first inventor, and blown forwards by thousands more.' I asked him once if he believed the story of the destruction of Lisbon by an earthquake when it first happened: 'Oh! not for six months (said he) at least: I *did* think that story too dreadful to be credited, and can hardly yet persuade myself that it was true to the full extent we all of us have heard [1].'

Among the numberless people however whom I heard him grossly and flatly contradict, I never yet saw any one who did not take it patiently excepting Dr. Burney, from whose habitual softness of manners I little expected such an exertion of spirit: the event was as little to be expected. Mr. Johnson asked his pardon generously and genteelly, and when he left the room rose up to shake hands with him, that they might part in peace [2]. On another occasion, when he had violently provoked Mr. Pepys [3], in a different but perhaps not a less offensive manner, till something much too like a quarrel was grown up between them, the moment he was gone, 'Now (says Dr. Johnson) is Pepys gone home hating me, who love him better than I did before; he spoke in defence of his dead friend [4]; but though I hope *I* spoke better who spoke against him, yet all my eloquence will gain me nothing but an honest man for an enemy!' He did not however

[1] He wrote, I have no doubt, the review in the *Literary Magazine* for 1756 (p. 22), of *A True Account of Lisbon since the Earthquake*, in which it is stated that the destruction was grossly exaggerated. After quoting the writer at length, he concludes:—'Such then is the actual, real situation of *that place which once was* Lisbon, and has been since gazetically and pamphletically quite destroyed, consumed, annihilated!' See *Life*, i. 309, *n.* 3.

[2] *Ib.* iv. 49, *n.* 3.

[3] William Weller Pepys, a Master in Chancery, brother of Sir Lucas Pepys (*Life*, iv. 169), and father of Lord Chancellor Cottenham. Samuel Pepys, the author of the *Diary*, was of the same family. *Letters*, ii. 136, *n.* 1.

[4] The 'dead friend' was Lord Lyttelton. For Miss Burney's account of this quarrel see Mme. D'Arblay's *Diary*, ii. 45, 82, 290, and *Life*, iv. 65, *n.* 1.

ever cordially love Mr. Pepys, though he respected his abilities. 'I knew the dog[1] was a scholar (said he, when they had been disputing about the classics for three hours together one morning at Streatham); but that he had so much taste and so much knowledge I did *not* believe: I might have taken Barnard's word though, for Barnard[2] would not lie.'

We had got a little French print among us at Brighthelmstone, in November 1782, of some people skaiting, with these lines written under:

Sur un mince cristal l'hiver conduit leurs pas,
Le précipice est sous la glace;
Telle est de nos [vos] plaisirs la légère surface;
Glissez, mortels, n'appuyez pas[3].

And I begged translations from every body: Dr. Johnson gave me this;

O'er ice the rapid skaiter flies,
With sport above and death below;
Where mischief lurks in gay disguise,
Thus lightly touch and quickly go.

He was however most exceedingly enraged when he knew that in the course of the season I had asked half a dozen acquaintance to do the same thing, and said, it was a piece of treachery, and done to make every body else look little when compared to my favourite friends the *Pepyses*, whose translations were unquestionably the best. I will insert them, because he *did* say so. This is the distich given me by Sir Lucas, to whom I owe more solid obligations, no less than the power of thanking him for the life he saved[4], and whose least valuable praise is the correctness of his taste:

O'er the ice as o'er pleasure you lightly should glide;
Both have gulphs which their flattering surfaces hide.

[1] For instances of Johnson's use of *dog* see *Life*, vi. 298, to which I must add 'the dog was never good for much' (said of his imperfect eye), *ib.* i. 41, *n.* 2. The definition in his *Dictionary* of *dog*, in its third sense, as *a reproachful name for a man*, does not cover all his uses of the word. The reproach is often mixed with good humour.

[2] *Ante*, p. 168.

[3] 'Un charmant quatrain écrit par le poète Roy au bas d'une gravure de Larmessin.' *Grammaire Littéraire* par P. Larousse, 1880, p. 101.

[4] Pepys knew that her illness in

This

This other more serious one was written by his brother:

Swift o'er the level how the skaiters slide,
  And skim the glitt'ring surface as they go:
Thus o'er life's specious pleasures lightly glide,
  But pause not, press not on the gulph below.

Dr. Johnson seeing this last, and thinking a moment, repeated,

O'er crackling ice, o'er gulphs profound,
  With nimble glide the skaiters play;
O'er treacherous pleasure's flow'ry ground
  Thus lightly skim, and haste away.

Though thus uncommonly ready both to give and take offence, Mr. Johnson had many rigid maxims concerning the necessity of continued softness and compliance of disposition[1]: and when I once mentioned Shenstone's idea, that some little quarrel among lovers, relations, and friends was useful, and contributed to their general happiness upon the whole, by making the soul feel her elastic force, and return to the beloved object with renewed delight[2]:—'Why, what a pernicious maxim is this now (cries Johnson), *all* quarrels ought to be avoided studiously, particularly conjugal ones, as no one can possibly tell where they may end; besides that lasting dislike is often the consequence of occasional disgust, and that the cup of life is surely bitter enough, without squeezing in the hateful rind of resentment.' It was upon something like the same principle, and from his general hatred of refinement, that when I told him how Dr. Collier[3], in order to keep the servants in humour with his favourite dog, by

1783-4 was caused by her love for Piozzi. Hayward's *Piozzi*, i. 220, ii. 53, and Mme. D'Arblay's *Diary*, ii. 284.

[1] 'Were I to write the Life of Dr. Johnson,' said Reynolds, 'I would labour this point, to separate his conduct that proceeded from his passions, and what proceeded from his reason, from his natural disposition seen in his quiet hours.' Leslie and Taylor's *Reynolds*, ii. 462.

[2] 'Were a person to make use of art in procuring the affection of his mistress it were perhaps his most effectual method to contrive a slight estrangement, and then, as it were imperceptibly, bring on a reconciliation. The soul here discovers a kind of elasticity; and being forced back returns with an additional violence.' Shenstone's *Works*, ed. 1791, ii. 213.

[3] Dr. Arthur Collier. *Letters*, ii. 69, *n*. 5, and Hayward's *Piozzi*, ii. 18, 35.

seeming rough with the animal himself on many occasions, and crying out, Why will nobody knock this cur's brains out? meant to conciliate their tenderness towards Pompey; he returned me for answer, 'that the maxim was evidently false, and founded on ignorance of human life: that the servants would kick the dog the sooner for having obtained such a sanction to their severity: and I once (added he) chid my wife for beating the cat before the maid, who will now (said I) treat puss with cruelty perhaps, and plead her mistress's example [1].'

I asked him upon this, if he ever disputed with his wife? (I had heard that he loved her passionately.) 'Perpetually (said he): my wife had a particular reverence for cleanliness, and desired the praise of neatness in her dress and furniture, as many ladies do, till they become troublesome to their best friends, slaves to their own besoms, and only sigh for the hour of sweeping their husbands out of the house as dirt and useless lumber: a clean floor is *so* comfortable, she would say sometimes, by way of twitting; till at last I told her, that I thought we had had talk enough about the *floor*, we would now have a touch at the *ceiling*.'

On another occasion I have heard him blame her for a fault many people have, of setting the miseries of their neighbours half unintentionally, half wantonly before their eyes, shewing them the bad side of their profession, situation, &c.[2] He said, 'she would lament the dependence of pupillage to a young heir, &c., and once told a waterman who rowed her along the Thames in a wherry, that he was no happier than a galley-slave,

[1] 'I never shall forget the indulgence with which he treated Hodge, his cat: for whom he himself used to go out and buy oysters, lest the servants having that trouble should take a dislike to the poor creature.' *Life*, iv. 197.

[2] 'No one ought to remind another of misfortunes of which the sufferer does not complain, and which there are no means proposed of alleviating.' *Rambler*, No. 75. 'Unnecessarily to obtrude unpleasing ideas is a species of oppression.' *Ib.* No. 98. See *Life*, iii. 310, iv. 171 for occasions where Boswell angered Johnson by making him think of some great dignity to which he might have attained.

one

one being chained to the oar by authority, the other by want [1]. I had however (said he, laughing), the wit to get her daughter on my side always before we began the dispute [2]. She read comedy better than any body he ever heard (he said); in tragedy she mouthed too much.'

Garrick told Mr. Thrale however, that she was a little painted puppet, of no value at all, and quite disguised with affectation, full of odd airs of rural elegance; and he made out some comical scenes, by mimicking her in a dialogue he pretended to have overheard: I do not know whether he meant such stuff to be believed or no, it was so comical; nor did I indeed ever see him represent her ridiculously, though my husband did [3]. The intelligence I gained of her from old Levett, was only perpetual illness and perpetual opium. The picture I found of her at Litchfield was very pretty, and her daughter Mrs. Lucy Porter said it was like [4]. Mr. Johnson has told me, that her hair was eminently beautiful, quite *blonde* like that of a baby; but

[1] 'Un jour, en me promenant sur la Tamise, l'un de mes rameurs, voyant que j'étais Français, se mit à m'exalter, d'un air fier, la liberté de son pays, et me dit, en jurant Dieu, qu'il aimait mieux être batelier sur la Tamise qu'archevêque en France.' *Œuvres de Voltaire*, ed. 1821, xliii. 157.

[2] The daughter, Lucy Porter, only lived with them for about two years. She never visited London. *Life*, ii. 462.

[3] Boswell, after giving the description of her which he received from Garrick, continues:—'He probably, as is the case in all such representations, considerably aggravated the picture.' *Ib.* i. 99. See *post* in Percy's *Anecdotes*.

[4] This portrait is in the possession of Colonel G. F. Pearson, of Nantlys, St. Asaph, who had it from his grandfather, the Rev. J. B. Pearson, the husband of the lady who was Lucy Porter's heir. In an interleaved copy of Harwood's *Lichfield*, in the Bodleian, at p. 450, is a picture of Mrs. Johnson, as well as an engraving by T. Cook (1807) of Hogarth's picture of Joseph Porter.

The author of the Memoirs of the *Life and Writings of Dr. Johnson*, (ed. 1785, p. 25), who had some of his information from Mrs. Desmoulins the daughter of Johnson's godfather, says that Mrs. Porter was still handsome at the time of her second marriage. He adds (p. 111):—'She was a lady of great sensibility and worth; so shrewd and cultivated that in the earlier part of their connection he was fond of consulting her in all his literary pursuits, and so handsome that his associates in letters and wit were often very pleasant with him on the strange disparity which, in this respect, subsisted between husband and wife.'

but that she fretted about the colour, and was always desirous to dye it black, which he very judiciously hindered her from doing. His account of their wedding we used to think ludicrous enough—'I was riding to church (says Johnson), and she following on another single horse: she hung back however, and I turned about to see whether she could get her steed along, or what was the matter. I had however soon occasion to see it was only coquetry, and *that I despised*, so quickening my pace a little, she mended hers; but I believe there was a tear or two——pretty dear creature[1]!'

Johnson loved his dinner exceedingly, and has often said in my hearing, perhaps for my edification, 'that wherever the dinner is ill got there is poverty, or there is avarice, or there is stupidity; in short, the family is somehow grossly wrong: for (continued he) a man seldom thinks with more earnestness of any thing than he does of his dinner[2]; and if he cannot get that well dressed, he should be suspected of inaccuracy in other things.' One day when he was speaking upon the subject, I asked him, if he ever huffed his wife about his dinner? 'So often (replied he), that at last she called to me, and said, Nay, hold Mr. Johnson, and do

[1] See *Life*, i. 96, for the account of the ride which Boswell had from Johnson. They rode from Birmingham to Derby, a distance of forty miles. They would pass through Lichfield. Faujas Saint-Fond, who went over the same road more than forty years later, thus describes it:—'Nous partîmes à midi de Derby, et comme les chemins sont encore fort mauvais sur toute cette route, nous eûmes beaucoup de peine à arriver ce jour-là à Birmingham: il était plus de neuf heures du soir lorsque nous entrâmes dans l'auberge, après avoir traversé des bruyères noires et arides et un pays extrêmement sauvage.' *Voyage en Angleterre*, ii. 393.

[2] 'At supper this night he talked of good eating with uncommon satisfaction. "Some people (said he,) have a foolish way of not minding, or pretending not to mind, what they eat. For my part, I mind my belly very studiously, and very carefully; for I look upon it, that he who does not mind his belly will hardly mind anything else."' *Life*, i. 467.

'He who makes his belly his business will quickly come to have a conscience of as large a swallow as his throat.' South's *Sermons*, ii. 283.

'He wrote to Mrs. Thrale on April 15, 1784, at a time when after a long illness his appetite was inordinate:—'I have now an inclination to luxury which even your table did not excite; for till now my talk was more about the dishes than my thoughts.' *Letters*, ii. 389.

not

not make a farce of thanking God for a dinner which in a few minutes you will protest not eatable.'

When any disputes arose between our married acquaintance however, Mr. Johnson always sided with the husband, 'whom (he said) the woman had probably provoked so often, she scarce knew when or how she had disobliged him first. Women (says Dr. Johnson) give great offence by a contemptuous spirit of non-compliance on petty occasions. The man calls his wife to walk with him in the shade, and she feels a strange desire just at that moment to sit in the sun: he offers to read her a play, or sing her a song, and she calls the children in to disturb them, or advises him to seize that opportunity of settling the family accounts. Twenty such tricks will the faithfullest wife in the world not refuse to play, and then look astonished when the fellow fetches in a mistress[1]. Boarding-schools were established (continued he) for the conjugal quiet of the parents: the two partners cannot agree which child to fondle, nor how to fondle them, so they put the young ones to school, and remove the cause of contention. The little girl pokes her head[2], the mother reproves her sharply: Do not mind your mamma, says the father, my dear, but do your own way. The mother complains to me of this: Madam (said I), your husband is right all the while; he is with you but two hours of the day perhaps, and then you teize him by making the child cry. Are not ten hours enough for tuition? And are the hours of pleasure so frequent in life, that

[1] 'Johnson used to say that in all family disputes the odds were in favour of the husband from his superior knowledge of life and manners.' Johnson's *Works* (1787), xi. 210.

Talking to Boswell he said:—'A wife should study to reclaim her husband by more attention to please him. Sir, a man will not, once in a hundred instances, leave his wife and go to a harlot, if his wife has not been negligent of pleasing.' *Life*, ii. 56.

'Sae, whensoe'er they slight their
 maiks[1] at hame,
'Tis ten to ane their wives are
 maist to blame.'
Allan Ramsay's *Gentle Shepherd*, Act i. sc. 2.

[2] The only definition given by Johnson of *poke* is 'to feel in the dark; to search anything with a long instrument.'

[1] Mates.

when

when a man gets a couple of quiet ones to spend in familiar chat with his wife, they must be poisoned by petty mortifications? Put missey to school; she will learn to hold her head like her neighbours, and you will no longer torment your family for want of other talk.'

The vacuity of life had at some early period of his life struck so forcibly on the mind of Mr. Johnson, that it became by repeated impression his favourite hypothesis, and the general tenor of his reasonings commonly ended there, wherever they might begin. Such things therefore as other philosophers often attribute to various and contradictory causes, appeared to him uniform enough; all was done to fill up the time, upon his principle[1]. I used to tell him, that it was like the Clown's answer in All's well that ends well[2], of 'Oh Lord, Sir!' for that it suited every occasion. One man, for example, was profligate and wild, as we call it, followed the girls, or sat still at the gaming-table. 'Why, life must be filled up (says Johnson), and the man who is not capable of intellectual pleasures must content himself with such as his senses can afford.' Another was a hoarder: 'Why, a fellow must do something; and what so easy to a narrow mind as hoarding halfpence till they turn into sixpences.'—Avarice was a vice against which, however, I never much heard Mr. Johnson disclaim[3], till one represented it to him connected with cruelty, or some such disgraceful companion. 'Do not (said he) discourage your children from hoarding, if they have a taste to it: whoever lays up his penny rather than part with it for a cake, at least is not the slave of gross appetite; and shews besides

[1] 'When I, in a low-spirited fit, was talking to him with indifference of the pursuits which generally engage us in a course of action, and inquiring a *reason* for taking so much trouble; "Sir (said he, in an animated tone) it is driving on the system of life."' *Life*, iv. 112.

[2] Act ii. sc. 2.

[3] 'The prospect of penury in age is so gloomy and terrifying, that every man who looks before him must resolve to avoid it; and it must be avoided generally by the science of sparing.' *Rambler*, No. 57.

To Boswell, who had come into his inheritance, he wrote:—'Do not think your estate your own, while any man can call upon you for money which you cannot pay; therefore begin with timorous parsimony. Let it be your first care not to be in any man's debt.' *Life*, iv. 154.

besides a preference always to be esteemed, of the future to the present moment [1]. Such a mind may be made a good one; but the natural spendthrift, who grasps his pleasures greedily and coarsely, and cares for nothing but immediate indulgence, is very little to be valued above a negro.' We talked of Lady Tavistock, who grieved herself to death for the loss of her husband [2] —'She was rich and wanted employment (says Johnson), so she cried till she lost all power of restraining her tears: other women are forced to outlive their husbands, who were just as much beloved, depend on it; but they have no time for grief: and I doubt not, if we had put my Lady Tavistock into a small chandler's shop, and given her a nurse-child to tend, her life would have been saved. The poor and the busy have no leisure for sentimental sorrow [3].' We were speaking of a gentleman who loved his friend—'make him prime minister (says Johnson), and see how long his friend will be remembered [4].' But he had a rougher answer for me, when I commended a sermon preached by an intimate acquaintance of our own at the trading end of the town.

[1] 'Whatever withdraws us from the power of our senses, whatever makes the past, the distant, or the future predominate over the present, advances us in the dignity of thinking beings.' *Life*, v. 334; *Works*, ix. 145.

[2] Horace Walpole wrote on March 19, 1767:—'Lord Tavistock, the Duke of Bedford's only son, has killed himself by a fall and kick of his horse, as he was hunting.... No man was ever more regretted; the honesty, generosity, humility, and moderation of his character endeared him to all the world. The desolation of his family is extreme. Lady Tavistock, passionately in love with him, is six months gone with child.' Walpole's *Letters*, v. 43. She died at Lisbon on Nov. 1, 1768. *Gentleman's Magazine*, 1768, p. 542. The child was Lord William Russell, who, on May 6, 1840, was murdered by his Swiss valet, Courvoisier. Burke's *Peerage*.

[3] 'Dr. Johnson told me the other day he hated to hear people whine about metaphysical distresses, when there was so much want and hunger in the world. I told him I supposed then he never wept at any tragedy but Jane Shore, who had died for want of a loaf. He called me a saucy girl, but did not deny the inference.' Hannah More's *Memoirs*, i. 249. *Jane Shore* is by Nicholas Rowe. Johnson's *Works*, vii. 410, and *post*, p. 284.

[4] See *Life*, iii. 2, where Johnson 'shewed that a man who has risen in the world, must not be condemned too harshly for being distant to former acquaintance, even though he may have been much obliged to them.'

For *prime minister* see *Life*, ii. 355, *n.* 2, and *Letters*, i. 92, *n.* 2.

town. 'What was the subject, Madam (says Dr. Johnson)?' Friendship, Sir (replied I). 'Why now, is it not strange that a wise man, like our dear little Evans [1], should take it in his head to preach on such a subject, in a place where no one can be thinking of it?' Why, what are they thinking upon, Sir (said I)? 'Why, the men are thinking on their money I suppose, and the women are thinking of their mops.'

Dr. Johnson's knowledge and esteem of what we call low or coarse life was indeed prodigious; and he did not like that the upper ranks should be dignified with the name of *the world*. Sir Joshua Reynolds said one day, that nobody *wore* laced coats now [2]; and that once every body wore them. 'See now (says Johnson) how absurd that is; as if the bulk of mankind consisted of fine gentlemen that came to him to sit for their pictures. If every man who wears a laced coat (that he can pay for) was extirpated, who would miss them?' With all this haughty contempt of gentility, no praise was more welcome to Dr. Johnson than

[1] Miss Hawkins (*Memoirs*, i. 65), mentions 'the Rev. Mr. Evans, who having the living of St. Olave's, Tooley Street, was frequently a guest at Mrs. Thrale's table.'

[2] 'Greek, Sir (said Johnson), is like lace; every man gets as much of it as he can.' *Life*, iv. 23. When, in 1749, his *Irene* was acted 'he appeared in one of the side boxes in a scarlet waistcoat, with rich gold lace, and a gold-laced hat.' *Ib.* i. 200. Ruddiman, the Scotch grammarian and Librarian of the Faculty of Advocates, is thus described in 1747:—'His coat was of cloth and of a mixed orange colour; his waistcoat of scarlet-cloth and decorated with broad gold lace. His shirt was ornamented with very deep ruffles.' Chalmers's *Life of Ruddiman*, p. 274.

Lord Chesterfield, writing in 1747 to his son, a boy of about fifteen or sixteen, says:—'If I am rightly informed, I am now writing to a fine Gentleman in a scarlet coat laced with gold, a brocade waistcoat, and all other suitable ornaments.' *Letters to his Son*, i. 261.

When Joseph Andrews had to choose a dress from the wardrobe of his new brother-in-law, Squire Booby, 'the plainest he could find was a blue coat and breeches, with a gold edging, and a red waistcoat with the same.' *Joseph Andrews*, Bk. iv. ch. 4.

Bentham, writing of about the year 1756, says:—'At dinner [at the Duke of Leeds'] my attention was excited by a Mr. Trimmer, an humble dependant of the family, who sat at the bottom of the table and wore gold lace like the rest; for everybody wore gold lace then; but narrow was the gold lace worn by Mr. Trimmer.' Bentham's *Works*, x. 31.

than that which he said had the notions or manners of a gentleman[1]: which character I have heard him define with accuracy, and describe with elegance. 'Officers (he said) were falsely supposed to have the carriage of gentlemen; whereas no profession left a stronger brand behind it than that of a soldier; and it was the essence of a gentleman's character to bear the visible mark of no profession whatever[2].' He once named Mr. Berenger[3] as the standard of true elegance; but some one objecting that he too much resembled the gentleman in Congreve's comedies, Mr. Johnson said, 'We must fix them upon the famous Thomas Hervey[4], whose manners were polished even to acuteness and brilliancy, though he lost but little in solid power of reasoning, and in genuine force of mind.' Mr. Johnson had however an avowed and scarcely limited partiality for all who bore the name or boasted the alliance of an Aston or a Hervey[5]; and when

[1] Mrs. Piozzi, I conjecture, meant to say, 'that which said he had,' &c.

[2] 'Dr. Johnson denied that military men were always the best bred men. "Perfect good breeding, he observed, consists in having no particular mark of any profession, but a general elegance of manners; whereas, in a military man, you can commonly distinguish the *brand* of a soldier, *l'homme d'épée*."' *Life*, ii. 82.

In a note on *All's Well that Ends Wells*, Act ii. sc. 1, he says:—'Every man has observed something peculiar in the strut of a soldier.'

[3] 'Richard Berrenger, Esq., many years Gentleman of the Horse, and first Equerry to his present Majesty.' *Life*, iv. 90. His salary as Gentleman of the Horse was £256. *Court and City Calendar*, 1766, p. 91. His *History and Art of Horsemanship* is reviewed in the *Annual Register* for 1771, ii. 260. In Dodsley's *Collection of Poems*, ed. 1758, vi. 271, are some verses of his *To Mr. Grenville on his intended Resignation*. He compares Grenville to a man intending to drown himself, who hears a voice exclaiming:—

'Consider well, pray, what you do,
And think what numbers live in you;
If you go drown, your woes to ease,
Pray who will keep your lice and fleas?'

The poem ends:—

'Oh, Grenville, then this tale apply,
Nor drown yourself lest I should die;
Compassionate your louse's case,
And keep your own to save his place.'

He seems a strange 'standard of true elegance.'

[4] 'Tom Hervey,' said Johnson, 'though a vicious man, was one of the genteelest men that ever lived.' *Life*, ii. 341. See also *ib.* ii. 32.

[5] Thomas Hervey's brother Henry had married Catherine Aston. *Ib.* i. 83, *n.* 4. Of him Johnson said:—'He was a vicious man, but very kind to me. If you call a dog Hervey I shall love him.' *Ib.* i. 106.

Mr.

Mr. Thrale once asked him which had been the happiest period of his past life? he replied, 'it was that year in which he spent one whole evening with M—y As—n [1]. That indeed (said he) was not happiness, it was rapture; but the thoughts of it sweetened the whole year.' I must add, that the evening alluded to was not passed *tête-à-tête*, but in a select company, of which the present Lord Killmorey [2] was one. 'Molly (says Dr. Johnson) was a beauty and a scholar, and a wit and whig; and she talked all in praise of liberty: and so I made this epigram upon her—She was the loveliest creature I ever saw!!!

Liber ut esse velim, suasisti pulchra Maria,
Ut maneam liber—pulchra Maria, vale!'

Will it do this way in English, Sir (said I)?

Persuasions to freedom fall oddly from you;
If freedom we seek—fair Maria, adieu!

'It will do well enough (replied he); but it is translated by a lady, and the ladies never loved M—y As—n.' I asked him what his wife thought of this attachment? 'She was jealous to be sure (said he), and teized me sometimes when I would let her; and one day, as a fortune-telling gipsey passed us when we were walking out in company with two or three friends in the country, she made the wench look at my hand, but soon repented her curiosity; for (says the gipsey) Your heart is divided, Sir, between a Betty and a Molly: Betty loves you best, but you take most delight in Molly's company: when I turned about to laugh, I saw my wife was crying. Pretty charmer! she had no reason!'

It was, I believe, long after the currents of life had driven him to a great distance from this lady, that he spent much of his time with Mrs. F—zh—b—t [3], of whom he always spoke with esteem

[1] Molly Aston. She was the daughter of Sir Thomas Aston, and wife of Captain Brodie of the navy. *Life*, i. 83; ii. 466. She explained to Johnson a question in political economy which puzzled him and Lord Kames. *Ib.* iii. 340.

[2] Johnson, with the Thrales, visited his house in 1774. 'Lord Kilmorey,' he wrote, 'shewed the place with too much exultation.' *Ib.* v. 433.

[3] Fitzherbert. 'Of her Dr. Johnson said that she had the best understanding he ever met with in any

esteem and tenderness, and with a veneration very difficult to deserve. 'That woman (said he) loved her husband as we hope and desire to be loved by our guardian angel. F—tz-h—b—t was a gay good-humoured fellow, generous of his money and of his meat, and desirous of nothing but cheerful society among people distinguished in *some* way, in *any way*, I think; for Rousseau and St. Austin would have been equally welcome to his table and to his kindness [1]: the lady however was of another way of thinking; her first care was to preserve her husband's soul from corruption; her second, to keep his estate entire for their children: and I owed my good reception in the family to the idea she had entertained, that I was fit company for F—tz-h—b—t, whom I loved extremely [2]. They dare not (said she) swear, and take other conversation-liberties before *you*.' I asked if her husband returned her regard? 'He felt her influence too powerfully (replied Mr. Johnson): no man will be fond of what forces him daily to feel himself inferior. She stood at the door of her Paradise in Derbyshire, like the angel with the flaming sword, to keep the devil at a distance [3]. But she was not immortal, poor dear! she died, and her husband felt at once afflicted and released.' I enquired if she was handsome? 'She

human being.' *Life*, i. 83. See also *ib.* iv. 33, and *Letters*, i. 45, *n.* 6. In the *Gentleman's Magazine* for 1753, p. 148, is a notice of her death, written perhaps by Johnson:—'March 12. Wife of Wm. Fitzherbert of Derby, Esq., in the flower of her age, distinguished for her piety and fine accomplishments.'

[1] Miss Hill Boothby wrote of him to Johnson on Aug. 20, 1755:—'Mr. Fitzherbert and his company arrived here [at Tissington] on Thursday last, all at a loss what to do with themselves in *still life*. They set out yesterday to Derby race, and return on Friday with some forty more people, to eat a turtle." *An Account of the Life of Dr. Johnson*, &c., 1805, p. 113.

[2] 'There was (said Johnson) no sparkle, no brilliancy in Fitzherbert; but I never knew a man who was so generally acceptable. He made every body quite easy, overpowered nobody by the superiority of his talents, made no man think worse of himself by being his rival, seemed always to listen, did not oblige you to hear much from him, and did not oppose what you said.' *Life*, iii. 148. 'What eminence he had was by a felicity of manner; he had no more learning than what he could not help.' *Ib.* iii. 386. He hanged himself in a fit of insanity, after going to see some convicts executed in the morning. *Ib.* ii. 228, *n.* 3.

[3] It is not said either in the Bible or in *Paradise Lost* that it was the devil who was kept at a distance by the flaming sword.

would

would have been handsome for a queen (replied the panegyrist); her beauty had more in it of majesty than of attraction, more of the dignity of virtue than the vivacity of wit.' The friend of this lady, Miss B—thby[1], succeeded her in the management of Mr. F—tzh—b—t's family, and in the esteem of Dr. Johnson; though he told me she pushed her piety to bigotry, her devotion to enthusiasm; that she somewhat disqualified herself for the duties of *this* life, by her perpetual aspirations after the *next*: such was however the purity of her mind, he said, and such the graces of her manner, that Lord Lyttelton and he used to strive for her preference with an emulation that occasioned hourly disgust, and ended in lasting animosity[2]. 'You may see (said he to me, when the Poets Lives were printed), that dear B—thby is at my heart still. She *would* delight in that fellow Lyttelton's company though, all that I could do; and I cannot forgive even his memory the preference given by a mind like her's[3].' I have heard Baretti say, that when this lady died, Dr. Johnson was almost distracted with his grief; and that the friends about him had much ado to calm the violence of his emotion[4]. Dr. Taylor too related once to Mr. Thrale and me, that when he lost his wife, the negro Francis ran away, though in the middle of the night, to Westminster, to fetch Dr. Taylor to his master, who

[1] Miss Hill Boothby. Her mother was a Fitzherbert. *Letters*, i. 45, *n*. 6. For Johnson's letters to her see *ib*. i. 45-53.

[2] Boswell carelessly says that 'Mrs. Thrale suggests that Johnson was offended by *Molly Aston's* preference of his Lordship to him.' *Life*, iv. 57.

[3] Miss Boothby died in 1756 at the age of forty-seven. *An Account of the Life of Dr. Johnson*, &c., p. 143. *The Life of Lyttelton* was published in 1781. It is incredible that Johnson, in whom malice never dwelt, should have nursed a petty resentment so long. He was unwilling to write the *Life*, and tried to get it done by Lyttelton's brother. On his refusal he wrote to him:—'I shall certainly not wantonly nor willingly offend.' *Letters*, ii. 188.

The Rev. John Hussey says in a marginal note on the *Life*, iv. 57:—'Johnson said to me many years before he published his Preface[1], "Lord Lyttelton was a worthy, good man, but so ungracious that he did not know how to be a Gentleman."'

[4] *Ante*, p. 18, and *Letters*, i. 52.

[1] The 'Preface' was the *Life of Lyttelton*. Johnson wrote 'a Preface, biographical and critical, to each Authour.' *Life*, iii. 108.

was all but wild with excess of sorrow, and scarce knew him when he arrived[1]: after some minutes however, the doctor proposed their going to prayers[2], as the only rational method of calming the disorder this misfortune had occasioned in both their spirits. Time, and resignation to the will of God, cured every breach in his heart before I made acquaintance with him[3], though he always persisted in saying he never rightly recovered the loss of his wife. It is in allusion to her that he records the observation of a female critic, as he calls her, in Gay's Life[4]; and the lady of great beauty and elegance, mentioned in the criticisms upon Pope's epitaphs, was Miss Molly Aston[5]. The person spoken of in his strictures upon Young's poetry[6], is the writer of these Anecdotes, to whom he likewise addressed the following verses when he was in the Isle of Sky with Mr. Boswell[7]. The letters written in his journey, I used to tell him, were better than the printed book; and he was not displeased at my having taken the pains to copy them all over[8].

[1] *Life*, i. 238. It was not Francis who took the message, for he did not enter Johnson's service till about a fortnight after Mrs. Johnson's death. *Ib.* i. 239.

[2] According to the account given by Taylor to Boswell, 'Johnson requested him to join with him in prayer.' *Ib.* i. 238.

[3] Five years after he made acquaintance with Mrs. Thrale he recorded of his wife:—'When I recollect the time in which we lived together my grief for her departure is not abated.' *Ante*, p. 51.

[4] 'As a poet he cannot be rated very high. He was, as I once heard a female critick remark, "of a lower order."' *Works*, viii. 70.

[5] 'I once heard a lady of great beauty and excellence object to the fourth line, that it contained an unnatural and incredible panegyrick. Of this let the ladies judge.' *Ib.* viii. 355. The fourth line is in the epitaph on Mrs. Corbet:—

'No arts essay'd, but not to be admir'd.'

[6] 'When he lays hold of an illustration he pursues it beyond expectation, sometimes happily, as in his parallel of Quicksilver with Pleasure, which I have heard repeated with approbation by a lady of whose praise he would have been justly proud, and which is very ingenious, very subtle and almost exact.' *Ib.* viii. 461.

'Pleasures are few, and fewer we enjoy;
Pleasure, like quicksilver, is bright and coy;
We strive to grasp it with our utmost skill;
Still it eludes us, and it glitters still;
If seiz'd at last, compute your mighty gains;
What is it but rank poison in your veins.'

The Universal Passion, Satire v.

[7] *Life*, v. 158; *Letters*, i. 284.

[8] 'Do you keep my letters?' he

Here

Here is the Latin ode:

Permeo terras, ubi nuda rupes
Saxeas miscet nebulis ruinas,
Torva ubi rident steriles coloni
Rura labores.

Pervagor gentes hominum ferorum,
Vita ubi nullo decorata cultu
Squallet informis, tugurique fumis
Fœda latescit.

Inter erroris salebrosa longi,
Inter ignotæ strepitus loquelæ,
Quot modis mecum, quid agat, requiro
Thralia dulcis?

Seu viri curas pia nupta mulcet,
Seu fovet mater sobolem benigna,
Sive cum libris novitate pascit
Sedula mentem:

Sit memor nostri, fideique merces
Stet fides constans, meritoque blandum
Thraliæ discant resonare nomen
Littora Skiæ[1].

On another occasion I can boast verses from Dr. Johnson.—As I went into his room the morning of my birth-day once, and said to him, Nobody sends me any verses now, because I am five-and-thirty years old[2]; and Stella was fed with them till forty-six[3], I remember. My being just recovered from illness and confinement will account for the manner in which he burst out suddenly, for so he did without the least previous hesitation whatsoever, and without having entertained the smallest intention towards it half a minute before:

wrote to her two years later. 'I am not of your opinion that I shall not like to read them hereafter.' *Letters*, i. 361.

[1] For Lord Houghton's version of these lines see *Life*, v. 424.

[2] In one of her memorandum books she gives 1776 as the date of these verses, and in *Thraliana*, 1777. According to an entry in the possession of Mr. Salusbury, she was baptized on January 16, 1740, O. S. (January 27, 1741, N. S.). Hayward's *Piozzi*, i. 40.

[3] Stella was not quite forty-six when she died. Swift wrote verses on her last birth-day, March 13, 1726-7. Swift's *Works*, ed. 1803, xi. 21.

Oft in danger, yet alive,
We are come to thirty-five;
Long may better years arrive,
Better years than thirty-five.
Could philosophers contrive
Life to stop at thirty-five,
Time his hours should never drive
O'er the bounds of thirty-five.
High to soar, and deep to dive,
Nature gives at thirty-five.
Ladies, stock and tend your hive,
Trifle not at thirty-five:
For howe'er we boast and strive,
Life declines from thirty-five[1]:
He that ever hopes to thrive
Must begin by thirty-five;
And all who wisely wish to wive
Must look on Thrale at thirty-five.

'And now (said he, as I was writing them down), you may see what it is to come for poetry to a Dictionary-maker; you may observe that the rhymes run in alphabetical order exactly.'—— And so they do.

Mr. Johnson did indeed possess an almost Tuscan power of improvisation[2]: when he called to my daughter, who was consulting with a friend about a new gown and dressed[3] hat she thought of wearing to an assembly, thus suddenly, while she hoped he was not listening to their conversation,

Wear the gown, and wear the hat,
  Snatch thy pleasures while they last;
Hadst thou nine lives like a cat,
  Soon those nine lives would be past.

[1] Johnson wrote to Mrs. Thrale on August 14, 1780:—'If you try to plague me I shall tell you that, according to Galen, life begins to decline from *thirty-five*.' *Letters*, ii. 192. Dr. John Carlyle, in a note on the first line of Dante's *Inferno*, says:—'Dante speaks of our life as an arch, which we ascend and descend; and in which the highest, or middle point, "is at the thirty-fifth year in men of perfect constitution."'

[2] This word is not in Johnson's *Dictionary*.

[3] 'Your father intends you six suits (three of them dressed suits) at his own expense.' *Clarissa*, ed. 1810, i. 305. I conjecture that 'dress clothes' was originally 'dressed clothes.'

It

It is impossible to deny to such little sallies the power of the Florentines, who do not permit their verses to be ever written down though they often deserve it, because, as they express it, *cosi se perderebbe la poca gloria* [1].

As for translations, we used to make him sometimes run off with one or two in a good humour. He was praising this song of Metastasio,

Deh, se piacer mi vuoi,
Lascia i sospetti tuoi;
Non mi turbar conquesto
Molesto dubitar [2]*:*
Chi ciecamente crede,
Impegna a serbar fede;
Chi sempre inganno aspetta,
Alletta ad ingannar.

Should you like it in English (said he) thus?'

Would you hope to gain my heart,
Bid your teizing doubts depart;
He who blindly trusts, will find
Faith from every generous mind:
He who still expects deceit,
Only teaches how to cheat.

Mr. Baretti coaxed him likewise one day at Streatham out of a translation of Emirena's speech to the false courtier Aquileius [3], and it is probably printed before now, as I think two or three people took copies; but perhaps it has slipt their memories.

Ah! tu in corte invecchiasti, e giurerei
Che fra i pochi non sei tenace ancora

[1] Mrs. Piozzi says in her *Journey through Italy*, i. 239:—'The whole secret of improvisation seems to consist in this—that extempore verses are never written down, and one may easily conceive that much may go off well with a good voice in singing which no one would read if they were once registered by the pen.'

[2] 'Non mi stancar con questo
Molesto-dubitar.'
La Clemenza di Tito, Act 1. sc. 2.

[3] Aquilio. The speech is in Metastasio's *Adriano*, Act ii. sc. 1. It was first inserted in a later edition than that of 1748.

Dell'

Dell' antica onestà[1] *Quando bisogna,*
Saprai sereno in volto
Vezzeggiare un nemico; acciò vi cada,
Aprirgli innanzi un [*il*] *precipizio, e poi*
Piangerne la caduta. Offrirti a tutti,
E non esser che tuo; di false lodi
Vestir le accuse, ed aggravar le colpe
Nel farne la difesa; ognor dal trono
I buoni allontanar; d'ogni castigo
Lasciar l'odio allo scettro, e d'ogni dono
Il merito usurpar: tener nascosto
Sotto un zelo apparente un empio fine;
Ne fabbricar che sulle altrui rouine[2].

Grown old in courts, thou art not surely one
Who keeps the rigid rules of ancient honour;
Well skill'd to sooth a foe with looks of kindness,
To sink the fatal precipice before him,
And then lament his fall with seeming friendship:
Open to all, true only to thyself,
Thou know'st those arts which blast with envious praise,
Which aggravate a fault with feign'd excuses,
And drive discountenanc'd virtue from the throne:
That leave the blame of rigour to the prince,
And of his every gift usurp the merit;
That hide in seeming zeal a wicked purpose,
And only build upon another's ruin.

These characters Dr. Johnson however did not delight in reading, or in hearing of: he always maintained that the world was not half as wicked as it was represented[3]; and he might very well continue in that opinion, as he resolutely drove from him every story that could make him change it; and when Mr. Bickerstaff's flight confirmed the report of his guilt[4], and my husband said in answer to Johnson's astonishment, that he

[1] 'Tu che in corte invecchiasti,
Non dovresti invidiarne. Io giurerei
Che fra 'pochi non sei tenaci ancora
Dell' antica onestà.'

Horace Walpole says of Mrs. Piozzi's *Journey*:—'Her Latin, French and Italian too are so miserably spelt that she had better have studied her own language before she floundered into other tongues.' Walpole's *Letters*, ix. 179.

[2] 'Nè fabbricar que su l'altrui ruine.'

[3] *Ante*, p. 208.

[4] *Life*, ii. 82, *n*. 3.

had

had long been a suspected man: 'By those who look close to the ground, dirt will be seen, Sir (was the lofty reply): I hope I see things from a greater distance.'

His desire to go abroad, particularly to see Italy, was very great[1]; and he had a longing wish too to leave some Latin verses at the Grand Chartreux[2]. He loved indeed the very act of travelling[3], and I cannot tell how far one might have taken him in a carriage before he would have wished for refreshment. He was therefore in some respects an admirable companion on the road, as he piqued himself upon feeling no inconvenience, and on despising no accommodations[4]. On the other hand however, he expected no one else to feel any, and felt exceeding inflamed with anger if any one complained of the rain, the sun, or the dust. 'How (said he) do other people bear them[5]?' As for general uneasiness, or complaints of long confinement in a carriage, he considered all lamentations on their account as proofs of an empty head, and a tongue desirous to talk without materials of conversation[6]. 'A mill that goes without grist (said he) is as good a companion as such creatures.'

I pitied a friend before him, who had a whining wife that found every thing painful to her and nothing pleasing—'He

[1] In the *Life*, iii. 453, I have examined Lord Macaulay's wild assertion that 'of foreign travel . . . Johnson spoke with the fierce and boisterous contempt of ignorance.'

[2] He was perhaps stirred by the Alcaic Ode which Gray, in August, 1741, had written in the Album of the Grande Chartreuse. Mason's *Gray*, ed. 1807, i. 275.

[3] 'In the afternoon, as we were driven rapidly along in the post-chaise, he said to me, "Life has not many things better than this."' *Life*, ii. 453. See also *ib.* iii. 162.

[4] Boswell wrote of the hovel in which they lodged at Glenelg:—'Our bad accommodation here made me uneasy, and almost fretful. Dr. Johnson was calm. I said, he was so from vanity. JOHNSON. "No, Sir, it is from philosophy." It pleased me to see that the *Rambler* could practise so well his own lessons.' *Ib.* v. 146. See, however, *ib.* iv. 284 for his ill-humour over an inn-dinner.

[5] *Ante*, p. 218.

[6] Of the drive from Monboddo to Aberdeen Boswell says:—'We had tedious driving this afternoon, and were somewhat drowsy.' *Life*, v. 83. Of the same drive Johnson writes:—'We did not affect the impatience we did not feel, but were satisfied with the company of each other, as well riding in the chaise as sitting at an inn.' *Works*, ix. 10.

does not know that she whimpers (says Johnson); when a door has creaked for a fortnight together, you may observe—the master will scarcely give sixpence to get it oiled.'

Of another lady, more insipid than offensive, I once heard him say, 'She has some softness indeed, but so has a pillow.' And when one observed in reply, that her husband's fidelity and attachment were exemplary, notwithstanding this low account at which her perfections were rated—'Why, Sir (cries the Doctor), being married to those sleepy-souled women, is just like playing at cards for nothing: no passion is excited, and the time is filled up. I do not however envy a fellow one of those honey-suckle wives for my part, as they are but *creepers* at best, and commonly destroy the tree they so tenderly cling about.'

For a lady of quality, since dead, who received us at her husband's seat in Wales with less attention than he had long been accustomed to, he had a rougher denunciation: 'That woman (cries Johnson) is like sour small-beer, the beverage of her table, and produce of the wretched country she lives in: like that, she could never have been a good thing, and even that bad thing is spoiled [1].' This was in the same vein of asperity, and I believe with something like the same provocation, that he observed of a Scotch lady, 'that she resembled a dead nettle; were she alive (said he), she would sting.'

Mr. Johnson's hatred of the Scotch is so well known [2], and so many of his *bons mots* expressive of that hatred have been

[1] This lady, according to Mrs. Piozzi's marginal note, was Lady Catherine Wynne. Hayward's *Piozzi*, i. 293. Johnson recorded in his *Tour to Wales* on Aug. 21, 1774:—'We went to dinner at Sir Thomas Wynne's,—the dinner mean, Sir Thomas civil, his Lady nothing.' *Life*, v. 449.

[2] 'That he was to some degree of excess a *true-born Englishman*, so as to have entertained an undue prejudice against both the country and the people of Scotland must be allowed. But it was a prejudice of the head, and not of the heart.' *Ib.* ii. 301. See *ib.* ii. 306 for his justification of his feelings. Reynolds says of him:—'The chief prejudice in which he indulged himself was against Scotland, though he had the most cordial friendship with individuals of that country.' Taylor's *Reynolds*, ii. 460.

already

already repeated in so many books and pamphlets, that 'tis perhaps scarcely worth while to write down the conversation between him and a friend of that nation who always resides in London, and who at his return from the Hebrides asked him, with a firm tone of voice, What he thought of his country? 'That it is a very vile country to be sure, Sir [1],' (returned for answer Dr. Johnson.) Well, Sir! replies the other somewhat mortified, God made it. 'Certainly he did (answers Mr. Johnson again); but we must always remember that he made it for Scotchmen, and comparisons are odious, Mr. S—— [2]; but God made hell.'

Dr. Johnson did not I think much delight in that kind of conversation which consists in telling stories: 'every body (said he) tells stories of me, and I tell stories of nobody [3]. I do not recollect (added he), that I have ever told *you*, that have been always favourites, above three stories; but I hope I do not play the Old Fool, and force people to hear uninteresting narratives, only because I once was diverted with them myself.' He was [not] however an enemy to that sort of talk from the famous Mr. Foote, 'whose happiness of manner in relating was such (he said) as subdued arrogance and roused stupidity [4]: *His* stories were truly like those of Biron in Love's Labour Lost [5], so *very* attractive,

> That aged ears play'd truant with [at] his tales,
> And younger hearings were quite ravish'd;
> So sweet and voluble was his discourse.

[1] 'Seeing Scotland,' said Johnson, 'is only seeing a worse England. It is seeing the flower gradually fade away to the naked stalk.' *Life*, iii. 248.

[2] Perhaps Mr. Strahan.

[3] *Ante*, p. 226.

[4] 'Foote,' he said, 'is very entertaining, with a kind of conversation between wit and buffoonery.' *Life*, ii. 155. 'He has a great range for wit; he never lets truth stand between him and a jest, and he is sometimes mighty coarse.' *Ib.* iii. 69. See *ib.* for the way in which he pleased Johnson against his will; *Letters*, ii. 55, where Johnson wishes for a Footeana, and *ante*, p. 225.

[5] *Love's Labour's Lost*, Act ii. sc. 1. l. 74.

These lines with the preceding ones were inscribed by Beauclerk under Garrick's portrait. *Life*, iv. 96.

Of

'Of all conversers however (added he), the late Hawkins Browne was the most delightful with whom I ever was in company: his talk was at once so elegant, so apparently artless, so pure, and so pleasing, it seemed a perpetual stream of sentiment, enlivened by gaiety, and sparkling with images [1].' When I asked Dr. Johnson, who was the *best* man he had ever known? 'Psalmanazar,' was the unexpected reply: he said, likewise, 'that though a native of France, as his friend imagined, he possessed more of the English language than any one of the other foreigners who had separately fallen in his way. Though there was much esteem however, there was I believe but little confidence between them; they conversed merely about general topics, religion and learning, of which both were undoubtedly stupendous examples; and, with regard to true Christian perfection, I have heard Johnson say, 'that George Psalmanazar's piety, penitence, and virtue exceeded almost what we read as wonderful even in the lives of saints [2].'

I forget in what year it was that this extraordinary person lived and died at a house in Old-street [3], where Mr. Johnson was witness to his talents and virtues, and to his final preference of the church of England, after having studied, disgraced, and adorned so many forms of worship [4]. The name he went by, was

[1] 'Isaac Hawkins Browne,' said Johnson, 'one of the first wits of this country, got into Parliament and never opened his mouth.' *Life*, ii. 339. 'Dr. Johnson told us that Browne drank freely for thirty years, and that he wrote his poem *De Animi Immortalitate* in some of the last of these years.' *Ib.* v. 156. 'The pretty Mrs. Cholmondely said she was soon tired of him, because the first hour he was so dull there was no bearing him; the second he was so witty there was no bearing him; the third he was so drunk there was no bearing him.' Hayward's *Piozzi*, i. 294. See *Letters*, ii. 324, *n.* 1, for his gluttony, and Campbell's *British Poets* for specimens of his verses.

[2] 'Once talking of George Psalmanazar, whom he reverenced for his piety, he said:—"I should as soon think of contradicting a Bishop."' *Life*, iv. 274.

I have examined Psalmanazar's penitence in Appendix A to vol. iii. of the *Life*.

[3] He died in Ironmonger Row, Old Street, on May 3, 1763. *Gentleman's Magazine*, 1763, p. 257.

[4] He belonged only to the Church of Rome and the Church of England, though 'he invented an awkward show of worship, turning his face to the rising or setting sun, and pleased to be taken notice of for so doing.' *Life*, iii. 447.

not

not supposed by his friend to be that of his family, but all enquiries were vain; his reasons for concealing his original were penitentiary[1]; he deserved no other name than that of the impostor, he said. That portion of the Universal History[2] which was written by him, does not seem to me to be composed with peculiar spirit, but all traces of the wit and the wanderer were probably worn out before he undertook the work.—His pious and patient endurance of a tedious illness, ending in an exemplary death, confirmed the strong impression his merit had made upon the mind of Mr. Johnson. 'It is so *very* difficult (said he, always) for a sick man not to be a scoundrel[3]. Oh! set the pillows soft, here is Mr. Grumbler o'coming: Ah! let no air in for the world, Mr. Grumbler will be here presently.'

This perpetual preference is so offensive where the privileges of sickness are besides supported by wealth, and nourished by dependence, that one cannot much wonder that a rough mind is revolted by them. It was however at once comical and *touchant*[4] (as the French call it), to observe Mr. Johnson so habitually watchful against this sort of behaviour, that he was often ready to suspect himself of it; and when one asked him gently, how he did?—'Ready to become a scoundrel, Madam (would commonly be the answer): with a little more spoiling you will, I think, make me a complete rascal[5].'

His desire of doing good was not however lessened by his aversion to a sick chamber: he would have made an ill man well by

[1] Mrs. Piozzi means, I suppose, 'penitential.' To his concealment he thought himself obliged, he says, 'out of respect to his country and family.' The excuse seems unsatisfactory, for he tells enough to shew that he came from the South of France, while for his family there was no need of care. It was, he writes, 'ancient but decayed,' and he was the only surviving child. Of his father and mother he had heard nothing since he started on the career of a pious rogue. They must have been dead very many years by the time his *Memoirs* were given to the world. *Life*, iii. 446.

[2] *Letters*, ii. 432.

[3] 'He that contents a sick man,' he wrote, 'a man whom it is impossible to please, has surely done his part well.' *Ib.* ii. 400.

[4] This use of *touchant* seems to show that *touching* was not yet in common use. Johnson gives it in his *Dictionary*, but without any authority.

[5] Quoted in the *Life*, iii. 1.

by any expence or fatigue of his own, sooner than any of the canters. Canter indeed was he none: he would forget to ask people after the health of their nearest relations, and say in excuse, 'That he knew they did not care: why should they? (says he:) every one in this world has as much as they can do in caring for themselves, and few have leisure really to *think* of their neighbours distresses, however they may delight their tongues with *talking* of them [1].'

The natural depravity of mankind and remains of original sin were so fixed in Mr. Johnson's opinion [2], that he was indeed a most acute observer of their effects; and used to say sometimes, half in jest half in earnest, that they were the remains of his old tutor Mandeville's instructions [3]. As a book however, he took care always loudly to condemn the Fable of the Bees, but not without adding, 'that it was the work of a thinking man.'

I have in former days heard Dr. Collier of the Commons [4] loudly condemned for uttering sentiments, which twenty years after I have heard as loudly applauded from the lips of Dr. Johnson, concerning the well-known writer of that celebrated work: but if people will live long enough in this capricious world, such instances of partiality will shock them less and less, by frequent repetition. Mr. Johnson knew mankind, and wished to mend them: he therefore, to the piety and pure religion, the untainted integrity, and scrupulous morals of my earliest and most disinterested friend, judiciously contrived to join a cautious

[1] On April 28, 1768, he wrote to Mrs. Thrale:—'Yet when any man finds himself disposed to complain with how little care he is regarded, let him reflect how little he contributes to the happiness of others, and how little, for the most part, he suffers from their pains . . . Nor can we wonder that, in a state in which all have so much to feel of their own evils, very few have leisure for those of another.' *Letters*, i. 141.

[2] 'Lady Macleod asked if no man was naturally good. JOHNSON. "No, Madam, no more than a wolf." BOSWELL. "Nor no woman, Sir?" JOHNSON. "No, Sir." Lady Macleod started at this, saying in a low voice, "This is worse than Swift."' *Life*, v. 211.

[3] *Ante*, p. 207.

[4] *Ante*, p. 246.

not

attention to the capacity of his hearers, and a prudent resolution not to lessen the influence of his learning and virtue, by casual freaks of humour, and irregular starts of ill-managed merriment. He did not wish to confound, but to inform his auditors[1]; and though he did not appear to solicit benevolence, he always wished to retain authority, and leave his company impressed with the idea, that it was his to teach in this world, and theirs to learn. What wonder then that all should receive with docility from Johnson those doctrines, which propagated by Collier they drove away from them with shouts! Dr. Johnson was not grave however because he knew not how to be merry. No man loved laughing better, and his vein of humour was rich, and apparently inexhaustible[2]; Though Dr. Goldsmith said once to him, We should change companions oftener, we exhaust one another, and shall soon be both of us worn out[3]. Poor Goldsmith was to him indeed like the earthen pot to the iron one in Fontaine's fables; it had been better for *him* perhaps, that they had changed companions oftener; yet no experience of his antagonist's strength hindered him from continuing the contest[4]. He used to remind me always of that verse in Berni,

> *Il pover uomo che non sen' èra accorto,*
> *Andava combattendo—ed era morto.*

Mr. Johnson made him a comical answer one day, when seeming to repine at the success of Beattie's Essay on Truth[5]—'Here's such a stir (said he) about a fellow that has written one book,

[1] *Ante*, p. 213.

[2] 'In the talent of humour,' writes Hawkins, 'there hardly ever was Johnson's equal, except perhaps among the old comedians.' Hawkins's *Johnson*, p. 139. See *post*, pp. 287, 345.

[3] 'Dr. Goldsmith said once to Dr. Johnson, that he wished for some additional members to the LITERARY CLUB, to give it an agreeable variety; for (said he,) there can now be nothing new among us; we have travelled over one another's minds. Johnson seemed a little angry, and said, "Sir, you have not travelled over *my* mind, I promise you."' *Life*, iv. 183.

[4] Boswell speaks of that 'vanity which often excited Goldsmith to occasional competition' with Johnson. *Ib.* i. 417; ii. 216, 257. He admits, however, that 'he was often very fortunate in his witty contests, even when he entered the lists with Johnson himself.' *Ib.* ii. 231.

[5] *Ib.* ii. 201; *Letters of Hume to Strahan*, p. 269.

and

and I have written many.' Ah, Doctor (says his friend), there go two-and-forty sixpences you know to one guinea[1].

They had spent an evening with Eaton Graham[2] too, I remember hearing it was at some tavern; his heart was open, and he began inviting away; told what he could do to make his college agreeable, and begged the visit might not be delayed. Goldsmith thanked him, and proposed setting out with Mr. Johnson for Buckinghamshire in a fortnight; 'Nay hold, Dr. *Minor* (says the other), I did not invite you[3].'

Many such mortifications arose in the course of their intimacy to be sure, but few more laughable than when the newspapers had tacked them together as the pedant and his flatterer in Love's Labour lost[4]. Dr. Goldsmith came to his friend, fretting and foaming, and vowing vengeance against the printer, &c. till Mr. Johnson, tired of the bustle, and desirous to think of something else, cried out at last, 'Why, what would'st thou have, dear Doctor! who the plague is hurt with all this nonsense? and how is a man the worse I wonder in his health, purse, or character, for being called *Holofernes*?' I do not know (replies the other) how you may relish being called Holofernes, but I do not like at least to play *Goodman Dull*[5].

Dr. Johnson was indeed famous for disregarding public abuse. When the people criticised and answered his pamphlets, papers, &c. 'Why now, these fellows are only advertising my book (he would say); it is surely better a man should be abused than forgotten.

[1] 'Le maréchal de Rochefort, capitaine des gardes-du-corps, mourut. Il était le favori de M. de Louvois, qui à la mort de M. de Turenne l'avait fait faire maréchal de France avec les autres, dont le Français, fertile en bons mots, disait que le roi avait changé une pièce d'or en monnaie.' *Mémoires du Duc de Saint-Simon*, ed. 1829, iii. 386.

[2] Rev. George Graham of Eton College.

[3] See *Life*, v. 97, for Johnson's account of this incident.

[4] *Love's Labour's Lost.*

[5] Prior in his *Life of Goldsmith*, ii. 283, quotes the article in which the two men had been thus ridiculed. It is found, he says, in the *St. James's Chronicle*, June 14, 1770. This number is not in the British Museum.

forgotten[1].' When Churchill nettled him however, it is certain he felt the sting, or that poet's works would hardly have been left out of the edition. Of that however I have no right to decide;

[1] *Life*, ii. 335; iii. 375; v. 273, 400.

Johnson, as Boswell believed, only once in his life replied to an attack. *Ib.* i. 314. To the instances of authors who laid down this rule, given *ib.* ii. 61, *n.* 4, I would add the following:—'Silence or a negligent indifference has a deeper way of wounding than opposition; because opposition proceeds from an anger that has a sort of generous sentiment for the adversary mingling along with it, while it shows that there is some esteem in your mind for him; in short that you think him worth while to contest with: but silence, or a negligent indifference, proceeds from anger, mixed with a scorn that shows another he is thought by you too contemptible to be regarded.' *The Spectator*, No. 538.

'De quelque source que partent ces outrages, il est sûr qu'un homme qui n'est attaqué que dans ses écrits ne doit jamais répondre aux critiques; car si elles sont bonnes, il n'a autre chose à faire qu'à se corriger; et si elles sont mauvaises, elles meurent en naissant. Souvenous-nous de la fable du Boccalini, "Un voyageur, dit-il, était importuné, dans son chemin, du bruit des cigales; il s'arrêta pour les tuer; il n'en vint pas à bout, et ne fit que s'écarter de sa route: il n'avait qu'à continuer paisiblement son voyage; les cigales seraient mortes d'elles-mêmes au bout de huit jours."' *Œuvres de Voltaire*, ed. 1819, ii. 329.

'Addison knew the policy of literature too well to make his enemy important by drawing the attention of the public upon a criticism which, though sometimes intemperate, was often irrefragable.' Johnson's *Works*, vii. 436. 'If we can suppose Dryden vexed [by Prior and Montague's attack] it would be hard to deny him sense enough to conceal his uneasiness.' *Ib.* viii. 2.

Hume wrote in 1762:—'As I had fixed a resolution, in the beginning of my life, always to leave the public to judge between my adversaries and me, without making any reply, I must adhere inviolably to this resolution.' Burton's *Hume*, ii. 118.

Sir Walter Scott wrote on Jan. 31, 1817:—'I considered always that, by subjecting myself to the irritability which much greater authors have felt on occasions of literary dispute, I should be laying in a plentiful stock of unhappiness for the rest of my life. I therefore made it a rule never to read the attacks made upon me.' Lockhart's *Scott*, ed. 1839, v. 187. A year later he wrote:—'I am so deeply fixed in the opinion that a man lowers his estimation in the public eye by engaging in such controversy, that since I have been dipped in ink I have suffered no personal attacks to provoke me to reply.' *Ib.* v. 301.

'I rejoice,' wrote Charles Darwin, 'that I have avoided controversies, and this I owe to Lyell, who many years ago strongly advised me never to get entangled in a controversy, as it rarely did any good and caused a miserable loss of time and temper.' *Life of Charles Darwin*, ed. 1887, i. 89. He only twice departed from his rule, and in one of the cases he afterwards regretted it. *Ib.* i. 159, *n.*

decide[1]; the booksellers perhaps did not put Churchill on their list. I know Mr. Johnson was exceedingly zealous to declare how very little he had to do with the selection[2]. Churchill's works too might possibly be rejected by him upon a higher principle; the highest indeed, if he was inspired by the same laudable motive which made him reject every authority for a word in his dictionary that could only be gleaned from writers dangerous to religion or morality[3]—'I would not (said he) send people to look for words in a book, that by such a casual seizure of the mind might chance to mislead it for ever.' In consequence of this delicacy, Mrs. Montague[4] once observed, That were an angel to give the *imprimatur*, Dr. Johnson's works were among those very few which would not be lessened by a line. That such praise from such a lady should delight him, is not strange; insensibility in a case like that, must have been the result alone of arrogance acting on stupidity. Mr. Johnson had indeed no dislike to the commendations which he knew he deserved: 'What signifies protesting so against flattery (would he cry)! when a person speaks well of one, it must be either true or false, you know; if true, let us rejoice in his good opinion; if he lies, it is a proof at least that he loves more to please me, than to sit silent when he need say nothing[5].'

[1] Nevertheless she has decided it by her certainty.

[2] 'I was somewhat disappointed in finding that the edition of *The English Poets* for which he was to write Prefaces and Lives, was not an undertaking directed by him; but that he was to furnish a Preface and Life to any poet the booksellers pleased. I asked him if he would do this to any dunce's works, if they should ask him. JOHNSON. "Yes, Sir; and *say* he was a dunce."' *Life*, iii. 137. Johnson was charged with not including Goldsmith in the *Lives*, whereas his exclusion was due to the bookseller who had the copyright of *She Stoops to Conquer*. *Ib.* iii. 100, *n.* 1. For Churchill's attack on Johnson see *ib.* i. 319, 406, 419, *n.* 1; iii. 1, *n.* 2.

[3] Boswell makes the same statement, borrowing it, no doubt, from Mrs. Piozzi. *Ib.* i. 189. I have there shown that it is not true.

[4] *Post*, p. 287.

[5] 'JOHNSON. "Nay, Sir, flattery pleases very generally. In the first place, the flatterer may think what he says to be true: but, in the second place, whether he thinks so or not, he certainly thinks those whom he flatters of consequence enough to be flattered."' *Life*, ii. 364.

'*Tu m'aduli, ma tu mi piaci* (you flatter me but you please me) is a very true Italian saying, which self-love, if sincere, would confess.' Chesterfield's *Misc. Works*, iv. 366.

That

That natural roughness of his manner, so often mentioned, would, notwithstanding the regularity of his notions, burst through them all from time to time; and he once bade a very celebrated lady, who praised him with too much zeal perhaps, or perhaps too strong an emphasis (which always offended him), 'consider what her flattery was worth before she choaked *him* with it [1].' A few more winters passed in the talking world shewed him the value of that friend's commendations however, and he was very sorry for the disgusting speech he made her.

I used to think Mr. Johnson's determined preference of a cold monotonous talker over an emphatical and violent one, would make him quite a favourite among the men of *ton*, whose insensibility, or affectation of perpetual calmness, certainly did not give to him the offence it does to many. He loved 'conversation without effort (he said);' and the encomiums I have heard him so often pronounce on the manners of Topham Beauclerc in society, constantly ended in that peculiar praise, that 'it was without *effort* [2].'

We were talking of Richardson who wrote Clarissa: 'You think I love flattery (says Dr. Johnson), and so I do; but a little too much always disgusts me: that fellow Richardson, on the contrary, could not be contented to sail quietly down the stream

[1] For 'the genuine anecdote' see *Life*, iv. 341. The lady was Hannah More.

[2] He disliked a man to be in his talk 'a rapturist,' 'an enthusiast by rule.' *Ib.* ii. 41, *n.*; iv. 33. 'The happiest conversation,' he said, 'is that of which nothing is distinctly remembered but a general effect of pleasing impression.' *Ib.* iv. 50.

'BOSWELL. "Beauclerk has a keenness of mind which is very uncommon." JOHNSON. "Yes, Sir; and everything comes from him so easily. It appears to me that I labour, when I say a good thing." BOSWELL. "You are loud, Sir; but it is not an effort of mind."' *Ib.* v. 76.

Macaulay wrote of Talleyrand:—'There is a poignancy without effort in all that he says which reminded me a little of the character which the wits of Johnson's circle give of Beauclerk.' Trevelyan's *Macaulay*, ed. 1877, i. 235.

Beauclerk, through Charles II, was descended from Henry IV of France, of whom 'Matthieu dit qu'aucun de ses courtisans n'entendait aussi bien que lui à rendre un conte d'une manière plaisante.' *Mémoires de Sully*, ed. 1788, viii. 11, *n.*

of

of reputation, without longing to taste the froth from every stroke of the oar[1].'

With regard to slight insults from newspaper abuse, I have already declared his notions[2]: 'They sting one (says he) but as a fly stings a horse[3]; and the eagle will not catch flies.' He once told me however, that Cummyns the famous Quaker, whose friendship he valued very highly, fell a sacrifice to their insults, having declared on his death-bed to Dr. Johnson, that the pain of an anonymous letter, written in some of the common prints of the day, fastened on his heart, and threw him into the slow fever of which he died[4].

Nor was Cummyns the only valuable member so lost to society: Hawkesworth, the pious, the virtuous, and the wise, for want of that fortitude which casts a shield before the merits of his friend, fell a lamented sacrifice to wanton malice and cruelty, I know not how provoked[5]; but all in turn feel the lash of censure

[1] Mrs. Piozzi says, in a marginal note on one of Johnson's letters:—'Dr. Johnson said, that if Mr. Richardson had lived till *I* came out, my praises would have added two or three years to his life. "For," says Dr. Johnson, "that fellow died merely for want of change among his flatterers; he perished for want of more, like a man obliged to breathe the same air till it is exhausted."' Hayward's *Piozzi*, ii. 77.

[2] *Ante*, p. 270.

[3] Speaking of the attack made by Edwards in his *Canons of Criticism* on Warburton, Johnson said:—'A fly, Sir, may sting a stately horse and make him wince; but one is but an insect, and the other is a horse still.' *Life*, i. 263, *n*. 3.

[4] 'In 1745 my friend Tom Cumming the Quaker, said he would not fight, but he would drive an ammunition cart.' *Ib.* iv. 212. See also *ib.* v. 98, 230.

[5] Hawkesworth was charged with impiety in doubting the efficacy of prayer. According to Malone the attacks made on him 'affected him so much that from low spirits he was seized with a nervous fever, which on account of the high living he had indulged in had the more power on him; and he is supposed to have put an end to his life by intentionally taking an immoderate dose of opium.' Prior's *Malone*, p. 441.

'But what, we are told, completed his chagrin was the notice frequently given in an infamous magazine published at that time, that—"All the amorous passages and descriptions in Dr. Hawk—th's *Collection of Voyages* should be selected and illustrated with a suitable plate." And this, in defiance of public decency, was actually done; and he, whose fame had been raised on his labours in the cause of piety and morals was

censure in a country where, as every baby is allowed to carry a whip, no person can escape except by chance. The unpublished crimes, unknown distresses, and even death itself, however, daily occurring in less liberal governments and less free nations, soon teach one to content one's self with such petty grievances, and make one acknowledge that the undistinguishing severity of newspaper abuse may in some measure diminish the diffusion of vice and folly in Great Britain, and while they fright delicate minds into forced refinements and affected insipidity, they are useful to the great causes of virtue in the soul, and liberty in the state; and though sensibility often sinks under the roughness of their prescriptions, it would be no good policy to take away their licence [1].

Knowing the state of Mr. Johnson's nerves, and how easily they were affected, I forbore reading in a new Magazine one day, the death of a Samuel Johnson who expired that month; but my companion snatching up the book, saw it himself, and contrary to my expectation—'Oh (said he)! I hope that Death will now be glutted with Sam. Johnsons [2], and let me alone for

thus dragged into a partnership in the most detestable depravity that the human mind can invent.' Chalmers's *British Essayists*, xix. Preface, p. 25.

A man who had received, as he had, £6,000 for a mere compilation was scarcely justified in putting an end to his life. He should have left suicide to his publishers, who were great losers by him. See Hume's *Letters to Strahan*, p. 283.

[1] Horace Walpole wrote on Dec. 31, 1769 (*Letters*, v. 211):—'The licentiousness of abuse surpasses all example. The most savage massacre of private characters passes for sport.' Burke wrote two years later:—'Distinction of character seemed at an end; and that powerful incentive to all public and private virtue of establishing a fair fame and of gaining popular applause, which to noble minds is the highest of all rewards, seemed now to be totally cut off, and no longer to be hoped for.' *Annual Register*, 1771, i. 60. A young German, travelling in England in 1782, recorded:—'It is shocking to a foreigner to see what violent satires on men, rather than on things, daily appear in the newspapers, of which they tell me there are at least a dozen, if not more, published every day.' Moritz's *Travels in England*, p. 184. See also *Life*, i. 116, *n.* 1.

[2] Among the contemporaries of Johnson bearing the same name are the following:—

1. Rev. Samuel Johnson, Librarian of St. Martin's in the Fields. *Life*, i. 135.

2. and 3. Rev. William Samuel

some

some time to come: I read of another namesake's departure last week.'—Though Mr. Johnson was commonly affected even to agony at the thoughts of a friend's dying, he troubled himself very little with the complaints they might make to him about ill health [1]. 'Dear Doctor [2] (said he one day to a common acquaintance, who lamented the tender state of his *inside*), do not be like the spider, man; and spin conversation thus incessantly out of thy own bowels.'—I told him of another friend who suffered grievously with the gout—'He will live a vast many years for that (replied he), and then what signifies how much he suffers? but he will die at last, poor fellow, there's the misery; gout seldom takes the fort by a coup-de-main, but turning the siege into a blockade, obliges it to surrender at discretion.'

A lady he thought well of, was disordered in her health—'What help has she called in (enquired Johnson)?' Dr. James [3], Sir; was the reply. 'What is her disease?' Oh, nothing positive, rather a gradual and gentle decline. 'She will die, then, pretty dear (answered he)! When Death's pale horse [4] runs away with persons on full speed, an active physician may possibly give them a turn; but if he carries them on an even slow pace, down hill too! no care nor skill can save them!'

When Garrick was on his last sick-bed, no arguments, or recitals of such facts as I had heard, would persuade Mr. Johnson of his danger [5]: he had prepossessed himself with a notion, that to

Johnson of Connecticut, with whom Johnson corresponded (*Letters*, i. 209), and his son Samuel. G. M. Berkeley's *Poems*, Introduction, p. 452.

4. Samuel Johnson, author of *Hurlo Thrumbo*. Croker's *Boswell*, p. 366, *n.* 6.

5. Samuel Johnson of the Secretary's Office of the India House. *Anecdotes of John Hoole*, by Samuel Hoole, 1803, p. 12.

[1] *Ante*, p. 267.

[2] According to Mrs. Piozzi's marginal note Dr. Delap (*ante*, p. 234). Hayward's *Piozzi*, i. 294.

[3] *Ante*, p. 166.

[4] 'And I looked, and behold a pale horse: and his name that sat on him was Death.' Rev. vi. 8.

[5] Johnson wrote a few weeks after Garrick's death:—'Poor David had doubtless many futurities in his head, which death has intercepted, a death, I believe, totally unexpected; he did not in his last hour seem to think his life in danger.' *Letters*, ii. 86.

to say a man was sick, was very near wishing him so; and few things offended him more, than prognosticating even the death of an ordinary acquaintance. 'Ay, ay (said he), Swift knew the world pretty well, when he said, that

> Some dire misfortune to portend,
> No enemy can match a friend[1].'

The danger then of Mr. Garrick, or of Mr. Thrale, whom he loved better, was an image which no one durst present before his view[2]; he always persisted in the possibility and hope of their recovering [from] disorders from which no human creatures by human means alone ever did recover. His distress for their loss was for that very reason poignant to excess[3]; but his fears of his own salvation were excessive: his truly tolerant spirit, and Christian charity, which *hopeth all things*, and *believeth all things*, made him rely securely on the safety of his friends, while his earnest aspiration after a blessed immortality made him cautious of his own steps, and timorous concerning their consequences. He knew how much had been given, and filled his mind with fancies of how much would be required, till his impressed imagination was often disturbed by them, and his health suffered from the sensibility of his too tender conscience: a real Christian is *so* apt to find his task above his power of performance[4]!

[1] 'Some great misfortune to portend,
No enemy can match a friend.'
Swift's *Works*, ed. 1803, xi. 243.

[2] He wrote to Mrs. Thrale the autumn before Mr. Thrale's death:—'The chief wish that I form is, that Mr. Thrale could be made to understand his true state; to know that he is tottering upon a point, &c.' *Letters*, ii. 200. See *ante*, p. 96, where he records:—'I had constantly prayed for him some time before his death,' and *ib.* for the warnings he had given him.

[3] Murphy says, though certainly with exaggeration, that 'after Garrick's death Johnson never talked of him without a tear in his eye.' Murphy's *Johnson*, p. 145. For his grief for Mr. Thrale see *ante*, p. 205, *n.* 3.

[4] In the last year of his life he wrote to Mrs. Thrale:—'March 10, 1784 . . . Goodness, always wishing to be better, and imputing every deficience to criminal indulgence and every fault to voluntary corruption, never dares to suppose the condition of forgiveness fulfilled, nor what is wanting in the crime supplied by the penitence.' *Letters*, ii. 380. 'March 20, 1784 . . . Write to me no more about *dying with a grace*; when you feel what I have felt in approaching eternity—in fear of soon hearing the sentence of which there is no revocation, you will know the folly.' *Ib.* p. 384.

Mr.

Mr. Johnson did not however give in to ridiculous refinements either of speculation or practice, or suffer himself to be deluded by specious appearances. 'I have had dust thrown in my eyes too often (would he say), to be blinded so. Let us never confound matters of belief with matters of opinion.'—Some one urged in his presence the preference of hope to possession; and as I remember, produced an Italian sonnet on the subject. 'Let us not (cries Johnson) amuse ourselves with subtleties and sonnets, when speaking about hope, which is the follower of faith and the precursor of eternity[1]; but if you only mean those air-built hopes which to-day excites and to-morrow will destroy, let us talk away, and remember that we only talk of the pleasures of hope; we feel those of possession, and no man in his senses would change the last for the first: such hope is a mere bubble, that by a gentle breath may be blown to what size you will almost, but a rough blast bursts it at once. Hope is an amusement rather than a good, and adapted to none but very tranquil minds[2].' The truth is, Mr. Johnson hated what we call unprofitable chat; and to a gentleman who had disserted some time about the natural history of the mouse—'I wonder what such a one would have said (cried Johnson), if he had ever had the luck to see a *lion*[3]!'

I well remember that at Brighthelmstone once, when he was not present, Mr. Beauclerc asserted that he was afraid of spirits; and I, who was secretly offended at the charge, asked him, the first opportunity I could find, What ground he had ever given to the world for such a report? 'I can (replied he) recollect nothing nearer it, than my telling Dr. Lawrence many years ago, that a long time after my poor mother's death, I heard her

[1] 'BOSWELL. "But may not a man attain to such a degree of hope as not to be uneasy from the fear of death?" JOHNSON. "A man may have such a degree of hope as to keep him quiet. You see I am not quiet, from the vehemence with which I talk; but I do not despair."' *Life*, iv. 299.

[2] 'Hope,' he wrote, 'is itself a species of happiness, and perhaps the chief happiness which this world affords.' *Ib.* i. 368. See also *ib.* ii. 350.

[3] Mrs. Piozzi, who had this anecdote from Boswell, spoilt it in the telling. *Ib.* ii. 194.

voice

voice call *Sam*[1]!' What answer did the doctor make to your story, Sir, said I? 'None in the world,' (replied he;) and suddenly changed the conversation. Now as Mr. Johnson had a most unshaken faith, without any mixture of credulity, this story must either have been strictly true, or his persuasion of its truth the effect of disordered spirits. I relate the anecdote precisely as he told it me; but could not prevail on him to draw out the talk into length for further satisfaction of my curiosity.

As Johnson was the firmest of believers without being credulous[2], so he was the most charitable of mortals without being what we call an active friend. Admirable at giving counsel, no man saw his way so clearly; but he would not stir a finger for the assistance of those to whom he was willing enough to give advice: besides that, he had principles of laziness, and could be indolent by rule. To hinder your death, or procure you a dinner, I mean if really in want of one; his earnestness, his exertions could not be prevented, though health and purse and ease were all destroyed by their violence. If you wanted a slight favour, you must apply to people of other dispositions; for not a step would Johnson move to obtain a man a vote in a society, to repay a compliment which might be useful or pleasing, to write a letter of request, or to obtain a hundred pounds a year more for a friend, who perhaps had already two or three. No force could urge him to diligence, no importunity could conquer his resolution of standing still[3].

[1] This is most likely an inaccurate report of the following incident which happened a long time before his mother's death:—'Dr. Johnson said, that one day at Oxford, as he was turning the key of his chamber, he heard his mother distinctly call *Sam*. She was then at Lichfield; but nothing ensued.' *Life*, iv. 94.

[2] 'I would be a Papist if I could (he said); but an obstinate rationality prevents me.' *Ib.* iv. 289. He longed for more evidence of the spiritual world (*ib.* iv. 299); but he had to admit that 'it is still undecided whether or not there has ever been an instance of the spirit of any person appearing after death. All argument is against it; but all belief is for it.' *Ib.* iii. 230. He was 'willing to believe in second sight; but I never could,' he said, 'advance my curiosity to conviction.' *Ib.* ii. 10, *n.* 3.

[3] Boswell quotes most of this paragraph and refers to Mrs. Piozzi's own contradiction of her assertion (*ante*, p. 180). He continues:—'I

'What

'What good are we doing with all this ado (would he say)? dearest Lady, let's hear no more of it!' I have however more than once in my life forced him on such services, but with extreme difficulty.

We parted at his door one evening when I had teized him for many weeks to write a recommendatory letter of a little boy to his school-master; and after he had faithfully promised to do this prodigious feat before we met again—Do not forget dear Dick, Sir, said I, as he went out of the coach: he turned back, stood still two minutes on the carriage-step—'When I have written my letter for Dick, I may hang myself, mayn't I?'—and turned away in a very ill humour indeed [1].

Though apt enough to take sudden likings or aversions to people he occasionally met, he would never hastily pronounce upon their character; and when seeing him justly delighted with Solander's [2] conversation, I observed once that he was a man of great parts who talked from a full mind—'It may be so (said Mr. Johnson), but you cannot know it yet, nor I neither: the pump works well, to be sure! but how, I wonder, are we to decide in so very short an acquaintance, whether it is supplied by a spring or a reservoir?'—He always made a great difference in his

am certain that a more active friend has rarely been found in any age.' *Life*, iv. 344. 'Johnson,' says Murphy (*Essay*, *&c.*, p. 96), 'felt not only kindness but zeal and ardour for his friends.'

[1] 'Dick' was no doubt Richard Burney. Boswell says that in 1778, 'Dr. Johnson not only wrote to Dr. Joseph Warton in favour of Dr. Burney's youngest son, who was to be placed in the college of Winchester, but accompanied him when he went thither.' *Life*, iii. 367. See also *Early Diary of Frances Burney*, ii. 284.

[2] Dr. Solander was a Swede who, with Joseph Banks, accompanied Captain Cook in his first voyage round the world. *Life*, v. 328. Professor Südenberg of the University of Lunde tells me that *Solander* is an artificially formed name after a fashion still common in Sweden, when a man of humble origin rises to a learned profession. Probably Solander or his father had a name which began with *Sol*, to which was added the Greek termination *ander*. Professor Südenberg gave me the following instance of this usage. A clergyman whom he knows is named Evander. He came from the parish of Efocslöf. *Ef* he changed into *Ev*, and added *ander*.

his esteem between talents and erudition; and when he saw a person eminent for literature, though wholly unconversable, it fretted him [1]. 'Teaching such tonies [2] (said he to me one day), is like setting a lady's diamonds in lead, which only obscures the lustre of the stone, and makes the possessor ashamed on't.' Useful and what we call every-day knowledge had the most of his just praise. 'Let your boy learn arithmetic [3], dear Madam,' was his advice to the mother of a rich young heir: 'he will not then be a prey to every rascal which this town swarms with: teach him the value of money, and how to reckon it; ignorance to a wealthy lad of one-and-twenty, is only so much fat to a sick sheep: it just serves to call the *rooks* about him.'

> And all that prey in [on] vice or folly
> Joy to see their quarry fly;
> Here the gamester light and jolly,
> There the lender grave and sly.

These improviso lines, making part of a long copy of verses which my regard for the youth on whose birth-day they were written obliges me to suppress lest they should give him pain [4], shew a mind of surprising activity and warmth; the more so as he was past seventy years of age when he composed them: but nothing more certainly offended Mr. Johnson, than the idea of a man's faculties (mental ones I mean) decaying by time; 'It is not true, Sir (would he say); what a man could once do, he would always do, unless indeed by dint of vicious indolence, and compliance with the nephews and nieces who crowd round an old

[1] *Post*, p. 289.

[2] Webster defines *Tony* as *a simpleton*.

> 'In short, a Pattern and companion fit
> For all the keeping Tonyes of the Pit.'
> Dryden. Prologue to *All For Love*, l. 15.

[3] Writing to one of Mrs. Thrale's daughters he says:—'Nothing amuses more harmlessly than computation, and nothing is oftener applicable to real business or speculative enquiries.' *Letters*, ii. 321. See *post*, p. 295.

[4] The youth was Sir John Lade. *Ante*, p. 213, *n.* 2, and Hayward's *Piozzi*, i. 78. Eight years later Mrs. Piozzi published these lines in her *British Synonomy*, i. 359, whence Boswell copied them for the third edition of the *Life*, iv. 412, *n.* 2. She adds to the wonder by making them 'improviso.' Johnson wrote to her on Aug. 8, 1780:—'You have heard in the papers how . . . is come to age; I have enclosed a short song of congratulation, which you must not show to anybody.' *Letters*, ii. 190. See *post*, in Mr. Hoole's *Anecdotes*.

old fellow, and help to tuck him in, till he, contented with the exchange of fame for ease, e'en resolves to let them set the pillows at his back, and gives no further proof of his existence than just to suck the jelly that prolongs it [1].'

For such a life or such a death Dr. Johnson was indeed never intended by Providence: his mind was like a warm climate, which brings every thing to perfection suddenly and vigorously, not like the alembicated [2] productions of artificial fire, which always betray the difficulty of bringing them forth when their size is disproportionate to their flavour. *Je ferois un Roman tout comme un autre, mais la vie n'est point un Roman*, says a famous French writer; and this was so certainly the opinion of the Author of the Rambler, that all his conversation precepts tended towards the dispersion of romantic ideas, and were chiefly intended to promote the cultivation of

> That which before thee [us] lies in daily life.
> MILTON [3].

And when he talked of authors, his praise went spontaneously to such passages as are sure in his own phrase to leave something behind them useful on common occasions, or observant of common manners. For example, it was not the two *last*, but the two *first*, volumes of Clarissa that he prized; 'For give me a sick bed, and a dying lady (said he), and I'll be pathetic myself: but Richardson had picked the kernel of life (he said), while Fielding was contented with the husk [4].' It was not King

[1] 'There is nothing,' said Johnson, 'against which an old man should be so much upon his guard as putting himself out to nurse.' *Life*, ii. 474. Writing to Mrs. Thrale of her husband he says:—'Every man has those about him who wish to soothe him into inactivity and delitescence, nor is there any semblance of kindness more vigorously to be repelled than that which voluntarily offers a vicarious performance of the tasks of life, and conspires with the natural love of ease against diligence and perseverance.' *Letters*, i. 401.

[2] This word apparently is of Mrs. Piozzi's coining. She seems to be speaking of fruit grown in a hothouse. It is a pity that she forgot to include *alembicated* in her *British Synonymy*.

[3] *Paradise Lost*, viii. 193.

[4] 'In comparing those two writers, he used this expression: 'that there was as great a difference between them as between a man who knew

Lear

Lear cursing his daughters, or deprecating the storm, that I remember his commendations of; but Iago's ingenious malice, and subtle revenge [1]; or prince Hal's gay compliance with the vices of Falstaff, whom he all along despised. Those plays had indeed no rivals in Johnson's favour: 'No man but Shakespeare (he said) could have drawn Sir John [2].'

His manner of criticising and commending Addison's prose, was the same in conversation as we read it in the printed strictures, and many of the expressions used have been heard to fall from him on common occasions [3]. It was notwithstanding observable enough (or I fancied so), that he did never like, though he always thought fit to praise it; and his praises resembled those of a man who extols the superior elegance of high painted porcelain, while he himself always chuses to eat off *plate*. I told him so one day, and he neither denied it nor appeared displeased.

Of the pathetic in poetry he never liked to speak, and the only passage I ever heard him applaud as particularly tender

how a watch was made, and a man who could tell the hour by looking on the dial-plate.' *Life*, ii. 49. See also *ib.* ii. 174. Smollett speaks of 'an amazing knowledge and command of human nature' found in Richardson. *Hist. of England*, v. 382.

[1] 'The fiery openness of Othello, magnanimous, artless, and credulous, boundless in his confidence, ardent in his affection, inflexible in his resolution, and obdurate in his revenge; the cool malignity of Iago, silent in his resentment, subtle in his designs, and studious at once of his interest and his vengeance; the soft simplicity of Desdemona, confident of merit, and conscious of innocence, her artless perseverance in her suit, and her slowness to suspect that she can be suspected, are such proofs of Shakespeare's skill in human nature as, I suppose, it is vain to seek in any modern writer.' Johnson's *Shakespeare*, viii. 472.

[2] 'But Falstaff, unimitated, unimitable Falstaff, how shall I describe thee? Thou compound of sense and vice; of sense which may be admired, but not esteemed, of vice which may be despised, but hardly detested. Falstaff is a character loaded with faults, and with those faults which naturally produce contempt. He is a thief, and a glutton, a coward, and a boaster, always ready to cheat the weak and prey upon the poor; to terrify the timorous and insult the defenceless. . . . Yet the man thus corrupt, thus despicable, makes himself necessary to the Prince that despises him by the most pleasing of all qualities, perpetual gaiety, by an unfailing power of exciting laughter . . .' *Ib.* iv. 356.

[3] *Ante*, p. 233.

in

in any common book, was Jane Shore's exclamation in the last act,

Forgive me! *but* forgive me[1]!

It was not however from the want of a susceptible heart that he hated to cite tender expressions, for he was more strongly and more violently affected by the force of words representing ideas capable of affecting him at all, than any other man in the world I believe; and when he would try to repeat the celebrated *Prosa Ecclesiastica pro Mortuis*[2], as it is called, beginning *Dies iræ, Dies illa*, he could never pass the stanza ending thus, *Tantus labor non sit cassus*[3], without bursting into a flood of tears; which sensibility I used to quote against him when he would inveigh against devotional poetry, and protest that all religious verses were cold and feeble, and unworthy the subject, which ought to be treated with higher reverence, he said, than either poets or painters could presume to excite or bestow[4]. Nor can any thing be a stronger proof of Dr. Johnson's piety than such an expression; for his idea of poetry was magnificent indeed,

[1] 'What she answers to her husband when he asks her movingly,—

"Why dost thou fix thy dying eyes upon me
With such an earnest, such a piteous look,
As if thy heart was full of some sad meaning
Thou couldst not speak!"

is pathetic to a great degree.

"Forgive me! *but* forgive me!" These few words far exceed the most pompous declamations of Cato.' J. Warton's *Essay on Pope*, ed. 1762, i. 273.

'Johnson says of Rowe's *Jane Shore*: — "This play, consisting chiefly of domestic scenes and private distress, lays hold upon the heart."' *Works*, vii. 410. See *ante*, p. 252, *n.* 3.

[2] In Daniel's *Thesaurus*, ii. 103, the *Dies Irae* is called *Prosa de Mortuis*.

[3] 'Quaerens me sedisti lassus.
Redemisti crucem passus:
Tantus labor non sit cassus.'

[4] 'Watts's devotional poetry is, like that of others, unsatisfactory. The paucity of its topics enforces perpetual repetition, and the sanctity of the matter rejects the ornaments of figurative diction. It is sufficient for Watts to have done better than others what no man has done well.' *Works*, viii. 386. See also *ib.* vii. 213 (*The Life of Waller*), where Johnson explains why 'poetical devotion cannot often please.'

'Moses Browne published in verse a series of devout contemplations called *Sunday Thoughts*. Johnson, who for the purpose of religious meditation seemed to think one day as proper as another, read them with cold approbation, and said he had a great mind to write and publish *Monday Thoughts*.' Nichols's *Lit. Anec.* v. 51.

and

and very fully was he persuaded of its superiority over every other talent bestowed by heaven on man. His chapter upon that particular subject in his Rasselas[1], is really written from the fulness of his heart, and quite in his best manner I think. I am not so sure that this is the proper place to mention his writing that surprising little volume in a week or ten days' time, in order to obtain money for his journey to Lichfield when his mother lay upon her last sickbed[2].

Promptitude of thought indeed, and quickness of expression, were among the peculiar felicities of Johnson: his notions rose up like the dragon's teeth sowed by Cadmus all ready clothed, and in bright armour too, fit for immediate battle[3]. He was therefore (as somebody is said to have expressed it) a tremendous converser[4], and few people ventured to try their skill against an antagonist with whom contention was so hopeless. One gentleman however, who dined at a nobleman's house in his company and that of Mr. Thrale, to whom I was obliged for the anecdote, was willing to enter the lists in defence of King William's character[5], and having opposed and contradicted Johnson two or three times petulantly enough; the master of the house began to feel uneasy, and expected disagreeable consequences: to avoid which he said, loud enough for the Doctor to hear, Our friend here has no meaning now in all this, except just to relate at club to-morrow how he teized Johnson at dinner to-day—this is all to do himself *honour*. No, upon my word, replied the other, I see no *honour* in it, whatever you may do. 'Well, Sir! (returned Mr. Johnson sternly) if you do not *see* the *honour*, I am sure I *feel* the *disgrace*.'

[1] Chapter x.

[2] Johnson probably began *Rasselas* in order to obtain money for his journey to Lichfield, but he did not get it finished in time. *Life*, i. 341; *Letters*, i. 79.

[3] 'Sir Joshua observed to me the extraordinary promptitude with which Johnson flew upon an argument. "Yes, (said I,) he has no formal preparation, no flourishing with his sword; he is through your body in an instant."' *Life*, ii. 365.

[4] George Garrick called him 'a tremendous companion.' *Ib.* i. 496, *n.* 1; iii. 139.

[5] Johnson called William III 'one of the most worthless scoundrels that ever existed.' *Ib.* ii. 342. See also *ib.* v. 255.

A young

A young fellow, less confident of his own abilities, lamenting one day that he had lost all his Greek—'I believe it happened at the same time, Sir (said Johnson), that I lost all my large estate in Yorkshire.'

But however roughly he might be suddenly provoked to treat a harmless exertion of vanity, he did not wish to inflict the pain he gave, and was sometimes very sorry when he perceived the people to smart more than they deserved [1]. How harshly you treated that man to-day, said I once, who harangued us so about gardening—'I am sorry (said he) if I vexed the creature, for there certainly is no harm in a fellow's rattling a rattle-box, only don't let him think that he thunders.'—The Lincolnshire lady [2] who shewed him a grotto she had been making, came off no better as I remember: Would it not be a pretty cool habitation in summer? said she, Mr. Johnson! 'I think it would, Madam (replied he),—for a toad.'

All desire of distinction indeed had a sure enemy in Mr. Johnson. We met a friend driving six very small ponies, and stopt to admire them. 'Why does nobody (said our doctor) begin the fashion of driving six spavined [3] horses, all spavined of the same leg? it would have a mighty pretty effect, and produce the distinction of doing something worse than the common way.'

When Mr. Johnson had a mind to compliment any one, he did it with more dignity to himself, and better effect upon the company, than any man. I can recollect but few instances indeed, though perhaps that may be more my fault than his. When Sir Joshua Reynolds left the room one day, he said, 'There goes a man not to be spoiled by prosperity [4].' And

[1] He wrote to Dr. Taylor on Nov. 18, 1756:—'When I am musing alone I feel a pang for every moment that any human being has by my peevishness or obstinacy spent in uneasiness.' *Letters*, i. 72.

[2] In 1764 he paid a visit to the Langton family at their seat of Langton in Lincolnshire. *Life*, i. 476. In the Taylor Gallery in Oxford there is a water-colour drawing of the house.

[3] *Spavined* is not in Johnson's *Dictionary*. He only gives *Spavin*.

[4] 'Sir Joshua Reynolds, Sir, is the most invulnerable man I know; the

when

when Mrs. Montague shewed him some China plates which had once belonged to Queen Elizabeth, he told her, 'that they had no reason to be ashamed of their present possessor, who was so little inferior to the first[1].' I likewise remember that he pronounced one day at my house a most lofty panegyric upon Jones the Orientalist, who seemed little pleased with the praise, for what cause I know not[2]. He was not at all offended, when comparing all our acquaintance to some animal or other, we pitched upon the elephant for his resemblance, adding that the proboscis of that creature was like his mind most exactly, strong to buffet even the tyger, and pliable to pick up even the pin. The truth is, Mr. Johnson was often good-humouredly willing to join in childish amusements, and hated to be left out of any innocent merriment that was going forward. Mr. Murphy always said, he was incomparable at buffoonery; and I verily think, if he had had good eyes, and a form less inflexible, he would have made an admirable mimic[3].

He certainly rode on Mr. Thrale's old hunter with a good firmness

man with whom if you should quarrel, you would find the most difficulty how to abuse.' *Life*, v. 102.

[1] Mrs. Montagu's name was Elizabeth. For Johnson's praise of her conversation see *ib.* iv. 275, and for her pretence to learning, *ib.* iii. 244. It was mainly by reason of her wealth that she was famous for her wit and writings. Johnson said of her:—'Mrs. Montagu has dropped me. Now, Sir, there are people whom one should like very well to drop, but would not wish to be dropped by.' *Ib.* iv. 73.

To her might be applied what Macaulay wrote of Rogers, far inferior to him though she was as a writer. 'That such men as Lord Granville, Lord Holland, Hobhouse, Lord Byron, and others of high rank in intellect, should place Rogers, as they do, above Southey, Moore, and even Scott himself, is what I cannot conceive. But this comes of being in the highest society of London. What Lady Jane Granville [in Miss Edgeworth's *Patronage*] called the Patronage of Fashion can do as much for a middling poet as for a plain girl like Miss Arabella Falconer.' Trevelyan's *Macaulay*, ed. 1877, i. 219.

[2] Sir William Jones was famous for his modesty, if we can trust Dean Barnard's line:—

'Jones teach me modesty—and Greek.' *Life*, iv. 433.

[3] 'Dr. Johnson has more fun, and comical humour, and love of nonsense about him than almost anybody I ever saw.' Mme. D'Arblay's *Diary*, i. 204. 'Gesticular mimicry and buffoonery Johnson hated, and would often huff Garrick for exercising it in his presence.' Hawkins's *Johnson*, p. 386. See *ante*, p. 269, *post*, p. 345.

firmness, and though he would follow the hounds fifty miles an end sometimes, would never own himself either tired or amused [1]. 'I have now learned (said he), by hunting, to perceive, that it is no diversion at all, nor ever takes a man out of himself for a moment: the dogs have less sagacity than I could have prevailed on myself to suppose; and the gentlemen often call to me not to ride over them. It is very strange, and very melancholy, that the paucity of human pleasures should persuade us ever to call hunting one of them [2].'—He was however proud to be amongst the sportsmen; and I think no praise ever went so close to his heart, as when Mr. Hamilton [3] called out one day upon Brighthelmstone Downs, Why Johnson rides as well, for aught I see, as the most illiterate fellow in England.

Though Dr. Johnson owed his very life to air and exercise, given him when his organs of respiration could scarcely play, in the year 1766 [4], yet he ever persisted in the notion, that neither of them had any thing to do with health [5]. 'People live as long

[1] 'Dr. Johnson told us at breakfast that he rode harder at a fox chace than anybody.' *Life*, v. 253. Writing to Mrs. Thrale on August 27, 1777, in the midst of an abundant harvest, he says:—'Barley, malt, beer, and money. There is the series of ideas. The deep logicians call it a *sorites*. I hope my master will no longer endure the reproach of not keeping me a horse.' *Letters*, ii. 25.

'Riding had no tendency to raise Johnson's spirits; and he once told me that in a journey on horseback he fell asleep.' Hawkins's *Johnson*, p. 458.

[2] 'The public pleasures of far the greater part of mankind are counfeit.' *The Idler*, No. 18.

[3] William Gerard Hamilton.

[4] *Ante*, p. 234.

[5] In the *Rambler*, No. 85, he points out 'how much happiness is gained, and how much misery escaped, by frequent and violent agitation of the body. . . . Exercise cannot secure us from that dissolution to which we are decreed: but while the soul and body continue united, it can make the association pleasing, and give probable hopes that they shall be disjoined by an easy separation.'

He wrote to Dr. Taylor:—'I hope you are diligent to take as much exercise as you can bear. . . . I take the true definition of exercise to be labour without weariness.' *Letters*, ii. 102. 'Exercise short of great fatigue must be your great medicine.' *Ib.* ii. 355. He urged Mr. Thrale to ride. *Ib.* ii. 73, 106.

He recommended to Boswell as a remedy against melancholy 'a great deal of exercise.' *Life*, i. 446.

Though in his strength he ridiculed the notion that weather much affects us (*Ib.* i. 332, 452; ii. 358), nevertheless when ill he owned the effect of change of air. In 1773 he wrote:—'My cold was once so bad that I

(said

(said he) in Pepper-alley[1] as on Salisbury-plain; and they live so much happier, that an inhabitant of the first would, if he turned cottager, starve his understanding for want of conversation, and perish in a state of mental inferiority[2].'

Mr. Johnson indeed, as he was a very talking man himself, had an idea that nothing promoted happiness so much as conversation. A friend's erudition was commended one day as equally deep and strong—'He will not talk, Sir (was the reply), so his learning does no good, and his wit, if he has it, gives us no pleasure: out of all his boasted stores I never heard him force but one word, and that word was *Richard*[3].' With a contempt not inferior he received the praises of a pretty lady's face and behaviour: 'She says nothing, Sir (answers Johnson); a talking blackamoor were better than a white creature who adds nothing to life, and by sitting down before one thus desperately silent, takes away the confidence one should have in the company of her chair if she were once out of it.'—No one was however less willing to begin any discourse than himself: his friend

began to think of country air.' *Letters*, i. 208. In 1782:—'I am now harassed by a catarrhous cough, from which my purpose is to seek relief by change of air.' *Life*, iv. 151. See also *ib.* iv. 336, 348.

[1] Three alleys of this name are mentioned in Dodsley's *London and its Environs*.

'JOHNSON. "I'll take you five children from London, who shall cuff five Highland children. Sir, a man bred in London will carry a burthen, or run, or wrestle, as well as a man brought up in the hardiest manner in the country."' *Life*, ii. 101.

[2] '"Yet Sir (said I) there are many people who are content to live in the country." JOHNSON. "Sir, it is in the intellectual world as in the physical world: we are told by natural philosophers that a body is at rest in the place that is fit for it; they who are content to live in the country, are *fit* for the country."' *Ib.* iv. 338.

[3] 'Demosthenes Taylor, as he was called, (that is, the Editor of Demosthenes) was the most silent man, the merest statue of a man that I have ever seen. I once dined in company with him, and all he said during the whole time was no more than *Richard*. How a man should say only Richard, it is not easy to imagine. But it was thus: Dr. Douglas was talking of Dr. Zachary Grey, and ascribing to him something that was written by Dr. Richard Grey. So, to correct him, Taylor said, (imitating his affected sententious emphasis and nod,) "*Richard*."' *Ib.* iii. 318.

It was Taylor who said that 'to be one of the Trustees of the British Museum should be the blue ribband of literary men.' Nichols's *Lit. Hist.* vi. 304. See *ante*, p. 281.

Mr. Thomas Tyers said, he was like the ghosts, who never speak till they are spoken to: and he liked the expression so well, that he often repeated it [1]. He had indeed no necessity to lead the stream of chat to a favourite channel, that his fulness on the subject might be shewn more clearly, whatever was the topic; and he usually left the choice to others. His information best enlightened, his argument strengthened, and his wit made it ever remembered. Of him it might have been said, as he often delighted to say of Edmund Burke, 'that you could not stand five minutes with that man beneath a shed while it rained, but you must be convinced you had been standing with the greatest man you had ever yet seen [2].'

As we had been saying one day that no subject failed of receiving dignity from the manner in which Mr. Johnson treated it, a lady at my house said, she would make him talk about love; and took her measures accordingly, deriding the novels of the day because they treated about love. 'It is not (replied our philosopher) because they treat, as you call it, about love, but because they treat of nothing, that they are despicable: we must not ridicule a passion which he who never felt never was happy, and he who laughs at never deserves to feel—a passion which has caused the change of empires, and the loss of worlds—a passion which has inspired heroism and subdued avarice [3].' He thought he had already said too much. 'A passion, in short (added he, with an altered tone), that consumes me away for my pretty Fanny here, and she is very cruel (speaking of another lady in the room).' He told us however in the course of the same chat, how his negro Francis had been eminent for his success among the girls. Seeing us all laugh, 'I must have you

[1] *Life*, iii. 307; v. 73, and *ante*, p. 160. For Tyers see *Life*, iii. 308.

[2] 'Yes, Sir; if a man were to go by chance at the same time with Burke under a shed to shun a shower, he would say, "this is an extraordinary man." If Burke should go into a stable to see his horse dressed, the ostler would say, "we have had an extraordinary man here."' *Ib.* iv. 275. See also v. 34, and *post*, p. 309.

[3] 'Of the passion of love Dr. Johnson remarked, that its violence and ill effects were much exaggerated; for who knows any real sufferings on that head, more than from the exorbitancy of any other passion?' *Life*, ii. 122.

know,

know, ladies (said he), that Frank has carried the empire of Cupid further than most men. When I was in Lincolnshire so many years ago, he attended me thither; and when we returned home together, I found that a female haymaker[1] had followed him to London for love.' Francis was indeed no small favourite with his master, who retained however a prodigious influence over his most violent passions.

On the birth-day of our eldest daughter, and that of our friend Dr. Johnson, the 17th and 18th of September[2], we every year made up a little dance and supper, to divert our servants and their friends, putting the summer-house[3] into their hands for the two evenings, to fill with acquaintance and merriment. Francis and his white wife were invited of course. She was eminently pretty, and he was jealous, as my maids told me. On the first of these days amusements (I know not what year) Frank took offence at some attentions paid his Desdemona, and walked away next morning to London in wrath. His master and I driving the same road an hour after, overtook him. 'What is the matter, child (says Dr. Johnson), that you leave Streatham to-day? *Art sick?*' He is jealous (whispered I). 'Are you jealous of your wife, you stupid blockhead (cries out his master in another tone)?' The fellow hesitated; and, *To be sure Sir, I don't quite approve Sir*, was the stammering reply. 'Why, what do they *do* to her, man? do the footmen kiss her?' No Sir, no!—Kiss my *wife Sir!—I hope not Sir*. 'Why, what *do* they do to her, my lad?' Why nothing Sir, I'm sure Sir. 'Why then go back directly and dance you dog, do; and let's hear no more of such empty lamentations.' I believe however that Francis was scarcely as much the object of Mr. Johnson's personal kindness, as the representative of Dr. Bathurst[4], for whose sake he would have loved any body, or any thing.

[1] The 'haymaker' must be due to Mrs. Piozzi's lively invention. Johnson visited Langton in the winter of 1764 and was back in London in February. *Life*, i. 477.

[2] *Ante*, p. 92.

[3] It was to the summer-house that Johnson on August 9, 1781 'retired, to plan a life of greater diligence.' *Ante*, p. 99.

[4] *Life*, i. 239, *n.* 1.

When he spoke of negroes[1], he always appeared to think them of a race naturally inferior, and made few exceptions in favour of his own; yet whenever disputes arose in his household among the many odd inhabitants of which it consisted, he always sided with Francis against the others, whom he suspected (not unjustly, I believe) of greater malignity. It seems at once vexatious and comical to reflect, that the dissentions those people chose to live constantly in, distressed and mortified him exceedingly. He really was oftentimes afraid of going home, because he was so sure to be met at the door with numberless complaints[2]; and he used to lament pathetically to me, and to Mr. Sastres[3] the Italian master, who was much his favourite, that they made his life miserable from the impossibility he found of making theirs happy, when every favour he bestowed on one was wormwood to the rest. If, however, I ventured to blame their ingratitude, and condemn their conduct, he would instantly set about softening the one and justifying the other; and finished commonly by telling me, that I knew not how to make allowances for situations I never experienced.

> To thee no reason who know'st only good,
> But evil hast not try'd. MILTON[4].

Dr. Johnson knew how to be merry with mean people too, as well as to be sad with them; he loved the lower ranks of humanity with a real affection: and though his talents and learning kept him always in the sphere of upper life, yet he never lost sight of the time when he and they shared pain and pleasure in common[5]. A borough election[6] once shewed me

[1] *Life*, ii. 478.

[2] *Ib.* iii. 461; *Letters*, ii. 74-5, 77, 122, 128; *ante*, p. 205; *post*, in Percy's *Anecdotes.*

[3] *Letters*, ii. 414.

[4] *Paradise Lost*, iv. 895.

[5] 'In our Tour, I observed that he was disgusted whenever he met with coarse manners. He said to me, "I know not how it is, but I cannot bear low life: and I find others, who have as good a right as I to be fastidious, bear it better, by having mixed more with different sorts of men. You would think that I have mixed pretty well too."' *Life*, v. 307.

[6] Mrs. Piozzi means no doubt an election in the Borough of Southwark for which Mr. Thrale was member from Dec. 1765, to the dissolution of 1780. Mr. Matthews, stationer, of St. Giles', Oxford, showed me a fragment of a MS. with the following

his

his toleration of boisterous mirth, and his content in the company of people whom one would have thought at first sight little calculated for his society. A rough fellow one day on such an occasion, a hatter by trade, seeing Mr. Johnson s beaver in a state of decay, seized it suddenly with one hand, and clapping him on the back with the other; Ah, Master Johnson (says he), this is no time to be thinking about *hats*. 'No, no, Sir (replies our Doctor in a cheerful tone), hats are of no use now, as you say, except to throw up in the air and huzza with;' accompanying his words with the true election halloo [1].

But it was never against people of coarse life that his contempt was expressed, while poverty of sentiment in men who considered themselves to be company for *the parlour* [2], as he called it, was what he would not bear. A very ignorant young fellow, who had plagued us all for nine or ten months, died at last consumptive:

entry:—'1754, April 15. Mr. Morton was chosen for Abingdon, after a long opposition of first Collington Esq. who left ye town and his Debts unpaid. Next Thrale Esq., who notwithstanding ye Superfluity of his money was rejected to ye Honour of Abingdon.'

[1] Johnson wrote to Mrs. Thrale in 1780:—'The voters of the Borough are too proud and too little dependant to be solicited by deputies; they expect the gratification of seeing the candidate bowing or curtseying before them. If you are proud they can be sullen.' *Letters*, ii. 153.

[2] Johnson defines *Drawingroom* as *the room in which company assembles at court* and *Parlour* as *a room in houses on the first floor, elegantly furnished for reception or entertainment.*

Mrs. Raine Ellis in a note on Miss Burney's *Early Diary* (ii. 157) says that 'Fanny does not seem to have said "drawing-room" until she went to Court, as she writes in her Windsor diary, "the *drawing-room*," as they call it *here*." Mrs. Delany, in 1755, speaks of her "*dining-room, vulgarly so called.*" The old words were *parlour* for any sitting-room; *eating-* or *dining-parlour* and *chamber* or *bed-chamber* for rooms distinct from those of reception.' In New England *parlour* has not been supplanted by drawing-room.

'Upon a visit to me at a country lodging near Twickenham,' writes Dr. Maxwell, 'Johnson asked what sort of society I had there. I told him, but indifferent; as they chiefly consisted of opulent traders, retired from business. He said, he never much liked that class of people; "For, Sir (said he,) they have lost the civility of tradesmen, without acquiring the manners of gentlemen."' *Life*, ii. 120.

'The lower class of the gentry and the higher of the mercantile world are in reality the worst-bred part of mankind.' *Joseph Andrews*, Bk. iii. ch. 3.

sumptive: 'I think (said Mr. Johnson when he heard the news), I am afraid, I should have been more concerned for the death of the *dog*: but —— (hesitating a while) I am not wrong now in all this, for the dog acted up to his character on every occasion that we know; but that dunce of a fellow helped forward the general disgrace of humanity.' Why dear Sir (said I), how odd you are! you have often said the lad was not capable of receiving further instruction. 'He was (replied the Doctor) like a corked bottle, with a drop of dirty water in it, to be sure; one might pump upon it for ever without the smallest effect; but when every method to open and clean it had been tried, you would not have me grieve that the bottle was broke at last.'

This was the same youth who told us he had been reading Lucius Florus; *Florus Delphini* was the phrase; and my mother (said he) thought it had something to do with Delphos: but of that I know nothing [1]. Who founded Rome then (enquired Mr. Thrale)? The lad replied, Romulus. And who succeeded Romulus (said I)? A long pause, and apparently distressful hesitation, followed the difficult question. 'Why will you ask him in terms that he does not comprehend (said Mr. Johnson enraged)? You might as well bid him tell you who phlebotomised Romulus. This fellow's dulness is elastic (continued he), and all we do is but like kicking at a woolsack.'

The pains he took however to obtain the young man more patient instructors, were many, and oftentimes repeated. He was put under the care of a clergyman in a distant province [2]; and Mr. Johnson used both to write and talk to his friend concerning his education. It was on that occasion that I remember his saying, 'A boy should never be sent to Eton or Westminster school before he is twelve years old at least; for if in his years of babyhood he 'scapes that general and transcendent [3] know-

[1] The youth had been reading the edition of Florus 'In Usum Serenissimi Delphini.'

[2] He was perhaps the pupil about whom Johnson wrote to the Master of Abingdon Grammar School. *Letters*, i. 157.

[3] Perhaps he said *transcendental*, of which in his *Dictionary* he gives as the first definition:—*General, pervading many particulars.*

ledge

ledge without which life is perpetually put to a stand, he will never get it at a public school, where if he does not learn Latin and Greek, he learns nothing [1].' Mr. Johnson often said, 'that there was too much stress laid upon literature as indispensably necessary: there is surely no need that every body should be a scholar, no call that every one should square the circle. Our manner of teaching (said he) cramps and warps many a mind, which if left more at liberty would have been respectable in some way, though perhaps not in that. We lop our trees, and prune them, and pinch them about (he would say), and nail them tight up to the wall, while a good standard is at last the only thing for bearing healthy fruit, though it commonly begins later. Let the people learn necessary knowledge; let them learn to count their fingers, and to count their money, before they are caring for the classics [2]; for (says Mr. Johnson) though I do not quite agree with the proverb, that *Nullum numen abest si sit prudentia*, yet we may very well say, that *Nullum numen adest—ni sit prudentia* [3].'

We had been visiting at a lady's house, whom as we returned some of the company ridiculed for her ignorance: 'She is not ignorant (said he), I believe, of any thing she has been taught, or of any thing she is desirous to know; and I suppose if one wanted a little *run tea*, she might be a proper person enough to apply to [4].'

[1] 'We must own,' said Johnson, 'that neither a dull boy, nor an idle boy, will do so well at a great school as at a private one. For at a great school there are always boys enough to do well easily, who are sufficient to keep up the credit of the school; and after whipping being tried to no purpose, the dull or idle boys are left at the end of a class, having the appearance of going through the course, but learning nothing at all. Such boys may do good at a private school, where constant attention is paid to them, and they are watched. So that the question of publick or private education is not properly a general one; but whether one or the other is best for *my son*.' *Life*, v. 85. See also *ib.* iii. 12; iv. 312.

[2] *Ante*, p. 281.

[3] 'I heard Johnson once say, "Though the proverb *Nullum numen abest, si sit prudentia*, does not always prove true, we may be certain of the converse of it, *Nullum numen adest, si sit imprudentia*."' *Life*, iv. 180. See Juvenal, *Satires*, x. 365.

[4] *Life*, v. 449, *n.* 1.

When

When I relate these various instances of contemptuous behaviour shewn to a variety of people, I am aware that those who till now have heard little of Mr. Johnson will here cry out against his pride and his severity; yet I have been as careful as I could to tell them, that all he did was gentle, if all he said was rough. Had I given anecdotes of his actions instead of his words, we should I am sure have nothing on record but acts of virtue differently modified, as different occasions called that virtue forth: and among all the nine biographical essays or performances which I have heard will at last be written about dear Dr. Johnson[1], no mean or wretched, no wicked or even slightly culpable action will I trust be found[2], to produce and put in the scale against a life of seventy years, spent in the uniform practice of every moral excellence and every Christian perfection; save humility alone, says a critic, but that I think *must* be excepted. He was not however wanting even in that to a degree seldom attained by man, when the duties of piety or charity called it forth[3].

[1] 1. *A Biographical Sketch of Dr. Samuel Joh son*, by Thomas Tyers, Esq. *Gentleman's Magazine*, December, 1784.

2. *The Life of Samuel Johnson, LL.D.* G. Kearsley, 1785.

3. *Memoirs of the Life and Writings of the late Dr. Samuel Johnson.* J. Walker, 1785.

4. *Anecdotes of the late Samuel Johnson, LL.D.*, by H. L. Piozzi. T. Cadell, 1786.

5. *An Essay on the Life, Character, and Writings of Dr. Samuel Johnson*, by Joseph Towers, 1786.

6. *The Life of Dr. Samuel Johnson*, by Sir John Hawkins, Knight, 1787.

7. *The Life of Samuel Johnson, LL.D.*, by James Boswell. C. Dilly, 1791.

8. *An Essay on the Life and Genius of Samuel Johnson, LL.D.*, by Arthur Murphy. T. Longman, &c., 1792.

9. *The Life of Samuel Johnson, LL.D., with critical Observations on his Works*, by Robert Anderson, M.D., Edinburgh, 1795.

Dr. Parr projected a Life of Johnson. *Life*, iv. 444.

[2] 'Whatever record leap to light
He never shall be shamed.'
Tennyson. *Ode on the Death of the Duke of Wellington.*

[3] 'The solemn text, "of him to whom much is given, much will be required," seems to have been ever present to his mind, in a rigorous sense, and to have made him dissatisfied with his labours and acts of goodness, however comparatively great; so that the unavoidable consciousness of his superiority was, in that respect, a cause of disquiet.' *Life*, iv. 427.

On his death-bed he said to one present:—'Live well, I conjure you; and you will not feel the compunction at the last, which I now feel.' 'So

Lowly

Lowly towards God, and docile towards the church; implicit in his belief of the gospel, and ever respectful towards the people appointed to preach it; tender of the unhappy, and affectionate to the poor, let no one hastily condemn as proud, a character which may perhaps somewhat justly be censured as arrogant. It must however be remembered again, that even this arrogance was never shewn without some intention, immediate or remote, of mending some fault or conveying some instruction. Had I meant to make a panegyric on Mr. Johnson's well-known excellencies, I should have told his deeds only, not his words—sincerely protesting, that as I never saw him once do a wrong thing, so we had accustomed ourselves to look upon him almost as an excepted [1] being; and I should as much have expected injustice from Socrates or impiety from Paschal, as the slightest deviation from truth and goodness in any transaction one might be engaged in with Samuel Johnson. His attention to veracity was without equal or example [2]: and when I mentioned Clarissa as a perfect character; 'On the contrary (said he), you may observe there is always something which she prefers to truth. Fielding's Amelia was the most pleasing heroine of all the romances (he said); but that vile broken nose never cured [3], ruined the sale of perhaps the only book, which being printed off betimes one morning, a new edition was called for before night [4].'

truly humble,' adds Nichols, 'were the thoughts which this great and good man entertained of his own approaches to religious perfection.' *Life*, iv. 410.

[1] I do not find any instances of *excepted* as here used. A writer of the present day would perhaps have said *exceptional*—a word not in Johnson's *Dictionary*.

[2] *Ante*, p. 225.

[3] 'The injury done to her beauty by the overturning of a chaise, by which, as you may well remember, her lovely nose was beat all to pieces, gave me an assurance that the woman who had been so much adored for the charms of her person deserved a much higher adoration to be paid to her mind.' *Amelia*, Bk. ii. c. 1.

[4] Mrs. Piozzi must mean 'which being *published* betimes,' &c.

Wraxhall (*Memoirs*, i. 54), says that Cadell told him that his predecessor Andrew Millar, who gave Fielding £800 for the copyright of *Amelia*, was advised 'to get rid of it as soon as he could. At the first sale which he made to the Trade he said, "Gentlemen, I have several works to put up for which I shall be glad if you will bid; but as to *Amelia* every copy is already bespoke." This manœuvre had

Mr.

Mr. Johnson's knowledge of literary history was extensive and surprising: he knew every adventure of every book you could name almost, and was exceedingly pleased with the opportunity which writing the Poets' Lives gave him to display it. He loved to be set at work, and was sorry when he came to the end of the business he was about [1]. I do not feel so myself with regard to these sheets: a fever which has preyed on me while I wrote them over for the press, will perhaps lessen my power of doing well the first, and probably the last work I should ever have thought of presenting to the Public. I could doubtless wish so to conclude it, as at least to shew my zeal for my friend, whose life, as I once had the honour and happiness of being useful to, I should wish to record a few particular traits of, that those who read should emulate his goodness; but seeing the necessity of making even virtue and learning such as *his* agreeable, that all should be warned against such coarseness of manners, as drove even from *him* those who loved, honoured, and esteemed him. His wife's daughter, Mrs. Lucy Porter of Litchfield, whose veneration for his person and character has ever been the greatest possible [2], being opposed one day in conversation by a clergyman who came often to her house, and feeling somewhat offended, cried out suddenly, Why, Mr. Pearson [3], said she, 'you are just like Dr. Johnson, I think: I do not mean that you are a man of the greatest capacity in all the world like Dr.

its effect. All the booksellers were anxious to get their names put down for copies of it, and the edition, though very large, was immediately sold.'

[1] About a revised edition of his *Dictionary* he wrote:—'I am now within a few hours of being able to send the whole dictionary to the press, and though I often went sluggishly to the work I am not much delighted at the completion.' *Letters*, i. 191.

[2] Boswell says of her:—'she reverenced Johnson, and he had a parental tenderness for her.' *Life*, ii. 462. Nevertheless such passages as the following in his letters must have shown Mrs. Thrale that the veneration was sometimes veiled. 'July 20, 1767. Miss Lucy is more kind and civil than I expected.' *Letters*, i. 129. 'Lucy is a philosopher, and considers me as one of the external and accidental things that are to be taken and left without emotion.' *Ib.* i. 180. 'Aug. 1, 1775. Fits of tenderness with Mrs. Lucy are not common; but she seems now to have a little paroxysm, and I was not willing to counteract it.' *Ib.* i. 359. 'Oct. 31, 1781. She never was so civil to me before.' *Ib.* ii. 232.

[3] *Letters*, i. 85, *n.* 2; ii. 86, *n.* 4.

Dr. Johnson, but that you contradict one every word one speaks, just like him.

Mr. Johnson told me the story: he was present at the giving of the reproof. It was however observable that with all his odd severity, he could not keep even indifferent people from teizing him with unaccountable confession of silly conduct which one would think they would scarcely have had inclination to reveal even to their tenderest and most intimate companions; and it was from these unaccountable volunteers in sincerity that he learned to warn the world against follies little known, and seldom thought on by other moralists.

Much of his eloquence, and much of his logic have I heard him use to prevent men from making vows on trivial occasions[1]; and when he saw a person oddly perplexed about a slight difficulty, 'Let the man alone (he would say), and torment him no more about it; there is a vow in the case, I am convinced; but is it not very strange that people should be neither afraid nor ashamed of bringing in God Almighty thus at every turn between themselves and their dinner?' When I asked what ground he had for such imaginations, he informed me, 'That a young lady once told him in confidence, that she could never persuade herself to be dressed against the bell rung for dinner, till she had made a vow to heaven that she would never more be absent from the family meals.'

[1] 'BOSWELL. "But you would not have me to bind myself by a solemn obligation?" JOHNSON. (much agitated) "What! a vow—O, no, Sir, a vow is a horrible thing, it is a snare for sin."' *Life*, iii. 357. See also *ib.* ii. 21, and *Letters*, i. 217.

'Biron amidst his extravagancies speaks with great justness against the folly of vows. They are made without sufficient regard to the variations of life, and are therefore broken by some unforeseen necessity. They proceed commonly from a presumptuous confidence and a false estimate of human power.' Johnson's *Shakespeare*, ed. 1765, ii. 118.

'Lear, who is characterized as hot, heady, and violent, is, with very just observation of life, made to entangle himself with vows, upon any sudden provocation to vow revenge, and then to plead the obligation of a vow in defence of implacability.' *Ib.* vi. 12.

The

The strangest applications in the world were certainly made from time to time towards Mr. Johnson, who by that means had an inexhaustible fund of anecdote, and could, if he pleased, tell the most astonishing stories of human folly and human weakness that ever were confided to any man not a confessor by profession.

One day when he was in a humour to record some of them, he told us the following tale: 'A person (said he) had for these last five weeks often called at my door, but would not leave his name, or other message; but that he wished to speak with me. At last we met, and he told me that he was oppressed by scruples of conscience: I blamed him gently for not applying, as the rules of our church direct, to his parish priest or other discreet clergyman [1]; when, after some compliments on his part, he told me, that he was clerk to a very eminent [2] trader, at whose warehouses much business consisted in packing goods in order to go abroad: that he was often tempted to take paper and packthread enough for his own use, and that he had indeed done so so often, that he could recollect no time when he ever had bought any for himself.—But probably (said I), your master was wholly indifferent with regard to such trivial emoluments; you

[1] 'If there be any of you who by this means cannot quiet his own conscience herein, but requireth further comfort or counsel, let him come to me, or to some other discreet and learned Minister of God's Word, and open his grief.' *Book of Common Prayer*. The Communion.

[2] *Eminent* was a favourite word last century; the following instances show its use.

'What would a stranger say of the English nation, in which on the day of marriage all the men are *eminent*?' Johnson's *Works*, iv. 186.

'Mr. Samuel Vandewall, an eminent merchant, was married to the relict of Mr. Harris Neate.' *Gentleman's Magazine*, 1745, p. 51. 'The Rev. and eminent Mr. Warburton to Miss Tucker of Bath.' *Ib.* p. 502.

'An eminent personage, however, he [Cromwell] was in many respects, and even a superior genius.' Hume's *History of England*, ed. 1773, vii. 290.

'The son of Mr. Galliard, an eminent Turkey merchant, is the man with whom she has made this exchange.' *Sir Charles Grandison*, ed. 1754, ii. 239.

'He had been an eminent man for many years for cursing, swearing, drinking,' &c. Wesley's *Journal*, ed. 1830, ii. 133. 'One of the most eminent drunkards in all the town.' *Ib.* ii. 226.

had

had better ask for it at once, and so take your trifles with consent.—Oh, Sir! replies the visitor, my master bid me have as much as I pleased, and was half angry when I talked to him about it.—Then pray Sir (said I), teize me no more about such airy nothings[1]—and was going on to be very angry, when I recollected that the fellow might be mad perhaps; so I asked him, When he left the counting-house of an evening?—At seven o'clock, Sir.—And when do you go to-bed, Sir?—At twelve o'clock.—Then (replied I) I have at least learned thus much by my new acquaintance;—that five hours of the four-and-twenty unemployed are enough for a man to go mad in; so I would advise you Sir, to study algebra, if you are not an adept already in it[2]: your head would get less *muddy*[3], and you will leave off tormenting your neighbours about paper and packthread, while we all live together in a world that is bursting with sin and sorrow. It is perhaps needless to add, that this visitor came no more.'

Mr. Johnson had indeed a real abhorrence of a person that had ever before him treated a little thing like a great one: and he quoted this scrupulous person with his packthread very often, in ridicule of a friend who, looking out on Streatham Common from our windows one day, lamented the enormous wickedness of the times, because some bird-catchers were busy there one fine Sunday morning. 'While half the Christian world is permitted (said he) to dance and sing, and celebrate Sunday as a day of festivity, how comes your puritanical spirit so offended with frivolous and empty deviations from exactness[4]? Whoever

[1] 'And as imagination bodies forth
The forms of things unknown, the poet's pen
Turns them to shape, and gives to airy nothing
A local habitation and a name.'
A Midsummer Night's Dream, Act v. sc. 1.

[2] 'When Mr. Johnson felt his fancy, or fancied he felt it, disordered, his constant recurrence was to the study of arithmetic.' *Ante*, p. 200. The clerk no doubt had arithmetic enough in the counting-house, and so was advised not to have recourse to it, but to algebra.

[3] 'Dost think I am so muddy, so unsettled,
To appoint myself in this vexation?'
The Winter's Tale, Act i. sc. 2. See *Life*, ii. 362, *n*. 3.

[4] 'Dr. Johnson enforced the strict observance of Sunday. "It should

loads

loads life with unnecessary scruples [1], Sir (continued he), provokes the attention of others on his conduct, and incurs the censure of singularity without reaping the reward of superior virtue.'

I must not, among the anecdotes of Dr. Johnson's life, omit to relate a thing that happened to him one day, which he told me of himself. As he was walking along the Strand a gentleman stepped out of some neighbouring tavern, with his napkin [2] in his hand and no hat, and stopping him as civilly as he could—I beg your pardon, Sir; but you are Dr. Johnson, I believe. 'Yes, Sir.' We have a wager depending on your reply: Pray, Sir, is it irrèparable or irrepàirable that one should say? 'The *last* I think, Sir (answered Dr. Johnson), for the adjective ought to follow the verb; but you had better consult my dictionary than me [3], for that was the result of more thought than you will now give me time for.' No, no, replied the gentleman gaily, the book I have no certainty at all of; but here is the *author*, to whom I referred: Is he not, Sir? to a friend with him: I have won my twenty guineas quite fairly, and am much obliged to you, Sir; so shaking Mr. Johnson kindly by the hand, he went back to finish his dinner or desert.

Another strange thing he told me once which there was no danger of forgetting: how a young gentleman called on him one morning, and told him that his father having, just before his death, dropped suddenly into the enjoyment of an ample fortune, he, the son, was willing to qualify himself for genteel society by adding some literature to his other endowments, and wished to

be different (he observed) from another day. People may walk, but not throw stones at birds. There may be relaxation, but there should be no levity."' *Life*, v. 69.

[1] *Ante*, p. 38, *n.* 5.

[2] A napkin in a London tavern must have been a rare thing in those days. Arthur Young, writing in 1790, says:—'The idea of dining without a napkin seems ridiculous to a Frenchman, but in England we dine at the tables of people of tolerable fortune without them.' *Travels in France*, ed. 1890, p. 307.

[3] *Irréparable* in the *Dictionary*. Mrs. Piozzi seems to have thought that the syllable *pa* in *paro* was long.

be

be put in an easy way of obtaining it. Johnson recommended the university: 'for you read Latin, Sir, with *facility*[1].' I read it a little to be sure, Sir. 'But do you read it *with facility*, I say?' Upon my word, Sir, I do not very well know, but I rather believe not. Mr. Johnson now began to recommend other branches of science, when he found languages at such an immeasurable distance, and advising him to study natural history, there arose some talk about animals, and their divisions into oviparous and viviparous; And the cat here, Sir, said the youth who wished for instruction, pray in which class is she? Our doctor's patience and desire of doing good began now to give way to the natural roughness of his temper. 'You would do well (said he) to look for some person to be always about you, Sir, who is capable of explaining such matters, and not come to us (there were some literary friends present as I recollect) to know whether the cat lays eggs or not: get a discreet man to keep you company, there are so many who would be glad of your table and fifty pounds a year.' The young gentleman retired, and in less than a week informed his friends that he had fixed on a preceptor to whom no objections could be made; but when he named as such one of the most distinguished characters in our age or nation, Mr. Johnson fairly gave himself up to an honest burst of laughter; and seeing this youth at such a surprising distance from common knowledge of the world, or of any thing in it, desired to see his visitor no more.

He had not much better luck with two boys that he used to tell of, to whom he had taught the classics, 'so that (he said) they were no incompetent or mean scholars:' it was necessary however that something more familiar should be known, and he bid them read the history of England. After a few months had elapsed he asked them, 'If they could recollect who first destroyed the monasteries in our island?' One modestly replied, that he did not know; the other said, *Jesus Christ*[2].

[1] Windham records 'Johnson's opinion that I could not name above five of my college acquaintance who read Latin with sufficient ease to make it pleasurable.' *Letters*, ii. 440.

[2] Hawkins (p. 471) tells a similar story.

Of

Of the truth of stories which ran currently about the town concerning Dr. Johnson, it was impossible to be certain, unless one asked him himself; and what he told, or suffered to be told before his face without contradicting, has every possible mark I think of real and genuine authenticity [1]. I made one day very minute enquiries about the tale of his knocking down the famous Tom Osborne with his own Dictionary in the man's own house. And how was that affair, in earnest? do tell me, Mr. Johnson? 'There is nothing to tell, dearest Lady, but that he was insolent and I beat him, and that he was a blockhead and told of it, which I should never have done; so the blows have been multiplying, and the wonder thickening for all these years, as Thomas was never a favourite with the Public. I have beat many a fellow, but the rest had the wit to hold their tongues [2].'

[1] 'I once got from one of his friends a list, [of his works] which there was pretty good reason to suppose was accurate, for it was written down in his presence by this friend, who enumerated each article aloud, and had some of them mentioned to him by Mr. Levett, in concert with whom it was made out; and Johnson, who heard all this, did not contradict it. But when I shewed a copy of this list to him, and mentioned the evidence for its exactness, he laughed, and said, "I was willing to let them go on as they pleased, and never interfered."' *Life*, iii. 321.

[2] 'It has been confidently related, with many embellishments, that Johnson one day knocked Osborne down in his shop, with a folio, and put his foot upon his neck. The simple truth I had from Johnson himself. "Sir, he was impertinent to me, and I beat him. But it was not in his shop: it was in my own chamber."' *Life*, i. 154.

'The identical book with which Johnson knocked down Osborne (Biblia Græca Septuaginta, fol. 1594, Frankfort; the note written by the Rev. — Mills) I saw in February, 1812, at Cambridge, in the possession of J. Thorpe, bookseller; whose Catalogue, since published, contains particulars authenticating this assertion.' Nichols's *Lit. Anec.* viii. 446. This folio is not mentioned in the Sale Catalogue of Johnson's Library. It is scarcely likely that Osborne brought it to Johnson's chamber, as schoolboys used to provide the birch rods with which they were beaten.

In Sir Henry Irving's collection is a copy of The Shakespeare Folio (The Second Impression) in which are the following three inscription:—

(1) 'Bo^{t} at Dr. Johnson's Sale Feb. 18, 1785. S. J.'

(2) 'This book at the death [in 1744] of Theobald the editor of Shakespear came into the hands of Osbourn ye bookseller of Gray's Inn —who soon after presented it to the late Dr. Johnson.

S. J. Feb. 25, 1785.'

(3) [This is a printed cutting pasted in.] 'In the late sale of Dr. Johnson's books there were several

I have

I have heard Mr. Murphy[1] relate a very singular story, while he was present, greatly to the credit of his uncommon skill and knowledge of life and manners: When first the Ramblers came out in separate numbers, as they were the objects of attention to multitudes of people, they happened, as it seems, particularly to attract the notice of a society who met every Saturday evening during the summer at Rumford in Essex, and were known by the name of The Bowling-green club. These men seeing one day the character of Leviculus the fortune-hunter, or Tetrica the old maid: another day some account of a person who spent his life in hoping for a legacy, or of him who is always prying into other folks affairs[2], began sure enough to think they were betrayed; and that some of the coterie sate down to divert himself by giving to the Public the portrait of all the rest. Filled with wrath against the traitor of Rumford, one of them resolved to write to the printer and enquire the author's name; Samuel Johnson, was the reply. No more was necessary; Samuel Johnson was the name of the curate[3], and soon did each begin to load him with reproaches for turning his friends into ridicule in a manner so cruel and unprovoked. In vain did the guiltless curate protest his innocence; one was sure that Aliger meant Mr. Twigg, and that Cupidus was but another name for neighbour Baggs[4]: till the poor parson, unable to contend any longer, rode to London, and brought them full satisfaction concerning the writer, who from his own knowledge of general

articles which sold wonderfully cheap, particularly the following—a folio edition of Shakespeare, the second, with a large number of notes, MS., in the margin, Johnson's own handwriting. The book has the further incidental circumstances enhancing its value, that it had been the property of Theobald, and had many notes also written by him. The title and part of another leaf were wanting. These were the only articles on the *per contra* side; and the book, thus extremely curious, sold for only a guinea!'

Sir Henry Irving informs me that he paid a hundred pounds for it.

Lort, the antiquary, sending a pamphlet to Bishop Percy, says:—'You will observe it, in Tom Osborne's phrase, *paululum spoliatum in margine.*' Nichols's *Lit. Hist.* vii. 458.

[1] *Life*, i. 215.

[2] These characters are in Nos. 74, 103, 182, and 197.

[3] A curate of that name is mentioned in the *Life*, i. 135.

[4] Aliger is in No. 201, and Cupidus in No. 73.

 manners,

manners, quickened by a vigorous and warm imagination, had happily delineated, though unknown to himself, the members of the Bowling-green Club.

Mr. Murphy likewise used to tell before Dr. Johnson, of the first time *they* met, and the occasion of their meeting, which he related thus: That being in those days engaged in a periodical paper, he found himself at a friend's house out of town; and not being disposed to lose pleasure for the sake of business, wished rather to content his bookseller by sending some unstudied essay to London by the servant, than deny himself the company of his acquaintance, and drive away to his chambers for the purpose of writing something more correct. He therefore took up a French *Journal Literaire* that lay about the room, and translating something he liked from it, sent it away without further examination. Time however discovered that he had translated from the French a Rambler of Johnson's, which had been but a month before taken from the English [1]; and thinking it right to make him his personal excuses, he went next day, and found our friend all covered with soot like a chimney-sweeper, in a little room, with an intolerable heat and strange smell, as if he had been acting Lungs in the Alchymist, making *æther* [2]. 'Come, come (says Dr. Johnson),

[1] *Life*, i. 356. It was in the *Gray's Inn Journal* for June 15, 1754, that the *Rambler*, No. 190, appeared in its retranslation. Johnson's opening paragraph is as follows:—'Among the emirs and visiers, the sons of valour and of wisdom, that stand at the corners of the Indian throne, to assist the counsels or conduct the wars of the posterity of Timur, the first place was long held by Morad the son of Hanuth.' This is given by Murphy:—'Among the Visiers and Ministers who figured round the Indian throne, and supported by their Prudence and Valour the Lustre and Dignity of the illustrious Race of Timur, Morad, the son of Hanuth, held the most conspicuous rank.'

[2] It was not *aether* but *elixir* that was made. '*Lungs* was a term of art for the under-operators in chemistry, whose business principally was to take care of the fire. So Cowley, in his sketch of a philosophic college, in the number of its members reckons two *lungs* or chemical servants; and afterwards, assigning their salaries, "To each of the *lungs* twelve pounds."' Note on *The Alchemist*, Ben Jonson's *Works*, ed. 1756, iii. 31. 'As to alchymy Johnson was not a positive unbeliever.' *Life*, ii. 376. 'Philosophy, with the aid of experience, has at length banished the

dear

dear Mur[1], the story is black enough now; and it was a very happy day for me that brought you first to my house, and a very happy mistake about the Ramblers.'

Dr. Johnson was always exceeding fond of chemistry; and we made up a sort of laboratory at Streatham one summer, and diverted ourselves with drawing essences and colouring liquors[2]. But the danger Mr. Thrale found his friend in one day when I was driven to London, and he had got the children and servants round him to see some experiments performed, put an end to all our entertainment; so well was the master of the house persuaded, that his short sight would have been his destruction in a moment, by bringing him close to a fierce and violent flame. Indeed it was a perpetual miracle that he did not set himself on fire reading a-bed, as was his constant custom, when exceedingly unable even to keep clear of mischief with our best help; and accordingly the fore-top of all his wigs were [*sic*] burned by the candle down to the very net-work. Mr. Thrale's valet-de-chambre, for that reason, kept one always in his own hands, with which he met him at the parlour-door when the bell had called him down to dinner, and as he went up stairs to

study of alchymy.' Gibbon's *Decline and Fall*, ed. 1802, ii. 138.

[1] 'Johnson had a way of contracting the names of his friends, as Beauclerk, Beau; Boswell, Bozzy; Langton, Lanky: Murphy, Mur; Sheridan, Sherry.' *Life*, ii. 258.

[2] He wrote to Mrs. Thrale on July 24, 1771: 'Be pleased to make my compliments to Mr. Thrale, and desire that his builders will leave about a hundred loose bricks. I can at present think of no better place for chymistry in fair weather than the pump-side in the kitchen-garden.' *Letters*, i. 183. For his love of chemistry see *Life*, i. 140, 436; iii. 398; iv. 237. He defines *chymist* as *a philosopher by fire.*

Smollett, writing of the reign of George II, says:—'Natural philosophy became a general study; and the new doctrine of electricity grew into fashion... The art of chemistry was perfectly understood and assiduously applied to the purposes of sophistication.' *History of England*, ed. 1800, v. 375. (Johnson defines *Sophistication*; *adulteration.*)

Watson, at his chemical lectures at Cambridge (1766-9), had very crowded audiences 'of persons of all ages and degrees in the University.' *Life of Bishop Watson*, i. 46, 53.

Gibbon, after the publication of the first volume of his History, attended a course of anatomy and some lessons on chemistry. 'The anatomist and chemist,' he says, 'may sometimes track me in their own snow.' *Misc. Works*, i. 229.

sleep in the afternoon, the same man constantly followed him with another.

Future experiments in chemistry however were too dangerous, and Mr. Thrale insisted that we should do no more towards finding the philosopher's stone.

Mr. Johnson's amusements were thus reduced to the pleasures of conversation merely[1]: and what wonder that he should have an avidity for the sole delight he was able to enjoy? No man conversed so well as he on every subject; no man so acutely discerned the reason of every fact, the motive of every action, the end of every design. He was indeed often pained by the ignorance or causeless wonder of those who knew less than himself, though he seldom drove them away with apparent scorn, unless he thought they added presumption to stupidity: And it was impossible not to laugh at the patience he shewed, when a Welch parson of mean abilities, though a good heart, struck with reverence at the sight of Dr. Johnson, whom he had heard of as the greatest man living, could not find any words to answer his inquiries concerning a motto round somebody's arms which adorned a tomb-stone in Ruabon church-yard. If I remember right the words were,

Heb Dw, Heb Dym,
Dw o' diggon[2].

And though of no very difficult construction, the gentleman seemed wholly confounded, and unable to explain them; till Mr. Johnson having picked out the meaning by little and little, said to the man, '*Heb* is a preposition, I believe Sir, is it not?' My countryman recovering some spirits upon the sudden question, cried out, So I humbly presume Sir, very comically.

Stories of humour do not tell well in books; and what made impression on the friends who heard a jest, will seldom much delight the distant acquaintance or sullen critic who reads it. The cork model of Paris is not more despicable as a resemblance of a great city, than this book, *levior cortice*[3], as a specimen of

[1] *Post*, p. 324.

[2] 'The Welsh words, which are the Myddelton motto, mean, "Without God, without all. God is all-sufficient."' *Life*, v. 450, *n.* 2.

[3] Horace, *Odes*, iii. 9. 22.

Johnson's

Johnson's character. Yet every body naturally likes to gather little specimens of the rarities found in a great country; and could I carry home from Italy square pieces of all the curious marbles which are the just glory of this surprising part of the world, I could scarcely contrive perhaps to arrange them so meanly as not to gain some attention from the respect due to the places they once belonged to.——Such a piece of motley Mosaic work will these Anecdotes inevitably make: but let the reader remember that he was promised nothing better, and so be as contented as he can.

An Irish trader at our house one day heard Dr. Johnson launch out into very great and greatly deserved praises of Mr. Edmund Burke[1]: delighted to find his countryman stood so high in the opinion of a man he had been told so much of, Sir (said he), give *me* leave to tell something of Mr. Burke now. We were all silent, and the honest Hibernian began to relate how Mr. Burke went to see the collieries in a distant province; and he would go down into the bowels of the earth (in a bag), and he would examine every thing: he went in a bag Sir, and ventured his health and his life for knowledge; but he took care of his clothes, that they should not be spoiled, for he went down in a bag[2]. 'Well Sir (says Mr. Johnson good-humouredly), if our friend Mund should die in any of these hazardous exploits, you and I would write his life and panegyric together; and your chapter of it should be entitled thus: *Burke in a Bag*.'

He had always a very great personal regard and particular affection for Mr. Edmund Burke, as well as an esteem difficult for me to repeat, though for him only easy to express. And when at the end of the year 1774 the general election called us all different ways, and broke up the delightful society in which we had spent some time at Beconsfield, Dr. Johnson shook the hospitable master of the house kindly by the hand, and said, 'Farewell my dear Sir, and remember that I wish you all the

[1] *Ante*, p. 290.

[2] The bag apparently was not the vehicle in which he went down, but a covering for his clothes. *Sack* was used of 'a woman's loose robe.' Johnson's *Dictionary*.

success

success which ought to be wished you, which can possibly be wished you indeed—*by an honest man*[1].'

I must here take leave to observe, that in giving little memoirs of Mr. Johnson's behaviour and conversation, such as I saw and heard it, my book lies under manifest disadvantages, compared with theirs, who having seen him in various situations, and observed his conduct in numberless cases, are able to throw stronger and more brilliant lights upon his character. Virtues are like shrubs, which yield their sweets in different manners according to the circumstances which surround them: and while generosity of soul scatters its fragrance like the honeysuckle, and delights the senses of many occasional passengers, who feel the pleasure, and half wonder how the breeze has blown it from so far, the more sullen but not less valuable myrtle waits like fortitude to discover its excellence, till the hand arrives that will *crush* it, and force out that perfume whose durability well compensates the difficulty of production.

I saw Mr. Johnson in none but a tranquil uniform state[2], passing the evening of his life among friends, who loved, honoured, and admired him: I saw none of the things he did, except such acts of charity as have been often mentioned in this book, and such writings as are universally known. What he said is all I can relate; and from what he said, those who think it worth while to read these Anecdotes, must be contented to gather his character. Mine is a mere *candle-light* picture of his latter days, where every thing falls in dark shadow except the face, the index of the mind; but even that is seen unfavourably, and with a paleness beyond what nature gave it.

When I have told how many follies Dr. Johnson knew of others, I must not omit to mention with how much fidelity he

[1] Johnson and the Thrales on their return from a trip to Wales stayed at Beconsfield. Johnson, as his Journal shows, had arrived there on September 24. *Life*, v. 460. Parliament was dissolved on September 30.

[2] This is not true. After Mr. Thrale's death the tranquillity was more and more disturbed. *Life*, iv. 158, *n.* 4; 159, *n.* 3. It was partly disturbed by her neglect of him. *Letters*, ii. 300, 303.

would

would always have kept them concealed, could they of whom he knew the absurdities have been contented, in the common phrase, to keep their own counsel. But returning home one day from dining at the chaplain's[1] table, he told me, that Dr. Goldsmith had given a very comical and unnecessarily exact recital there, of his own feelings when his play was hissed[2]; telling the company how he went indeed to the Literary Club at night, and chatted gaily among his friends, as if nothing had happened amiss; that to impress them still more forcibly with an idea of his magnanimity, he even sung his favourite song about an old woman tossed in a blanket seventeen times as high as the moon; but all this while I was suffering horrid tortures (said he), and verily believe that if I had put a bit into my mouth it would have strangled me on the spot, I was so excessively ill; but I made more noise than usual to cover all that, and so they never perceived my not eating, nor I believe at all imaged to themselves the anguish of my heart: but when all were gone except Johnson here, I burst out a-crying, and even swore by —— that I would never write again. 'All which, Doctor (says Mr. Johnson, amazed at his odd frankness), I thought had been a secret between you and me! and I am sure I would not have said any thing about it for the world. Now see (repeated he when he told the story) what a figure a man makes who thus unaccountably chuses to be the frigid narrator of his own disgrace[3]. *Il volto sciolto, ed i pensieri stretti*[4], was a proverb made

[1] No doubt Percy, who was chaplain to George III. *Letters*, i. 414, *n.*

[2] *The Good Natured Man.* Though there was a good deal of hissing, especially at the 'uncommonly low language' of the scene of the bailiffs, yet 'it was played ten consecutive nights.' Forster's *Goldsmith*, ii. 98.

'It [the tragedy of *Agamemnon*] struggled with such difficulty through the first night that Thomson, coming late to his friends with whom he was to sup, excused his delay by telling them how the sweat of his distress had so disordered his wig that he could not come till he had been refitted by a barber.' Johnson's *Works*, viii. 372.

[3] 'A man (said Johnson) should be careful never to tell tales of himself to his own disadvantage. People may be amused and laugh at the time, but they will be remembered, and brought out against him upon some subsequent occasion.' *Life*, ii. 472.

[4] 'At Sienna I was tabled in the house of one Alberto Scipioni, an old Roman courtier in dangerous times . . . At my departure towards

on

on purpose for such mortals, to keep people, if possible, from being thus the heralds of their own shame: for what compassion can they gain by such silly narratives? No man should be expected to sympathise with the sorrows of vanity. If then you are mortified by any ill usage, whether real or supposed, keep at least the account of such mortifications to yourself, and forbear to proclaim how meanly you are thought on by others, unless you desire to be meanly thought of by all.'

The little history of another friend's superfluous ingenuity will contribute to introduce a similar remark. He had a daughter of about fourteen years old, as I remember, fat and clumsy: and though the father adored, and desired others to adore her, yet being aware perhaps that she was not what the French call *paitrie des graces*[1], and thinking I suppose that the old maxim, of beginning to laugh at yourself first where you have any thing ridiculous about you, was a good one[2], he comically enough called his girl *Trundle* when he spoke of her; and many who bore neither of them any ill-will felt disposed to laugh at the happiness of the appellation[3]. 'See now (says Dr. Johnson) what haste people are in to be hooted. Nobody ever thought of this fellow nor of his daughter, could he but have been quiet himself, and forborne to call the eyes of the world on his dowdy and her deformity. But it teaches one to see at least, that if

Rome I had won confidence enough to beg his advice how I might carry myself securely there, without offence of others, or of mine own conscience. "Signor Arrigo mio," says he, "i pensieri stretti ed il viso sciolto," that is, "your thoughts close and your countenance loose," will go safely over the whole world.' Milton's *Prose Works*, ed. 1806, vii. 88. See Johnson's *Works*, vii. 72.

'The height of abilities is to have *volto sciolto* and *pensieri stretti*; that is a frank, open and ingenuous exterior, with a prudent and reserved interior.' Chesterfield's *Letters to his Son*, ii. 90.

[1] Pétrie des grâces.

[2] 'If it be a natural impediment, as a red nose, squint eyes, crooked legs, or any such imperfection, infirmity, disgrace, reproach, the best way is to speak of it first thyself, and so thou shalt surely take away all occasions from others to jest at or contemn, that they may perceive thee to be careless of it.' Burton's *Anatomy of Melancholy*, ed. 1660, p. 359.

[3] Johnson defines *Trundle* as 'any round rolling thing.'

nobody

nobody else will nickname one's children, the parents will e'en do it themselves.'

All this held true in matters to Mr. Johnson of more serious consequence. When Sir Joshua Reynolds had painted his portrait looking into the slit of his pen, and holding it almost close to his eye, as was his general custom, he felt displeased, and told me 'he would not be known by posterity for his *defects* only, let Sir Joshua do his worst [1].' I said in reply, that Reynolds had no such difficulties about himself, and that he might observe the picture which hung up in the room where we were talking [2], represented Sir Joshua holding his ear in his hand to catch the sound. 'He may paint himself as deaf if he chuses (replied Johnson); but I will not be *blinking Sam* [3].'

It is chiefly for the sake of evincing the regularity and steadiness of Mr. Johnson's mind that I have given these trifling memoirs, to show that his soul was not different from that of another person, but, as it was, greater; and to give those who did not know him a just idea of his acquiescence in what we call vulgar prejudices, and of his extreme distance from those notions which the world has agreed, I know not very well why, to call romantic. It is indeed observable in his preface to Shakespeare, that while other critics expatiate on the creative powers and vivid imagination of that matchless poet, Dr. Johnson commends him for giving so just a representation of human manners, 'that from his scenes a hermit might estimate the value of society, and a confessor predict the progress of the passions [4].' I have not the book with me here, but am pretty sure that such is his expression.

[1] Northcote (*Life of Reynolds*, ii. 3) and Leslie and Taylor (*Life*, ii. 143) assign this anecdote to the portrait of Johnson reading. According to Northcote, Johnson said to Sir Joshua :—' It is not friendly to hand down to posterity the imperfections of any man.'

[2] The Library at Streatham which was hung with Reynolds's portraits of Mr. Thrale's friends.' *Life*, iv. 158, *n.* 1; *Letters*, i. 232, *n.* 1; *post*, p. 342.

[3] *Post*, in Miss Reynolds's *Recollections*.

[4] 'This therefore is the praise of Shakespeare, that his drama is the mirrour of life; that he who

The

The general and constant advice he gave too, when consulted about the choice of a wife, a profession, or whatever influences a man's particular and immediate happiness, was always to reject no positive good from fears of its contrary consequences. 'Do not (said he) forbear to marry a beautiful woman if you can find such, out of a fancy that she will be less constant than an ugly one; or condemn yourself to the society of coarseness and vulgarity for fear of the expences or other dangers of elegance and personal charms, which have been always acknowledged as a positive good, and for the want of which there should be always given some weighty compensation. I have however (continued Mr. Johnson) seen some prudent fellows who forbore to connect themselves with beauty lest coquetry should be near, and with wit[1] or birth lest insolence should lurk behind them, till they have been forced by their discretion to linger life away in tasteless stupidity, and chuse to count the moments by remembrance of pain instead of enjoyment of pleasure.'

When professions were talked of, 'Scorn (said Mr. Johnson) to put your behaviour under the dominion of canters[2]; never think it clever to call physic a mean study, or law a dry one; or ask a baby of seven years old which way *his genius* leads him, when we all know that a boy of seven years old has no *genius*[3] for any thing except a peg-top and an apple-pye; but fix on some business where much money may be got and little virtue risqued: follow that business steadily, and do not live as Roger

has mazed his imagination in following the phantoms which other writers raise up before him may here be cured of his delirious extasies by reading human sentiments in human language; by scenes from which a hermit may estimate the transactions of the world, and a confessor predict the progress of the passions.' Shakespeare's *Works*, ed. 1765, Preface, p. xii.

[1] 'Some cunning men choose fools for their wives, thinking to manage them, but they always fail. . . . Depend upon it no woman is the worse for sense and knowledge.' *Life*, v. 226.

[2] *Canter* Johnson here uses in a different sense from that given in his *Dictionary*—'a term of reproach for hypocrites, who talk formally of religion without obeying it.' He talks of 'the cant of an author,' and 'the cant of sensibility.' *Works*, viii. 238, 248. For other instances of *cant* see *Life*, iv. 221, *n.* 1.

[3] *Ib.* ii. 437, *n.* 2. 'Genius,' said Johnson, 'is in fact knowing the use of tools.' *Memoirs of Dr. Burney*, iii. 5.

Ascham

Ascham says the wits do, *Men know not how; and at last die obscurely, men mark not where*[1].'

Dr. Johnson had indeed a veneration for the voice of mankind beyond what most people will own; and as he liberally confessed that all his own disappointments proceeded from himself, he hated to hear others complain of general injustice[2]. I remember when lamentation was made of the neglect shewed to Jeremiah Markland[3], a great philologist as some one ventured to call him—'He is a scholar undoubtedly Sir (replied Dr. Johnson), but remember that he would run from the world, and that it is not the world's business to run after him. I hate a fellow whom pride, or cowardice, or laziness drives into a corner, and [who] does nothing when he is there but sit and *growl*; let him come out as I do, and *bark*[4]. The world (added he) is chiefly unjust and ungenerous in this, that all are ready to encourage a man who once talks of leaving it, and few things do really provoke me more, than to hear people prate of retirement, when they have neither skill to discern their own motives, or penetration to estimate the consequences: but while a fellow is active to gain

[1] Ascham is not writing of 'the wits' in the eighteenth century sense of the term, but of 'quick wits,' those who at school 'take their lesson readily;' who 'commonly be apt to take, unapt to keep; soon hot, and desirous of this and that, as cold, and soon weary of the same again;' who are 'ever quick, hasty, rash, heady and brain-sick.' Of them he says:—'In youth also they be ready scoffers, privy mockers, and ever over-light and merry; in age, soon testy, very waspish and always over-miserable. And yet few of them come to any great age by reason of their misordered life when they were young; but a great deal fewer of them come to show any great countenance, or bear any great authority abroad in the world, but either live obscurely, men know not how, or die obscurely, men mark not when.' Ascham's *Works*, ed. 1864, iii. 99.

[2] *Life*, iv. 172.

[3] *Ib.* iv. 161; *Letters*, ii. 276.

[4] Markland is perhaps alluded to in the following passage:—'All the complaints which are made of the world are unjust. I never knew a man of merit neglected: it was generally by his own fault that he failed of success. A man may hide his head in a hole: he may go into the country, and publish a book now and then, which nobody reads, and then complain he is neglected. There is no reason why any person should exert himself for a man who has written a good book: he has not written it for any individual. I may as well make a present to the postman who brings me a letter.' *Life*, iv. 172.

either

either power or wealth (continued he), every body produces some hindrance to his advancement, some sage remark, or some unfavourable prediction; but let him once say slightly, I have had enough of this troublesome bustling world, 'tis time to leave it now: Ah, dear Sir! cries the first old acquaintance he meets, I am glad to find you in this happy disposition: yes, dear friend! *do* retire and think of nothing but your own ease: there's Mr. William will find it a pleasure to settle all your accounts and relieve you from the fatigue; Miss Dolly makes the charmingest chicken broth in the world, and the cheesecakes we eat of her's once, how good they were: I will be coming every two or three days myself to chat with you in a quiet way; *so snug!* and tell you how matters go upon 'Change, or in the House, or according to the blockhead's first pursuits, whether lucrative or politic, which thus he leaves; and lays himself down a voluntary prey to his own sensuality and sloth, while the ambition and avarice of the nephews and nieces, with their rascally adherents, and coadjutors, reap the advantage, while they fatten their fool [1].'

As the votaries of retirement had little of Mr. Johnson's applause, unless that he knew that the motives were merely devotional, and unless he was convinced that their rituals were accompanied by a mortified state of the body, the sole proof of their sincerity which he would admit, as a compensation for such fatigue as a worldly life of care and activity requires [2]; so of the various states and conditions of humanity, he despised none more I think than the man who marries for a maintenance: and of a friend who made his alliance on no higher principles, he said once, 'Now has that fellow (it was a nobleman of whom we were speaking) at length obtained a certainty of three meals a day, and for that certainty, like his brother dog in the fable, he will get his neck galled for life with a collar [3].'

[1] 'Every man has those about him who wish to soothe him into inactivity and delitescence, nor is there any semblance of kindness more vigorously to be repelled than that which voluntarily offers a vicarious performance of the tasks of life, and conspires with the natural love of ease against diligence and perseverance.' *Letters*, i. 401. See *Life*, ii. 337; iii. 176, *n*. 1.

[2] *Ib*. v. 62; *ante*, p. 209.

[3] This nobleman was Lord Sandys. Hayward's *Piozzi*, i. 296. 'He mar-

That

That poverty was an evil to be avoided by all honest means however, no man was more ready to avow: concealed poverty particularly, which he said was the general corrosive that destroyed the peace of almost every family; to which no evening perhaps ever returned without some new project for hiding the sorrows and dangers of the next day[1]. 'Want of money (says Dr. Johnson) is sometimes concealed under pretended avarice, and sly hints of aversion to part with it; sometimes under stormy anger, and affectation of boundless rage; but oftener still under a shew of thoughtless extravagance and gay neglect—while to a penetrating eye, none of these wretched veils suffice to keep the cruel truth from being seen. Poverty is *hic et ubique* (says he), and if you do shut the jade out of the door, she will always contrive in some manner to poke her pale lean face in at the window.'

I have mentioned before, that old age had very little of Mr. Johnson's reverence: 'a man commonly grew wickeder as he grew older (he said), at least he but changed the vices of youth; headstrong passion and wild temerity, for treacherous caution, and desire to circumvent. I am always (said he) on the young people's side, when there is a dispute between them and the old ones: for you have at least a chance for virtue till age has withered its very root[2].' While we were talking, my mother's spaniel, whom he never loved, stole our toast and butter; Fye Belle! said I, you used to be upon honour: 'Yes

ried the widow of W. P. King, Esq., who left his whole estate to her, by which means she brought a large fortune to her second husband.' Burke's *Peerage*. Johnson visited him with the Thrales in 1774. *Life*, v. 455.

[1] 'Poverty, my dear friend, is so great an evil, and pregnant with so much temptation, and so much misery, that I cannot but earnestly enjoin you to avoid it.' *Ib.* iv. 149. 'Poverty takes away so many means of doing good, and produces so much inability to resist evil, both natural and moral, that it is by all virtuous means to be avoided.' *Ib.* p. 152. 'Resolve not to be poor: whatever you have, spend less. Poverty is a great enemy to human happiness; it certainly destroys liberty, and it makes some virtues impracticable, and others extremely difficult.' *Ib.* p. 157.

[2] 'I believe men may be generally observed to grow less tender as they advance in age.' *Rambler*, No. 78.

Madam

Madam (replies Johnson), *but Belle grows old.*' His reason for hating the dog was, 'because she was a professed favourite (he said), and because her Lady ordered her from time to time to be washed and combed: a foolish trick (said he) and an assumption of superiority that every one's nature revolts at; so because one must not wish ill to the Lady in such cases (continued he), one curses the cur.' The truth is, Belle was not well behaved, and being a large spaniel, was troublesome enough at dinner with frequent solicitations to be fed. 'This animal (said Dr. Johnson one day) would have been of extraordinary merit and value in the state of Lycurgus; for she condemns one to the exertion of perpetual vigilance.'

He had indeed that strong aversion felt by all the lower ranks of people towards four-footed companions very completely[1], notwithstanding he had for many years a cat which he called Hodge, that kept always in his room at Fleet-street; but so exact was he not to offend the human species by superfluous attention to brutes, that when the creature was grown sick and old, and could eat nothing but oysters, Mr. Johnson always went out himself to buy Hodge's dinner, that Francis the Black's delicacy might not be hurt, at seeing himself employed for the convenience of a quadruped[2].

No one was indeed so attentive not to offend in all such sort of things as Dr. Johnson; nor so careful to maintain the ceremonies of life: and though he told Mr. Thrale once, that he had never sought to please till past thirty years old, considering the matter as hopeless, he had been always studious not to make enemies, by apparent preference of himself[3]. It happened very comically, that the moment this curious conversation past, of which I was a silent auditress, was in the coach, in some distant province, either Shropshire or Derbyshire I believe[4]; and as soon as it was over, Mr. Johnson took out of his pocket a little book and

[1] If this was once true how great a change came over 'the lower ranks' in the next hundred years.

[2] *Life*, iv. 197.

[3] *Ante*, p. 169.

[4] They passed through these counties on their tour to Wales in 1774. *Life*, v. 427–460.

read,

read, while a gentleman of no small distinction for his birth and elegance, suddenly rode up to the carriage, and paying us all his proper compliments, was desirous not to neglect Dr. Johnson; but observing that he did not see him, tapt him gently on the shoulder—'Tis Mr. Ch—lm—ley, says my husband;—'Well, Sir! and what if it is Mr. Ch—lm—ley!' says the other sternly, just lifting his eyes a moment from his book, and returning to it again with renewed avidity [1].

He had sometimes fits of reading very violent; and when he was in earnest about getting through some particular pages, for I have heard him say he never read but one book, which he did not consider as obligatory, through in his whole life [2] (and Lady Mary Wortley's Letters [3] was the book); he would be quite lost to company, and withdraw all his attention to what he was reading, without the smallest knowledge or care about the noise made round him. His deafness made such conduct less odd and less difficult to him than it would have been to another man; but his advising others to take the same method, and pull a little book out when they were not entertained with what was going forward in society, seemed more likely to advance the growth of science than of polished manners, for which he always pretended extreme veneration [4].

[1] For Boswell's comment on this story see *Life*, iv. 345.

[2] 'Mr. Elphinston talked of a new book that was much admired, and asked Dr. Johnson if he had read it. JOHNSON. "I have looked into it." "What (said Elphinston,) have you not read it through?" Johnson, offended at being thus pressed, and so obliged to own his cursory mode of reading, answered tartly, "No, Sir, do *you* read books *through*?"' *Ib.* ii. 226.

He read *Amelia* through without stopping (*Ib.* iii. 43), and rejoiced at finding that *Clarissa* was not to be curtailed. *Letters*, i. 21. A few months before his death, having had the *Memoirs of Captain Carleton* sent to him when 'he was going to bed, he sat up till he had read it through.' *Life*, iv. 334. A year earlier he said:—'I have this year read all Virgil through. I read a book of the *Æneid* every night, so it was done in twelve nights, and I had great delight in it.' *Ib.* iv. 218.

[3] First published in 1763.

[4] 'Before dinner Dr. Johnson seized upon Mr. Charles Sheridan's *Account of the late Revolution in Sweden*, and seemed to read it ravenously, as if he devoured it, which was to all appearance his method of studying.' *Ib.* iii. 284.

Mr.

Mr. Johnson indeed always measured other people's notions of every thing by his own, and nothing could persuade him to believe, that the books which he disliked were agreeable to thousands, or that air and exercise which he despised were beneficial to the health of other mortals [1]. When poor Smart, so well known for his wit and misfortunes, was first obliged to be put in private lodgings [2], a common friend of both lamented in tender terms the necessity which had torn so pleasing a companion from their acquaintance—'A madman must be confined, Sir [3], (replies Dr. Johnson;) but, says the other, I am now apprehensive for his general health, he will lose the benefit of exercise. 'Exercise!' (returns the Doctor) I never heard that he used any: he might, for aught I know, walk *to* the alehouse; but I believe he was always *carried* home again.'

It was however unlucky for those who delighted to echo Johnson's sentiments, that he would not endure from them to-day what perhaps he had yesterday, by his own manner of treating the subject, made them fond of repeating; and I fancy

[1] *Ante*, p. 288.

[2] 'On the first attack of lunacy it is usual to confine the unhappy objects in private custody under the direction of their nearest friends and relations; but when the disorder is grown permanent, and the circumstances of the party will bear such additional expense, it is thought proper to apply to the royal authority to warrant a lasting confinement.' Blackstone's *Commentaries*, ed. 1775, i. 305. 'By the vagrant acts a method is chalked out for imprisoning, chaining and sending them to their proper homes.' *Ib.* iv. 25.

[3] Johnson said of his confinement:—'I did not think he ought to be shut up. His infirmities were not noxious to society. He insisted on people praying with him; and I'd as lief pray with Kit Smart as any one else. Another charge was, that he did not love clean linen; and I have no passion for it.' *Life*, i. 397.

One of Kit Smart's infirmities was like that of Mrs. Quickly's man. 'His worst fault is that he is given to prayer; he is something peevish that way; but nobody but has his fault; but let that pass.' *Merry Wives of Windsor*, Act i. sc. 4.

Smart died in the King's Bench Prison in 1770. Miss Burney says that not long before his death he wrote to her father to ask his assistance for a fellow-sufferer, adding 'that he had himself assisted him according to his willing poverty.' In another letter to Dr. Burney, who had raised a fund for his relief, he wrote:—'I bless God for your good nature, which please take as a receipt.' *Early Diary of F. Burney*, i. 127.

Mr.

Mr. B—— has not forgotten, that though his friend one evening in a gay humour talked in praise of wine as one of the blessings permitted by heaven, when used with moderation, to lighten the load of life, and give men strength to endure it; yet, when in consequence of such talk *he* thought fit to make a Bacchanalian discourse in its favour, Mr. Johnson contradicted him somewhat roughly as I remember; and when to assure himself of conquest he added these words, You must allow me, Sir, at least that it produces truth; *in vino veritas*, you know, Sir— 'That (replied Mr. Johnson) would be useless to a man who knew he was not a liar when he was sober [1].'

When one talks of giving and taking the lie familiarly, it is impossible to forbear recollecting the transactions between the editor of Ossian and the author of the Journey to the Hebrides. It was most observable to me however, that Mr. Johnson never bore his antagonist the slightest degree of ill-will. He always kept those quarrels which belonged to him as a writer, separate from those which he had to do with as a man; but I never did hear him say in private one malicious word of a public enemy; and of Mr. Macpherson I once heard him speak respectfully [2], though his reply to the friend who asked him if *any man living* could have written such a book, is well known, and has been often repeated: 'Yes, Sir; many men, many women, and many children [3].'

I enquired of him myself if this story was authentic, and he said it was. I made the same enquiry concerning his account of the state of literature in Scotland, which was repeated up and down at one time by every body—'How knowledge was divided

[1] Boswell, after relating the genuine anecdote, adds in a note:—'Mrs. Piozzi, in her *Anecdotes*, has given an erroneous account of this incident, as of many others. She pretends to relate it from recollection, as if she herself had been present; when the fact is that it was communicated to her by me. She has represented it as a personality, and the true point has escaped her.' *Life*, ii. 188.

[2] He had written to him:—'I will not desist from detecting what I think a cheat from any fear of the menaces of a ruffian.' *Ib.* ii. 297, *n.* 2.

[3] *Ib.* i. 396.

 among

among the Scots, like bread in a besieged town, to every man a mouthful, to no man a bellyful [1].' This story he likewise acknowledged, and said besides, 'that some officious friend had carried it to Lord Bute, who only answered—'Well, well! never mind what he says—he will have the pension all one.'

Another famous reply to a Scotsman who commended the beauty and dignity of Glasgow, till Mr. Johnson stopped him by observing, 'that he probably had never yet seen Brentford [2],' was one of the jokes he owned: and said himself, 'that when a gentleman of that country once mentioned the lovely prospects common in his nation, he could not help telling him, that the view of the London road was the prospect in which every Scotsman most naturally and most rationally delighted [3].'

Mrs. Brook received an answer not unlike this, when expatiating on the accumulation of sublime and beautiful objects, which form the fine prospect UP the river St. Lawrence in North America; 'Come Madam (says Dr. Johnson), confess that nothing ever equalled your pleasure in seeing that sight reversed; and finding yourself looking at the happy prospect DOWN the river St. Lawrence [4].' The truth is, he hated to hear about

[1] 'Their learning is like bread in a besieged town: every man gets a little, but no man gets a full meal.' *Life*, ii. 363.

[2] 'I once reminded him that when Dr. Adam Smith was expatiating on the beauty of Glasgow, he had cut him short by saying, "Pray, Sir, have you ever seen Brentford?" and I took the liberty to add, "My dear Sir, surely that was *shocking*." "Why then, Sir (he replied), you have never seen Brentford."' *Ib.* iv. 186; v. 369.

[3] For the correct version of this story see *ib.* i. 425.

[4] Frances Brooke. *Life*, iii. 259, *n.* 1. Her husband, Rev. John Brooke, D.D., was chaplain to the garrison at Quebec, whither they went soon after their marriage, about 1756. *Dict. Nat. Biog.*

'The evening before her departure to Canada some friends met at her apartments to take their farewell, Miss Hannah More, Miss Seward, Mr. Keate, Dr. Johnson and Mr. Boswell were among her visitors. As Dr. Johnson was obliged to leave the company early he rose, and wishing her health and happiness went seemingly away. In a few minutes a servant came to acquaint her that a gentleman in the parlour wished to speak with her. She accordingly went down stairs, where she found the Doctor, who said to her, "Madam, I sent for you down stairs that I might kiss you, which I did not choose to do before so much com-

prospects

prospects and views, and laying out ground and taste in gardening[1]: 'That was the best garden (he said) which produced most roots and fruits; and that water was most to be prized which contained most fish.' He used to laugh at Shenstone most unmercifully for not caring whether there was any thing good to *eat* in the streams he was so fond of, 'as if (says Johnson) one could fill one's belly with hearing soft murmurs, or looking at rough cascades[2]!'

He loved the sight of fine forest trees however, and detested Brighthelmstone Downs, 'because it was a country so truly desolate (he said), that if one had a mind to hang one's self for desperation at being obliged to live there, it would be difficult to find a tree on which to fasten the rope.' Walking in a wood when it rained, was, I think, the only rural image he pleased his fancy with[3]; 'for (says he) after one has gathered the apples in an orchard, one wishes them well baked, and removed to a London eating-house for enjoyment.'

With such notions, who can wonder he passed his time uncomfortably enough with us, whom he often complained of for living so much in the country; 'feeding the chickens (as he said I did) till I starved my own understanding. Get however (said he) a book about gardening, and study it hard, since you will pass your life with birds and flowers, and learn to raise the *largest* turnips,

pany."' *European Magazine*, xv. 100.

If there is any truth in this story it is wrong in its particulars, for at this time Boswell and Hannah More did not know Johnson.

[1] 'I have a notion,' writes Boswell, 'that he at no time has had much taste for rural beauties. I have myself very little.' *Life*, v. 112. See *ante*, p. 215.

[2] 'We talked of Shenstone. Dr. Johnson said he was a good layer-out of land, but would not allow him to approach excellence as a poet.' *Life*, v. 267. After describing him as 'a layer-out of land' Johnson continues:—'Perhaps a surly and a sullen speculator may think such performances rather the sport than the business of human reason.' *Works*, viii. 409. 'Nothing raised Shenstone's indignation more than to ask if there were any fishes in his water.' *Ib.* p. 410.

[3] When he was kept in town by his *Lives of the Poets* he wrote to Mr. Thrale:—'I hope to see standing corn in some part of the earth this summer, but I shall hardly smell hay or suck clover-flowers.' *Letters*, ii. 163.

turnips, and to breed the *biggest* fowls.' It was vain to assure him that the goodness of such dishes did not depend upon their size; he laughed at the people who covered their canals[1] with foreign fowls, 'when (says he) our own geese and ganders are twice as large: if we fetched better animals from distant nations, there might be some sense in the preference; but to get cows from Alderney, or water-fowl from China, only to see nature degenerating round one, is a poor ambition indeed.'

Nor was Mr. Johnson more merciful with regard to the amusements people are contented to call such: 'You hunt in the morning (says he), and crowd to the public rooms at night, and call it *diversion*[2]; when your heart knows it is perishing with poverty of pleasures, and your wits get blunted for want of some other mind to sharpen them upon. There is in this world no real delight (excepting those of sensuality), but exchange of ideas in conversation[3]; and whoever has once experienced the full flow of London talk, when he retires to country friendships and rural sports, must either be contented to turn baby again and play with the rattle, or he will pine away like a great fish in a little pond, and die for want of his usual food[4].'—'Books without the knowledge of life are useless (I have heard him say); for what should books teach but the art of *living*? To study manners however only in coffee-houses, is more than equally imperfect; the minds of men who acquire no solid learning, and only

[1] Johnson's first definition of *Canal* is *a bason of water in a garden.*

[2] '*Diversion* seems to be something lighter than *amusement* and less forcible than *pleasure.*' Johnson's *Dictionary.* 'The publick pleasures of far the greater part of mankind are counterfeit.' *Idler*, No. 18.

[3] *Ante*, p. 308.

[4] 'Talking of a London life, he said, "The happiness of London is not to be conceived but by those who have been in it. I will venture to say, there is more learning and science within the circumference of ten miles from where we now sit, than in all the rest of the kingdom."' *Life*, ii. 75.

'I observed to Dr. Johnson, that I had a most disagreeable notion of the life of country gentlemen; that I left Mr. Fraser just now, as one leaves a prisoner in a jail. Dr. Johnson said, that I was right in thinking them unhappy; for that they had not enough to keep their minds in motion.' *Ib.* v. 108. Mrs. Thrale writing to him in 1777, says:—'You would rather be sick in London than well in the country.' *Piozzi Letters*, i. 394.

exist

exist on the daily forage that they pick up by running about, and snatching what drops from their neighbours as ignorant as themselves, will never ferment into any knowledge valuable or durable[1]; but like the light wines we drink in hot countries, please for the moment though incapable of keeping. In the study of mankind much will be found to swim as froth, and much must sink as feculence, before the wine can have its effect, and become that noblest liquor which rejoices the heart, and gives vigour to the imagination.'

I am well aware that I do not, and cannot give each expression of Dr. Johnson with all its force or all its neatness; but I have done my best to record such of his maxims, and repeat such of his sentiments, as may give to those who knew him not, a just idea of his character and manner of thinking. To endeavour at adorning, or adding, or softening, or meliorating such anecdotes, by any tricks my inexperienced pen could play, would be weakness indeed[2]; worse than the Frenchman who presides over the porcelain manufactory at Seve[3]; to whom when some Greek vases were given him as models, he lamented *la tristesse de telles formes*; and endeavoured to assist them by clusters of flowers, while flying Cupids served for the handles of urns originally intended to contain the ashes of the dead. The misery is, that I can recollect so few anecdotes, and that I have recorded no more axioms of a man whose every word merited attention, and whose every sentiment did honour to human nature. Remote from affectation as from error or falsehood, the comfort a reader has in looking over these papers, is the certainty that those were *really* the opinions of Johnson, which are related as such.

Fear of what others may think, is the great cause of affectation; and he was not likely to disguise his notions out of

[1] See *Life*, iii. 308, *n.* 3, for Tom Restless.

[2] 'I besought Boswell's tenderness for our virtuous and most revered departed friend, and begged he would mitigate some of his asperities. He said roughly: "He would not cut off his claws, nor make a tiger a cat, to please anybody."' H. More's *Memoirs*, i. 403.

[3] The Thrales and Johnson visited Sèvres in 1775. *Life*, ii. 397.

cowardice.

cowardice. He hated disguise, and nobody penetrated it so readily[1]. I shewed him a letter written to a common friend, who was at some loss for the explanation of it: 'Whoever wrote it (says our Doctor) could, if he chose it, make himself understood; but 'tis the letter of an *embarrassed man, Sir*;' and so the event proved it to be.

Mysteriousness in trifles offended him on every side[2]: 'it commonly ended in guilt (he said); for those who begin by concealment of innocent things, will soon have something to hide which they dare not bring to light.' He therefore encouraged an openness of conduct, in women particularly, 'who (he observed) were often led away when children, by their delight and power of surprising.' He recommended, on something like the same principle, that when one person meant to serve another, he should not go about it slily, or as we say underhand, out of a false idea of delicacy, to surprise one's friend with an unexpected favour, 'which, ten to one (says he), fails to oblige your acquaintance, who had some reasons against such a mode of obligation, which you might have known but for that superfluous cunning which you think an elegance. Oh! never be seduced by such silly pretences (continued he); if a wench wants a good gown, do not give her a fine smelling-bottle, because that is more delicate: as I once knew a lady[3] lend the key of her library to a poor scribbling dependant, as if she took the woman for an ostrich that could digest iron.' He said indeed, 'that women were very difficult to be taught the proper

[1] 'Dr. Johnson talked of that studied behaviour which many have recommended and practised. He disapproved of it; and said, "I never considered whether I should be a grave man, or a merry man, but just let inclination, for the time, have its course."' *Life*, i. 470.

'La gravité est un mystère du corps, inventé pour cacher les défauts de l'esprit.' LA ROCHEFOUCAULD, *Maximes*, No. 265.

'Gravity is of the very essence of imposture.' Shaftesbury's *Characteristicks*, ed. 1714, i. 11.

'Ciceron laissait aux petits esprits leur constante gravité, qui n'est que la masque de la médiocrité.' VOLTAIRE: quoted in Warton's *Pope's Works*, iv. 222.

[2] Horace Walpole (*Letters*, iii. 371) calls mystery 'the wisdom of blockheads.'

[3] 'This lady was Mrs. Montagu.' Hayward's *Piozzi*, i. 296.

manner

manner of conferring pecuniary favours ; that they always gave too much money or too little; for that they had an idea of delicacy accompanying their gifts, so that they generally rendered them either useless or ridiculous.'

He did indeed say very contemptuous things of our sex ; but was exceedingly angry when I told Miss Reynolds that he said, 'It was well managed of some one to leave his affairs in the hands of his wife, because, in matters of business (said he), no woman stops at integrity[1].' This was, I think, the only sentence I ever observed him solicitous to explain away after he had uttered it[2]. He was not at all displeased at the recollection of a sarcasm thrown on a whole profession at once; when a gentleman leaving the company, somebody who sate next Dr. Johnson, asked him, who he was? 'I cannot exactly tell you Sir (replied he), and I would be loth to speak ill of any person who I do not know deserves it, but I am afraid he is an *attorney*[3].' He did not however encourage general satire[4], and for the most part professed himself to feel directly contrary to Dr. Swift ; 'who (says he) hates the world, though he loves John and Robert, and certain individuals.'

Johnson said always, 'that the world was well constructed, but that the particular people disgraced the elegance and beauty of the general fabric.' In the same manner I was relating once

[1] His anger at this being told to Miss Reynolds was probably due to his high opinion of her virtue. See *ante*, p. 207.

[2] 'JOHNSON (who, from drinking only water, supposed every body who drank wine to be elevated,) "I won't argue any more with you, Sir. You are too far gone." SIR JOSHUA. "I should have thought so indeed, Sir, had I made such a speech as you have now done." "JOHNSON (drawing himself in, and, I really thought, blushing,) "Nay, don't be angry. I did not mean to offend you."' *Life*, iii. 329.

[3] 'Much enquiry having been made concerning a gentleman, who had quitted a company where Johnson was, and no information being obtained ; at last Johnson observed, that "he did not care to speak ill of any man behind his back, but he believed the gentleman was an *attorney*."' *Life*, ii. 126. When we see how this sarcasm has been spoilt in the telling by Mrs. Piozzi, we may quote Mr. Fitzherbert's saying, 'It is not every man that can carry a bon-mot.' *Ib.* ii. 350.

[4] See *ante*, p. 223 for his 'aversion to general satire.'

to him, how Dr. Collier[1] observed, that the love one bore to children was from the anticipation one's mind made while one contemplated them: 'We hope (says he) that they will some time make wise men, or amiable women; and we suffer 'em to take up our affection beforehand. One cannot love *lumps of flesh*, and little infants are nothing more. On the contrary (says Johnson), one can scarcely help wishing, while one fondles a baby, that it may never live to become a man; for it is *so* probable that when he becomes a man, he should be sure to end in a scoundrel[2].' Girls were less displeasing to him; 'for as their temptations were fewer (he said), their virtue in this life, and happiness in the next, were less improbable[3]; and he loved (he said) to see a knot of little misses dearly.'

Needle-work had a strenuous approver in Dr. Johnson, who said, 'that one of the great felicities of female life, was the general consent of the world, that they might amuse themselves with petty occupations, which contributed to the lengthening their lives, and preserving their minds in a state of sanity.' A man cannot hem a pocket-handkerchief (said a lady of quality to him one day), and so he runs mad, and torments his family and friends. The expression struck him exceedingly, and when one acquaintance grew troublesome, and another unhealthy, he used to quote Lady Frances's observation, 'That a man cannot hem a pocket-handkerchief[4].'

The nice people[5] found no mercy from Mr. Johnson; such I mean as can dine only at four o'clock, who cannot bear to be waked at an unusual hour, or miss a stated meal without inconvenience.

[1] *Ante*, p. 246.

[2] Johnson could never have said 'it is so probable that he should be sure.' For his use of the word *scoundrel* see *Life*, iii. 1.

[3] 'Women,' said Johnson, 'have not the same temptations that we have: they may always live in virtuous company; men must mix in the world indiscriminately.' *Ib.* iii. 287.

[4] 'Women have a great advantage that they may take up with little things, without disgracing themselves: a man cannot, except with fiddling. Had I learnt to fiddle, I should have done nothing else.' *Ib.* iii. 242.

[5] *Nice* in the sense in which it is commonly used at the present time is not given in Johnson's *Dictionary*.

venience. *He* had no such prejudices himself[1], and with difficulty forgave them in another. 'Delicacy does not surely consist (says he) in impossibility to be pleased, and that is false dignity indeed which is content to depend upon others.'

The saying of the old philosopher, who observes, That he who wants least is most like the gods, who want nothing[2]; was a favourite sentence with Dr. Johnson, who on his own part required less attendance, sick or well, than ever I saw any human creature[3]. Conversation was all he required to make him happy; and when he would have tea made at two o'clock in the morning, it was only that there might be a certainty of detaining his companions round him[4]. On that principle it was that he preferred winter to summer, when the heat of the weather gave people an excuse to stroll about, and walk for pleasure in the shade, while he wished to sit still on a chair, and chat day after day, till somebody proposed a drive in the coach; and that was the most delicious moment of his life[5]. 'But the carriage must stop sometime (as he said), and the people would come home at last;' so his pleasure was of short duration.

I asked him why he doated on a coach so? and received for answer, 'That in the first place, the company was shut in with him *there*; and could not escape, as out of a room: in the next place, he heard all that was said in a carriage, where it was my turn to be deaf:' and very impatient was he at my occasional

[1] 'JOHNSON. I never felt any difference upon myself from eating one thing rather than another . . . There are people, I believe, who feel a difference; but I am not one of them. And as to regular meals, I have fasted from the Sunday's dinner to the Tuesday's dinner without any inconvenience. I believe it is best to eat just as one is hungry; but a man who is in business, or a man who has a family, must have stated meals.' *Life*, iii. 305.

[2] Socrates. Ἐγὼ δὲ νομίζω τὸ μὲν μηδενὸς δεῖσθαι θεῖον εἶναι, τὸ δ' ὡς ἐλαχίστων, ἐγγυτάτω τοῦ θείου. *Memorabilia*, i. 6. 10.

'Deum quem a teneris coluit cum primis imitatus est paucis egendo.' Epitaph on Dr. Barrow. *Life of Seth Ward*, p. 168.

[3] 'There is nothing,' he said, 'against which an old man should be so much upon his guard as putting himself to nurse.' *Life*, ii. 474.

[4] *Ante*, p. 231.

[5] *Life*, iii. 5, 162.

difficulty

difficulty of hearing. On this account he wished to travel all over the world [1]; for the very act of going forward was delightful to him, and he gave himself no concern about accidents, which he said never happened: nor did the running-away of the horses on the edge of a precipice between Vernon and St. Denys in France [2] convince him to the contrary; 'for nothing came of it (he said), except that Mr. Thrale leaped out of the carriage into a chalk-pit, and then came up again, looking *as white!*' When the truth was, all their lives were saved by the greatest providence ever exerted in favour of three human creatures; and the part Mr. Thrale took from desperation was the likeliest thing in the world to produce broken limbs and death.

Fear was indeed a sensation to which Mr. Johnson was an utter stranger, excepting when some sudden apprehensions seized him that he was going to die [3]; and even then he kept all his wits about him, to express the most humble and pathetic petitions to the Almighty: and when the first paralytic stroke [4] took his speech from him, he instantly set about composing a prayer in Latin, at once to deprecate God's mercy, to satisfy himself that his mental powers remained unimpaired, and to keep them in exercise, that they might not perish by permitted stagnation. This was after we parted; but he wrote me an account of it, and I intend to publish that letter [5], with many more.

[1] For his love of travelling see *Life*, iii. 449.

[2] Johnson's Journal for this part of his tour is missing.

[3] 'JOHNSON. "Fear is one of the passions of human nature of which it is impossible to divest it. You remember that the Emperour Charles V, when he read upon the tomb-stone of a Spanish nobleman, 'Here lies one who never knew fear,' wittily said, 'Then he never snuffed a candle with his fingers.'"' *Life*, ii. 81. 'Johnson feared death, but he feared nothing else, not even what might occasion death.' *Ib.* ii. 298.

'It was the saying of one of the bravest men in this age, to one who told him he feared nothing, "Shew me but a certain danger, and I shall be as much afraid as any of you."' Pope's *Iliad*, ed. 1760, vi. 19, *n.*

'Daniel Webster, the day he died, said, "No man who is not a brute can say that he is not afraid of death."' Curtis's *Webster*, ii. 697.

[4] It does not seem that he had more than one stroke. For his prayer in Latin see *Life*, iv. 230, *n.* 1.

[5] His letter begins:—'I am sitting down in no cheerful solitude to write a narrative which would once have affected you with tenderness and sorrow, but which you will perhaps

When

When one day he had at my house taken tincture of antimony instead of emetic wine, for a vomit, he was himself the person to direct us what to do for him, and managed with as much coolness and deliberation as if he had been prescribing for an indifferent person. Though on another occasion, when he had lamented in the most piercing terms his approaching dissolution, and conjured me solemnly to tell him what I thought, while Sir Richard Jebb[1] was perpetually on the road to Streatham, and Mr. Johnson seemed to think himself neglected if the physician left him for an hour only, I made him a steady, but as I thought a very gentle harangue, in which I confirmed all that the Doctor had been saying, how no present danger could be expected; but that his age and continued ill health must naturally accelerate the arrival of that hour which can be escaped by none[2]: 'And this (says Johnson, rising in great anger) is the voice of female friendship I suppose, when the hand of the hangman would be softer.'

Another day, when he was ill, and exceedingly low-spirited, and persuaded that death was not far distant, I appeared before him in a dark-coloured gown, which his bad sight, and worse apprehensions, made him mistake for an iron-grey. 'Why do you delight (said he) thus to thicken the gloom of misery that surrounds me? is not here sufficient accumulation of horror without anticipated mourning?' This is not mourning Sir (said I), drawing the curtain, that the light might fall upon the silk, and shew it was a purple mixed with green. 'Well, well (replied he, changing his voice), you little creatures should never wear those sort of clothes however; they are unsuitable in every way. What! have not all insects gay colours[3]!' I relate these instances

pass over now with the careless glance of frigid indifference.' *Letters*, ii. 300.

[1] *Ib.* ii. 148, *n.* 2.

[2] Another time, when he was very ill, she had written to him 'about dying with a grace.' *Ib.* ii. 384.

[3] Quoted in the *Life*, i. 495.

'A lady who met her on her way to Wynnstay in January, 1803 [when she was sixty-two years old], describes her as "skipping about like a kid, quite a figure of fun, in a tiger skin shawl, lined with scarlet, and *only* five colours upon her head-dress—on the top of a flaxen wig a bandeau of blue velvet, a bit of tiger ribbon, a white beaver hat and plume of black feathers—as gay as a lark."' Hayward's *Piozzi*, i. 346.

instances chiefly to shew that the fears of death itself could not suppress his wit, his sagacity, or his temptation to sudden resentment.

Mr. Johnson did not like that his friends should bring their manuscripts for him to read, and he liked still less to read them when they were brought: sometimes however when he could not refuse he would take the play or poem, or whatever it was, and give the people his opinion from some one page that he had peeped into. A gentleman carried him his tragedy, which, because he loved the author[1], Johnson took, and it lay about our rooms some time. What answer did you give your friend, Sir? said I, after the book had been called for. 'I told him (replied he), that there was too much *Tig* and *Tirry* in it.' Seeing me laugh most violently, 'Why what would'st have, child?' (said he.) I looked at nothing but the dramatis [personæ], and there was *Tig*ranes and *Tiri*dates, or Teribazus, or such stuff[2]. A man can tell but what he knows, and I never got any further than the first page. Alas, Madam! (continued he) how few books are there of which one ever can possibly arrive at the *last* page! Was there ever yet any thing written by mere man that was wished longer by its readers, excepting Don Quixote, Robinson Crusoe[3], and the Pilgrim's Progress[4]?' After Homer's Iliad,

[1] Arthur Murphy, whom Johnson 'very much loved.' *Life*, ii. 127.

[2] In Murphy's tragedy of *Zenobia* two of the characters are Teribazus and Tigranes.

[3] Smollett describes the author 'as one Daniel de Foe, a scurrilous party-writer, in very little estimation.' *History of England*, ed. 1800, i. 420.

[4] *Ante*, p. 319. For Johnson's admiration of Bunyan see *Life*, ii. 238. I have collected the following instances of the estimate set on the *Pilgrim's Progress* last century.

1710. Addison. 'I never yet knew an author that had not his admirers. Bunyan and Quarles have passed through several editions, and please as many readers as Dryden and Tillotson.' *The Whig Examiner*, No. 2.

1720. Swift. 'I have been better entertained and more informed by a few pages in the *Pilgrim's Progress* than by a long discourse upon the will and the intellect and simple or complex ideas.' *A Letter to a Young Clergyman. Works*, ed. 1803, viii. 20.

1741. *Gentleman's Magazine*, p. 488. 'Take it all together there never was an Allegory better designed or better supported.'

1758. Mrs. Montagu. 'Bunyan and Quarles, those classics of the artificers

Mr.

Mr. Johnson confessed that the work of Cervantes was the greatest in the world, speaking of it I mean as a book of entertainment; and when we consider that every other author's admirers are confined to his countrymen, and perhaps to the literary classes among *them*, while Don Quixote is a sort of common property, an universal classic, equally tasted by the court and the cottage, equally applauded in France and England as in Spain, quoted by every servant, the amusement of every age from infancy to decrepitude; the first book you see on every shelf, in every shop, where books are sold, through all the states of Italy; who can refuse his consent to an avowal of the

in leather.' *Letters of Mrs. Montagu*, iv. 78.

1759. Burke. 'The admirer of *Don Bellianis* perhaps does not understand the refined language of the Eneid, who, if it was degraded into the style of the *Pilgrim's Progress*, might feel it in all its energy on the same principle which made him an admirer of *Don Bellianis*.' *On the Sublime and Beautiful*, ed. 1759, p. 25.

1765. *Gentleman's Magazine*, p. 168. '*The Pilgrim's Progress* is certainly a work of original and uncommon genius.'

1776. Beattie. 'Certain it is that fables in which there is neither love nor gallantry may be made highly interesting even to the fancy and affections of a modern reader. This appears not only from the writings of Shakespeare and other great authors, but from the *Pilgrim's Progress* of Bunyan, and the *History of Robinson Crusoe*.' *Essays on Poetry and Music*, ed. 1779, p. 191.

1782. Horace Walpole. 'Dante was extravagant, absurd, disgusting, in short a Methodist Parson in Bedlam. Ariosto was a more agreeable Amadis de Gaul, and Spenser, John Bunyan in rhyme.' Walpole's *Letters*, viii. 235.

1785. Cowper:—

'I name thee not, lest so despised a name
Should move a sneer at thy deserved fame,
Yet ev'n in transitory life's late day
That mingles all my brown with sober grey,
Revere the man whose *Pilgrim* marks the road
And guides the *Progress* of the soul to God.'

Tirocinium. Poems, 1786, ii, 298.

Macaulay, in 1830, wrote:—'Cowper said forty or fifty years ago that he dared not name John Bunyan in his verse for fear of moving a sneer. To our refined forefathers, we suppose, Lord Roscommon's Essay on Translated Verse, and the Duke of Buckinghamshire's Essay on Poetry, appeared to be compositions infinitely superior to the allegory of the preaching tinker. We live in better times,' &c. *Essays*, ed. 1843, i. 424. Not six years after Macaulay wrote this, the *Pilgrim's Progress* was described in the *Penny Cyclopaedia*, vi. 20, as a 'coarse allegory . . . mean, jejune and wearisome.'

superiority

superiority of Cervantes to all other modern writers? Shakespeare himself has, till lately, been worshipped only at home, though his plays are now the favourite amusements of Vienna; and when I was at Padua some months ago, Romeo and Juliet was acted there under the name of *Tragedia Veronese*; while engravers and translators *live* by the Hero of La Mancha in every nation, and the sides of miserable inns all over England and France, and I have heard Germany too, are adorned with the exploits of Don Quixote. May his celebrity procure my pardon for a digression in praise of a writer who, through four volumes of the most exquisite pleasantry and genuine humour, has never been seduced to overstep the limits of propriety, has never called in the wretched auxiliaries of obscenity or profaneness; who trusts to nature and sentiment alone, and never misses of that applause which Voltaire and Sterne labour to produce [1], while honest merriment bestows her unfading crown upon Cervantes.

Dr. Johnson was a great reader of French literature, and delighted exceedingly in Boileau's works [2]. Moliere I think he had hardly sufficient taste of; and he used to condemn me for preferring La Bruyère to the Duc de Rochefoucault, 'who (he said) was the only *gentleman* writer who wrote like a professed author.' The asperity of his harsh sentences, each of them a sentence of condemnation, used to disgust me however; though it must be owned, that, among the necessaries of human life, a *rasp* is reckoned one as well as a *razor*.

Mr. Johnson did not like any one who said they were happy, or who said any one else was so. 'It is all *cant* (he would cry), the dog knows he is miserable all the time [3].' A friend whom

[1] Goldsmith called Sterne 'a bawdy blockhead.' *Citizen of the World*, *Letter* 74; *Life*, ii. 173, *n*. 2. When he said that he was 'a very dull fellow' Johnson replied, 'Why no Sir.' *Ib*. ii. 222. Later on however, Johnson said:—'Nothing odd will do long. *Tristram Shandy* did not last.' *Ib*. ii. 449.

[2] 'S'il m'est permis de parler pour moi-même, Boileau est un des hommes qui m'ont le plus occupé depuis que je fais de la critique, et avec qui j'ai le plus vécu en idée.' Sainte-Beuve, *Causeries de Lundi*, vi. 495.

[3] 'The world in its best state is nothing more than a larger assembly

he

he loved exceedingly, told him on some occasion notwithstanding, that his wife's sister was *really* happy, and called upon the lady to confirm his assertion, which she did somewhat roundly as we say, and with an accent and manner capable of offending Mr. Johnson, if her position had not been sufficient, without any thing more, to put him in very ill humour. 'If your sister-in-law is really the contented being she professes herself Sir (said he), her life gives the lie to every research of humanity; for she is happy without health, without beauty, without money, and without understanding.' This story he told me himself; and when I expressed something of the horror I felt, 'The same stupidity (said he) which prompted her to extol felicity she never felt, hindered her from feeling what shocks you on repetition. I tell you, the woman is ugly, and sickly, and foolish, and poor; and would it not make a man hang himself to hear such a creature say, it was happy?'

'The life of a sailor was also a continued scene of danger and exertion (he said); and the manner in which time was spent on shipboard would make all who saw a cabin envy a gaol [1].' The roughness of the language used on board a man of war, where he passed a week on a visit to Capt. Knight, disgusted him terribly. He asked an officer what some place was called, and received for answer, that it was where the loplolly man kept his loplolly [2]: a reply he considered, not unjustly, as disrespectful,

of beings, combining to counterfeit happiness which they do not feel.' *Works*, iv. 120. See *Life*, ii. 350; iii. 53.

[1] 'He said, "No man will be a sailor who has contrivance enough to get himself into a jail; for being in a ship is being in a jail, with the chance of being drowned." And at another time, "A man in a jail has more room, better food, and commonly better company."' *Life*, i. 348.

'There is no slavery worse than that sailors are subjected to.' Franklin's *Works*, ed. 1889, iv. 73. Yet even their lot was better than the soldiers'. 'The son of a creditable labourer or artificer may frequently go to sea with his father's consent; but if he inlists as a soldier it is always without it.' *Wealth of Nations*, ed. 1811, i. 148.

[2] Johnson and Reynolds visited Plymouth in 1762. *Life*, i. 378. Mr. Croker says that Captain Knight of the *Belleisle* lay for a couple of months in 1762 in Plymouth Sound. Croker's *Boswell*, p. 480. It seems unlikely that Johnson passed a whole

gross,

gross, and ignorant; for though in the course of these Memoirs I have been led to mention Dr. Johnson's tenderness towards *poor* people, I do not wish to mislead my readers, and make them think he had any delight in *mean* manners or coarse expressions[1]. Even dress itself, when it resembled that of the vulgar, offended him exceedingly; and when he had condemned me many times for not adorning my children with more show than I thought useful or elegant, I presented a little girl to him who came o'visiting one evening covered with shining ornaments, to see if he would approve of the appearance she made. When they were gone home, Well Sir, said I, how did you like little miss? I hope she was *fine* enough. 'It was the finery of a beggar (said he), and you know it was; she looked like a native of Cow-lane dressed up to be carried to Bartholomew-fair[2].'

His reprimand to another lady for crossing her little child's handkerchief before, and by that operation dragging down its head oddly and unintentionally, was on the same principle. 'It is the beggar's fear of cold (said he) that prevails over such parents, and so they pull the poor thing's head down, and give it the look of a baby that plays about Westminster-Bridge, while the mother sits shivering in a *niche*[3].'

I commended a young lady for her beauty and pretty behaviour one day however, to whom I thought no objections could have been made. 'I saw her (says Dr. Johnson) take a pair of scissars in her left hand though; and for all her father is now

week on ship-board. *Loplolly*, or *Loblolly*, is explained in *Roderick Random*, chap. xxvii. Roderick, when acting as the surgeon's assistant on a man of war, 'suffered,' he says, 'from the rude insults of the sailors and petty officers, among whom I was known by the name of *Loblolly Boy*.'

[1] *Ante*, p. 292, *n* 5.

[2] Five Cow Lanes are mentioned in Dodsley's *London*, 1761, ii. 197.

The fair was held in Smithfield 'at Bartholomew-tide.' *Ib.* vi. 29.

[3] Johnson defines *niche* 'a hollow in which a statue may be placed.' In many of the recesses on the Bridge were 'pedestals on which was intended [*sic*] a group of figures.' *Ib.* vi. 286.

become

become a nobleman, and as you say excessively rich [1], I should, were I a youth of quality ten years hence, hesitate between a girl so neglected, and a *negro*.'

It was indeed astonishing how he *could* remark such minutenesses with a sight so miserably imperfect; but no accidental position of a ribband escaped him, so nice was his observation, and so rigorous his demands of propriety [2]. When I went with him to Litchfield and came down stairs to breakfast at the inn [3], my dress did not please him, and he made me alter it entirely before he would stir a step with us about the town, saying most satirical things concerning the appearance I made in a riding-habit; and adding, ''Tis very strange that such eyes as yours cannot discern propriety of dress: if I had a sight only half as good, I think I should see to the centre.'

My compliances however were of little worth: what really surprised me was the victory he gained over a Lady little accustomed to contradiction, who had dressed herself for church at Streatham one Sunday morning, in a manner he did not approve, and to whom he said such sharp and pungent things concerning her hat, her gown, &c. that she hastened to change them, and returning quite another figure received his applause, and thanked him for his reproofs, much to the amazement of her husband, who could scarcely believe his own ears.

[1] Perhaps Lord Sandys (*ante*, p. 316, *n*. 3), who became a nobleman a year after his marriage.

[2] 'I supposed him,' writes Boswell, 'to be only near-sighted; and indeed I must observe, that in no other respect could I discern any defect in his vision; on the contrary, the force of his attention and perceptive quickness made him see and distinguish all manner of objects, whether of nature or of art, with a nicety that is rarely to be found. . . . The ladies with whom he was acquainted agree, that no man was more nicely and minutely critical in the elegance of female dress.' *Life*, i. 41.

'His blindness,' wrote Miss Burney, 'is as much the effect of absence [of mind] as of infirmity, for he sees wonderfully at times. He can see the colour of a lady's top-knot, for he very often finds fault with it.' Mme. D'Arblay's *Diary*, ii. 174.

[3] The Swan. *Life*, v. 428. Boswell and Johnson in 1776 stayed at the Three Crowns. *Ib*. ii. 461. In 1779 Boswell passed a night at the George. *Ib*. iii. 411. All three inns still exist.

Another

Another lady, whose accomplishments he never denied, came to our house one day covered with diamonds, feathers, &c.[1] and he did not seem inclined to chat with her as usual. I asked him why? when the company was gone. 'Why; her head looked so like that of a woman who shews puppets (said he), and her voice so confirmed the fancy, that I could not bear her to-day; when she wears a large cap, I can talk to her.'

When the ladies wore lace trimmings to their clothes, he expressed his contempt of the reigning fashion in these terms: 'A Brussels trimming is like bread sauce (said he), it takes away the glow of colour from the gown, and gives you nothing instead of it; but sauce was invented to heighten the flavour of our food, and trimming is an ornament to the manteau[2], or it is nothing. Learn (said he) that there is propriety or impropriety in every thing how slight soever, and get at the general principles of dress and of behaviour; if you then transgress them, you will at least know that they are not observed.'

All these exactnesses in a man who was nothing less than exact himself, made him extremely impracticable as an inmate, though most instructive as a companion, and useful as a friend. Mr. Thrale too could sometimes over-rule his rigidity, by saying

[1] Most likely Mrs. Montagu. 'The Queen of the *bas bleus*, Mrs. Montagu, crowned her *toupet*, and circled her neck with diamonds, when she received an assembly of foreigners, literati, and maccaronis, in her dressing-room, the walls of which were newly painted with "bowers of roses and jessamines, entirely inhabited by little cupids."' *Early Diary of F. Burney*, i. Preface, p. 85. Miss Burney speaks of her 'parade and ostentation.' Mme. D'Arblay's *Diary*, i. 325.

'Daddy' Crisp wrote of Mrs. Montagu to Miss Burney in 1780:—'I believe I have told you of several letters the Duchess of Portland shewed me of hers formerly, so full of affectation, refinement, attempts to philosophize, talking metaphysics—in all which particulars she so bewildered and puzzled herself and her readers, and showed herself so superficial, nay, really ignorant in the subjects she paraded on—that in my own private mind's pocket-book I set her down for a vain, empty, conceited pretender, and little else.' *Early Diary*, i. Preface, p. 34, *n.* 2. For her pretentious *Essay on Shakespeare*, see *Life*, ii. 88. See also *ante*, p. 287.

[2] *Manteau* is not in Johnson's *Dictionary*.

coldly, There, there, now we have had enough for one lecture, Dr. Johnson; we will not be upon education any more till after dinner, if you please—or some such speech [1]: but when there was nobody to restrain his dislikes, it was extremely difficult to find any body with whom he could converse, without living always on the verge of a quarrel, or of something too like a quarrel to be pleasing [2]. I came into the room, for example, one evening, where he and a gentleman, whose abilities we all respect exceedingly, were sitting; a lady who walked in two minutes before me had blown 'em both into a flame, by whispering something to Mr. S——d, which he endeavoured to explain away, so as not to affront the Doctor, whose suspicions were all alive. 'And have a care, Sir (said he), just as I came in; the Old Lion will not bear to be tickled.' The other was pale with rage, the Lady wept at the confusion she had caused [3], and I could only say with Lady Macbeth,

> Soh! you've displac'd the mirth, broke the good meeting
> With most admir'd disorder [4].

Such accidents however occurred too often, and I was forced to take advantage of my lost lawsuit [5], and plead inability of

[1] 'I know no man (said Johnson) who is more master of his wife and family than Thrale. If he but holds up a finger he is obeyed.' *Life*, i. 494. He was, it seems, master also of his guest, even when his guest was Johnson.

[2] See *ante*, p. 310, where she writes:—'I saw Mr. Johnson in none but a tranquil uniform state, passing the evening of his life among friends who loved, honoured, and admired him.'

[3] Mr. S—d was no doubt William Seward (*Life*, iii. 123), and the lady who wept was most probably Sophy Streatfield.

'"I'm sure," said Mrs. Thrale, "when she cried for Seward I never saw her look half so lovely."

'"For Seward?" cried Sir Philip [Clerk]; "did she cry for Seward?"

'"Seward," said Mrs. Thrale, "had affronted Johnson, and then Johnson affronted Seward, and then the S. S. cried."

'SIR PHILIP. "But what did Seward do? was he not melted?"

'MRS. THRALE. "Not he; he was thinking only of his own affront and taking fire at that."' Mme. D'Arblay's *Diary*, i. 227.

[4] 'You have displaced' &c. *Macbeth*, Act iii. sc. 5. 'Soh!' is Mrs. Thrale's addition.

[5] Mrs. Piozzi seems to have thought that her lost lawsuit was known to all the world. What it was is shown by the following entries. 'My uncle's widow, Lady Salusbury, had

purse to remain longer in London or its vicinage. I had been crossed in my intentions of going abroad [1], and found it convenient, for every reason of health, peace, and pecuniary circumstances, to retire to Bath, where I knew Mr. Johnson would not follow me, and where I could for that reason command some little portion of time for my own use; a thing impossible while I remained at Streatham or at London, as my hours, carriage, and servants had long been at his command, who would not rise in the morning till twelve o'clock perhaps [2], and oblige me to make

threatened to seize upon my Welsh estate if I did not repay *her* money lent by Sir Thomas Salusbury to my father; money in effect which poor papa had borrowed to give *him* when he was a student at Cambridge, and your little friend just born. This debt, however, not having been cancelled, stood against me as heiress.' Hayward's *Piozzi*, ii. 57. 'Aug. 22, 1782. My lawsuit with Lady Salusbury turns out worse in the event and infinitely more costly than I could have dreamed on; £8,000 is supposed necessary to the payment of it.' *Ib.* i. 169. 'Jan. 29, 1783. I told Dr. Johnson and Mr. Crutchley three days ago . . . that I would go and live in a little way at Bath till I had paid all my debts and cleared my income. . . . I may in six or seven years be freed from all incumbrances, and carry a clear income of £2500 a year and an estate of £500 in land to the man of my heart.' *Ib.* i. 195.

[1] 'Dec. 1. 1782. The guardians have met upon the scheme of putting our girls in Chancery. I was frighted at the project, not doubting but the Lord Chancellor would stop us from leaving England, as he would certainly see no joke in three young heiresses, his ward, quitting the kingdom to frisk away with their mother into Italy. . . . Nobody much applauded my resolution in going, but Johnson and Cator said they would not concur in stopping me by violence. . . . Jan. 29, 1783. I told Dr. Johnson and Mr. Crutchley three days ago that I had determined—seeing them so averse to it—that I would not go abroad.' *Ib.* i. 192–195.

[2] See *ante*, p. 37, where he recorded in 1766 that he had that year persisted in the habit of early rising, till 'I went to Mr. Thrale's; the irregularity of that family broke my habit of rising.' As for his call on her servants she herself has said, 'Dr. Johnson on his own part required less attendance, sick or well, than ever I saw any human creature.' *Ante*, p. 329.

According to Baretti: 'he wanted nothing else from her servants than to be shaved once in three days, as he was almost beardless; and as for her carriage never once during the whole time of their acquaintance did he borrow, much less *command* it, for any purpose of his own. . . . During his acquaintance with the Thrale family he got the habit of rising as early as other folks, nor ever made Mr. Thrale stay a single moment for his breakfast, knowing that his business called him away about ten o'clock every morning.' Croker's *Boswell*, ed. 1844, x. 36. Baretti left Streatham in June, 1776,

breakfast

breakfast for him till the bell rung for dinner, though much displeased if the toilet was neglected, and though much of the time we passed together was spent in blaming or deriding, very justly, my neglect of œconomy, and waste of that money which might make many families happy. The original reason of our connection, his *particularly disordered health and spirits*, had been long at an end [1], and he had no other ailments than old age and general infirmity [2], which every professor of medicine was ardently zealous and generally attentive to palliate, and to contribute all in their power for the prolongation of a life so valuable. Veneration for his virtue, reverence for his talents, delight in his conversation, and habitual endurance of a yoke my husband first put upon me, and of which he contentedly bore his share for sixteen or seventeen years, made me go on so long with Mr. Johnson; but the perpetual confinement I will own to have been terrifying in the first years of our friendship, and irksome in the last; nor could I pretend to support it without help, when my coadjutor was no more [3]. To the assistance we gave him, the shelter our house afforded to his uneasy fancies, and to the pains we took to sooth or repress them, the world perhaps is indebted for the three political pamphlets [4], the new edition and correction of his Dictionary, and for the Poets' Lives, which he would scarce have lived, I think, and kept his faculties entire, to have written, had not incessant care been exerted at the time of

having lived with the Thrales five years and a half. *Letters*, i. 403, *n*.6. He cannot therefore speak of the time after Mr. Thrale's death. The cheerfulness of the Streatham life during the life-time of its master is shown in Miss Burney's *Diaries*.

[1] *Ante*, p. 234. What had come to an end was the life of Mr. Thrale who, perhaps chiefly from compassion, had at first made Johnson an inmate of his house, but who came to take so much delight in his company that, as his wife said, 'he would go no-where that he could help without him.' *Life*, iii. 28, *n*.

[2] Her readers would hardly infer that he had had a stroke of palsy, a dangerous sarcocele, asthma, and dropsy.

[3] Boswell, quoting this passage, continues:—'Alas! how different is this from the declarations which I have heard Mrs. Thrale make in his life-time, without a single murmur against any peculiarities, or against any one circumstance which attended their intimacy.' *Ib.* iv. 340.

[4] He wrote four political pamphlets.

his

his first coming to be our constant guest in the country; and several times after that, when he found himself particularly oppressed with diseases incident to the most vivid and fervent imaginations. I shall for ever consider it as the greatest honour which could be conferred on any one, to have been the confidential friend of Dr. Johnson's health; and to have in some measure, with Mr. Thrale's assistance, saved from distress at least, if not from worse, a mind great beyond the comprehension of common mortals, and good beyond all hope of imitation from perishable beings [1].

Many of our friends were earnest that he should write the lives of our famous prose authors; but he never made any answer that I can recollect to the proposal, excepting when Sir Richard Musgrave once was singularly warm about it, getting up and intreating him to set about the work immediately; he coldly replied, '*Sit down, Sir* [2] *!*'

When Mr. Thrale built the new library at Streatham, and hung up over the books the portraits of his favourite friends, that of Dr. Johnson was last finished, and closed the number [3]. It was

[1] Writing of him and her mother she says:—'excellent as they both were, far beyond the excellence of any other man and woman I ever yet saw.' *Ante*, p. 235.

[2] Miss Burney describes Musgrave as 'a caricature of Mr. Boswell, who is a caricature of all others of Dr. Johnson's admirers.... The incense he paid Dr. Johnson by his solemn manner of listening, by the earnest reverence with which he eyed him, and by a theatric start of admiration every time he spoke, joined to the Doctor's utter insensibility to all these tokens, made me find infinite difficulty in keeping my countenance.' Mme. D'Arblay's *Diary*, ii. 84.

He published in 1802 *Memoirs of the Rebellions in Ireland.*

[3] 'The whole of them were sold by auction in the spring of 1816. According to Mrs. Piozzi's marked catalogue they fetched the following prices:—Lord Sandys, £36. 15; Lord Lyttelton [W. H. Lyttelton, afterwards Lord Westcote], £43. 1; Mrs. Piozzi and her daughter, £81. 18; Goldsmith (duplicate of the original), £133. 7; Sir J. Reynolds, £128. 2; Sir R. Chambers, £84; David Garrick, £183. 15; Baretti, £31. 10; Dr. Burney, £84; Edmund Burke, £252; Dr. Johnson, £378; "Mr. Murphy was offered £102. 18, but I bought it in."' Hayward's *Piozzi*, ii. 171. 'In 1780,' continues Mr. Hayward, 'Reynolds raised the price of his portraits (three-quarter size) from thirty-five to fifty guineas, which, Mrs. Piozzi complains, made the

almost

almost impossible *not* to make verses on such an accidental combination of circumstances, so I made the following ones: but as a character written in verse will for the most part be found imperfect as a character, I have therefore written a prose one, with which I mean, not to complete, but to conclude these Anecdotes of the best and wisest man that ever came within the reach of my personal acquaintance, and I think I might venture to add, that of all or any of my readers:

Gigantic in knowledge, in virtue, in strength,
Our company closes with JOHNSON at length;
So the Greeks from the cavern of Polypheme past,
When wisest, and greatest, Ulysses came last.
To his comrades contemptuous, we see him look down,
On their wit and their worth with a general frown.
Since from Science' proud tree the rich fruit he receives,
Who could shake the whole trunk while they turn'd a few leaves.
His piety pure, his morality nice—
Protector of virtue, and terror of vice;
In these features Religion's firm champion display'd,
Shall make infidels fear for a modern crusade.
While th' inflammable temper, the positive tongue,
Too conscious of right for endurance of wrong,
We suffer from JOHNSON, contented to find,
That some notice we gain from so noble a mind;
And pardon our hurts, since so often we've found
The balm of instruction pour'd into the wound.
'Tis thus for its virtues the chemists extol
Pure rectified spirit, sublime alcohol;
From noxious putrescence, preservative pure,
A cordial in health, and in sickness a cure;
But expos'd to the sun, taking fire at his rays,
Burns bright to the bottom, and ends in a blaze.

It is usual, I know not why, when a character is given, to begin with a description of the person; that which contained the

Streatham portraits in many instances cost more than they fetched, as she had to pay for them after Mr. Thrale's death at the increased price.'

Only three of the portraits fetched less than fifty guineas—those of W. H. Lyttelton, Sandys and Baretti. Lyttelton was painted in 1772, Sandys in 1773 (Leslie and Taylor's *Reynolds*, i. 507, 523), and Baretti in 1774 (*ib.* ii. 76). Leslie says that 'the portrait of Baretti is among the finest Reynolds ever painted.'

For the library at Streatham see *ante*, p. 109, and *Life*, iv. 158.

soul

soul of Mr. Johnson deserves to be particularly described [1]. His stature was remarkably high, and his limbs exceedingly large: his strength was more than common I believe, and his activity had been greater I have heard than such a form gave one reason to expect: his features were strongly marked, and his countenance particularly rugged; though the original complexion had certainly been fair, a circumstance somewhat unusual: his sight was near, and otherwise imperfect; yet his eyes, though of a light-grey colour, were so wild, so piercing, and at times so fierce, that fear was I believe the first emotion in the hearts of all his beholders. His mind was so comprehensive, that no language but that he used could have expressed its contents; and so ponderous was his language, that sentiments less lofty and less solid than his were, would have been encumbered, not adorned by it.

Mr. Johnson was not intentionally however a pompous converser; and though he was accused of using big words as they are called, it was only when little ones would not express his meaning as clearly, or when perhaps the elevation of the thought would have been disgraced by a dress less superb [2]. He used to say,

[1] In her *Thraliana* she records:—'One evening as I was giving my tongue liberty to praise Mr. Johnson to his face, a favour he would not often allow me, he said, in high good humour, "Come, you shall draw up my character your own way, and shew it me, that I may see what you will say of me when I am gone." At night I wrote as follows:—(Here follows the character in the text). When I shewed him his Character next day, for he would see it, he said, "It was a very fine piece of writing, and that I had improved upon *Young*," who he saw was my model, he said, "for my flattery was still stronger than his, and yet, somehow or other, less hyperbolical."' Hayward's *Piozzi*, 1st ed. ii. 345.

For her flattery of him see *Life*, ii. 349, and *Letters*, i. 200, 220, 221; ii. 308, and for Johnson's person, *Life*, i. 94; iv. 425; v. 18. How far Young could go in flattery is shown in the lines where, addressing the Deity, he says:—

''Tis Thou that lead'st our pow'rful armies forth,
And giv'st *Great Anne* Thy sceptre o'er the north.'
The Last Day, Book ii.

[2] Boswell told Johnson that 'Lord Monboddo disapproved of the richness of his language, and of his frequent use of metaphorical expressions. JOHNSON. "Why, Sir, this criticism would be just, if in my style, superfluous words, or words too big for the thoughts, could be pointed out; but this I do not believe can be done."' *Life*, iii. 173. 'Johnson

say, 'that the size of a man's understanding might always be justly measured by his mirth;' and his own was never contemptible. He would laugh at a stroke of genuine humour, or sudden sally of odd absurdity, as heartily and freely as I ever yet saw any man; and though the jest was often such as few felt besides himself, yet his laugh was irresistible, and was observed immediately to produce that of the company, not merely from the notion that it was proper to laugh when he did, but purely out of want of power to forbear it [1]. He was no enemy to splendour of apparel or pomp of equipage—'Life (he would say) is barren enough surely with all her trappings; let us therefore be cautious how we strip her [2].' In matters of still higher moment he once observed, when speaking on the subject of sudden innovation,—'He who plants a forest may doubtless cut down a hedge; yet I could wish methinks that even he would wait till he sees his young plants grow.'

With regard to common occurrences Mr. Johnson had, when I first knew him, looked on the still-shifting scenes of life [3] till he was weary; for as a mind slow in its own nature, or unenlightened by information, will contentedly read in the same book

once said to me, in a pleasant humour, "Sir, if Robertson's style be faulty, he owes it to me; that is, having too many words, and those too big ones."' *Life*, iii. 173.

[1] 'Garrick remarked to me of him, "Rabelais and all other wits are nothing compared with him. You may be diverted by them; but Johnson gives you a forcible hug, and shakes laughter out of you whether you will or no."' *Ib.* ii. 231. 'I passed many hours with him on the 17th, of which I find all my memorial is "much laughing." It should seem he had that day been in a humour for jocularity and merriment, and upon such occasions I never knew a man laugh more heartily.' *Ib.* ii. 378. See also *ib.* ii. 262, for his peals of laughter 'that in the silence of the night seemed to resound from Temple Bar to Fleet Ditch.' See also *ante*, p. 269.

[2] At Inverary Castle he said:—'What I admire here is the total defiance of expense.' *Life*, v. 355. 'Sir' (he said), 'were I to have any thing fine, it should be very fine. Were I to wear a ring, it should not be a bauble, but a stone of great value. Were I to wear a laced or embroidered waistcoat, it should be very rich. I had once a very rich laced waistcoat, which I wore the first night of my tragedy.' *Ib.* v. 364.

[3] 'Remark each anxious toil, each eager strife,
And watch the busy scenes of crowded life.'
The Vanity of Human Wishes, l. 3.

book for twenty times perhaps, the very act of reading it being more than half the business, and every period being at every reading better understood; while a mind more active or more skilful to comprehend its meaning is made sincerely[1] sick at the second perusal; so a soul like his, acute to discern the truth, vigorous to embrace, and powerful to retain it, soon sees enough of the world's dull prospect, which at first, like that of the sea, pleases by its extent, but soon, like that too, fatigues from its uniformity; a calm and a storm being the only variations that the nature of either will admit.

Of Mr. Johnson's erudition the world has been the judge, and we who produce each a score of his sayings, as proofs of that wit which in him was inexhaustible, resemble travellers who having visited Delhi or Golconda, bring home each a handful of Oriental pearl to evince the riches of the Great Mogul. May the Public condescend to accept my *ill-strung* selection with patience at least, remembering only that they are relics of him who was great on all occasions, and, like a cube in architecture, you beheld him on each side, and his size still appeared undiminished.

As his purse was ever open to almsgiving[2], so was his heart tender to those who wanted relief, and his soul susceptible of gratitude, and of every kind impression; yet though he had refined his sensibility, he had not endangered his quiet, by encouraging in himself a solicitude about trifles, which he treated with the contempt they deserve.

It was well enough known before these sheets were published, that Mr. Johnson had a roughness in his manner which subdued the saucy, and terrified the meek[3]: this was, when I knew him, the prominent part of a character which few durst venture to approach so nearly; and which was for that reason in many respects grossly and frequently mistaken; and it was perhaps peculiar to him, that the lofty consciousness of his own superiority,

[1] I know no other instance of this strange use of *sincerely*.

[2] *Ante*, p. 204.

[3] 'He was always indulgent to the young, he never attacked the unassuming, nor meant to terrify the diffident.' Mme. D'Arblay's *Diary*, ii. 343.

superiority, which animated his looks, and raised his voice in conversation[1], cast likewise an impenetrable veil over him when he said nothing. His talk therefore had commonly the complexion of arrogance, his silence[2] of superciliousness. He was however seldom inclined to be silent when any moral or literary question was started: and it was on such occasions, that, like the sage in Rasselas, he spoke, and attention watched his lips; he reasoned, and conviction closed his periods[3]: if poetry was talked of, his quotations were the readiest; and had he not been eminent for more solid and brilliant qualities, mankind would have united to extol his extraordinary memory[4]. His manner of repeating deserves to be described, though at the same time it defeats all power of description; but whoever once heard him repeat an ode of Horace, would be long before they could endure to hear it repeated by another[5].

His equity in giving the character of living acquaintance[6] ought not undoubtedly to be omitted in his own, whence partiality and prejudice were totally excluded, and truth alone presided in his tongue: a steadiness of conduct the more to be commended, as no man had stronger likings or aversions. His

[1] Miss Hawkins (*Memoirs*, i. 79), says that 'Mrs. Piozzi [Mrs. Thrale, she should have said], when living much with Johnson, had his tones, which sat very ill on her little French person.'

[2] 'Having taken the liberty, this evening, to remark to Dr. Johnson, that he very often sat quite silent for a long time, even when in company with only a single friend, which I myself had sometimes sadly experienced, he smiled and said, "It is true, Sir. Tom Tyers described me the best. He once said to me, 'Sir, you are like a ghost: you never speak till you are spoken to.'"' *Life*, v. 73. See also *ib.* iii. 307, and *ante*, p. 290.

[3] *Rasselas*, chap. xvii. This passage is quoted in the *Life*, iv. 346.

'Opposite a passage [in the *Anecdotes*] descriptive of Johnson's conversation Mrs. Piozzi has written:—"We used to say to one another familiarly at Streatham Park, Come, let us go into the library, and make Johnson speak Ramblers."' Hayward's *Piozzi*, i. 297.

[4] *Life*, i. 39; iii. 318, *n.* 1.

[5] 'His recitation was grand and affecting, and, as Sir Joshua Reynolds has observed to me, had no more tone than it should have.' *Ib.* v. 115. 'His manner of reciting verses was wonderfully impressive.' Murphy's *Johnson*, p. 145. See *post* in Anecdotes of W. Cooke.

[6] 'The person with whom we are acquainted. In this sense the plural is in some authours *acquaintance*, in others *acquaintances*.' Johnson's *Dictionary*.

veracity

veracity was indeed, from the most trivial to the most solemn occasions, strict, even to severity; he scorned to embellish a story with fictitious circumstances, which (he used to say) took off from its real value. 'A story (says Johnson) should be a specimen of life and manners; but if the surrounding circumstances are false, as it is no more a representation of reality, it is no longer worthy our attention [1].'

For the rest—That beneficence which during his life increased the comforts of so many, may after his death be perhaps ungratefully forgotten; but that piety which dictated the serious papers in the Rambler, will be for ever remembered; for ever, I think, revered. That ample repository of religious truth, moral wisdom, and accurate criticism, breathes indeed the genuine emanations of its great Author's mind, expressed too in a style so natural to him, and so much like his common mode of conversing [2], that I was myself but little astonished when he told me, that he had scarcely read over one of those inimitable essays before they went to the press [3].

I will add one or two peculiarities more, before I lay down my pen.——Though at an immeasurable distance from content in

[1] 'Johnson said, "The value of every story depends on its being true. A story is a picture either of an individual or of human nature in general; if it be false, it is a picture of nothing. For instance: suppose a man should tell that Johnson, before setting out for Italy, as he had to cross the Alps, sat down to make himself wings. This many people would believe; but it would be a picture of nothing. ******* used to think a story, a story, till I shewed him that truth was essential to it.' *Life*, ii. 433. See *ante*, p. 225.

[2] 'I could not help remarking how very like Dr. Johnson is to his writing, and how much the same thing it was to hear or to read him; but that nobody could tell that without coming to Streatham, for his language was generally imagined to be laboured and studied, instead of the mere common flow of his thoughts. "Very true," said Mrs. Thrale, "he writes and talks with the same ease, and in the same manner."' Mme. D'Arblay's *Diary*, i. 120.

[3] 'He told us, "almost all his *Ramblers* were written just as they were wanted for the press; that he sent a certain portion of the copy of an essay, and wrote the remainder, while the former part of it was printing. When it was wanted, and he had fairly sat down to it, he was sure it would be done."' *Life*, iii. 42. He carefully revised them for the collected edition. *Ib.* i. 203, *n.* 6.

the

the contemplation of his own uncouth form and figure, he did not like another man much the less for being a coxcomb [1]. I mentioned two friends who were particularly fond of looking at themselves in a glass—'They do not surprise me at all by so doing (said Johnson): they see, reflected in that glass, men who have risen from almost the lowest situations in life; one to enormous riches, the other to every thing this world can give—rank, fame, and fortune. They see likewise, men who have merited their advancement by the exertion and improvement of those talents which God had given them; and I see not why they should avoid the mirror [2].'

The other singularity I promised to record, is this: That though a man of obscure birth himself, his partiality to people of family was visible on every occasion; his zeal for subordination warm even to bigotry [3]; his hatred to innovation [4], and reverence

[1] 'Johnson said foppery was never cured; it was the bad stamina of the mind, which like those of the body were never rectified, once a coxcomb, and always a coxcomb.' *Life*, ii. 128.

[2] The first of these men, Mrs. Piozzi says, was John Cator, one of her husband's executors, and the second Alexander Wedderburne, Lord Loughborough and Earl of Rosslyn. Hayward's *Piozzi*, i. 296. Cator, likely enough, was the man mentioned in the following passage:—'Mrs. Thrale mentioned a gentleman who had acquired a fortune of four thousand a year in trade, but was absolutely miserable, because he could not talk in company; so miserable, that he was impelled to lament his situation in the street to ****** [? Seward], whom he hates, and who he knows despises him. "I am a most unhappy man (said he). I am invited to conversations. I go to conversations; but, alas! I have no conversation." JOHNSON. "Man commonly cannot be successful in different ways. This gentleman has spent, in getting four thousand pounds a year, the time in which he might have learnt to talk; and now he cannot talk." Mr. Perkins made a shrewd and droll remark: "If he had got his four thousand a year as a mountebank, he might have learnt to talk at the same time that he was getting his fortune."' *Life*, iv. 83. For a specimen of his talk see *Letters*, ii. 217, *n.* 1.

Of Wedderburne's rise Boswell says:—'When I look back on this noble person at Edinburgh, in situations so unworthy of his brilliant powers, and behold LORD LOUGHBOROUGH at London, the change seems almost like one of the metamorphoses in *Ovid*.' *Life*, i. 387.

[3] 'I heard Dr. Johnson once say, "I have great merit in being zealous for subordination and the honours of birth; for I can hardly tell who was my grandfather."' *Ib.* ii. 261.

[4] 'He said to Sir William Scott, "The age is running mad after innovation; all the business of the world

for

for the old feudal times[1], apparent, whenever any possible manner of shewing them occurred. I have spoken of his piety, his charity, and his truth, the enlargement of his heart, and the delicacy of his sentiments; and when I search for shadow to my portrait, none can I find but what was formed by pride, differently modified as different occasions shewed it; yet never was pride so purified as Johnson's, at once from meanness and from vanity. The mind of this man was indeed expanded beyond the common limits of human nature, and stored with such variety of knowledge, that I used to think it resembled a royal pleasure-ground, where every plant, of every name and nation, flourished in the full perfection of their powers, and where, though lofty woods and falling cataracts first caught the eye, and fixed the earliest attention of beholders, yet neither the trim parterre nor the pleasing shrubbery, nor even the antiquated ever-greens, were denied a place in some fit corner of the happy valley.

is to be done in a new way; men are to be hanged in a new way; Tyburn itself is not safe from the fury of innovation."' *Life*, iv. 188.

[1] Johnson, had he read this, might have reproached Mrs. Piozzi, as he reproached the Earl of Chatham, with 'feudal gabble.' *Ib.* ii. 134, *n.* 'I said,' writes Boswell, 'I believed mankind were happier in the ancient feudal state of subordination, than they are in the modern state of independency. JOHNSON. "To be sure, the *Chief* was: but we must think of the number of individuals. That *they* were less happy, seems plain; for that state from which all escape as soon as they can, and to which none return after they have left it, must be less happy; and this is the case with the state of dependance on a chief or great man."' *Ib.* v. 106. See also *ib.* ii. 177; iii. 3.

POSTSCRIPT.

Naples, Feb. 10, 1786.

SINCE the foregoing went to the press, having seen a passage from Mr. Boswell's Tour to the Hebrides, in which it is said, that *I could not get through Mrs. Montagu's Essay on Shakespeare*, I do not delay a moment to declare, that, on the contrary, I have always commended it myself, and heard it commended by every one else; and few things would give me more concern than to be thought incapable of tasting, or unwilling to testify my opinion of its excellence [1].

[1] 'I spoke of Mrs. Montague's very high praises of Garrick. JOHNSON. "Sir, it is fit she should say so much, and I should say nothing. Reynolds is fond of her book, and I wonder at it; for neither I, nor Beauclerk, nor Mrs. Thrale could get through it."' *Life*, v. 245.

For Boswell's reply to Mrs. Piozzi's Postscript see *ib. n.* 2.

AN ESSAY

ON

THE LIFE AND GENIUS

OF

SAMUEL JOHNSON, LL.D.

BY ARTHUR MURPHY, ESQ.[1]

[LONDON: MDCCXCII.]

[1] 'For this slight Essay the Booksellers paid Mr. Murphy £300.' Nichols's *Literary Anecdotes*, ix. 159.

ESSAY

ON

JOHNSON'S LIFE AND GENIUS

WHEN the works of a great Writer, who has bequeathed to posterity a lasting legacy, are presented to the world, it is naturally expected, that some account of his life should accompany the edition [1]. The Reader wishes to know as much as possible of the Author. The circumstances that attended him, the features of his private character, his conversation, and the means by which he rose to eminence, become the favourite objects of enquiry. Curiosity is excited; and the admirer of his works is eager to know his private opinions, his course of study, the particularities of his conduct, and, above all, whether he pursued the wisdom which he recommends, and practised the virtue which his writings inspire. A principle of gratitude is awakened in every generous mind. For the entertainment and instruction which genius and diligence have provided for the world, men of refined and sensible tempers are ready to pay their tribute of praise, and even to form a posthumous friendship with the author.

In reviewing the life of such a writer, there is, besides, a rule of justice to which the publick have an undoubted claim. Fond admiration and partial friendship should not be suffered to represent his virtues with exaggeration; nor should malignity be allowed, under a specious disguise, to magnify mere defects, the usual failings of human nature, into vice or gross deformity.

[1] Published in 1792 in 12 volumes octavo.

The lights and shades of the character should be given; and, if this be done with a strict regard to truth, a just estimate of Dr. Johnson will afford a lesson perhaps as valuable as the moral doctrine that speaks with energy in every page of his works.

The present writer enjoyed the conversation and friendship of that excellent man more than thirty years. He thought it an honour to be so connected, and to this hour he reflects on his loss with regret: but regret, he knows, has secret bribes, by which the judgement may be influenced, and partial affection may be carried beyond the bounds of truth. In the present case, however, nothing needs to be disguised, and exaggerated praise is unnecessary. It is an observation of the younger Pliny, in his Epistle to his Friend of Tacitus [*sic*], that history ought never to magnify matters of fact, because worthy actions require nothing but the truth. *Nam nec historia debet egredi veritatem, et honeste factis veritas sufficit*[1]. This rule the present biographer promises shall guide his pen throughout the following narrative.

It may be said, the death of Dr. Johnson kept the public mind in agitation beyond all former example[2]. No literary character ever excited so much attention; and, when the press has teemed with anecdotes, apophthegms, essays, and publications of every kind, what occasion now for a new tract on the same threadbare subject[3]? The plain truth shall be the answer. The

[1] *Epistolae*, vii. 33. 10.

[2] 'His death,' writes Hannah More, 'made a kind of era in literature.' *Memoirs*, i. 394.

Miss Martineau (*Autobiography*, i. 438) records that Miss Berry, who died in 1852, used to tell 'how the world of literature was perplexed and distressed—as a swarm of bees that have lost their queen—when Dr. Johnson died.'

[3] The Rev. Dr. W. Barrow, 'a coarse north-countryman but a very good scholar,' as Boswell described him, to whose academy in Soho Square he sent his son James (*Letters to Temple*, p. 315), wrote on Jan. 26, 1786:—'The reviews and papers will tell you better than I can that the booksellers are engaged in a contest who shall publish the first and best edition of Johnson's Dictionary, and that his friends are running a race who shall be foremost in giving, or rather selling, to the world some scrap or fragment of our literary Leviathan—an anecdote, a letter, or a character, a sermon, a prayer, or

proprietors

proprietors of Johnson's Works thought the life, which they prefixed to their former edition, too unwieldy for republication [1]. The prodigious variety of foreign matter, introduced into that performance, seemed to overload the memory of Dr. Johnson, and in the account of his own life to leave him hardly visible [2]. They wished to have a more concise, and, for that reason, perhaps a more satisfactory account, such as may exhibit a just picture of the man, and keep him the principal figure in the foreground of his own picture. To comply with that request is the design of this essay, which the writer undertakes with a trembling hand. He has no discoveries, no secret anecdotes, no occasional controversy, no sudden flashes of wit and humour, no private conversation, and no new facts to embellish his work. Every thing has been gleaned. Dr. Johnson said of himself, 'I am not uncandid, nor severe: I sometimes say more than I mean, in jest, and people are apt to think me serious [3].' The exercise of that

a bon-mot.' *Letters of Radcliffe and James*, p. 266.

Romilly wrote from London on Aug. 20, 1790:—'I have been surprised, and I own a little indignant, to observe how little impression Adam Smith's death has made here. Scarce any notice has been taken of it, while for above a year together, after the death of Dr. Johnson, nothing was to be heard of but panegyrics of him. Lives, Letters, and Anecdotes, and even at this moment there are two more Lives of him about to start into existence.' Romilly's *Memoirs*, i. 404. The two *Lives* were Boswell's and Murphy's.

[1] By Sir John Hawkins. It was prefixed to an edition of Johnson's *Works* in eleven volumes, published in 1787 at £3 6*s*.

[2] Boswell, who in his text attacks Hawkins's *Life*, says in a note:—'Let me add, that though I doubt I should not have been very prompt to gratify Sir John Hawkins with any compliment in his life-time, I do now frankly acknowledge, that, in my opinion, his volume, however inadequate and improper as a life of Dr. Johnson, and however discredited by unpardonable inaccuracies in other respects, contains a collection of curious anecdotes and observations, which few men but its author could have brought together.' *Life*, i. 27.

[3] 'A friend was one day, about two years before his death, struck with some instance of Dr. Johnson's great candour. "Well, Sir, (said he,) I will always say that you are a very candid man." "Will you, (replied the Doctor,) I doubt then you will be very singular. But, indeed, Sir, (continued he,) I look upon myself to be a man very much misunderstood. I am not an uncandid, nor am I a severe man. I sometimes say more than I mean, in jest; and people are apt to believe me serious: however, I am more candid than I was when I was younger."' *Life*, iv. 239.

that privilege, which is enjoyed by every man in society, has not been allowed to him. His fame has given importance even to trifles, and the zeal of his friends has brought every thing to light. What should be related, and what should not, has been published without distinction. *Dicenda tacenda locuti*[1]*!* Every thing that fell from him has been caught with eagerness by his admirers, who, as he says in one of his letters, have acted with the diligence of spies upon his conduct[2]. To some of them the following lines, in Mallet's Poem on Verbal Criticism, are not inapplicable:

> Such that grave bird in Northern seas is found,
> Whose name a Dutchman only knows to sound[3],
> Where-e'er the king of fish moves on before,
> This humble friend attends from shore to shore;
> With eye still earnest, and with bill inclin'd [declin'd],
> He picks up what his patron drops behind,
> With those choice cates his palate to regale,
> And is the careful TIBBALD of A WHALE[4].

After so many essays and volumes of *Johnsoniana,* what remains for the present writer? Perhaps, what has not been attempted; a short, yet full, a faithful, yet temperate history of Dr. Johnson.

SAMUEL JOHNSON was born at Lichfield, September 7, 1709, O.S.[5] His father, Michael Johnson, was a bookseller in that city; a man of large athletic make, and violent passions; wrongheaded, positive, and at times afflicted with a degree of melancholy,

[1] 'Ut ventum ad caenam est, dicenda tacenda locutus,
Tandem dormitum dimittitur.'
'Behold him now at supper, where he said,
Or right or wrong, what came into his head.'
Francis's *Horace*, *Epis*. i. 7. 72.

[2] 'You never told me, and I omitted to enquire, how you were entertained by Boswell's Journal. One would think the man had been hired to be a spy upon me.' *Letters*, i. 330.

[3] 'This remarkable bird is called the Strundt Jager. See a *Collection of Voyages in the North*.' Note by MALLET. 'Struntjäger; Stercorarius Crepidatus; Richardson's Strua.' Dresser's *Birds of Europe*, vol. viii.

[4] *Poems on Several Occasions*, by David Mallet. London, 1743, p. 184. Lewis Theobald, or Tibbald as his name was pronounced, was the ingenious editor of Shakespeare, most unjustly libelled by a far inferior editor Pope.

[5] September 18, N. S. *Ante*, p. 129.

melancholy, little short of madness [1]. His mother was sister to Dr. Ford, a practising physician, and father of Cornelius Ford, generally known by the name of PARSON FORD, the same who is represented near the punch-bowl in Hogarth's Modern Midnight Conversation [2]. In the Life of Fenton, Johnson says, that 'his abilities, instead of furnishing convivial merriment to the voluptuous and dissolute, might have enabled him to excel among the virtuous and the wise.' Being chaplain to the Earl of Chesterfield, he wished to attend that nobleman on his embassy to the Hague. Colley Cibber has recorded the anecdote [3]. 'You should go,' said the witty peer, 'if to your many vices you would add one more.' 'Pray, my Lord, what is that?' 'Hypocrisy, my dear Doctor.' Johnson had a younger brother named Nathaniel, who died at the age of twenty-seven or twenty-eight [4]. Michael Johnson, the father, was chosen in the year 1718 Under Bailiff of Lichfield, and in the year 1725 he served the office of the Senior Bailiff [5]. He had a brother of the name of Andrew, who, for some years, kept the ring at Smithfield, appropriated to wrestlers and boxers. Our author used to say, that he was never thrown or conquered [6]. Michael, the father, died December 1731, at the age of seventy-six [7]; his mother at eighty-nine, of a gradual decay, in the year 1759. Of the family nothing more can be related worthy of notice. Johnson did not

[1] *Ante*, p. 148.

[2] *Ante*, p. 154.

[3] Murphy probably got this anecdote from the *Monthly Review*, 1787, p. 275, where it is assigned to Colley Cibber. I do not think that it is in his *Apology*.

'When parson Ford, an infamous fellow, but of much off-hand and conversation wit, besought Lord Chesterfield to carry him over with him as his chaplain, when he went ambassador to Holland, he said to him, "I would certainly take you, if you had one vice more than you already have." "My lord," said Ford, "I thought I should never be reproached for my deficiency that way." "True," replied the earl, "but if you had still one more, almost worse than all the rest put together, it would hinder these from giving scandal."' Jonathan Richardson's *Richardsoniana*, p. 225.

Chesterfield was minister at the Hague from 1728 to 1732. His chaplain, Richard Chenevix, was afterwards Bishop of Waterford. Chesterfield's *Misc. Works*, i. 91.

[4] He was born in 1712, and died in 1737. *Life*, iv. 393, *n*. 2.

[5] *Ib*. i. 36, *n*. 4.

[6] *Ante*, p. 149.

[7] Seventy-five. *Life*, iv. 393, *n*. 2.

delight in talking of his relations. 'There is little pleasure,' he said to Mrs. Piozzi, 'in relating the anecdotes of beggary [1].'

Johnson derived from his parents, or from an unwholesome nurse, the distemper called the King's Evil. The Jacobites at that time believed in the efficacy of the royal touch; and accordingly Mrs. Johnson presented her son, when two years old, before Queen Anne, who, for the first time, performed that office, and communicated to her young patient all the healing virtue in her power [2]. He was afterwards cut for that scrophulous humour, and the under part of his face was seamed and disfigured by the operation. It is supposed, that this disease deprived him of the sight of his left eye, and also impaired his hearing. At eight years old, he was placed under Mr. Hawkins, at the Free-school at Lichfield, where he was not remarkable for diligence or regular application [3]. Whatever he read, his tenacious memory made his own [4]. In the fields with his school-fellows he talked more to himself than with his companions [5]. In 1725, when he was about sixteen years old, he went on a visit to his cousin Cornelius Ford, who detained him for some months, and in the mean time assisted him in the classics. The general direction for his studies, which he then received, he related to Mrs. Piozzi.

[1] *Ante*, p. 148.

[2] *Ante*, pp. 133, 152.

[3] *Ante*, p. 138.

[4] In the *Life of Johnson* published by Kearsley, said to be written by 'Conversation' Cooke (Nichols's *Lit. Hist.* vii. 467), it is stated (p. 107) that Hawkesworth read his *Ode on Life* to Johnson, 'and asked him for his opinion, "Why, Sir, (says Johnson,) I can't well determine on a first reading, second thoughts are best." Hawkesworth complied, after which Johnson read it himself and returned it. Next morning at breakfast Johnson said he had but one objection to make to it, which was that he doubted its originality. Hawkesworth alarmed at this challenged him to the proof; when the Doctor repeated the whole of the poem with only the omission of a very few lines. "What do you say now, Hawkey?" says the Doctor. "Only this," replied the other, "that I shall never repeat anything I write before you again, for you have a memory that would convict any author of plagiarism in any court of literature in the world." The poem contains 68 lines.'

[5] 'Mr. Hector relates that "he could not oblige him more than by sauntering away the hours of vacation in the fields, during which he was more engaged in talking to himself than to his companion."' *Life*, i. 48, and Hawkins's *Johnson*, p. 7.

'Obtain,'

'Obtain,' says Ford, 'some general principles of every science: he who can talk only on one subject, or act only in one department, is seldom wanted, and, perhaps, never wished for; while the man of general knowledge can often benefit, and always please[1].' This advice Johnson seems to have pursued with a good inclination. His reading was always desultory, seldom resting on any particular author, but rambling from one book to another, and, by hasty snatches, hoarding up a variety of knowledge. It may be proper in this place to mention another general rule laid down by Ford for Johnson's future conduct: 'You will make your way the more easily in the world, as you are contented to dispute no man's claim to conversation-excellence: they will, therefore, more willingly allow your pretensions as a writer[2].' 'But,' says Mrs. Piozzi, 'the features of peculiarity, which mark a character to all succeeding generations, are slow in coming to their growth.' That ingenious lady adds, with her usual vivacity, 'Can one, on such an occasion, forbear recollecting the predictions of Boileau's father, who said, stroking the head of the young satirist, "this little man has too much wit, but he will never speak ill of any one"[3]?'

On Johnson's return from Cornelius Ford, Mr. Hunter, then Master of the Free-school at Lichfield, refused to receive him again on that foundation[4]. At this distance of time, what his reasons were, it is vain to enquire: but to refuse assistance to a lad of promising genius must be pronounced harsh and illiberal. It did not, however, stop the progress of the young student's education. He was placed at another school, at Stourbridge in Worcestershire, under the care of Mr. Wentworth[5]. Having gone through the rudiments of classic literature, he returned to his father's house, and was probably intended for the trade of a bookseller. He has been heard to say that he could bind

[1] *Ante*, p. 155.

[2] It was not a general rule laid down by Ford, but his observation of Johnson's character. He said:—'You will make your way the more easily in the world, *I see*,' &c. *Ante*, ib.

[3] According to Mrs. Piozzi, Boileau's father said:—'Ce petit bon homme n'a point trop d'esprit,' &c. *Ante*, p. 155.

[4] Hawkins's *Johnson*, p. 8.

[5] *Ante*, p. 159, *n*. 3.

a book.

a book [1]. At the end of two years, being then about nineteen, he went to assist the studies of a young gentleman, of the name of Corbet, to the University of Oxford ; and on the 31st of October, 1728, both were entered of Pembroke College; Corbet as a gentleman-commoner, and Johnson as a commoner [2]. The college tutor, Mr. Jordan, was a man of no genius ; and Johnson, it seems, shewed an early contempt of mean abilities, in one or two instances behaving with insolence to that gentleman [3]. Of his general conduct at the university there are no particulars that merit attention, except the translation of Pope's Messiah, which was a college exercise imposed upon him as a task by Mr. Jordan [4]. Corbet left the university in about two years, and Johnson's salary ceased [5]. He was, by consequence, straitened in his circumstances; but he still remained at college. Mr. Jordan, the tutor, went off to a living; and was succeeded by Dr. Adams, who afterwards became head of the college, and was esteemed through life for his learning, his talents, and his amiable character. Johnson grew more regular in his attendance. Ethics, theology, and classic literature were his favourite studies [6]. He

[1] *Life*, i. 56, *n.* 2; *Letters*, ii. 89.

[2] Corbet had entered the year before. *Life*, i. 58, *n.* 1.

[3] *Ante*, p. 164. 'He had a love and respect for Jorden, not for his literature, but for his worth. "Whenever (said he) a young man becomes Jorden's pupil, he becomes his son."' *Life*, i. 61.

[4] Boswell recorded in his notebook in March 1776:—'Mr. Hector told me that the Master of Pembroke used to see him idling away his time in the quadrangle, and that he set him a task to turn Pope's *Messiah* into Latin (wrong, he was asked very civilly by Jorden to do it) upon which Mr. Johnson produced his admirable version of that poem.' *Morrison Autographs*, 2nd Series, i. 368. See *Life*, i. 61.

[5] Murphy gets this statement from Hawkins, p. 9. Dr. Taylor told Boswell that though Corbet's father had promised to support Johnson at Oxford 'in the character of his son's companion, in fact he never received any assistance whatever from that gentleman.' *Life*, i. 58.

Corbet, as the books of the College show, entered in 1727. In October, 1728, his charges became irregular, and ceased altogether in the following December, when no doubt he left College. Johnson, as I have shown, was only fourteen months in College, leaving in December, 1729. *Ib.* i. 78, *n.* 2. Adams was only 'his nominal tutor.' *Ib.* p. 79.

[6] Hawkins, p. 11. 'He told me what he read *solidly* at Oxford was Greek . . . that the study of which he was the most fond was Metaphysicks, but he had not read much even in that way.' *Life*, i. 70.

discovered,

discovered, notwithstanding, early symptoms of that wandering disposition of mind which adhered to him to the end of his life. His reading was by fits and starts, undirected to any particular science [1]. General philology, agreeably to his cousin Ford's advice, was the object of his ambition. He received, at that time, an early impression of piety [2], and a taste for the best authors ancient and modern. It may, notwithstanding, be questioned whether, except his Bible, he ever read a book entirely through. Late in life, if any man praised a book in his presence, he was sure to ask, 'Did you read it through?' If the answer was in the affirmative, he did not seem willing to believe it [3]. He continued at the university till the want of pecuniary supplies obliged him to quit the place. He obtained, however, the assistance of a friend, and returning in a short time was able to complete a residence of three years [4]. The history of his exploits at Oxford, he used to say, was best known to Dr. Taylor and Dr. Adams [5]. Wonders are told of his memory, and, indeed, all who knew him late in life can witness that he retained that faculty in the greatest vigour [6].

From the university Johnson returned to Lichfield. His father died soon after, December 1731; and the whole receipt out of his effects, as appeared by a memorandum in the son's hand-writing, dated 15th June, 1732, was no more than twenty pounds [7]. In

[1] Hawkins, p. 12.

[2] Hawkins (p. 18) fathers these 'sentiments of piety' on 'the order and discipline of a college life . . . the early calls to prayers, the frequent instructions from the pulpit, with all the other means of religious and moral improvement.' Johnson told Boswell that it was reading Law's *Serious Call to a Holy Life* which 'was the first occasion of his thinking in earnest of religion after he became capable of rational inquiry.' *Life*, i. 68.

[3] *Ante*, p. 319.

[4] Hawkins (p. 16), in accounting for this second period of residence, which never took place, attributes Johnson's maintenance at college to 'the bounty, as it is supposed, of some one or more of the members of the Cathedral [of Lichfield].' Murphy goes a step further and speaks positively of a friend.

[5] *Ante*, p. 166.

[6] See *Life*, v. 368, for a singular proof of his memory at the age of sixty-four, and *ante*, p. 437.

[7] The entry of this is remarkable for his early resolution to preserve through life a fair and upright character:—'1732, Junii 15. Undecim aureos deposui, quo die, quidquid ante matris funus (quod serum sit

this

this exigence, determined that poverty should neither depress his spirit nor warp his integrity, he became under-master of a Grammar-school at Market Bosworth in Leicestershire. That resource, however, did not last long. Disgusted by the pride of Sir Wolstan Dixie, the patron of that little seminary, he left the place in discontent, and ever after spoke of it with abhorrence[1]. In 1733 he went on a visit to Mr. Hector, who had been his school-fellow, and was then a surgeon at Birmingham, lodging at the house of Warren, a bookseller[2]. At that place Johnson

precor) de paternis bonis sperare licet, viginti scilicet libras, accepi. Usque adeo mihi mea fortuna fingenda est interea, et ne paupertate vires animi languescant, ne in flagitia egestas adigat, cavendum.' *Note* by Murphy. Boswell gives the date Julii 15; for *sperare* he has *sperari*, and he thus gives the last paragraph:—'Usque adeo mihi fortuna fingenda est. Interea, ne paupertate vires animi languescant, nec in flagitia egestas abigat, cavendum.' *Life*, i. 80. Hawkins (p. 21) differs both from Murphy and Boswell.

[1] *Life*, i. 84; *Letters*, i. 2.

Boswell recorded in his note-book at Lichfield in March, 1776:—'After leaving Oxford Mr. Johnson lived at home. Then, as Miss Porter informed me, he got the school of Bosworth. He was very unhappy there, with Sir Woolston Dixey, an abandoned brutal rascal. Dr. Taylor told me this, and said Dr. Johnson did not like to recollect that dissagreeable [*sic*] period of his life, that he said to him that it was uneasy to him to see that side of the town (I suppose of Ashburn) which leads to Bosworth; that he could not bear the horrid disgust of that state, and threw up the school. He then was tutor to the son of Mr. Whitby. His pupil did not live to inherit the estate.' *Morrison Autographs*, 2nd Series, i. 369. In Dixey's house Johnson is said 'to have officiated as a kind of domestick chaplain, so far, at least, as to say grace at table.' *Life*, i. 84. Addison, in the *Guardian*, No. 163, gives a letter from a young nobleman's chaplain, who writes:—'I have, with much ado, maintained my post hitherto at the dessert, and every day eat tart in the face of my patron, but how long I shall be invested with this privilege I do not know. For the servants, who do not see me supported as I was in my old lord's time, begin to brush very familiarly by me, and thrust aside my chair when they set the sweetmeats on the table.' South (*Sermons*, iv. 136) describes how 'some keep chaplains, not out of any concern for religion, but as it is a piece of grandeur something above keeping a coach; though in such cases he who serves at the altar has generally as much contempt and disdain passed upon him as he who serves in the kitchen.'

[2] *Life*, i. 85.

'Miss Porter told me the Birmingham people could not bear Mr. Johnson, and he did not say why. I suppose from envy of his parts, though I do not see how traders could envy such qualities.' *Morrison Autographs*, 2nd Series, i. 369.

translated

translated a Voyage to Abyssinia, written by Jerome Lobo, a Portugueze missionary. This was the first literary work from the pen of Dr. Johnson. His friend Hector was occasionally his amanuensis. The work was, probably, undertaken at the desire of Warren, the bookseller, and was printed at Birmingham; but it appears in the Literary Magazine, or History of the Works of the Learned, for March, 1735, that it was published by Bettesworth and Hitch, Pater-noster-row [1]. . .

Having finished this work, Johnson returned in February, 1734, to his native city, and, in the month of August following, published Proposals for printing by subscription, the Latin Poems of Politian, with the History of Latin Poetry, from the Æra of Petrarch to the time of Politian; and also the Life of Politian, to be added by the Editor, Samuel Johnson [2]. The book to be printed in thirty octavo sheets, price five shillings. It is to be regretted that this project failed for want of encouragement. Johnson, it seems, differed from Boileau, Voltaire, and D'Alembert, who have taken upon them to proscribe all modern efforts to write with elegance in a dead language [3]. For a decision, pronounced in so high a tone, no good reason can be assigned. The interests of learning require, that the diction of

[1] *Life*, i. 87.

Major (afterwards Sir Francis) Head accused Johnson of having translated Lobo to injure the sale of Bruce's *Travels*. *Gentleman's Magazine*, 1830, ii. 482. These *Travels* were published six years after Johnson's death.

I omit ten pages containing an extract from the preface given in the *Life*, i. 88, and an abstract of the book.

[2] '*Angeli Politiani Poemata Latina, quibus, Notas cum historiâ Latinæ poeseos, à Petrarchæ ævo ad Politiani tempora deductâ, et vitâ Politiani fusius quam antehac enarratâ, addidit* SAM. JOHNSON.' *Life*, i. 90. Petrarch was born in 1304; Politian died in 1494. What young scholar of the present age would dream of writing the history of this late period of Latin poetry?

[3] Johnson in his last work shows his fondness for modern Latin poetry. He says:—'Pope had sought for images and sentiments in a region not known to have been explored by many other of the English writers; he had consulted the modern writers of Latin poetry, a class of authors whom Boileau endeavoured to bring into contempt, and who are too generally neglected.' *Works*, viii. 299.

Boileau ridicules them in a *Fragment de Dialogue*, where the *Interlocuteurs* are 'Apollon, Horace, des Muses, des Poètes.' *Œuvres*, ed. 1747, iii. 55.

Greece

Greece and Rome should be cultivated with care; and he who can write a language with correctness, will be most likely to understand its idiom, its grammar, and its peculiar graces of style. What man of taste would willingly forego the pleasure of reading *Vida*, *Fracastorius*, *Sannazaro*, *Strada* [1], and others, down to the late elegant productions of Bishop Lowth [2]? The history which Johnson proposed to himself would, beyond all question, have been a valuable addition to the history of letters; but his project failed. His next expedient was to offer his assistance to Cave, the original projector of the Gentleman's Magazine. For this purpose he sent his proposals in a letter, offering, on reasonable terms, occasionally to fill some pages with poems and inscriptions never printed before; with fugitive pieces that deserved to be revived, and critical remarks on authors ancient and modern. Cave agreed to retain him as a correspondent and contributor to the Magazine [3]. What the conditions were cannot now be known; but, certainly, they were not sufficient to hinder Johnson from casting his eyes about him in quest of other employment. Accordingly, in 1735, he made overtures to the reverend Mr. Budworth, Master of a Grammar-school

[1] 'Upon the whole Erasmus is rather a versifier than a poet, and is not to be ranked amongst the Italian poets of those days, Sannazarius, Fracastorius, Vida, &c., many of whom wrote better than any of the ancients, except Lucretius, Virgil, Horace and a few more.' Jortin's *Erasmus*, i. 601.

Addison, in the *Guardian*, Nos. 115, 119, writes about Strada's *Prolusion*, describing it as 'one of the most entertaining as well as the most just pieces of criticism that I have ever read.'

The Earl of Aberdeen (the Prime-minister), when a Cambridge undergraduate of eighteen years old, wrote to a friend in 1802:—'I will in some sort defend Vida when we meet, but meanwhile do you read Sannazarius. You will be pleased with him and also with Fracastorius.' *The Earl of Aberdeen*, 1893, p. 8.

For a charge brought against Sir Walter Scott of stealing from one of Vida's poems see *Life*, i. 230, *n*. 1.

[2] Lowth's 'incomparable *Praelectiones* on the Poetry of the Hebrews' (Gibbon's *Misc. Works*, ed. 1814, i. 51) were published in 1753. 'All Scotland,' said Johnson, 'could not muster learning enough for Lowth's *Prelections*.' *Life*, v. 57, *n*. 3.

[3] Murphy follows Hawkins (p. 29) in this statement. The letter was written on Nov. 25, 1734, and was answered on Dec. 2. 'But whether,' says Boswell, 'anything was done in consequence of it we are not informed.' *Ib*. i. 92. 'His first performance in the *Gentleman's Magazine* was a copy of Latin verses in March, 1738.' *Ib*. p. 113.

school at Brerewood, in Staffordshire, to become his assistant. This proposition did not succeed. Mr. Budworth apprehended, that the involuntary motions, to which Johnson's nerves were subject, might make him an object of ridicule with his scholars, and, by consequence, lessen their respect for their master [1]. Another mode of advancing himself presented itself about this time. Mrs. Porter, the widow of a mercer in Birmingham, admired his talents. It is said that she had about eight hundred pounds; and that sum to a person in Johnson's circumstances was an affluent fortune [2]. A marriage took place; and, to turn his wife's money to the best advantage, he projected the scheme of an academy for education [3]. Gilbert Walmsley, at that time Register of the Ecclesiastical Court of the Bishop of Lichfield, was distinguished by his erudition and the politeness of his manners. He was the friend of Johnson, and, by his weight and influence, endeavoured to promote his interest [4]. The celebrated Garrick, whose father, Captain Garrick, lived at Lichfield, was placed in the new seminary of education by that gentleman's advice. Garrick was then about eighteen years old. An accession of seven or eight pupils was the most that could be obtained [5], though notice was given by a public advertisement [6], that at

[1] Hawkins, p. 32; *Life*, iv. 407, *n.* 4.

In the same year he applied for the mastership of Solihull Grammar School in Warwickshire. The 'Fœofees' did not approve of him, as 'he has the character of being a very haughty, ill-natured gent, and y^{t} he has such a way of distorting his Face (w^{h} though he can't help) ye gent. think it may affect some young ladds.' *Ib.* vi. *Addenda*, p. 44.

[2] Murphy here follows Hawkins (p. 33), who, in his turn, followed the anonymous author of *Memoirs of the Life &c. of Dr. Johnson*, ed. 1785, p. 25. Boswell speaks of the marriage as 'a very imprudent scheme both on account of their disparity of years and her want of fortune.' *Life*, i. 95. There is no doubt that she had some property. *Ib. n.* 3.

[3] By the fineness of his language Murphy, like Milton's biographers, seems to shrink from stating that Johnson thought of starting a boarding-school. A few lines lower down he calls it 'a seminary of education.' Johnson defines *Academy* as 'a place of education, in contradistinction to the universities or public schools.'

[4] Hawkins, p. 35; *Life*, i. 81.

[5] Hawkins, p. 36. According to Boswell (*Life*, i. 97) there were only three pupils.

[6] *Gent. Mag.*, 1736, pp. 360, 428. Pembroke College has lately acquired a desk which belonged to Johnson at Edial.

Edial,

Edial, near Lichfield, in Staffordshire, young Gentlemen are boarded and taught the Latin and Greek Languages, by Samuel Johnson.

The undertaking proved abortive. Johnson, having now abandoned all hopes of promoting his fortune in the country, determined to become an adventurer in the world at large. His young pupil, Garrick, had formed the same resolution[1]; and, accordingly, in March, 1737, they arrived in London together. Two such candidates for fame perhaps never, before that day, entered the metropolis together. Their stock of money was soon exhausted[2]. In his visionary project of an academy Johnson had probably wasted his wife's substance; and Garrick's father had little more than his half-pay. The two fellow-travellers had the world before them, and each was to chuse his road to fortune and to fame. They brought with them genius, and powers of mind, peculiarly formed by nature for the different vocations to which each of them felt himself inclined. They acted from the impulse of young minds, even then meditating great things, and with courage anticipating success. Their friend Mr. Walmsley, by a letter to the Rev. Mr. Colson, who, it seems, was a great mathematician, exerted his good offices in their favour. He gave notice of their intended journey[3]. 'Davy Garrick,' he said, 'will be with you next week; and Johnson, to try his fate with a tragedy, and to get himself employed in some translation either from the Latin or French. Johnson is a very good scholar and a poet, and, I have great hopes, will turn out a fine tragedy-writer. If it should be in your way, I doubt not but you will be ready to recommend and assist your countrymen.' Of Mr. Walmsley's merits and the excellence of his character, Johnson has left a beautiful testimonial at the end of the Life of Edward Smith[4]. It is reasonable to conclude, that a mathematician, absorbed in abstract speculations, was not able to find a sphere of

[1] Garrick's intention was 'to complete his education and follow the profession of the law.' *Life*, i. 101.

[2] *Ib. n.* 1.

[3] *Ib.* i. 102. Murphy does not quote the letter accurately.

[4] Edmund Smith. *Works*, vii. 380; *Life*, i. 81.

action

action for two men who were to be the architects of their own fortune. In three or four years afterwards Garrick came forth with talents that astonished the publick. He began his career at Goodman's-fields[1], and there, *monstratus fatis Vespasianus*[2] *!* he chose a lucrative profession, and consequently soon emerged from all his difficulties. Johnson was left to toil in the humble walks of literature. A tragedy, as appears by Walmsley's letter, was the whole of his stock. This, most probably, was IRENE[3]; but, if then finished, it was doomed to wait for a more happy period. It was offered to Fleetwood, and rejected. Johnson looked round him for employment. Having, while he remained in the country, corresponded with Cave under a feigned name, he now thought it time to make himself known to a man whom he considered as a patron of literature[4]. Cave had announced, by public advertisement, a prize of fifty pounds for the best

[1] On Oct. 19, 1741. Murphy's *Garrick*, pp. 13, 16.

[2] Tacitus, *Agricola*, c. 13. 'Destiny learnt to know its favourite.' Church and Brodribb's *Translation*.

[3] It was *Irene*. *Life*, i. 100.

Boswell recorded in his note-book:—'Peter Garrick told me that Mr. Johnson went first to London, to see what could be made of his tragedy of *Irene*; that he remembers his borrowing the *Turkish History* (I think Peter said of *him*) in order to take the story of his play out of it; that he and Mr. Johnson went to the Fountain Tavern by themselves, and Mr. Johnson read it to him. This, Mr. Peter Garrick told me at Lichfield, Sunday, 24 March, 1778. Mr. Porter, son to Mrs. Johnson, was by, and objected that the Fountain was a notorious bawdy-house. Peter said it might be so, but that people might be decently there, as well as anywhere else; that he belonged to a West India club kept there, at which a dozen of Madeira used to be set before the fire to toast, and that they never had women with them.' *Morrison Autographs*, i. 369.

For the Fountain Tavern see *Life*, i. 111, and for the rejection of *Irene* by Fleetwood, the patentee of Drury Lane Theatre, see *ib.* i. 111, 153, and *Letters*, i. 5.

In the advertisement at the end of *Theatrical Records*, 1756, are eight tragedies published by Dodsley, *Irene* among them—each at eighteen-pence. On p. 103 is mentioned *Irene or the Fair Greek*, a Tragedy by Charles Goring, 1708.

Gilbert Swinhoe, in 1658, published *The Tragedy of the unhappy fair Irene*. Lowndes's *Biblio. Man.* p. 2562.

[4] Murphy in this is following Hawkins. Johnson had not written 'under a feigned name.' He had said:—'Your letter by being directed to *S. Smith*, to be left at the Castle Inn, Birmingham will reach your humble servant.' *Life*, i. 92. His letter, to which Murphy now refers (*Ib.* i. 107), clearly shows that the first had had no result.

Poem on Life, Death, Judgement, Heaven, and Hell[1]; and this circumstance diffused an idea of his liberality. Johnson became connected with him in business, and in a close and intimate acquaintance. Of Cave's character it is unnecessary to say anything in this place, as Johnson was afterwards the biographer of his first and most useful patron[2]. To be engaged in the translation of some important book was still the object which Johnson had in view. For this purpose he proposed to give the History of the Council of Trent, with copious notes then lately added to a French edition. Twelve sheets of this work were printed[3], for which Johnson received forty-nine pounds, as appears by his receipt in the possession of Mr. Nichols, the compiler of that entertaining and useful work, the Gentleman's Magazine. Johnson's translation was never completed; a like design was offered to the publick, under the patronage of Dr. Zachary Pearce; and by that contention both attempts were frustrated[4]. Johnson had been commended by Pope for the translation of the Messiah into Latin verse; but he knew no approach to so eminent a man[5]. With one, however, who was connected with Pope, he became acquainted at St. John's Gate; and that person was no other than the well-known Richard Savage, whose life was afterwards written by Johnson with great elegance, and a depth of moral reflection. Savage was a man of considerable talents. His address, his various

[1] 'Cave sometimes offered subjects for poems, and proposed prizes for the best performers. The first prize was fifty pounds, for which, being but newly acquainted with wealth, and thinking the influence of fifty pounds extremely great, he expected the first authors of the kingdom to appear as competitors; and offered the allotment of the prize to the universities. But when the time came, no name was seen among the writers that had ever been seen before; the universities and several private men rejected the province of assigning the prize.' Johnson's *Works*, vi. 432; *Life*, i. 91.

[2] *Ib.* i. 256.

[3] Only six sheets. 'A few copies were intended to be reserved; but they were so carefully put by as to be lost in the mass of Mr. Cave's papers deposited in St. John's Gate.' *Gentleman's Magazine*, 1787, p. 345.

[4] *Life*, i. 107, 135.

[5] 'It was shown to Pope by a son of Dr. Arbuthnot, then a gentleman-commoner of Christ Church. He returned it with this encomium:—"The writer of this poem will leave it a question for posterity whether his or mine be the original."' Hawkins, p. 13.

accomplishments,

accomplishments, and, above all, the peculiarity of his misfortunes recommended him to Johnson's notice. They became united in the closest intimacy. Both had great parts, and they were equally under the pressure of want. Sympathy joined them in a league of friendship. Johnson has been often heard to relate, that he and Savage walked round Grosvenor-square till four in the morning; in the course of their conversation reforming the world, dethroning princes, establishing new forms of government, and giving laws to the several states of Europe, till, fatigued at length with their legislative office, they began to feel the want of refreshment; but could not muster up more than four pence halfpenny[1]. Savage, it is true, had many vices; but vice could never strike its roots in a mind like Johnson's, seasoned early with religion, and the principles of moral rectitude. His first prayer was composed in the year 1738[2]. He had not at that time renounced the use of wine[3]; and, no doubt, occasionally enjoyed his friend and his bottle. The love of late hours, which followed him through life, was, perhaps, originally

[1] 'Johnson told Sir Joshua Reynolds, that one night in particular, when Savage and he walked round St. James's-square for want of a lodging, they were not at all depressed by their situation; but in high spirits and brimful of patriotism, traversed the square for several hours, inveighed against the minister, and "resolved they would *stand by their country*."' *Life*, i. 164. In Grosvenor Square, when the Thrales were living there, he had his own room (*Ib.* iv. 72, *n.* 1), and recalling the old days, thought perhaps how 'the whirligig of time brings in his revenge.'

[2] *Ante*, p. 7.

[3] Boswell, writing of Johnson's first visit to London in 1737, says:—'He at this time, I believe, abstained entirely from fermented liquors.' *Life*, i. 103.

Johnson describing his dinner at the Pine Apple, in New Street, said:—'It used to cost the rest a shilling, for they drank wine; but I had a cut of meat for six-pence, and bread for a penny, and gave the waiter a penny; so that I was quite well served, nay, better than the rest, for they gave the waiter nothing.' *Ib.* i. 103.

In a marginal note Leigh Hunt says:—'Lord Byron, in repeating this story, of which he was fond, used to dwell upon these particular words, "a cut of meat," with great and pleasant gusto.' *A Shelf of Old Books*, by Mrs. James T. Fields, p. 174. The price of wine is shown in the following quotation:—'Her spirits grew very low; and she was once or twice going to ring the bell, to send her maid for half a pint of white wine; but checked her inclination, in order to save the little sum of sixpence.' *Amelia*, Bk. x. ch. v. 'White wine' is sherry.

contracted

contracted in company with Savage. However that may be, their connection was not of long duration. In the year 1738, Savage was reduced to the last distress. Mr. Pope, in a letter to him, expressed his concern for 'the miserable withdrawing of his pension after the death of the Queen[1];' and gave him hopes that, 'in a short time, he should find himself supplied with a competence, without any dependance on those little creatures, whom we are pleased to call the Great[2].' The scheme proposed to him was, that he should retire to Swansea in Wales, and receive an allowance of fifty pounds a year, to be raised by subscription; Pope was to pay twenty pounds[3]. This plan, though finally established, took more than a year before it was carried into execution. In the mean time, the intended retreat of Savage called to Johnson's mind the third satire of Juvenal, in which that poet takes leave of a friend, who was withdrawing himself from all the vices of Rome. Struck with this idea, he wrote that well-known Poem, called London. The first lines manifestly point to Savage[4].

> Though grief and fondness in my breast rebel,
> When injured Thales bids the town farewell;
> Yet still my calmer thoughts his choice commend;
> I praise the hermit, but regret the friend.
> Resolv'd at length from Vice and London far,
> To breathe in distant fields a purer air;
> And, fix'd on Cambria's solitary shore,
> Give to St. David one true Briton more.

[1] 'Savage,' said Adam Smith, 'was but a worthless fellow; his pension of fifty pounds never lasted him above a few days. As a sample of his economy you may take a circumstance that Johnson himself told me. It was, at that period, fashionable to wear scarlet cloaks trimmed with gold lace: the Doctor met him one day, just after he had received his pension, with one of these cloaks upon his back, while, at the same time, his naked toes were peeping through his shoes.' *Buchan MSS.* quoted in Croker's *Boswell*, x. 122.

[2] This letter, I think, is not extant. The passages quoted in the text are given, without Pope's name, in Johnson's *Works*, viii. 169.

[3] *Ib.* viii. 318.

[4] Boswell denies this. In a note I have examined the question. *Life*, i. 125, *n.* 4.

Mr. Hussey (*Life*, iii. 369), in a MS. note in the *Life*, says:—'Johnson told me that London was written *many years* before he was acquainted with Savage, and that it was even *published before* he knew him—of which I informed Mr. Boswell, who did not think proper to believe me.—Johnson also said that by Thales he did not mean any particular person.'

Johnson

Johnson at that time lodged at Greenwich[1]. He there fixes the scene, and takes leave of his friend; who, he says in his Life, parted from him with tears in his eyes[2]. The poem, when finished, was offered to Cave[3]. It happened, however, that the late Mr. Dodsley was the purchaser at the price of ten guineas[4]. It was published in 1738; and Pope, we are told, said, 'The author, whoever he is, will not be long concealed;' alluding to the passage in Terence, *Ubi, ubi est, diu celari non potest*[5]. Notwithstanding that prediction, it does not appear that, besides the copy-money, any advantage accrued to the author of a poem, written with the elegance and energy of Pope. Johnson, in August 1738[6], went, with all the fame of his poetry, to offer himself a candidate for the mastership of the school at Appleby, in Leicestershire. The statutes of the place required, that the person chosen should be a master of arts. To remove this objection, the late Lord Gower was induced to write to a friend, in order to obtain for Johnson a master's degree in the University of Dublin, by the recommendation of Dr. Swift[7].

. . . .

This scheme miscarried. There is reason to think, that Swift declined to meddle in the business; and to that circumstance Johnson's known dislike of Swift has been often imputed[8].

[1] He had lodged at Greenwich a year earlier. *Life*, i. 107. He was living in Castle Street, Cavendish Square, when he wrote *London*. *Ib.* p. 120.

[2] 'Savage left London in July, 1739, having taken leave with great tenderness of his friends, and parted from the author of this narrative with tears in his eyes.' *Works*, viii. 173.

[3] *Life*, i. 120.

[4] *Ib.* p. 124.

[5] *Eunuchus*, ii. 3, 4. 'Pope said, "he will soon be déterré."' *Life*, i. 129. 'Pope recollected perhaps a passage recorded of Milton, who, seeing a beautiful young lady pass him whom he never had seen before, turned to look at her and said, "Whoever thou art, thou canst not long be concealed."' Hawkins, p. 60. Perhaps he recollected the line in *Le Misanthrope*, Act iii. sc. 8:—

'Un mérite éclatant se déterre lui-même.'

Johnson never saw Pope, as the following note by Mr. Hussey shows:—'Asking Johnson if he had ever been in Mr. Pope's company he replied, "No, Sir, I never *saw* Pope."' Yet Pope lived seven years after Johnson's first visit to London.

[6] It was in 1739 that Johnson went to Appleby. *Life*, i. 132, *n.* 1; *Letters*, i. 3, *n.* 1.

[7] For Lord Gower's letter, which I omit, see *Life*, i. 133.

[8] 'I once took the liberty to ask

It

It is mortifying to pursue a man of merit through all his difficulties; and yet this narrative must be, through many following years, the history of Genius and Virtue struggling with Adversity. Having lost the school at Appleby, Johnson was thrown back on the metropolis. Bred to no profession, without relations, friends, or interest, he was condemned to drudgery in the service of Cave, his only patron. In November 1738 was published a translation of Crousaz's Examen of Pope's Essay on Man; 'containing a succinct View of the System of the Fatalists, and a Confutation of their Opinions; with an Illustration of the Doctrine of Free Will; and an Enquiry, what view Mr. Pope might have in touching upon the Leibnitzian Philosophy, and Fatalism. By Mr. Crousaz, Professor of Philosophy and Mathematics at Lausanne.' This translation has been generally thought a production of Johnson's pen; but it is now known, that Mrs. Elizabeth Carter has acknowledged it to be one of her early performances[1]. It is certain, however, that Johnson was eager to promote the publication. He considered the foreign philosopher as a man zealous in the cause of religion; and with him he was willing to join against the system of the Fatalists, and the doctrine of Leibnitz[2]. It is well known that Warburton wrote a vindication of Mr. Pope[3]; but there is reason to think, that Johnson conceived an early prejudice against the Essay on Man; and what once took root in a mind like his, was not easily eradicated. His letter to

Johnson if Swift had personally offended him, and he told me he had not.' *Life*, v. 44.

'Johnson attributed the Tale of a Tub to Arbuthnot. He thought Swift not equal to it.' MS. note by Mr. Hussey. See *post* in Percy's *Anecdotes*.

[1] *Life*, i. 137.

Her father wrote to her on June 25, 1738:—'You mention Johnson; but that is a name with which I am utterly unacquainted. Neither his scholastic, critical, or poetical character ever reached my ears. I a little suspect his judgment if he is very fond of Martial.' *Memoirs of Mrs. Carter*, i. 39.

[2] 'No, Sir; Leibnitz was as paltry a fellow as I know.' *Life*, v. 287.

[3] 'The Rev. Mr. Strahan clearly recollects having been told by Johnson, that the King observed that Pope made Warburton a Bishop. "True, Sir, (said Johnson,) but Warburton did more for Pope; he made him a Christian:" alluding, no doubt, to his ingenious Comments on the *Essay on Man*.' *Ib.* ii. 37, *n.* 1; *Works*, viii. 289.

Cave

Cave on this subject is still extant, and may well justify Sir John Hawkins, who inferred that Johnson was the translator of Crousaz [1]. The conclusion of the letter is remarkable. 'I am yours, IMPRANSUS.' If by that Latin word was meant that he had not dined, because he wanted the means, who can read it, even at this hour, without an aching heart [2]?

With a mind naturally vigorous, and quickened by necessity, Johnson formed a multiplicity of projects; but most of them proved abortive. A number of small tracts issued from his pen with wonderful rapidity; such as 'MARMOR NORFOLCIENSE; or an Essay on an ancient prophetical Inscription, in Monkish Rhyme, [lately] discovered at Lynn [near Lynne] in Norfolk. By *Probus Britannicus*.' This was a pamphlet against Sir Robert Walpole. According to Sir John Hawkins, a warrant was issued to apprehend the Author, who retired with his wife to an obscure lodging near Lambeth Marsh, and there eluded the search of the messengers [3]. But this story has no foundation in truth. Johnson was never known to mention such an incident in his life; and Mr. Steele (late of the Treasury) caused diligent search to be made at the proper offices, and no trace of such a proceeding could be found [4]. In the same year (1739) the Lord Chamberlain prohibited the representation of a tragedy, called GUSTAVUS VASA, by Henry Brooke. Under the mask of irony Johnson published, 'A Vindication of the Licencer from the malicious and scandalous Aspersions of Mr. Brooke [5].' Of these two pieces Sir John Hawkins says, 'they have neither learning nor wit; not a single ray of that genius which has since blazed forth [6];' but as they have been lately re-printed,

[1] Hawkins, p. 67.

[2] *Life*, i. 137. The original of this letter, owing to this one word *impransus*, was sold in 1888 for £46. *Letters*, i. 3.

[3] Hawkins, p. 72.

Pennant, in his *London* (1790, p. 30), writes:—'From Lambeth I returned by the water-side, near the end of Westminster Bridge, along a tract once a dreary marsh, and still in parts called *Lambeth Marsh*. . . . Most of this tract is become firm land, and covered with most useful buildings, even to the edge of the river.'

[4] *Life*, i. 141.

[5] *Ib.* i. 140.

[6] Hawkins, p. 78. Murphy's quotation is inaccurate.

the reader, who wishes to gratify his curiosity, is referred to the fourteenth volume of Johnson's works, published by Stockdale[1]. The lives of Boerhaave, Blake, Barratier, Father Paul, and others, were, about that time, printed in the Gentleman's Magazine[2]. The subscription of fifty pounds a year for Savage was completed[3]; and in July, 1739, Johnson parted with the companion of his midnight-hours, never to see him more. The separation was, perhaps, an advantage to him, who wanted to make a right use of his time, and even then beheld, with self-reproach, the waste occasioned by dissipation. His abstinence from wine and strong liquors began soon after the departure of Savage[4]. What habits he contracted in the course of that acquaintance cannot now be known. The ambition of excelling in conversation, and that pride of victory, which, at times, disgraced a man of Johnson's genius, were, perhaps, native blemishes[5]. A fierce spirit of independence, even in the midst of poverty, may be seen in Savage; and, if not thence transfused by Johnson into his own manners, it may, at least, be supposed to have gained strength from the example before him. During that connection there was, if we believe Sir John Hawkins, a short separation between our author and his wife[6]; but a reconciliation soon took place. Johnson loved her, and shewed his affection in various modes of gallantry, which Garrick used to render ridiculous by his mimicry. The affectation of soft and fashionable airs did not become an unwieldy figure: his admiration was received by the wife with the flutter of an antiquated coquette; and both, it is well known, furnished matter for the lively genius of Garrick[7].

[1] *Works*, v. 329; vi. 89.

[2] *Life*, i. 139, 140, 147, 153.

[3] Johnson, in his *Life of Savage*, says, 'the subscription did not amount to fifty pounds a year;' in his *Life of Pope* he states that Pope raised for him forty pounds. *Works*, viii. 173, 318.

[4] It had begun before, though it might have been interrupted. *Ante*, p. 371, *n.* 3.

[5] Murphy makes 'the ambition of excelling in conversation' a blemish.

[6] 'While he was in a lodging in Fleet Street she was harboured by a friend near the Tower.' Hawkins, p. 89. See *Life*, i. 163, *n.* 2. In 'the exact list of his places of residence' which he gave to Boswell (*Ib.* iii. 405, *n.* 6) he does not mention Fleet Street.

[7] *Ib.* i. 99.

It is a mortifying reflection, that Johnson, with a store of learning and extraordinary talents, was not able, at the age of thirty, to force his way to the favour of the publick. *Slow rises worth by poverty depress'd*[1]. 'He was still,' as he says himself, 'to provide for the day that was passing over him[2].' He saw Cave involved in a state of warfare with the numerous competitors[3], at that time struggling with the Gentleman's Magazine; and gratitude for such supplies as Johnson received, dictated a Latin Ode on the subject of that contention[4]. The first lines,

> Urbane, nullis fesse laboribus,
> Urbane, nullis victe calumniis,

put one in mind of Casimir's Ode to Pope Urban:

> Urbane, regum maxime, maxime
> Urbane vatum.—

The Polish poet was, probably, at that time in the hands of a man who had meditated the history of the Latin poets[5].

[1] 'This mournful truth is everywhere confess'd;
Slow rises worth by poverty depress'd.'
Johnson parodied the first line in the following verse:—
'Yet hear, alas! this mournful truth,
Nor hear it with a frown;—
Thou canst not make the tea so fast
As I can gulp it down.'
Letters, ii. 113, *n.* 3.

[2] 'Much of my life has been lost under the pressures of disease; much has been trifled away; and much has always been spent in provision for the day that was passing over me.' *Works*, v. 49.

[3] The chief rivals, according to Hawkins (p. 90), were 'a knot of booksellers, the proprietors of the *London Magazine*.' He adds (p. 92) that 'the check which the increasing demand for the *Gentleman's Magazine* gave to the sale of its rival was so great as to throw back no fewer than 70,000 copies on the hands of the proprietors.' To make up this vast number he must have added together the surplus copies of many months, if not years. Cave was libelled as a madman. By way of reply he merely reprinted in his own Magazine the most scurrilous of the attacks.

[4] *Life*, i. 113.

[5] *Ante*, p. 365.

'Casimir Sarbiewski, whose name has been Latinised into Sarbievius (1646). His contemporaries considered him as the greatest rival of Horace that had appeared, and he received a gold medal from the Pope, who made him his laureate. Many of his works were translated into English by Dr. Watts.' Morfill's *Poland*, p. 278.

Johnson describes him as 'a writer who has many of the beauties and faults of Cowley.' *Works*, vii. 39.

Guthrie

Guthrie, the historian[1], had from July 1736 composed the parliamentary speeches for the Magazines; but, from the beginning of the session which opened on the 19th of November 1740, Johnson succeeded to that department, and continued it from that time to the debate on spirituous liquors, which happened in the House of Lords in February, 1742-3[2]. The eloquence, the force of argument, and the splendor of language, displayed in the several speeches, are well known, and universally admired. The whole has been collected in two volumes by Mr. Stockdale, and may form a proper supplement to this edition. 'That Johnson was the author of the debates during that period was not generally known; but the secret transpired several years afterwards, and was avowed by himself on the following occasion. Mr. Wedderburne (now Lord Loughborough), Dr. Johnson, Dr. Francis (the translator of Horace)[3], the present writer, and others, dined with the late Mr. Foote. An important debate towards the end of Sir Robert Walpole's administration being mentioned, Dr. Francis observed, 'That Mr. Pitt's speech, on that occasion, was the best he had ever read.' He added, 'That he had employed eight years of his life in the study of Demosthenes, and finished a translation of that celebrated orator, with all the decorations of style and language within the reach of his capacity; but he had met with nothing equal to the speech above-mentioned.' Many of the company remembered the debate; and some passages were cited, with the approbation and applause of all present. During the ardour of conversation Johnson remained silent. As soon as the warmth of praise subsided, he opened with these words: 'That speech I wrote in a garret in Exeter-street.' The company was struck with astonishment. After staring at each other in silent amaze, Dr. Francis asked, 'How that speech could be written by him?'

[1] *Life*, i. 116; ii. 52; iv. 30.

[2] *Ib.* i. 150, 501-512.

[3] Gibbon, who at the age of fourteen was Francis's pupil, says:—'The translator of Horace might have taught me to relish the Latin poets, had not my friends discovered in a few weeks that he preferred the pleasures of London to the instruction of his pupils.' It was this discovery which carried Gibbon at so early an age to Oxford. *Misc. Works*, i. 40.

'Sir,'

'Sir,' said Johnson, 'I wrote it in Exeter-street. I never had been in the gallery of the House of Commons but once. Cave had interest with the door-keepers [1]. He, and the persons employed under him, gained admittance: they brought away the subject of discussion, the names of the speakers, the side they took, and the order in which they rose, together with notes of the arguments advanced in the course of the debate. The whole was afterwards communicated to me, and I composed the speeches in the form which they now have in the Parliamentary debates [2].' To this discovery Dr. Francis made answer: 'Then, Sir, you have exceeded Demosthenes himself; for to say, that you have exceeded Francis's Demosthenes, would be saying nothing.' The rest of the company bestowed lavish encomiums on Johnson: one, in particular, praised his impartiality; observing, that he dealt out reason and eloquence with an equal hand to both parties. 'That is not quite true,' said Johnson; 'I saved appearances tolerably well; but I took care that the WHIG DOGS should not have the best of it [3].' The sale of the Magazine was

[1] Some of the speeches had been previously given in the *Political State of Great Britain*. 'These for the most part were taken by stealth, and were compiled from the information of listeners and the under-officers and door-keepers of either house; but Cave had an interest with some of the members of both, arising from an employment he held in the post-office, that of inspector of the franks. . . . I have been informed by some who were much about him that, taking with him a friend or two, he found means to procure admission into the gallery of the House of Commons, or to some concealed station in the other, and that then they privately took down notes of the several speeches. Thus furnished they would adjourn to a neighbouring tavern, and compare and adjust their notes.' Hawkins, p. 94.

[2] In Appendix A to vol. i. of the *Life*, I have examined the whole question of Johnson's *Debates*. On the above passage I say:—'Murphy wrote from memory. This dinner with Foote must have taken place at least nineteen years before this account was published, for so many years had Dr. Francis been dead. At the time when Johnson was living in Exeter-street he was not engaged on the magazine. Nevertheless, the main facts may be true enough. Johnson himself told Boswell (*Life*, iii. 351) that in Lord Chesterfield's *Miscellaneous Works* (ii. 319) there were two speeches ascribed to Chesterfield which he had himself entirely written. Horace Walpole (*Letters*, i. 147) complained that the published report of his own first speech "did not contain one sentence of the true one."'

[3] Sir Robert Walpole, speaking in the House on January 24, 1738 (before Johnson had begun to write the Debates), said:—'I have read

greatly

greatly increased by the Parliamentary debates[1], which were continued by Johnson till the month of March, 1742-3. From that time the Magazine was conducted by Dr. Hawkesworth[2].

In 1743-4, Osborne, the bookseller, who kept a shop in Gray's-Inn, purchased the Earl of Oxford's library, at the price of thirteen thousand pounds. He projected a catalogue in five octavo volumes, at five shillings each. Johnson was employed in that painful drudgery[3]. He was likewise to collect all such small tracts, as were in any degree worth preserving, in order to reprint and publish the whole in a collection, called 'The Harleian Miscellany[4].' The catalogue was completed; and the Miscellany in 1749 was published in eight quarto volumes. In this business Johnson was a day-labourer for immediate subsistence, not unlike Gustavus Vasa working in the mines of Dalecarlia. What Wilcox, a bookseller of eminence in the Strand, said to Johnson, on his first arrival in town, was now almost confirmed. He lent our author five guineas, and then asked him, 'How do you mean to earn your livelihood in this town?' 'By my literary labours,' was the answer. Wilcox, staring at him, shook his head: 'By your literary labours!—You had better buy a porter's knot.' Johnson used to tell this anecdote to Mr. Nichols; but he said, 'Wilcox was one of my best friends, and he meant well[5].' In fact, Johnson, while employed

debates wherein all the wit, learning, and argument have been thrown into one side, and on the other nothing but what was low, mean, and ridiculous . . . If any gentleman will take the trouble, which, I own, I very seldom do, to look into these magazines, he will find four pages wrote against the government for one that is in its favour.' Coxe's *Walpole*, i. 570-2.

[1] The sale, according to Hawkins (p. 123), rose from ten to fifteen thousand copies a month.

The Private Journal of Dr. John Byrom mentions that, in 1739, 10,000 copies were printed; and of the *London Magazine*, 7,000 copies. *Gentleman's Magazine*, 1857, i. 149.

[2] The Magazine was, I believe, still conducted by Cave. Hawkesworth wrote the Debates. Hawkins, p. 132. He probably in other ways supplied Johnson's place, who, after 1743, wrote very little in it.

[3] *Life*, i. 153.

[4] *Ib.* i. 175; Hawkins, pp. 132-150.

[5] *Life*, i. 102, *n.* 2.

'Any porter has the liberty of bringing goods into London; but may not carry any out of the city, or from one part of it to another, unless he be a freeman; otherwise he is liable to be arrested.' Dodsley's *London*, 1761, v. 206. See also W. C. Hazlitt's *Livery Companies*, 1892, p. 154.

in

in Gray's-Inn, may be said to have carried a porter's knot. He paused occasionally, to peruse the book that came to his hand. Osborne thought that such curiosity tended to nothing but delay, and objected to it with all the pride and insolence of a man, who knew that he paid daily wages. In the dispute that of course ensued, Osborne, with that roughness which was natural to him, enforced his argument by giving the lie. Johnson seized a folio, and knocked the bookseller down[1]. This story has been related as an instance of Johnson's ferocity; but merit cannot always take the spurns of the unworthy with a patient spirit.

That the history of an author must be found in his works is, in general, a true observation[2]; and was never more apparent than in the present narrative. Every æra of Johnson's life is fixed by his writings. In 1744, he published the Life of Savage; and then projected a new edition of Shakspeare. As a prelude to this design, he published, in 1745, *Miscellaneous Observations on the Tragedy of Macbeth, with Remarks on Sir Thomas Hanmer's Edition; to which were prefixed, Proposals for a new Edition of Shakspeare, with a Specimen.* Of this pamphlet Warburton, in the Preface to Shakspeare, has given his opinion: 'As to all those things, which have been published under the title of Essays, Remarks, Observations, &c. on Shakspeare, if you except some critical notes on *Macbeth*, given as a specimen of a projected edition, and written, as appears, by a man of parts and genius, the rest are absolutely below a serious notice[3].' But the attention of

[1] Murphy gets the story from Hawkins, who places the scene in Osborne's shop. 'The simple truth,' says Boswell, 'I had from Johnson himself. "Sir, he was impertinent to me, and I beat him. But it was not in his shop; it was in my own chamber.' *Life*, i. 154. See also *ante*, p. 304.

[2] *Life*, iv. 98.

[3] 'Johnson always remembered with gratitude that he had been praised by Warburton at a time (1745) when, as Macaulay says, to be praised by Warburton was no light thing. And he did not know the contemptuous and brutal language in which Warburton had written of him to Hurd only two years after the "praise." "Of this Johnson you and I, I believe, think much alike. His remarks have in them as much folly as malignity."' Pattison's *Essays*, ed. 1889, ii. 158.

Warburton's letter was written on the

the publick was not excited; there was no friend to promote a subscription; and the project died, to revive at a future day[1]. A new undertaking, however, was soon after proposed; namely, an English Dictionary, upon an enlarged plan. Several of the most opulent booksellers had meditated a work of this kind; and the agreement was soon adjusted between the parties[2]. Emboldened by this connection, Johnson thought of a better habitation than he had hitherto known. He had lodged with his wife in courts and alleys about the Strand[3]; but now, for the purpose of carrying on his arduous

Oct. 31, 1765, not two, but twenty years after this 'praise.' It was provoked by the severe criticisms of his Shakespeare by Johnson in the edition which.he had just published. *Letters from a Late Eminent Prelate*, 1st ed., p. 272.

[1] Dr. Anderson, in his *Life of Johnson*, 1815, p. 106, gives a letter dated April 11, 1745, in which Tonson threatens Cave with a Chancery suit if he prints Shakespeare. That, he says, 'will be the method we shall take with any one who shall attack our property in this or any other copy that we have fairly bought and paid for.' The University of Oxford, it was true, had lately published Hanmer's edition; but, 'if you call on me,' Tonson continues, 'I will give my reasons why we rather chuse to proceed with the University by way of reprisal for their scandalous invasion of our rights than by law.'

Lord Camden, in the judgment which he gave in the House of Lords on Feb. 22, 1774, on the great copyright case says: — 'Shakespeare's works, which he left carelessly behind him in town when he retired from it, were surely given to the public if ever author's were; but two prompters, or players behind the scenes, laid hold of them, and the present proprietors pretend to derive that copy from them, for which the author himself never received a farthing.' *Parl. Hist.*, xvii. 1000.

For the booksellers' claim of copyright see *Life*, i. 437, and *Letters of Hume to Strahan*, p. 275, where I have examined it at some length.

They had undertaken to publish Warburton's Shakespeare which appeared in 1747, and so would not in 1745 suffer a rival edition. In 1756 they themselves engaged Johnson as editor. *Life*, i. 175, 318; Hawkins, p. 361.

'Warburton (said Quin the player) ought to have stuck to his own Bible, and not to have meddled with ours.' Nichols, *Lit. Hist.*, ii. 840.

[2] *Life*, i. 182. Hawkins, who had seen the original contract, says that it was dated June 18, 1746. Hawkins, p. 345. I had not noticed this fact when I wrote my note 2 on vol. i. p. 176 of the *Life*, where 1774 is a misprint for 1747. It adds to the absurdity of Croker's suspicion that Johnson was at this time absent or concealed on account of some difficulties which had arisen through the rebellion of 1745.

[3] For a list of his lodgings, which had not all been about the Strand, see *Life*, iii. 405, *n*. 6.

undertaking,

undertaking, and to be near his printer and friend Mr. Strahan, he ventured to take a house in Gough-square, Fleet-street [1]. He was told that the Earl of Chesterfield was a friend to his undertaking; and, in consequence of that intelligence, he published, in 1747, *The Plan of a Dictionary of the English Language, addressed to the Right Honourable Philip Dormer, Earl of Chesterfield, one of his Majesty's principal Secretaries of State* [2]. Mr. Whitehead, afterwards Poet Laureat, undertook to convey the manuscript to his Lordship: the consequence was an invitation from Lord Chesterfield to the author [3]. A stronger contrast of characters could not be brought together; the Nobleman, celebrated for his wit, and all the graces of polite behaviour; the Author, conscious of his own merit, towering in idea above all competition, versed in scholastic logic, but a stranger to the arts of polite conversation, uncouth, vehement, and vociferous. The coalition was too unnatural [4]. Johnson expected a Mæcenas, and was disappointed [5]. No patronage, no assistance followed. Visits were repeated; but the reception was not cordial. Johnson one day was left a full hour, waiting in an anti-chamber, till a gentleman should retire, and leave his Lordship at leisure. This was the famous Colley Cibber. Johnson saw him go, and, fired with indignation, rushed out of the house [6]. What Lord Chesterfield thought of his visitor

[1] *Life*, i. 188. Strahan lived at No. 10, Little New Street, Shoe Lane. Napier's *Boswell*, iii. 560.

[2] For the 'casual excuse for laziness' which led Johnson to address his *Plan* to the Earl of Chesterfield, see *Life*, i. 183.

[3] 'Dr. Taylor told me, that Johnson sent his *Plan* to him in manuscript, for his perusal; and that when it was lying upon his table, Mr. William Whitehead happened to pay him a visit, and being shewn it, was highly pleased with such parts of it as he had time to read, and begged to take it home with him, which he was allowed to do; that from him it got into the hands of a noble Lord, who carried it to Lord Chesterfield.' *Ib.* i. 184.

[4] 'In a short time the moral, pious Johnson and the gay, dissipated Beauclerk were companions. "What a coalition!" said Garrick when he heard of this.' *Ib.* i. 249.

[5] Of Andrew Millar, the printer, Johnson said 'he is the Mæcenas of the age.' *Ib.* i. 287, *n.* 3.

[6] Hawkins (p. 189) tells the same story, which had long been current. 'But,' writes Boswell, 'Johnson himself assured me, that there was not the least foundation for it. He told me, that there never was any particular incident which produced a quarrel between Lord Chesterfield

may

may be seen in a passage in one of that Nobleman's letters to his son (Letter CCXII). 'There is a man, whose moral character, deep learning, and superior parts, I acknowledge, admire, and respect; but whom it is so impossible for me to love, that I am almost in a fever whenever I am in his company. His figure (without being deformed) seems made to disgrace or ridicule the common structure of the human body. His legs and arms are never in the position which, according to the situation of his body, they ought to be in, but constantly employed in committing acts of hostility upon the Graces. He throws any where, but down his throat, whatever he means to drink; and only mangles what he means to carve. Inattentive to all the regards of social life, he mistimes or misplaces every thing. He disputes with heat and indiscriminately, mindless of the rank, character, and situation of those with whom he disputes; absolutely ignorant of the several gradations of familiarity and respect, he is exactly the same to his superiors, his equals, and his inferiors; and therefore, by a necessary consequence, absurd to two of the three. Is it possible to love such a man? No. The utmost I can do for him is, to consider him a respectable Hottentot [1].' Such was the idea entertained

and him; but that his Lordship's continued neglect was the reason why he resolved to have no connection with him.' *Life*, i. 257.

[1] I have shewn that it was not of Johnson but of George Lyttelton that Chesterfield was writing. *Life*, i. 267; *Dr. Johnson, His Friends and his Critics*, p. 214.

'Johnson said to me many years before he published his Preface [to Lyttelton's Poems], "Lord Lyttelton was a worthy good man, but so ungracious that he did not know how to be a Gentleman."' MS. note by Mr. Hussey, in Mr. H. Symonds's copy of the *Life*.

I do not know when *Hottentot* first came into common use. Addison, in the *Freeholder* for Jan. 6, 1716, describes how a Hottentot, who had been brought to England, and 'in a great measure polished out of his natural barbarity, upon being carried back to the Cape of Good Hope, mixed in a kind of transport with his countrymen, brutalized with them in their habits and manners, and would never again return to his foreign acquaintance.'

Dr. Watts, in the first page of his Logick, published in 1724, says that 'the improvement of reason hath raised the learned and the prudent in the European world almost as much above the Hottentots, and other savages of Africa, as those savages are by nature superior to the birds, the beasts, and the fishes.

Fielding, in *Tom Jones* (Bk. xvi. ch. 8), describes Lady Bellaston as being 'much better pleased with the

by

by Lord Chesterfield. After the incident of Colley Cibber, Johnson never repeated his visits. In his high and decisive tone, he has been often heard to say, 'Lord Chesterfield is a Wit among Lords, and a Lord among Wits [1].'

In the course of the year 1747, Garrick, in conjunction with Lacy, became patentee of Drury-lane Playhouse [2]. For the opening of the theatre, at the usual time, Johnson wrote for his friend the well-known prologue [3], which, to say no more of it, may at least be placed on a level with Pope's to the tragedy of Cato. The play-house being now under Garrick's direction,

prospect of making the proposals to a woman of sense, and who knew the world, than to a gentleman whom she honoured with the appellation of Hottentot.'

Horace Walpole, writing of 'theatric genius,' says:—'In Southern it seemed a genuine ray of nature and Shakspeare, but falling on an age still more Hottentot was stifled in those gross and barbarous productions, tragi-comedies.' Quoted in Warton's Pope's *Works*, iv. 198.

'The young men of this day are quite Hottentots,' wrote in 1797 the author of the Life of G. M. Berkeley. Berkeley's *Poems*, p. 313.

A Hottentot was a good deal lower than a Goth.

[1] 'This man (said he) I thought had been a Lord among wits; but, I find, he is only a wit among Lords!' *Life*, i. 266.

[2] The partnership lasted till 1773. Davies's *Life of Garrick*, i. 100; ii. 289.

[3] *Life*, i. 181; *Works*, i. 23.

In this Prologue Johnson, speaking of 'the wits of Charles,' says:—

'Themselves they studied, as they felt they writ,
Intrigue was plot, obscenity was wit;
. . . .
Yet bards like these aspir'd to lasting praise,
And proudly hoped to pimp in future days.'

He concludes:—

'Bid scenick virtue form the rising age,
And truth diffuse her radiance from the stage.'

This contrasts oddly with an attempt made by Garrick only two years later. Johnson says that Otway's *Friendship in Fashion* 'was, upon its revival at Drury Lane in 1749, hissed off the stage for immorality and obscenity.' *Works*, vii. 174.

'The wits of Charles' is perhaps borrowed from *The Spectator*, No. 5, where Addison writes of 'the wits of King Charles's time.'

The Prologue, writes Hawkins (p. 198), 'failed in a great measure of its effect; the town, it is true, submitted to the revival of Shakespeare's plays, recommended, as they were, by the exquisite acting of Mr. Garrick; but in a few winters they discovered an impatience for pantomimes and ballad-farces. Mr. Garrick gave up the hope of correcting the public taste, and became so indifferent about it, that he once told me that, if the town required him to exhibit the *Pilgrim's Progress* in a drama, he would do it.'

Johnson thought the opportunity fair to think of his tragedy of Irene, which was his whole stock on his first arrival in town, in the year 1737. That play was accordingly put into rehearsal in January 1749. As a precursor to prepare the way, and awaken the public attention, *The Vanity of Human Wishes*, a Poem in Imitation of the Tenth Satire of Juvenal, by the Author of *London*, was published in the same month[1]. In the Gentleman's Magazine, for February, 1749, we find that the tragedy of *Irene* was acted at Drury-lane, on Monday, February the 6th, and from that time, without interruption, to Monday, February the 20th, being in all thirteen nights[2]. Since that time it has not been exhibited on any stage. *Irene* may be added to some other plays in our language, which have lost their place in the theatre, but continue to please in the closet. During the representation of this piece, Johnson attended every night behind the scenes. Conceiving that his character, as an author, required some ornament for his person, he chose, upon that occasion, to decorate himself with a handsome waistcoat, and a gold-laced hat. The late Mr. Topham Beauclerc, who had had a great deal of that humour which pleases the more for seeming undesigned[3], used to give a pleasant description of this Green-room finery, as related by the author himself; 'But,' said

[1] *Life*, i. 192.

Irene and *Tom Jones* are announced in the *Gentleman's Magazine* for February, p. 96.

[2] In the *Gentleman's Magazine* for 1749, p. 76, it is stated that '*Irene* was acted from Monday, Feb. 6, to Monday, Feb. 20, inclusive.' According to Boswell and Hawkins, it was only acted nine nights. *Life*, i. 197; Hawkins, p. 199.

Gibbon, in a note to the *Decline and Fall*, ed. 1802, xii. 223, attacks 'the extravagance of the rant' in one of Mahomet's speeches. 'His passion soars above sense and reason.'

The winter season was a trying time for a new play, as is shown in Cibber's *Lives of the Poets*, v. 339, where it is stated that 'George Lillo rather chose *George Barnwell* should take its fate in the summer than run the more hazardous fate of encountering the winter criticks.'

[3] Johnson, speaking of Beauclerk, said, that 'no man ever was so free when he was going to say a good thing, from a *look* that expressed that it was coming; or, when he had said it, from a look that expressed that it had come.' *Life*, iii. 425.

Another time he said:—'Everything comes from him so easily. It appears to me that I labour when I say a good thing.' *Ib.* v. 76.

Johnson,

Johnson, with great gravity, 'I soon laid aside my gold-laced hat, lest it should make me proud[1].' The amount of the three benefit nights for the tragedy of *Irene*, it is to be feared, was not very considerable, as the profit, that stimulating motive, never invited the author to another dramatic attempt[2]. Some years afterwards, when the present writer was intimate with Garrick, and knew Johnson to be in distress, he asked the manager why he did not produce another tragedy for his Lichfield friend? Garrick's answer was remarkable: 'When Johnson writes *tragedy, declamation roars, and passion sleeps*[3]: when Shakspeare wrote, he dipped his pen in his own heart.'

There may, perhaps, be a degree of sameness in this regular way of tracing an author from one work to another, and the reader may feel the effect of a tedious monotony; but in the life of Johnson there are no other landmarks. He was now forty years old, and had mixed but little with the world[4]. He followed no profession, transacted no business, and was a stranger to what is called a town-life. We are now arrived at the brightest period he had hitherto known. His name broke out upon mankind with a degree of lustre that promised a triumph over all his difficulties. The Life of Savage was admired as

[1] 'He humourously observed to Mr. Langton, "that when in that dress he could not treat people with the same ease as when in his usual plain clothes."' *Life*, i. 200.

[2] Mr. Croker says that 'it appears by a MS. note in Isaac Reed's copy of Murphy's *Life*, that the receipts of the third, sixth, and ninth nights, after deducting sixty guineas a night for the expenses of the house, amounted to £195 17*s.*: Johnson cleared therefore, with the copyright, very nearly £300.'

By his *London* and *Vanity of Human Wishes* he only made twenty-five guineas. *Life*, i. 124, 193, *n.*

[3] 'From bard to bard the frigid caution crept,
Till declamation roared whilst passion slept.'
Johnson's *Prologue on the Opening of Drury Lane Theatre*.

[4] Boswell, writing of this time, says:—'Nothing can be more erroneous than the notion which some persons have entertained, that Johnson was then a retired authour, ignorant of the world; and, of consequence, that he wrote only from his imagination when he described characters and manners. He said to me, that before he wrote that work [*The Rambler*], he had been "running about the world," as he expressed it, more than almost any body.' *Life*, i. 215.

 a beautiful

a beautiful and instructive piece of biography. The two Imitations of Juvenal were thought to rival even the excellence of Pope; and the tragedy of *Irene*, though uninteresting on the stage, was universally admired in the closet, for the propriety of the sentiments, the richness of the language, and the general harmony of the whole composition. His fame was widely diffused; and he had made his agreement with the booksellers for his English Dictionary at the sum of fifteen hundred guineas; part of which was to be, from time to time, advanced in proportion to the progress of the work[1]. This was a certain fund for his support, without being obliged to write fugitive pieces for the petty supplies of the day. Accordingly we find that, in 1749, he established a club, consisting of ten in number, at Horseman's, in Ivy-lane, on every Tuesday evening[2]. This is the first scene of social life to which Johnson can be traced out of his own house. The members of this little society were, Samuel Johnson; Dr. Salter[3] (father of the late Master of the Charter-house); Dr. Hawkesworth[4]; Mr. Ryland[5], a merchant; Mr. Payne[6], a bookseller,

[1] *Post*, p. 406; *Life*, i. 183, 304; *Letters*, i. 25, 27.

[2] *Life*, i. 190; *Letters*, ii. 359, 363-4; 388, 390; Hawkins, pp. 219-235, 250-259. 'Thither,' says Hawkins (p. 219), 'he constantly resorted, and with a disposition to please and be pleased would pass those hours in a free and unrestrained interchange of sentiments which otherwise had been spent at home in painful reflection.' 'It required,' Hawkins adds (p. 250), 'on the part of us who considered ourselves as his disciples some degree of compliance with his political prejudices; the greater part of our company were Whigs, and I was not a Tory, and we all saw the prudence of avoiding to call the then late adventurer in Scotland, or his adherents, by those names which others hesitated not to give them, or to bring to remembrance what had passed a few years before on Tower Hill.' Bathurst, who was 'a very good hater,' and who 'hated a Whig,' must have had here to veil his hate.

[3] 'Dr. Samuel Salter was a Cambridge divine. He could carry his recollection back to the time when Dr. Samuel Clarke was yet a member of that University, and would frequently entertain us with particulars respecting him.' Hawkins, p. 220.

[4] *Life*, i. 190, *n.* 3; *Letters*, i. 412; ii. 7; Hawkins, pp. 220, 252, 310. *Ante*, p. 166.

[5] John Ryland was Hawkesworth's brother-in-law, and one of Johnson's correspondents. *Letters*, i. 56, *n.* 3.

[6] John Payne, afterwards chief accountant of the Bank of England. Hawkins, p. 220; *Letters*, ii. 363, *n.* 1. Johnson, when he himself was rapidly sinking, wrote to Ryland:—'To hear that dear Payne is better gives me great delight.' *Ib.* ii. 428.

a bookseller, in Paternoster row; Mr. Samuel Dyer, a learned young man; Dr. William M'Ghie[1], a Scotch physician; Dr. Edmund Barker[2], a young physician; Dr. Bathurst, another young physician; and Sir John Hawkins. This list is given by Sir John, as it should seem, with no other view than to draw a spiteful and malevolent character of almost every one of them. Mr. Dyer, whom Sir John says he loved with the affection of a brother[3], meets with the harshest treatment, because it was his maxim, that *to live in peace with mankind, and in a temper to do good offices, was the most essential part of our duty*[4]. That notion of moral goodness gave umbrage to Sir John Hawkins, and drew down upon the memory of his friend the bitterest imputations.

Ryland and Payne were among the four survivors of the old Club who dined together a few times in 1783-4. *Letters*, ii. 358, 363, 388, 390.

[1] M'Ghie had served as a volunteer on the side of government in 1745. 'He was a learned, ingenious and modest man, and one of those few of his country whom Johnson could endure. To say the truth, he treated him with great civility, and may almost be said to have loved him.' Hawkins, p. 233.

[2] Barker, like Dyer, had studied at Leyden. 'He was an excellent classical scholar, a deep metaphysician, and had read the Italian poets; but he was a thoughtless young man, and in all his habits of dress and appearance so slovenly as made him the jest of all his companions. Physicians in his time were used to be full dressed; and in his garb of a full suit, a brown tye-wig with a knot over one shoulder, and a long yellow-hilted sword, and his hat under his arm he was a caricature. In his religious principles he professed himself an Unitarian, for which Johnson so often snubbed him, that his visits to us became less and less frequent.' *Ib.* p. 233.

[3] Hawkins writes (p. 230), 'whom I once loved with the affection of a brother.'

[4] Hawkins is malignant enough, but Murphy does not quote him fairly. He had described how Dyer, who had been brought up for the dissenting ministry, had sunk into sloth and materialism. He came at last to think 'that those mistook their interest and shewed their ignorance of human life who abstained from any pleasure that disturbed not the quiet of families or the order of society; that natural appetites required gratification; that the indulgence of the irascible passions alone was vice; and that to live in peace with all mankind, &c.,' p. 230.

Hawkins, in this character of Dyer, according to Malone (Prior's *Life of Malone*, p. 419) aims a stab at the two Burkes. Dyer, he says, lost his fortune 'by contracting a fatal intimacy with some persons of desperate fortunes who were dealers in India stock.' These persons, says Malone, were Edmund Burke and his cousin. Dyer met Edmund Burke at the Literary Club, of which they were both members. *Life*, i. 478.

imputations. Mr. Dyer, however, was admired and loved through life. He was a man of literature [1]. Johnson loved to enter with him into a discussion of metaphysical, moral, and critical subjects; in those conflicts, exercising his talents, and, according to his custom, always contending for victory [2]. Dr. Bathurst was the person on whom Johnson fixed his affection. He hardly ever spoke of him without tears in his eyes [3]. It was from him, who was a native of Jamaica, that

[1] On a point of Latinity Johnson once said to him:—'Sir, I beg to have your judgement, for I know your nicety.' *Life*, iv. 11. Burke described him as 'a man of profound and general erudition.' *Ib. n.* 1.

[2] *Ante*, p. 376. 'He owned he sometimes talked for victory.' *Life*, v. 17. 'Care must be taken to distinguish between Johnson when he "talked for victory," and Johnson when he had no desire but to inform and illustrate.' *Ib.* iv. 111.

Dyer was little likely to have entered into such a contest. According to Malone 'he was so modest and reserved, that he frequently sat silent in company for an hour, and seldom spoke unless appealed to.' *Ib.* iv. 11, *n.* 1.

[3] *Ib.* i. 190, 242, *n.* 1; *Letters*, i. 32; *ante*, p. 158. 'Bathurst thought of becoming an eminent London physician, and omitted no means to attain that character: he studied hard, dressed well, and associated with those who were likely to bring him forward, but he failed in his endeavours, and shortly before his leaving England [for the Havannah] confessed to Johnson that in the course of ten years' exercise of his faculty he had never opened his hand to more than one guinea.' Hawkins, p. 235.

Johnson, who 'had in general a peculiar pleasure in the company of physicians' (*Life*, iv. 293), had three of them in his Club. Of these, 'M'Ghie, failing in his hope of getting forward in his profession, died of a broken heart, and was buried by a contribution of his friends' (Hawkins, p. 233); Barker 'died in obscurity' (*Ib.* p. 234), and Bathurst, 'missing of success,' went as 'physician to the army that was sent on the expedition against the Havannah,' where he died of fever (*ib.* p. 235). According to Hawkins, Bathurst's failure drew from Johnson the following reflection which many years later he inserted in his *Life of Akenside*: 'A physician in a great city seems to be the mere plaything of fortune; his degree of reputation is for the most part totally casual; they that employ him know not his excellence; they that reject him know not his deficience. By any acute observer, who had looked on the transactions of the medical world for half a century, a very curious book might be written on the *Fortune of Physicians*.' *Works*, viii. 471.

'Hawkins, remarking on 'the very many ignorant men who have been known to succeed in the profession,' adds in a note, 'so ignorant as to request of the College [of Physicians] the indulgence of an examination in English.'

Johnson

Johnson received into his service Frank, the black servant, whom, on account of his master, he valued to the end of his life [1]. At the time of instituting the club in Ivy-lane, Johnson had projected the *Rambler* [2]. The title was most probably suggested by the *Wanderer*; a poem which he mentions, with the warmest praise, in the Life of Savage [3]. With the same spirit of independence with which he wished to live, it was now his pride to write. He communicated his plan to none of his friends [4]: he desired no assistance, relying entirely on his own fund, and the protection of the Divine Being, which he implored in a solemn form of prayer, composed by himself for the occasion [5]. Having formed a resolution to undertake a work that might be of use and honour to his country, he thought, with Milton, that this was not to be obtained 'but by devout prayer to that Eternal Spirit that [who] can enrich with all utterance and knowledge, and send [sends] out his seraphim with the hallowed fire of his altar, to touch and purify the lips of whom he pleases [6].'

[1] *Life*, i. 239; iv. 401; *ante*, p. 291. 'Soon after the decease of Mrs. Johnson the father of Dr. Bathurst arrived in England from Jamaica, and brought with him a negro-servant, a native of that island, whom he caused to be baptised and named Francis Barber, and sent for instruction to Barton upon Tees in Yorkshire; upon the decease of Captain Bathurst, for so he was called, Francis went to live with his son, who willingly parted with him to Johnson. The uses for which he was intended to serve this his last master were not very apparent, for Diogenes himself never wanted a servant less than he seemed to do . . . He placed him at a school at Bishop Stortford, and kept him there five years; and, as Mrs. Williams was used to say, who would frequently reproach him with his indiscretion in this instance, expended £300 in an endeavour to have him taught Latin and Greek.' Hawkins, pp. 326–8. Francis entered Johnson's service a fortnight after Mrs. Johnson's death. *Life*, i. 239.

[2] According to Nichols (*Lit. Anec.* ix. 501) the Club was known as the Ramblers' Club. If so the name must have been given some time after its foundation.

See *Life*, i. 202 for the origin of the name of *The Rambler*. In the list of Periodical Publications in Nichols's *Lit. Anec.* viii. 495 is a paper under this name published in 1712.

[3] 'From a poem so diligently laboured, and so successfully finished, it might be reasonably expected that he should have gained considerable advantage; nor can it without some degree of indignation and concern be told, that he sold the copy for ten guineas.' *Works*, viii. 131.

[4] Hawkins, p. 265.

[5] *Ante*, p. 9.

[6] *The Reason of Church Govern-*

Having

Having invoked the special protection of Heaven, and by that act of piety fortified his mind, he began the great work of the *Rambler*. The first number was published on Tuesday, March the 20th, 1750; and from that time was continued regularly every Tuesday and Saturday for the space of two years, when it was finally closed on Saturday, March 14, 1752[1]. As it began with motives of piety, so it appears, that the same religious spirit glowed with unabating ardour to the last. His conclusion is: 'The Essays professedly serious, if I have been able to execute my own intentions, will be found exactly conformable to the precepts of Christianity, without any accommodation to the licentiousness and levity of the present age. I therefore look back on this part of my work with pleasure, which no [blame or praise of] man shall diminish or augment. I shall never envy the honours which wit and learning obtain in any other cause, if I can be numbered among the writers who have given ardour to virtue, and confidence to truth.' The whole number of Essays amounted to two hundred and eight[2]. Addison's, in the Spectator, are more in number, but not half in point of quantity[3]. Addison was not bound to publish on stated days; he could watch the ebb and flow of his genius, and send his paper to the press when his own taste was satisfied. Johnson's case was very different. He wrote singly and alone. In the whole progress of the work he did not receive more than ten essays. This was a scanty contribution. For the rest, the author has described his situation: 'He that condemns himself to compose on a stated day, will often bring to his task an attention dissipated, a memory embarrassed, an imagination overwhelmed, a mind distracted with anxieties, a body languishing with disease: he will labour on a barren topic, till it is too late to change it; or, in the ardour of invention, diffuse his

ment, &c., Book II. Introduction. Milton's *Works*, ed. 1806, i. 122. Quoted in Johnson's *Life of Milton*, *Works*, vii. 78.

[1] *Life*, i. 203, *n.* 1.

[2] Of these, four whole numbers and part of a fifth were by other hands. *Ib.* i. 203.

[3] Addison wrote about 240 *Spectators*, of about 112 lines to a number. In ninety-two weeks he wrote, roughly speaking, 26,680 lines, or 292 lines a week. Johnson wrote 203 *Ramblers* in 103 weeks, which, at 167 lines to a number, give 33,901 lines, or 329 a week.

thoughts

thoughts into wild exuberance, which the pressing hour of publication cannot suffer judgement to examine or reduce[1].' Of this excellent production the number sold on each day did not amount to five hundred: of course the bookseller, who paid the author four guineas a week, did not carry on a successful trade. His generosity and perseverance deserve to be commended; and happily, when the collection appeared in volumes, were amply rewarded. Johnson lived to see his labours flourish in a tenth edition[2]. His posterity, as an ingenious French writer has said on a similar occasion, began in his lifetime.

In the beginning of 1750, soon after the *Rambler* was set on foot, Johnson was induced by the arts of a vile impostor to lend his assistance, during a temporary delusion, to a fraud not to be paralleled in the annals of literature. One LAUDER, a native of Scotland, who had been a teacher in the University of EDINBURGH, had conceived a mortal antipathy to the name and character of Milton[3]. His reason was, because the prayer of

[1] *Rambler*, No. 208. In this number he says:—'I have never complied with temporary curiosity, nor enabled my readers to discuss the topick of the day.' There is a curious instance of this in his passing over in silence the great earthquake scare of April 8, 1750, when 'the open fields that skirt the metropolis were filled with an incredible number of people assembled in chairs, in chaises and coaches, as well as on foot, who waited in the most fearful suspense until morning.' Smollett's *History of England*, iii. 293. See also Walpole's *Letters*, ii. 201. Johnson's next number was on 'Retirement natural to a great mind.'

[2] In the closing number Johnson says:—'I have never been much a favourite with the public.' The bookseller was Cave. *Life*, i. 203, *n.* 6. It is stated in Chalmers's *British Essayists*, vol. xvi. Preface, p. 14, that 'the only number which had a prosperous sale' was 97—contributed by Richardson. A second impression however was required of the first numbers, as I have shown in the Introduction to *Select Essays of Johnson* (Dent & Co., 1889), p. 21.

Each edition, according to Hawkins (p. 269), consisted of 1,250 copies. Johnson soon parted with the copyright. *Letters*, i. 29, *n.* 1.

[3] Lauder had scarcely left college when he was struck on the knee by a golf-ball on Bruntsfield Links; through neglect of the wound he had to have the leg amputated. In spite of considerable merit he failed to get one or two appointments which he sought. This soured his temper, and 'at length drove him in an unlucky hour from Edinburgh to London. Here his folly working on his necessities induced him to detract from the fame of Milton by publishing forgeries. The public indignation

Pamela,

Pamela, in Sir Philip Sidney's Arcadia, was, as he supposed, maliciously inserted by the great poet in an edition of the Eikon Basilike, in order to fix an imputation of impiety on the memory of the murdered king[1]. Fired with resentment, and willing to reap the profits of a gross imposition, this man collected from several Latin poets, such as Masenius the Jesuit, Staphorstius a Dutch divine, Beza, and others, all such passages as bore any kind of resemblance to different places in the Paradise Lost; and these he published, from time to time, in the Gentleman's Magazine, with occasional interpolations of lines, which he himself translated from Milton. The public credulity swallowed all with eagerness; and Milton was supposed to be guilty of plagiarism from inferior modern writers. The fraud succeeded so well, that Lauder collected the whole into a volume, and advertised it under the title of '*An Essay on Milton's Use and Imitation of the Moderns, in his Paradise Lost; dedicated to the Universities of Oxford and Cambridge.*' While the book was in the press, the proof-sheets were shewn to Johnson at the Ivy-lane Club, by Payne, the bookseller, who was one of the members. No man in that society was in possession of the authors from whom Lauder professed to make his extracts. The

at length forced him to look for refuge and subsistence in Barbadoes, where he died in poverty and neglect about 1771. He had a sallow complexion, large rolling fiery eyes, a stentorian voice and a sanguine temper.' Ruddiman, who had given him some help in his *Poetarum Scotorum Musae Sacrae*, says in a manuscript note, 'I was so sensible of the weakness and folly of that man that I shunned his company as far as I decently could.' *Life of Ruddiman*, by G. Chalmers, 1794, p. 146.

[1] It was in 1747 that Lauder began his forgeries; in 1750 he collected them into a pamphlet. *Life*, i. 230. It was not till 1754, three years after his detection and retractation, that he published his pamphlet about the *Eikon Basilike*, under the title of *The General Impostor detected, or Milton convicted of forgery against King Charles I. Gent. Mag.* 1754, p. 97. There is no reason to believe that, as Murphy says, 'he supposed' that Milton was guilty.

Johnson repeated the charge in his *Life of Milton. Works*, vii. 84. 'A century after Milton's death it was safe for the most popular writer of the day to say that the prayer from the *Arcadia* had been interpolated in the *Eikon* by Milton himself, and then by him charged upon the King as a plagiarism.' Pattison's *Milton*, p. 103.

For Pamela's prayer see Milton's *Works*, ed. 1806, ii. 408.

charge

charge was believed, and the contriver of it found his way to Johnson, who is represented by Sir John Hawkins, not indeed as an accomplice in the fraud, but, through motives of malignity to Milton, delighting in the detection, and exulting that the poet's reputation would suffer by the discovery [1]. More malice to a deceased friend cannot well be imagined. Hawkins adds, '*that he wished well to the argument, must be inferred from the preface, which indubitably was written by him.*' The preface, it is well known, was written by Johnson, and for that reason is inserted in this edition [2]. But if Johnson approved of the argument, it was no longer than while he believed it founded in truth. Let us advert to his own words in that very preface. 'Among the enquiries to which the [this] ardour of criticism has naturally given occasion, none is more obscure in itself, or more worthy of rational curiosity, than a retrospection of the progress of this mighty genius in the construction of his work; a view of the fabric gradually rising, perhaps from small beginnings, till its foundation rests in the centre, and its turrets sparkle in the skies; to trace back the structure, through all its varieties, to the simplicity of the [its] first plan; to find what was [first] projected, whence the scheme was taken, how it was improved, by what assistance it was executed, and from what stores the materials were collected; whether its founder dug them from the quarries of nature, or demolished other buildings to embellish his own.' These were the motives that induced Johnson to assist Lauder with a preface: and are not these the motives of a critic and a scholar? What reader of taste, what man of real knowledge, would not think his time well employed in an enquiry so curious, so interesting, and instructive? If Lauder's facts were really true, who would not be glad, without the smallest tincture of malevolence, to receive real information? It is painful to be thus obliged to vindicate a man who, in his heart, towered above

[1] 'I could all along observe that Johnson seemed to approve not only of the design but of the argument, and seemed to exult in a persuasion that the reputation of Milton was likely to suffer by this discovery.' Hawkins, p. 276. See *Life*, i. 230. The Whig members of the Club, some of them sound scholars, do not seem to have suspected the fraud.

[2] *Works*, v. 267.

the

the petty arts of fraud and imposition, against an injudicious biographer, who undertook to be his editor, and the protector of his memory. Another writer, Dr. Towers, in an Essay on the Life and Character of Dr. Johnson, seems to countenance this calumny. He says, *It can hardly be doubted, but that Johnson's aversion to Milton's politics was the cause of that alacrity with which he joined with Lauder in his infamous attack on our great epic poet, and which induced him to assist in that transaction*[1]. These words would seem to describe an accomplice, were they not immediately followed by an express declaration, that Johnson was *unacquainted with the imposture.* Dr. Towers adds, *It seems to have been by way of making some compensation to the memory of Milton, for the share he had in the attack of Lauder, that Johnson wrote the prologue, spoken by Garrick, at Drury-lane Theatre, in* 1750, *on the performance of the Masque of Comus, for the benefit of Milton's grand-daughter*[2]. Dr. Towers is not free from prejudice; but, as Shakspeare has it, 'he begets a temperance, to give it smoothness[3].' He is, therefore, entitled to a dispassionate answer. When Johnson wrote the prologue, it does [? not] appear that he was aware of the malignant artifices practised by Lauder. In the postscript to Johnson's preface, a subscription is proposed, for relieving the grand-daughter of the author of Paradise Lost[4]. Dr. Towers will agree that this shews Johnson's alacrity in doing good. That alacrity shewed

[1] P. 57. This Essay was published in 1786. See *Life*, iv. 41, *n.* 1.

[2] *Life*, i. 228; *Works*, i. 115. Johnson, in his *Life of Milton*, says:—'The profits of the night were only £130. . . . This was the greatest benefaction that *Paradise Lost* ever procured the author's descendants; and to this he who has now attempted to relate his life had the honour of contributing a Prologue.' *Works*, vii. 118.

[3] 'You must acquire and beget a temperance that may give it smoothness.' *Hamlet*, iii. 2. 8.

[4] 'It is yet in the power of a great people to reward the poet whose name they boast, and from their alliance to whose genius they claim some kind of superiority to every other nation of the earth; that poet, whose works may possibly be read when every other monument of British greatness shall be obliterated; to reward him, not with pictures or with medals, which, if he sees, he sees with contempt, but with tokens of gratitude, which he, perhaps, may even now consider as not unworthy the regard of an immortal spirit.' *Life*, i. 230.

itself

itself again in the letter printed in the European Magazine, January, 1785, and there said to have appeared originally in the General Advertiser, 4th April, 1750, by which the publick were invited to embrace the opportunity of paying a just regard to the illustrious dead, united with the pleasure of doing good to the living [1]. The letter adds, 'To assist industrious indigence, struggling with distress, and debilitated by age, is a display of virtue, and an acquisition of happiness and honour. Whoever, therefore [then], would be thought capable of pleasure in reading the works of our incomparable Milton, and not so destitute of gratitude as to refuse to lay out a trifle, in a rational and elegant entertainment, for the benefit of his living remains, for the exercise of their own virtue, the increase of their reputation, and the [pleasing] consciousness of doing good, should appear at Drury-lane Theatre, to-morrow, April 5, when COMUS will be performed for the benefit of Mrs. Elizabeth Foster, grand-daughter to the author, and the only surviving branch of his family. *Nota bene*, there will be a new prologue on the occasion written by the author of Irene, and spoken by Mr. Garrick.' The man, who had thus exerted himself to serve the grand-daughter, cannot be supposed to have entertained personal malice to the grand-father. It is true, that the malevolence of Lauder, as well as the impostures of Archibald Bower, were fully detected by the labours, in the cause of truth, of the Rev. Dr. Douglas, now Lord Bishop of Salisbury [2].

> 'Diram qui contudit Hydram,
> Notaque fatali portenta labore subegit [3].'

But the pamphlet, entituled, *Milton vindicated from the Charge of Plagiarism brought against him by Mr. Lauder, and Lauder himself convicted of several Forgeries and gross Impositions on the Publick. By John Douglas, M.A. Rector of Eaton Constantine, Salop*, was not published till the year 1751. In that work, p. 77, Dr. Douglas says: 'It is to be hoped, nay, it is *expected*, that the elegant and nervous writer, whose judicious

[1] *Life*, i. 227. [2] *Ib.* i. 228.
[3] 'Who crush'd the Hydra when to life renew'd,
And monsters dire with fated toil subdu'd.'
Francis, *Hor.*, *Ep.* ii. 1. 10.

sentiments

sentiments and inimitable style point out the author of Lauder's preface and postscript, will no longer allow A MAN [one] to *plume himself with his feathers*, who appears so little to have deserved his assistance; an assistance which I am persuaded would never have been communicated, had there been the least suspicion of those facts, which I have been the instrument of conveying to the world.' We have here a contemporary testimony to the integrity of Dr. Johnson throughout the whole of that vile transaction [1]. What was the consequence of the requisition made by Dr. Douglas? Johnson, whose ruling passion may be said to be the love of truth, convinced Lauder, that it would be more for his interest to make a full confession of his guilt, than to stand forth the convicted champion of a lye; and for this purpose he drew up, in the strongest terms, a recantation in a Letter to the Rev. Mr. Douglas, which Lauder signed, and published in the year 1751 [2]. That piece will remain a lasting memorial of the abhorrence with which Johnson beheld a violation of truth. Mr. Nichols, whose attachment to his illustrious friend was unwearied, shewed him in 1780 a book, called *Remarks on Johnson's Life of Milton*, in which the affair of Lauder was renewed with virulence [3], and a *poetical scale* in the Literary Magazine 1758 (when Johnson had ceased to write in that collection) was urged as an additional proof of deliberate malice. He read the libellous passage with attention, and instantly wrote on the margin: '"In the business of Lauder I was deceived, partly by thinking the man too frantic to be fraudulent." Of the *poetical scale* quoted from the Magazine I am not the author. I fancy it was put in after I had quitted that work; for I not only did not write it, but I do not remember it [4].' As a critic and a scholar, Johnson

[1] *Life*, i. 229, *n*. 1. [2] *Ib*.

[3] *Post*, p. 486.

Remarks on Johnson's Life of Milton, 1780, formed a part of *The Memoirs of Thomas Hollis*, published anonymously, but written by Archdeacon Blackburne. Nichols, *Lit. Anec.* viii. 57. The passage referred to is on vol. ii. p. 537, of those *Memoirs*.

[4] In this *Poetical Scale* little injustice is done to Milton:—'The point of perfection is supposed to be twenty degrees. Shakespeare is estimated to be in genius 19, judgment 14, learning 14, versification 19. Milton, in genius 18, judgment 16, learning 17, versification 18.' But in the 'remarks' it is said ... 'Shakespeare's faults were those of a great

was

was willing to receive what numbers at the time believed to be true information: when he found that the whole was a forgery, he renounced all connection with the author [1].

In March 1752, he felt a severe stroke of affliction in the death of his wife. The last number of the Rambler, as already mentioned, was on the 14th of that month. The loss of Mrs. Johnson was then approaching, and, probably, was the cause that put an end to those admirable periodical essays. It appears that she died on the 28th of March: in a memorandum, at the foot of the Prayers and Meditations, that is called her Dying Day [2]. She was buried at Bromley, under the care of Dr. Hawkesworth [3]. Johnson placed a Latin inscription on her tomb, in which he celebrated her beauty [4]. With the singularity of his prayers for

poet; those of Milton of a little pedant.' Prior's *Goldsmith*, i. 233. *The Literary Magazine* for 1758 is not in the British Museum. Johnson did not write for it after 1757. *Life*, i. 307.

[1] Porson says that it was his 'opinion that the writer of the preface, postscript and letter of contrition for *W. Lauder* was neither willingly undeluded, nor forward in exposing the *atrocity* of those hideous interpolations by which it had been vainly contrived to obscure the splendor of Milton's PARADISE LOST.' Porson's *Tracts*, p. 379.

Mark Pattison went far beyond Porson. 'Dr. Johnson,' he writes, 'conspired with one William Lauder to stamp out Milton's credit by proving him to be a wholesale plagiarist.' He calls them 'this pair of literary bandits.' On the next page he writes:—'Johnson, who was not concerned in the cheat, and was only guilty of indolence and party spirit, saved himself by sacrificing his comrade. He afterwards took ample revenge for the mortification of this exposure, in his *Lives of the Poets*, in which he employed all his vigorous powers and consummate skill to write down Milton.' *Milton*, by Mark Pattison, pp. 217–219. Both Porson and Pattison must have known that Johnson in the postscript to Lauder's pamphlet spoke of Milton as 'that poet whose works may possibly be read when every other monument of British greatness shall be obliterated,' and that he ends his *Life* of him by saying that 'his great works were performed under discountenance and in blindness: but difficulties vanished at his touch; he was born for whatever is arduous; and his work is not the greatest of heroick poems only because it is not the first.' *Works*, v. 271; vii. 142.

[2] She died three days after the publication of the last *Rambler*, on March 17 O. S., 28 N. S. I do not know to what memorandum Murphy refers.

[3] Hawkesworth lived at Bromley. *Life*, i. 241.

[4] It was not till a few months before his death that he placed this inscription. 'Shall I ever be able

his

his deceased wife, from that time to the end of his days, the world is sufficiently acquainted. On Easter-day, 22d April, 1764, his memorandum says: 'Thought on Tetty, poor dear Tetty[1]! with my eyes full. Went to Church. After sermon I recommended Tetty in a prayer by herself; and my father, mother, brother, and Bathurst, in another. I did it only once, so far as it might be lawful for me.' In a prayer, January 23, 1759, the day on which his mother was buried, he commends, as far as may be lawful, her soul to God, imploring for her whatever is most beneficial to her in her present state[2]. In this habit he persevered to the end of his days. The Rev. Mr. Strahan, the editor of the Prayers and Meditations, observes, 'That Johnson, on some occasions, prays that the Almighty *may have had mercy* on his wife and Mr. Thrale: evidently supposing their sentence to have been already passed in the Divine Mind; and, by consequence, proving, that he had no belief in a state of purgatory, and no reason for praying for the dead that could impeach the sincerity of his profession as a Protestant.' Mr. Strahan adds, 'That, in praying for the regretted tenants of the grave, Johnson conformed to a practice which has been retained by many learned members of the Established Church, though the Liturgy no longer admits it. *If where the tree falleth, there it shall be*[3]; if our state, at the close of life, is to be the measure of our final sentence, then prayers for the dead, being visibly fruitless, can be regarded only as the vain oblations of superstition. But of all superstitions this, perhaps, is one of the least unamiable, and most incident to a good mind. If our sensations of kindness be intense, those, whom we have revered and loved, death cannot wholly seclude from our concern. It is true, for the reason just mentioned, such evidences of our surviving affection may be thought ill-judged; but surely they are generous, and some natural tenderness is due even to a superstition, which thus

to bear the sight of this stone?' he wrote to his friend Ryland. 'In your company I hope I shall.' *Letters*, ii. 429. See also *ib.* ii. 411; *Life*, i. 241, *n.*; iv. 351, 394. He gave the wrong date of the year of her death. *Letters*, ii. 429.

[1] *Ante*, p. 11, *n.* 1.

[2] *Ante*, pp. 23, 29; *Life*, i. 240.

[3] Ecclesiastes xi. 3; for Johnson's explanation of the text, see *Life*, iv. 225.

originates

originates in piety and benevolence [1].' These sentences, extracted from the Rev. Mr. Strahan's preface, if they are not a full justification, are, at least, a beautiful apology. It will not be improper to add what Johnson himself has said on the subject. Being asked by Mr. Boswell, what he thought of purgatory, as believed by the Roman Catholics? His answer was, 'It is a very harmless doctrine. They are of opinion, that the generality of mankind are neither so obstinately wicked as to deserve everlasting punishment; nor so good as to merit being admitted into the society of blessed spirits; and, therefore, that God is graciously pleased to allow a middle state, where they may be purified by certain degrees of suffering. You see [Sir] there is nothing unreasonable in this'; [BOSWELL. 'But then, Sir, their masses for the dead?' JOHNSON. 'Why, Sir] if it be once established that there are souls in purgatory, it is as proper to pray for them, as for our brethren of mankind, who are yet in this life [2].' This was Dr. Johnson's guess into futurity; and to guess is the utmost that man can do. *Shadows, clouds, and darkness, rest upon it* [3].

Mrs. Johnson left a daughter, Lucy Porter, by her first husband. She had contracted a friendship with Mrs. Anne Williams, the daughter of Zachary Williams, a physician of eminence in South Wales, who had devoted more than thirty years of a long life to the study of the longitude, and was thought to have made great advances towards that important discovery. His letters to Lord Halifax, and the Lords of the Admiralty, partly corrected and partly written by Dr. Johnson, are still extant in the hands of Mr. Nichols [4]. We there find Dr. Williams, in the eighty-third year of his age, stating, that he

[1] *Prayers and Meditations*, Preface, pp. 10–13. Murphy's extracts are not accurately made.

[2] *Life*, ii. 104.

[3] Addison, *Cato*, Act v. sc. 1.

'Mr. Speaker, I cannot prevail upon myself to hurry over this great consideration.' *It is good for us to be here.* We stand where we have an immense view of what is and what is past. *Clouds*, indeed, and *darkness rest upon the future*.' Burke's *Speech on Conciliation*. Payne's *Burke*, i. 172.

[4] Published in the *Gentleman's Magazine*, 1787, pp. 757, 1041. *Life*, i. 274, *n.* 2, 301.

had

had prepared an instrument, which might be called an epitome or miniature of the terraqueous globe, shewing, with the assistance of tables constructed by himself, the variations of the magnetic needle, and ascertaining the longitude for the safety of navigation [1]. It appears that this scheme had been referred to Sir Isaac Newton [2]; but that great philosopher excusing himself on account of his advanced age, all applications were useless till 1751, when the subject was referred. by order of Lord Anson [3], to Dr. Bradley, the celebrated professor of Astronomy [4]. His report was unfavourable, though it allows that a considerable progress had been made. Dr. Williams, after all his labour and expence, died in a short time after, a melancholy instance of unrewarded merit [5]. His daughter possessed uncommon talents,

[1] 'It was no new thing then when Columbus, as he sailed westward, marked the variation [of the needle] proceeding from the north-east more and more westerly; but it was a revelation when he came to a position where the magnetic north and the north star stood in conjunction, as they did on this 13th of September, 1492. As he still moved westerly the magnetic line was found to move farther and farther away from the pole, as it had before the 13th approached it. To an observer of Columbus's quick perceptions, there was a ready guess to possess his mind. This inference was that this line of no variation was a meridian line, and that divergences from it east and west might have a regularity which would be found to furnish a method of ascertaining longitude far easier and surer than tables or water-clocks.' Justin Winsor's *Christopher Columbus*, 1891, p. 200.

[2] According to the *Gentleman's Magazine*, p. 1042, in 1729; but Newton died in 1727.

[3] First Commissioner of the Admiralty; *ante*, p. 195.

[4] James Bradley, Savilian Professor of Astronomy at Oxford, and third Astronomer Royal.

[5] His merit was not great, as Bradley reported that in some cases the difference between his tables and the best observations amounted to ten, fifteen, or twenty degrees! *Gentleman's Magazine*, 1787, p. 1042.

Johnson, no doubt, had him in mind in the *Rambler*, No. 67, when in the Garden of Hope he placed one 'who was on the point of discovering the longitude.' Addison, nearly forty years earlier, in a letter from a member of the Tall Club, said:—'I must add, to the honour of our Club, that it is one of our society who is now finding out the longitude.' *The Guardian*, No. 108.

Williams had first taken orders, and later on 'was a surgeon, physician, and projector.' Some of his projects are given in the *Gentleman's Magazine*, 1787, p. 1157. He was admitted to the Charter-House, but he was expelled in 1749, at the age of seventy-eight, in consequence of attacks on the management of that Institution. In a letter to General Oglethorpe he describes how 'this

and,

and, though blind, had an alacrity of mind that made her conversation agreeable, and even desirable. To relieve and appease melancholy reflections, Johnson took her home to his house in Gough-square [1]. In 1755, Garrick gave her a benefit-play, which produced two hundred pounds [2]. In 1766, she published, by subscription, a quarto volume of Miscellanies, and increased her little stock to three hundred pounds [3]. That fund, with Johnson's protection, supported her through the remainder of her life [4].

During the two years in which the Rambler was carried on, the Dictionary proceeded by slow degrees. In May 1752, having composed a prayer preparatory to his return from tears and sorrow to the duties of life [5], he resumed his grand design, and went on with vigour, giving, however, occasional assistance to his friend Dr. Hawkesworth in the Adventurer, which began soon after the Rambler was laid aside. Some of the most valuable essays in that collection were from the pen of Johnson [6]. The Dictionary was completed towards the end of 1754; and, Cave being then no more [7], it was a mortification to the author

great and goodly hospital is become a den of thieves! the master a tyrannical oppressor; the servants fraudulent managers, and the poor gentlemen-pensioners great sufferers from their first entrance even to their graves.' *Gent. Mag.*, 1787, p. 1158.

[1] Murphy misrepresents the motive of Johnson's kindness. *Life*, i. 232.

[2] *Life*, i. 393, *n.* 1; *Letters*, i. 53-6.

[3] *Life*, ii. 26; *Letters*, ii. 334, *n.* 3.

[4] For many years she had a small pension from Mrs. Montagu. *Letters*, ii. 336.

[5] *Ante*, p. 12.

[6] *Life*, i. 252. Dr. Warton says that 'the title *The Adventurer*, it seems, alluded to its being a kind of Knight Errantry to attack the vices and follies of men.' Warton's Pope's *Works*, ix. 345.

According to Percy, 'Hawkesworth usually sent Johnson each paper to prefix a motto before it was printed.' Anderson's *Johnson*, ed. 1815, p. 190. Chalmers (*British Essayists*, vol. xix. Preface, p. 38) states that 'Johnson revised his *Adventurers* for the second edition with the same attention he bestowed on the *Rambler*.' This is untrue; scarcely a change can be found.

[7] Cave died on January 10, 1754. *Letters*, i. 56, *n.* 2. According to the *Life of Johnson*, published by Kearsley in 1785, p. 47, Cave was the husband of the woman 'who fraudulently made a purse for herself' (*Life*, iv. 319). The money she had laid out in India bonds.

of that noble addition to our language, that his old friend did not live to see the triumph of his labours. In May 1755, that great work was published [1]. Johnson was desirous that it should come from one who had obtained academical honours; and for that purpose, his friend the Rev. Thomas Warton obtained for him, in the preceding month of February, a diploma for a master's degree from the University of Oxford [2]. Garrick, on the publication of the Dictionary, wrote the following lines.

'Talk of war with a Briton, he'll boldly advance,
That one English soldier can [will] beat ten of France.
Would we alter the boast from the sword to the pen,
Our odds are still greater, still greater our men.
In the deep mines of science though Frenchmen may toil,
Can their strength be compar'd to Locke, Newton, or [and] Boyle?
Let them rally their heroes, send forth all their pow'rs,
Their versemen and prosemen, then match them with ours.
First Shakspeare and Milton [Milton and Shakspeare], like Gods
in the fight,
Have put their whole drama and epic to flight.
In satires, epistles, and odes, would they cope?
Their numbers retreat before Dryden and Pope.
And Johnson well arm'd, like a hero of yore,
Has beat Forty French, and will beat Forty more [3].

It is, perhaps, needless to mention, that Forty was the number of the French Academy, at the time when their Dictionary was published to settle their language [4].

[1] *Life*, i. 290, *n.* 1. I have seen a letter from Mr. John P. Anderson of the British Museum, the author of the *Bibliography* at the end of Colonel F. Grant's *Johnson*, to Mr. J. Dewitt Miller, of Philadelphia, a great Johnsonian collector, in which it is stated:—'The first edition appeared on April 17, 1755. What I called a second edition was a weekly re-issue, same type, &c., which began on June 17 of the same year. The second edition appeared in 1760, in 2 vols. octavo. I have discovered this from the advertisement to the *London Evening Post*. Some authorities give the date of the second edition as 1755, others 1756, but they are all wrong. The advertisement of the first edition gives the date—"This day is published"—April 17, not as usually accepted, April 15.'

My edition of the *Dictionary*, called the second, is dated 1755 in the first volume, and 1756 in the second. The sheets are numbered from i to clxv.

[2] *Life*, i. 275, 283.

[3] *Ib.* i. 300.

[4] *Ib.* i. 186.

In

In the course of the winter preceding this grand publication, the late Earl of Chesterfield gave two essays in the periodical Paper, called THE WORLD, dated November 28, and December 5, 1754, to prepare the publick for so important a work. The original plan, addressed to his Lordship in the year 1747, is there mentioned in terms of the highest praise[1]; and this was understood, at the time, to be a courtly way of soliciting a dedication of the Dictionary to himself. Johnson treated this civility with disdain. He said to Garrick and others, 'I have sailed a long and painful voyage round the world of the English language; and does he now send out two cock-boats to tow me into harbour[2]?' He had said, in the last number of the Rambler, 'that, having laboured to maintain the dignity of virtue, I will not now degrade it by the meanness of dedication[3].' Such a man, when he had finished his 'Dictionary, not,' as he says himself, 'in the soft obscurities of retirement, or under the shelter of academic bowers, but amidst inconvenience and distraction, in sickness and in sorrow, and without the patronage of the great[4],' was not likely to be caught by the lure thrown out by Lord Chesterfield. He had in vain sought the patronage of that nobleman;

[1] 'Perfection is not to be expected from man; but if we are to judge by the various works of Mr. Johnson already published, we have good reason to believe that he will bring this as near to perfection as any man could do.' *Life*, i. 258.

[2] Murphy perhaps gets this story from the *Memoirs of the Life and Writings of Dr. Johnson*, ed. 1785, p. 120, where it is also stated that to Edward Moore, the editor of *The World*, and 'the creature of Lord Chesterfield,' who had come from his Lordship, Johnson replied:—'I am under obligations to no great man, and of all others Chesterfield ought to know me better than to think me capable of contracting myself into a dwarf that he may be thought a giant.' See also *Life*, i. 259.

[3] 'The loftiness of Johnson's mind prevented him from ever dedicating in his own person.' *Ib.* ii. 1.

Dr. Franklin wrote in June, 1782:—'I never made a dedication and I never desired that one should be made to me.' Franklin's *Works*, ed. 1888, vii. 475. Gibbon, in the Preface to vol. vii. of the *Decline and Fall*, artfully dedicates without a dedication. 'Were I ambitious of any other Patron than the Public, I would inscribe this work to a Statesman,' &c.

[4] '*The English Dictionary* was written with little assistance of the learned, and without any patronage of the great; not in the soft obscurities,' &c. *Works*, v. 51. Murphy mars that passage which Horne Tooke said he 'could never read without shedding a tear.' *Life*, i. 297, *n.* 2.

nobleman; and his pride, exasperated by disappointment, drew from him the following letter, dated in the month of February, 1755[1].

It is said, upon good authority, that Johnson once received from Lord Chesterfield the sum of ten pounds. It were to be wished that the secret had never transpired. It was mean to receive it[2], and meaner to give it. It may be imagined, that for Johnson's ferocity, as it has been called, there was some foundation in his finances; and, as his Dictionary was brought to a conclusion, that money was now to flow in upon him. The reverse was the case. For his subsistence, during the progress of the work, he had received at different times the amount of his contract; and when his receipts were produced to him at a tavern-dinner, given by the booksellers, it appeared, that he had been paid a hundred pounds and upwards more than his due[3]. The

[1] For this letter, which I omit, see *Life*, i. 261.

Mr. Hussey says:—'Enquiring of Dr. Johnson if it were true that Lord Chesterfield had been much offended at the receipt of his letter, the Doctor replied, "so far from it his Lordship expressed himself obliged to me for it, and did me the honour to say it was the letter of a Scholar and a Gentleman."' 'Dr. Johnson once spoke to me very warmly in recommendation of Lord Chesterfield, and said that he was the politest man he ever knew; but added "Indeed he did not think it worth his while to treat *me* like a Gentleman."'

'On telling him Voltaire's opinion, that "if ever Lord Chesterfield published anything he would expose his ignorance," Johnson replied, "His Letters betray no want of abilities, but the bad use he has made of them."' Marginal notes in Mr. H. P. Symonds's copy of the *Life*.

Voltaire said of the *Letters*:—'Je ne sais si ce n'est pas le meilleur livre d'éducation qu'on ait jamais fait.' *Œuvres de Voltaire*, ed. 1821, lvi. 399.

Davies, in his *Life of Garrick*, i. 92, shows how at Dublin Chesterfield did not think it worth his while to treat Garrick like a gentleman.

[2] *Life*, i. 261, *n*. 3.

Murphy, if we can trust Rogers's account of him, was not entitled to pass so harsh a judgment. Towards the close of his life, till he received a pension of £200 from the King, he was in great pecuniary difficulties. He had eaten himself out of every tavern from the other side of Temple-Bar to the west end of the town.' He owed Rogers a large sum of money, which he never repaid. 'He assigned over to me the whole of his works; and I soon found that he had already disposed of them to a bookseller.' Rogers's *Table-Talk*, p. 106.

[3] Hawkins, p. 345; *Life*, i. 304; *ante*, p. 388.

In 1781 one-eightieth share of the

author

author of a book, called *Lexiphanes*, written by a Mr. Campbell, a Scotchman, and purser of a man of war, endeavoured to blast his laurels, but in vain[1]. The world applauded, and Johnson never replied. 'Abuse,' he said, 'is often of service: there is nothing so dangerous to an author as silence; his name, like a shuttlecock, must be beat backward and forward, or it falls to the ground[2].' Lexiphanes professed to be an imitation of the pleasant manner of Lucian; but humour was not the talent of the writer of Lexiphanes[3]. As Dryden says, 'He has too much horse-play in his raillery[4].'

It was in the summer 1754, that the present writer became acquainted with Dr. Johnson. The cause of his first visit is related

folio edition sold for £11. Mr. H. P. Symonds's MSS.

Boswell recorded in his note-book on Sept. 22, 1777:—'Dr. Johnson told me in the forenoon that he had six amanuenses when he composed his Dictionary, that eighty paper books of two quires each, 160 quires, were first used, and as they were written on both sides, it afterwards cost him twenty pounds for paper to have them transcribed, to be written only on one page. (This must be a mistake were it only 1*s*. a quire) . . . He said it was remarkable that, when he revised and improved the last edition of his Dict'y, the printer was never kept waiting.' *Morrison Autographs*, 2nd Series, i. 367.

See *Life*, i. 189. It is strange that Johnson, who was now an author of some years standing, should have had the paper written on both sides.

[1] This mention of *Lexiphanes* is premature as it was not published till 1767. *Life*, ii. 44.

'As well as for the malignancy of his heart as his terrific countenance he was called horrible Campbell.' Hawkins, p. 347. Another Scotchman, Dr. Robertson the historian, 'told Johnson that he had fairly perused his *Dictionary* twice over.' *Ib.* p. 346. Macaulay says that 'it was hailed with an enthusiasm such as no similar work has ever excited. It was indeed the first dictionary which could be read with pleasure. The definitions show so much acuteness of thought and command of language, and the passages quoted from poets, divines, and philosophers are so skilfully selected, that a leisure hour may always be very agreeably spent in turning over the pages.' Macaulay's *Misc. Works*, ed. 1871, p. 382.

[2] 'Dr. Johnson said, "It is advantageous to an authour, that his book should be attacked as well as praised. Fame is a shuttlecock. If it be struck only at one end of the room, it will soon fall to the ground. To keep it up, it must be struck at both ends."' *Life*, v. 400.

[3] The book is as dull as it is indecent.

[4] 'He is too much given to horse-play in his raillery, and comes to battle like a dictator from the plough.' *Preface to the Fables*, Dryden's *Poems*, Aldine ed. iii. 198.

related by Mrs. Piozzi nearly in the following manner[1]. 'Mr. Murphy being engaged in a periodical paper, the Gray's-Inn Journal, was at a friend's house in the country, and, not being disposed to lose pleasure for business, wished to content his bookseller by some unstudied essay. He therefore took up a French *Journal Litéraire*, and translating something he liked, sent it away to town. Time, however, discovered that he translated from the French a Rambler, which had been taken from the English without acknowledgement. Upon this discovery Mr. Murphy thought it right to make his excuses to Dr. Johnson. He went next day, and found him covered with soot, like a chimney-sweeper, in a little room, as if he had been acting Lungs in the Alchymist, *making æther*. This being told by Mr. Murphy in company, "Come, come," [dear Mur.] said Dr. Johnson, "the story is black enough; but it was a happy day that brought you first to my house."' After this first visit, the author of this narrative by degrees grew intimate with Dr. Johnson. The first striking sentence, that he heard from him, was in a few days after the publication of Lord Bolingbroke's posthumous works. Mr. Garrick asked him, 'If he had seen them?' 'Yes, I have seen them.' 'What do you think of them?' 'Think of them!' He made a long pause, and then replied: 'Think of them! A scoundrel and a coward! A scoundrel, who spent his life in charging a gun against Christianity; and a coward, who was afraid of hearing the report of his own gun; but left half a crown to a hungry Scotchman to draw the trigger after his death[2].' His mind, at this time strained and over-laboured by constant exertion, called for an interval of repose

[1] *Ante*, p. 306.

[2] The 'hungry' or 'beggarly Scotchman' as he is in the *Life*, i. 268, was David Mallet. Bolingbroke left him the copyright of all his published works, 'and all the books which, at the time of my decease, shall be in the room called my library.' Bolingbroke's *Works*, ed. 1809, i. Introduction, p. 219.

'So sanguine was Mallet in his expectations that he rejected the offer of £3,000 which Millar offered him for the copyright, although he was at this time so distressed for money that he was forced to borrow some of Millar to pay the stationer and printer. He had reason to repent his refusal as the edition was not sold off in twenty years.' Chalmers's *Biog. Dict.*, xxi. 196.

and

and indolence. But indolence was the time of danger: it was then that his spirits, not employed abroad, turned with inward hostility against himself[1]. His reflections on his own life and conduct were always severe; and, wishing to be immaculate, he destroyed his own peace by unnecessary scruples. He tells us, that when he surveyed his past life, he discovered nothing but a barren waste of time, with some disorders of body, and disturbances of mind, very near to madness[2]. His life, he says, from his earliest years, was wasted in a morning bed[3]; and his reigning sin was a general sluggishness, to which he was always inclined, and, in part of his life, almost compelled, by morbid melancholy, and weariness of mind. This was his constitutional malady, derived, perhaps, from his father, who was, at times, overcast with a gloom that bordered on insanity[4]. When to this it is added, that Johnson, about the age of twenty, drew up a description of his infirmities, for Dr. Swinfen, at that time an eminent physician in Staffordshire; and received an answer to his letter, importing, that the symptoms indicated a future privation of reason[5]; who can wonder that he was troubled with melancholy and dejection of spirit? An apprehension of the worst calamity that can befal human nature hung over him all the rest of his life, like the sword of the tyrant suspended over his guest. In his sixtieth year he had a mind to write the history of his melancholy; but he desisted, not knowing whether it would not too much disturb him[6]. In a Latin poem, however, to which he has prefixed as a title, ΓΝΩΘΙ ΣΕΑΥΤΟΝ, he has left a picture, of himself, drawn with as much truth, and as firm a hand, as can be seen in the portraits of Hogarth or Sir Joshua Reynolds. The learned reader will find the original poem in

[1] Hawkins, p. 350.

[2] *Ante*, p. 78.

[3] *Ante*, p. 72.

[4] '"I inherited, (said he,) a vile melancholy from my father, which has made me mad all my life, at least not sober." Lady M'Leod wondered he should tell this. "Madam, (said I,) he knows that with that madness he is superior to other men."' *Life*, v. 215.

[5] Murphy improves on Hawkins, who says (p. 288) that the physician said that 'he could think nothing better of his disorder than that it had a tendency to insanity; and without great care might possibly terminate in the deprivation of his rational faculties.' See *Life*, i. 64.

[6] *Ante*, p. 48.

this

this volume, p. 178[1]; and it is hoped, that a translation, or rather imitation, of so curious a piece will not be improper in this place.

KNOW YOURSELF.

(AFTER REVISING AND ENLARGING THE ENGLISH LEXICON, OR DICTIONARY.)

When Scaliger, whole years of labour past,
Beheld his Lexicon complete at last,
And weary of his task, with wond'ring eyes,
Saw from words pil'd on words a fabric rise,
He curs'd the industry, inertly strong,
In creeping toil that could persist so long,
And if, enrag'd he cried, Heav'n meant to shed
Its keenest vengeance on the guilty head,
The drudgery of words the damn'd would know,
Doom'd to write Lexicons in endless woe[2].

Yes, you had cause, great Genius! to repent;
'You lost good days, that might be better spent;'
You well might grudge the hours of ling'ring pain,
And view your learned labours with disdain.
To you were giv'n the large expanded mind,
The flame of genius, and the taste refin'd.
'Twas yours on eagle wings aloft to soar,
And amidst rolling worlds the Great First Cause explore;
To fix the aeras of recorded time,
And live in ev'ry age and ev'ry clime;
Record the Chiefs, who propt their Country's cause;
Who founded Empires, and establish'd Laws;
To learn whate'er the Sage with virtue fraught,
Whate'er the Muse of moral wisdom taught.
These were your quarry; these to you were known,
And the world's ample volume was your own.

Yet warn'd by me, ye pigmy Wits, beware,
Nor with immortal Scaliger compare.

[1] *Works*, i. 164; *Life*, i. 298, *n*. 4.

[2] 'JOSEPHI SCALIGERI EPIGRAMMA.
Si quem dura manet sententia judicis, olim
Damnatum aerumnis suppliciisque caput,
Hunc neque fabrili lassent ergastula massa,
Nec rigidas vexent fossa metalla manus:
Lexica contexat, nam caetera quid moror?
Paenarum facies hic labor unus habet.'
Gentleman's Magazine, 1748, p. 8.

For

For me, though his example strike my view,
Oh! not for me his footsteps to pursue.
Whether first Nature, unpropitious, cold,
This clay compounded in a ruder mould;
Or the slow current, loit'ring at my heart,
No gleam of wit or fancy can impart;
Whate'er the cause, from me no numbers flow,
No visions warm me, and no raptures glow.

A mind like Scaliger's, superior still,
No grief could conquer, no misfortune chill.
Though for the maze of words his native skies
He seem'd to quit, 'twas but again to rise;
To mount once more to the bright source of day,
And view the wonders of th' ætherial way.
The love of Fame his gen'rous bosom fir'd;
Each Science hail'd him, and each Muse inspir'd,
For him the Sons of Learning trimm'd the bays,
And Nations grew harmonious in his praise.

My task perform'd, and all my labours o'er,
For me what lot has Fortune now in store?
The listless will succeeds, that worst disease,
The rack of indolence, the sluggish ease.
Care grows on care, and o'er my aching brain
Black Melancholy pours her morbid train.
No kind relief, no lenitive at hand,
I seek at midnight clubs, the social Band;
But midnight clubs, where wit with noise conspires,
Where Comus revels, and where wine inspires,
Delight no more; I seek my lonely bed,
And call on Sleep to sooth my languid head.
But Sleep from these sad lids flies far away;
I mourn all night, and dread the coming day,
Exhausted, tir'd, I throw my eyes around,
To find some vacant spot on classic ground;
And soon, vain hope! I form a grand design;
Languor succeeds, and all my pow'rs decline.
If Science open not her richest vein,
Without materials all our toil is vain.
A form to rugged stone when Phidias gives,
Beneath his touch a new creation lives.
Remove his marble, and his genius dies;
With Nature then no breathing statue vies.

Whate'er I plan, I feel my pow'rs confin'd
By Fortune's frown and penury of mind.

I boast

I boast no knowledge glean'd with toil and strife,
That bright reward of a well-acted life.
I view myself, while Reason's feeble light
Shoots a pale glimmer through the gloom of night,
While passions, error, phantoms of the brain,
And vain opinions, fill the dark domain;
A dreary void, where fears with grief combin'd
Waste all within, and desolate the mind.

What then remains? Must I in slow decline
To mute inglorious ease old age resign?
Or, bold ambition kindling in my breast,
Attempt some arduous task? Or, were it best
Brooding o'er Lexicons to pass the day,
And in that labour drudge my life away?

Such is the picture for which Dr. Johnson sat to himself. He gives the prominent features of his character; his lassitude, his morbid melancholy, his love of fame, his dejection, his tavern-parties, and his wandering reveries, *Vacuæ mala somnia mentis*[1], about which so much has been written; all are painted in miniature, but in vivid colours, by his own hand. His idea of writing more Dictionaries was not merely said in verse. Mr. Hamilton, who was at that time an eminent printer[2], and well acquainted with Dr. Johnson, remembers that he engaged in a Commercial Dictionary, and, as appears by the receipts in his possession, was paid his price for several sheets; but he soon relinquished the undertaking[3]. It is probable, that he found himself not sufficiently versed in that branch of knowledge.

[1] 'Nascuntur curis curæ, vexatque dolorum
Importuna cohors, vacuæ mala somnia mentis.'
From Johnson's Poem.

[2] 'On Monday, April 19, Dr. Johnson called on me with Mrs. Williams, in Mr. Strahan's coach.... A printer having acquired a fortune sufficient to keep his coach, was a good topick for the credit of literature. Mrs. Williams said, that another printer, Mr. Hamilton, had not waited so long as Mr. Strahan, but had kept his coach several years sooner. JOHNSON. "He was in the right. Life is short. The sooner that a man begins to enjoy his wealth the better."' *Life*, ii. 226.

[3] Johnson in 1761 contributed the Preface to Rolt's *Dictionary of Trade and Commerce*. *Life*, i. 358. It is possible that he at first had undertaken the whole work.

He

He was again reduced to the expedient of short compositions for the supply of the day. The writer of this narrative has now before him a letter in Dr. Johnson's hand-writing, which shews the distress and melancholy situation of the man, who had written the Rambler, and finished the great work of his Dictionary. The letter is directed to Mr. Richardson (the author of Clarissa), and is as follows:

'SIR,

I am obliged to entreat your assistance. I am now under an arrest for five pounds eighteen shillings. Mr. Strahan, from whom I should have received the necessary help in this case, is not at home; and I am afraid of not finding Mr. Millar. If you will be so good as to send me this sum, I will very gratefully repay you, and add it to all former obligations. I am Sir,

Your most obedient
and most humble servant,
SAMUEL JOHNSON.
Gough Square, 16 March [1].'

In the margin of this letter there is a memorandum in these words: 'March 16, 1756. Sent six guineas. Witness, Wm. Richardson.' For the honour of an admired writer it is to be regretted, that we do not find a more liberal entry. To his friend in distress he sent eight shillings more than was wanted. Had an incident of this kind occurred in one of his Romances, Richardson would have known how to grace his hero; but in fictitious scenes generosity costs the writer nothing.

About this time Johnson contributed several papers to a periodical Miscellany, called The VISITOR, from motives which are highly honourable to him, a compassionate regard for the late Mr. Christopher Smart [2]. The criticism on Pope's Epitaphs appeared in that work [3]. In a short time after, he became a reviewer in the Literary Magazine [4], under the auspices

[1] *Life*, i. 303, *n.* 1; *Letters*, i. 61. Strahan was the printer and Millar one of the publishers of the *Dictionary*. *Life*, i. 287; iv. 321.

[2] *Ib.* ii. 345. See *ante*, p. 320.

[3] They were afterwards added first to his *Idler* and later on to his *Life of Pope*.

[4] *Life*, i. 307.

of

of the late Mr. Newbery, a man of a projecting head, good taste, and great industry[1]. This employment engrossed but little of Johnson's time. He resigned himself to indolence, took no exercise, rose about two, and then received the visits of his friends. Authors, long since forgotten, waited on him as their oracle, and he gave responses in the chair of criticism. He listened to the complaints, the schemes, and the hopes and fears of a crowd of inferior writers, 'who,' he said, in the words of Roger Ascham, 'lived, *men knew not how, and died obscure, men marked not when*[2].' He believed, that he could give a better history of Grub-street than any man living[3]. His house was filled with a succession of visitors till four or five in the evening. During the whole time he presided at his tea-table[4]. Tea was his favourite beverage; and, when the late Jonas Hanway[5] pronounced his anathema against the use of tea, Johnson rose in defence of his habitual practice, declaring himself 'in that article a hardened sinner, who had for years diluted his meals with the infusion of that fascinating plant; whose tea-kettle had no time to cool; who with tea solaced the midnight hour, and with tea welcomed the morning[6].'

[1] Murphy borrows from Hawkins, p. 364, who describes Newbery as 'a man of a projecting head, a good understanding, and great integrity, who by a fortunate connexion with Dr. James, the physician, and the honest exertions of his own industry, became the founder of a family.' He was the vendor of James's powder. *Life*, iii. 4, *n.* 2. See also *Letters*, i. 22.

[2] *Ante*, p. 315.

[3] Grub Street he defined in his *Dictionary* as 'the name of a street in London, much inhabited by writers of small histories, dictionaries, and temporary poems; whence any mean production is called *Grub-street*.' *Life*, i. 296. He told Miss Burney that he had never visited it. Mme. D'Arblay's *Diary*, i. 415.

There were two streets of this name, one by Fore Street, Cripplegate, the other by Market Street, Westminster. Dodsley's *London*, iii. 100. It was to the former street that the name was given. A writer in the *Gentleman's Magazine* for 1735, p. 206, says that John Fox of the *Book of Martyrs* lived there. 'The Papists often called him by way of contempt the Grub-street Author.'

[4] *Life*, i. 247.

[5] *Ib.* i. 313.

[6] 'A hardened and shameless tea-drinker, who has for twenty years diluted his meals with only the infusion of this fascinating plant; whose kettle has scarcely time to cool; who with tea amuses the evening, with tea solaces the midnight, and with tea welcomes the morning.' *Works*, vi. 21.

Hawkins (p. 561) blames Johnson's

The proposal for a new edition of Shakspeare, which had formerly miscarried[1], was resumed in the year 1756. The bookseller readily agreed to his terms, and subscription-tickets were issued out[2]. For undertaking this work, money, he confessed, was the inciting motive[3]. His friends exerted themselves to promote his interest; and, in the mean time, he engaged in a new periodical production called THE IDLER[4]. The first number appeared on Saturday, April 15, 1758; and the last, Apri 5, 1760. The profits of this work, and the subscriptions for the new edition of Shakspeare, were the means by which he supported himself for four or five years. In 1759 was published Rasselas, Prince of Abyssinia. His translation of Lobo's Voyage to Abyssinia seems to have pointed out that country for the scene of action; and *Rassila Christos*[5], the General of *Sultan Segued*, mentioned in that work, most probably suggested the name of the prince. The author wanted to set out on a journey to Lichfield, in order to pay the last offices of filial piety to his mother, who, at the age of ninety, was then near her dissolution; but money was necessary. Mr. Johnston, a bookseller who has long since left off business, gave one hundred pounds for the copy[6]. With this supply Johnson set out for Lichfield; but did not arrive in time to close the eyes of a parent whom he loved. He attended the funeral, which, as

'*unmanly* thirst for tea.' He mentions however without dispraise the fact that 'Bishop Burnet for many years drank sixteen large cups of it every morning.' Hawkins, p. 355. Bentham in his old age described tea as 'that fountain of faculties.' Bentham's *Works*, x. 506.

[1] *Ante*, p. 381.

[2] *Life*, i. 318. One of these tickets I give in a note on the *Letters*, i. 68.

[3] On finishing it he wrote to Dr. Warton:—'To tell the truth as I felt no solicitude about this work I receive no great comfort from its conclusion.' *Ib.* i. 123. According to Hawkins (p. 361) it was the booksellers who 'found out for him' this piece of work.

[4] Johnson had 'promised his Shakespeare should be published before Christmas, 1757'—four months before he began *The Idler*. *Life*, i. 319.

[5] Rassela Christos.

[6] According to Boswell, 'Mr. Strahan, Mr. Johnston, and Mr. Dodsley, purchased it for £100, but afterwards paid him £25 more when it came to a second edition.' *Life*, i. 341. But Johnson wrote to Strahan:—'The bargain which I made with Mr. Johnson [*sic*] was seventy-pounds (or guineas) a volume, and twenty-five pounds for the second edition.' *Letters*, i. 80.

appears

appears among his memorandums, was on the 23d of January, 1759[1].

Johnson now found it necessary to retrench his expences. He gave up his house in Gough-square. Mrs. Williams went into lodgings. He retired to Gray's-Inn[2], and soon removed to chambers in the Inner Temple-lane, where he lived in poverty, total idleness, and the pride of literature[3]. *Magni stat nominis umbra*[4]. Mr. Fitzherbert (the father of Lord St. Helen's, the present minister at Madrid) a man distinguished through life for his benevolence and other amiable qualities[5], used to say, that he paid a morning visit to Johnson, intending from his chambers to send a letter into the city; but, to his great surprise, he found an author by profession without pen, ink, or paper. The present Bishop of Salisbury[6] was also among those who endeavoured, by constant attention, to sooth the cares of a mind which he knew to be afflicted with gloomy apprehensions. At one of the parties made at his house, Boscovich[7], the Jesuit, who had then lately introduced the Newtonian philosophy at Rome, and, after publishing an elegant Latin poem on the subject, was made a Fellow of the Royal Society, was one of the company invited to meet Dr. Johnson. The conversation at first was mostly in French. Johnson, though thoroughly versed in that language, and a professed admirer of Boileau and La Bruyère[8], did not

[1] He did not go to Lichfield. He was on the point of setting out when the news came of her death. *Life*, i. 514; *Letters*, i. 81; *ante*, p. 22.

[2] He moved first to Staple Inn, on March 23, 1759. *Letters*, i. 86. He was in Gray's Inn in the following December (*ib.* p. 88) and in Inner Temple Lane in June, 1760. *Life*, i. 350. In neither of the two Inns are his rooms known.

[3] 'I have been told,' says Hawkins (p. 383), 'by his neighbour at the corner, that during the time he dwelt there more inquiries were made at his shop for Mr. Johnson than for all the inhabitants put together of both the Inner and Middle Temple.'

[4] 'Stat magni nominis umbra.' *Pharsalia*, i. 135. Windham (*Diary*, p. 18) jotting down Johnson's talk at Ashbourne, writes:—'*Stat magni nominis umbra* would construe as *Umbra quae est magni nom. h. e. celebrata*.'

[5] *Life*, i. 82; iii. 148; *Letters*, i. 45, *n.* 6; *ante*, p. 256.

[6] Dr. Douglas. *Ante*, p. 397.

[7] Boscovitch. *Life*, ii. 125, *n.* 5.

[8] See *ante*, p. 334, where he condemned Mrs. Thrale for preferring La Bruyère to the Duke of Rochefoucault.

understand

understand its pronunciation, nor could he speak it himself with propriety. For the rest of the evening the talk was in Latin. Boscovich had a ready current flow of that flimsy phraseology with which a priest may travel through Italy, Spain, and Germany. Johnson scorned what he called colloquial barbarisms. It was his pride to speak his best. He went on, after a little practice, with as much facility as if it was his native tongue. One sentence this writer well remembers. Observing that Fontinelle at first opposed the Newtonian philosophy, and embraced it afterwards, his words were: *Fontinellus, ni fallor, in extremâ senectute fuit transfuga ad castra Newtoniana*[1].

We have now travelled through that part of Dr. Johnson's life which was a perpetual struggle with difficulties. Halcyon days[2] are now to open upon him. In the month of May 1762, his Majesty, to reward literary merit, signified his pleasure to grant to Johnson a pension of three hundred pounds a year. The Earl of Bute was minister[3]. Lord Loughborough, who, perhaps, was originally a mover in the business[4], had authority to

[1] In a note on the fourteenth of Voltaire's *Lettres sur les Anglais* we read:—'Lorsque cet article a été écrit (1728) plus de quarante ans après la publication du livre des *Principes*, toute la France était encore cartésienne.' On Newton's death in 1727 Fontenelle spoke the 'Éloge' on him in the Academy of Sciences. 'On attendait en Angleterre son jugement comme une déclaration solennelle de la supériorité de la philosophie anglaise; mais quand on a vu que non seulement il s'était trompé en rendant compte de cette philosophie, mais qu'il comparait Descartes à Newton, toute la Société royale de Londres s'est soulevée.' *Œuvres de Voltaire*, ed. 1819, xxiv. 67. In 1738 Voltaire was refused in France the *imprimatur* for his *Élémens de Newton*. He printed it in Holland. *Ib.* xlvii. pp. 141, 165.

'In a Latin conversation with the Père Boscovitch,' writes Dr. Maxwell, 'at the house of Mrs. Cholmondeley, I heard Johnson maintain the superiority of Sir Isaac Newton over all foreign philosophers, with a dignity and eloquence that surprized that learned foreigner.' *Life*, ii. 125.

[2] 'When great Augustus made
war's tempests cease,
His halcyon days brought forth
the arts of peace.'
Denham; quoted in Johnson's *Dictionary*.

[3] It was in the month of July. On July 24, Johnson wrote to Miss Porter:—'Last Monday I was sent for by the Chief Minister the Earl of Bute, who told me that the King had empowered him to do something for me,' &c. *Letters*, i. 92. See also *Life*, i. 376.

[4] Lord Bute told me,' writes Boswell, 'that Mr. Wedderburne, now Lord Loughborough, was the person

 mention

mention it. He was well acquainted with Johnson; but, having heard much of his independent spirit, and of the downfall of Osborne the bookseller, he did not know but his benevolence might be rewarded with a folio on his head [1]. He desired the author of these memoirs to undertake the task [2]. This writer thought the opportunity of doing so much good the most happy incident in his life. He went, without delay, to the chambers in the Inner Temple-lane, which, in fact, were the abode of wretchedness. By slow and studied approaches the message was disclosed. Johnson made a long pause: he asked if it was seriously intended? He fell into a profound meditation, and his own definition of a pensioner occurred to him [3]. He was told, 'That he, at least, did not come within the definition.' He desired to meet next day, and dine at the Mitre Tavern [4]. At that meeting he gave up all his scruples. On the following day Lord Loughborough conducted him to the Earl of Bute. The conversation that passed was in the evening related to this writer by Dr. Johnson. He expressed his sense of his Majesty's bounty, and thought himself the more highly honoured, as the favour was not bestowed on him for having dipped his pen in faction. 'No, Sir,' said Lord Bute, 'it is not offered to you for having dipped your pen in faction, nor with a *design* that you ever should [5].' Sir John Hawkins will have it, that, after this interview,

who first mentioned this subject to him.' *Life*, i. 373. For Wedderburne's going on errands for Lord Bute, see *ib.* ii. 354.

[1] *Ante*, p. 381.

[2] 'Mr. Murphy and the late Mr. Sheridan severally contended for the distinction of having been the first who mentioned to Mr. Wedderburne that Johnson ought to have a pension.' *Life*, i. 374.

[3] *Pension.* 'An allowance made to any one without an equivalent. In England it is generally understood to mean pay given to a state hireling for treason to his country.' *Pensioner.* 'One who is supported by an allowance paid at the will of another; a dependant.' These definitions remain in the fourth edition, corrected by Johnson in 1773.

[4] 'I had learnt that his place of frequent resort was the Mitre tavern in Fleet-street, where he loved to sit up late, and I begged I might be allowed to pass an evening with him there soon, which he promised I should.' *Ib.* i. 399.

[5] In the review of Hawkins's *Johnson* in the *Monthly Review*, lxxvi. 375, no doubt written by Murphy, it is not *design* but *desire.* Murphy adds:—'On the next day Mr. Murphy was in the Temple soon after nine; *he got Johnson up and dressed in due time*; and saw him set off at eleven.'

Johnson

Johnson was often pressed to wait on Lord Bute, but with a sullen spirit refused to comply[1]. However that be, Johnson was never heard to utter a disrespectful word of that nobleman[2]. The writer of this essay remembers a circumstance which may throw some light on this subject. The late Dr. Rose, of Chiswick, whom Johnson loved and respected, contended for the pre-eminence of the Scotch writers; and Ferguson's book on Civil Society, then on the eve of publication, he said, would give the laurel to North Britain. 'Alas! what can he do upon that subject?" said Johnson: 'Aristotle, Polybius, Grotius, Puffendorf, and Burlamaqui, have reaped in that field before him.' 'He will treat it,' said Dr. Rose, 'in a new manner.' 'A new manner! Buckinger had no hands, and he wrote his name with his toes at Charing-cross, for half a crown apiece; that was a new manner of writing[3]!' Dr. Rose replied, 'If that will not satisfy you, I will name a writer, whom you must allow to be the best in the kingdom.' 'Who is that?' 'The Earl of Bute, when he wrote an order for your pension.' 'There, Sir,' said Johnson, 'you have me in the toil: to Lord Bute I must allow whatever praise you may claim for him[4].' Ingratitude was no part of Johnson's character.

Being now in the possession of a regular income, Johnson left his chambers in the Temple, and once more became master of

[1] Murphy misrepresents Hawkins, who says (p. 393):—'It was by Johnson and his friends thought fit that he should return thanks for this distinguishing mark of the royal favour, and that Lord Bute was the proper person to convey them. Accordingly he waited on his Lordship, and being admitted to him testified his sense of the obligation; but having done this he thought he had done enough, and never after could be prevailed on to knock at his door.'

[2] He reproached Bute with 'shewing an undue partiality to Scotchmen.' *Life*, ii. 354. The author of the *Memoirs of Dr. Johnson* (1785, p. 136), who had his information from James Elphinston, says that 'Johnson dined at Mr. Elphinston's but a few days before the pension was proposed. He was there asked why he had shown such dislike to the minister; because, said he, he gave the King a wrong education. He had only taught him, added Johnson, *to draw a tree*.'

[3] *Ante*, p. 188.

[4] Boswell mentions this story as 'having been circulated both in conversation and in print.... When I mentioned it to Johnson, "Sir, (said he) if Rose said this I never heard it."' *Life*, iv. 168, *n*. 1.

a house

a house in Johnson's-court, Fleet-street [1]. Dr. Levet, his friend and physician in ordinary, paid his daily visits with assiduity; made tea all the morning, talked what he had to say, and did not expect an answer. Mrs. Williams had her apartment in the house, and entertained her benefactor with more enlarged conversation. Chemistry was part of Johnson's amusement. For this love of experimental philosophy, Sir John Hawkins thinks an apology necessary. He tells us, with great gravity, that curiosity was the only object in view; not an intention to grow suddenly rich by the philosopher's stone, or the transmutation of metals [2]. To enlarge his circle, Johnson once more had recourse to a literary club. This was at the Turk's Head, in Gerrard-street, Soho, on every Tuesday evening through the year [3]. The members were, besides himself, the right honourable Edmund Burke, Sir Joshua Reynolds, Dr. Nugent, Dr. Goldsmith, the late Mr. Topham Beauclerk, Mr. Langton, Mr. Chamier, Sir John Hawkins, and some others [4]. Johnson's affection for Sir Joshua was founded on a long acquaintance, and a thorough

[1] *Life*, ii. 5. For his house in Bolt Court into which he moved in the winter of 1775-6 he paid £40 a year rent. Wheatley's *London*, i. 216.

[2] Hawkins, p. 413. Hawkins adds that 'Johnson had for a laboratory the garret over his chambers in the Inner Temple; he furnished that with an alembic, with retorts, receivers, and other vessels adapted to the cheapest processes. . . . From the dregs of strong beer he was able to extract a strong but very nauseous spirit, which all might smell, but few chose to taste.' See *ante*, pp. 307, 408.

[3] It was on Monday evening that the Club met. In Dec. 1772 the night was changed to Friday. *Life*, i. 478, *n*. 3; Hawkins, p. 415.

'The object of all clubs is either drinking or gaming, but commonly both.' Chesterfield's *Letters*, ed. 1845, ii. 425.

If this is true Johnson and Reynolds instituted a new kind of club.

[4] The original members were the nine mentioned. *Ante*, p. 230. For those who joined afterwards, see *Life*, i. 478, *n*. 2, 479.

In the *Malone MSS.* in the British Museum, in No. 36, which contains two lists of the members, are the following entries.

'9. Sir John Hawkins.
Sent to Coventry
Withdrew s— [MS. imperfect].'

'Sr John Hawkins *sent to*
Coventry and
expelled.'

According to Sir Joshua Reynolds, Hawkins 'one evening attacked Mr. Burke in so rude a manner that all the company testified their displeasure; and at their next meeting his reception was such that he never came again.' *Life*, i. 479. For Hawkins's 'dark allusion' to Burke see *ib.*, *n*. 1.

knowledge

knowledge of the virtues and amiable qualities of that excellent artist [1]. He delighted in the conversation of Mr. Burke [2]. He met him for the first time at Mr. Garrick's several years ago. On the next day he said, 'I suppose, Murphy, you are proud of your countryman. CUM TALIS SIT UTINAM NOSTER ESSET!' From that time his constant observation was, 'That a man of sense could not meet Mr. Burke by accident, under a gateway to avoid a shower, without being convinced that he was the first man in England [3].' Johnson felt not only kindness, but zeal and ardour for his friends [4]. He did every thing in his power to advance the reputation of Dr. Goldsmith. He loved him, though he knew his failings, and particularly the leaven of envy which corroded the mind of that elegant writer, and made him impatient, without disguise, of the praises bestowed on any person whatever [5]. Of this infirmity, which marked Goldsmith's character, Johnson gave a remarkable instance. It happened that he went with Sir Joshua Reynolds and Goldsmith to see the Fantoccini, which were exhibited some years ago in or near the Haymarket. They admired the curious mechanism by which the puppets were made to walk the stage, draw a chair to the

[1] 'Sir Joshua Reynolds,' writes Boswell, 'was truly his *dulce decus.*' *Life*, i. 244. Sir Pearce Edgcumbe of Somerleigh Court, Dorchester, the great-grandson of Sir Joshua's sister Mary, has pointed out to me how many of the great painter's relations were University men. On the paternal side, his grandfather was a B.A. of Exeter; his father a Fellow of Balliol; his uncle Joshua a Fellow of Corpus; and his cousin William a Fellow of Exeter, Oxford; while his uncle John was a Fellow of King's College, Cambridge, and of Eton College. His mother's grandfather, the Rev. Thomas Baker, an eminent mathematician, was a Scholar of Wadham. This connection with the two universities, especially with Oxford, would have endeared him all the more to Johnson.

[2] He praised its 'affluence.' *Ib.* ii. 181. 'His stream of mind is perpetual.' *Ib.* ii. 450. 'Burke is the only man whose common conversation corresponds with the general fame which he has in the world. Take up whatever topic you please, he is ready to meet you.' *Ib.* iv. 19. 'His talk is the ebullition of his mind; he does not talk from a desire of distinction, but because his mind is full.' *Ib.* iv. 167. 'He is never what we call hum-drum; never unwilling to begin to talk, nor in haste to leave off.' *Ib.* v. 33.

[3] 'If a man were to go by chance at the same time with Burke under a shed to shun a shower, he would say—"this is an extraordinary man."' *Ib.* iv. 275. See also *ib.* v. 34, and *ante*, p. 290.

[4] *Ante*, p. 279.

[5] *Life*, i. 413; ii. 260; iii. 271.

table,

table, sit down, write a letter, and perform a variety of other actions with such dexterity, that *though Nature's journeymen made the men, they imitated humanity* to the astonishment of the spectator[1]. The entertainment being over, the three friends retired to a tavern. Johnson and Sir Joshua talked with pleasure of what they had seen; and says Johnson, in a tone of admiration, 'How the little fellow brandished his spontoon[2]!' 'There is nothing in it,' replied Goldsmith, starting up with impatience; 'give me a spontoon; I can do it as well myself[3].'

Enjoying his amusements at his weekly club[4], and happy in a state of independence, Johnson gained in the year 1765 another resource, which contributed more than any thing else to exempt him from the solicitudes of life. He was introduced to the late Mr. Thrale and his family. Mrs. Piozzi has related the fact, and it is therefore needless to repeat it in this place[5]. The author of this narrative looks back to the share he had in that business with self-congratulation, since he knows the tenderness which from that time soothed Johnson's cares at Streatham, and prolonged a valuable life[6]. The subscribers to Shakspeare began to despair of ever seeing the promised edition[7]. To acquit himself of this obligation, he went to work unwillingly, but proceeded with vigour. In the month of October 1765, Shakspeare was published[8]; and, in a short time after, the University of

[1] 'I have thought some of Nature's journeymen had made men and not made them well, they imitated humanity so abominably.' *Hamlet*, Act iii. sc. 2. l. 37.

[2] *Spontoon* is not in Johnson's *Dictionary*.

[3] According to Boswell 'Goldsmith went home with Mr. Burke to supper; and broke his shin by attempting to exhibit to the company how much better he could jump over a stick than the puppets.' *Life*, i. 414, *n*. 4.

[4] 'The hours which Johnson spent in this society seemed to be the happiest of his life; he would often applaud his own sagacity in the selection of it, and was so constant at our meetings as never to absent himself. It is true he came late, but then he stayed late.' Hawkins, p. 424. He was in later years irregular in his attendance. *Ante*, p. 229, *n*. 4.

[5] *Ante*, p. 232.

[6] In his last letter to her Johnson speaks of 'that kindness which soothed twenty years of a life radically wretched.' *Letters*, ii. 407.

[7] For Churchill's taunt on the delay, see *Life*, i. 319.

[8] *Life*, i. 496. For the first edition he received £375, and for the second, £100. *Gentleman's Magazine*, 1787, p. 76.

Dublin

Dublin sent over a diploma, in honourable terms, creating him a Doctor of Laws [1]. Oxford in eight or ten years afterwards followed the example; and till then Johnson never assumed the title of Doctor [2]. In 1766 his constitution seemed to be in a rapid decline, and that morbid melancholy, which often clouded his understanding, came upon him with a deeper gloom than ever. Mr. and Mrs. Thrale paid him a visit in this situation, and found him on his knees, with Dr. Delap, the rector of Lewes, in Sussex, beseeching God to continue to him the use of his understanding [3]. Mr. Thrale took him to his house at Streatham; and Johnson from that time became a constant resident in the family. He went occasionally to the club in Gerrard-street; but his head quarters were fixed at Streatham [4]. An apartment was fitted up for him, and the library was greatly enlarged. Parties were constantly invited from town; and Johnson was every day at an elegant table, with select and polished company. Whatever could be devised by Mr. and Mrs. Thrale to promote the happiness, and establish the health of their guest, was studiously performed from that time to the end of Mr. Thrale's life [5]. Johnson accompanied the family in all their summer excursions to Brighthelmstone, to Wales [6], and to Paris [7]. It is but justice to Mr. Thrale to say, that a more ingenuous frame of mind no man possessed. His education at Oxford gave him the habits of a gentleman [8]; his amiable temper recommended his

[1] *Life*, i. 488.

[2] The Oxford degree was conferred in 1775. *Ib.* ii. 331. According to Hawkins (p. 446):—'His attachment to Oxford prevented Johnson from receiving this honour [the Dublin degree] as it was intended, and he never assumed the title which it conferred.'

Boswell states:—'It is remarkable that he never, so far as I know, assumed his title of *Doctor*, but called himself *Mr.* Johnson.' *Life*, ii. 332, *n.* 1. In this Boswell was not perfectly accurate. *Ib.*

[3] *Ante*, p. 234.

[4] He had his apartment also in Mr. Thrale's house in Southwark. *Life*, i. 493.

[5] Had Mr. Thrale lived only four years longer how different would have been the closing scene of Johnson's life!

[6] *Life*, ii. 285; v. 427.

[7] *Ib.* ii. 384.

[8] Murphy perhaps is thinking of Boswell, who writing of Thrale had said:—'There may be some who think that a new system of gentility might be established upon principles totally different from what have hitherto prevailed. . . . Such are the specious, but false arguments for a proposition which always will find

conversation,

conversation, and the goodness of his heart made him a sincere friend. That he was the patron of Johnson, is an honour to his memory.

In petty disputes with contemporary writers, or the wits of the age, Johnson was seldom entangled. A single incident of that kind may not be unworthy of notice, since it happened with a man of great celebrity in his time. A number of friends dined with Garrick on a Christmas day[1]. Foote was then in Ireland. It was said at table, that the modern Aristophanes (so Foote was called) had been horse-whipped by a Dublin apothecary, for mimicking him on the stage. 'I wonder,' said Garrick, 'that any man should shew so much resentment to Foote; he has a patent for such liberties; nobody ever thought it *worth his while* to quarrel with him in London.' 'I am glad,' said Johnson, 'to find that the *man is rising in the world*.' The expression was afterwards reported to Foote; who, in return, gave out, that he would produce the *Caliban of literature*[2] on the stage. Being informed of this design, Johnson sent word to Foote, 'That the theatre being intended for the reformation of vice, he would step from the boxes on the stage, and correct him before the audience[3].' Foote knew the intrepidity of his antagonist, and abandoned the design. No ill-will ensued. Johnson used to say, 'That, for broad-faced mirth, Foote had not his equal[4].'

Dr. Johnson's fame excited the curiosity of the King. His Majesty expressed a desire to see a man of whom extraordinary

numerous advocates, in a nation where men are every day starting up from obscurity to wealth. To refute them is needless. The general sense of mankind cries out, with irresistible force, "*Un gentilhomme est toujours gentilhomme*."' *Life*, i. 491.

Johnson described Thrale as 'a regular scholar.' *Ib.* p. 494. Miss Burney, on first seeing him, wrote:—'He is a very tall, well-looking man, very well-bred, but shy and reserved.' *Early Diary of Frances Burney*, ii. 256, *n.* 2.

[1] Murphy, who tells this story in the *Monthly Review*, vol. 76, p. 374, places it in 1760.

[2] 'Being told that Gilbert Cooper called him the Caliban of literature, "Well, (said Johnson) I must dub him the Punchinello."' *Life*, ii. 129.

Cooper 'was the last of the *benevolists* or sentimentalists.' *Ib.* iii. 149, *n.* 2.

[3] *Ib.* ii. 95, 299.

[4] *Ante*, p. 265.

things

things were said. Accordingly, the librarian at Buckingham-house invited Johnson to see that elegant collection of books, at the same time giving a hint of what was intended [1]. His Majesty entered the room; and, among other things, asked the author, 'If he meant to give the world any more of his compositions?' Johnson answered, 'That he thought he had written enough.' 'And I should think so too,' replied his Majesty, 'if you had not written so well [2].'

Though Johnson thought he had written enough, his genius, even in spite of bodily sluggishness, could not lie still. In 1770 we find him entering the lists as a political writer. The flame of discord that blazed throughout the nation on the expulsion of Mr. Wilkes, and the final determination of the House of Commons, that Mr. Luttrell was duly elected by 206 [3] votes against 1143, spread a general spirit of discontent. To allay the tumult, Dr. Johnson published *The False Alarm.* Mrs. Piozzi informs us, 'That this pamphlet was written at her house, between eight o'clock on Wednesday night and twelve on Thursday night [4].' This celerity has appeared wonderful to many, and some have doubted the truth [5]. It may, however, be placed within the bounds of probability. Johnson has observed that there are different methods of composition. Virgil was used to pour out a great number of verses in the morning, and pass the day in retrenching the exuberances, and correcting inaccuracies; and it was Pope's custom to write his first thoughts in his first words, and gradually to amplify, decorate, rectify, and refine them [6]. Others employ at once memory and invention, and,

[1] Johnson had been in the habit of reading in the Library. *Life*, ii. 33.

Gibbon, writing in 1779, says:—'The greatest city in the world is still destitute of a public library; and the writer, who has undertaken to treat any large historical subject, is reduced to the necessity of purchasing for his private use a numerous and valuable collection of the books which must form the basis of his work.' *Misc. Works*, iv. 591.

[2] *Life*, ii. 35.

[3] 296 votes. *Ib.* ii. 111, *n.* 2.

[4] *Ante*, p. 173.

[5] Speaking of his *Debates* he said:—'Three columns of the *Magazine* in an hour was no uncommon effort, which was faster than most persons could have transcribed that quantity.' *Life*, iv. 409.

[6] The whole paragraph is borrowed with alterations from Johnson's *Life of Pope*. *Works*, viii. 321.

with

with little intermediate use of the pen, form and polish large masses by continued meditation, and write their productions only, when, in their opinion, they have completed them. This last was Johnson's method. He never took his pen in hand till he had weighed well his subject, and grasped in his mind the sentiments, the train of argument, and the arrangement of the whole. As he often thought aloud, he had, perhaps, talked it over to himself. This may account for that rapidity with which, in general, he dispatched his sheets to the press, without being at the trouble of a fair copy[1]. Whatever may be the logic or eloquence of *The False Alarm*, the House of Commons have since erased the resolution from the Journals[2]. But whether they have not left materials for a future controversy may be made a question.

In 1771 he published another tract, on the subject of FALKLAND ISLANDS. The design was to shew the impropriety of going to war with Spain for an island thrown aside from human use, stormy in winter, and barren in summer[3]. For this work it is apparent that materials were furnished by direction of the minister[4].

At the approach of the general election in 1774, he wrote a short discourse, called THE PATRIOT, not with any visible application to Mr. Wilkes[5]; but to teach the people to reject the leaders of the opposition, who called themselves patriots. In 1775 he undertook a pamphlet of more importance, namely, *Taxation no Tyranny*[6], in answer to the Resolutions and Address of the American Congress. The scope of the argument was, that distant colonies, which had, in their assemblies, a legislature of their own, were, notwithstanding, liable to be taxed in a British Parliament, where they had neither peers in one house, nor representatives in the other. He was of opinion, that this country was strong enough to enforce obedience. 'When an

[1] *Life*, i. 71; iii. 62, *n*. 1.
[2] *Ib*. ii. 112.
[3] Murphy quotes the pamphlet. *Works*, vi. 198.
[4] *Life*, ii. 134.
[5] *Ib*. ii. 286. Wilkes is mentioned in it. *Works*, vi. 216.
[6] *Life*, ii. 312.

Englishman,

Englishman, he says, 'is told that the Americans shoot up like the hydra, he naturally considers how the hydra was destroyed [1].' The event has shewn how much he and the minister of that day were mistaken.

The Account of the Tour to the Western Islands of Scotland, which was undertaken in the autumn of 1773, in company with Mr. Boswell, was not published till some time in the year 1775 [2]. This book has been variously received; by some extolled for the elegance of the narrative, and the depth of observation on life and manners; by others, as much condemned, as a work of avowed hostility to the Scotch nation [3]. The praise was, beyond all question, fairly deserved; and the censure, on due examination, will appear hasty and ill-founded. That Johnson entertained some prejudices against the Scotch, must not be dissembled. It is true, as Mr. Boswell says, '*that he thought their success in England* [rather] *exceeded their proportion of real merit, and he could not but see in them that nationality which* [I believe] *no liberal-minded Scotsman will deny* [4].' The author of these memoirs well remembers, that Johnson one day asked him, 'Have you observed the difference between your own country impudence and Scottish impudence?' The answer being in the negative: 'Then I will tell you,' said Johnson. 'The impudence of an Irishman is the impudence of a fly, that buzzes about you, and you put it away, but it returns again, and flutters and teazes you. The impudence of a Scotsman is the impudence of a leech, that fixes and sucks your blood [5].' Upon another occasion, this writer went with him into the shop of Davies the

[1] 'When it is urged that they will shoot up,' &c. *Works*, vi. 227.

[2] *Life*, ii. 290.

[3] *Ib.* ii. 300.

[4] *Ib.* v. 20.

Hannah More (*Memoirs*, iv. 193) records 'the answer some one made to a minister who asked whether he could do anything for him—"Nothing," he replied, "unless you could make me a Scotchman." She goes on to tell how two Englishmen, arriving at Tunbridge Wells, got shaved by a barber of the place, whom their Scotch companion declined to employ. They heard the waiter whisper to him, "Sir, I have found a Scotch barber," to which he replied, "Oh! very good, let him walk in."'

[5] *Life*, ii. 307; iv. 12.

bookseller,

bookseller, in Russel-street, Covent-garden. Davies came running to him almost out of breath with joy: 'The Scots gentleman is come, Sir; his principal wish is to see you; he is now in the back-parlour.' 'Well, well, I'll see the gentleman,' said Johnson. He walked towards the room. Mr. Boswell was the person. This writer followed with no small curiosity. 'I find,' said Mr. Boswell, 'that I am come to London at a bad time, when great popular prejudice has gone forth against us North Britons; but when I am talking to you, I am talking to a large and liberal mind, and you know that I cannot *help coming from Scotland*.' 'Sir,' said Johnson, 'no more can the rest of your countrymen [1].'

He had other reasons that helped to alienate him from the natives of Scotland. Being a cordial well-wisher to the constitution in Church and State, he did not think that Calvin and John Knox [2] were proper founders of a national religion. He made, however, a wide distinction between the Dissenters of Scotland [3]

[1] 'Mr. Murphy, in his *Essay on the Life and Genius of Dr. Johnson*, has given an account of this meeting considerably different from mine, I am persuaded without any consciousness of errour. His memory, at the end of nearly thirty years, has undoubtedly deceived him, and he supposes himself to have been present at a scene, which he has probably heard inaccurately described by others. In my note *taken on the very day*, in which I am confident I marked every thing material that passed, no mention is made of this gentleman; and I am sure, that I should not have omitted one so well known in the literary world.' *Life*, i. 391, *n*. 4.

Boswell's account is as follows:—'Mr. Davies mentioned my name, and respectfully introduced me to him. I was much agitated; and recollecting his prejudice against the Scotch, of which I had heard much, I said to Davies, "Don't tell where I come from."—"From Scotland," cried Davies roguishly. "Mr. Johnson, (said I) I do indeed come from Scotland, but I cannot help it." .... He retorted, "That, Sir, I find is what a very great many of your countrymen cannot help."'

The President of St. John's College, Oxford, remembers a London merchant named Lindsey, who, on being introduced to Johnson, told him that he came from Scotland. 'There is no need to tell me that,' was the reply.

[2] *Life*, v. 61.

[3] By 'the Dissenters of Scotland' Murphy means not the Episcopalians nor the Roman Catholics, but the members of the Established Church. Johnson was intolerant enough to refuse to attend the parish-church at Auchinleck. *Ib*. v. 384. Of Dr. Robertson he said:—'I will hear him if he will get up into a tree and preach; but I will not give a sanction by my presence to a Presbyterian assembly.' *Ib*. v. 121. For an

and

and the Separatists of England. To the former he imputed no disaffection, no want of loyalty. Their soldiers and their officers had shed their blood with zeal and courage in the service of Great Britain; and the people, he used to say, were content with their own established modes of worship, without wishing, in the present age, to give any disturbance to the Church of England. This he was at all times ready to admit; and therefore declared, that whenever he found a Scotchman to whom an Englishman was as a Scotchman, that Scotchman should be as an Englishman to him [1]. In this, surely, there was no rancour, no malevolence. The Dissenters on this side the Tweed appeared to him in a different light. Their religion, he frequently said, was too worldly, too political, too restless and ambitious. The doctrine of *cashiering* kings, and erecting on the ruins of the constitution a new form of government, which lately issued from their pulpits [2], he always thought was, under a calm disguise, the principle that lay lurking in their hearts. He knew that a wild democracy had overturned King, Lords, and Commons; and that a set of Republican Fanatics, who would not bow at the name of JESUS, had taken possession of all the livings and all the parishes in the kingdom [3]. That those scenes of horror might never be renewed, was the ardent wish of Dr. Johnson; and though he apprehended no danger from Scotland, it is probable that his dislike of Calvinism mingled sometimes with his reflections on the natives of that country. The association of ideas could not be easily broken; but it is well known that he loved and respected many gentlemen from that part of the island. Dr. Robertson's History of Scotland [4], and Dr. Beattie's

Englishman to give a sanction to the Established Church of another country is absurd enough.

[1] *Life*, ii. 306.

[2] 'The ceremony of cashiering kings of which these gentlemen talk so much at their ease can rarely, if ever, be performed without force.' Burke's *Works*, ed. 1808, v. 73. It was a sermon preached by Dr. Price that Burke attacked. *Ib.* p. 40.

[3] Apparently Murphy is speaking of the men of the Commonwealth.

[4] 'Thinking that I now had him in a corner, and being solicitous for the literary fame of my country, I pressed him for his opinion on the merit of Dr. Robertson's *History of Scotland*. But, to my surprize, he escaped.—"Sir, I love Robertson, and I won't talk of his book."' *Life*, ii. 53. See also *ib.* ii. 236, where he attacks 'the *verbiage* of Robertson' and calls his History a romance.

Essays,

Essays [1], were subjects of his constant praise. Mr. Boswell, Dr. Rose of Chiswick, Andrew Millar, Mr. Hamilton the printer, and the late Mr. Strahan, were among his most intimate friends [2]. Many others might be added to the list. He scorned to enter Scotland as a spy [3]; though Hawkins, his biographer, and the professing defender of his fame, allowed himself leave to represent him in that ignoble character. He went into Scotland to survey men and manners [4]. Antiquities, fossils, and minerals, were not within his province. He did not visit that country to settle the station of Roman camps, or the spot where Galgacus fought the last battle for public liberty [5]. The people, their customs, and the progress of literature, were his objects. The civilities which he received in the course of his tour have been repaid with grateful acknowledgement, and, generally, with great elegance of expression [6]. His crime is, that he found the country bare of trees, and he has stated the fact. This, Mr. Boswell, in his Tour to the Hebrides, has told us, was resented by his countrymen with anger inflamed to rancour; but he admits that there are few trees on the east side of Scotland [7]. Mr. Pennant, in his Tour, says, that in some parts of the eastern side of the country, he saw several large plantations of pine planted by gentlemen near their seats; and in this respect such a laudable spirit prevails that, *in another half century*, it never shall be said, '*To spy the nakedness of the land are you come* [8].' Johnson

[1] Of Beattie's *Essay on Truth* he wrote:—'It is, I believe, every day more liked; at least I like it more as I look more upon it.' *Life*, ii. 202.

[2] *Ib.* ii. 121, 306.

Percy said that 'Johnson's invectives against Scotland in common conversation were more in pleasantry and sport than real and malignant; for no man was more visited by natives of that country, nor were there any for whom he had a greater esteem.' Anderson's *Johnson*, ed. 1815, p. 285.

[3] The Scotch, Hawkins says (p. 486), 'had reason to look on Johnson rather as a spy than a traveller, and might have said to him—"To discover [see] the nakedness of the land are ye [ye are] come. [Genesis, xlii. 12]."'

[4] *Life*, v. 112.

[5] Tacitus, *Agricola*, c. 29. It was left for Jonathan Oldbuck to prove that it was on the Kaim of Kinprunes that this battle was fought. *The Antiquary*, c. 4.

[6] *Life*, ii. 303.

[7] *Ib.* ii. 301, 304, 311; v. 69, 75.

[8] Sir A. Gordon, describing how his father, the Earl of Aberdeen, on attaining his majority in 1805, went down to his ancestral home, says:—

could

could not wait for that half century, and therefore mentioned things as he found them. If in any thing he has been mistaken, he has made a fair apology in the last paragraph of his book, avowing with candour, 'That he may have been surprized by modes of life, and appearances of nature, that are familiar to men of wider survey, and more varied conversation. Novelty and ignorance must always be reciprocal; and he is conscious that his thoughts [1] on national manners are the thoughts of one, who has seen but little.'

The Poems of Ossian made a part of Johnson's enquiry during his residence in Scotland and the Hebrides. On his return to England, November 1773, a storm seemed to be gathering over his head; but the cloud never burst, and the thunder never fell. Ossian, it is well known, was presented to the publick as a translation from the *Earse*; but that this was a fraud, Johnson declared without hesitation [2]. 'The *Earse*,' he says, 'was always oral only, and never a written language. The Welch and the Irish were more cultivated. In *Earse* there was not in the world

'He had not revisited Aberdeenshire since he left it as a child of eight years of age, with a child's illusions as to the surroundings of a home which has been his world. He was wholly unprepared for the rough awakening which awaited him, and on the rare occasions on which he could be induced to speak of his own early days, he dwelt with great force on the sensations he experienced when brought face to face with the reality before him. The backward condition of agriculture, the miserable dwellings and half-savage habits of the people, the ignorance and coarseness of the gentry, the inclemency of the climate, the ugliness and monotony of the country — bare, undulating, and treeless—were all very unlike his dreams and filled him with dismay.' *The Earl of Aberdeen*, 1893, p. 11.

[1] 'I cannot but be conscious that my thoughts,' &c.

[2] *Life*, ii. 302, 309, 347, 383.

The following note is in Anderson's *Johnson*, ed. 1815, p. 342:—'The Bishop of Dromore (Dr. Percy) has allowed Dr. Anderson to declare, that he repeatedly received the most positive assurances from Sir John Elliot, the confidential friend of Macpherson, that all the poems published by him as translations of Ossian were entirely of his own composition.'

Elliot was a physician of whom Walpole wrote on Feb. 5, 1785 (*Letters*, viii. 542):—He had happened to attend my housemaid, and would not take a fee; to prevail, I pretended to talk on my own gout, and he was so tractable, and suffered me to prescribe to him what he should prescribe to me . . . that I continued to see him.'

a single

a single manuscript a hundred years old. Martin, who in the last century published an Account of the Western Islands, mentions *Irish*, but never *Earse* manuscripts, to be found in the islands in his time. The bards could not read ; if they could, they might probably have written. But the bard was a barbarian among barbarians, and, knowing nothing himself, lived with others that knew no more. If there is a manuscript from which the translation was made, in what age was it written, and where is it? If it was collected from oral recitation, it could only be in detached parts and scattered fragments: the whole is too long to be remembered [1].' Who put it together in its present form? For these, and such like reasons, Johnson calls the whole an imposture. He adds, 'The editor, or author, never could shew the original, nor can it be shewn by any other. To revenge reasonable incredulity, by refusing evidence, is a degree of insolence with which the world is not yet acquainted; and stubborn audacity is the last refuge of guilt [2].' This reasoning carries with it great weight. It roused the resentment of Mr. Macpherson. He sent a threatening letter to the author; and Johnson answered him in the rough phrase of stern defiance [3]. The two heroes frowned at a distance, but never came to action.

In the year 1777, the misfortunes of Dr. Dodd excited his compassion [4]. He wrote a speech for that unhappy man, when called up to receive judgement of death [5]; besides two petitions, one to the King, and another to the Queen [6]; and a sermon to be preached by Dodd to the convicts in Newgate [7]. It may appear trifling to add, that about the same time he wrote a prologue to the comedy of A Word to the Wise, written by *Hugh Kelly* [8]. The play, some years before, had been damned by a party on the first night. It was revived for the benefit of the author's widow. Mrs. Piozzi relates, that when Johnson

[1] These extracts are an abridgment of Johnson's *Works*, ix. 112–115.

[2] *Ib.* p. 115.

[3] *Life*, ii. 297.

[4] *Ib.* iii. 139–148.

[5] *Ib.* p. 141.

[6] *Ib.* p. 142.

[7] *Ib.* p. 167. Johnson wrote to Mrs. Thrale from Lichfield on Aug. 9, 1777:—'Lucy [Porter] said, "When I read Dr. Dodd's sermon to the prisoners, I said, Dr. Johnson could not make a better."' *Letters*, ii. 18.

[8] *Life*, iii. 113.

was

was rallied for these exertions, so close to one another, his answer was, *When they come to me with a dying Parson, and a dead Stay-maker, what can a man do*[1]*?* We come now to the last of his literary labours. At the request of the Booksellers he undertook the Lives of the Poets. The first publication was in 1779, and the whole was compleated in 1781[2]. In a memorandum of that year he says, some time in March he finished the Lives of the Poets, which he wrote in his usual way, dilatorily and hastily, unwilling to work, yet working with vigour and haste[3]. In another place, he hopes they are written in such a manner as may tend to the promotion of piety[4]. That the history of so many men, who, in their different degrees, made themselves conspicuous in their time, was not written recently after their deaths, seems to be an omission that does no honour to the Republic of Letters. Their contemporaries in general looked on with calm indifference, and suffered Wit and Genius to vanish out of the world in total silence, unregarded, and unlamented. Was there no friend to pay the tribute of a tear? No just observer of life, to record the virtues of the deceased? Was even Envy silent? It seemed to have been agreed, that if an author's works survived, the history of the man was to give no moral lesson to after-ages. If tradition told us that BEN JONSON went to the Devil Tavern[5]; that SHAKSPEARE stole deer, and held the stirrup at playhouse doors[6]; that DRYDEN

[1] *Ante*, p. 181.

[2] *Life*, iii. 109, 370; iv. 34.

[3] *Ante*, p. 96. The author of *The Life of Johnson*, published by Kearsley in 1785, says (p. 65), that 'the booksellers on going to press with the third edition of the *Lives* offered Johnson £200 for his reversion of the copyhold; but the Doctor, meeting the offer with the same generosity, after pausing some time replied, "Why, let me see—fourteen years[1] hence, why I shall be but eighty-six then—no—I'll even keep the reversion as a nest-egg for old age."'

[4] *Ante*, p. 88.

[5] *Life*, iv. 254, *n*. 4.

'And each true Briton is to Ben so civil,
He swears the Muses met him at the Devil.'

Pope, *Imitations of Horace*, *Epis*. ii. 1. 41.

[6] Johnson's *Shakespeare*, ed. 1765, Introduction, pp. 147, 172.

[1] 'The term of years allowed by the Act of Queen Anne for an author's resumption of his works not exclusively disposed of.'

frequented Button's Coffee-house[1]; curiosity was lulled asleep, and Biography forgot the best part of her function, which is to instruct mankind by examples taken from the school of life. This task remained for Dr. Johnson, when years had rolled away; when the channels of information were, for the most part, choaked up, and little remained besides doubtful anecdote, uncertain tradition, and vague report.

'Nunc situs informis premit et deserta Vetustas[2].'

The value of Biography has been better understood in other ages, and in other countries. Tacitus informs us, that to record the lives and characters of illustrious men was the practice of the Roman authors, in the early periods of the Republic[3]. In France the example has been followed. *Fontenelle*, *D'Alembert*, and *Monsieur Thomas*[4], have left models in this kind of composition. They have *embalmed* the dead[5]. But it is true, that they had incitements and advantages, even at a distant day, which could not, by any diligence, be obtained by Dr. Johnson. The wits of France had ample materials. They lived in a nation of critics, who had at heart the honour done to their country by their Poets, their Heroes, and their Philosophers. They had, besides, an *Academy of Belles Lettres*, where Genius was cultivated, refined, and encouraged. They had the tracts, the essays, and dissertations, which remain in the memories[6] of the Academy, and they had the speeches of the several members, delivered at their first admission to a seat in that learned Assembly. In those speeches the new Academician did ample justice to the

[1] It was at Will's coffee-house that Dryden 'had a particular chair for himself.' *Life*, iii. 71; *Works*, vii. 300. Button opened his coffee-house after Dryden's time, under the patronage of Addison. *Ib.* p. 449.

[2] Though now deform'd by dust
and cover'd o'er with mould.'
FRANCIS. HORACE, *Epis.* ii. 2. 118.

[3] *Agricola*, c. 1.

[4] Voltaire wrote on Sept. 23, 1765:—'Je viens de lire le sublime *Éloge de Descartes*, par M. Thomas. J'aime mieux lire, je vous jure, le panégyriste que le héros. C'est un homme d'un rare mérite que ce Thomas; et ni Thomas d'Aquin, ni Thomas Didyme, ni Thomas de Cantorbéry, n'approchent de lui.' *Œuvres de Voltaire*, 1821, liii. 171.

[5] 'Those tears eternal that embalm
the dead.'
Pope, *Epistle to Mr. Jervas.*

[6] Apparently Murphy's translation of *Mémoires*, unless *memories* is a misprint for *memoirs*.

memory

memory of his predecessor; and though his harangue was decorated with the colours of eloquence, and was, for that reason, called panegyric, yet being pronounced before qualified judges, who knew the talents, the conduct, and morals of the deceased, the speaker could not, with propriety, wander into the regions of fiction. The truth was known, before it was adorned[1]. The Academy saw the marble, before the artist polished it. But this country has had no Academy of Literature. The public mind, for centuries, has been engrossed by party and faction; *by the madness of many for the gain of a few*[2]; by civil wars, religious dissentions, trade and commerce, and the arts of accumulating wealth. Amidst such attentions, who can wonder that cold praise has been often the only reward of merit? In this country Doctor Nathaniel Hodges, who, like the good bishop of Marseilles, *drew purer breath*[3] amidst the contagion of the plague in London, and, during the whole time, continued in the city, administering medical assistance, was suffered, as Johnson used to relate with tears in his eyes, to die for debt in a gaol[4]. In this country, the man who brought the New River to London was ruined by that noble project[5]; and in this country Otway died for want on Tower Hill[6]; Butler, the great author of Hudibras, whose name can only die with the English language,

[1] Hannah More in 1786 read 'an Eloge on the humility of the Virgin Mary, delivered at the Academie Françaises by one of the Quarante. Mons. Tourreuil informs her [the Virgin] that her humility is still further rewarded, by her having the honour of being made the subject for the prize of eloquence by the most enlightened Academy in the world.' More's *Memoirs*, ii. 44.

[2] 'Party is the madness of many for the gain of a few.' Pope, *Thoughts on Various Subjects*. Warton's Pope's *Works*, 1822, vi. 381.

[3] 'Why drew Marseille's good bishop purer breath
When nature sicken'd, and each gale was death?'

Pope, *Essay on Man*, iv. 107.

'In the plague of Marseilles, in the year 1720, the Bishop distinguished himself by his zeal and activity, being the pastor, the physician, and the magistrate of his flock whilst that horrid calamity prevailed.' NOTE BY WARTON.

[4] *Life*, ii. 341, *n.* 3.

[5] 'Myddelton, though never a rich man, and much impoverished by his work on the New River, was enabled to end his days in comfort, and leave a respectable patrimony to his children.' Colonel Myddelton, whom Johnson visited at Gwaynynog (*Life*, v. 443), was of the same family. *Dict. Nat. Biog.*

[6] Johnson's *Works*, vii. 176.

 was

was left to languish in poverty, the particulars of his life almost unknown, and scarce a vestige of him left except his immortal poem [1]. Had there been an Academy of Literature, the lives, at least, of those celebrated persons would have been written for the benefit of posterity. Swift, it seems, had the idea of such an institution, and proposed it to Lord Oxford [2]; but Whig and Tory were more important objects. It is needless to dissemble, that Dr. Johnson, in the Life of Roscommon, talks of the inutility of such a project. 'In this country,' he says, 'an Academy could be expected to do but little. If an academician's place were profitable, it would be given by interest; if attendance were gratuitous, it would be rarely paid, and no man would endure the least disgust. Unanimity is impossible, and debate would separate the assembly.' To this it may be sufficient to answer, that the Royal Society has not been dissolved by sullen disgust; and the modern Academy at Somerset-house has already performed much, and promises more [3]. Unanimity is not necessary to such an assembly. On the contrary, by difference of opinion, and collision of sentiment, the cause of Literature would thrive and flourish. The true principles of criticism, the secret of fine writing, the investigation of antiquities, and other interesting subjects, might occasion a clash of opinions; but in that contention Truth would receive illustration, and the essays of the several members would supply the Memoirs of the Academy. But, says Dr. Johnson, 'suppose the philological decree made and promulgated, what would be its authority? In absolute governments there is sometimes a general reverence paid to all that

[1] 'In this mist of obscurity passed the life of Butler, a man whose name can only perish with his language. The mode and place of his education are unknown; the events of his life are variously related, and all that can be told with certainty is that he was poor.' *Works*, vii. 148.

[2] *Ib.* vii. 167; viii. 202. See also v. 48; viii. 4, and Swift's *Proposal for correcting, &c., the English Tongue. Works*, ed. 1803, vi. 43.

Sir G. Trevelyan, describing the last summer of Macaulay's life, says:—'I remember our sitting at the window through the best part of an afternoon, looking across Windermere, and drawing up under his superintendence a list of forty names for an imaginary English Academy.' Trevelyan's *Macaulay*, ed. 1877, ii. 477.

[3] The Royal Academy in 1780 for the first time held its Exhibition in Somerset House. *Letters*, ii. 150.

has

has the sanction of power, and the countenance of greatness. How little this is the state of our country needs not to be told. ... The edicts of an English academy would probably be read by many, only that they might be sure to disobey them. ... The present manners of the nation would deride authority, and therefore nothing is left but that every writer should criticize himself[1].' This surely is not conclusive. It is by the standard of the best writers that every man settles for himself his plan of legitimate composition; and since the authority of superior genius is acknowledged, that authority, which the individual obtains, would not be lessened by an association with others of distinguished ability. It may, therefore, be inferred, that an Academy of Literature would be an establishment highly useful, and an honour to Literature. In such an institution profitable places would not be wanted. *Vatis avarus haud facile est animus*[2]; and the minister, who shall find leisure from party and faction, to carry such a scheme into execution, will, in all probability, be respected by posterity as the Mæcenas of letters[3].

We now take leave of Dr. Johnson as an author. Four volumes of his Lives of the Poets were published in 1778[4], and the work was completed in 1781. Should Biography fall again into

[1] *Works*, vii. 167. 'JOHNSON. Subordination is sadly broken down in this age. No man now has the same authority which his father had—except a gaoler. No master has it over his servants; it is diminished in our colleges; nay in our Grammar-schools.' *Life*, iii. 262.

It is strange that Matthew Arnold in his *Literary Influence of Academies* (*Essays in Criticism*, ed. 1889, p. 42), nowhere mentions Johnson's opinion.

[2] 'Vatis avarus
Non temere est animus.'
Horace, *Epis.* ii. 1. 119.
'Rarely avarice taints the tuneful mind.'
Pope, *Imitations of Horace*, I. 192.

[3] Macaulay recorded on Dec. 10, 1850:—'I met Sir Bulwer Lytton. He is anxious about some scheme for some association of literary men. I detest all such associations. I hate the notion of gregarious authors. The less we have to do with each other the better.' Trevelyan's *Macaulay*, ed. 1877, ii. 289.

[4] Murphy had correctly stated (*ante*, p. 433) that they were published in 1779. Hawkins, writing but six years after the publication of the last six volumes of the *Lives*, says that 'they came abroad in 1778 in ten small volumes.' p. 534.

disuse,

disuse, there will not always be a Johnson to look back through a century, and give a body of critical and moral instruction. In April 1781, he lost his friend Mr. Thrale. His own words, in his diary, will best tell that melancholy event[1]. 'On Wednesday the 11th of April, was buried my dear friend Thrale, who died on Wednesday the 4th, and with him were buried many of my hopes and pleasures. About five, I think, on Wednesday morning he expired. I felt almost the last flutter of his pulse, and looked for the last time upon the face, that for fifteen years had never been turned upon me but with respect and benignity. Farewel: may God, that delighteth in mercy, have *had* mercy on thee. I had constantly prayed for him [some time] before his death. The decease of him, from whose friendship I had obtained many opportunities of amusement, and to whom I turned my thoughts as to a refuge from misfortunes, has left me heavy. But my business is with myself.' From the close of his last work, the malady, that persecuted him through life, came upon him with alarming severity, and his constitution declined apace. In 1782 his old friend *Levet* expired without warning, and without a groan[2]. Events like these reminded Johnson of his own mortality. He continued his visits to Mrs. Thrale at Streatham, to the 7th day of October, 1782, when having first composed a prayer for the happiness of a family, with whom he had for many years enjoyed the pleasures and comforts of life, he removed to his own house in town. He says he was up early in the morning, and read fortuitously in the Gospel [gospels], *which was his parting use of the library*[3]. The merit of the family is manifested by the sense he had of it, and we see his heart overflowing with gratitude. He leaves the place with regret, and *casts a lingering look behind*[4].

The few remaining occurrences may be soon dispatched. In the month of June, 1783, Johnson had a paralytic stroke, which affected his speech only[5]. He wrote to Dr. Taylor of Westminster; and to his friend Mr. Allen, the printer, who lived at

[1] *Life*, iv. 84. *Ante*, p. 96.
[2] *Life*, iv. 137. *Ante*, p. 102.
[3] *Ib.* iv. 158. *Ante*, p. 109.
[4] 'Nor cast one longing lingering look behind.' Gray's *Elegy*, l. 88.
[5] *Ante*, p. 111.

the

the next door. Dr. Brocklesby arrived in a short time, and by his care, and that of Dr. Heberden, Johnson soon recovered. During his illness the writer of this narrative visited him, and found him reading Dr. Watson's Chemistry [1]. Articulating with difficulty, he said, 'From this book, he who knows nothing may learn a great deal; and he who knows, will be pleased to find his knowledge recalled to his mind in a manner highly pleasing.' In the month of August he set out for Lichfield, on a visit to Mrs. Lucy Porter, the daughter of his wife by her first husband; and in his way back paid his respects to Dr. Adams at Oxford [2]. Mrs. Williams died at his house in Bolt-court in the month of September, during his absence [3]. This was another shock to a mind like his, ever agitated by the thoughts of futurity. The contemplation of his own approaching end was constantly before his eyes; and the prospect of death, he declared, was terrible [4]. For many years, when he was not disposed to enter into the conversation going forward, whoever sat near his chair, might hear him repeating, from Shakspeare,

> Ay, but to die and go we know not where;
> To lie in cold obstruction and to rot;
> This sensible warm motion to become
> A kneaded clod, and the delighted spirit
> To bathe in fiery floods [5].

And from Milton,

> Who would lose,
> For fear of pain, this intellectual being [6]?

[1] 'Murphy is just gone from me; he visits me very kindly.' *Letters*, ii. 313. For Dr. Watson see *Life*, iv. 118; *Letters*, i. 183, *n.* 1.

[2] Johnson did not visit Lichfield or Oxford this year. Murphy has been misled, perhaps, by an error on Mrs. Thrale's part, who misdates by a year one of Johnson's letters written at Oxford, and fabricates her answer to include both it and one written twelve months and two days later. *Letters*, ii. 257, *n.* 2, 258, *n.* 3.

[3] He was at Heale, near Salisbury, when she died. *Life*, iv. 235.

[4] *Ib.* ii. 106, 298; *Letters*, ii. 369, 380.

[5] *Measure for Measure*, Act iii. sc. 1.

[6] '*Though full* of pain, &c.' *Paradise Lost*, ii. 146.

'Talking to himself was, indeed, one of Johnson's singularities ever since I knew him. I was certain that he was frequently uttering pious ejaculations; for fragments of the Lord's Prayer have been distinctly overheard.' *Life*, i. 483.

By

By the death of Mrs. Williams he was left in a state of destitution, with nobody but Frank, his black servant, to sooth his anxious moments[1]. In November 1783, he was swelled from head to foot with a dropsy[2]. Dr. Brocklesby, with that benevolence with which he always assists his friends, paid his visits with assiduity. The medicines prescribed were so efficacious, that in a few days, Johnson, while he was offering up his prayers, was suddenly obliged to rise, and, in the course of the day, discharged twenty pints of water[3].

Johnson, being eased of his dropsy, began to entertain hopes that the vigour of his constitution was not entirely broken. For the sake of conversing with his friends, he established a conversation club, to meet on every Wednesday evening; and, to serve a man whom he had known in Mr. Thrale's household for many years, the place was fixed at his house in Essex street near the Temple[4]. To answer the malignant remarks of Sir John Hawkins on this subject, were a wretched waste of time. Professing to be Johnson's friend, that biographer has raised more objections to his character, than all the enemies of that excellent man[5]. Sir John had a root of bitterness that *put rancours in the*

[1] 'Last month died Mrs. Williams, who had been to me for thirty years in the place of a sister; her knowledge was great and her conversation pleasing. I now live in cheerless solitude.' *Letters*, ii. 348.

[2] *Life*, iv. 255.

[3] It was not till February 19 that Johnson had this relief. *Letters*, ii. 384; *Life*, iv. 261, 271; Hawkins, p. 565.

[4] Murphy was a member of the Essex Head Club; yet his account is inaccurate. 'We meet thrice a week,' wrote Johnson. *Life*, iv. 254. In the Rules it is laid down that 'the meetings shall be on the Monday, Thursday, and Saturday of every week; but in the week before Easter there shall be no meeting.' *Ib. n.* 5.

[5] Hawkins (p. 567) thus writes of the formation of the Club:—'I was not made privy to this his intention, but all circumstances considered, it was no matter of surprise to me when I heard that the great Dr. Johnson had, in the month of December 1783, formed a sixpenny club at an ale-house in Essex-street, and that though some of the persons thereof were persons of note, strangers, under restrictions, for three pence each night might three nights in a week hear him talk and partake of his conversation.'

Miss Hawkins (*Memoirs*, i. 103) says:—'Boswell was well justified in his resentment of my father's designation of this club as a sixpenny club, meeting at an ale-house. . . . Honestly speaking, I daresay my

vessel

vessel of his peace[1]. Fielding, he says, was the inventor of a cant phrase, *Goodness of heart, which means little more than the virtue of a horse or a dog*[2]. He should have known that kind affections are the essence of virtue; they are the will of God implanted in our nature, to aid and strengthen moral obligation; they incite to action; a sense of benevolence is no less necessary than a sense of duty. Good affections are an ornament not only to an author but to his writings. He who shews himself upon a cold scent for opportunities to bark and snarl throughout a volume of six hundred pages, may, if he will, pretend to moralize; but GOODNESS OF HEART, or, to use that politer phrase, the *virtue of a horse or a dog*, would redound more to his honour. But Sir John is no more: our business is with Johnson. The members of his club were respectable for their rank, their talents, and their literature[3]. They attended with punctuality till about Midsummer 1784, when, with some appearance of health, Johnson went into Derbyshire, and thence to Lichfield[4]. While he was in that part of the world, his friends in town were labouring for his benefit. The air of a more southern climate they thought might prolong a valuable life. But a pension of £300 a year was a slender fund for a travelling valetudinarian, and it was not then known that he had saved a moderate sum of money[5]. Mr. Boswell and Sir Joshua Reynolds undertook to solicit the patronage of the Chancellor[6]. With Lord Thurlow, while he was at the bar, Johnson was well acquainted. He was often heard to say, 'Thurlow is a man of such vigour of mind, that I never knew I was to meet him but—I was going to say, I was

father did not like being passed over.'

[1] *Macbeth*, Act iii. sc. i. l. 67.

[2] Hawkins, p. 215.

'Had not Thwackum too much neglected virtue, and Square religion, in the composition of their several systems, and had not both utterly discarded all natural goodness of heart, they had never been represented as the objects of derision in this history.' *Tom Jones*, Bk. iii. ch. 4.

[3] *Life*, iv. 254, 438.

[4] *Ib.* iv. 353.

[5] He left at least £2,000 (*Ib.* iv. 402, *n.* 2); but so little did he know the amount of his property that a few months before his death he said to Boswell:—'I have (said he) about the world I think above a thousand pounds, which I intend shall afford Frank an annuity of seventy pounds a year.' *Ib.* iv. 284.

[6] *Ib.* iv. 326, 348.

afraid,

afraid, but that would not be true, for I never was afraid of any man; but I never knew that I was to meet Thurlow, but I knew I had something to encounter[1].' The Chancellor undertook to recommend Johnson's case, but without success[2]. To protract if possible the days of a man, whom he respected, he offered to advance the sum of five hundred pounds[3]. Being informed of this at Lichfield[4], Johnson wrote the following letter.

'My Lord,

'After a long and not inattentive observation of mankind, the generosity of your Lordship's offer raises in me not less wonder than gratitude. Bounty, so liberally bestowed, I should gladly receive if my condition made it necessary; for to such a mind who would not be proud to own his obligations? But it has pleased God to restore me to so great a measure of health, that if I should now appropriate so much of a fortune destined to do good, I could not escape from myself the charge of advancing a false claim. My journey to the continent, though I once thought it necessary, was never much encouraged by my physicians; and I was very desirous that your Lordship should be told of it by Sir Joshua Reynolds as an event very uncertain; for, if I grew much better, I should not be willing; if much worse, not able to migrate. Your Lordship was first solicited without my knowledge; but when I was told that you were pleased to honour me with your patronage, I did not expect to hear of a refusal; yet, as I have had no long time to brood hopes, and have not rioted in imaginary opulence, this cold reception has been scarce a disappointment; and from your Lordship's kindness I have received a benefit which only men like you

[1] 'Depend upon it, Sir, it is when you come close to a man in conversation that you discover what his real abilities are; to make a speech in a publick assembly is a knack. Now I honour Thurlow, Sir; Thurlow is a fine fellow; he fairly puts his mind to yours.' *Life*, iv. 179; see also *Ib.* iv. 327.

[2] *Ib.* iv. 350, *n.* 1.

[3] *Ib.* iv. 348. Horace Walpole says that in 1770 'the Seals were valued at £13,000 a year.' *Memoirs of George III*, iv. 45. On March 5, 1783, an annuity of £2,680 was granted to Thurlow. *Annual Register*, 1783, i. 198.

[4] Ashbourne. *Life*, iv. 348.

you are able to bestow. I shall now live *mihi carior*[1], with a higher opinion of my own merit.

'I am, my Lord,
'your Lordship's most obliged,
'most grateful,
'and most humble servant,
'SAMUEL JOHNSON.
'September, 1784.'

We have in this instance the exertion of two congenial minds; one, with a generous impulse relieving merit in distress[2], and the other, by gratitude and dignity of sentiment rising to an equal elevation.

It seems, however, that greatness of mind is not confined to greatness of rank. Dr. Brocklesby was not content to assist with his medical art; he resolved to *minister* to his patient's *mind*, and *pluck from his memory the sorrow*[3] which the late refusal from a high quarter might occasion. To enable him to visit the south of France in pursuit of health, he offered from his own funds an annuity of one hundred pounds, payable quarterly[4].

[1] Perhaps Johnson had in mind Juvenal's line (*Sat.* x. l. 350)—
'Carior est illis homo quam sibi.'

[2] Thurlow's neglect of Cowper is alluded to in the *Epistle to Joseph Hill.* Southey's *Cowper*, ix. 269, *n.* See also *ib.* iv. 208, 256. On the other hand he treated Crabbe with generosity, who, on being at first neglected by him, had sent him 'some strong, but not disrespectful lines.' He invited the young poet to breakfast, and said, 'The first poem you sent me, Sir, I ought to have noticed—and I heartily forgive the second.' On parting he put into his hand a sealed packet containing a bank-note for a hundred pounds. Crabbe's *Works*, 1834, i. 56, 101.

[3] 'About eight or ten days before his death, when Dr. Brocklesby paid him his morning visit, he seemed very low and desponding, and said, "I have been as a dying man all night." He then emphatically broke out in the words of Shakspeare,—

"Can'st thou not minister to a mind diseas'd;
Pluck from the memory a rooted sorrow;
Raze out the written troubles of the brain;
And, with some sweet oblivious antidote,
Cleanse the stuff'd bosom of that perilous stuff,
Which weighs upon the heart?"

To which Dr. Brocklesby readily answered, from the same great poet:—

"——— therein the patient
Must minister to himself."'

Macbeth, Act v. sc. 3. *Life*, iv. 400.

[4] *Life*, iv. 338.

This

This was a *sweet oblivious antidote*, but it was not accepted for the reasons assigned to the Chancellor. The proposal, however, will do honour to Dr. Brocklesby, as long as liberal sentiment shall be ranked among the social virtues.

In the month of October, 1784, we find Dr. Johnson corresponding with Mr. Nichols, the intelligent compiler of the Gentleman's Magazine, and, in the langour of sickness, still desirous to contribute all in his power to the advancement of science and useful knowledge. He says, in a letter to that gentleman, dated Lichfield, October 20, that he should be glad to give so skilful a lover of Antiquities any information [1]. He adds, 'At Ashburne, where I had very little company, I had the luck to borrow Mr. Bowyer's Life [2], a book so full of contemporary history, that a literary man must find some of his old friends. I thought that I could now and then have told you some hints [3] worth your notice: and perhaps we may talk a life over. I hope we shall be much together. You must now be to me what you were before, and what dear Mr. Allen [4] was besides. He was taken unexpectedly away, but I think he was a very good man. I have made little progress in recovery. I am very weak, and very sleepless; but I live on and hope.'

In that languid condition, he arrived, on the 16th of November, at his house in Bolt-court [5], there to end his days. He laboured with the dropsy and an asthma. He was attended by

[1] 'Any information about my native place.' *Life*, iv. 369.

[2] Nichols published in 1782 *Anecdotes of William Bowyer*, Printer. In 1812–15 he brought out this work, recast and enlarged, under the title of *Literary Anecdotes of the Eighteenth Century*.

[3] In the original not *hints* but *names*.

[4] A printer, his landlord, and next neighbour in Bolt Court. *Life*, iii. 141. On July 31, Johnson, who had heard of his death, writes:—'I have lost one of my best and tenderest friends.' *Ib.* iv. 354.

[5] *Ib.* iv. 377.

In the register of the Library of Lichfield Cathedral are the following entries:—

'July 17, 1784.

Sir John Floyer on the Asthma. Dr. Johnson. ret[urned] November 9.

Oct. 5, 1784.

Fuller's Worthies. Dr. Sam. Johnson. ret[urned] November 9.'

For Floyer see *Life*, iv. 353.

Dr.

Dr. Heberden, Dr. Warren, Dr. Brocklesby, Dr. Butter, and Mr. Cruikshank, the eminent surgeon[1]. Eternity presented to his mind an aweful prospect, and, with as much virtue as perhaps ever is the lot of man, he shuddered at the thought of his dissolution. His friends awakened the comfortable reflection of a well-spent life[2]; and, as his end drew near, they had the satisfaction of seeing him composed, and even chearful[3], insomuch that he was able, in the course of his restless nights, to make translations of Greek epigrams from the Anthologia[4]; and to compose a Latin epitaph for his father, his mother, and his brother Nathaniel[5]. He meditated, at the same time, a Latin inscription to the memory of Garrick, but his vigour was exhausted[6].

His love of Literature was a passion that stuck to his last sand[7]. Seven days before his death he wrote the following letter to his friend Mr. Nichols.

'SIR,

'The late learned Mr. Swinton[8] of Oxford having one day remarked that one man, meaning, I suppose, no man but himself, could assign all the parts of the Ancient Universal History to their proper authors, at the request of Sir Robert Chambers, or

[1] *Life*, iv. 399.

[2] Hawkins (p. 584) records on November 29:—'Mr. Langton, who had spent the evening with him, reported that his hopes were increased, and that he was much cheered upon being reminded of the general tendency of his writings and of his example.' See *Life*, iv. 414, *n.* 2.

[3] 'November 30, I saw him in the evening and found him chearful.' Hawkins, p. 584.

[4] On April 19 he had borrowed from Mrs. Thrale's library the Greek Anthology. 'When I lay sleepless,' he wrote, 'I used to drive the night along by turning Greek epigrams into Latin. I know not if I have not turned a hundred.' *Letters*, ii. 391.

On December 1, Hawkins records (p. 584):—'He gave to Mr. Langton and another person to fair copy some translations of the Greek epigrams which he had made in the preceding nights and transcribed the next morning.' See also *Life*, iv. 384, and *Works*, i. 175. Hawkins says (p. 579) Johnson alledged as a reason for these renderings 'that Henry Stephens, Buchanan, Grotius, and others had paid a like tribute to literature.'

[5] *Life*, iv. 393.

[6] Hawkins, p. 579.

[7] 'Time that on all things lays his lenient hand
Yet tames not this; it sticks to our last sand.'
Pope's *Moral Essays*, i. 224.

[8] *Life*, i. 273.

myself,

myself, gave the account which I now transmit to you in his own hand, being willing that of so great a work the history should be known, and that each writer should receive his due proportion of praise from posterity.

'I recommend to you to preserve this scrap of literary intelligence in Mr. Swinton's own hand, or to deposit it in the Museum [1], that the veracity of this account may never be doubted.

'I am, Sir,

'Your most humble servant,

Dec. 6, 1784. 'SAM. JOHNSON [2].'

On the morning of Dec. 7, Dr. Johnson requested to see Mr. Nichols [3]. A few days before, he had borrowed some of the early volumes of the Magazine, with a professed intention to point out the pieces which he had written in that collection. The books lay on the table, with many leaves doubled down, and in particular those which contained his share in the Parliamentary Debates. Such was the goodness of Johnson's heart, that he then declared, that 'those debates were the only parts of his writings which gave him any compunction; but that at the time he wrote them he had no conception that he was imposing upon the world, though they were frequently written from very slender materials, and often from none at all, the mere coinage of his own imagination [4].' He added, 'that he never wrote any part of his work with equal velocity. Three columns of the Magazine in an hour,' he said, 'was no uncommon effort; which was faster than most persons could have transcribed that quantity.

[1] It is there deposited. J. N. [Note by Murphy.]

[2] *Life*, iv. 381. In note 1 on *Letters*, ii. 431, I wrongly state that this letter was first published in Malone's *Boswell*. It appeared earlier in Murphy's *Essay*.

The list of authors which I omit will be found in *Letters*, ii. 432.

[3] Boswell gives part of what follows but not all; on the other hand he inserts particulars which Murphy has omitted. *Life*, iv. 407.

[4] *Ib.* i. 501. Nichols, in the Preface to the *Gentleman's Magazine* for 1784, says:—'It must indeed be owned that the Debates in Parliament, since they have been retailed genuine day after day in the newspapers, have become much less interesting than when formerly fabricated by "Dr. Johnson in his garret."'

In

In one day in particular, and that not a very long one, he wrote twelve pages, more in quantity than he ever wrote at any other time, except in the Life of Savage, of which forty-eight pages in octavo were the production of one long day, including a part of the night [1].'

In the course of the conversation, he asked, whether any of the family of Faden the printer were living. Being told that the geographer near Charing-cross was Faden's son, he said, after a short pause, 'I borrowed a guinea of his father near thirty years ago; be so good as to take this, and pay it for me [2].'

Wishing to discharge every duty, and every obligation, Johnson recollected another debt of ten pounds, which he had borrowed from his friend Mr. Hamilton [3] the printer, about twenty years before. He sent the money to Mr. Hamilton at his house in Bedford Row, with an apology for the length of time. The Reverend Mr. Strahan was the bearer of the message, about four or five days before Johnson breathed his last.

Mr. Sastres (whom Dr. Johnson esteemed and mentioned in his will [4]) entered the room during his illness. Dr. Johnson, as soon as he saw him, stretched forth his hand, and, in a tone of lamentation, called out, JAM MORITURUS [5]! But the love of life

[1] 'I wrote forty-eight of the printed octavo pages of the *Life of Savage* at a sitting; but then I sat up all night. I have also written six sheets in a day of translation from the French.' *Life*, v. 67. Six sheets would be ninety-six octavo pages.

[2] *Ib.* iv. 440; Nichols's *Lit. Anec.*, ii. 554. Faden the printer was the editor of *The Literary Magazine*, for which Johnson wrote in 1756. Hawkins, p. 252.

[3] *Ante*, p. 412.

[4] 'To Mr. Sastres, the Italian master, the sum of five pounds to be laid out in books of piety for his own use.' *Life*, iv. 402, *n.* 2.

[5] Hawkins records on December 13 (p. 590):—'At eight in the evening word was brought me by Mr. Sastres, to whom in his last moments he uttered these words, "Jam moriturus," that at a quarter past seven he had without a groan, or the least sign of pain or uneasiness, yielded his last breath.'

According to the account which Boswell had received, the last words he uttered were to a young lady, who asked his blessing. 'He turned himself in his bed and said, "God bless you, my dear."' *Life*, iv. 418. That his words to her were not quite his last words is shown by Mr. Hoole's account. Croker's *Boswell*, ix. 191.

was

was still an active principle. Feeling himself swelled with the dropsy, he conceived that, by incisions in his legs, the water might be discharged. Mr. Cruikshank apprehended that a mortification might be the consequence; but, to appease a distempered fancy, he gently lanced the surface. Johnson cried out, 'Deeper, deeper; I want length of life, and you are afraid of giving me pain, which I do not value [1].'

On the 8th of December, the Reverend Mr. Strahan drew his will [2], by which, after a few legacies, the residue, amounting to about fifteen hundred pounds, was bequeathed to Frank, the Black servant, formerly consigned to the testator by his friend Dr. Bathurst [3].

The history of a death-bed is painful. Mr. Strahan informs us, that the strength of religion prevailed against the infirmity of nature; and his foreboding dread of the Divine Justice subsided into a pious trust and humble hope of mercy at the Throne of Grace [4]. On Monday the 13th day of December (the last of his existence on this side the grave), the desire of life returned with all its former vehemence. He still imagined, that, by puncturing his legs relief might be obtained. At eight in the morning he tried the experiment, but no water followed [5]. In an hour or two after, he fell into a doze, and about seven in the evening, expired without a groan.

On the 20th of the month his remains, with due solemnities, and a numerous attendance of his friends, were buried in Westminster Abbey, near the foot of Shakspeare's monument,

[1] *Life*, iv. 399; Hawkins, p. 592. To Dr. Brocklesby a few days earlier he had said:—'How many men in a year die through the timidity of those whom they consult for health! I want length of life, and you fear giving me pain, which I care not for.' Hawkins, p. 588. See *Life*, iv. 409.

[2] Strahan was only his amanuensis. Hawkins records on December 9 (p. 588):—'I found him dictating to Mr. Strahan another will, the former [*ib.* pp. 576, 580–3] being, as he had said at the time of making it, a temporary one.'

[3] *Life*, iv. 401, 441.

[4] *Prayers and Meditations*, Preface, p. 15; *Life*, iv. 416.

[5] *Life*, iv. 399, 418, *n.* 1.

and close to the grave of the late Mr. Garrick [1]. The funeral service was read by his friend Dr. Taylor [2].

A black marble over his grave has the following inscription:

SAMUEL JOHNSON, LL.D.
obiit XIII die Decembris,
Anno Domini
MDCCLXXXIV.
Ætatis suæ LXXV.

If we now look back, as from an eminence, to view the scenes of life, and the literary labours in which Dr. Johnson was engaged, we may be able to delineate the features of the man, and to form an estimate of his genius.

As a man, Dr. Johnson stands displayed in open day-light. Nothing remains undiscovered [3]. Whatever he said is known; and without allowing him the usual privilege of hazarding

[1] *Life*, iv. 419; *Letters*, ii. 434.

Close to Johnson's grave is one to Sir Archibald Campbell, who, among other distinctions, was 'heretable usher of the white rod.' In Chester's *Westminster Abbey Registry*, p. 438, the entry next before Johnson's interment is, 'Dec. 18 Elizabeth Broughton, wife of John Broughton the celebrated pugilist.' She was buried in the cloisters. The pugilist himself was buried there a few years later. In 1750 he had been beaten in 'a grand boxing-match by Slack the butcher of Norwich.' *Gentleman's Magazine*, 1750, p. 184.

[2] In a note on Johnson's last letter to Taylor dated October 23, 1784 (*Letters*, ii. 426), I quote Taylor's endorsement:—'My answer . . . he resented extremely.' I add Mrs. Piozzi's statement that on account of this answer, 'Dr. Johnson quarrelled with his truest friend, Dr. Taylor.' The quarrel had been made up. See *post*, in Mr. Hoole's *Anecdotes*.

'A dissatisfaction was expressed in the public papers that he was not buried with all possible funeral rites and honours. The executors did not think themselves justified in doing more than they did. For only a little cathedral service, accompanied with light and music, would have raised the price of interment. In this matter fees run high. His funeral expenses amounted to more than £200.' *Gentleman's Magazine*, 1785, p. 86.

It was owing to the expense of the funeral that Goldsmith's body lies in an unknown grave in the Temple Churchyard, and not in Westminster Abbey. Goldsmith's *Works*, ed. 1801, i. 115.

[3] *Ante*, p. 296.

 sentiments,

sentiments, and advancing positions, for mere amusement, or the pleasure of discussion, Criticism has endeavoured to make him answerable for what, perhaps, he never seriously thought [1]. His diary, which has been printed, discovers still more. We have before us the very heart of the man, with all his inward consciousness. And yet neither in the open paths of life, nor in his secret recesses, has any one vice been discovered. We see him reviewing every year of his life, and severely censuring himself, for not keeping resolutions, which morbid melancholy, and other bodily infirmities, rendered impracticable. We see him for every little defect imposing on himself voluntary penance, going through the day with only one cup of tea without milk [2], and to the last, amidst paroxysms and remissions of illness, forming plans of study and resolutions to amend his life [3]. Many of his scruples may be called weaknesses; but they are the weaknesses of a good, a pious, and most excellent man.

His person, it is well known, was large and unwieldy [4]. His

[1] 'He appeared to have a pleasure in contradiction, especially when any opinion whatever was delivered with an air of confidence; so that there was hardly any topick, if not one of the great truths of Religion and Morality, that he might not have been incited to argue, either for or against.' *Life*, iii. 24.

[2] 'His prayers for the dead and his minute account of the rigour with which he observed church fasts, whether he drank tea or coffee, whether with sugar or without, and whether one or two dishes of either, are the most important items to be found in this childish register of the great Johnson, supreme dictator in the chair of literature, and almost a driveller in his closet.' Cowper's *Works*, ed. 1836, v. 152.

'Yet he was himself under the tyranny of scruples as unreasonable as those of Hudibras or Ralpho. . . . He has gravely noted down in his diary that he once committed the sin of drinking coffee on Good Friday. . . . . With what a storm of invective he would have overwhelmed any man who had blamed him for celebrating the redemption of mankind with sugarless tea and butterless buns.' Macaulay's *Essays*, ed. 1843, i. 394.

Cowper was unaware that his own state was far worse than Johnson's, whose superstition was tempered by great laxness of practice. 'The *sin* of drinking coffee' is in Macaulay's article but not in Johnson's diary. See *ante*, p. 75.

[3] *Life*, iv. 134. *Ante*, p. 99.

In 1764 he recorded:—'I have now spent fifty-five years in resolving.' *Ante*, p. 31.

[4] The author of the *Life of Dr. Johnson*, published by Kearsley, says, p. 87:—'His face was composed of large coarse features, which from a studious turn when composed looked

nerves

nerves were affected by that disorder, for which, at two years of age, he was presented to the royal touch[1]. His head shook, and involuntary motions made it uncertain that his legs and arms would, even at a tea-table, remain in their proper place[2]. A person of Lord Chesterfield's delicacy might in his company be in a fever[3]. He would sometimes of his own accord do things inconsistent with the established modes of behaviour. Sitting at table with the celebrated Mrs. Cholmondeley, who exerted herself to circulate the subscription for Shakspeare[4], he took hold of her hand in the middle of dinner, and held it close to his eye, wondering at the delicacy and the whiteness, till with a smile she asked, *Will he give it to me again when he has done with it?* The exteriors of politeness did not belong to Johnson. Even that civility which proceeds, or ought to proceed, from the mind, was sometimes violated. His morbid melancholy had an effect on his temper; his passions were irritable; and the pride of science, as well as of a fierce independent spirit, inflamed him on some occasions above all bounds of moderation. Though not in the shade of academic bowers[5], he led a scholastic life; and the habit of pronouncing decisions to his friends and visitors gave him a dictatorial manner, which was much enforced by a voice naturally loud, and often overstretched[6]. Metaphysical discussion, moral theory, systems of religion, and anecdotes of literature, were his favourite topics[7]. General history had little of his regard. Biography was his delight[8]. *The proper study of mankind is*

sluggish, yet awful and contemplative. . . . His face however was capable of great expression both in respect to *intelligence* and *mildness*, as all those can witness who have seen him in the flow of conversation or under the influence of grateful feelings.'

[1] *Ante*, pp. 133, 152.

[2] *Life*, i. 144; v. 18.

[3] Chesterfield, in the passage wrongly applied to Johnson (*ante*, p. 384), describing Lord Lyttelton, had said:—'I am almost in a fever whenever I am in his company.' Chesterfield's *Letters to his Son*, iii. 129.

[4] To get subscribers, that is to say, for his edition of *Shakespeare*. *Letters*, i. 68. For Mrs. Cholmondely, see *ib.* ii. 186, *n.* 3; *Life*, iii. 318.

[5] 'Under the shelter of academic bowers.' *Works*, v. 51. *Ante*, p. 405.

[6] Boswell mentions 'his deliberate and strong utterance.' *Life*, ii. 326; 'his loud voice and slow deliberate utterance.' *Ib.* iv. 429.

[7] *Ante*, p. 201.

[8] 'MONBODDO. "The history of manners is the most valuable. I never set a high value on any other history." JOHNSON. "Nor I; and

 man.

man[1]. Sooner than hear of the Punic war, he would be rude to the person that introduced the subject[2].

Johnson was born a logician; one of those, to whom only books of logic are said to be of use. In consequence of his skill in that art, he loved argumentation. No man thought more profoundly, nor with such acute discernment. A fallacy could not stand before him: it was sure to be refuted by strength of reasoning, and a precision both in idea and expression almost unequalled. When he chose by apt illustration to place the argument of his adversary in a ludicrous light, one was almost inclined to think *ridicule the test of truth*[3]. He was surprized to be told, but it is certainly true, that, with great powers of mind, wit and humour were his shining talents[4]. That he often argued for the sake of a triumph over his adversary, cannot be dissembled[5]. Dr. Rose[6], of Chiswick, has been heard to tell of a friend of his, who thanked him for introducing him to Dr. Johnson, as he had been convinced, in the course of a long dispute, that an opinion which he had embraced as a settled truth, was no better than a vulgar error. This being reported

therefore I esteem biography, as giving us what comes near to ourselves, what we can turn to use."' *Life*, v. 79. 'The biographical part of literature,' he said, 'is what I love most.' *Ib.* i. 425.

[1] Pope, *Essay on Man*, ii. 2.

[2] *Ante*, p. 202.

[3] 'Truth, 'tis suppos'd, may bear *all* Lights: and one of those principal Lights or natural Mediums by which Things are to be view'd, in order to a thorow Recognition, is *Ridicule* it-self, or that Manner of Proof by which we discern whatever is liable to just Raillery in any subject. . . . . Without Wit and Humour *Reason* can hardly have its proof, or be distinguish'd.' Shaftesbury's *Characteristics*, ed. 1714, i. 61, 73.

For Warburton's argument that 'reason is the test of ridicule and not ridicule the test of truth,' see *The Divine Legation*, ed. 1765, i. Dedication, p. 15.

'It is commonly said, and more particularly by Lord Shaftesbury, that ridicule is the best test of truth, for that it will not stick where it is not just. I deny it. A truth learned in a certain light, and attacked in certain words, by men of wit and humour, may, and often doth, become ridiculous, at least so far that the truth is only remembered and repeated for the sake of the ridicule.' Chesterfield's *Letters*, iii. 260.

'Akenside adopted Shaftesbury's foolish assertion of the efficacy of ridicule for the discovery of truth.' Johnson's *Works*, viii. 470.

[4] *Ante*, p. 287.

[5] *Ante*, p. 185.

[6] *Ante*, p. 419.

to

to Johnson, 'Nay,' said he, 'do not let him be thankful, for he was right, and I was wrong.' Like his uncle Andrew, in the ring at Smithfield, Johnson, in a circle of disputants, was determined *neither to be thrown nor conquered*[1]. Notwithstanding all his piety, self-government, or the command of his passions in conversation, does not seem to have been among his attainments. Whenever he thought the contention was for superiority, he has been known to break out with violence, and even ferocity. When the fray was over, he generally softened into repentance, and, by conciliating measures, took care that no animosity should be left rankling in the breast of his antagonist[2]. Of this defect he seems to have been conscious. In a letter to Mrs. Thrale[3], he says, 'Poor Baretti! do not quarrel with him; to neglect him a little will be sufficient. He means only to be frank and manly, and independent, and, perhaps, as you say, a little wise. To be frank, he thinks, is to be cynical; and to be independent, is to be rude. Forgive him, dearest lady, the rather, because of his misbehaviour I am afraid he learned part of me. I hope to set him hereafter a better example.' For his own intolerant and overbearing spirit he apologized by observing, that it had done some good; obscenity and impiety were repressed in his company[4].

It was late in life before he had the habit of mixing, otherwise than occasionally, with polite company[5]. At Mr. Thrale's he

[1] *Ante*, p. 49.

[2] 'Goldsmith sat silently brooding over Johnson's reprimand to him after dinner. Johnson perceived this, and said aside to some of us, "I'll make Goldsmith forgive me;" and then called to him in a loud voice, "Dr. Goldsmith,—something passed to-day where you and I dined; I ask your pardon." Goldsmith answered placidly, "It must be much from you, Sir, that I take ill." And so at once the difference was over.' *Life*, ii. 256. See *post*, in Miss Reynolds's *Recollections*, and in Sir Joshua Reynolds's *Character of Johnson*.

[3] *Letters*, i. 350.

[4] *Life*, iv. 295.

[5] 'Before his arrival in town he was but little accustomed to free conversation with his superiors.' Hawkins, p. 164. Boswell, speaking of the best families at Lichfield, says:—'In these families he passed much time in his early years. In most of them he was in the company of ladies . . . so that the notion which has been industriously circulated and believed that he never was in good company till late in life . . . is wholly without foundation.' *Life*, i. 82. See *post*, in Percy's *Anecdotes*.

saw

saw a constant succession of well-accomplished visitors. In that society he began to wear off the rugged points of his own character. He saw the advantages of mutual civility, and endeavoured to profit by the models before him [1]. He aimed at what has been called by Swift the *lesser morals*, and by Cicero *minores virtutes* [2]. His endeavour, though new and late, gave pleasure to all his acquaintance. Men were glad to see that he was willing to be communicative on equal terms and reciprocal complacence. The time was then expected when he was to cease being what George Garrick, brother to the celebrated actor, called him the first time he heard him converse, 'A TREMENDOUS COMPANION [3].' He certainly wished to be polite, and even thought himself so [4]; but his civility still retained something uncouth and harsh. His manners took a milder tone, but the endeavour was too palpably seen. He laboured even in trifles [5]. He was a giant gaining a *purchase* [6] to lift a feather.

It is observed by the younger Pliny, that in the confines of virtue and great qualities there are generally vices of an opposite nature. In Dr. Johnson not one ingredient can take the name of vice. From his attainments in literature grew the pride of

[1] *Life*, i. 495; iii. 325; *ante*, p. 318.

[2] 'Those inferiour duties of life, which the French call *les petites morales*, or the smaller morals, are with us distinguished by the name of good manners or breeding.' Swift, *Tatler*, No. 20.

'Great talents and great virtues (if you should have them) will procure you the respect and the admiration of mankind; but it is the lesser talents, the *leniores virtutes*, which must procure you their love and affection.' Chesterfield's *Letters*, ii. 304.

'To kinder skies, where gentler
manners reign,
I turn.' *The Traveller*, l. 239.

[3] *Life*, iii. 139. George Garrick had been Johnson's pupil. *Ib.* i. 97. 'He died two days after his brother's funeral. His first question on his entering the theatre after a temporary absence was invariably, "Has my brother wanted me?" Old Charles Bannister, with a sort of tender pleasantry, when he heard of his death said, "His brother wanted him."' *Garrick Corres.*, vol. i. Preface, p. 62.

[4] '"Sir, I look upon myself as a very polite man;" and he was right in a proper manly sense of the word.' *Life*, v. 363. See also *ib.* iii. 337, and *ante*, p. 168.

[5] 'It appears to me that I labour when I say a good thing.' *Ib.* v. 76.

[6] *Purchase* used in this sense is not in Johnson's *Dictionary*.

of knowledge; and from his powers of reasoning, the love of disputation and the vain-glory of superior vigour. His piety, in some instances, bordered on superstition. He was willing to believe in preternatural agency, and thought it not more strange that there should be evil spirits than evil men [1]. Even the question about second-sight held him in suspense. 'Second-sight,' Mr. Pennant tells us, 'is a power of seeing images impressed on the organs of sight by the power of fancy, or on the fancy by the disordered spirits operating on the mind. It is the faculty of seeing spectres or visions, which represent an event actually passing at a distance, or likely to happen at a future day. In 1771, a gentleman, the last who was supposed to be possessed of this faculty, had a boat at sea in a tempestuous night, and, being anxious for his freight, suddenly started up, and said his men would be drowned, for he had seen them pass before him with wet garments and dropping locks. The event corresponded with his disordered fancy. And thus,' continues Mr. Pennant, 'a distempered imagination, clouded with anxiety, may make an impression on the spirits; as persons, restless and troubled with indignation, see various forms and figures while they lie awake in bed [2].' This is what Dr. Johnson was not willing to reject [3]. He wished for some positive proof of communications with another world [4]. His benevolence embraced the whole race of man, and yet was tinctured with particular prejudices. He was pleased with the minister in the Isle of Sky, and loved him so much that he began to wish him not a Presbyterian [5].

[1] *Life*, v. 45.

[2] Apparently quoted from Pennant's *Tour in Scotland*, 1769, 4th ed., p. 198.

[3] Johnson (*Works*, ix. 107) thus sums up his examination of second-sight:—'There is against it, the seeming analogy of things confusedly seen, and little understood; and for it, the indistinct cry of natural persuasion, which may be, perhaps, resolved at last into prejudice and tradition. I never could advance my curiosity to conviction; but came away at last only willing to believe.'

[4] Speaking of 'Thomas Lord Lyttelton's vision' he said:—'"I am so glad to have every evidence of the spiritual world that I am willing to believe it." DR. ADAMS. "You have evidence enough; good evidence, which needs not such support." JOHNSON. "I like to have more."' *Life*, iv. 298.

[5] Johnson wrote of the ministers:—'I saw not one in the islands whom I had reason to think either deficient in learning, or irregular in life; but found several with whom I could not converse without wishing, as my re-

To that body of Dissenters his zeal for the Established Church made him in some degree an adversary; and his attachment to a mixed and limited Monarchy led him to declare open war against what he called a sullen Republican [1]. He would rather praise a man of Oxford than of Cambridge [2]. He disliked a Whig, and loved a Tory. These were the shades of his character, which it has been the business of certain party-writers to represent in the darkest colours [3].

Since virtue, or moral goodness, consists in a just conformity of our actions to the relations in which we stand to the Supreme Being and to our fellow-creatures, where shall we find a man who has been, or endeavoured to be, more diligent in the discharge of those essential duties? His first prayer was composed in 1738; he continued those fervent ejaculations of piety to the end of his life. In his meditations we see him scrutinizing himself with severity, and aiming at perfection unattainable by man. His duty to his neighbour consisted in universal benevolence, and a constant aim at the production of happiness. Who was more sincere and steady in his friendships? It has been said that there was no real affection between him and Garrick [4]. On the part of the latter, there might be some corrosions of jealousy. The character of PROSPERO, in the Rambler, N°. 200, was, beyond all question, occasioned by Garrick's ostentatious display of furniture and Dresden china [5]. It was surely fair to take from this incident a hint for a moral

spect increased, that they had not been Presbyterians.' *Works*, ix. 102.

It was the Rev. Donald M'Queen whom he loved so much. *Life*, v. 257.

[1] 'Milton's political notions were those of an acrimonious and surly republican.' *Works*, vii. 116.

[2] *Ante*, p. 168.

[3] 'Against his *Life of Milton* the hounds of Whiggism have opened in full cry.' *Life*, iv. 40.

[4] Hawkins, p. 425; Hawkins adds (p. 426), that 'Johnson's behaviour to Garrick was ever austere, like that of a schoolmaster to one of his scholars.' Percy says that 'Johnson kept Garrick much in awe.' *Life*, i. 99, *n*. 1. Boswell describes how one evening 'Garrick played round Johnson with a fond vivacity, taking hold of the breasts of his coat, and, looking up in his face with a lively archness, complimented him on the good health which he seemed then to enjoy; while the sage, shaking his head, beheld him with a gentle complacency.' *Ib*. ii. 82.

[5] *Ib*. i. 216.

essay;

essay; and, though no more was intended, Garrick, we are told, remembered it with uneasiness. He was also hurt that his Lichfield friend did not think so highly of his dramatic art as the rest of the world. The fact was, Johnson could not see the passions as they rose and chased one another in the varied features of that expressive face; and by his own manner of reciting verses, which was wonderfully impressive [1], he plainly shewed that he thought there was too much of artificial tone and measured cadence in the declamation of the theatre. The present writer well remembers being in conversation with Dr. Johnson near the side of the scenes during the tragedy of King Lear: when Garrick came off the stage, he said, 'You two talk so loud you destroy all my feelings.' 'Prithee,' replied Johnson, 'do not talk of feelings, Punch has no feelings [2].' This seems to have been his settled opinion; admirable as Garrick's imitation of nature always was, Johnson thought it no better than mere mimickry. Yet it is certain that he esteemed and loved Garrick; that he dwelt with pleasure on his praise; and used to declare, that he deserved his great success, because on all applications for charity he gave more than was asked [3].' After

[1] *Ante*, p. 347.

[2] *Life*, iv. 7, 243; v. 38. *Post*, in Reynolds's *Dialogues*.

Johnson in two notes on *A Midsummer Night's Dream*, Act i. sc. 4, ridicules the players. 'Bottom, who is generally acknowledged the principal actor, declares his inclination to be for a tyrant, for a part of fury, tumult and noise, such as every young man pants to perform when he first steps upon the stage. The same Bottom, who seems bred in a tiring-room, has another histrionical passion. He is for engrossing every part, and would exclude his inferiors from all possibility of distinction. . . . Here Bottom again discovers a true genius for the Stage by his solicitude for propriety of dress, and his deliberation which beard to chuse among many beards all unnatural.'

Adam Smith wrote of players:—'It seems absurd at first sight that we should despise their persons, and yet reward their talents with the most profuse liberality.' *Wealth of Nations*, Bk. i. ch. 10. See also *ib.*, Bk. ii. ch. 3.

This was written, though not published, before he joined the Literary Club, where he met Garrick, who pronounced his conversation *flabby*. *Life*, iv. 24, *n.* 2. In *Gil Blas*, Bk. iii. chs. 11 and 12, is shown why an author so often despises actors.

[3] Murphy (*Life of Garrick*, p. 378) says:—'Dr. Johnson often said that, when he saw a worthy family in distress, it was his custom to collect charity among such of his friends as he knew to be affluent; and on those occasions he received from Garrick more than from any other person,

Garrick's

Garrick's death he never talked of him without a tear in his eyes [1]. He offered, if Mrs. Garrick would desire it of him, to be the editor of his works and the historian of his life [2]. It has been mentioned that on his death-bed he thought of writing a Latin inscription to the memory of his friend [3]. Numbers are still living who know these facts, and still remember with gratitude the friendship which he shewed to them with unaltered affection for a number of years [4]. His humanity and generosity, in proportion to his slender income, were unbounded. It has been truly said, that the lame, the blind, and the sorrowful, found in his house a sure retreat [5]. A strict adherence to truth he considered as a sacred obligation, insomuch that, in relating the most minute anecdote, he would not allow himself the smallest addition to embellish his story [6]. The late Mr. Tyers, who knew Dr. Johnson intimately, observed, 'that he always talked as if he was talking upon oath [7].' After a long acquaintance with this excellent man, and an attentive retrospect to his whole conduct, such is the light in which he appears to the writer of this essay. The following lines of Horace may be deemed his picture in miniature:

> Iracundior est paulo; minus aptus acutis
> Naribus horum hominum; rideri possit, eo quod
> Rusticius tonso toga defluit, et male laxus
> In pede calceus hæret; at est bonus, ut melior vir
> Non alius quisquam; at tibi amicus; at ingenium ingens
> Inculto latet hoc sub corpore [8].

and always more than he expected.' See also *Life*, iii. 70, 264, 387.

[1] The statement—allowing that one tear can be in two eyes—like some others of Murphy's about Johnson, is an exaggeration.

[2] Murphy (*Life of Garrick*, p. 374) says:—'Shortly after Garrick's death Johnson was told in a large company, "You are recent from the *Lives of the Poets*; why not add your friend Garrick to the number?" Johnson's answer was, "I do not like to be officious; but if Mrs. Garrick will desire me to do it, I shall be very willing to pay that last tribute to the memory of a man I loved."' Murphy adds that he himself took care that Mrs. Garrick was informed of what Johnson had said, but that no answer was ever received.

[3] *Ante*, p. 445.

[4] *Ante*, pp. 279, 421.

[5] *Ante*, p. 205.

[6] *Ante*, p. 225.

[7] *Life*, ii. 434; iii. 308.

[8] 'Your friend is passionate; perhaps unfit
For the brisk petulance of modern wit.

It

It remains to give a review of Johnson's works; and this, it is imagined, will not be unwelcome to the reader.

Like Milton and Addison, he seems to have been fond of his Latin poetry[1]. Those compositions shew that he was an early scholar; but his verses have not the graceful ease that gave so much suavity to the poems of Addison. The translation of the Messiah labours under two disadvantages; it is first to be compared with Pope's inimitable performance[2], and afterwards with the Pollio of Virgil. It may appear trifling to remark, that he has made the letter *o*, in the word *Virgo*, long and short in the same line; VIRGO, VIRGO PARIT[3]. But the translation has great merit, and some admirable lines[4]. In the odes there

His hair ill cut, his robe that aukward flows,
Or his large shoes, to raillery expose
The man you love; yet is he not possess'd
Of virtues, with which very few are blest?
While underneath this rude uncouth disguise
A genius of extensive knowledge lies.'

Francis's Horace, Book i. Sat. 3. l. 29.

'On the frame of Johnson's portrait, Mr. Beauclerk had inscribed,—

"——— *Ingenium ingens*
Inculto latet hoc sub corpore."

After Mr. Beauclerk's death, when it became Mr. Langton's property, he made the inscription be defaced. Johnson said complacently, "It was kind in you to take it off;" and then after a short pause added, "and not unkind in him to put it on."' *Life*, iv. 180.

'His versibus indicari ac velut pingi Virgilium tradit vetus interpres.' *Delphine Horace.*

[1] 'Milton was at this time [in his student days] eminently skilled in the Latin tongue; and he himself, by annexing the dates to his first compositions . . . . seems to commend the earliness of his own proficiency to the notice of posterity.' *Works*, vii. 67. 'Addison's Latin compositions seem to have had much of his fondness.' *Ib.* p. 421.

[2] *Ante*, p. 362.

Pope is reported to have said:—'The writer of this poem will leave it a question for posterity, whether his or mine be the original.' Hawkins, p. 13.

[3] *Works*, i. 155, l. 10.

[4] 'This translation has been praised and magnified beyond its merits. In it are many hard and unclassical expressions, a great want of harmony, and many unequal and un-virgilian lines. I was once present at a dispute on this subject betwixt a person of great political talents, and a scholar who had spent his life among the Greek and Roman classics. Both were intimate friends of Johnson. The former, after many objections had been made to this translation by the latter, quoted a line which he thought equal to any he ever had read:—

"—juncique tremit variabilis umbra.
The green reed trembles—"

The Scholar (Pedant if you will)

is

is a sweet flexibility, particularly, To his worthy friend Dr. Laurence[1]; on himself at the theatre, March 8, 1771[2]; the Ode in the isle of Sky[3]; and that to Mrs. Thrale from the same place[4].

His English poetry is such as leaves room to think, if he had devoted himself to the Muses, that he would have been the rival of Pope. His first production in this kind was LONDON[5], a poem in imitation of the third satire of Juvenal. The vices of the metropolis are placed in the room of antient manners. The author had heated his mind with the ardour of Juvenal, and, having the skill to polish his numbers, he became a sharp accuser of the times. The VANITY OF HUMAN WISHES[6] is an imitation of the tenth satire of the same author. Though it is translated by Dryden, Johnson's imitation approaches nearest to the spirit of the original. The subject is taken from the ALCIBIADES of PLATO, and has an intermixture of the sentiments of SOCRATES concerning the object of prayers offered up to the Deity. The general proposition is, that good and evil are so little understood by mankind, that their wishes when granted are always destructive. This is exemplified in a variety of instances, such as riches, state-preferment, eloquence, military glory, long life, and the advantages of form and beauty. Juvenal's conclusion is worthy of a Christian poet, and such a pen

said there is no such word as *variabilis* in any classical writer. "Surely," said the other; "in Virgil; *variabile semper femina*." "You forget," said the opponent; "it is *varium et mutabile*."' Warton's Pope's *Works*, ed. 1822, i. 159. It is not unlikely that the two disputants were either Dr. Warton himself or his brother, and Burke.

'As we were leaving Pembroke College' (writes Thomas Warton) 'Johnson said, "Here I translated Pope's Messiah. Which do you think is the best line in it?—My own favourite is,

'*Vallis aromaticas fundit Saronica nubes.*'"

I told him, I thought it a very sonorous hexameter. I did not tell him, it was not in the Virgilian style.' *Life*, i. 272.

Johnson or Warton misquoted the line. It stands:—

'Mittit aromaticas vallis Saronica nubes.'

Husbands' *Miscellany*, p. 112, and Johnson's *Works*, i. 156.

[1] *Life*, iv. 143, *n.* 2; *Works*, i. 165.

[2] *Ante*, p. 197.

[3] *Life*, v. 155.

[4] *Ib.* v. 158; *Letters*, i. 284.

[5] *Ante*, p. 372.

[6] *Ante*, p. 386.

as

as Johnson's. 'Let us,' he says, 'leave it to the Gods to judge what is fittest for us. Man is dearer to his Creator than to himself. If we must pray for special favour, let it be for a sound mind in a sound body. Let us pray for fortitude, that we may think the labours of Hercules and all his sufferings preferable to a life of luxury and the soft repose of SARDANAPALUS. This is a blessing within the reach of every man; this we can give ourselves. It is virtue, and virtue only, that can make us happy.' In the translation the zeal of the Christian conspired with the warmth and energy of the poet; but Juvenal is not eclipsed[1]. For the various characters in the original the reader is pleased, in the English poem, to meet with Cardinal Wolsey, Buckingham stabbed by Felton, Lord Strafford, Clarendon, Charles XII. of Sweden; and for Tully and Demosthenes, Lydiat, Galileo, and Archbishop Laud. It is owing to Johnson's delight in biography that the name of LYDIAT is called forth from obscurity. It may, therefore, not be useless to tell, that LYDIAT was a learned divine and mathematician in the beginning of the last century. He attacked the doctrine of Aristotle and Scaliger, and wrote a number of sermons on the harmony of the Evangelists. With all his merit, he lay in the prison of *Bocardo* at Oxford, till Bishop Usher, Laud, and others, paid his debts. He petitioned Charles I. to be sent to Ethiopia to procure manuscripts. Having spoken in favour of monarchy and bishops, he was plundered by the Puritans, and twice carried away a prisoner from his rectory. He died very poor in 1646[2].

The Tragedy of Irene[3] is founded on a passage in KNOLLES'S

[1] 'It is in truth not easy to say whether the palm belongs to the ancient or to the modern poet. . . . It must be owned that in the concluding passage the Christian moralist has not made the most of his advantages, and has fallen decidedly short of the sublimity of his Pagan model. On the other hand, Juvenal's Hannibal must yield to Johnson's Charles; and Johnson's vigorous and pathetic enumeration of the miseries of a literary life must be allowed to be superior to Juvenal's lamentation over the fate of Demosthenes and Cicero.' Macaulay's *Misc. Works*, ed. 1871, p. 379.

[2] Murphy follows the account given as a note in the Supplement to the *Gentleman's Magazine* for 1748, quoted in the *Life*, i. 194, *n.* 2.

[3] 'A manuscript page of Macaulay's *History*, thickly scored with dashes and erasures—it is the passage

History

History of the Turks; an author highly commended in the Rambler, N°. 122[1]. An incident in the Life of Mahomet the Great, first emperor of the Turks, is the hinge on which the fable is made to move. The substance of the story is shortly this. In 1453 Mahomet laid siege to Constantinople, and, having reduced the place, became enamoured of a fair Greek, whose name was IRENE. The sultan invited her to embrace the law of the Prophet, and to grace his throne. Enraged at this intended marriage, the Janizaries formed a conspiracy to dethrone the emperor. To avert the impending danger, Mahomet, in a full assembly of the grandees, 'Catching with one hand,' as KNOLLES relates it, 'the fair Greek by the hair of her head, and drawing his falchion with the other, he, at one blow, struck off her head, to the great terror of them all; and, having so done, said unto them, Now, by this, judge whether your emperor is able to bridle his affections or not[2].' The story is simple, and it remained for the author to amplify it with proper episodes, and give it complication and variety. The catastrophe is changed, and horror gives place to terror and pity. But, after all, the fable is cold and languid. There is not, throughout the piece, a single situation to excite curiosity, and raise a conflict of passions. The diction is nervous, rich, and elegant; but splendid language, and melodious numbers, will make a fine poem, not a tragedy. The sentiments are beautiful, always happily expressed, but seldom appropriated to the character, and generally too philosophic. What Johnson has said of the Tragedy of *Cato* may be applied to Irene: 'it is rather a poem in dialogue

in the twenty-fifth chapter where Sir Hans Sloane is mentioned as "the founder of the magnificent museum which is one of the glories of our country"—is preserved at that museum in a cabinet, which may truly be called the place of honour. . . . There may be seen Nelson's hasty sketch of the line of battle at the Nile; and the sheet of paper on which Wellington computed the strength of the cavalry regiments that were to fight at Waterloo; and the note-book of Locke; and the autographs of Samuel Johnson's *Irene*, and Ben Jonson's *Masque of Queens*; and the rough copy of the translation of the Iliad, written, as Pope loved to write, on the margin of frayed letters and the backs of tattered envelopes.' Trevelyan's *Macaulay*, ed. 1877, ii. 396.

[1] *Life*, i. 100.

[2] *The General History of the Turkes*, by Richard Knolles, ed. 1603, p. 353.

than

than a drama; rather a succession of just sentiments in elegant language, than a representation of natural affections. . . . Nothing here "excites or assuages emotion." . . . The events are expected without solicitude, and are remembered without joy or sorrow. Of the agents we have no care; we consider not what they are doing, or what they are suffering; we wish only to know what they have to say. . . . It is unaffecting elegance, and chill philosophy[1].' The following speech, in the mouth of a Turk, who is supposed to have heard of the British constitution, has been often selected from the numberless beauties with which IRENE abounds:

'If there be any land, as fame reports,
Where common laws restrain the prince and subject;
A happy land, where circulating pow'r
Flows through each member of th' embodied state;
Sure, not unconscious of the mighty blessing,
Her grateful sons shine bright with ev'ry virtue;
Untainted with the LUST OF INNOVATION[2];
Sure all unite to hold her league of rule
Unbroken as the sacred chain of nature,
That links the jarring elements in peace[3].'

These are British sentiments. Above forty years ago they found an echo in the breast of applauding audiences, and to this hour they are the voice of the people, in defiance of the *meta-physics* and the *new lights* of certain politicians, who would gladly find their private advantage in the disasters of their country[4]; a race of men, *quibus nulla ex honesto spes.*

The Prologue to Irene is written with elegance, and, in a peculiar strain, shews the literary pride and lofty spirit of the author[5]. The Epilogue, we are told in a late publication, was written by Sir William Young. This is a new discovery, but

[1] *Works*, vii. 456.
'*Cato* is a fine dialogue on liberty and the love of one's country.' Warton's *Essay on Pope*, ed. 1762, i. 259.

[2] For 'the fury of innovation' from which 'Tyburn itself is not safe' see *ante*, p. 349, *n.* 4.

[3] *Irene*, Act i. sc. 2.

[4] Perhaps Priestley is one of these politicians. See *Life*, iv. 238, *n.* 1 for Boswell's attack on his doctrine of Philosophical Necessity. The *metaphysics* and the *new lights* may be a reference to Hudibras and his squire Ralph.

[5] *Life*, i. 196.

by

by no means probable[1]. When the appendages to a Dramatic Performance are not assigned to a friend, or an unknown hand, or a person of fashion, they are always supposed to be written by the author of the Play. It is to be wished, however, that the Epilogue in question could be transferred to any other writer. It is the worst *Jeu d'Esprit* that ever fell from Johnson's pen[2].

An account of the various pieces contained in this edition, such as miscellaneous tracts, and philological dissertations, would lead beyond the intended limits of this essay. It will suffice to say, that they are the productions of a man who never wanted decorations of language, and always taught his reader to think. The life of the late king of Prussia, as far as it extends[3], is a model of the biographical style. The Review of THE ORIGIN OF EVIL was, perhaps, written with asperity; but the angry epitaph, which it provoked from SOAME JENYNS, was an ill-timed resentment, unworthy of the genius of that amiable author[4].

[1] Boswell in the first edition of the *Life* says:—'The Epilogue was written by Sir William Yonge.' To the second edition he added, no doubt in answer to Murphy, 'as Johnson informed me.' *Ib.* i. 197, *n.* 4.

[2] The wonder is that Johnson accepted this Epilogue, which is a little coarse and a little profane. Chesterfield writes of Yonge as a man 'with a most sullied, not to say blasted character.' *Letters*, iv. 53.

[3] It ends with the year 1745. It was published in 1756 in *The Literary Magazine. Life*, i. 308; *Works*, vi. 435. Carlyle, in his *Frederick the Great* (ed. 1862, iii. 276), has the following about the English Lives of that king:—'One Dilworth, an innocent English soul, writing on the spot some years after Voltaire, has this useful passage:—"It is the great failing of a strong imagination to catch greedily at wonders. Voltaire was misinformed, and would perhaps learn by a second inquiry a truth less amusing and splendid. A Contribution was by News-writers, upon their own authority, fruitlessly proposed. It ended in nothing: the Parliament voted a supply." . . . "Fruitlessly by News-writers on their own authority," that is the sad fact.' In a footnote Carlyle adds:—'A poor little Book, one of many coming out on that subject just then, which contains, if available now, the above sentence and no more. Indeed its brethren, one of them by Samuel Johnson (*impransus*, the imprisoned giant) do not even contain that, and have gone wholly to zero.'

It is strange Carlyle did not see Johnson's hand in the one sentence. Dilworth stole it from him, and slightly spoilt it in the stealing. See *Works*, vi. 455; *Life*, i. 498, *n.* 4.

[4] *Life*, i. 316; *Gentleman's Magazine*, 1786, pp. 428, 696.

The

The Rambler may be considered as Johnson's great work. It was the basis of that high reputation which went on increasing to the end of his days. The circulation of those periodical essays was not, at first, equal to their merit. They had not, like the Spectators, the art of charming by variety; and indeed how could it be expected? The wits of queen Anne's reign sent their contributions to the Spectator; and Johnson stood alone. A stage-coach, says Sir Richard Steele, must go forward on stated days, whether there are passengers or not [1]. So it was with the Rambler, every Tuesday and Saturday, for two years. In this collection Johnson is the great moral teacher of his countrymen; his essays form a body of ethics; the observations on life and manners are acute and instructive; and the papers, professedly critical, serve to promote the cause of literature. It must, however, be acknowledged, that a settled gloom hangs over the author's mind; and all the essays, except eight or ten [2], coming from the same fountain-head, no wonder that they have the raciness of the soil from which they sprung. Of this uniformity Johnson was sensible. He used to say, that if he had joined a friend or two, who would have been able to intermix papers of a sprightly turn, the collection would have been more miscellaneous, and, by consequence, more agreeable to the generality of readers. This he used to illustrate by repeating two beautiful stanzas from his own Ode to Cave, or *Sylvanus Urban* [3]:

Non ulla Musis pagina gratior,
Quam quæ severis ludicra jungere
  Novit, fatigatamque nugis
    Utilibus recreare mentem.

Texente nymphis serta Lycoride,
Rosæ ruborem sic viola adjuvat
  Immista, sic Iris refulget
    Æthereis variata fucis.

[1] 'When a man has engaged to keep a stage-coach he is obliged, whether he has passengers or not, to set out. Thus it fares with us weekly historians.' *The Tatler*, No. 12.

'Such histories as these do in reality very much resemble a newspaper, which consists of just the same number of words, whether there be any news in it or not. They may likewise be compared to a stage-coach, which performs constantly the same course, empty as well as full.' *Tom Jones*, bk. ii. c. 1.

[2] *Ante*, p. 392.

[3] *Life*, i. 113; *ante*, p. 377.

It is remarkable, that the pomp of diction, which has been objected to Johnson, was first assumed in the Rambler. His Dictionary was going on at the same time, and, in the course of that work, as he grew familiar with technical and scholastic words, he thought that the bulk of his readers were equally learned; or at least would admire the splendour and dignity of the style [1]. And yet it is well known, that he praised in Cowley the ease and unaffected structure of the sentences [2]. Cowley may be placed at the head of those who cultivated a clear and natural style. Dryden [3], Tillotson [4], and Sir William Temple [5], followed. Addison, Swift, and Pope, with more correctness, carried our language well nigh to perfection [6]. Of Addison,

[1] *Life*, i. 217.

[2] 'No author ever kept his verse and his prose at a greater distance from each other. His thoughts are natural, and his style has a smooth and placid equability which has never yet obtained its due commendation. Nothing is far-sought or hard-laboured.' *Works*, vii. 55.

[3] 'Dryden does not appear to have any art other than that of expressing with clearness what he thinks with vigour. His style could not easily be imitated, either seriously or ludicrously; for being always equable and always varied it has no prominent or discriminative characters.' *Ib.* vii. 307.

[4] 'JOHNSON. I should not advise a preacher at this day to imitate Tillotson's style: though I don't know; I should be cautious of objecting to what has been applauded by so many suffrages.' *Life*, iii. 247. 'There is nothing peculiar to the language of Archbishop Tillotson, but his manner of writing is inimitable; for one who reads him wonders why he himself did not think and speak it in that very manner.' Goldsmith, *The Bee*, Nov. 24, 1759.

[5] 'Temple wrote always like a man of sense and a gentleman; and his style is the model by which the best prose writers in the reign of Queen Anne formed theirs.' Goldsmith, *The Bee*, Nov. 24, 1759.

'I have heard,' writes Dr. Warton, 'that, among works of prose, Pope was most fond of the second part of Sir William Temple's *Miscellanies*.' Warton's Pope's *Works*, i. Preface, p. 3.

Boswell recorded in his note-book: 'Dr. Johnson told me that what made him first think of forming his style as we find it was reading Sir William Temple, and of about twenty lines by Chambers of a proposal for his Dictionary.' *Morrison Autographs*, 2nd Series, i. 372. See also *Life*, i. 218, and iii. 257, where he says, 'Temple was the first writer who gave cadence to English prose.' Perhaps he had in mind Boileau's lines—

'Enfin Malherbe vint, et, le premier en France,
Fit sentir dans les vers une juste cadence.'
L'Art poëtique, c. i.

[6] For Johnson's estimate of Addison's style see *Life*, i. 225; *Works*, vii. 472; of Swift's, *Life*, ii. 191; *Works*, viii. 220; of Pope's, *Ib.* viii. 324.

Johnson

Johnson was used to say, *He is the Raphael of Essay Writers.* How he differed so widely from such elegant models is a problem not to be solved, unless it be true that he took an early tincture from the writers of the last century, particularly Sir Thomas Browne[1]. Hence the peculiarities of his style, new combinations, sentences of an unusual structure, and words derived from the learned languages. His own account of the matter is, 'When common words were less pleasing to the ear, or less distinct in their signification, I have familiarized the terms of philosophy, by applying them to popular ideas[2].' But he forgot the observation of Dryden: *If too many foreign words are poured in upon us, it looks as if they were designed, not to assist the natives, but to conquer them*[3]. There is, it must be admitted, a swell of language, often out of all proportion to the sentiment[4]; but there is, in general, a fullness of mind, and the thought seems to expand with the sound of the words. Determined to discard colloquial barbarisms and licentious idioms, he forgot the elegant simplicity that distinguishes the writings of Addison. He had what Locke calls a round-about view of his subject[5]; and, though he was never tainted, like many modern wits, with the ambition of shining in paradox[6], he may be fairly called an ORIGINAL THINKER. His reading was extensive. He treasured in his mind whatever was worthy of notice, but he added to it from his own meditation. He collected, *quæ reconderet, auctaque promeret*[7]. Addison was not so profound a thinker. He was *born to write, converse, and live with ease*[8]; and he found an early patron in Lord Somers[9]. He depended, however, more

[1] *Life*, i. 221.

[2] *Ib.* i. 218; *Rambler*, No. 208.

[3] Dryden's *Works*, ed. 1808, xiv. 223.

[4] Francis Horner, speaking of Johnson's style in the *Rambler*, says:—'The rhythm dictates what is said.' Horner's *Memoirs*, ii. 454.

[5] 'Those sincerely follow reason, but for want of having large, sound, roundabout sense, have not a full view of all that relates to the question.' Locke, quoted in Johnson's *Dictionary*.

[6] *Life*, iii. 376, *n.* 1.

[7] Tacitus, *Annals*, i. 69.

[8] Pope, *Prol. Sat.*, l. 196.

[9] 'King William had no regard to elegance or literature; his study was only war; yet by a choice of ministers whose disposition was very different from his own he procured without intention a very liberal patronage to poetry. Addison was

upon a fine taste, than the vigour of his mind. His Latin Poetry shews, that he relished, with a just selection, all the refined and delicate beauties of the Roman classics; and when he cultivated his native language, no wonder that he formed that graceful style, which has been so justly admired; simple, yet elegant; adorned, yet never over-wrought; rich in allusion, yet pure and perspicuous; correct, without labour, and, though sometimes deficient in strength, yet always musical. His essays, in general, are on the surface of life; if ever original, it was in pieces of humour. Sir Roger de Coverley, and the Tory Fox-hunter [1], need not to be mentioned. Johnson had a fund of humour, but he did not know it [2], nor was he willing to descend to the familiar idiom and the variety of diction which that mode of composition required. The letter, in the Rambler, N°. 12, from a young girl that wants a place, will illustrate this observation. Addison possessed an unclouded imagination, alive to the first objects of nature and of art. He reaches the sublime without any apparent effort. When he tells us, 'If we consider the fixed stars as so many vast oceans of flame, that are each of them attended with a different set of planets; and still discover new firmaments and new lights, that are sunk farther in those unfathomable depths of æther, so as not to be seen by the strongest of our telescopes, we are lost in such a labyrinth of suns and world, and confounded with the immensity and magnificence of nature;' the ease, with which this passage rises to unaffected grandeur, is the secret charm that captivates the reader [3]. Johnson is always lofty; he seems, to use Dryden's phrase, to be o'er-inform'd with meaning [4], and his words do not appear to himself adequate to his conception. He moves in state, and his periods are always harmonious. His Oriental Tales are in the true style of Eastern magnificence [5],

caressed both by Somers and Montague.' Johnson's *Works*, vii. 423.

Addison, in *The Freeholder*, No. 39, finely describes Somers's character.

[1] *The Freeholder*, Nos. 22, 44, 47.

[2] *Ante*, pp. 287, 452.

[3] In quoting this passage, which is found in *The Spectator*, No. 420, Murphy made five errors which I have corrected.

[4] Murphy, I suppose, refers to the line in *Absalom and Achitophel*—

'And o'er-inform'd the tenement of clay.'

[5] *The Rambler*, Nos. 120, 190, 204, 205; *Idler*, Nos. 75, 99. Percy 'heard Johnson say that he thought

and

and yet none of them are so much admired as the Visions of Mirza[1]. In matters of criticism, Johnson is never the echo of preceding writers. He thinks and decides for himself. If we except the Essays on the Pleasures of Imagination, Addison cannot be called a philosophical critic[2]. His moral Essays are beautiful; but in that province nothing can exceed the Rambler, though Johnson used to say, that the Essay on *The burthens of mankind* (in the Spectator, N°. 558) was the most exquisite he had ever read. Talking of himself, Johnson said, 'Topham Beauclerk has wit, and every thing comes from him with ease; but when I say a good thing, I seem to labour[3].' When we compare him with Addison, the contrast is still stronger. Addison lends grace and ornament to truth; Johnson gives it force and energy. Addison makes virtue amiable[4]; Johnson represents it as an awful duty. Addison insinuates himself with an air of modesty; Johnson commands like a dictator[5]; but a dictator in his splendid robes, not labouring at the plough. Addison is the Jupiter of Virgil, with placid serenity talking to Venus:

'Vultu, quo cœlum tempestatesque serenat[6].'

The Vision of Theodore the Hermit was the best thing he ever wrote.' *Life*, i. 192.

[1] *Spectator*, No. 159. Unfortunately Addison's promise was never fulfilled, and of 'The Visions of Mirzah' he gave but one.

[2] *Ib.* Nos. 411-421. 'Addison is now to be considered as a critick; a name which the present generation is scarcely willing to allow him. His criticism is condemned as tentative or experimental rather than scientifick; and he is considered as deciding by taste rather than by principles.' *Works*, vii. 469. Johnson was referring to Warburton, who said that 'Addison was but an ordinary poet and a worse critic,' and to Hurd, who condemned his want of the 'chastised philosophical spirit.' Warton's Pope's *Works*, ed. 1822, i. 230; iv. 179.

[3] *Life*, v. 76.

[4] 'Addison has dissipated the prejudice that had long connected gaiety with vice, and easiness of manners with laxity of principles. . . . All the enchantment of fancy and all the cogency of argument are employed to recommend to the reader his real interest, the care of pleasing the author of his being. . . . Truth wears a thousand dresses, and in all is pleasing.' *Works*, vii. 451, 472.

[5] 'As it has been my principal design to inculcate wisdom or piety, I have allotted few papers to the idle sports of imagination. . . . Scarcely any man is so steadily serious as not to complain that the severity of dictatorial instruction has been too seldom relieved.' *Rambler*, No. 208.

[6] *Aeneid*, i. 255.

Johnson is JUPITER TONANS: he darts his lightning, and rolls his thunder, in the cause of virtue and piety. The language seems to fall short of his ideas; he pours along, familiarizing the terms of philosophy [1], with bold inversions, and sonorous periods; but we may apply to him what Pope has said of Homer: 'It is the sentiment that swells and fills out the diction, which rises with it, and forms itself about it; .... like glass in the furnace, which grows to a greater magnitude, ... as the breath within is more powerful, and the heat more intense [2].'

It is not the design of this comparison to decide between those two eminent writers. In matters of taste every reader will chuse for himself [3]. Johnson is always profound, and of course gives the fatigue of thinking. Addison charms while he instructs; and writing, as he always does, a pure, an elegant, and idiomatic style, he may be pronounced the safest model for imitation.

The essays written by Johnson in the Adventurer may be called a continuation of the Rambler [4]. The IDLER, in order to be consistent with the assumed character, is written with abated vigour, in a style of ease and unlaboured elegance. It is the Odyssey after the Iliad [5]. Intense thinking would not become the IDLER. The first number presents a well-drawn portrait of an

[1] 'When common words were less pleasing to the ear, or less distinct in their signification, I have familiarized the terms of philosophy by applying them to popular ideas.' *Rambler*, No. 208.

[2] Pope's Homer's *Iliad*, ed. 1760, i. Preface, p. 20.

[3] Johnson wrote in 1781:—'Whoever wishes to attain an English style, familiar but not coarse, and elegant but not ostentatious, must give his days and nights to the volumes of Addison.' *Works*, vii. 473. Hawkins, in 1787 (p. 270), said:—'The characteristics of Mr. Addison's style are feebleness and inanity.' Four years later Boswell wrote:—'It has of late been the fashion to compare the style of Addison and Johnson, and to depreciate, I think very unjustly, the style of Addison as nerveless and feeble, because it has not the strength and energy of that of Johnson.' *Life*, i. 224. Macaulay wrote in 1856:—'On the question of precedence between Addison and Johnson, a question which seventy years ago was much disputed, posterity has pronounced a decision from which there is no appeal.' *Misc. Works*, ed. 1871, p. 381.

[4] *Life*, i. 255.

[5] 'The *Idler* may be described as a second part of the *Rambler*, somewhat livelier and somewhat weaker than the first part.' Macaulay's *Misc. Works*, p. 383.

an Idler, and from that character no deviation could be made. Accordingly, Johnson forgets his austere manner, and plays us into sense. He still continues his lectures on human life, but he adverts to common occurrences, and is often content with the topic of the day. An advertisement in the beginning of the first volume informs us, that twelve entire Essays were a contribution from different hands [1]. One of these, N°. 33, is the journal of a Senior Fellow at Cambridge, but, as Johnson, being himself an original thinker, always revolted from servile imitation, he has printed the piece, with an apology, importing that the journal of a citizen in the *Spectator* almost precluded the attempt of any subsequent writer [2]. This account of the Idler may be closed, after observing, that the author's mother being buried on the 23d of January 1759, there is an admirable paper, occasioned by that event, on Saturday the 27th of the same month, N°. 41 [3]. The reader, if he pleases, may compare it with another fine paper in the Rambler, N°. 54, on the conviction that rushes on the mind at the bed of a dying friend [4].

'Rasselas,' says Sir John Hawkins, 'is a specimen of our language scarcely to be paralleled; it is written in a style refined to a degree of *immaculate purity*, and displays the whole force of *turgid* eloquence [5].' One cannot but smile at this encomium. Rasselas is undoubtedly both elegant and sublime. It is a view of human life, displayed, it must be owned, in gloomy colours. The author's natural melancholy, depressed, at the time, by the approaching dissolution of his mother, darkened the picture [6]. A tale, that should keep curiosity awake by the artifice of unexpected incidents, was not the design of a mind pregnant with better things. He, who reads the heads of the chapters, will find, that it is not a course of adventures that invites him forward, but a discussion of interesting questions; Reflections on Human Life; the History of *Imlac*, the Man of Learning; a Dissertation upon Poetry; the Character of a wise and happy Man, who dis-

[1] *Life*, i. 330.

[2] *Spectator*, No. 317. The author of the Journal in the *Idler* was Thomas Warton.

[3] *Life*, i. 331.

[4] *Ib.* i. 214.

[5] Hawkins, p. 368.

[6] *Ante*, p. 415.

courses

courses with energy on the government of the passions, and on a sudden, when Death deprives him of his daughter, forgets all his maxims of wisdom and the eloquence that adorned them, yielding to the stroke of affliction with all the vehemence of the bitterest anguish. It is by pictures of life, and profound moral reflection, that expectation is engaged and gratified throughout the work. The History of the Mad Astronomer, who imagines that, for five years, he possessed the regulation of the weather, and that the sun passed from tropic to tropic by his direction, represents in striking colours the sad effects of a distempered imagination. It becomes the more affecting, when we recollect that it proceeds from one, who lived in fear of the same dreadful visitation; from one who says emphatically, 'Of the uncertainties of our present state, the most dreadful and alarming is the uncertain continuance of reason [1].' The enquiry into the cause of madness, and the dangerous prevalence of imagination, till, in time, some particular train of ideas fixes the attention, and the mind recurs constantly to the favourite conception, is carried on in a strain of acute observation; but it leaves us room to think, that the author was transcribing from his own apprehensions. The discourse on the nature of the soul gives us all that philosophy knows, not without a tincture of superstition [2]. It is remarkable that the vanity of human pursuits was, about the same time, the subject that employed both Johnson and Voltaire [3]; but *Candide* is the work of a lively imagination, and Rasselas, with all its splendour of eloquence, exhibits a gloomy picture. It should, however, be remembered, that the world has known the WEEPING as well as the LAUGHING philosopher.

The Dictionary does not properly fall within the province of this essay [4]. The preface, however, will be found in this

[1] *Rasselas*, ch. 43; *Life*, i. 66.

[2] *Rasselas*, ch. 48. There is not a single line in which a believer in the immortality of the soul would find this 'tincture.'

[3] *Life*, i. 342; vi. Addenda, p. 29; *Letters*, i. 79.

[4] Boswell, after quoting some humorous definitions, adds that Johnson said to him:—'You know, Sir, Lord Gower forsook the old Jacobite interest. When I came to the word *Renegado*, after telling that it meant "one who deserts to the enemy, a revolter," I added, *Sometimes we say a* GOWER. Thus it went to the

edition

edition. He who reads the close of it, without acknowledging the force of the pathetic and sublime, must have more insensibility in his composition than usually falls to the share of man[1]. The work itself, though in some instances abuse has been loud, and in others malice has endeavoured to undermine its fame, still remains the MOUNT ATLAS of English Literature.

> Though storms and tempests thunder on its brow,
> And oceans break their billows at its feet,
> It stands unmov'd, and glories in its height[2].

That Johnson was eminently qualified for the office of a commentator on Shakspeare, no man can doubt; but it was an office which he never cordially embraced[3]. The publick expected more than he had diligence to perform; and yet his edition has been the ground on which every subsequent commentator has chose to build. One note, for its singularity, may be thought worthy of notice in this place. Hamlet says, *For if the sun breed maggots in a dead dog, being a God-kissing carrion*[4]. In this Warburton discovered the *origin of evil.* Hamlet, he says, breaks off in the middle of the sentence; but the learned commentator knows what he was going to say, and, being unwilling to keep the secret, he goes on in a train of philosophical reasoning that leaves the reader in astonishment. Johnson, with true piety, adopts the fanciful hypothesis, declaring it to be a noble emendation, which almost sets the critic on a level with the author[5]. The general observations

press; but the printer had more wit than I, and struck it out.' *Life*, i. 296. This is made clearer by the following passage in the *Lives of the Norths*, ed. 1826, iii. 73:—'Many of the Turks think that Gowers [Giaours] or unbelievers are unworthy of the knowledge of their sublime state.'

Johnson, in his *Dictionary*, under the word *Bottle* has, I think, a hit at himself. 'Bottle,' he writes, 'is often compounded with other words; as *bottle-friend*, a drinking-friend; bottle-companion. "Sam, who is a very good *bottle-companion*, has been the diversion of his friends." *Addison.*'

Stock-jobber he defines as *a low wretch who gets money by buying and selling shares in the funds.* For other definitions see *Life*, i. 294.

[1] *Ib.* i. 297, *n.* 2; *ante*, p. 405, *n.* 4.

[2] 'Thou hast seen Mount Atlas;
While storms and tempests thunder on its brows,' &c.
Addison, *Cato*, Act ii. sc. 6.

[3] *Ante*, p. 415.

[4] *Hamlet*, Act ii. sc. 2. l. 181.

[5] Warburton corrected the old

at

at the end of the several plays, and the preface, will be found in this edition. The former, with great elegance and precision, give a summary view of each drama. The preface is a tract of great erudition and philosophical criticism [1].

Johnson's political pamphlets, whatever was his motive for writing them, whether gratitude for his pension, or the solicitation of men in power [2], did not support the cause for which they were undertaken. They are written in a style truly harmonious, and with his usual dignity of language. When it is said that he advanced positions repugnant to the *common rights of mankind*, the virulence of party may be suspected. It is, perhaps, true that in the clamour raised throughout the kingdom Johnson over-heated his mind; but he was a friend to the rights of man [3], and he was greatly superior to the littleness of spirit that might incline him to advance what he did not think and firmly believe. In the *False Alarm*, though many of the most eminent men in the kingdom concurred in petitions to the throne, yet Johnson, having well surveyed the mass of the people, has given, with great humour and no less truth, what may be called, *the birth, parentage, and education of a remonstrance* [4]. On the subject of Falkland's islands, the fine dissuasive from too hastily involving the world in the calamities of war [5], must extort applause even from the party that wished, at that time, for scenes of tumult and commotion.

reading, 'Being a *good* kissing carrion,' by changing *good* into *God*. Johnson says nothing of the hypothesis, but merely remarks 'this is a noble emendation,' &c. Murphy, doubtless, is right in attributing the exaggerated praise to his piety. Mr. Dyce says:—'Warburton's emendation, if over-praised by Johnson, at least has the merit of conveying something like a meaning.'

[1] The general observations are the worst part of the edition—they are sometimes almost absurd.

'The preface, though it contains some good passages, is not in his best manner. The most valuable notes are those in which he had an opportunity of showing how attentively he had during many years observed human life and human nature. The best specimen is the note on the character of Polonius. Nothing so good is to be found even in Wilhelm Meister's admirable examination of Hamlet.' Macaulay's *Misc. Works*, 1871, p. 385.

[2] *Life*, ii. 317.

[3] *Ib.* i. 424; ii. 170.

[4] *Ib.* ii. 90, *n.* 5; *Works*, vi. 172.

[5] *Life*, ii. 134; *Works*, vi. 199.

It

It was in the same pamphlet that Johnson offered battle to JUNIUS; a writer, who, by the uncommon elegance of his style, charmed every reader, though his object was to inflame the nation in favour of a faction. Junius fought in the dark; he saw his enemy and had his full blow, while he himself remained safe in obscurity. But let us not, said Johnson, mistake the venom of the shaft for the vigour of the bow [1]. The keen invective which he published on that occasion, promised a paper-war between two combatants, who knew the use of their weapons. A battle between them was as eagerly expected as between Mendoza and Big Ben [2]. But Junius, whatever was his reason, never returned to the field. He laid down his arms, and has, ever since, remained as secret as the MAN IN THE MASK in Voltaire's History [3].

The account of his journey to the Hebrides or Western Isles of Scotland, is a model for such as shall hereafter relate their travels. The author did not visit that part of the world in the character of an Antiquary, to amuse us with wonders taken from the dark and fabulous ages; nor as a Mathematician, to measure a degree, and settle the longitude and latitude of the several islands. Those, who expected such information,

[1] *Works*, vi. 205.

[2] 'Big Ben (Mr. George C. Boase writes to me) was Benjamin Brain or Bryan, champion of England in 1790. I do not think he ever fought with Mendoza; but Mendoza succeeded him as champion in 1791. Big Ben was never beaten.' It was probably after him that the Warden of Wadham College, Oxford, of my undergraduate days, Dr. Benjamin Symons, was called 'Big Ben.'

In the *Gentleman's Magazine*, for 1787, p. 361, an account is given of a fight between Mendoza a Jew, and one Martin, a Bath butcher, in the presence of some of the first personages of the kingdom. It was decided in favour of the Jew. A year later the Prince of Wales witnessed a fight at Brighton, in which one of the men was killed. *Ib.* 1788, p. 745.

Horace Walpole wrote on June 20, 1760:—'It is a comfortable reflection to me that all the victories of last year have been gained since the suppression of the Bear Garden and prize-fighting; as it is plain, and nothing else would have made it so, that our valour did not singly and solely depend upon these two Universities.' *Letters*, iii. 320. If prize-fighting was suppressed for a time, it soon revived.

[3] *Siècle de Louis XIV*, ch. 25; *ante*, p. 172.

expected

expected what was never intended. *In every work regard the writer's end*[1]. Johnson went to see men and manners, modes of life, and the progress of civilization[2]. His remarks are so artfully blended with the rapidity and elegance of his narrative, that the reader is inclined to wish, as Johnson did with regard to GRAY, that *to travel, and to tell his travels, had been more of his employment*[3].

As to Johnson's Parliamentary Debates, nothing with propriety can be said in this place. They are collected in two volumes by Mr. Stockdale[4], and the flow of eloquence which runs through the several speeches is sufficiently known.

It will not be useless to mention two more volumes, which may form a proper supplement to this edition. They contain a set of Sermons left for publication by John Taylor, LL.D. The Reverend Mr. Hayes, who ushered these Discourses into the world, has not given them as the composition of Dr. Taylor. All he could say for his departed friend was, that he left them in silence among his papers. Mr. Hayes knew them to be the production of a superior mind; and the writer of these Memoirs owes it to the candour of that elegant scholar[5], that he is now warranted to give an additional proof of Johnson's ardour in the cause of piety, and every moral duty. The last discourse in the collection was intended to be delivered by Dr. Taylor at the funeral of Johnson's wife; but that Reverend gentleman declined the office, because, as he told Mr. Hayes, the praise of the deceased was too much amplified[6]. He, who reads the piece, will find it a beautiful moral lesson, written with temper, and no where overcharged with ambitious ornaments. The rest of the Discourses were the fund, which

1 Pope, *Essay on Criticism*, l. 255.

2 *Ante*, p. 430.

3 *Works*, viii. 480.

4 *Life*, i. 190, *n.* 4.

5 *Ib.* iii. 181.

Samuel Hayes, 'Botch Hayes, as he was denominated, for the manner in which he mended his pupil's verses,' was Southey's tutor at Westminster. 'He had some skill and much facility in versifying.' He was 'a free, good-natured, fuddling companion, whose wig the boys stuck full of paper darts in school.' Southey's *Life, &c.*, ed. 1849, i. 135.

6 *Life*, i. 241.

Dr.

Dr. Taylor, from time to time, carried with him to his pulpit. He had the LARGEST BULL in England[1], and some of the best Sermons.

We come now to the Lives of the Poets, a work undertaken at the age of seventy, yet the most brilliant, and certainly the most popular of all our Author's writings[2]. For this performance he needed little preparation. Attentive always to the history of letters, and by his own natural bias fond of Biography, he was the more willing to embrace the proposition of the Booksellers. He was versed in the whole body of English Poetry, and his rules of criticism were settled with precision. The dissertation, in the Life of Cowley, on the metaphysical Poets[3] of the last century, has the attraction of novelty as well

[1] *Letters*, i. Preface, p. 13.

[2] He was sixty-seven when he undertook the work; sixty-nine when the first four volumes were published, and seventy-one when the last four. *Life*, iii. 109, 370; iv. 34.

Cowper wrote of the *Lives*:—'Johnson has a penetrating insight into character, and a happy talent of correcting the popular opinion upon all occasions where it is erroneous; and this he does with the boldness of a man who will think for himself, but, at the same time, with a justness of sentiment that convinces us he does not differ from others through affectation, but because he has a sounder judgment. This remark, however, has his narrative for its object, rather than his critical performance.' Cowper's *Works*, ed. 1836, v. 12.

'The Lives of the Poets are, on the whole, the best of Johnson's works. The narratives are as entertaining as any novel. The remarks on life and on human nature are eminently shrewd and profound. The criticisms are often excellent, and even when grossly and provokingly unjust, well deserve to be studied.' Macaulay's *Misc. Works*, ed. 1871, p. 392.

[3] Wordsworth writes of 'that class of curious thinkers whom Dr. Johnson has strangely styled metaphysical Poets.' Wordsworth's *Works*, ed. 1857, vi. 365. Johnson defines *metaphysical*, '1. versed in metaphysicks; relating to metaphysicks; 2. In Shakespeare it means *supernatural* or *preternatural*.' In speaking of an author's right to his own writings, he speaks of his having 'a metaphysical right, a right, as it were, of creation.' *Life*, ii. 259. I suppose he means that as 'creation' is beyond the nature of man, right derived from it is preternatural or metaphysical. He used the word in a very different sense when he told Hannah More that 'he hated to hear people whine about metaphysical distresses, when there was so much want and hunger in the world.' More's *Memoirs*, i. 249. South had used it in much the same sense when he writes:—'Those who neither do good turns, nor give good looks, nor speak good words, have a love

as

as sound observation[1]. The writers, who followed Dr. Donne, went in quest of something better than truth and nature. As Sancho says in Don Quixotte, they wanted better bread than is made with wheat. They took pains to bewilder themselves, and were ingenious for no other purpose than to err. In Johnson's review of Cowley's works, false wit is detected in all its shapes, and the Gothic[2] taste for glittering conceits, and far-fetched allusions, is exploded, never, it is hoped, to revive again.

An author, who has published his observations on the Life and Writings of Dr. Johnson[3], speaking of the Lives of the Poets, says, 'These [considered as] compositions, [and as] abounding in [with] strong and acute remarks, and with many fine and [some] even sublime passages, have unquestionably great merit; but if they be regarded merely as containing narrations of the lives, delineations of the characters, and strictures of the several authors, they are far from being always to be depended on.' He adds, 'The characters are sometimes partial, and there is sometimes TOO MUCH MALIGNITY [the capital letters are Murphy's] of misrepresentation, to which, perhaps, may be joined no inconsiderable portion of erroneous criticism.' The several clauses of this censure deserve to be answered as fully as the limits of this essay will permit.

strangely subtile and metaphysical; for other poor mortals of an ordinary capacity are forced to be ignorant of that which they can neither see, hear, feel, nor understand.' *Sermons*, ed. 1823, ii. 304.

Dr. Warton says that Johnson calls the poets *metaphysical* after Dryden. Warton's Pope's *Works*, i. 270.

'The designation,' writes Southey, 'is not fortunate, but so much respect is due to Johnson that it would be unbecoming to substitute, even if it were easy to propose, one which might be unexceptionable.' Southey's *Cowper*, ii. 127.

'Johnson had caught the cant of the age, in which it was usual to designate almost anything absurd or extravagant by the name of metaphysical.' Cary's *Lives of English Poets*, ed. 1846, p. 86.

[1] 'The Life of COWLEY he himself considered as the best of the whole, on account of the dissertation which it contains on the *Metaphysical Poets*.' *Life*, iv. 38.

[2] *Gothic* is not in Johnson's *Dictionary*. It was commonly used for *mediaeval* or *barbarous*. *Ante*, p. 384, *n*. 1.

[3] *An Essay on the Life, Character, &c., of Dr. Samuel Johnson*, 1786, p. 53. It was published anonymously, but it was by Dr. Joseph Towers.

In

In the first place, the facts are related upon the best intelligence, and the best vouchers that could be gleaned, after a great lapse of time[1]. Probability was to be inferred from such materials as could be procured, and no man better understood the nature of historical evidence than Dr. Johnson; no man was more religiously an observer of truth. If his History is any where defective, it must be imputed to the want of better information, and the errors of uncertain tradition.

Ad nos vix tenuis famæ perlabitur aura[2].

If the strictures on the works of the various authors are not always satisfactory, and if erroneous criticism may sometimes be suspected, who can hope that in matters of taste all shall agree? The instances in which the public mind has differed from the positions advanced by the author, are few in number. It has been said, that justice has not been done to Swift; that Gay and Prior are undervalued; and that Gray has been harshly treated[3]. This charge, perhaps, ought not to be disputed. Johnson, it is well known, had conceived a prejudice against Swift[4]. His friends trembled for him when he was writing that life, but were pleased, at last, to see it executed with temper and moderation. As to Prior, it is probable that he gave his real opinion, but an opinion that will not be adopted by men of lively fancy[5]. With regard

[1] 'Dr. Johnson,' writes Boswell, 'was by no means attentive to minute accuracy in his Lives of the Poets.' *Life*, iii. 359, *n.* 2. See also, *ib.* iv. 51, *n.* 2. He trusted greatly to his memory. If he did not retain anything exactly, he did not think himself bound to look it up. *Ib.* iv. 36, *n.* 3.

[2] *Aeneid*, vii. 646.

[3] *Life* i. 404; iv. 64.

Cowper wrote on Jan. 17, 1782 (*Works*, ed. 1836, iv. 175):—'Prior's reputation as an author who, with much labour indeed, but with admirable success, has embellished all his poems with the most charming ease, stood unshaken till Johnson thrust his head against it.' 'The supposed injury done by him to the memory of Gray is resented by the whole university of Cambridge.' Hawkins, p. 538. 'Among the Lives the very worst is, beyond all doubt, that of Gray.' Macaulay's *Misc. Works*, ed. 1871, p. 392.

[4] *Life*, iv. 61; v. 44; *ante*, p. 373.

[5] 'His numbers are such as mere diligence may attain; they seldom offend the ear, and seldom soothe it; they commonly want airiness, lightness, and facility: what is smooth

to

to Gray, when he condemns the apostrophe, in which Father Thames is desired to tell who drives the hoop, or tosses the ball, and then adds, that Father Thames had no better means of knowing than himself; when he compares the abrupt beginning of the first stanza of the bard to the ballad of JOHNNY ARMSTRONG, '*Is there ever a man in all Scotland*[1];' there are, perhaps, few friends of Johnson, who would not wish to blot out both the passages. It may be questioned whether the remarks on Pope's Essay on Man can be received without great caution. It has been already mentioned[2], that Crousaz, a professor in Switzerland, eminent for his Treatise of Logic, started up a professed enemy to that poem. Johnson says, 'his mind was one of those, in which philosophy and piety are happily united. He looked with distrust upon all metaphysical systems of theology, and was persuaded, that the positions of Pope were intended to draw mankind away from Revelation, and to represent the whole course of things as a necessary concatenation of indissoluble fatality[3].' This is not the place for a controversy about the Leibnitzian system. Warburton, with all the powers of his large and comprehensive mind, published a Vindication of Pope; and yet Johnson says, that 'in many passages a religious eye may easily discover expressions not very favourable to morals, or to liberty[4].' This sentence is severe, and, perhaps, dogmatical. Crousaz wrote an Examen of THE ESSAY ON MAN, and afterwards a Commentary on every remarkable passage; and though it now appears that Mrs. Elizabeth Carter translated the foreign Critic[5], yet it is certain that Johnson encouraged the work, and, perhaps, imbibed those early prejudices which adhered to him to the end of his life. He shuddered at the idea of irreligion. Hence we are told in the Life of Pope, 'Never were penury of knowledge and vulgarity of sentiment so happily

is not soft. His verses always roll but they seldom flow.' *Works*, viii. 22.

[1] *Life*, i. 403; *Works*, viii. 483, 486.

[2] *Ante*, p. 374.

[3] *Works*, viii. 287. The quotation is abridged and altered.

[4] *Ib.* p. 288.

[5] *Ante*, p. 374. Dryden spells the word *critick*; Addison, *critique*; Pope, *critique* and *critick*. Johnson's *Dictionary*.

disguised

disguised; Pope, in the chair of wisdom, tells much that every man knows, and much that he did not know himself; and gives us comfort in the position, that *though man's a fool, yet God is wise*[1]; that human advantages are unstable; that our true honour is, not to have a great part, but to act it well; that virtue only is our own, and that happiness is always in our power. The reader, when he meets all this in its new array, no longer knows the talk of his mother and his nurse[2].' But may it not be said, that every system of ethics must or ought to terminate in plain and general maxims for the use of life? and, though in such axioms no discovery is made, does not the beauty of the moral theory consist in the premises, and the chain of reasoning that leads to the conclusion? May not truth, as Johnson himself says, be conveyed to the mind by a new train of intermediate images? Pope's doctrine about the ruling passion does not seem to be refuted, though it is called, in harsh terms, pernicious as well as false, tending to establish a kind of moral predestination, or over-ruling principle, which cannot be resisted[3]. But Johnson was too easily alarmed in the cause of religion. Organized as the human race is, individuals have different inlets of perception, different powers of mind, and different sensations of pleasure and pain.

> All spread their charms, but charm not all alike,
> On different senses different objects strike;
> Hence different passions more or less inflame,
> As strong or weak the organs of the frame;
> And hence one master-passion in the breast,
> Like Aaron's serpent swallows up the rest[4].

Brumoy says, Pascal from his infancy felt himself a geometrician; and Vandyke, in like manner, was a painter. Shakspeare, who of all poets had the deepest insight into human nature, was aware of a prevailing bias in the operations

[1] *Essay on Man*, ii. 294.
[2] *Works*, viii. 339. The quotation is abridged and altered.
[3] *Ib.* viii. 293.
[4] *Essay on Man*, ii. 127.

of every mind. By him we are told, '*Masterless passion sways us to the mood of what it likes or loaths*[1].'

It remains to enquire, whether in the lives before us the characters are partial, and too often drawn with malignity of misrepresentation. To prove this it is alleged, that Johnson has misrepresented the circumstances relative to the translation of the first Iliad, and maliciously ascribed that performance to Addison, instead of Tickell, with too much reliance on the testimony of Pope, taken from the account in the papers left by Mr. Spence[2]. For a refutation of the fallacy imputed to Addison, we are referred[3] to a note in the *Biographia Britannica*, written by the late *Judge Blackstone*[4], who, it is said, examined the whole matter with accuracy, and found that the first regular statement of the accusation against Addison was published by Ruffhead in his Life of Pope, from the materials which he received from Dr. Warburton. But, with all due deference to the learned Judge, whose talents deserve all praise, this account is by no means accurate.

Sir Richard Steele, in a dedication of the Comedy of the Drummer to Mr. Congreve, gave the first insight into that business. He says, in a style of anger and resentment, 'If

[1] 'For affection,
Mistress of passion, sways it to the mood,' &c.
Merchant of Venice, Act. iv. sc. 1. l. 50.

Some editors read 'Master of passion.'

Johnson must have had these lines in mind when he described Goldsmith as

'Sive risus essent movendi,
Sive lacrymæ,
Affectuum potens at lenis dominator.' *Life*, iii. 83.

[2] *Works*, viii. 87.

'Mr. Watts, the printer,' writes Dr. Warton, 'a man of integrity, assured a friend of Mr. Nicols [? Nichols] that the translation of the First Book of the Iliad was in Tickell's handwriting, but much corrected and interlined by Addison.' Warton's Pope's *Works*, i. Preface, p. 20.

[3] By Dr. Towers, *An Essay on the Life*, &c., p. 91.

[4] Dr. Kippis, editor of the *Biog. Britan.*, ed. 1778, thus introduces this note:—'We are now happy in having the difference between him and Mr. Pope very fully discussed by a gentleman of considerable rank, to whom the Public is obliged for works of much higher importance.' i. 56.

that

that gentleman (Mr. Tickell) thinks himself injured [1], I will allow I have wronged him upon this issue, that (if the reputed translator of the first book of Homer shall please to give us another book) there shall appear another good judge in poetry, besides Mr. Alexander Pope, who shall like it.' The authority of Steele outweighs all opinions founded on vain conjecture, and, indeed, seems to be decisive, since we do not find that Tickell, though warmly pressed, thought proper to vindicate himself.

But the grand proof of Johnson's malignity, is the manner in which he has treated the character and conduct of Milton [2]. To enforce this charge, has wearied sophistry, and exhausted the invention of a party [3]. What they cannot deny, they palliate; what they cannot prove, they say is probable. But why all this rage against Dr. Johnson? Addison, before him, had said of Milton;

> Oh! had the Poet ne'er prophan'd his pen,
> To varnish o'er the guilt of faithless men [4]!

And had not Johnson an equal right to avow his sentiments? Do his enemies claim a privilege to abuse whatever is valuable to Englishmen, either in Church or State, and must the liberty of UNLICENSED PRINTING [5] be denied to the friends of the British constitution?

It is unnecessary to pursue the argument through all its artifices, since, dismantled of ornament and seducing language,

[1] 'If a certain gentleman is injured by it,' &c. Addison's *Works*, ed. 1856, v. 153.

[2] Malone wrote to Lord Charlemont on April 5, 1779:—'Johnson's political principles break out in all his compositions. In his life of Waller having occasion to mention Hampden, his uncle, he has no other epithet for him than "the zealot of rebellion." I have not seen his Milton, but he told me, "we have had too many honey-suckle lives of Milton, and that his should be in another strain." These prejudices, however, do not appear to affect his criticisms, which are in general in my opinion extremely just.' *Hist. MSS. Com.*, Twelfth Report, App. x. 345.

[3] *Ante*, p. 394; *Life*, iv. 40.

[4] *An Account of the Greatest English Poets.* Addison's *Works*, ed. 1862, i. 25.

[5] Murphy alludes to Milton's *Areopagitica*: *A Speech for the Liberty of Unlicensed Printing.*

 the

the plain truth may be stated in a narrow compass. Johnson knew that Milton was a republican; he says, 'an acrimonious, and surly republican [1], for which it is not known that he gave any better reason, than that a popular government was the most frugal; for the trappings of a monarchy would set up an ordinary commonwealth.' Johnson knew that Milton talked aloud of the danger of READMITTING KINGSHIP in this nation [2]; and when Milton adds, 'that a commonwealth was commended, or rather ENJOINED, by our Saviour himself to all Christians, not without a remarkable disallowance, and the brand of Gentilism UPON KINGSHIP [3],' Johnson thought him no better than a wild enthusiast. He knew, as well as Milton, 'that the happiness of a nation must needs be firmest and certainest in a full and free council of their own electing, where no single person, but reason only sways [4];' but the example of all the republics, recorded in the annals of mankind, gave him no room to hope that REASON ONLY would be heard. He knew that the republican form of government, having little or no complication, and no consonance of parts by a nice mechanism forming a regular whole, was too simple to be beautiful even in theory. In practice it, perhaps, never existed. In its most flourishing state, at Athens, Rome, and Carthage, it was a constant scene of tumult and commotion. From the mischiefs of a wild democracy, the progress has ever been to the dominion of an aristocracy; and the word aristocracy fatally includes the boldest and most turbulent citizens, who rise by their crimes, and call themselves the best men in the State. By intrigue, by cabal, and faction, a pernicious oligarchy is sure to succeed, and end at last in the tyranny of a single ruler. Tacitus, the great master of political wisdom, saw, under the mixed authority of king, nobles, and people, a better form of government than

[1] 'His political notions were those of an acrimonious,' &c. *Works*, vii. 116.

[2] Murphy is referring to Milton's work—'*The Ready and Easy Way to establish a Free Commonwealth, and the Excellence thereof, compared with the Inconveniencies and Dangers of readmitting Kingship in this Nation.*' Milton's *Works*, ed. 1806, iii. 401.

[3] *Ib.* p. 407.

[4] *Ib.* p. 409.

Milton's

Milton's boasted republic; and what Tacitus admired in theory, but despaired of enjoying, Johnson saw established in this country. He knew that it had been overturned by the rage of frantic men; but he knew that, after the iron rod of Cromwell's usurpation, the constitution was once more restored to its first principles. Monarchy was established, and this country was regenerated. It was regenerated a second time at the Revolution: the rights of men were then defined, and the blessings of good order and civil liberty have been ever since diffused through the whole community.

The peace and happiness of society were what Dr. Johnson had at heart. He knew that Milton called his Defence of the Regicides, a defence of the people of England[1], but, however glossed and varnished, he thought it an apology for murder. Had the men, who, under a shew of liberty, brought their king to the scaffold, proved by their subsequent conduct, that the public good inspired their action, the end might have given some sanction to the means; but usurpation and slavery followed. Milton undertook the office of secretary under the despotic power of Cromwell, offering the incense of adulation to his master, with the titles of *Director of public Councils, the Leader of unconquered Armies, the Father of his Country*[2]. Milton declared, at the same time, that *nothing is more pleasing to God, or more agreeable to reason, than that the highest mind should have the sovereign power*[3]. In this strain of servile flattery

[1] Milton's *Works*, iii. 103. It was in writing this Defence—'In Liberty's defence, my glorious task,' that the poet lost his sight. This Defence Charles Lamb describes as 'uniformly great, and such as is befitting the very mouth of a great nation, speaking for itself.' Lamb's *Letters*, ed. 1888, i. 191.

[2] 'Dux publici consilii, fortissimorum exercituum imperator, pater patriae.' 'The leader of our councils, the general of our armies, and the father of your country.' Milton's *Works*, v. 258; vi. 435; Johnson's *Works*, vii. 88.

[3] 'Nihil esse in societate hominum magis vel Deo gratum, vel rationi consentaneum, esse in civitate nihil aequius, nihil utilius, quam potiri rerum dignissimum.' 'Nothing in the world is more pleasing to God, more agreeable to reason, more politically just, or more generally useful than that the supreme power should be vested in the best and the wisest of men.' *Ib.*

Milton

Milton gives us the right divine of tyrants[1]. But it seems, in the same piece, he exhorts Cromwell 'not to desert those great principles of liberty which he had professed to espouse; for it would be a grievous enormity, if, after having successfully opposed tyranny, he should himself act the part of a tyrant, and betray the cause that he had defended[2].' This desertion of every honest principle the advocate for liberty lived to see. Cromwell acted the tyrant; and, with vile hypocrisy, told the people, that he had consulted the Lord, and the Lord would have it so[3]. Milton took an under part in the tragedy. Did that become the defender of the people of England? Brutus saw his country enslaved; he struck the blow for freedom, and he died with honour in the cause. Had he lived to be secretary under Tiberius what would now be said of his memory[4]?

But still, it seems, the prostitution with which Milton is charged, since it cannot be defended, is to be retorted on the character of Johnson. For this purpose a book has been published, called *Remarks on Dr. Johnson's Life of Milton, to which are added Milton's Tractate of Education, and Areopagitica.* In this laboured tract we are told, 'There is one performance ascribed to the pen of the Doctor, where the prostitution is of so singular a nature, that it would be difficult to select an adequate motive for it out of the mountainous heap of conjectural causes of human passions, or human caprice. It is the speech of the late unhappy Dr. William Dodd, when he was about to hear the sentence of the law pronounced upon him, in consequence of an indictment for forgery. The voice of the publick has given the honour of manufacturing this speech to Dr. Johnson; and the style and configuration of the speech itself confirm the imputation. . . . But it is hardly possible to divine what could

[1] 'Caesar, when he assumed the perpetual dictatorship, had not more servile or elegant flattery.' Johnson's *Works*, vii. 88.

[2] This seems an abridgement of a passage in Milton's *Works*, v. 259; vi. 436-7.

[3] Murphy refers, I think, to Cromwell's speech on dissolving his first parliament. Carlyle's *Cromwell*, ed. 1857, iii. 71.

[4] Dante has put him with Judas Iscariot in the lowest gulf in Hell. He could not have put him lower even had he been Tiberius's secretary.

be

be his motive for accepting the office. A man, to express the precise state of mind of another, about to be destined to an ignominious death for a capital crime, should, one would imagine, have some consciousness, that he himself had incurred some guilt of the same kind [1].' In all the schools of sophistry is there to be found so vile an argument? In the purlieus of Grub-street is there such another mouthfull of dirt? In the whole quiver of Malice is there so envenomed a shaft?

After this it is to be hoped, that a certain class of men will talk no more of Johnson's malignity. The last apology for Milton is, that he acted according to his principles. But Johnson thought those principles detestable; pernicious to the constitution in Church and State, destructive of the peace of society, and hostile to the great fabric of civil policy, which the wisdom of ages has taught every Briton to revere, to love, and cherish [2]. He reckoned Milton in that class of men, of whom the Roman historian says, when they want, by a sudden convulsion, to overturn the government, they roar and clamour for liberty; if they succeed, they destroy liberty itself. *Ut imperium evertant, Libertatem præferunt; si perverterint, libertatem ipsam aggredientur* [3]. Such were the sentiments of Dr. Johnson; and it may be asked, in the language of Bolingbroke, 'Are these sentiments, which any man, who is born a Briton, in any circumstances, in any situation, ought to be ashamed, or afraid to avow [4]?' Johnson has done ample justice to Milton's poetry: the Criticism on Paradise Lost is a sublime composition. Had he thought the author as good and pious a citizen as Dr. Watts, he would have been ready, notwithstanding his non-conformity, to do equal honour to the memory of the man [5].

[1] *Ante*, p. 432; *Memoirs of Thomas Hollis*, ii. 579.

[2] *Life*, iv. 41.

[3] Tacitus, *Annals*, xvi. 22.

[4] 'Are these designs,' &c. Bolinbroke's *Works*, ed. 1809, iii. 4.

[5] 'Happy will be that reader whose mind is disposed by his [Dr. Watts's] verses or his prose to imitate him in all but his nonconformity, to copy his benevolence to man and his reverence to God.' *Works*, viii. 387. See also *Life*, i. 312; iii. 126.

It

It is now time to close this essay, which the author fears has been drawn too much into length. In the progress of the work, feeble as it may be, he thought himself performing the last human office to the memory of a friend, whom he loved, esteemed, and honoured.

> His saltem accumulem donis, et fungar inani
> Munere[1].——

The author of these memoirs has been anxious to give the features of the man, and the true character of the author. He has not suffered the hand of partiality to colour his excellencies with too much warmth; nor has he endeavoured to throw his singularities too much into shade. Dr. Johnson's failings may well be forgiven for the sake of his virtues. His defects were spots in the sun. His piety, his kind affections, and the goodness of his heart, present an example worthy of imitation. His works will remain a monument of genius and of learning. Had he written nothing but what is contained in this edition, the quantity shews a life spent in study and meditation. If to this we add the labour of his Dictionary and other various productions, it may be fairly allowed, as he used to say of himself, that he has written his share[2]. In the volumes here presented to the publick, the reader will find a perpetual source of pleasure and instruction. With due precautions, authors may learn to grace their style with elegance, harmony and precision; they may be taught to think with vigour and perspicuity; and, to crown the whole, by a diligent attention to these books all may advance in virtue.

[1] *Aeneid*, vi. 885.

[2] 'BOSWELL. "But, Sir, why don't you give us something in some other way?" GOLDSMITH. "Ay, Sir, we have a claim upon you." "JOHNSON. "No, Sir, I am not obliged to do any more. No man is obliged to do as much as he can do. A man is to have part of his life to himself."' *Life*, ii. 15. See also ii. 35, where the King urged him to continue his labours.

END OF VOL. I.